"Performance management and control is an important and rapidly-evolving field; this companion combines extensive literature surveys and stimulating new material to provide a wide-ranging guide to recent developments that will be of great interest to students, practitioners, new researchers and established scholars looking for further insights."

– Brian A Rutherford, Emeritus Professor of Accounting, Kent Business School, University of Kent, UK

"This edited book is great reading for people who want to learn about the latest developments in performance management and control. The quality of the contributors to the book is outstanding."

– Antonio Dávila, Professor of Entrepreneurship and Accounting and Control, IESE Business School, University of Navarra, Spain

The Routledge Companion to Performance Management and Control

Performance management is key to the ongoing success of any organization, allowing it to meet its strategic objectives by designing and implementing management control systems.

This book goes beyond the usual discussion of performance management in accounting and finance, to consider strategic management, human behaviour and performance management in different countries and contexts. With a global mix of world-renowned researchers, this book systematically covers the *what*, the *who*, the *where* and the *why* of performance management and control (PMC) systems.

A comprehensive, state-of-the-art collection edited by a leading expert in the field, this book is a vital resource for all scholars, students and researchers with an interest in business, management and accounting.

Elaine Harris is Professor of Accounting and Management at the University of Roehampton, London and Chair of the Management Control Association, UK.

Routledge Companions in Business, Management and Accounting

Routledge Companions in Business, Management and Accounting are prestige reference works providing an overview of a whole subject area or sub-discipline. These books survey the state of the discipline including emerging and cutting edge areas. Providing a comprehensive, up to date, definitive work of reference, Routledge Companions can be cited as an authoritative source on the subject.

A key aspect of these Routledge Companions is their international scope and relevance. Edited by an array of highly regarded scholars, these volumes also benefit from teams of contributors which reflect an international range of perspectives.

Individually, Routledge Companions in Business, Management and Accounting provide an impactful one-stop-shop resource for each theme covered. Collectively, they represent a comprehensive learning and research resource for researchers, postgraduate students and practitioners.

Published titles in this series include:

The Routledge Companion to Contemporary Brand Management
Edited by Francesca Dall'Olmo Riley, Jaywant Singh and Charles Blankson

The Routledge Companion to Banking Regulation and Reform
Edited by Ismail Ertürk and Daniela Gabor

The Routledge Companion to the Makers of Modern Entrepreneurship
Edited by David B. Audretsch and Erik E. Lehmann

The Routledge Companion to Business History
Edited by Abe de Jong, Steven Toms, John Wilson and Emily Buchnea

The Routledge Companion to Qualitative Accounting Research
Edited by Zahirul Hoque, Lee D. Parker, Mark A. Covaleski and Kathryn Haynes

The Routledge Companion to Accounting and Risk
Edited by Margaret Woods and Philip Linsley

The Routledge Companion to Wellbeing at Work
Edited by Sir Cary L. Cooper and Michael P. Leiter

The Routledge Companion to Performance Management and Control
Edited by Elaine Harris

The Routledge Companion to Performance Management and Control

Edited by Elaine Harris

Routledge
Taylor & Francis Group
LONDON AND NEW YORK

First published 2018
by Routledge
2 Park Square, Milton Park, Abingdon, Oxon OX14 4RN

and by Routledge
711 Third Avenue, New York, NY 10017

Routledge is an imprint of the Taylor & Francis Group, an informa business

British Library Cataloguing-in-Publication Data
A catalogue record for this book is available from the British Library

Library of Congress Cataloging-in-Publication Data
Names: Harris, Elaine Pamela, editor.
Title: The Routledge companion to performance management and control / edited by Elaine Harris. Description: Abingdon, Oxon; New York, NY: Routledge, 2017. | Series: Routledge companions in business, management and accounting |
Includes bibliographical references and index.
Identifiers: LCCN 2017004198 | ISBN 9781138913547 (hardback) | ISBN 9781315691374 (ebook)
Subjects: LCSH: Performance—Management. | Performance technology.
Classification: LCC HF5549.5.P35 R68 2017 | DDC 658.3/12—dc23
LC record available at https://lccn.loc.gov/2017004198

ISBN: 978-1-138-91354-7 (hbk)
ISBN: 978-1-315-69137-4 (ebk)

Typeset in Bembo
by codeMantra

Contents

List of figures, tables, and appendices

Figures

Tables

Appendices

Contributors

Ralph W. Adler is Professor of Accounting and Director of the Centre for Organisational Performance Measurement and Management at the University of Otago. His research interests are in performance management, strategic management accounting, organisational effectiveness and business education. He is a Senior Associate Editor of *Accounting Education* and the convenor of the Performance Measurement Association of Australasia.

Damminda Alahakoon is Professor of Business Analytics and leads the Centre for Data Analytics and Cognitive Computing at the Business School, La Trobe University, Australia. His research interests are in data mining, machine learning, artificial intelligence, cognitive computing and text analytics. His work laid the foundation for a Melbourne-based technology start up called 'Conscious Machines'.

Chandana Alawattage is a Senior Lecturer in accounting at the University of Aberdeen and the Accounting and Finance Research and PhD Coordinator. He has a PhD in Management Control from Keele University. His research focuses on the way western managerial discourses and calculative technologies implicate on the social and organisational reformations in less-developed countries.

Maria Argyropoulou is a Programme Director at Laureate Online Education International and a member of adjunct faculty at the Hellenic Open University. She received her PhD from Brunel Business School, UK. She is a consultant in Business Process Re-engineering and Information Systems specializing in Operations Management, Global Supply Chains and International Trade.

Rachel Argyropoulou is a Lecturer at the Hellenic Army Academy. She has a PhD in chemical engineering from the National Technical University of Athens, Greece. Her research interests focus on environmental chemistry, green supply chain and the production of advanced materials. She has worked as a consultant in companies specialized in analysis, inspection and certification of products.

Tony Berry began his career as an aeronautical engineer working on Concorde in the UK and later in Seattle, where he began his management studies. He gained a PhD at Manchester Business School. His research interests include management control, leadership and financial management. He has had extensive academic and consultancy experience.

Georgia Birch attended the University of Otago from where she received a Post Graduate Diploma endorsed in Psychology. Georgia worked for 3 and a half years at Deloitte in the audit division in Auckland where she qualified as a chartered accountant. In May 2016 Georgia moved to London for international work experience and is working as a finance associate at Argent Group Europe.

Karen Brickman is a Senior Lecturer in the Business Faculty at the University of Greenwich. Her research is in the area of Management Control and Risk in the Financial Services Sector. Karen started her career as a Chartered Management Accountant (CIMA) at a London-based Investment Bank. She is also on the panel of reviewers of academic bids for CIMA ad-hoc funding.

Jane Broadbent is Emerita Professor of Accounting at Royal Holloway University of London. She trained as an accountant in the NHS, working mainly in management accounting, which informed her academic career and research interest in management control in the Public Services. She has also written on issues relating to accounting and gender. As a distinguished professor, she has worked nationally and internationally on a number of research assessment exercises.

Rhoda Brown is a Senior Lecturer in Financial Reporting at Loughborough University. Her research interests are in performance management and measurement and earnings management. She started her career with a Big4 accounting firm, is a member of the ICAEW and her PhD (University of Warwick) was in the economic effects of accounting policy choice.

David Carter is an Associate Professor in Law and Associate Dean of Research in the Faculty of Business, Government and Law at the University of Canberra, Australia. His research focuses on three main pillars: the ontological politics of information, the nature of governance and regulation and the discourses of capital. His research applies a range of post-structural theory (including Laclau, Lazzarato and Hardt and Negri) to current social problems in business, accounting and law.

Robert H. Chenhall is Emeritus Professor at Monash University. His research has focused mainly on theory-based, empirical studies in management accounting employing organizational and behavioural frameworks. His research has included examining conditions in which different types of management control systems are effective and how those systems are implicated in strategic and organizational change using survey-based, case-based and experimental approaches.

David Dugdale, Emeritus Professor of Management Accounting at the University of Bristol, received a lifetime achievement award from the British Accounting and Finance Association in 2014. His research interests include costing, investment appraisal, budgeting and performance management and he continues to serve on CIMA's Research Board.

Mark Ellul is the Registrar and formerly Head of and Director of Planning at the University of Roehampton. Educated at the University of Sussex, he graduated with a degree in Physics with Computational Physics. He has worked extensively in both FE and HE across London.

Lin Fitzgerald is Emeritus Professor of Management Accounting at Loughborough University. Her research interests are in performance management in service businesses. She qualified as a Chartered Management Accountant whilst working for British Telcomm and has maintained strong links with the Chartered Institute of Management Accountants (CIMA) throughout her career and continues to serve on both CIMA Council and the Research Board of CIMA.

Tharusha Gooneratne is Senior Lecturer in Accounting at the Faculty of Management and Finance of the University of Colombo, Sri Lanka. She received her PhD degree from La Trobe University. Her research interests include management accounting and control systems.

Matthew Hall is Professor of Accounting at Monash University. His research interests relate to management accounting and performance measurement, with a specific focus on non-profits, social enterprise and the third sector. His work has been published in a variety of leading journals in the accounting, management and non-profit fields.

Elaine Harris is Professor of Accounting and Management at Roehampton University, having also been the Director of the Business School from 2010 to 2014. She started her career in accountancy practice and has held various management positions in higher education in the last 30 years. She is chair of the Management Control Association and has published books and papers on strategic investment appraisal and project risk. She is associate editor of the *British Accounting Review.*

Julie Harrison is a Senior Lecturer in the Department of Accounting and Finance at the University of Auckland. Her research interests include performance measurement, data envelopment analysis, revenue management and transfer pricing. Prior to joining the University she worked as a tax accountant and management accountant in New Zealand, Australia and the United Kingdom.

Geoffrey Heath is a Fellow in Public Sector Accounting at Keele University, having been a lecturer there and at Staffordshire University. Previously he worked in NHS finance, qualifying as a chartered management accountant. He has been engaged for many years in collaborative research and evaluation in the public sector.

Ian Herbert is Deputy Director of the Centre for Global Sourcing and Services at Loughborough University. His main research interest is the transformation of the finance function through new organisational forms, particularly, the way in which the digitalised knowledge-based economy is creating challenges for the career paths of finance professionals.

Zahirul Hoque is Professor of Management Accounting/Public Sector and Executive Director of the Centre for Public Sector Governance, Accountability and Performance at La Trobe University, Melbourne, Australia. He is also the Founding Editor-in-Chief of the *Journal of Accounting & Organizational Change.* His research interests include management accounting, performance management, public sector accounting and interdisciplinary research on management control.

Robin Jarvis is Professor of Accounting at Brunel University and Special Advisor to the European Federation of Accountants and Auditors for SMEs. Robin was awarded the British Accounting and Finance Association (BAFA) Lifetime Achievement Award in 2013. He is a member of the IASB's IFRS for SMEs Implementation Group and for 12 years was on the EFRAG Supervisory Board.

Ruth King was, prior to retirement, Director of Programme Quality at Loughborough University and a lecturer in accounting and financial management. Her research interests are in performance measurement, financial reporting, accounting education and corporate governance.

Ivo De Loo is Professor of Management Accounting and Control at Nyenrode Business University, where he was previously Associate Professor of Research Methods and Methodology and Associate Professor of Management Accounting and Control at the Open University of the Netherlands. His research interests include management control as practice, the role of management accountants in organizations, management accounting discourse and research methodology.

Alan Lowe is Professor of Management Accounting at RMIT, Melbourne. He is also joint Editor of the *British Accounting Review*. Alan's research has included management controls, ERP and internet reporting using case studies and interpretive methodology. Recent projects include due diligence in private equity, control systems in a food oil refinery, paradoxical forces in Government Audit and the study of consultants in an international recruitment group based in The Netherlands and UK.

Xuan Thuy Mai is Lecturer in Accounting at the School of Accounting and Auditing of the National Economics University, Vietnam and currently pursuing her PhD degree in Performance Management in the higher education sector at La Trobe University. She obtained her master's degree in accounting and finance from the University of Manchester. Her research interests include behavioural issues in performance measurement.

Tony Mancini is the Director of Academic Affairs Operations at Laureate Online Education International. He received an MBA from Concordia University in Montreal, Canada, where he has since lectured in operations, project management and statistics. He held senior roles in the telecoms industry in network services; corporate services and human resources. His interests are in business forecasting, supply chain management, enterprise risk assessment, process re-engineering and TQM.

Craig Marsh is Director of Lincoln International Business School and Pro Vice Chancellor for International Partnerships at the University of Lincoln. He is a member of the Institute of Directors with 30 years of experience in the military, the private sector, academia and consulting. He has a PhD in management learning from Lancaster and his research interests are in leadership.

Ruth Mattimoe lectures in Management Accounting at DCU Business School, Dublin. Her PhD on hotel room rate pricing, under Professor Bob Scapens at Manchester, was awarded a CIMA Research Foundation grant. Her research concerning real life issues of decision-making and performance measurement in hotel and tourism firms has been supported by CIMA and Fáilte Ireland.

Laurie McAulay was, prior to retirement, a Reader in Management Accounting at Loughborough University with research interests in management control systems and performance measurement; short-termism; climate change; management learning and information systems.

Anette Mikes is Professor of Accounting and Control at the University of Lausanne, Switzerland. She researches risk management, man-made disasters and the role of risk expertise and management control in settings in which multiple and conflicting objectives, values and interests are at stake. Her research documentary on a man-made disaster (the Kursk Submarine Rescue Mission) won the Most Outstanding Short Film Award at the Global Risk Forum in Davos in 2014.

Pascal Nevries is Professor and Head of Management Accounting and Control at Kassel University. Previously he held a similar position at Witten/Herdecke University and served as Managing Director of the Center for Controlling and Management at WHU – Otto Beisheim School of Management. His research focuses on controllership, performance measurement and management control systems.

Rick Payne is ICAEW's expert on building effective finance functions, business partnering and the role of the Chief Financial Officer. His current role includes building links between academia and practice. He qualified as a chartered accountant with KPMG and then worked in senior roles in the wholesale financial services sector.

Martin Quinn is Senior Lecturer and Head of Accounting at Dublin City University Business School. He has worked for over a decade in accounting roles. He joined academia in 2006 and researches and publishes on accounting change, accounting and information systems and accounting history.

James Radcliffe is a Fellow of Staffordshire University based in the Faculty of Health Sciences. He has written on a variety of issues including British central government and environmental politics. More recently his work has centred on health care management and policy.

Paul Rouse is Professor of Management Accounting at the University of Auckland. His research areas include performance and productivity measurement (with a focus on Data Envelopment Analysis (DEA)), revenue and cost management, cost-benefit and evaluation methods. Recent work has focused on primary and community healthcare involving case mix for primary care and the use of DEA in setting Government funding for large, tertiary hospitals. He is an Editor of *Pacific Accounting Review*.

Will Seal has held chairs at the universities of Essex, Birmingham and Southampton. He is currently Professor of Accounting & Management at Loughborough University. He has published extensively and his main research interests are the relationship between theory and practice in management, strategic control, shared services and lean operations.

Chaturika Seneviratne is a Senior Lecturer in Accounting at the Faculty of Management Studies and Commerce of University of Sri Jayewardenepura, Sri Lanka and currently pursuing her PhD at La Trobe University. She is a merit holder and gold medalist in her

MBA at University of Colombo. Her research interests include management accounting, performance management and control systems.

Paul Shantapriyan is the Academic Advocate for ISACA at the University of Tasmania. He has previously worked at the Universities of the South Pacific, New South Wales, Otago. He is a certified SAP consultant in Strategic Enterprise Management and a Certified Practicing Accountant (CPA Australia). He is also a member of the International Society of Engineered Asset Management.

David Smith is Professor of Management Accounting at the University of Queensland. His research interests are in the area of management control systems, with a particular interest in performance measurement and impact assessment in the NGO sector. He is currently a member of the board of directors of the Accounting and Finance Association of Australia and New Zealand (AFAANZ).

Frank Stadtherr is a PhD student and Research Assistant in the Department of Economics and Management at the Karlsruhe Institute of Technology, Germany. His research interest is in cost management methods of modular product families. He aims to develop new controlling instruments with a German car company to manage component costs during product development.

Erik Strauss is Professor of Accounting and Control at Witten/Herdecke University. His research interests are in management control systems, management accounting change, organizational routines. He is a member of the editorial board of *Qualitative Research in Accounting and Management* and *Corporate Ownership and Control.*

Carolyn Stringer is a Senior Lecturer in the Department of Accountancy and Finance at the University of Otago. She is a Fellow of CPA Australia and a Chartered Accountant (NZICA). Her research examines performance management processes and involves case studies, surveys and archival research. She is a founding member of the Centre for Organisational Performance Measurement and Management and Performance Measurement Association Australasia.

John Paul Tivnan, BA (Accounting and Finance, DCU), MBS (Accounting, DCU), Chartered Tax Advisor, FCA, MICS (Chartered Shipbroker), is Senior Vice President and Chief Financial Officer of Ardmore Shipping Corporation and a former Senior Tax Manager in Ernst and Young, Dublin.

Shahzad Uddin is Professor of Accounting and the Director of Essex Accounting Centre. Shahzad has published on management accounting, accounting and development issues, new public management, corporate governance and corporate social responsibility in a wide variety of contexts including Greece, China, Japan, Indonesia, Sri Lanka, Bangladesh, Pakistan, Mexico, Ghana and Uganda.

Paresh Wankhade is Professor of Leadership and Management at Edge Hill University Business School, UK. He is also the Editor-In-Chief of the *International Journal of Emergency Services.* His research and publications have focused on the analyses of strategic leadership, organisational culture, organisational change and interoperability within different emergency services settings.

Liz Warren is Director of Learning and Teaching at the Business School, University of Greenwich, where she teaches management accounting and strategy. She gained her PhD at Southampton and continues to research in the areas of decision making, control and regulatory change. Liz is a member of CIMA's Expert Review Group.

Danture Wickramasinghe has been in academia over 33 years teaching and researching management accounting. Presently, he is the chair in management accounting at Adam Smith Business School, Glasgow. Among others, he has published in *Critical Perspectives on Accounting, Auditing, Accountability Journal, Accounting and Business Research* and *Financial Management (UK).*

Piyumini Wijenayake is a PhD student at the Business School, La Trobe University, Australia. Her PhD research is focused on the integration of multi-source data to build a holistic view of a business situation for improved real-time decision making. She is collaborating with the ICT Business Intelligence unit at La Trobe University to enhance its business intelligence tasks.

Marc Wouters is Professor of Management Accounting at the Karlsruhe Institute of Technology, Germany and Visiting Professor at the University of Amsterdam, the Netherlands. His research and teaching focuses on management accounting within the context of operations, marketing, entrepreneurship and innovation, especially in companies where technology plays an important role. His research is both quantitative and qualitative and often with researchers from other fields.

Maria Zhivitskaya was awarded a PhD in Risk Management from the London School of Economics in 2015. Her research focused on risk governance and oversight in UK financial institutions since the global financial crisis. She then worked for Goldman Sachs in a risk oversight role before joining Prudential plc.

1

Introduction to performance management and control

Elaine Harris

The objective of this book is to provide a reference work that offers students and researchers an insight into the current scholarship in organisational performance management and control (PMC). As a companion volume, the book offers a collection of work from more than 50 authors in the field and includes a variety of different perspectives on this key area of management. The aim of this chapter is to introduce the content of the book in terms of its subject matter, to explain the rationale for the book and how it is structured, and to give a brief taste of what each chapter contributes.

Defining performance management and control

In introducing the subject matter of the book's content, the title and key terms will first be defined in order to position the work in its academic domain. There are many possible definitions of both performance management and management control as they relate to organisations. One might start with an organisation in mind, whether it is a business enterprise with a profit motive or some other kind of organisation that perhaps has a social or educational motive, to define performance management as a practice that seeks to identify what the organisation exists to do and to measure and control how effectively it does it. For the purpose of this book, performance management is defined as the design and implementation of management control systems in organisations to ensure that the strategic objectives are met.

Performance management therefore relates to a critical management practice that usually involves measurement of the key indicators of the organisational goals and achievements. Management control may be more broadly defined to include all the systems and procedures established and action taken by managers to ensure that the organisational goals are met. This implies more than the measurement of target and actual performance, and extends to the allocation of resources and the efficiency with which those resources are deployed in pursuance of organisational goals. Where the prime motive of an organisation is concerned with value creation defined in financial terms, it is clear that performance measurement is likely to be seen as the responsibility of the accounting and finance function. However, in other organisations, it may be that human resources are seen as being equally or more important to effective performance management, so management control may be focussed on managing people and their behaviour. Thus, performance management can be focussed at an individual level, where organisational members have their own specific objectives to achieve. This perspective is examined in Chapter 15 on leadership and control.

The key to PMC therefore starts with understanding what the organisation seeks to do (its strategic goals) and how it aims to deliver those goals (strategic plans) by utilising the resources available to it (effective management). Management control is concerned with the ways in which organisational managers encourage and motivate people in the organisation to work towards common goals. It also deals with how the organisation is seen to perform by a range of outside stakeholders such as providers of its finance, market regulators, consumers of its goods and services, and suppliers of its bought in goods and services. Thus, enterprise risk management and supply chain management (SCM) may be seen as part of management control (see Chapters 11 and 17).

As can be seen in the final chapter, a body of literature on PMC has developed considerably over the last 50 or so years, that seeks to explain and possibly to enhance management practice. Much of the research and scholarship in this period has been conducted in Business Schools, but there are overlaps with the social sciences, technology and engineering; thus, the authors who have contributed to this book are not all from a single discipline or background. Equally, they are not all academics. The authors include many academics who gained practical experience in accounting and business before entering academia and some non-academics who are and remain practitioners in organisations. This gives the book a richer context and a more practical feel than either standard textbooks or academic journals may have, with the aim of making it more accessible to a wider audience.

Structure of the book

The book is divided into four sections that take the reader through a logical set of questions about the theory and practice of PMC and how the relevant body of literature has been researched. The first section on the design of PMC systems deals with ***what*** gets measured and ***how*** PMC systems are designed. The second section on people and management control explores the human dimension of ***who*** gets involved in PMC and ***how*** they behave. The third section on PMC in different contexts examines ***where*** PMC takes place in a variety of countries, sectors and organisational settings and ***how*** these contexts shape PMC. The last section aimed at researchers in PMC (especially those new to the subject matter or to academia) is devoted to the matter of ***how*** research in PMC may be conducted, ***why*** it is important and *what* challenges the researcher may face along the way.

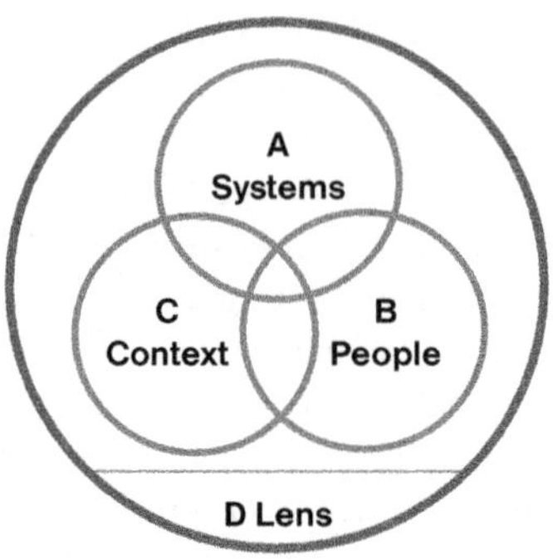

Figure 1.1 PMC conceptual model

Figure 1.1 depicts the conceptual model underlying the book, which the structure follows. Some of the chapters could have been placed in more than one section as they shed light on more than one question or dimension of PMC. However, they have been organised into sections according to their focus. The first section focusses on performance management ***systems*** (PMS) design, the metrics, data and technologies that organisations need to effectively measure and monitor performance. The second section illuminates the role of ***people***, the organisational actors and their formal and informal uses of PMS in management control. The third section explores a variety of alternative ***contexts*** for PMC through case- and sector-based studies. The last section has an entirely different focus, and it aims to help researchers entering or re-entering this academic field by examining some alternative approaches to conducting PMC research, the ***lens*** through which the researcher may view themselves and their evidence and what impact their research might have on PMC practice.

The remainder of this chapter introduces the content and highlights of each contribution.

Introduction to the chapters

Part I: Design of performance management and control systems

Dugdale (Chapter 2) introduces us to management control theory before comparing PMC in action in three case organisations in manufacturing, insurance and banking. He illustrates organisational objectives, strategies and key success factors, targets and key performance indicators (KPIs), cost control and the role of company culture and structure (decentralisation), incentives and motivation. This chapter could have been positioned in Section 3, but the focus here is on PMC design, and he provides a gentle introduction to both the theory and lessons for practice, ideal for the non-expert reader to get a feel for the subject of PMC. He "suggests that there is scope for integration of contemporary performance management insights with established organisation theory" (page 36).

The focus of enquiry for Adler (Chapter 3) is on the fourth of eight functional questions posed by Ferreira and Otley (2009) in PMS design introduced by Dugdale ("What is the organisation structure and how does it affect the strategy and control?"). Adler presents an interesting case study of a Japanese manufacturing company using what is termed "amoeba" management, which is based on breaking the organisation down into very small operational units for management control purposes. He shows how this "radically decentralised organisation structure" has been operationalised to address the challenges in the competitive environment. Adler used Simons' three levers of beliefs, diagnostic and interactive controls (Simons, 1995) to analyse the case evidence and found that the belief systems were the key to Kyocera's success in making amoeba management work.

Wouters and Stadherr (Chapter 4), by contrast, take us on a detailed journey through the design of a cost management system in the motor vehicle industry, where a product modularity strategy is adopted to improve financial performance. Their case study demonstrates that a modular design strategy goes beyond target costing and is more far-reaching than simply having a product portfolio that shares common components, having implications for all aspects and functions of the business. They position their case in relation to the literature on new product development and demonstrate how both innovation and accountability can improve when modularity is fully embraced.

Rouse and Harrison (Chapter 5) explain the issues that need to be addressed when composite measures are used to combine multiple measures of performance into indices for internal or external benchmarking purposes. They explain how reflective or formative metrics may be collected from a number of decision-making units and how fixed or free weights may be applied to incorporate them into a single measure. They illustrate the construction of composite measures with reference to their research in the healthcare sector. They acknowledge the mistrust of some league tables such as those used to publish university rankings and recommend "that any such measure is accompanied by a careful explanation of how it is compiled and the rationale for the weighting systems employed" (page 104).

Warren and Brickman (Chapter 6) continue on a theme of industry benchmarks by considering the external influences on metrics used in PMC systems in regulated industries. They analyse five case studies drawn from the financial services and utilities sectors, both heavily regulated in the UK. They consider the design of PMS in each case and show the benefits (for example the learning value) and issues (such as stifling innovation) involved in external benchmarking. They conclude that when using external data sources in designing internal PMS, it is important "to ensure that a system is flexible enough to withstand change" (page 121).

Quinn and Strauss (Chapter 7) consider the (largely enabling) role information technology has played in the development of PMS and the actual and potential impact it has had on PMC with the growing use of cloud technologies in organisations and society. They explore the advantages and challenges for managers and accountants working with cloud technologies and identify risks (not least issues of data security) that arise from using cloud technologies in the design and operation of PMS.

Leading on from the issues identified by Quinn and Strauss, Alahakoon and Wijenayake (Chapter 8) pick up on the management challenges of working with so much data availability in the design of PMS and consider how organisations can make the best use of 'big data'. An extension to maturity models in PMS is presented. They also give a flavour of the current research going on in the data analytics field and the development of a dynamic form of Self-Organising Map (SOM) to help organisations harness data analytics technologies to gain competitive advantage.

Part II: People and management control

Nevries and Payne (Chapter 9) explore the changing role of the financial professional in PMC. First, they use the Ferreira and Otley (2009) framework (see Figure 9.1, page 160) to analyse the role of finance professionals (those working in the finance function of organisations). Then, they consider the factors that drive successful finance departments, from both a personnel profile perspective (knowledge, skills and behaviours) and a relational perspective (trust and collaboration). A typical career path is presented, and country-specific differences are considered. They conclude that more research is needed on the changing role of finance professionals (especially in light of the challenges of managing 'big data') and that the future success of those embarking on careers in finance in organisations depends on effective collaboration and co-creation across domains.

Harris and Ellul (Chapter 10) use a case study in higher education to illustrate how another kind of (non-financially qualified) professional, the strategic planner, might take up the challenges of managing 'big data' (see Chapter 8) in contributing to the organisation's PMC. This study also used the Ferreira and Otley (2009) framework (see Figure 9.1, page 160) to analyse professional practice, but from the shared experience of two organisational members, one professionally qualified in accounting (though working as an academic manager, not in the finance function) and the other not. Whilst they found that the role of the Director of Planning was expanding and becoming more strategic in a highly competitive environment, it was not taking over the work previously undertaken in the finance function. Rather, the two departments (finance and planning) were seen as operating side by side in a complementary way.

Mikes and Zhivitskaya (Chapter 11) respond to Berry *et al.*'s (2009) call for more research on risk management as an essential part of management control with their focus on enterprise risk management and the management of ambiguity as part of PMC. They explore the developing role of the chief risk officer (CRO) in the UK financial services industry. They make a case for how the development of CROs may contribute (given the financial crisis and the damage to the reputation of banks and other providers of financial services in society) to a greater sense of control being exercised more professionally in this sector.

Mai and Hoque (Chapter 12) provide a useful analysis of performance management research that has focussed on the behavioural aspects in their literature review. The review covers the period from 1992 to 2015, contributing to the literature on PMS by assessing the behavioural causes and consequences of PMS. They examine the link between the theories underlying such research, especially those drawn from psychology, and methodological issues in the literature surveyed. There are useful indications of gaps in our knowledge and potential for future research in this field. They also provide some salient warnings about the potential pitfalls of qualitative studies in behavioural PMS research.

Carter (Chapter 13) identifies the key challenges that managing in organisations employing 'knowledge workers' provides for management accounting by examining two case studies. One case analyses research management practice in higher education, and the other looks at billing practices in professional law and accountancy firms. He provides a critique of current practice, largely based on management accounting techniques that were originally designed to control manufacturing operations and involve mainly numeric measures. In the contexts of these two cases, Carter illustrates how adopting a PMS that counts inputs (6-minute time slots) or outputs (numbers of publications in a time period) may lead to game-playing and mistrust and stifle creativity. Carter considers options for identifying new approaches to managing what he calls 'the immaterial' in organisations where intellectual capital is more important than financial capital.

Fitzgerald *et al.* (Chapter 14) explore the role of a company-wide mantra named the '4Cs' (Compliance; Cycle Time; Customer Service; and Cash) of PMC in their case study of Network Rail. The mantra of the 4Cs provides a common vocabulary for organisational members to align their actions and decisions to the corporate strategy. Like Adler, they focus on the interactive controls and the role of values and beliefs. However, unlike Adler's case of decentralisation, Fitzgerald *et al.*'s study takes place within the context of an organisation that has centralised its financial shared services function in an attempt to make cost savings. The case study highlights the use of visual aids to remind people about key elements of the PMS.

Marsh (Chapter 15) draws on his professional experience as a 'scholar practitioner' to illustrate the two issues that appear as the seventh and eighth questions in Ferreira and Otley's (2009) framework (see Figure 9.1, page 160), namely the evaluation of individual and group performance against target measures and the consequences (rewards and penalties) of such evaluation. Marsh provides two distinct and competing organisational narratives to suggest that performance appraisal systems based on the traditional precepts of performance ratings and performance-related pay are perhaps outmoded. The staff in the second scenario were at the same time 'agency' staff and 'educational professionals' who took pride in their work, so one could see how a policy of 'engagement' and the use of a customer-focussed 'dashboard' might be effective in this context. It is worth noting here the contrast between the PMC practice presented by Marsh and the immaterial labour example of academic staff management presented by Carter (Chapter 13) in a public-sector environment.

Part III: PMC in different contexts

Alawattage *et al.* (Chapter 16) take us on a journey through the critical accounting literature of the past few decades to enhance our understanding of management accounting practices in less-developed countries (LDCs). They focus on how (popular) theorisation has changed over time. They identify key authors (who I will call the 4Hs) who influenced their work in the 2000s and subsequent scholars, Hopwood's work on behavioural accounting in the 1970s, Hofstede's work on culture in the 1980s, Hopper's work on the political economic context of LDCs, and Hoque's case study work in Bangladesh in the 1990s. They also note Hopper's role in the Berry *et al.* (1985) project in the National Coal Mines as an important influence on Hopper's subsequent work with Alawattage *et al.* in developing a critical theorisation of accounting and control in LDCs. This review chapter sets the scene for the chapters that follow in this section, though perhaps less in a theoretical sense and more from a methodological viewpoint, as we see a tradition of case studies becoming more popular in management accounting to explore the differences between PMC studied in different geographical contexts and varying business sectors.

Mancini *et al.* (Chapter 17) provide a literature review of performance measurement frameworks (PMF) in use according to the SCM papers published since 2010. They begin by introducing key developments in PMFs in the 1990s, the performance pyramid (Lynch and Cross, 1991), balanced scorecard (Kaplan and Norton, 1992), the results and determinants matrix (Fitzgerald *et al.*, 1991), and the frameworks specific to SCM (SCOR and GSCF). They update a study conducted in 2000–2011 by analysing 27 journal articles and identify which systems and frameworks work best along multi-echelon supply chains and across national boundaries.

Adler *et al.* (Chapter 18) present a case study of AirAsia, a low-cost airline established in Malaysia, and the effect on the design of their PMS of following a hybrid strategy of cost leadership and differentiation. From prior research based on contingency theory, they argue that strategy is a key determinant of PMS design. The case study gives an insight into how one player in the highly competitive world of the airline industry adopted a PMS to fit their 'new world' carrier strategy. They point to the trendy and informal culture of the company and its use of social media as part of the 'people's airline' image it sought to foster. They found that the collaborative culture, flat organisational structure, team-based incentives and interactive planning systems combined to enable AirAsia to perform well (as shown by operational performance measures for 2008–2012) despite tough competition.

Gooneratne and Hoque (Chapter 19) present a comparative analysis of two banks under different types of ownership (public and private) in their case study of management control systems. They adopt an actor network theory approach to examine the extensive interview data they collected from a cross section of organisational members. Their cross-case comparison presented in Table 19.1 (page 339) showing the internal actors, external forces, use of management control information and future direction shows that despite the difference in ownership and need for external legitimacy of the state-owned bank, both banks rely on traditional budgetary control mechanisms rather than balanced scorecards or more innovative PMS.

Jarvis (Chapter 20) examines the literature on PMS in small and medium size entities (SMEs), using a European Commission definition (employees, turnover and balance sheet value) of an SME. He notes the neglect of SMEs in performance management textbooks and research. Other authors in this volume have pointed out the need to align PMS with organisational strategies, and case study researchers tend to examine PMC practice in the specific context of the organisation being studied. Thus, the context and strategic goals of

SMEs (personal motives of owner–managers) that may be more concerned with survival and sustainability than growth and profitability would be expected to shape their PM practice. Jarvis found that a typical performance measure revealed in a grounded theory-based study of micro-entities was the concept of 'busyness' – an interesting yardstick.

Mattimoe and Tivnan's study (Chapter 21) on PMC in hotel management is set in the economically important hospitality industry in Ireland. The chapter provides an extensive review of generic and industry-specific literature enriched by empirical evidence from a small-scale survey. They find that in theory, there are numerous measures and several sources of external benchmarking data that hotels can use in their PMS. However, it seems likely that only the large hotel chains use multiple measures in more sophisticated dashboards. They found that a small number of mainly revenue-based performance measures are actually used by the sample of small- and medium-sized hotels that responded to their survey. Measures such as average room rate and occupancy (a measure of 'busyness') were monitored on a daily basis.

Chenhall *et al.* (Chapter 22) consider the design of PMS in non-governmental organisations (NGOs) where the organisational goals are typically non-financial, i.e. humanitarian or social welfare objectives, and may be ambiguous or conflicting. The size and structure of NGOs varies, but they share common factors such as the need to preserve social capital and the mobilisation of volunteer workers, which bring different challenges to the design of PMS. The chapter explores how these challenges might be met by NGOs, drawing on two specific case organisations studied by Chenhall *et al.* in Australia and the UK. The key to success for PMS in NGOs appears to be an acknowledgement and respect for the plurality of personal values and beliefs of the people who are vital to the effectiveness of the programmes and the ability to demonstrate effective use of resources to funders and donors.

Heath *et al.* (Chapter 23) also examine PMS in a social welfare–oriented organisation, but in the English ambulance service (public sector) where performance measurement is a critical element of new public management and governance. The changing role of the paramedic in the ambulance service, especially the emergency care practitioners, has impacted on how services are delivered and therefore how outcomes should be measured. Heath *et al.* employ Simons' levers of control in their analysis of the new PMS. The adoption of a 'top-down' dashboard in the service at a time when 'quality accounts' are demanding 'bottom-up' reporting to be scrutinised by the National Audit Office has produced interesting results.

Seneviratne and Hoque (Chapter 24) present the results of a structured literature review of research on management control systems in public-sector universities. They analyse a total of 48 relevant papers published in 18 accounting and management journals from the commencement of those journals (mostly after 2000) up to 2015. They also list in Appendix 24.1 (page 452) a further 13 journals that might have been expected to publish such articles, but did not. Of the 48 papers, they highlight 20 that were focussed on performance (systems generally, balanced scorecard specifically or appraisal schemes). More than half of all papers were based on qualitative research, but less than half identified any explicit theory. They conclude that these papers have made a significant contribution to management accounting literature, but identify growing potential for further studies (e.g. building on the university case study in Chapter 10).

Part IV: PMC research: the lens through which PMC may be viewed

This section is not intended to cover the full range of possible methodologies that may be used to research PMC as there are sufficient research methods texts available that already do that job, some extremely well. In the specific fields of accounting (Humphrey and Lee, 2004) and management (Thorpe and Holt, 2008), there are contributions from some of the authors of chapters in this volume. It is not the editor's intention to advocate particular research approaches. However, in compiling this volume, the opportunity has been taken to include two chapters by experienced researchers that provide a thoughtful explanation of how PMC research may be conducted in a qualitative paradigm. They offer insights into how the 'story' may be told and what the respective roles of interviewees and researchers are in collecting and presenting fieldwork evidence. It is hoped that these two chapters will encourage future researchers to be more reflexive on their own as well as their participants' practice.

Seal (Chapter 25) makes a case for adopting an actor-reality perspective (ARP) to bridge the theory practice gap in management control research. ARP, a conceptual framework based on facts, values, logics and communication, is differentiated from actor network theory (ANT) as the actors are all human, where ANT has both human and non-human 'actants'. ARP operationalises a different form of constructivism, recognising organisational members as knowledgeable individuals who can sense 'what works' and provide a pragmatic narrative. Seal offers an illustration of using an ARP research design, arguing how this leads to a richer picture of Simons' (1995) levers of control at work in the hospitality industry than might otherwise have been found.

De Loo and Lowe (Chapter 26) deal with the role of the researcher in interpretive research and use two recent papers as examples where the authors appear to see the results they report from their interviews quite differently. In one, De Loo and Lowe argue that the authors portray their interpretation of the evidence from interviews as if it were objective and may be expected to represent the interviewees' views and narrative (implicitly assuming the researcher to be neutral). In the second example, they find that the authors deal more explicitly with how they interpreted the interviews and acknowledge their own role in the interpretation of the evidence. This provides a useful lesson for (would be) interpretive researchers. The penultimate chapter (27) by Broadbent also offers a view of some of the problems of conducting research on PMC and argues for a relational approach to research that may actually help organisations to improve their practice. In this way, Broadbent argues that research should have a positive impact on the practices studied, rather than simply making observations or generating theories for an academic audience. She then turns her attention to the transactional approach taken in the way that research is assessed in the UK research excellence framework (REF) and finds this measurement of impact to be dysfunctional as a PMS in terms of the unintended consequences it has produced.

Finally, Berry and Harris (Chapter 28) summarise the key milestones in the developing field of PMC research, presenting references to some seminal work in chronological order (Appendix 28.2, page 511). They then offer tips and advice for researchers embarking on new journeys of discovery, from their own and their Management Control Association (MCA)[1] colleagues' experience of working in this field.

Note

1 www.managementcontrolassociation.ac.uk

References

Berry, A. J., Capps, T., Cooper, D., Ferguson, P., Hopper, T. and Lowe, E. A. (1985) Management control in an area of the NCB: rationales of accounting practices in a public enterprise. *Accounting, Organizations and Society* 10 (1), 3–28.

Berry, A. J., Coad, A. F., Harris, E. P., Otley, D. T. and Stringer, C. (2009) Emerging themes in management control: a review of recent literature. *The British Accounting Review* 41, 2–20.
Ferreira, A. and Otley, D. A. (2009) The design and use of management control systems: an extended framework for analysis. *Management Accounting Research* 20, 263–282.
Fitzgerald, L., Johnston, R., Brignall, T. J., Silvestro, R. and Voss, C. (1991) *Performance Measurement in Service Businesses*, London: The Chartered Institute of Management Accountants.
Humphrey, C. and Lee, B. (Eds.) (2004) *The Real Life Guide to Accounting Research: A Behind-the-Scenes View of Using Qualitative Research Methods*, Kiddlington: Elsevier.
Kaplan, R. S. and Norton, D. P. (1992) The balanced scorecard: measures that drive performance. *Harvard Business Review* 70 (1) (January–February), 71–79.
Lynch, R. L. and Cross, K. F. (1991) *Measure Up – The Essential Guide to Measuring Business Performance*, London: Mandarin.
Simons, R. (1995) *Levers of Control: How Managers Use Innovative Control Systems to Drive Strategic Renewal*, Boston, MA: Harvard Business School Press.
Thorpe, R. and Holt, R. (Eds.) (2008) *The Sage Dictionary of Qualitative Management Research*, London: Sage.

Part I

Design of performance management and control systems

2

Management control systems

Theory and lessons from practice

David Dugdale

Introduction

This chapter begins with a review of contemporary theoretical contributions to management control theory. The specific aim is to show that overall goals and strategy, linked to performance measurement and target-setting, with further linking to rewards and incentives, permeate much of the management control literature. Three case studies are then described and their implications for theory discussed. In these cases, senior managers have consciously chosen *not* to set operational targets, and there are no incentives based on short-term operational performance. To some extent, the strategic concerns of senior managers are "decoupled" from the operating concerns of middle managers. It is concluded that for some companies, theory overemphasises the importance of linking organisational vision and goals through strategy and planning to the setting of targets, performance evaluation and incentives.

Berry *et al.* (2009: 6) identified that "three models of integrated performance management systems [that] have emerged in the literature: strategic performance measurement systems (SPMS) like Kaplan and Norton's balanced scorecard; Simons' levers of control; and Ferreira and Otley's performance management and control framework" (see Figure 9.1). These, together with Stern Stewart's economic value added (EVA), another theoretical contribution that has been taken seriously by major companies, are reviewed in the next section. It will be shown that a top-down approach to control and performance management is a theme that runs through all four performance management frameworks.

The Ferreira and Otley framework (see Figure 9.1) was useful in guiding interviews in the case companies and the three cases are set out below under headings loosely drawn from this framework. The chapter provides a comparative analysis of the three cases showing that although the three companies pay attention to overall aims, strategies and key success factors, they do not translate these into detailed performance targets. In the discussion and conclusion, it is argued that the performance frameworks discussed in the chapter understate the importance of social and cultural controls and fail to recognise that it can be advantageous to decouple strategic and operational control systems.

Management control theory

Historical context

Textbooks have often compared management control systems with mechanical models such as heating systems that control temperature by activating and deactivating a boiler in response to comparison between measured temperature and a preset, desired temperature level. This is feedback control where comparison between actual results is compared to preset plans and standards and deviations result in corrective action. This treatment of control can be traced back at least to the development of standard costing and budgeting in the early twentieth century, and these techniques have been widely adopted. Feedback control implies measurement–comparison–action, and this principle remains at the centre of much management control theory.

Strategic performance management

Strategic performance management systems, the best-known being the balanced scorecard, emerged as a response to perceived shortcomings in budget-based control systems. Budgeting had been criticised because a "budget-constrained" style can lead to unfortunate managerial behaviour and, in addition, overemphasis on *financial* performance became a major theme in the 1990s. Johnson and Kaplan (1987) had already called for more emphasis on forward-looking, non-financial measures, and Kaplan and Norton's (1992) balanced scorecard introduced three non-financial dimensions of performance: customers, internal processes, and learning and growth, that "balanced" the financial dimension. Kaplan and Norton (1992) set out a template that linked vision and strategy to actions in each of the dimensions through the identification of objectives, measures, targets and initiatives.

Kaplan and Norton (1996a) recommend that the vision and mission should be translated into "an integrated set of objectives and measures" (p. 4) with "ambitious goals" that guide resource allocation and priorities so as to further long-term strategic objectives. Feedback and learning then encourage "strategic learning" across all four dimensions of the scorecard. The development of the balanced scorecard follows in the tradition of feedback control but includes non-financial as well as financial measures and emphasises the importance of leading indicators such as market share and product innovation as well as lagging indicators such as financial results.

Subsequently, Kaplan and Norton (1996b, 2001, 2004) concentrated on the use of "strategy maps" in formulating a balanced scorecard and the importance of aligning and focusing resources on strategic priorities. They now emphasised the linkages between improving internal processes so as to meet customer needs more effectively and so deliver improved financial performance. However, this did not diminish the emphasis on identifying (strategy-driven) measures and setting targets for these. Strategy should be cascaded and disseminated from the corporate level, and "When individuals can construct their own Balanced Scorecards, then we have produced the clearest mechanism for aligning individual objectives to business unit and corporate objectives" (Kaplan and Norton, 2001: 244). Rewards and incentives receive little attention, although Kaplan and Norton report that companies they studied had either linked scorecard performance to rewards or were planning to do so. They concluded that "When all the individuals understand how their pay is linked to achieving strategic objectives ... strategy truly becomes everyone's day job" (pp. 270–271).

The balanced scorecard emerged from a year-long study of companies that were concerned to expand their performance reporting beyond the traditional emphasis on finance. This brief review shows how the balanced scorecard achieves this. It is taken for granted that strategy should drive operational measures and targets, that dissemination should be driven down through the organisation and the cycle of feedback control be completed by reporting versus targets.

The balanced scorecard is not the only strategic performance management system, and following its success, other models were also proposed such as the performance prism (Neely *et al.*, 2002). The performance prism expands the number of stakeholders to include, amongst others, employees, suppliers and regulators, and considers the development of strategies to not only meet their needs but also to ensure that they contribute to the organisation. Stakeholder contributions are to be transformed through organisational capabilities, processes and strategies into stakeholder satisfaction. Identifying the right measures is a key theme, and the "Measures Definition Template" (p. 35) lists the characteristics that should be considered for each measure: purpose, relates to, metric/formula, target level(s), frequency, source of data, who measures, who acts on the data (owner), and what do they do. Measurement, target-setting and feedback control are again central, and the authors set out to show how these principles can be applied to the management of relationships with investors, customers, employees, suppliers, regulators and the community.

Economic value added

If the balanced scorecard and its derivatives emphasise the importance of expanding the scope of performance management to include non-financial measures, Stern Stewart pursued a very different course in resurrecting the residual income measure as "economic value added", a single, clear (financial) measure that, they claimed, would align the interests of managers with those of shareholders. They argued that the first duty of a company is to create value for its shareholders, and in so doing, it would also serve wider society. The EVA calculation is more comprehensive than other financial metrics such as the price/earnings ratio and, mathematically, is consistent with the net present value calculation recommended for the appraisal of investment opportunities.

Stern Stewart marketed EVA as much more than a metric for evaluating businesses and guiding investment decisions: "EVA[1] must be coupled with a powerful change to management processes, including planning, portfolio management, strategic and tactical decision making, and compensation strategy" (Pettit, 2001). The aim is to cascade the use of EVA throughout the organisation so that all business units and profit centres are working towards the maximisation of EVA. The feedback loop is closed by linking managers' compensation to performance:

> Targets for compensation systems need to be derived from the long-term strategy and should not be renegotiated annually. The overall goal for each compensation system must be participation in true value creation; for example, measured by improvement in economic profit. Targets should be set in a top-down manner for each division and annual targets should be derived from the company's long-term target.
>
> *(Bischof et al., 2010: 6)*

The use of a "bonus bank" is intended to ensure that gaming is minimised and bonuses are linked to *long-term* economic performance. This is achieved by basing the bonus on comparison of EVA achieved versus target but paying out only a portion of any abnormal bonus in the year it is "earned". If there is poor performance, a negative bonus reduces the balance carried forward.

EVA systems are very different from the scorecard systems discussed in the previous section, but they again illustrate the importance of defining measures, setting targets, comparing performance to target and, especially, linking rewards to performance through a sophisticated remuneration scheme. Although the EVA system is intended to cascade targets throughout the organisation, Bischof *et al.* (2010) caution against embedding these in annual budgets. Instead, they recommend that the incentive target should be linked to the long-term organisational EVA target. Managers can then agree on budget stretch targets without these having an unfortunate impact on subsequent bonus payments.

Simons' levers of control

Another theoretical contribution that has had considerable impact is Simons' (1995) "Levers of Control". Based on a 10-year study of control systems in many US businesses, Simons was surprised to find that "the most innovative companies used their profit planning and control systems more intensively than did their less innovative counterparts" (p. ix). He concluded that successful organisations had achieved balance between four modes of control which he characterised as diagnostic, interactive, boundary and beliefs systems.

Diagnostic systems "are the backbone of traditional management control ... Three features distinguish diagnostic control systems: (1) the ability to measure the outputs of a process, (2) the existence of predetermined standards against which actual results can be compared, and (3) the ability to correct deviations from standards" (p. 59).

Interactive systems "provide frameworks, or agendas, for debate, and motivate information gathering outside of routine channels". Simons goes on to explain that an interactive system is "*not* a unique type of control system: many types of control systems can be used interactively by senior managers" (p. 96). Interactive systems are needed when businesses face competitive environments, and it is important to stimulate new ideas and experimentation throughout the organisation.

Boundary systems "delineate the acceptable domain of activity for organizational participants" (p. 39). Simons sees boundary systems as defining (and preventing) unacceptable behaviours such as accepting valuable gifts or contravening accounting standards.[2] Operational boundaries become especially important when there is high uncertainty and/or high performance pressure. Strategic boundaries can also be important and are "usually imposed when excessive search behaviour and experimentation have risked dissipating the firm's resources" (p. 48). Boundary systems are important in balancing both diagnostic systems that can generate performance pressure and interactive systems that can stimulate (excessive) search and experimentation.

Beliefs systems provide "basic values, purpose, and direction for the organization" (p. 34). Simons tends to equate beliefs systems with formal vision and mission statements that senior managers communicate formally and systematically throughout the organisation.

Simons himself emphasised that interactive "systems" are actually *uses* of the control system, and Tessier and Otley (2012) continued the analysis by pointing out that diagnostic and interactive "systems" are *uses*, boundary "systems" are a *purpose* and beliefs systems are a *type* of control system. This leads Tessier and Otley to reframe Simons' analysis differentiating purpose into performance and compliance; use into strategic and operational issues; and type into social and technical controls. Simons' classification has the merit of having been inductively derived by the study of how managers actually use their "levers of control", but Tessier and Otley force a more rigorous conceptualisation of Simons' ideas.

Tessier and Otley draw attention to two *types* of management control, and organisation theory has long recognised a major distinction between *technical* and *social* controls. Technical systems are linked to "scientific" management emphasising process analysis, specialisation, standardisation, clear job descriptions and lines of authority. This contrasts with the "human relations" school that relies on human interaction for coordination and control. Pugh (2007) refers to the dilemma of organisation theory because "organizers" and "behaviouralists" are both right: while organisation is necessary, it can lead to rigidity and apathy, and although interpersonal coordination and control can be highly motivating, it may be inefficient.

Simons' diagnostic and beliefs systems are readily categorised as technical and social systems, respectively (though organisational theory sees "social controls" as more wide-ranging, including social norms, culture and shared values as well as top-management-driven vision and mission statements). Both technical, diagnostic systems and social, beliefs systems can be used interactively to foster interaction and communication. Similarly, both technical and social control systems can be used to set boundaries: technical systems can make acceptable/unacceptable behaviour more explicit (for example through budgetary and authorisation limits), while social controls can help to shape a culture that is acceptable to wider society.

The Ferreira and Otley framework

The Ferreira and Otley (2009) performance management framework (see Figure 9.1) can be traced to Otley's (1999) framework that comprised five key questions relating to (1) organisational objectives and their evaluation; (2) strategies, plans and activities and how they are assessed and measured; (3) performance targets for the areas raised in (1) and (2); (4) rewards and penalties for achievement or failure to achieve the targets; and (5) feedback and feedforward loops so that the organisation can learn from experience and adapt behaviour in the light of that experience.

Otley (1999) "tested" the framework against three control systems: budgeting, the balanced scorecard and EVA. He concluded that none of these provide a *comprehensive* performance management system. Budgetary control concentrates only on financial objectives, does not consider links between means and ends, and does not explicitly consider rewards (although bonuses are often linked to budget-based targets). EVA has just a single financial objective, and it does not consider the link between means and ends, although appropriate incentive schemes are central to the method. The balanced scorecard considers both financial and non-financial performance measures that emerge from strategy but does not address how targets should be set or rewards structured.

Otley's analysis implicitly presumes that a management control system "should" address all the relevant issues: objectives, strategies, targets, feedback and rewards/penalties. While budgeting, EVA and the balanced scorecard provide valuable insights, none delivers a *comprehensive* system of control.

Otley found the framework useful when investigating performance management systems and, with Ferreira, developed it further, expanding the number of questions to 12 (Ferreira and Otley, 2009, see Figure 9.1). There are eight functional questions:

1 What is the vision and mission and how is it communicated?
2 What are the organisation's key success factors?
3 What strategies and plans and associated processes and activities are adopted?

4 What is the organisation structure and how does it affect strategy and the control?
5 What key performance indicators are derived from objectives and strategy?
6 What target performance is required in each of the above areas?
7 How is individual, group and organisational performance evaluated, what formal and informal information is used for this and with what consequences?
8 What rewards and penalties follow from meeting or failing to meet performance targets?

Broadbent and Laughlin (2009) pointed out that four of these questions (1, 2, 5, and 6) relate to ends and four relate to means (3, 4, 7, and 8). In addition to these eight functional questions, there are four further questions that concentrate on characteristics of the control system: feedback and feedforward information flows, uses of the system, how rapidly it changes and strength of the links between system components.

Collier (2005) used a longitudinal study of management control in an entrepreneurial organisation to evaluate the Simons and Ferreira and Otley frameworks (see Figure 9.1) and found Simons' framework more useful because social controls and boundary systems were important in his case. The Ferreira and Otley framework was "less helpful", although useful in drawing attention to the use of the performance management system, changes over time, and the strength and coherence of links in the performance management system. For Collier, "both Simons, and Ferreira and Otley ... pay too little attention to belief systems or, more precisely to socio-ideological (Ditillo, 2004) forms of control" (p. 337).

Ferreira and Otley (2009) responded to Collier's comments on an earlier draft of their framework by pointing out that the framework explicitly considers vision, mission, key success factors, strategies, plans and organisation structure, and these, "at the very least, influence belief systems, boundary systems or both" (p. 277). They add that as Collier's study focused on understanding the relationships between formal and informal controls, his conclusions were not unexpected. Ferreira and Otley nevertheless acknowledge that the framework may give the impression that its focus is on diagnostic and interactive systems (rather than on beliefs and boundary systems). While the framework can, no doubt, be used to uncover both formal and informal management controls, the Ferreira and Otley framework suggests rational, administrative control that links success factors through strategy and structure to performance targets, evaluation and rewards/penalties.

Discussion of contemporary control theory

This overview demonstrates the importance, in contemporary theory, of linking strategy to performance measurement and target-setting and, often, to rewards and incentives. Feedback control against targets is fundamental to budgeting and standard costing systems; targets for performance measures in each of the key dimensions are the means of converting strategy to performance in the balanced scorecard and the performance prism; the EVA target devolved throughout the organisation and linked to an incentive scheme is the essence of the Stern Stewart recommendation; and the Ferreira and Otley framework explicitly looks for links and feedback between strategy, performance measures, targets and rewards.

Simons' four "levers" of control is broader and explicitly recognises social control through the introduction of beliefs systems. However, the assumption that beliefs can be cascaded by senior managers using devices such as mission statements underplays the role of culture, social norms and peer pressure as informal controls. To some extent, Simons meets this criticism with his "interactive systems" that provide for communication throughout the organisation, although, even here, he tends to take a senior management perspective: "Some managers term these systems their 'personal hot buttons' … [to] … focus attention and force dialogue throughout the organization" (p. 96).

These performance management frameworks have widened the scope of management control considerably, both "horizontally" to include much more than just financial measures and "vertically" to link strategy through to operational performance and rewards. However, the emphasis is often on the importance of rational links, "stretch" targets and alignment of rewards with performance against these targets. In the following sections, three cases will be reviewed and some conclusions drawn about possible deficiencies in the "target-driven" management style that is endemic in much management control literature. First, however, it is acknowledged that theorists are well aware of the problems that control systems can create.

Control and dysfunctional behaviour

Neely *et al.* (2002) provide examples of the ways that measures and targets can lead to unfortunate behaviour. For example, one airline traced delays to (1) the gate (all passengers not checked in on time), (2) baggage handling (all bags not loaded on time), (3) cabin cleaning (failure to clean the aircraft on time), (4) flight attendants (failure to seat all passengers on time) and so on. The consequence was miscoding of delays due to the weather, air traffic control and external factors in general, while, paradoxically, there was *less* focus on the customer, as one employee observed: "Here … the ultimate goal is not the customers. It's the report card. You spend so much time filling out delay forms and fighting over a delay" (p. 43). Another example is drawn from the drinks industry. Glenmorangie, a whisky distiller, provided performance-related bonus incentives based on pushing products into the market. Unfortunately, the measure used was shipments to its local distributor, and its sales manager was therefore incentivised to ship as much as possible *to the distributor.* Senior management eventually discovered: "16,000 12-bottle cases of whisky … languishing undrunk in the distributor's warehouse" (p. 116).

A key aim of Stern Stewart's EVA is to overcome the problems associated with accounting-based measures such as earnings per share. Erhbar[3] (1998: 67) refers to the "cult of earnings per share" and cites ConAgra as a company that concentrated on this measure, even boasting in its 1997 annual report that "17 consecutive years of earnings per share growth at a compound rate better than 14% is unequalled by any major food company in the United States, and probably anywhere in the world. [However] … ConAgra had to fiddle the numbers to create the illusion of steadily increasing earnings". The fine print of the accounts disclosed the omission of a number of charges in the calculation of earnings per share. Erhbar goes on to note that there can be more substantive consequences. In a nice echo of the Glenmorangie example, he refers to the "common practice of … trade loading or channel stuffing. This refers to shipping unwanted merchandise to distributors and wholesalers near the end of a quarter in order to bolster reported sales and earnings, even though the final demand for the goods isn't there" (p. 68). Erhbar's examples highlight degrees of culpability from "fiddling" the accounting numbers as at ConAgra, to "channel stuffing" to, in extreme cases, outright fraud, for example: "A disk-drive manufacturer called Miniscribe filed for bankruptcy in 1990 after directors discovered that the company had literally been shipping bricks to distributors" (p. 68).

Otley (2003) recounted his early experiences working in the UK National Coal Board where managers would report production as being on budget throughout the week (thus avoiding awkward questions) with a "correcting" report at the end of the week. Also, if there was overproduction, there was a temptation to "hold back" some coal in the mine so as to make it easier to meet the target in the following week. Another example related to the optimum size of the transport fleet where calculations had indicated that a reduction in the size of the fleet from 60 to 50 vehicles was desirable. This was resisted by the transport manager, but it was only later discovered that this was probably motivated by the remuneration system: management of 55 vehicles or more meant a higher salary scale.

Simons (1995) discusses the difficulty, in diagnostic systems, of finding satisfactory measures. He noted that subjective measures need a high degree of trust, while objective measures run into different problems: an incomplete measure such as the number of sales calls per day can lead to dysfunctional behaviour as calls are maximised but large, important customers are ignored while a more "complete" measure such as earnings or economic profit subsumes so much activity that it is unlikely to be responsive to individual efforts or actions.

Three cases

Introduction

In this section, three cases will be described, all based on existing literature/presentations supplemented by interviews. The cases are drawn from a wider study that takes "Beyond Budgeting" as its theme and the interviews were undertaken by the author and a PhD student, Tauheed Ali. A modified version of the Ferreira and Otley framework (see Figure 9.1) was used to guide the interviews, and this framework therefore provides a common template for description of the cases. The cases are described individually, and then a further section provides a comparative cross-case analysis.

The examples were chosen because, in each case, managers expressed significant doubts about the use of targets to drive behaviour and generally felt that target-based incentive payments are counterproductive. In the previous section, it was concluded that although there was awareness of the dysfunctional behaviour targets and associated incentives could generate, there were nevertheless sound reasons for translating strategy into operational targets. In these cases, we will see that managers have consciously chosen *not* to create localised targets, preferring, instead, to decouple (to some extent) the strategic choices of senior managers from the operational concerns of middle and junior managers.

Case study 1 Manufacturing

Introduction

The first case is based on the book *Only Trends Matter* (Willcox, 2013) and an interview with the author (Willcox, 2014). The major theme of the book is that management accounting information, usually based on comparison of revenues and costs with budgeted month and year-to-date figures, is not as helpful as it might be. Willcox, a qualified accountant and CEO of a medium-sized engineering company, observed that board meetings often "degenerated into cross-questioning over historic variances from budget, and these discussions often became a witch hunt (much to the suppressed pleasure of those not under the spotlight)" (p. xxxiii).

Dissatisfied with his experience, Willcox (2013) asked managers how they would like information to be presented and found an overwhelming preference for graphical methods. Over a period of years, the management accounting department developed and tested a graphical presentation that combined graphs of historical month-by-month actual results with forecasts. The format included the previous and current years' actual results together with a forecast for the balance of the current year and the next financial year. The presentation therefore always included 3 years' actual/forecast data and avoided the common practice of losing valuable historical data by "wiping the slate clean" at the end of each financial year. The graphs were based on rolling annual totals, thus making long-run trends in the data plainly visible. The use of rolling annual totals had the added advantage, in this company, of eliminating seasonality from the trend data: particularly important in a company that supplied the construction industry where winter weather could easily affect sales.

Figure 2.1 illustrates the graphical presentation using some of the author's household spending as an example.

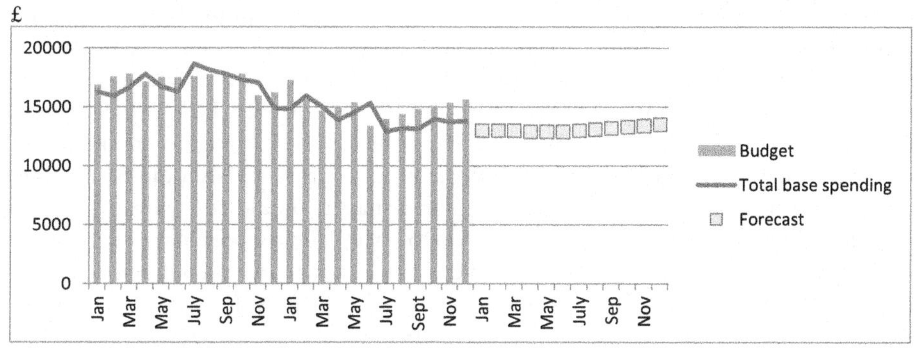

Figure 2.1 Household expenditure 2012–13, budgets 2012, 2013 and forecast 2014

Much of the book deals with the lessons learned in developing the graphical presentation of information, and Willcox explains how both actual and budget rolling totals should be calculated, which costs should be included in the rolling totals and how forecasting should be undertaken in order to reduce both optimistic and pessimistic biases. These issues are all interesting. However, the purpose, here, is to consider the impact of the revised presentation on the use of indicators and targets in the company.

Trends instead of targets for cost control

As the title of the book suggests, financial trends became a key focus of attention and the graphical presentations led to a very effective form of cost control. For each cost category, the annual moving total and its percentage of the annual moving total of revenue were charted and the latter compared with net profit as a percentage of revenue. Willcox refers to net profit as the "anchor point" in monitoring and controlling cost structure, and by tracking trends, it becomes clear whether net profit margin is improving or deteriorating and why. An example is presented where net profit margin falls from 10 per cent to 8 per cent, and the charts show increased material cost of sales percentage, rising from 13.5 per cent to 15 per cent and increased cost of external sales, rising from 15 per cent to 17 per cent. These are partially offset by the cost of administration, which fell from 7 per cent to 6 per cent, and the cost of accommodation, which fell from

(*Continued*)

11 per cent to 10 per cent. This sort of information, revealing trends in both absolute figures and cost structure percentages, became a vital aid to analysis and control.

The budget was still reported and shown on the graphs. However, comparisons to the budget were no longer the primary focus of cost control. Instead, an adverse trend in either absolute revenues/costs or costs as percentage of revenue quickly raised questions. Willcox added that even a rising trend, for example in sales of a new product, would give rise to action as the gradient became less steep, and it became clear that revenue was reaching its peak. The point is that although a budget was prepared, it was no longer central to cost control and neither budgets nor targets were needed in order to exercise control; simply examining graphical information was sufficient.

Key success factors and performance indicators

It was noted, in the previous section, that targets can lead to unintended (unfortunate) consequences. However, Willcox still thought it very important to identify key success factors and key performance indicators (KPIs), and he devotes a chapter in his book to the topic of non-financial performance indicators. However, he is not concerned with the "correct" indicators (which are dependent on industry and company) but on the manner in which they are used. Willcox argues that KPIs should be designed for different levels of management, and senior managers should concentrate on a few important indicators, resisting the temptation to "help" their subordinates by trying to solve operational problems. This provides our first example of "decoupling" the concerns of top management from those of operational managers. It is clear that Willcox expected junior managers to be free to solve operational problems *without* concerning themselves with meeting a plethora of imposed performance targets.

As an example, Willcox refers to one of his divisions that emphasised next-day, guaranteed delivery, and in order to monitor performance, the board now simply received notification of any instance of failure the following morning. Willcox compares this with the previous approach where "failures were reported by reason, lack of stock, goods lost in transit, staff shortage, showed in the stock records but not on the shelf, couldn't locate the customer, weather and so on" (p. 188). Top management did not have the time to take the right corrective action, and when they tried, they got it wrong and undermined responsible managers as well. "This task was the responsibility of those staff dealing with the issues every day and all that was needed from top management was to empower them to deal with it" (pp. 188–189).

Willcox emphasises the importance of matching the performance indicators to the degree of detail needed by the manager. When interviewed, he recalled that in his company, senior management concentrated on just a few KPIs: enquiries, conversion of enquiries to orders, revenue, net profit and margin percentages together with, of course, next-day delivery.

We asked whether KPIs were an input to or an output from the budgeting process. Willcox said that most indicators were neither. He used to chair meetings of middle managers where performance across a range of indicators was reviewed. The important issue was not whether indicators were "on target" but whether they were improving or not. This was not a simple matter because improvement in, for example, delivery might mean higher inventory. Willcox had to be involved because of inter-departmental interaction between indicators, which meant that individual directors could not easily adjudicate between completing claims.

Willcox makes an important point in relation to *presentation* of KPIs, suggesting that they be presented graphically, like the management accounts and across the same timescale. This presentation makes it possible to see whether a change in the trend of an indicator is leading to consequences for other indicators or financial results: it facilitates understanding of causality. This was most important in the relation between "new contract awards" in the construction industry, enquiries received and conversion of these enquiries into orders. This information became critical in the preparation of the quarterly forecasts.

Organisation and culture

In his interview responses, Willcox displayed slightly "old-fashioned" attitudes in that he felt clear (hierarchical) accountabilities were important and budgeting was desirable in that it gave the owners the opportunity to engage with company managers and for an agreement to be reached as to what was expected in the coming year. However, it was also clear that Willcox's management style involved making expectations clear but then allowing local managers the scope to deliver without undue interference from more senior managers. The graphical information generated by the management accountants was freely available, and a relatively open style was exemplified by the senior managers' decision to give up their offices (as they had been encouraging others to do), making themselves more obviously visible and available.

Incentives

There is little on the subject of incentives in *Only Trends Matter*, so we asked about this during the interview. During his career, Willcox had tried a variety of incentive schemes including personal targets, departmental targets and combinations of shared and personal targets, and had not been happy with the results. Targets could be set for some departments and individuals but not for others, and this caused dissent, jealousy and bad feeling.

When Willcox was appointed CEO in the early 1990s, the company was in trouble; recession in the construction industry had led to losses, and redundancies were necessary. Those that remained had to accept a wage freeze, and in the circumstances, a promise was made that should the company make a profit in the future, everyone would receive a profit share proportional to salary. The owners had no reason to object "as the company wasn't making a profit anyway". Willcox felt that over the years, as the company became increasingly profitable, this profit-sharing scheme helped to build morale and put peer pressure on those perceived not to be pulling their weight.

Lessons from the case

The major lessons from this case are that (1) in this company, local targets (if they existed) were set by local managers and senior management concentrated simply on their overall key success factors, instigating action when these signalled it was needed; (2) cost control was achieved not by comparison to a fixed budget or target but dynamically by monitoring trends; and (3) there was a profit-sharing scheme that rewarded shared endeavour rather than individual performance. There are also lessons concerning the use of budgets, graphical presentation of information and forecasting, but these are not our primary focus.

Case study 2 Insurance

Introduction

This case is based on a presentation (Wilson, 2013)[4] to the Beyond Budgeting Round Table (BBRT) and a subsequent interview with the presenter (Wilson, 2014). Wilson described the (previous) operation of call centres at Aviva where a rather "mechanical" approach to call centre management involved setting targets for speed in responding to calls, length of call, number of calls handled and so on. Operators were provided with standardised scripts to guide them in their responses to customers. However, often customers did not know exactly which product was appropriate, and call centre staff had to work out the best course of action before advising the potential customer. Operators' attempts to meet the needs of the customer while simultaneously sticking to the prescribed script and also meeting performance targets led to poor customer service. Wilson traced the problem to Chase's (1978) recommendation that service industries could learn from manufacturing by separating areas with high customer contact, the "front office", from low customer contact "back office" functions.[5]

Prescriptions from a manufacturing environment where product and process are well specified do not transfer easily to services such as insurance call centres where there is uncertainty that cannot easily be eliminated, not least because the caller may not know exactly what they want. The attempt to specialise, with different functions concentrating on sales, renewals, queries, etc. was unsuccessful, especially when efficiency incentives were also employed. The solution was to remove targets and incentives and to encourage call centre staff to handle a wide range of customer calls.

Removal of targets

Wilson's presentation provided examples of the dysfunctional behaviour encouraged by standards, targets and incentives. The "best" staff (who earned the highest incentive payments) were adept in passing on unpromising calls quickly: they were really "best" at gaming the system. In slack periods, staff would ring in with "dummy" requests in order to increase call volume. These calls would be handled very quickly, thus reducing the average time per call. When interviewed, Wilson (2014) provided further examples. An operator with experience of sales switched to renewals. When a customer wanted a new policy (a "sale"), the customer was immediately referred – even though the operator knew how to handle the call. A sale would take longer than a renewal and the system drove the operator's response: to hand the call over as quickly as possible. (The customer might, of course, be lost during the transfer.) Another example related to "failure demand". For example, a customer might call because of a problem with an on-line application. Having no incentive to help the customer, the operator would try to handle the call as quickly as possible, or would start the application all over again so as to take the credit for a telephone sale.

Wilson argues that top-down, functionally specialised, standard-based work design, treating workers as cogs in the machine to be incentivised by bonus payments for meeting detailed targets, is inappropriate when the task is to provide a service to the customer. The solution was based on well-informed call centre staff able to handle the (considerable) variety in callers' requests. Targets and incentives for the number of calls handled were removed and staff empowered to discuss customer requirements and recommend solutions. The change involved focusing on meeting customer needs, even if these were time-consuming to identify and, although the change involved much more investment in staff and depended on reduced staff turnover, it was very successful, sales increased and there was a vast improvement in customer satisfaction.

Broader issues relate to timescales, linkages and targets. There are annual budgets, and the call centres negotiate for budget resources, trading off service levels against efficiency/utilisation. The resources appear to be sufficient given that improvements are possible in typical call centre practices and this resource redundancy effectively decouples the budgeting process from short-term call centre management based on rolling forecasts. Call centre resourcing is organised, more or less, against a 3-month timescale. In day-to-day operations, a specialised, target-driven culture has been replaced by a service-oriented, employee-empowered, team-based culture. The removal of targets has taken rigidities out of the system so that responses are much more flexible.

Organisation and culture

We asked how, without target-based incentives, individuals were now motivated. Wilson's reply was telling. He felt that those at the front line did not need to be motivated to do a better job; to them "systems thinking" was simply common sense. It was enough to have them concentrate on the purpose of their operation (meeting the customer's needs) and to encourage cooperation. Operators naturally bought into the new ethos and became keen to learn more and widen their experience so that they could better serve the customer. It was more difficult for managers who, naturally, wondered what their role would become if the old ways of working were swept away. Previously, they had focused on "output" with daily meetings to consider performance on the previous day, despite the probability that good and bad "performance" might be explained by normal statistical variation. In the new organisation, team leaders had a key role in supporting staff and in working on system problems.

Key performance indicators

In the interview, Wilson was sensitive about reference to "key performance indicators" because they are often closely associated with targets. The removal of targets for call centre operators has been a major consequence of "systems thinking" in Aviva. However, the removal of targets did not mean the removal of key indicators. In fact, there are many measures. In his presentation to the BBRT, Wilson mentioned: failure demand (calls made because of policy problems and queries), end-to-end process time, cost per claim, account queries, handoffs (percentage of calls passed on to another operative), percentage of calls dealt with by a single operator (first point resolution), percentage of customers that would recommend Aviva (net of those that would not), customer satisfaction score and employee satisfaction score. In addition to these higher-level indicators, there are other, lower-level, measures such as the number of calls handled and sales made per operator and by team.

It is clear that there is extensive measurement of performance, and Wilson drew a number of graphs showing typical behaviour for these measures. The graphs illustrated interrelationships, variability, trends and outliers. (1) Interrelationships arise because it is not clear whether, for example, it is good that an operative handles more calls.

(Continued)

It may be efficient, but if the volume of calls is driven by failure demand or, worse, operator gaming generating phantom demand, it is not a good indicator. Even if calls are driven by genuine (renewal or sales) demand, dealing with a high volume would not be good if the operator was handing off calls that he/she did not want to deal with or was being overzealous in handling sensitive issues (such as a death claim) or pushing services that were not in the best interests of the customer. (2) Service industries face considerable variability in terms of volume and type of demand on a day-to-day basis. In the face of this uncertainty, it is not sensible to hold day-to-day (or even week-to-week) inquests over "good" or "bad" performance. Control charts have reduced this sort of overreaction considerably. (3) Although Wilson was dismissive of targets, he was very conscious of the need to monitor trends. While setting a target was likely to be unhelpful, it was reasonable to see an upward trend in sales as good and an upward trend in complaints as bad. (4) The use of control charts also allows good and poor performers (outliers) to be identified. If an operator is scoring significantly less than average, then the team leader should spend some time with that individual; similarly, if someone is significantly better than average, then it provides an opportunity for others to learn from their methods.

Dealing with poor performance

With the removal of targets and associated incentives, it was not clear (to us) how control was exercised in the revised operations. Wilson explained that the removal of targets did not mean the removal of performance monitoring. Statistics provided an indication of whether an operator was performing better or worse than others: the basis for assessment is comparative performance (over a sufficiently long period to eliminate normal statistical variation). Having allowed for the trade-off between indicators and how much experience the operator has, it might, for example, be concluded that there is a "skills gap" that needs to be overcome. In these circumstances, the team leader would listen to a sample of calls take by the operator and identify any issues that needed to be addressed.

Incentives

There has been a huge change in the approach to incentives in call centres. There were prizes, such as crates of wine or iPods, for beating targets by significant margins. However, Wilson felt that these did not motivate, and much more important was *fear of failing* to achieve satisfactory performance. A low "score" against targets could mean disciplinary action and, eventually, job loss.

Short-term incentive payments have been removed, and operators now receive a fixed salary. However, new starters are evaluated after 3 and 6 months with higher rates of pay for satisfactory progression. In addition, there is an annual "corporate" bonus, devolved to teams. Despite this being based on overall company performance, team leaders are expected to determine how much will be paid to each individual, and Wilson was unhappy with this. For the majority that did not receive an incentive payment, it was a de-motivator, not a motivator; individual incentive payments were counterproductive because overall performance depended on a team effort; and finally, a good performer on a poor team might stand out and be awarded a higher bonus than a similar performer on a good team: a perverse incentive to join a poorly performing team.

Lessons from the case

The major lessons from this case are that (1) in service industries where customer requirements are intrinsically unpredictable, employing standard methods and targets can be counterproductive; (2) linking incentives based on "performance" against such standards exacerbates the problem; (3) elimination of targets does not mean elimination of measures, and comprehensive monitoring of trends is sufficient to achieve control; (4) staff will respond to a change in culture that empowers them to focus on customer service; and (5) such changes are not easily accomplished, the roles of middle managers changed dramatically, and for these staff, the changes were unsettling and sometimes difficult.

Case study 3 Banking

Introduction

This case is based on the extensive Svenska Handelsbanken[6] literature (Hope and Fraser, 2003; Wallander, 2003; Lindsay and Libby, 2007; Kroner, 2009), a presentation to the BBRT by the CEO of Handelsbanken UK, Anders Bouvin (2014) and interviews at the headquarters of Handelsbanken UK (Winder, 2014) and at a UK branch (Dibble, 2014a).

Handelsbanken is well known for radical decentralisation and for abandoning budgets. Probably equally important is its conservative banking philosophy, set out in some detail by Kroner (2009). Handelsbanken is an "old-fashioned" bank, lending only to creditworthy, trusted clients. Loans are almost always repaid, with only 0.05–0.1 per cent of loans written off as bad debts.[7] Handelsbanken did not need government bailouts in the Swedish financial crisis of 1991–1992 or the wider "credit crunch" crisis of 2007–2008. "Responsible" banking is almost anachronistic in the twenty-first century, and answering a question from an investor, Kroner (2009) found the chief executive's reply: "illuminating … he was running the bank so it would do well over the next hundred years and he would refuse to do anything that put this future at risk" (pp. 128–129).

Aims and values

Bouvin (2014) emphasised the bank's two key aims: to generate higher return on equity and more satisfied customers than its competitors.[8] He spelt out the principles that underpin the way the bank pursues these aims:

relative not absolute goals based on benchmarking;
relationships not transactions;
taking the long-term view;
prudence and financial stability;
responsible member of the community;
values not command and control.

(Continued)

Wallander (2003, 24) emphasised the long-term orientation: "What is good in the short term is not always good in the long term and vice versa. For example, if the goal is to increase sales volume it may after a while turn out that although the goal has been attained, the result has also been to gain customers who cause major losses" (this was written 5 years before the credit crunch of 2008).

Key success factors and absence of targets

The bank avoids steering mechanisms that could conflict with its aims. For example, there are no product targets or bonuses: "If there were a product target there could be a temptation to sell a product that does not meet customer needs. The same goes for incentives, a temptation to maximise personal reward at the expense of customer satisfaction" (Bouvin, 2014).

Dibble was also very clear that Handelsbanken does not set targets. He said that a target could easily become a minimum acceptable level and limit ambition. In subsequent correspondence, he enlarged on the issue: "perhaps the central point [is] that we cannot say what a reasonable target will look like over any given period of time. Market conditions change, customer needs will be whatever they are, and we simply must therefore be in the best position to serve these needs and seize market opportunities as they emerge. This is the main reason we don't have targets" (Dibble, 2014b).

Return on equity is important to the bank overall, and it is a key measure for regional banks. Capital is allocated to regions as required, bearing in mind the associated risks. In the branches, "RoE could have been used but the C/I [cost/income] ratio drives business better and is easy to explain" (Bouvin, 2014). The conservative philosophy runs through the bank, and the key measures, return on equity and cost/income ratios, reinforce the underlying philosophy. These measures are *ratios* that emphasise earnings *quality* not profit maximisation.

Winder made it clear just how important the C/I ratio is and the effort that is expended in ensuring that branches are correctly charged for services received. Handelsbanken may not have budgets, but enormous effort goes into ensuring that accounting information is available, accurate and credible. *All* costs are charged to branches, "a great way to keep costs to essential levels".

C/I ratios and cost control

Wallander (2003) explains that control is achieved through impersonal league tables comparing the performance of branches and regional banks to internal and external peer organisations. Some regional bank managers claimed that conditions for doing bank business in their part of Sweden were poor, but "The reply was that, if this was really so, their resources should be moved to more favourable regions. Interest in this type of criticism soon died out" (p. 68).

C/I ratios are important but must be interpreted carefully. The ratio can even be *too good*: implying that costs are too tight, possibly compromising customer service or good housekeeping. Dibble (2014a) noted that "objectivity" must not be allowed to override common sense and league tables must be used with care. For example, it is normal for branches to improve over time as business builds up, so comparisons are between branches of similar age.

The emphasis on branch performance puts a premium on rapid, accurate reporting and on "fair" cost allocations. Dibble thought that the performance culture might be perceived as "soft" because of the lack of forecasts and targets, but this is not so. There are "robust" information systems that permit the branch to see its profit and loss account for the previous day together with its latest balance sheet. Branch managers can see any significant change in either the profit and loss (P&L) or the balance sheet almost immediately it has happened. A key part of the system is its consistency. The system has been fundamentally unchanged since its introduction in the UK 10 years ago.

Decentralisation

When Wallander joined Handelsbanken in the early 1970s, one of his first actions was to close down the special group working on a "modern budget system" (Wallander, 2003). Instead, "steering" was achieved by making profit and loss accounts and balance sheets available to business units "as often as is practicable" (p. 67). Comparisons between branches and between regions encourage those that are below average and keep pressure on the rest. Wallander's (2003) book *Decentralisation – Why and How to Make It Work* emphasises both the importance of decentralisation and the difficulty of implementing it. Arguments to be overcome included the following: staff would be incapable of taking extra responsibility, there would be loss of control and decision-making would suffer. There was also considerable resistance from head office functions such as marketing, personnel and accounting. Wallander's experience shows how difficult it is to force through the delegation of authority, and "if one is to succeed, one needs a firm and clear goal and one has to begin at the top. One has to begin with oneself" (p. 40).

The bank's "organisation chart" envisages central functions supporting and underpinning the branches, and the philosophy of radical decentralisation is central. A large banner at the company's London-based UK headquarters reminds staff that "The Branch is the Bank", and although in a large organisation there may be a temptation to insert another layer of management, the flat structure is "sacrosanct" (Dibble, 2014a).

The decentralised structure is reinforced by an internal market whereby central staff functions have to "sell" their services to regions and branches. "Branches select a group of representatives to negotiate with the central departments. There is a formal system which allows these representatives to scrutinise central costs, to understand the 'keys' used for charging costs to branches and to negotiate with the central departments" (Bouvin, 2014). "Regional and branch managers have every right to challenge these costs and even reject them" (Hope and Fraser, 2003: 64).

The considerable autonomy enjoyed by branches means that strong control mechanisms are also needed – to identify if something is going wrong. If there are problems, the reaction is to engage with the person involved, to discuss the issues and to provide support and guidance (Bouvin, 2014).

Culture

Winder referred to a "consensual" internal management style with responsibility for results devolved throughout the organisation. The absence of budgets and competing objectives was important as was extensive training, job rotation and acceptance of the Handelsbanken approach. He did not think that managers would adopt an autocratic

(Continued)

style of management given the emphasis, throughout the company, on "consensual" (rather than command and control) management. A quote from Wallander (2003, 23) reinforces this: "it is a bank manager's main job to make sure that the people who work in his or her office think it is a pleasure to go to work every morning".

A question to Anders Bouvin concerned the consequences of the "competitive league tables": why would branches help each other? The answer related to the "strong culture" where there is an "enormous sense of ownership" and a desire for "everyone to succeed". Part of this was the absence of bonuses, "You can trust me on that one" (Bouvin, 2014).

Incentives

The Handelsbanken management model includes a well-publicised profit-sharing scheme based on the performance of the whole bank; individuals can access their share of profit at the age of 60, so "It is not intended to be an incentive for individuals to pursue financial targets rather, it is intended as a reward for their collective effort and success" (Hope and Fraser, 2003: 62). As Dibble (2014a) noted, "It doesn't matter who [which branch] has the customer".

The profit-sharing scheme started in 1973, and an employee share of profit was paid into a union-controlled foundation, Oktogenen. The company makes payments into the fund in years when its return on equity is better than its peer group's with one-third of the "excess" profit being paid into the fund. "Each and every full-time employee, regardless of salary and position, would receive the same share of profit" (Wallander, 2003, 73). In 2002, each long-serving retiree received a payment of $430,000 from Oktogenen!

The interviews confirmed that the profit-sharing scheme remains an integral part of the Handelsbanken way with equal participation for all staff based on years of service and access to their share of the fund at the age of 60. It was emphasised that the profit share is not intended to be a pension scheme or a replacement for a pension scheme[9] (as is sometimes mistakenly assumed).

Asked about incentives in the bank, Winder admitted that there was a small group of investment bankers (about 200 in the company's total of about 11,500 employees) that receive bonuses ("variable commission"). The company needs this expertise particularly for share placements, and it is necessary to make individual incentive payments to attract staff. Even Handelsbanken is not untouched by the general banking culture!

Lessons from the case

The major lessons from this case are as follows: (1) radical decentralisation can work so long as it is promulgated consistently, staff are carefully recruited and the company's philosophy is constantly reaffirmed; (2) empowering staff can be successful so long as they are well trained, responsible and there are strong systems to ensure that unethical behaviour or poor performance can be quickly identified; (3) avoidance of budgets for control and performance targets as incentives can avoid dysfunctional behaviour; and (4) performance comparisons through "league tables", a cooperative, supportive culture and a (very) long-term, egalitarian, profit-sharing scheme can encourage high performance.

Comparative analysis of the three cases

Objectives, strategies and key success factors

The three companies have objectives and strategies, and these are translated into key success factors and performance measures. Handelsbanken explicitly adopts return on capital employed and customer satisfaction as objectives. Aviva places a heavy emphasis on a range of financial objectives, especially cash flow but also stresses customer satisfaction and employee engagement. The manufacturing company operated as a profit centre within a larger group, and the aim was to deliver a profitable business. Handelsbanken's long-term strategies are radical decentralisation and conservative banking. In Aviva's (UK) call centres, the (emergent) strategy is to prioritise customer service. In the manufacturing company, the strategy was to target particular customer segments: in the construction industry, responsiveness is highly valued, and one company division guaranteed next-day delivery.

The three companies pay attention to customers and employees as well as to financial performance and develop performance indicators in these areas. Each company had a clear sense of direction, and strategies led to the identification of key success factors such as next-day delivery performance in the manufacturing company, and at Aviva, increasing attention is paid to the proportion of customers that would recommend the company to others. The strategies and key success factors are translated into a range of performance indicators.

Performance indicators and targets

Although they develop strategies and performance indicators, these companies *do not* set performance targets. We saw earlier that targets, especially when linked to incentives, can lead to unfortunate behaviour including holding back output, creating false demand, manipulating accounting results and even outright fraud. The absence of targets and related incentives in these companies removes perverse incentives. Interestingly, the reasons for the absence of targets were different in the three companies. Handelsbanken has, for several decades, held to the view that targets could easily foster short-termism and opportunism. In Aviva's call centres, it was realised that attempting to dissect inherently uncertain customer demand into a target-driven process was counterproductive; customers often did not know what they wanted, so how could "standards" be set for each process step? In the manufacturing company, Willcox was sensitive to the interaction between performance measures, and he personally had to adjudicate trade-offs between them.

Cost control

The absence of budgets (Handelsbanken), the downplaying of budgets (manufacturing) and the removal of targets (Aviva) naturally lead one to ask how these companies are achieving cost control. The main method is the graphical presentation of key information. This is the major theme of Willcox's (2013) book, and at both Aviva and Handelsbanken, our interviewees emphasised the importance of measuring key metrics and monitoring trends in these. Graphical presentation allows managers to see whether trends are in the right or wrong direction and this is sufficient to stimulate action.[10] At Handelsbanken, comparative branch "league tables" based on C/I ratios also provide a powerful incentive to control costs.

While our interviewees were very obviously in favour of identifying, measuring and monitoring key metrics, they were acutely aware of the need to take care in interpreting and using the indicators. Even when these metrics are not used to set operational targets (thus removing one cause of manipulation), they need to be interpreted with care. At Handelsbanken, branches need to be compared with a "peer group" of similar age because profitability tends to increase over time and a C/I ratio can be "too good", possibly achieved at the expense of customer service or good administration. At Aviva, Wilson emphasised the need to allow for normal statistical variation so as to avoid overreacting to apparent poor (or good) performance. In the manufacturing company, Willcox was sensitive to the interaction between indicators, and his own involvement in reviewing these indicators was a reflection of his recognition that functional directors could not easily adjudicate on trade-offs between these metrics.

Information systems

The idea that decentralised, empowered organisations do not need sophisticated accounting and information systems is shown to be completely wrong in these cases. All three companies have sophisticated information systems. In manufacturing, a decade-long project saw the development of comprehensive charts that facilitated trend monitoring. At Aviva, a long and impressive list of performance metrics is monitored, not against targets but to identify trends and highlight both poor performance (for remedial action) and good performance (for learning). At Handelsbanken, very considerable effort is expended in creating branch income statements "as often as is practicable" and ensuring that these are credible through a sophisticated internal charging system that involves branch managers in agreeing the "keys" on which charges are based.

Motivation

Motivating staff in these companies did not seem difficult. In both the manufacturing and insurance companies, our interviewees felt that so long as company systems did not militate against it, staff would deliver highly motivated performance. In the manufacturing company, Willcox emphasised the importance of senior managers concentrating on their own performance indicators and not interfering in operations management. He gave a nice example of staff initiative: a power failure meant that achieving delivery next day appeared impossible, but staff used their car headlights to continue working and get the product delivered on time. In the insurance company, Wilson felt that releasing operators from the tyranny of standardised operations was sufficient to motivate much improved customer service. Handelsbanken have long fostered a decentralised, cooperative culture. Bank branches are evaluated using C/I statistics, but these are interpreted sensitively and there are no financial incentives associated with them.

Decentralisation

All three companies practice decentralised organisation structures to a greater or lesser degree. Handelsbanken has gone furthest with its insistence that "The Branch is the Bank", delegating "the overwhelming majority of *credit decisions* ... [to] ... branch office level" (Wallander, 2003: 51) together with the dismantling of corporate staffs and budgeting. However, the same theme can be observed in the other companies. In the same way that Handelsbanken aims to empower staff so that loans can be authorised by relatively junior staff, so in its call centres, Aviva has empowered staff to handle customer queries in a wide-ranging way that encourages initiative. Both at Aviva and in manufacturing, steps were taken to remove micro-management by performance metrics, targets and control.

While decentralisation can deliver considerable benefits, achieving it is not easy and Wallander's (2003) book is devoted to explaining why it is important, the problems that can be expected and how they might be overcome. The changes in Aviva call centres were met with consternation by some managers who were concerned about the changes to their roles. And, in manufacturing, Willcox conceded that the executive decision to give up their offices was neither quick nor easy.

Culture and incentives

In all three companies, social controls are important in helping to motivate (and control) staff. At Handelsbanken, recruitment of a branch manager can be time-consuming, and careful recruitment together with induction and ongoing communication ensures that branch managers buy into the ethos of conservative, responsible banking and the decentralised nature of the organisation. The bank even avoided expansion into some markets that were judged to be culturally difficult. In manufacturing, Willcox referred to the need for top management to "empower" operational managers. Managers were not to interfere in operational matters, but they were available, and the executive team gave up their offices as part of a drive for a cooperative culture. Willcox felt that the profit-sharing scheme also fostered more team spirit and generated peer pressure on underperformers. At Aviva, a cooperative, team-oriented approach had developed after the removal of individual incentives and the introduction of a more supportive role for team leaders.

However, to Wilson's disappointment, the company still employed an annual bonus system that forced team leaders to identify their "best" performers.

The management of uncertainty

Reflection on these cases leads one to the conclusion that in uncertain environments, imposing standard operating procedures and targets can be counterproductive. It may be better to free managers and staff to take advantage of opportunities and handle varied problems as they arise. Dealing with uncertainty is a key issue in organisational theory, and Grote (2004) set out to determine the appropriate mix of systems for a particular organisation at a particular point in time. In mechanistic, Taylorist, organisations every effort is made to *remove uncertainty* from the system by standardisation, formalisation, detailed forward planning and tight control versus standards and plans. The alternative is to *cope with uncertainty*: "instead of fighting uncertainties in an attempt to minimize the uncertainties themselves or at least their effect in the organization – to enable each and every member of an organization to handle uncertainties locally and to allow for feedback control ... From this perspective, planning is understood primarily as a resource for situated action" (Suchman, 1987 quoted by Grote, 2004: 268).

The three cases provide examples of planning for "situated action" best exemplified by Dibble (2014b): "perhaps the central point [is] that we cannot say what a reasonable target will look like over any given period of time. Market conditions change, customer needs will be whatever they are, and we simply must therefore be in the best position to serve these needs and seize market opportunities as they emerge. This is the main reason we don't have targets". This quotation could be almost a textbook exposition of the principle of planning for "situated action".

Discussion: uses of, and implications for, theory

This chapter has reviewed several contemporary performance management frameworks and described management control systems in three case companies. The focus has been on the lack of performance targets in these companies. The following discussion considers, first, the usefulness of performance management frameworks and, second, the implications of the cases for contemporary management control theory.

Usefulness of performance management frameworks

First, scorecard models are useful both as descriptive frameworks and as normative guides to strategy development. In these cases, considerable effort is expended in setting objectives, developing strategies and identifying key success factors. Thus, scorecard models can be helpful in identifying stakeholders, their contributions and objectives; in providing templates for strategic planning; and in guiding the development of KPIs. However, the cases do not support the typical scorecard assumption that companies "should" set targets for performance measures throughout the organisation and incentivise local managers through these. In fact, the cases provide counter-evidence: perhaps some companies should decouple strategic planning from their operational activities.

Second, it is noted that the EVA model is not directly relevant to these companies; none of the case companies employ the EVA measure. However, the recommendation that EVA targets should not be embedded in budgets *is* relevant. These companies emphasise longer-term incentives and avoid short-run targets, consistent with the EVA recommendation.

Third, it is concluded that Simons' analysis provides a useful descriptive and normative framework in the case companies. All the "levers of control" are employed. All three companies use "beliefs" systems with company culture being especially important at Handelsbanken. There are diagnostic control systems in the companies, although based on trend reporting of key cost ratios and performance indicators rather than comparison of actuals to targets. Boundary "systems" are embedded in both company values (such as conservative banking at Handelsbanken) and technical controls (such as budgetary limits on expenditure). Simons refers to interactive control as a *use* of the control systems. However, in these companies, there is plenty of evidence of "planned interaction" through, for example, 6-month reviews at Handelsbanken and a decision by Willcox and his executive team to give up their offices so as to foster increased availability and interaction. The "levers of control" provide a useful framework for investigation of company systems. However, the cases provide further empirical support for Collier's (2005) finding that belief systems can be much wider and deeper than Simons' emphasis on top management's use of company vision and mission statements.

Fourth, the Ferreira and Otley framework is also useful (see Figure 9.1), it is comprehensive and use of this framework in the interviews ensured a reasonably complete picture of the control systems. Although the framework has been criticised for its apparent emphasis on interactive and diagnostic systems, social and cultural controls were identified in the case companies (though this might reflect the researcher's sensitivity to their likely existence rather than the intrinsic characteristics of the Ferreira and Otley framework). The framework is not intended as a normative control model, and researchers should recognise that the absence of performance targets is not necessarily a "failure" of control.

Implications for management control theory

The balanced scorecard, Simons' levers of control and the Ferreira and Otley framework have been inductively derived from studies of practice, while the EVA recommendations and the "performance prism" stem from a more theoretical and deductive tradition. Whatever their source, the frameworks are often presented as "good" practice, intended to guide managers in strategic and operational planning and control and, implicit in much of this theory, is an assumption that strong linkages between strategy, performance indicators, targets and rewards are both logical and desirable. These cases provide counter-evidence.

These companies set objectives, develop strategies and identify key success factors, but there is a loose connection between this process and operational control with target-setting seen as counterproductive. In two companies, incentives are based on profit-sharing schemes in which all staff participate, and in the third company, rewards for hitting process targets have been removed (together with the associated targets). The pragmatic justification for these decisions is the removal of incentives to indulge in short-term, dysfunctional activity that could easily hinder achievement of company objectives. The theoretical justification is that uncertainty in local operations requires systems that recognise the need for flexible local response.

Flexible local response implies relatively autonomous local units, delegation to local managers and operators, and absence of performance targets that inhibit flexibility. In the absence of performance targets, the case companies have relied on good information flows, graphical presentation of key cost and performance measures, and a cooperative culture where managers and operatives aim for good customer service. The cases suggest that contemporary management accounting control theory underemphasises both the design of organisational structures in coping with uncertainty and the importance of social and cultural controls. Different organisational levels tend to operate to different timescales and need distinct systems to meet their different needs. Strategic plans can usually only be evaluated over a long timescale and, logically, should be linked to long-term incentives that recognise the contributions of many staff (as in the profit-sharing schemes in two of these companies). At operational levels, in these cases, organisational design ensures local autonomy and flexible responses to cope with market and operational uncertainties. Tight process specification with targets and incentives is not needed, and motivation of staff is achieved by developing appropriate supportive cultures.

Conclusion

It is concluded that, first, contemporary management control theory has considerable merit both in guiding managers and in providing frameworks for investigating researchers. However, contemporary theory tends to emphasise a top-down approach to strategy with rational, logical links between this and operational activity. Even where the importance of belief systems is recognised, as in Simons' levers of control, a top-down emphasis permeates the literature.

Second, these cases show that for some companies, especially those facing significant process or market uncertainties, decentralisation, delegation, empowerment and an operating culture that prioritises customer service, employee cooperation and support can be very successful. Staff are encouraged to respond flexibly to unpredictable problems and opportunities unencumbered by standardised processes and targets. Organisational success factors and strategic planning have been decoupled from local operational measures, and there is further "decoupling" of local performance from incentives. These companies thus avoid the various dysfunctional consequences that can be triggered by overzealous use of local targets exacerbated by linked incentive payments.

Third, radical decentralisation is not an easy process, and in these companies, delegation of significant responsibility has been linked with significant investment both in staff recruitment/development and in sophisticated information systems. Considerable effort has been expended identifying metrics such as the C/I ratio at Handelsbanken, the (net) percentage of customers that would recommend Aviva and next-day delivery percentage in manufacturing. There is rapid dissemination of information with graphically based trend analyses embedded in all three companies and branch financial statements at Handelsbanken. Freely available, credible information in a format that facilitates action is sufficient to ensure effective control.

Fourth, in these cases, the decoupling of operational issues means that there are separate systems for longer-term issues. In particular, there is "planning for situated action": the provision of human, financial and physical resources that enable flexible local response. This resource allocation process is based on rolling quarterly forecasts at Aviva, monthly review of trends in manufacturing and half-yearly planning meetings at Handelsbanken. It is noted, in passing, that these processes are not driven by annual budgeting.

Sixth, reflection on these cases suggests that there is scope for integration of contemporary performance management insights with established organisation theory. The analysis mirrors Anthony's (1965) longstanding categories of strategic planning, management control and operational control, and although Anthony's approach has been criticised for its apparently arbitrary divisions, it has the merit of explicitly recognising the different timescales associated with these activities. The balance between technical and social controls was the main theme of Burns and Stalker's (1961) seminal work, and finally, the idea of organisations as nested, relatively autonomous subunits within larger units was a key element of Beer's (1979, 1981, 1985) work on organisation theory.

Notes

1. EVA^{R} is a registered trademark of Stern Stewart & Co.
2. Simons draws his examples from the fields of accounting and banking, and more recent examples could include fixing LIBOR and exchange rates, miss-selling personal protection insurance and helping clients evade their tax liabilities.
3. Erhbar was a senior vice president at Stern Stewart & Co.
4. Rob Wilson was Systems Thinking Director at Aviva at the time of his presentation to the beyond Budgeting Round Table.
5. Front office functions are those that require interaction with customers, while back office functions refer to administrative and support activities that do not involve customer contact.
6. Henceforth referred to as "Handelsbanken", the company's preferred trade name in the UK.
7. Kroner (2009) sets out a convincing case in favour of the Handelsbanken model arguing that its philosophy (and specific actions) has helped it to avoid the "seven deadly sins of banking: asset/liability mismatches, supporting client asset/liability mismatches, lending to over-indebted customers, investing in non-core assets, dealing with the non-bank financial system, over-exposure to real estate and emerging markets and presuming that past trends will continue in the future".
8. Answering a question about whether these could conflict, Bouvin said that he did not think so (and the evidence supported his view). The emphasis on customer relationships meant that customers stayed with the bank and that reduced costs, and the culture of thrift meant that the bank has lower costs and could therefore please customers by offering competitive prices.
9. There is a separate defined contribution scheme where the company makes a significant contribution, a very generous, industry-leading, scheme in its own right.
10. Further examples of the power of trend analysis for cost control can readily be found. Bogsnes (2009: 80) reported that "Trend lines and '% change' numbers might not sound very advanced. Yet this constant reminder of being on a rising trend when we should have seen the opposite did something that we had never seen with traditional budget reporting: it focused attention and urgency on costs". Olesen (2014: 6) pointed out in Uno-X Automat report that "Trends on relative key figures (actuals)" and rolling 12-month figures were used to eliminate seasonality. Esberg (2015) confirmed that input and output were related by expressing costs as percentage of revenue.

References

Anthony, R. N. (1965) *Planning and Control Systems: A Framework for Analysis*, Harvard University, Graduate School of Business Administration, Boston, MA.

Beer, S. (1979) *The Heart of Enterprise*, John Wiley & Sons, Chichester, UK.

Beer, S. (1981) *Brain of the Firm, second edition*, John Wiley & Sons, Chichester, UK.

Beer, S. (1985) *Diagnosing the System for Organizations*, John Wiley & Sons, Chichester, UK.

Berry, A. J., Coad, A. F., Harris, E. P., Otley, D. T. and Stringer, C. (2009) Emerging themes in management control: a review of recent literature, *The British Accounting Review*, 41, 2–20.

Bischof, B., Essex, S. and Furtaw, P. (2010) Participating in Opportunities and Risks. Long Live the Bonus Bank! Stern Stewart Research// Volume 40 downloaded 14/02/2015 from: www.sternstewart.com/files/ssco_studie40_en.pdf.

Bogsnes, B. (2009) *Implementing beyond Budgeting: Unlocking the Performance Potential*, John Wiley & Sons, Inc, Hoboken, NJ.

Bouvin, A. (2014) Handelsbanken UK, *Beyond Budgeting: From Command and Control to Empower and Adapt*, Happy Ltd in association with BBRT, London, 22 October.

Broadbent, J. and Laughlin, R. (2009) Performance management systems: a conceptual model, *Management Accounting Research*, 20, 283–295.

Burns, T. and Stalker, G. M. (1961) *The Management of Innovation*, Tavistock Publications, London.

Chase, R. B. (1978) Where does the customer fit in a service operation?, *Harvard Business Review*, 56 (6) November–December, 137–142.

Collier, P. M. (2005) Entrepreneurial control and the construction of a relevant accounting, *Management Accounting Research*, 16, 321–339.

Dibble (2014a) Interview, Handelsbanken Bristol branch, August.

Dibble (2014b) Follow-up correspondence, September.

Ditillo, A. (2004) Dealing with uncertainty in knowledge-intensive firms: the role of management control systems as knowledge integration mechanisms, *Accounting, Organizations and Society*, 29, 401–421.

Erhbar, A. (1998) *Stern Stewart's EVA: the Real Key to Creating Wealth*, John Wiley & Sons, Inc, Hoboken, NJ.

Esberg, H. H. (2015) Uno-X Automat, *Presentation to the Beyond Budgeting Round Table*, London, March.

Ferreira, A. and Otley, D. A. (2009) The design and use of management control systems: an extended framework for analysis, *Management Accounting Research*, 20, 263–282.

Grote, G. (2004) Uncertainty management at the core of systems design, *Annual Reviews in Control*, 28, 267–274.

Hope, J. and Fraser, R. (2003) *Beyond Budgeting: How Managers Can Break Free from the Annual Performance Trap*, Harvard Business School Press, Boston, MA.

Johnson, H. T. and Kaplan, R. S. (1987) *Relevance Lost: the Rise and Fall of Management Accounting*, Harvard Business School Press, Boston, MA.

Kaplan, R. S. and Norton, D. P. (1992) The balanced scorecard: measures that drive performance, *Harvard Business Review*, 70 (1) (January–February), 71–79.

Kaplan, R. S. and Norton, D. (1996a) Putting the balanced scorecard to work, *Harvard Business Review*, January–February 3–13.

Kaplan, R. S. and Norton, D. (1996b) *The Balanced Scorecard*, Harvard Business School Press, Boston, MA.

Kaplan, R. S. and Norton, D. (2001) *The Strategy-Focused Organization*, Harvard Business School Press, Boston, MA.

Kaplan, R. S. and Norton, D. (2004) *Strategy Maps*, Harvard Business School Press, Boston.

Kroner, N. (2009) *A Blueprint for Better Banking: Svenska Handelsbanken and a Proven Model for More Stable and Profitable Banking*, Harriman House Ltd, Petersfield, Hampshire, UK.

Lindsay, R. M. and Libby, T. (2007) Svenska Handelsbanken: controlling a radically decentralized organization without budgets, *Issues in Accounting Education*, 22, 625–640.

Neely, A., Adams, C. and Kennerley, M. (2002) *The Performance Prism: The Scorecard for Measuring and Managing Business Success*, FT Prentice Hall, London.

Olesen, A. (2014) *Uno-X Automat: aiming for the most effective value driven organization*, Case report, Beyond Budgeting Round Table.

Otley, D. A. (2003) Management control and performance management: whence and whither?, *The British Accounting Review*, 35, 309–326.

Otley, D. T. (1999) Performance management: a framework for management control systems research, *Management Accounting Research*, 10, 363–382.

Pettit J. (2001) EVA and Strategy, Stern Stewart & Co. Research, downloaded 14/2/2015 from: www.sternstewart.com.br/publicacoes/pdfs/EVA_and_strategy.pdf.

Pugh, D. S. (2007) Introduction to the Fifth edition *in* Pugh, D. S. (ed.) *Organization Theory: Selected Classic Readings*, Penguin Books, London.

Simons, R. (1995) *Levers of Control: How Managers Use Innovative Control Systems to Drive Strategic Renewal*, Harvard Business School Press, Boston, MA.

Suchman, L. A. (1987) *Plans and Situated Actions: The Problem of Human Machine Communication*, Cambridge University Press, Cambridge.

Tessier, S. and Otley, D. (2012) A conceptual development of Simons' levers of control framework, *Management Accounting Research*, 23 (3), 171–185.

Wallander, J. (2003) *Decentralisation – Why and How to Make It Work: The Handelsbanken Way*, SNS Förlag, Stockholm, Sweden.

Willcox, D. (2013) *Only Trends Matter: A Step Change in Management Accounting*, Trafford Publishing, Bloomington, IN.

Willcox, D. (2014) Interview, Wales, January.

Wilson, R. (2013) *"Systems Thinking" – Changing the Way we Think about Operations Management*, Presentation to the Beyond Budgeting Round Table, London.

Wilson, R. (2014) Interview, Aviva Head Office, London, March.

Winder, R. (2014) Interview, Handelsbanken Head Office, London, July.

3

Kyocera's use of amoeba management as a performance management system

Why it works?

Ralph W. Adler

Introduction

Management control systems, or what the literature is increasingly calling performance management systems, comprise formal and informal mechanisms, processes, systems, and networks that help senior managers implement their organizations' strategies (Anthony, 1956) and, at least according to the performance management literature's more recent conceptualizations, assist with the formulation and control of strategy itself (Mintzberg, 1978; Merchant and Otley, 2007). As noted by Ferreira and Otley (2009), performance management systems play a crucial role in communicating key objectives and goals set by the organization's senior managers, helping employees throughout the organization manage performance (by instituting appropriate ongoing systems of planning, measurement, control, and reward), and supporting organizational programmes of learning and change.

Performance management is underpinned by the functioning of a number of distinct, but necessarily interconnected, organizational systems, including strategic planning systems, human resource planning systems, materials requirement planning systems, employee reward systems, and accounting information systems. As shown by Otley (1999), the aims of performance management cannot be achieved through reliance on any single organizational system or management approach alone. While it is true that Otley's (1999) conclusion derives from his studying a limited number of high-profile management practices – budgeting, economic value added, and the balanced scorecard – it is fair to say that even if he had included something like enterprise resource planning (ERP), which was quite new at the time he wrote his paper, his overall conclusion would not have changed. ERP might score strongly on communicating and tracking key performance measures and targets, but it would score weakly on facilitating an employee reward and incentive system that is free of distorted and dysfunctional behavioural effects.

Amoeba management is a relatively new (at least in the sense of it being discussed in English language academic journals) management technique. Both amoeba management's relative newness and its lack of presence beyond Japan would have contributed to its non-inclusion in Otley's (1999) study. The chapter argues, however, that amoeba management embodies all the central tenets of a comprehensive performance management system. As a performance management system, amoeba management appears especially adept at supporting the *simultaneous* pursuit of organizational efficiency and flexibility, a situation that Ahrens and Chapman (2004) highlight in their field study of a UK restaurant chain. For some organizations, a hybrid strategy that embodies a conservative/cost-focused strategic orientation and a flexible/entrepreneurially focused orientation is required. Accordingly, this chapter's contents are especially well suited for organizations that pursue a hybrid strategy, what some call a mixed-emphasis strategy (Campbell-Hunt, 2000) and others a confrontation strategy (Cooper, 1995).

The chapter is organized in the following manner. In the next section, a very brief history of Kyocera and the fundamental features of its amoeba management system are provided. The third section identifies and examines the factors behind amoeba management's success. These factors include amoeba management (1) representing the right organizational structure for the particular organizational strategy being pursued, (2) possessing the right balance of enabling and constraining factors, and (3) encouraging the selection of the right set of people to accept the responsibilities and challenges that characterize Kyocera's highly empowered work environment. The final section offers the chapter's conclusions, examining such issues as amoeba management's relevance for other firms operating in different industries and national cultures, as well as identifying future avenues of academic research.

Brief history of Kyocera and amoeba management

Kyocera Corporation is a very large and very successful Japanese multinational. The company began operations in 1959 as a producer of ceramic insulators for television sets. Today, it makes a wide range of ceramic and printing-related devices, with products ranging from automotive and semiconductor components to office equipment and mobile phones, and from dental implants to solar panels.

Kyocera operates on six continents, and as part of the Kyocera Group, it has annual sales of over €11 billion and a total workforce of over 68,000 employees. For its latest fiscal year end of March 2015, the company reported a net income of €860 million, which is a little under 8 per cent of net sales. This 8 per cent net income to net sales ratio is slightly on the low side of its long-run average. As further testament to Kyocera's outstanding financial performance, the company has reported a profit in every year of its 56 years of operations. Kyocera's financial performance clearly meets Michael Porter's definition of sustained success: above average rate of return (Porter, 1980: 35) sustained over a period of years (Porter, 1985: 11).

Kyocera's success is often attributed to its adoption of amoeba management. The company's managers certainly believe this, as the discussion later in this chapter will reveal. In addition, various organizational scholars, who customarily describe Kyocera's amoeba management as a showcase of exemplary business practice, also credit amoeba management for Kyocera's success (Kotter and Rothbard, 1991; Cooper, 1994; Miya, 1998; Mayo, Masako, and Mayuka, 2008).

Amoeba management was designed by and introduced into Kyocera by the company's founder Dr Kazuo Inamori. A central objective of amoeba management is the empowerment of employees. There were two main reasons Inamori wanted to promote employee empowerment. The first was his desire "to create an organization where every individual's ability could be utilized to the fullest" (Inamori, 1999: 57). The second reason was his hope that employee empowerment could be used as a way to overcome what he saw as his lack of preparation for his role as CEO. His previous business experience consisted of working 4 years as an electrical engineer at Shofu, a ceramics manufacturer that now specializes in dental products. During his early days as Kyocera's CEO, Inamori described feelings of intense loneliness and isolation. He lamented the fact that there was no one to mentor him, no one to share his/her business experience, provide management advice, or boost his confidence. Accordingly, he used amoeba management to create the business partners he so desperately craved.

Amoeba management uses a profit centre approach to structure a company into small, fast-responding, customer-focused, entrepreneurially oriented business units operating like independent companies that share a united purpose, i.e. the parent organization's goals and objectives. The amoebas are intended to act in coordinated independence from each other. The goal is to empower each amoeba to the point that each is akin to an independent company, with each seeking to manage its own profitability.

The use of the word "amoeba" is meant to capture the concept of an entity at its smallest, most elemental level, as well as to describe its life-like capability to "multiply and change shape in response to the environment" (Inamori, 1999: 57). In other words, amoeba management is intended to offer a spontaneous, homeostatic response to a business world that features rapid, dynamic change.

Amoebas typically consist of 5–50 employees. Within Kyocera, there are about 3,000 amoebas operating at any given time. The exact number fluctuates as individual amoebas divide, merge, and dissolve. All the production and sales departments are treated as amoebas with profit-oriented goals. Meanwhile, such departments as distribution, quality control, and research and development are treated as support departments and lack the same profit orientations as the production and sales amoebas.

Each amoeba is accountable for a meaningful organizational activity, an activity that is meant to mirror what currently exists (or could exist) in the outside, competitive environment. The amoeba leader and his/her employees are encouraged to act like the owner of a small, independent company. Accordingly, the manager is accountable for a wide range of activities, including the regular ongoing daily activities of purchasing raw materials and hiring and scheduling labour, as well as the more strategic activities of new product and new market development. Ultimately, the amoeba leader is meant to be accountable for managing his/her unit's profitability, and in the process, he/she becomes not just a valued and respected managerial decision maker, but also part of a network of *de facto* business partners.

Why amoeba management works at Kyocera

In seeking to explain why amoeba management works at Kyocera, a series of 21 semi-structured interviews were held with a variety of senior managers, plant managers, and amoeba leaders at various Kyocera locations, including its Kyoto headquarters, its Tokyo offices, a manufacturing plant in Kagoshima, Japan, and a manufacturing plant in San Diego, USA. The typical interview lasted about 2 hours, although some interviews well exceeded this time and lasted closer to 3 hours. Half of the interviews were attended by both researchers. One of the researchers is bilingual in English and Japanese, while the other relied upon a translator for the interviews conducted in Japanese. When permission was granted, the interviews were taped for later transcription and comparison with the researcher's set of field notes. A copy of the interview questions is included as Appendix 3.1.

The interview data were further complemented by various archival data, including financial statements and internal performance reports. This archival data offered opportunities to direct interview questions and facilitate further comments and clarifications during the course of the interviews. It also served to help corroborate the interview data.

In addition to the interviews and archival data, various meetings involving amoeba leaders, department heads, and divisional heads, as well as a monthly plant-wide morning assembly, were attended. A translator was available to offer real-time translation of the meetings attended in Japan.

The researcher provided opportunities for the interviewed managers to read and correct his field notes. Emails from the managers confirmed the field notes' accuracy. A summary copy of a working draft of the research was provided to Kyocera employees who had expressed an interest in receiving it. This allowed comments, especially in the way of corrections to any factual inaccuracies, to be received and corrections made. The protocols used to collect the data, including the procedures used to corroborate the field notes and allow for the correction of any factual inaccuracies, provide confidence in the data's validity and reliability.

The interviews and meetings revealed insights into two primary factors that underpin amoeba management's success at Kyocera. First, the use of a highly organic and horizontally differentiated organizational structure is the correct structure for the company's competitive environment. Second, Kyocera's amoeba management system features a number of integrating mechanisms that help ensure that the actions of the individual amoebas are coordinated and are supportive of the organization's overall goals and objectives. Each of these two factors is discussed more fully in the following.

Organizational structure and integrating mechanisms

Kyocera operates in an intensely competitive and dynamic environment. Since its inception, the company has been confronted with the challenge of competing in a technologically fast-changing environment, one that is characterized by quickly evolving technology and short product life cycles. As an example, the semiconductor industry's constant drive to miniaturize its products – whether these products are computers, printers, or mobile phones – means that the subcomponents Kyocera supplies to the semiconductor manufacturers must undergo parallel reductions in size. Capacitors that once were the size of a domino must now be a fraction of the size of a thumbnail, i.e. .6 mm × .3 mm × .3 mm.

In addition to the quickly changing product and manufacturing technology, Kyocera faces fierce competition. Each market that Kyocera operates in – whether it is the semiconductor industry, the automotive parts industry, the medical devices industry, etc. – features multiple competitors. Together with Kyocera, these competitors share a very limited and crowded competitive space, which in turn sees them all competing head to head on price, quality, and delivery.

The organizational sociology literature reveals that external environments characterized by high environmental uncertainty (which captures the environment faced by Kyocera) require organizations to adopt organic (Burns and Stalker, 1961) and more differentiated organizational structures (Lawrence and Lorsch, 1967). As described by Burns and Stalker (1961), organic structures are notable for their flexibility and adaptability. Organizations achieve these structures through the multiskilling of employees, the minimizing of management layers, the use of limited direct supervision, and the decentralization of decision-making. As will be discussed more fully in the following, these features are a centrepiece of amoeba management.

Lawrence and Lorsch (1967) observed the need for complex environments (i.e. ones featuring high competition, unpredictability, and/or turbulence) to be matched by complex organizational structures. In particular, they found that when faced with a complex environment, an organization, if it wants to succeed, must respond by dividing itself into separate functions (e.g. sales, production, and research and development). This process of organizational structuring is called horizontal differentiation. The need for horizontal differentiation is predicated on the different tasks, interpersonal skills, time perspectives, and type and extent of formalization demanded from each of the varied functions.

As Lawrence and Lorsch (1967) proceed to point out, the use of horizontal differentiation to meet the demands of a complex external environment is a necessary, but not a sufficient, organizational response. Organizations featuring greater horizontal differentiation are inevitably characterized by greater amounts of conflict than their less horizontally differentiated counterparts. Therefore, when using horizontal differentiation, senior managers need to ensure the presence of adequate conflict-resolving mechanisms.

To help manage conflict and promote organizational coherence and coordination, Lawrence and Lorsch (1967) encourage the use of what they term integrating mechanisms. Some typical examples are organizational roles dedicated to facilitating and sharing information between horizontally differentiated units; the operation of organizational systems and processes that require joint, interdepartmental participation – such as a negotiated transfer price system; and the use of interdepartmental meetings and forums. Ultimately, integrating mechanisms are intended to promote "collaboration" and "unity of effort" among the organization's horizontally differentiated units (Lawrence and Lorsch, 1967: 47). As described in the following, the use of differentiation and integration is vital to the effective operation of Kyocera's amoeba management system.

Integrating mechanisms and Simons' levers of control

Unified, common purpose of action is needed for an organization to achieve its goals and objectives. Simple organizations, especially ones that are small and have centralized structures, will have few challenges to maintaining coordinated organizational action. In particular, the small scale of operations and centralized organizational structure, assuming that this structure is appropriate for the type of environment, will mean that senior managers will be constantly aware of and in control of their employees' performance. It is during situations when the organization's size enlarges and/or its environment becomes complex that senior managers will need to adopt organizational structures featuring horizontal differentiation and, as a consequence, decide what organizational processes and systems to employ for ensuring unity of effort.

The idea of ensuring unity of effort is the focus of scholars who work in the field of performance management. Simons (1995: 5) refers to performance management as "the informal, information-based routines and procedures managers use to maintain or alter patterns in organizational activities". Simons (1995) proceeds to describe senior management's role as deciding the right emphasis to place on what he calls the "four levers of control". He labels the four levers belief, boundary, diagnostic, and interactive systems.

Belief systems comprise the inherent core values of an organization. These values are often a product of how senior managers define their particular organization's mission and view the relationships among its key stakeholders. An organization's values manifest themselves in the folklore, stories, symbols, and attitudes that are routinely expressed by the organization's members.

Boundary systems are commonly referred to as the "rules of the game". While Simons (1995) suggests that these rules of the game are best expressed in the negative, such as a statement like "the company will not source its inputs from sweatshops", these negative expressions can be readily seen as the flip side of positive expressions. For instance, the aforesaid negative expression can be reworded as "the company will only source its inputs from suppliers whose work practices include internationally acceptable standards of workers' rights and safeguards of employee health and safety". Accordingly, what most matters for boundary systems, especially if the organization seeks to promote employee initiative and creativity, is not whether the boundaries are negatively or positively stated, but that only the minimum number and most crucial set of boundaries are imposed. To do otherwise will constrain employee action and creativity.

Diagnostic systems are the set of measures that an organization routinely collects for the purpose of ensuring that the organization is on track for doing what it needs to do. The measures are meant to provide managers a quick assessment of how their organization is performing, with this performance generally being relative to a set of predetermined standards or benchmarks. Assuming that the measures indicate performance is near the benchmark or within certain prescribed parameters, then the employee needs to take no further action. It is only when the measures signify some type of abnormal performance that employee investigation and action is required.

Interactive systems consist of organizational procedures and processes that promote employee conversation and debate about the organizational challenges that are likely to significantly impact the organization's strategy and/or the implementation of it. As Simons notes, interactive systems cover the kinds of challenges that are likely to give managers sleepless nights. Managers and their employees must remain vigilant to these environmental opportunities and threats. They do so by ensuring that their organization, through the use of relevant surveillance systems, regularly and frequently gathers data about the direction and movement of these key challenges, and subsequently ensuring that the data serve to situate and motivate employee thinking and action.

In the specific case of Kyocera, its belief system is used to maintain boundaries on managerial activity. Accordingly, for the purpose of this chapter, Simons' three levers of beliefs, diagnostic and interactive controls are focused on.

Complex organizations, which are defined as organizations that have adopted horizontal differentiation to meet the demands of their external environment's high competition, unpredictability and/or turbulence, will require greater amounts of integration. If these organizations do not ensure integration, they will put their effectiveness at risk. In terms of the management control model presented by Simons' levers of control, senior managers of these complex organizations will find that they must develop a greater total mix of belief, diagnostic and interactive controls than senior managers of simple organizations. Generally speaking, this greater set of control will derive from the belief and diagnostic levers of control. Due to the intensive and time-consuming nature of interactive control, Simons argues that only the most critical imperatives should be made interactive. In other words, interactive control conforms to the features of a zero-sum phenomenon, whereby the addition of a further strategic imperative can only be achieved by jettisoning an existing imperative. This is the reason that complex organizations, which have substantial integration requirements, will feature large and extensive belief and diagnostic control systems.

For a company like Kyocera, its large size and highly competitive and turbulent environment mean that its adoption of an organic structure and use of horizontal differentiation are appropriate. Of course, Kyocera has chosen to operate a far from typical horizontally differentiated structure. Kyocera's use of horizontal differentiation featuring a host of organically structured amoebas in a near-constant state of interaction, with each amoeba emphasizing a profit motive as well as differentiated orientations and tasks, calls for a very strong presence of integrating systems. Without these integrating structures, Kyocera would likely disintegrate into a sea of chaos. The next three subsections of this chapter discuss the specific types of interactive, diagnostic and belief control systems that operate at Kyocera.

Interactive systems at Kyocera

The interviews with Kyocera's senior management identified four strategic imperatives. Three of the imperatives relate to how it competes against other companies in its industries. These three competitive imperatives are product price, quality, and timely delivery. Competing across all three of these product dimensions may sound particularly challenging, but companies like Kyocera are finding that they have no choice. Exacerbated by the consequences of today's fragile global economic environment, which is partly a function of national economies that are still working to recover from the Global Financial Crisis and partly the recent bursting of China's speculative bubble, Kyocera and its competitors are forever scrambling to maintain their customer bases. In the process, customers have increasingly come to learn that they are in a relatively strong bargaining position and can demand low prices, high quality, and quick deliveries.

The fourth strategic imperative revealed during the interviews relates to the ongoing inculcation of the company's core values to new and existing employees. Kyocera has high expectations of its employees, which is well captured by the company's corporate motto: *Kei Ten Ai Jin*. The literal translation of this motto is "respect the divine and love people". In practice, the motto is about the pursuit of meaning in one's life, which includes the devotion to one's work.

Together these four strategic imperatives dominate the daily conversations of management and employees. Much of the daily discourse is motivated and supported by the extensive set of meetings the company operates. For instance, at Kyocera's Kagoshima and San Diego manufacturing plants, formal meetings are a daily occurrence for every employee. A senior manager at the San Diego plant estimated that workers below the level of an amoeba leader, who were termed machine operators, had an average of 30 minutes of meetings per day. Meeting attendance was mandatory. Meanwhile, amoeba leaders and manufacturing VPs had about 45–60 minutes per day of formally scheduled meetings.

Formal meetings are used at the Kagoshima and San Diego manufacturing plants to present the upcoming month's budget (or what the company likes to call its monthly plan), compare the monthly plan to actual results, discuss the previous day's performance, brainstorm ideas for continuous improvement, and promote customer service. Invariably these meetings involve a cross section of employees from across product divisions, the sales division, and such support departments as distribution, quality control, and research and development.

Together these various meetings form an intricate web of internal communication. Hiromoto (2005) uses the term micro-macro loops (MMLs) to describe the interactively cycling information flows. In particular, he views the MMLs as Kyocera's critical means of ensuring the receipt and dissemination of information about organizational values, philosophy, and performance throughout the organization (Hiromoto, 2007: 98–102).

Diagnostic systems at Kyocera

The idea behind amoeba management is to empower workers to the point that they become independent owners and ultimately interconnected business partners of the organization.

One San Diego manager characterized amoeba management as "management by all". While this system of "management by all" has the advantage of what another manager saw as "bring[ing] everyone closer to the customer", it comes at a cost. In particular, Kyocera's workers, though possessing a good grasp of and familiarity with the raw production and sales data, do not necessarily possess some of the analytical skills commonly associated with decision makers. The skills gap is especially evident in their knowledge of financial measurement and evaluation. Inamori understands this limitation and has been willing to trade-off his workers' lower levels of financial literacy for their higher levels of work motivation.

When he first began designing his amoeba management system, Inamori sought to create an accounting and information system that was simple and easily understood. His beginning premise was that it should be patterned on the simplicity of the information a food stall seller would need. Accordingly, Inamori conceived a cash-basis accounting system, whereby the need for calculating inventories and accruals was avoided. Acting like independent companies, the amoebas negotiated transfer prices between themselves. Selling amoebas reflected revenues when the product shipped to another amoeba or an outside customer, while purchasing amoebas recorded an expense when product was shipped to it.[1] Such an uncomplicated system, believed Inamori, would allow the loosely coupled amoebas to readily manage their individual profitabilities.

When calculating the profit of an amoeba, Inamori deliberately chose to leave out the amoeba's labour costs. The labour expense-omitted profit figure was called hourly efficiency. Dividing the hourly efficiency by the amoeba's total number of labour hours produces a ratio that can be used as an index for evaluating any given amoeba's or combination of amoebas' performance. These hourly efficiency measures are captured in what are termed "per hour profit margin charts", which are indicative of dashboard indicators and ultimately diagnostic control. Table 3.1 provides an example of a generic hourly efficiency report.

Kyocera's accounting and information system features no such things as variance analysis, economic value added, or even customer profitability analysis. In fact, as one manager proudly reported, an amoeba in San Diego was divided into smaller amoebas, with

Table 3.1 Hourly efficiency report illustration

Gross production[1]	6,500,000 ($)
Production outside	4,000,000 ($)
Total internal sales	2,500,000 ($)
Total internal purchases[2]	2,200,000 ($)
Net production	4,300,000 ($)
Deductions	2,400,000 ($)
Added value[3]	1,900,000 ($)
Total working hours	35,000 (hours)
Hourly efficiency this month[4]	54.28 ($)
Production per hour	122.85 ($)

Source: Kazuo Inamori's official website at: http://global.kyocera.com/inamori/management/amoeba/system.html on 8 October 2015.

1 Gross production is the sum of production outside and internal sales.
2 Internal purchases are subtracted from gross production to calculate net production.
3 Added value is the difference between net production and deductions. These deductions include all expenses other than amoeba labour costs.
4 Hourly efficiency is calculated as added value divided by total working hours, and production per hour is the quotient obtained by dividing the total working hours into net production.

each resulting new amoeba being associated with production for a unique customer. This reorganization, reported the manager, meant that information could be obtained on the relative profitability of each customer. The idea that an amended accounting system could provide customer profitability information without the need for a structural change was seen as irrelevant. It was apparently the company's intent that costs and revenues should be simple and easily observable by the amoeba unit, rather than the product of management accounting alchemy.

Amoeba management is especially well suited to fast-paced, dynamic markets. As Inamori (2007) notes, under such environments, it is essential "to flexibly address these [environmental] changes and to make preemptive moves". For example, if the market price for the company's end product falls, then the amoeba management system is meant to create what the literature defines as a "reflexive", "spontaneous" reaction to the prices the company's amoebas charge one another. Of course, the changes in pricing are likely to also be accompanied by an equally "reflexive" and "spontaneous" change to the respective amoebas' production levels. It is for this reason that the sales order backlog data become a particularly important indicator of performance and management action. The sales order backlog provides essential data for developing future sales and production plans. Accordingly, sales order backlog becomes another important dashboard indicator that is used for diagnostic control.

Belief systems at Kyocera

Kyocera's amoeba management system is predicated upon and enabled by a set of powerful organizational values. In fact, these values form the bulk of Kyocera's set of integrating mechanisms. As previously noted, due to senior management time constraints, only the most critical success factors can be made interactive. Accordingly, interactive control at such a highly differentiated and decentralized company as Kyocera will fall well short of providing the integration required. Furthermore, because the accounting system has to be simple and easily understood by workers throughout the company, many of whom have only rudimentary financial skills, Kyocera's diagnostic system, even in combination with its interactive system, will never provide the level of integration needed. Instead, the most substantial component of Kyocera's integration comes from its belief system.

Kyocera's belief system is a joint product of Japan's national culture and, even more importantly, its founder, Inamori. While the influence of the national culture is more prevalent in Kyocera's Japanese operations, several fundamental traits of the Japanese culture also feature at its San Diego plant. For example, the willingness to work long hours is well engrained among San Diego employees. When asked to use various adjectives to describe the San Diego culture, one of the senior managers said "exhausting". He proceeded to say that all salaried employees worked very long days. The average engineer worked 50–60 hours per week, while he estimated that the average manager worked between 60 and 70 hours per week.

Japanese culture is notable for its high collectivity, whereby people are more willing to put the needs of their collective group ahead of any of their own personal needs (Hofstede, 1991). While US national culture is often described as individualistic, or the opposite of collective, the San Diego plant's employee selection policies ensure that its new recruits are more likely to embody the collectivist mindset of Japanese workers than the individualistic thinking of US workers. As one of the San Diego managers stated, the employee selection process includes assessing a prospective employee's ability to embrace Kyocera's philosophy of "humility, hard work, and selfless" attention to the customers' needs (whether these customers be internal or external). Accordingly, the collective orientation of the Japanese workers, which is often represented as the desire to "live up to the expectations of my family, friends, and society", appears to be similarly evidenced in the employees selected to work at Kyocera's San Diego plant. The collective orientation helps to ensure that the amoebas are working for the greater good of their company, and not just for their own self-interest.

Japanese workers' conceptions of what work is serve as a further salutary means of ensuring that amoebas act in coordinated fashion and not out of selfishness. Whereas it has been noted that Americans see work as a disutility, something that has to be done to acquire leisure, Japanese workers view work as a valued end in itself. In particular, as Sullivan (1992: 71) pointed out, for the Japanese, "work is what one does if one is a good person". The interviews with San Diego employees, as well as the worker behaviours revealed during the various meetings and assemblies attended by the researchers, tended to support Sullivan's observations.

Kyocera's Japanese workers therefore are more likely than their US counterparts to accept Akio Morita's, the founder of Sony, description of work as a useful tool for ensuring that the interests of owners, managers, employees, and even society are achieved. Such an idea is captured in Kyocera's mission statement, which states:

> *To provide opportunities for the material and intellectual growth of all employees, and through our joint effort, contribute to the advancement of society and mankind.*

The presence of such an idealistic view of work helps promote amoeba unit cohesion and harmony, which is called in this chapter organizational integration. Perhaps the lesser presence of this integrating mechanism in the US subsidiary explains the San Diego plant's slightly greater use of group-based worker incentives and rewards, which are seemingly being used to motivate or buy the harmonized, cooperative behaviour that occurs more naturally in Japan.

In addition to the role national culture plays in helping to promote amoeba cooperation and harmony, Kyocera's history and, in particular, the background of its founder, Inamori, provide a further key influence. Inamori's (1999) lack of managerial experience and low initial levels of confidence were fundamental drivers behind his quest to empower his employees and let them share in the responsibility of being an owner.

Inamori acutely understood that appointing people to management positions did not change the fact that his company sorely lacked management expertise. He further understood that there was no quick solution to obtaining this management expertise. Accordingly, soon after assuming his role as Kyocera's CEO, Inamori came to the conclusion that the best way to operate his company was to base management decisions on whether they were the "right thing to do as a human being", which Inamori (1995) further defined as the things that your parents and teachers taught you were right (p. 31). This, in turn, led him to adopt as the company's corporate motto: *Kei Ten Ai Jin*, which translates into "respect the divine and love people".

Kyocera's corporate motto is a key factor behind the success of its amoeba management system. First, it helped the company, including the CEO and his amoeba managers to overcome their collective lack of management expertise. More specifically, the corporate motto provides a clear framework on which management decisions can be based. The second benefit of the corporate motto is that it helps to preclude the occurrence of selfish amoeba behaviour. In particular, the corporate motto serves to instil in its employees the values of being "unselfish and noble" (Inamori, 1995: 28), and this helps ensure that the loosely coupled, entrepreneurially inspired amoebas will act for the greater good of the company.

There are two further parts to Kyocera's belief system that enhance amoeba management's ability to ensure organizational integration and unity of purpose: high trust and a customer-oriented philosophy. The strong Japanese work ethic noted earlier coupled with amoeba management's commitment to the philosophy of total quality management (TQM) help underpin and make possible the high trust and customer-oriented philosophy. Of course, at Kyocera, this commitment to customers goes well beyond the typical TQM philosophy.

Unlike the common western view, whereby employee behaviour and motivation are seen as a nexus of *quid pro quo* relationships between the organization and its employees (see, for example, Bernard Bass and his concept of transactional leadership), amoeba management views worker motivation as the product of a person's inherent desire to know that he/she has contributed to the good of the company and, by so doing, has earned the respect and appreciation of his/her peers (Bass, 1985: 59). The belief that workers are naturally striving to produce their best and the organization's best performance creates an environment of full trust and, in the process, helps transform workers from being simply empowered employees to being the business partners that Inamori so deeply craved when he set out to develop his amoeba management system.

Without full trust in the capabilities and motivations of his employees, Inamori would never have been successful in creating and implementing an amoeba management system. He had to believe that his employees shared his sense of duty for making high-quality products, ones that customers respected and valued. A lack of trust or a misplaced sense of trust is inimical to the use of an amoeba management system. Accordingly, Inamori insisted that all relevant company information must be provided to all organizational units, from the most aggregated unit to the smallest amoeba, so that these leaders could make informed decisions and act as valued business partners. In return, he required his managers and amoeba leaders to be completely open and candid about their business performance, and that they could do so without fear of reprisal or punitive actions. Furthermore, when a problem occurred, employees were responsible for identifying what went wrong and devising a plan for remedial action.

A customer-oriented philosophy is a further characteristic of Kyocera's belief system and an integral part to supporting the operation of its amoeba management. Inamori (1999: 41) describes the need for amoeba employees to be their "customers' servants". According to Inamori (1999: 41), this means not accepting the role with reluctance but doing so willingly and graciously. The amoebas are encouraged to produce "crisp" products, or what Inamori (1999: 43) refers to as "cutting edge quality that reminds our customers of the crisp touch of freshly-printed paper money". By striving to be their customers' servants, remember that these customers can be either internal or external to the company, the amoebas will find that they need to work in harmonious coordination.

People and empowerment

Employee empowerment resides at the very core of amoeba management. According to the organizational behaviour literature, empowerment produces satisfied, motivated, and high-performing employees. However, as Hackman and Oldham (1980) have demonstrated, the organizational outcomes from job enrichment and employee empowerment are not always simple and straightforward. They find that on some occasions, empowerment succeeds, and on other occasions, it fails.

Hackman and Oldham (1980) argue that individuals can be characterized on a scale they call growth need strength (GNS). A high GNS score indicates an individual with a high need for a sense of personal accomplishment and development, and people with high GNS tend to enjoy challenging tasks. Accordingly, they are not only accepting of the greater job responsibilities that are associated with a more empowered versus a less empowered work setting, but they actually thrive under such circumstances. People with low GNS dislike challenging tasks. They prefer work settings where someone else – generally their boss – plans, assigns, monitors, and evaluates their work. The practical implications of GNS are that empowerment works when employee GNS is high and fails when it is low.

Kyocera's managers, whether consciously or unconsciously, understand these implications. When recruiting, Kyocera selects employees for both their attitude and ability. Kyocera's reputation as a high-performing company means that it invariably attracts the most able job seekers. But managers at Kyocera are also keen to ensure that the individuals they hire have appropriate work attitudes. As stated by the plant manager at Kyocera's Kagoshima plant, job applicants are selected for their "intelligence, toughness, and hunger". The plant manager's further descriptions of what he meant by the words toughness and hunger revealed a striking similarity to Hackman and Oldham's high GNS employee.

Conclusion

Amoeba management works at Kyocera because it involves the right form of organizational structure, the right amount of performance management-derived organizational integration, and the right type of employees. Kyocera operates in an environment characterized by high competition and rapid technological change. Amoeba management represents a very shrewd way for successfully responding to this environment. Kyocera has matched a complex organizational structure to a complex environment. Due to the high, and even extreme, differentiation of its structure and decentralization of its decision-making, substantial integration is needed to maintain organizational coordination and success. Using Simons' model of management control, it was shown that this organizational integration is achieved through interactive, diagnostic, and belief systems of control. Belief systems proved to be the main control lever at Kyocera.

The use of amoeba management, as well as the role it plays as a performance management system, shares similarities with the performance management system observed by Ahrens and Chapman (2004) in their study of a UK restaurant chain. In particular, Ahrens and Chapman (2004) showed how a management control system could enhance the restaurant chain's effectiveness through a system of "enabled formalization", which allows formal structures and rules to operate without stripping away employee autonomy and responsibility. Kyocera's amoeba management system achieves a similar organizationally effective outcome through a performance management system – its amoeba management system – that showcases similar aspects of constraining and enabling characteristics. The amoeba management system calls for high employee empowerment, essentially encouraging the employees to act as the owners of their own independent business, while at the same time promoting shared, organizationally congruent behaviour through the operation of the company's compelling and forceful belief system.

The success of amoeba management is greatly dependent on the skill and attitude profile of its employees. Employee empowerment is at the heart of amoeba management. For this employee empowerment to succeed, employees must accept and even thrive on challenge. This fact explains why Kyocera includes in its recruitment criteria the need for employees to possess "intelligence, toughness, and hunger", with the last two criteria being especially well captured by Hackman and Oldham's concept of high GNS.

Whether amoeba management would be relevant to other organizations depends on a variety of factors, including the degree of competition faced and the complexity of the particular organization's internal and external environments. Of course, relevance is only one dimension that must be considered. The second dimension is whether the system can translate to the likely very different organizational cultures that exist at other organizations. For instance, can firms with cultures that are less collective/team-oriented than Kyocera be able to develop the belief systems needed to integrate the various amoebas? If Kyocera's San Diego plant is a suitable guide, it would appear that firms located outside Japan can successfully adopt amoeba management. To do so, however, may require the greater use of formalized systems, such as the use of performance measures and rewards, to motivate or buy the harmonized, cooperative behaviour that is required for amoeba management's success.

Acknowledgements

The author is grateful to employees throughout Kyocera for allowing access into their organization and their willingness to be interviewed.

Appendix 3.1

Interview Questions

1. What do you believe are the key order-winning criteria for Kyocera? In particular, what critical factors explain why a customer buys from Kyocera and not one of its competitors? Can you please rank the importance of the factors you have identified?
2. Do you believe that Kyocera's order-winning criteria, either the factors themselves or the ordering you have awarded them, are unique to the company or generic to the industry in which it operates? Assuming the criteria are unique, please contrast Kyocera's order-winning criteria with a major competitor's. If you believe that the order-winning criteria are generic, please discuss why you think this is the case.
3. What do you see as the main purpose(s) of amoeba management?
4. Please describe the structure of the amoeba management system at Kyocera. In this description, please discuss any company rules or policies relating to the formation of amoebas; the management of amoebas at their individual, group, and company levels (e.g. selection of amoeba heads, evaluation of amoebas and their managers, and replacement of amoeba heads); interactions between amoebas (e.g. the type and frequency of meetings, decisions about internal versus external sourcing, and amoeba dispute procedures); and disbanding of amoebas.
5. What do you believe are the amoeba management system's major strengths? What do you believe are the system's major weaknesses?
6. How does the amoeba management system differ from other organization's systems for controlling costs and stimulating innovation? Possible examples to use as points of comparison and contrast might be Kirin Brewery's use of profit centres and Higashimaru's price control system.
7. Some western academics believe that amoeba management is nothing more than a reconfiguring of an organization into profit centres. How would you respond to such an interpretation?

8 What do you believe are the critical factors for amoeba management success? Please list what you believe to be the 3–5 most important factors. Please rank their importance.
9 Thinking about how amoeba management currently operates at your company, what one change would you most like to see take place?
10 Are you aware of any competitors that use amoeba management or a system like it? If so, what are the points of similarity and contrast between your system and your competitor's? If not, why do you believe that none of your competitors have yet to adopt amoeba management or a system like it?
11 Assuming an organization wants to adopt amoeba management, what particular traps and pitfalls should it be aware of? Also, what do you believe an organization can do to prevent or minimize these traps and pitfalls?
12 Can you think of any settings where amoeba management is more or less difficult to introduce? For example, do you believe that the success of amoeba management is dependent on industry (e.g. manufacturing versus service and private versus public), organizational strategy (e.g. low cost versus differentiation and first developer versus imitator), and/or geographic location (e.g. perhaps due to political, social, or economic factors)?
13 Are you aware of any adoptions of amoeba management outside Japan? If so, can you please comment on these?

Note

1 Since Kyocera operates a just-in-time (JIT) production system, the cash-basis accounting system would in all likelihood be similar to an accrual system.

References

Ahrens, T. and Chapman, C. S. (2004) Accounting for flexibility and efficiency: a field study of management control systems in a restaurant chain, *Contemporary Accounting Research*, *21*(2), pp. 271–201.

Anthony, R. (1956) *Management Accounting: Text and Cases*, Homewood, IL: Irwin.

Bass, B. M. (1985) *Leadership and Performance beyond Expectations*, New York: Free Press.

Burns, T. and Stalker, G. M. (1961) *The Management of Innovation*, London: Tavistock.

Campbell-Hunt, C. (2000) What have we learned about generic competitive strategy: a meta-analysis, *Strategic Management Journal*, *21*(2), pp. 127–154.

Cooper, R. (1995) *Kyocera Corporation: The Amoeba Management System, HBS No. 195–064*, Boston: Harvard Business School Publishing.

Ferreira, A. and Otley, D. (2009). The design and use of performance management systems: an extended framework for analysis, *Management Accounting Research*, *20*(4), pp. 263–282.

Hackman, J. and Oldham, G. (1980) *Work Redesign*, Reading, MA: Addison-Wesley.

Hiromoto, T. (2005) Management accounting system as a micro-macro loop, *The Hitotsubashi Review* (Hitotsubashi University), *134*(5), pp. 58–88.

Hiromoto, T. (2007) *A Study on Business Organization and Management Accounting*, Japan Accounting Association.

Hofstede, G. (1991) *Cultures and Organizations*, London: McGraw-Hill.

Inamori, K. (1995) *A Passion for Success*, New York: McGraw-Hill.

Inamori, K. (1999) *Respect the Divine and Love People*, San Diego: University of San Diego Press.

Inamori, K. (2007) *A Passion for Success*, Singapore: McGraw-Hill.

Kotter, J. and Rothbard, N. (1991) *Kyocera Corporation, HBS No. 491–078*, Boston: Harvard Business School Publishing.

Kyocera. (2015) 1963: Establishing the Shiga Gamo Plant. Retrieved from http://global.kyocera.com/inamori/management/amoeba/system.html (Accessed 8 October 2015).

Lawrence, P. and Lorsch, J. (1967) *Organization and Environment*, Homewood, IL: Irwin.

Mayo, A., Masako, E. and Mayuka, Y. (2008) *"Kazuo Inamori, a Japanese Entrepreneur," HBS No. 408–039*, Boston: Harvard Business School Publishing.

Merchant, A. K. and Otley, D. (2007) A review of the literature on control and accountability, In Chapman C.S., Hopwood, A.G., and Shields, M.D. (Eds.), *Handbook of Management Accounting Research, Vol. 1*, UK: Elsevier Oxford, pp. 785–802.

Mintzberg, H. (1978) Patterns of strategy formulation, *Management Science*, *24*, pp. 934–948.

Miya, H. (1998) Micro-profit center system for empowerment: a case study of the amoeba system at the Kyocera corporation, *Gakushuin Economic Papers*, *35*(2), pp. 105–115.

Otley, D. (1999) Performance management: a framework for management control systems research, *Management Accounting Research*, *10*(4); pp. 363–382.

Porter, M. E. (1980) *Competitive Strategy: Techniques for Analyzing Industries and Competitors*, New York: Free Press.

Porter, M. E. (1985) *Competitive Advantage: Creating and Sustaining Superior Performance*, New York: Free Press.

Simons, R. (1995) *Levers of Control: How Managers Use Innovative Control Systems to Drive Strategic Renewal*, Cambridge: Harvard Business School Press.

Sullivan, J. J. (1992) Japanese management philosophies: from the vacuous to the brilliant, *California Management Review*, Winter, pp. 66–87.

4

Cost management and modular product design strategies

Marc Wouters and Frank Stadtherr

Introduction

This chapter discusses the use of product modularity for cost management purposes. We consider the context of firms offering a wide assortment of end products to their customers and which need to manage their costs to be able to offer such diversity efficiently. For example, German car manufacturers sell many different car models and individual configurations to customers, and managing the costs of that diversity is a big challenge. Modular design of products is a key approach they employ to be able to utilize economies of scale in development, purchasing, and manufacturing.[1] As we will discuss in the following section, modularity essentially involves mechanisms for coordinating technical design decisions across a large portfolio of products, with the aim of reducing the total costs and maximizing the total profit of that portfolio. Thus, it goes beyond target costing, which typically focuses on costs within the scope of only one product.

In the management accounting and control literature, there has been only limited attention paid to modularity, whereas much research on this topic has been published in the innovation and operations management literature (Wouters & Morales, 2014; Wouters et al., 2016). Many management accounting techniques are not necessarily compatible with modularity as a cost management approach. For example, Taipaleenmäki (2014) investigated the role of management accounting in new product development (NPD) based on several case studies. One of the companies used a product life-cycle profitability calculation, which aimed to reflect the NPD process and to cover the full product life cycle. However, "[product life-cycle profitability] was seen as an insufficient model for analyzing product variants, and no suitable method was available for *supporting modular development decisions*" (Taipaleenmäki, 2014, p. 304, emphasis added).

The purpose of this chapter is to look at various literatures and provide an overview of our current understanding of modularity for cost management purposes. So, even though the concept of modularity may also relate to organizational design or educational programs (Schilling, 2000), we will focus on modularity in the design of products and for the purpose of cost management.

Modularity and cost management in prior literature reviews

Several literature reviews have examined modularity from different points of view. Labro (2004) reviewed the operations management literature with respect to the effects of common components on various levels of cost divers, according to activity-based costing (ABC). Wouters and Morales (2014) and Wouters et al. (2016) addressed modularity, but not in that much detail, as this was one of many other cost management methods reviewed. Several other literature reviews concentrate on research and development (R&D) and manufacturing aspects of modularity, but they do not focus on cost management. Campagnolo and Camuffo (2009) reviewed 125 papers about modularity in a management or business context from a product design, process design, and organizational point of view. Fixson (2007) identified 160 studies within the engineering and management literature dealing with commonality and modularity, and analyzed these with respect to topic, investigated effects (such as costs), and applied research methods. Jiao et al. (2007) identified research and reflected on the current knowledge on product platforms and product family design. Their objective is to give a broad overview of the topic, and cost aspects are only briefly mentioned. Salvador (2007) screened management and engineering journals with the intention to discuss different definitions of modularity.

It is understandable that most of these prior reviews have not focused specifically on cost management, because most research does not go into much detail regarding cost impact. In some cases, general assumptions like "manufacturing costs always decline with the use of commonality" (Desai et al., 2001, p. 38) are too imprecise to capture the complex and sometimes opposed effects of modularity. Additionally, many studies mention the (supposed) benefits of modular design, platform usage, and common components rather broadly and not explicitly in financial terms, such as flexibility, risks, lead times, quality, or product variety (e.g., Ben Mahmoud-Jouini & Lenfle, 2010; Henke, 2000; Robertson & Ulrich, 1998). These effects are important, so we consider them and try to bridge their impact on costs, even if such effects are hard to quantify in some cases.

The current literature review

The contribution of the present literature review is that we focus on modularity and consider this as a *deliberate cost management strategy*. We extend the earlier literature review by Labro (2004) by reviewing later studies from similar journals and also by including several other aspects around modularity as a cost management strategy. Our objective is to create a detailed and differentiated review of the literature to get a better understanding of the multiple facets of modular design, component commonality, and product platforms as cost management strategies during the entire product life cycle.

Research method

We have included studies published in accounting as well as in innovations and operations management on the use of modularity for cost management purposes. We focus on all phases of a product life cycle, and thus on various kinds of costs (such as development costs, manufacturing, inventory holding, and after-sales service). There are many trade-offs involved when applying these methods, because cost savings in one phase of the life cycle or in one functional area can entail extra costs in another phase or area. The selection of sources has been a diverse process. We were aware of relevant literature through earlier research projects and structured literature searches we had been involved in, and so we realized in advance that the amount of research on modularity is very extensive.[2] A main challenge was to identify studies that specifically focus on cost management.

Keyword searches have been conducted to identify additional sources.[3] This included journals in accounting (the 37 journals listed by Bonner et al. (2006) complemented by *Advances in Management Accounting, Journal of Cost Management, European Accounting Review*, and *Management Accounting Research*) as well as journals in innovation and operations management (32 journals, consisting of the 23 journals listed in Wouters et al. (2016) plus *Production and Operations Management, Journal of Purchasing & Supply Chain Management, International Journal of Operations & Production Management, Engineering Management Journal, European Journal of Operational Research, Organization Studies, Journal of Management Studies, Journals of Management*, and *European Management Journal*).[4] Additional studies were found through the lists of references in key papers. The topic of modularity is huge, and the number of papers found quickly rose to an unmanageable number, even though many could very quickly be excluded because they were not addressing cost management and NPD. Gradually, we formulated the topics that are covered in this chapter and selected papers based on these. So, we do not claim to cover *all* papers on the intersection of modularity, cost management, and NPD, but we believe that we are including a significant part of the studies published in reputable academic journals for the specific topics covered in this review.

The remainder of this chapter is structured as follows. The next section discusses the relationship between cost management and modularity, and compares this to target costing. The following section goes into some of the terminology around modularity to become more specific on what this means for the scope of this chapter. The main section follows thereafter, looking at literature on the various ways in which these cost management methods have an impact on an organization's costs. After that, we consider a topic that has received far less attention in prior literature but is vital for cost management purposes, namely the role of cost allocation and other incentives for modularity. Next, we consider the organizational context of using modularity, in particular the problematic nature of accountability in this context.

Cost management through modularity: going beyond target costing

The management accounting literature has mainly addressed the topic of product design and cost management by looking at target costing (Wouters & Morales, 2014), and overall, management accounting research and practice have not focused that much on product development (Taipaleenmäki, 2014).

Target costing means that the allowable manufacturing costs of a product and of its components are determined at the beginning of an NPD project (Ansari et al., 2006). The starting point is to consider what kinds of products will be offered, at what sales price, and how these compare to competitors' products that are expected to be available, and the assumed sales prices of those. So, targets do not only relate to sales prices and costs derived from those, but also to the whole spectrum of functionality and performance of the product. Next, elements such as import duties, taxes, costs, and profit margins for various participants within the supply chain (for example, for car dealers and importing companies) are subtracted to arrive at the actual net earnings the *manufacturer* will receive. Deducing the target profit margin gives the allowable total unit cost for the manufacturer, from which the non-manufacturing costs (such as marketing, distribution, warranty, or development) need to be deducted to get the allowable manufacturing unit cost. This allowable cost can be broken down to obtain target costs for the major systems or even single components of the product.

Target costing can also be extended toward suppliers. The target cost of a component provides the maximum purchase price for the manufacturer. The manufacturer and supplier may also talk about the supplier's detailed cost breakdown for manufacturing the component (open-book accounting). Moreover, if product development requires significant resources and lead time, there will also be targets for the cost and lead time of that NPD project as such, potentially broken down into several stages (milestones) and cost categories.

Later into the NPD project, the maturing design of the new product can be reviewed after completion of each development phase. A design review is a milestone within a product development process whereby a design is evaluated against its requirements in order to verify the outcomes of previous activities and identify issues before committing to—and possibly re-prioritizing—further work. The manufacturing cost of the product and the components will be estimated, based on what is known about the semi-finished design. However, "does the estimated product cost meet the target cost?" is not the only question during these reviews. Similarly, the proposed product design will be examined in terms of the other targets for functionality and performance. Moreover, the cost and progress of the *NPD project* as such will be reviewed. Therefore, target costing should be seen in the wider context of stage-gate reviews (Hertenstein & Platt, 2000).

Thus, target costing is more elaborate than how it is often represented as "maximum allowable cost price = attainable selling price – required profit margin" (Dekker & Smidt, 2003). Inherently, several stages of the supply chain and various kinds of costs are involved. Clearly, there are multiple targets—not just costs—so there are complex trade-offs to be made among these targets. Obviously, all this planning needs a lot of forecasting, at least beyond the development time of the new product, so target costing is surrounded with considerable uncertainty. Evidently, with multiple models of the product, multiple sales channels, price erosion, and learning curves, these targets involve approximations, such as weighted-average sales prices and costs, and moreover, the targets will be dynamic (i.e., defined for several points in time). Understandably, estimating the cost of a product during the NPD project, when not everything has been determined, is challenging.

But apart from such complexities, the fundamental issue of target costing in the context of modularity is the focus on the product manufacturing cost within the *scope of one NPD project*. This is less relevant, or anyway not the whole story, in the context of modularity, because there the focus is on the costs and profitability of a *portfolio* of related products. In other words, "modular design ... entails a situation where the traditional product costing targeting at *product-level* (here meaning one good produced) cost information may become irrelevant. Instead, the focus seems to be frequently directed to the total profitability of technology or solution based *product lines* or profit responsible business units" (Granlund & Taipaleenmäki, 2005).

Beyond target costing

When a company is producing and selling a large number of different products and serving a large number of different customers, some costs are determined by the combined effect of design choices made in separate NPD projects. For example, the costs of warehousing products may be driven by the breadth of the product assortment (measured by the number of different stock-keeping units, or SKUs). The firm's R&D costs may be driven by the total number of different elements (i.e., parts, modules, designs, patterns, or versions) that need to be designed for all products. Or, purchasing transaction costs may be driven by the number of different suppliers the firm is doing business with for all its products. Purchase prices may be affected by the number of units purchased for all products in which a particular part is used. Similarly, manufacturing costs may be affected by the number of units produced per part and the number of production runs needed for producing that number of units. However, simply reducing the number of different parts, suppliers, or production batches may not result in lower costs, as the cost per part, supplier, or production batch may go up due to increased difficulty (Labro, 2004).

The point is that many of these "complexity-driven costs" can hardly be addressed within the scope of a single NPD project for developing only one product (Davila & Wouters, 2004). Structural cost management is required, that considers organizational design, product design and process design, in order to create an appropriate cost structure (Anderson & Dekker, 2009). For example, a car company will also have, next to target costing for each new model, programs in place across different car models to develop engines and other systems that are jointly used, and it will also develop platforms on the basis of which subsequent new car models need to be based.

As another example, consider Unilever in fast-moving consumer goods, such as home and personal care products, or ice cream. Different European country organizations within Unilever carried many local brands, developed their own new products, created marketing campaigns only for use in their own countries, and had their own manufacturing sites. The company went for a cost management strategy of complexity reduction. It decreased the number of different brands, formulations, packaging materials, suppliers, etc. that were used across Europe.[5] Also, *new global* brands were introduced, such as Magnum ice cream. As a result, fewer brands can be supported with larger budgets for product development and marketing (think of the very expensive commercials for Magnum ice cream). More commonality of products also allows lower inventories and better customer service, because a particular product can be sold in various countries, depending on actual demand. The company created more commonality across products as a deliberate cost management strategy, and this did not happen through target costing within separate NPD projects.

These examples illustrate that managing complexity-based costs requires additional cost management methods besides target costing.[6] That is the focus of methods such as component commonality, modular design, and product platforms, which, for brevity, we will simply refer to as "modularity."

Conceptualizations of modularity

Since modularity is a complex phenomenon, understood in many different ways, this section discusses various conceptualizations of modularity. The objective is to get confusion about the concept of modularity "out of the way" before we get to the heart of this literature review.

An NPD project concerns a distinct activity for the development and introduction of one or several new products that are added to the portfolio. The term "products" will refer here to the firm's market offerings that may consist of a combination of products and services that the firm offers to its customers (Ulaga & Reinartz, 2011). For example, a truck may be the core product, and additional services include financing, training, and maintenance.

A company will regularly develop and introduce new products and phase out old products, and so at any point in time, it offers a portfolio of products that are in different stages of their product life cycles. The NPD project requires various kinds of R&D costs, for internal resources such as staff and equipment, and for external contributions such as additional staff on a temporary basis, licenses and other intellectual property, and services (such as conducting tests or building prototypes). These R&D costs comprise one focus of the company's cost management efforts. The new product itself will require various kinds of manufacturing as well as non-manufacturing costs, and these product costs are the other focus of the company's cost management efforts.[7]

Several approaches to modularity can be distinguished, such as component commonality, modular design, and product platforms. Collectively, these are mechanisms for coordinating technical design decisions during NPD across a portfolio of products, with the aim of reducing the total costs over the total volume of these products (i.e., concerning all products, and over their entire life cycles) or maximizing the total profit of the firm. This is particularly relevant in the context of bringing a large portfolio of different end products to the market in a cost-efficient way. However, the terms modular design, commonality, and product platforms are often used in the literature without clearly defining or distinguishing them (Gershenson et al., 2003). For example, after reviewing about 100 papers dealing with product modularity, Salvador (2007) found about 40 different definitions. Also, a standard and accepted definition of the term "module" does not exist (Henke, 2000).

The close connection and difficulty in clearly distinguishing between these cost management methods become obvious in the attempt by Christopher (2000, p. 41) who includes all three concepts in one definition. He defines postponement or delayed configuration as "the principle of seeking to design products using common platforms, components, or modules, but where the final assembly or customization does not take place until the final market destination and/or customer requirement is known." Voss and Hsuan (2009, p. 543), on the other hand, include commonality in their definition of modularity as the "scheme by which interfaces shared among components in a given product architecture are standardized and specified to allow for greater reusability and commonality (or sharing) of components among product families."

We will compare and differentiate between several definitions and conclude with the definitions that are the basis for this chapter.

Component commonality

Labro (2004) and Mirchandani and Mishrah (2009) define component commonality simply as the usage of a same version of a component in the assembly of more than one different type of end product. This is comparable to "the replacement of several different components … by one component" (Eynan & Rosenblatt, 1996). These definitions are more referring to the static condition than to the dynamics of an NPD process, which is actually our focus. Therefore, Wouters and Morales (2014) define parts commonality as "limited sets of allowed materials, parts, components, packaging etc. that act as constraints during product design, in order to share these across a range of final products." This definition focuses on the NPD processes to enhance commonality among the product portfolio. When we talk about component commonality, we mean both the application of the same components of multiple products within a time period and the application of the same components from one product generation to the other, also called *reuse* (Ramdas et al., 2003).

Modular design

Although modular design promotes the application of the same component in several products, we will not equate the two methods. Modular design is a design philosophy, meaning that "products are designed in such a way, that a wide variety of final products can be produced using a limited number of modules that are adjusted and/or combined with different parts and other modules" (Wouters & Morales, 2014). Schilling (2000) describes modularity quite similarly as a general concept of a system, and its ability to separate and recombine its components.

Ulrich (1995) is one of the first researchers dealing with modularity from a technical point of view. He conceptualized the one-to-one mapping of functions to physical components as a fundamental characteristic of a modular product architecture. For an integral architecture, this mapping is complex and not one to one. If a functional feature of a product is executed by one specific component, and no interaction with other components is required to perform this function, we talk about a full modular product design. Another important technical key characteristic of modularity is standardized interface specifications, which minimize the interactions among the individual modules and create independence between them (Sanchez & Mahoney, 1996). Going into the same direction, Baldwin and Clark (2000, p. 63) define a module as "a unit whose structural elements are powerfully connected among themselves and relatively weakly connected to elements in other units."

This characteristic of modular design—which facilitates the decomposition of a modular system (Mikkola, 2007) due to standardized interfaces and therefore breaking the complex system down into smaller and simpler subsystems (Fine, 2009)—entails two important benefits. On the one hand, a product can be broken down into its functional components, and "single components can be developed and manufactured independently of what occurs in respect of other components" (Galvin, 1999, p. 467). The second important benefit is that exactly these standardized interfaces enable firms to reuse existing modules and build up a huge variety of different products: "Modularity … allows … creating product variety by changing some of the features of individual modules, while the basic architecture and relations among components are standardized" (Fredriksson & Gadde, 2005).

Fixson and Clark (2002, p. 131) go further and define modularity as "a bundle of product characteristics rather than a single dimension." They unbundle modularity in a multidimensional product architecture construct in order to measure differences in product architecture and operationalize modularity. As major dimensions of this construct, they identify the function–component mapping, i.e., the way functions are allocated to components, and interfaces, as the relations between the different components.

Pandremenos et al. (2009) distinguish between three fields of modularity: modularity in use, modularity in design, and modularity in production. This distinction deals with the various motives a firm has when applying a modular strategy. Modularity in use focuses on the customer's perspective (satisfying needs through individualization), modularity in design emphasizes the architectural dimension, and modularity in production underlines the flexibility of the manufacturing process.

The importance of the modules' independence grows with the complexity of the product. Langlois (2002, p. 19) describes modularity as a "set of principles for managing complexity." Standardized interfaces might be easier to implement in IT and software, or in a simple product like a chair or furniture, because the designer can overlook a manageable number of interdependencies. Yet, for a complex product such as a car, many physical and spatial restrictions reduce possibilities to implement standardized interfaces, so considerable coordination costs are unavoidable. Persson and Åhlström (2006) criticize that the literature focuses on rather simple products, and they conducted a case study at Volvo. Their key findings about difficulties in modularizing complex products concern the coordination process and the appropriate degree of modularity, and they suggest that it would be impossible to create a very complex product with a fully modular design.

Adding the term *mass customization*, also often mentioned in this context, "mass customization appears to presuppose product modularity, and the benefits heralded by move to modularity would likely be realized in a move to mass customization" (Ro et al., 2007). Duray et al. (2000) develop a conceptual typology about this topic and reason in a similar way. They define the term mass customization as "a paradox-breaking manufacturing reality that combines the unique products of craft manufacturing with the cost-efficient manufacturing methods of mass production" and "building products to customer specifications using modular components to achieve economies of scale" (Duray et al., 2000).

As shown earlier, the term modular design is multifaceted and can be defined in varied ways. Recognizing this ambiguity, Salvador (2007) screened management and engineering journals, and identified five definitional perspectives of the term product modularity: component commonality, component combinability, function binding, interface standardization, and loose coupling.

Product platform

A common example for product platforms is the automotive industry. Nowadays, many volume and premium car manufacturers create platforms as specific wheel bases on which several derivatives are based, like a sedan, a station wagon, and a cabriolet. Probably, the most widely known example is the Volkswagen group that also applies platforms across its brands (Paralikas et al., 2011).

Robertson and Ulrich (1998) give a general definition of platforms when they talk about a "collection of assets [i.e., components, processes, knowledge, people and relationships] that are shared by a set of products." Lehnerd and Meyer (1997) talk about a core technology, consisting of a set of subsystems and interfaces. This core technology results in a common structure that enables firms to develop and produce a stream of derivative products in an efficient way. Baldwin and Clark (1997) mention three aspects of product platforms: architecture (what modules with which function will be part of the system?), interfaces (how will the individual modules interact?), and standards (does the module conform to the system's design rules?).

Thus, a platform defines the core of a product and constitutes the physical base of a product family. It is a specific architecture that allows the shared use of processes, components, and knowledge among product sets (Davila & Wouters, 2004). Halman et al. (2003, p. 150) link platforms to product families and define a platform as the "common basis of all individual products within a product family. As a consequence, a platform is always linked to a product family."

Wortmann and Alblas (2009) discuss three types of platforms in their work: A *modular platform* reconfigures existing modules for a new variant. A *scalable platform* is variable with respect to the capacity, so deriving a product with the same function, but a divergent performance level, is eased. The focus of a *generational platform* lies on the time dimension, when deriving following product generations from an existing platform accelerates the product development process.

Modularity in this chapter

From our point of view, the perspectives of modularity and commonality are different. While modular design seems to be a more strategic and long-term oriented approach when a product family is conceptualized in an early development stage, the idea of component commonality is based on already developed and applied components used in existing product variants. When planning or developing a new derivative product, the question is this: are there already developed components existing products use that can be (re-)used for the new derivate product? So, commonality is medium-term oriented and focuses on the component: is a component particularly designed for and used in only one product, or is it used among a whole family of products? In contrast, modular design is long-term oriented and focuses on the design of a whole product family: if a modular approach is chosen, how can individual components be used and replaced independently among different derivative products?

Nonetheless, the two terms are closely connected: When a new derivative product is planned, and developers are willing to (re-)use already existing components developed for a present product, this product has to be constructed in a modular way. Otherwise, if products have an integral design, it becomes much more difficult to adopt components for the new derivative product. We argue, therefore, that component commonality is a consequence of modular design, or even modular design is a precondition to enable component commonality.

In addition, a product platform concerns the basic architecture of a product by describing the physical implementation of a functional design, and this becomes the basis for a series of derivative products.

For the purpose of this literature review, we developed the definitions shown in Table 4.1. These are based on common threads in the various definitions mentioned above and include the key characteristics of each method from our point of view.

Impact of modularity on costs

In this section, we review literature dealing with the impact of modularity on costs. First, we review some cases that describe modularity as an overall, strategic approach for NPD and cost management. Then, we look at studies that cover more detailed and specific design choices, for example, whether it would be better for a company to stick to the prescribed database of common parts, or to allow an exception and develop an individualized component for a particular product. We will also discuss that this literature implicitly assumes some form of centralized decision-making.

Table 4.1 Definitions used for this review

Component commonality	A constraint or requirement to use already developed components without adjusting or modifying them in an NPD project in order to increase the number of carry-over of parts.
Modular design	An architectural and strategic design philosophy that enables a firm to separate and recombine components within a product family or among products. Technical implementation is realized through functional independence and standardized interfaces among modules.
Product platform	A specification of a common technical base from which a high number of products with different performance characteristics and features are derived.

Holistic cases of cost management and modularity

Some of the empirical literature has studied the implementation of modularity in actual cases and describes quite comprehensive and pragmatic examples of how modularity can be implemented. A classic example of modularity implementation is IBM in the 1960s, described in *Harvard Business Review* (Baldwin & Clark, 1997). It describes how IBM introduced its first modular computer in 1964 and discusses the consequences for competitors, suppliers, innovation in general, and for IBM itself. Another classic example is Black & Decker in the 1970s, described in a book on product platforms (Rosenau & Rothberg, 2003). It tells the story of the big challenges regarding cost pressure and competiveness for Black & Decker in the 1970s, and how they solved it through a modular strategy. This led to large savings in material and labor costs, and it also brought considerable benefits in cycle time and new product introductions, which enabled Black & Decker to dominate the market for many years. Sanderson and Uzumeri (1995, p. 780) describe how Sony handled variety of its products, and one of the elements was modularity. Sony minimized its design costs by "building all of their models around key modules and platforms. Modular design and flexible manufacturing allowed Sony to produce a wide variety of models with high quality and low cost." It also enabled Sony to introduce many new products and achieve rapid model turnover. Hewlett-Packard is the focal example in the paper by Feitzinger and Lee (1997). The paper describes the effects when HP postponed "the task of differentiating [the] product for a specific customer until the latest possible point in the supply network" (p. 116) and reduced the number of different components in its LaserJets (a cost reduction in manufacturing, stocking, and delivering) and DeskJets (slightly higher manufacturing costs, but a considerable reduction in manufacturing, shipping, and inventory costs). Further examples talk about the development process of the "smart" by Daimler (Stephan et al., 2008) and more broadly about the US auto industry (Ro et al., 2007).[8] Other field studies address the limitations of modularity concepts and the problems and risks related to implementing these, for example, based on case studies of the three technology-driven companies ASML, Skil, and SDI (Halman et al., 2003); the automotive industry (Ben Mahmoud-Jouini & Lenfle, 2010; Persson & Åhlström, 2006; Sköld & Karlsson, 2012); and other empirical settings (Lau, 2011; Muffatto & Roveda, 2000).

The implicit assumption of centralized decision-making

Before going into more detail regarding the costs that are involved in specific design choices, it is helpful to consider the assumption that is implicit in the literature reviewed in the next section. Moving from an integral to a modular approach entails shifts in processes and organizational infrastructure, which requires additional costs the organization should be aware of. That these organizational costs are worth investing in is shown by Ramdas et al. (2003), who investigate *centralized versus decentralized decision-making.*

Their model considers a situation in which a firm offers a fixed and known number of products that are concurrently developed, and it includes two kinds of decisions: (1) which versions of each component should be developed for this defined product line, and (2) which version of each component should be used by each model in the line. Of course, there are all kinds of technical constraints, such as which components can be used together in a module, and which modules can be used for a particular product. Obviously, a lot of information is required, such as sales for each product, all feasible component versions (the existing versions and the versions that might be under consideration by any individual project team), the fixed costs of introducing a particular component version (such as for design, tooling, and after-sales support), and the variable costs when using a particular module on a particular product (such as for materials). The model assumes *centralized decision-making*, i.e., a cost minimization objective for the entire organization. Using the model, cost minimizing at the portfolio level can consider the cost trade-offs across all products (Ramdas et al., 2003).

Yet, often such an overall optimization may not be realistic, because not all information is available in one place at the same time, and not all decisions are taken simultaneously based on an overall cost minimization objective. *Decentralized decision-making* means that each project team independently (project by project) decides which components to develop for their product and which existing components to use, which have already been developed by another team. This approach results in higher costs for the entire portfolio. However, decentralized decision-making is not considered in this chapter. Here, we review research about the impact of modularity on different types of costs so as to better understand the trade-offs involved when using modularity as a cost management method. Implicitly, we consider centralized decision-making with an overall optimization objective. The issue of decentralized decision-making comes back toward the end of the chapter.

Table 4.2 illustrates the structure of the remainder of this section. We will deal with the numerous effects (mainly cost impacts) of modularity during the different life-cycle phases of a product. The table aggregates the effects we found, whereby we distinguish between cost rate and driver use regarding the several cost effects, as applied by Labro (2004). *F* indicates a favorable impact, so a cost reduction, and *U* means an unfavorable impact, so a cost increase. Please note that some papers discuss cost impact of modularity that can be either favorable or unfavorable, depending on the individual circumstances. Additionally, some papers deal with specific effects that cannot be categorized as favorable or unfavorable.

Table 4.2 Effects of modularity on various kinds of costs

Cost rate		*Driver use*		*Effects besides costs*	
Design, development, and innovation					
Initial development costs		**Number of development events**		**Individualization of components**	
(Mahmoud-Jouini & Lenfle, 2010)	U	(Mahmoud-Jouini & Lenfle, 2010)	F	(Fisher et al., 1999)	-
(Krishnan & Gupta, 2001)	U	(Fisher et al., 1999)	F	(Davila & Wouters, 2004)	-
(Davila & Wouters, 2004)	U	(Krishnan & Gupta, 2001)	F	(Chakravarty & Balakrishnan, 2001)	-
(Krishnan, Singh & T irupati, 1999)	U	(Krishnan, Singh & Tirupati, 1999)	F	**Manageability**	
				(Baldwin & Clark, 1997)	F
				(Langlois, 2002)	F
				Innovation level	
				(Kamrad et al., 2013)	F
				(Garud & Kumaraswamy, 1995)	F
				(Ramachandran & Krishnan, 2008)	F
				(Miozzo & Grimshaw, 2005)	U

(Continued)

Cost rate		*Driver use*		*Effects besides costs*	
Sourcing, manufacturing, and logistics					
Purchase pooling		**Manufacturing investments**		**Agility**	
(Fisher et al., 1999)	F			(Watanabe & Ane, 2004)	F
(Hu et al., 2013)	FU	(Fisher et al., 1999)	F		
Inventory costs		**Number of set-ups**		**Outsourcing**	
(Thomas & Warsing, 2009)	F	(Thonemann & Brandeau, 2000)	F	(Anderson & Parker, 2002)	F
(Hillier, 2002)	F			(Miozzo & Grimshaw, 2005)	U
Variable production costs					
(Ramdas et al., 2003)	U				
(Krishnan & Gupta, 2001)	U				
(Fisher et al., 1999)	U				
Marketing, sales, and distribution					
				Sales	
				(Nobeoka & Cusumano, 1997)	F
				Marketing research	
				(Sanchez, 1999)	-
				Pricing and cannibalisation	
				(Fisher et al., 1999)	-
				(Robertson & Ulrich, 1998)	-
				(Desai et al., 2001)	U
				(Subramanian et al., 2013)	F
				(Kim & Chhajed, 2000)	F
				Quality	
				(Fisher et al., 1999)	F
				(Ramdas & Randall, 2008)	FU
				Flexibility	
				(Cebon et al., 2008; Asan et al., 2008)	F
				Imitation	
				(Ethiraj et al., 2008)	U
Product use and maintenance					
Warranty costs				**Upgradeability**	
(Murthy & Blischke, 2000)	F			(Ramachandran & Krishnan, 2008)	F
				(Ülkü et al., 2012)	
Remanufacturing, recycling, and disposal					
Retirement costs				**Waste reduction**	
(Zhang & Gershenson, 2004)	-			(Kamrad et al., 2013)	F
Remanufacturing costs				(Fernández & Kekäle, 2005)	F
(Abbey et al., 2013)	F			(Sharma et al., 2010)	F
(Maslennikova & Foley, 2000)	F				
(Subramanian et al., 2013)	F				

It is our intention to offer a holistic view of the effects a modularity strategy can have on a firm's costs, so we also discuss two effects that are not mentioned in Table 4.2. These two effects cannot be clearly assigned to a specific life-cycle stage, or even arise in several stages. The first is *complexity costs*: Because the total number of different components to develop, purchase, manufacture, and store decreases, modularity reduces complexity (Davila & Wouters, 2004; Persson & Åhlström, 2006). Moreover, the disparity of processes declines (Garg & Tang, 1997). Furthermore, *coordination costs* affect several life-cycle stages, too. We argue that a higher coordination effort is needed almost throughout the whole life cycle when implementing a modular design strategy: in the development phase, when requirements of all products have to be considered or combined during products' conceptualization; during supplier negotiations, when an intensive coordination among the individual projects seems also important to realize economies of scale; and during manufacturing, when production systems are jointly used among several products. Fredriksson (2006) emphasizes the importance of coordination mechanisms for the efficient implementation of a modular strategy. Although both *complexity* and *coordination efforts* are hard to quantify in monetary terms, they have fundamental impact, an organization has to be aware of when pursuing a modular strategy.

Impact on design, development, and innovation

One of the most examined life-cycle stages concerning the effects of modularity is the product development phase. The literature has investigated multifaceted effects, which will be discussed next.

One argument is that a modular product architecture causes higher *initial development costs*. At the beginning of the development activities, when a component or a product platform is designed, additional costs arise to provide for the reusability for further product derivatives, compared to the development of a specific component or integral product. The requirements for a jointly used component are higher (or at least not lower) compared to a product-specific solution (Ben Mahmoud-Jouini & Lenfle, 2010; Davila & Wouters, 2004; Krishnan & Gupta, 2001; Krishnan et al., 1999). We compare two alternatives at this point: the development costs of a component suitable for one (integral) product versus the development cost of a component that can be used in more than one product. From our point of view, the firm increases its investment in product development at this stage to realize future development cost savings. The objective is to derive several products from the same platform in a cost-efficient way and consequently to avoid large development efforts for every single product.

Another argument deals with the *number of development events*: If components or platforms are shared among different products, fewer parts have to be designed and tested in total, which decreases overall development costs (Davila & Wouters, 2004; Fisher et al., 1999; Krishnan & Gupta, 2001; Krishnan et al., 1999). Therefore, even if the development effort for a platform might exceed the expenses for the development of the technical base of just one product, total development costs may decrease and lead times may be reduced when applying product platforms (Ben Mahmoud-Jouini & Lenfle, 2010; Muffatto & Roveda, 2000).

The practical challenge lies in the assessment of the technical feasibility, as well as in the estimation of the development expenses for each option, in order to handle this trade-off before taking the final decision. Krishnan and Gupta (2001) create a mathematical model to examine under which conditions a platform strategy outperforms an individual product development approach. They conclude that product platforms are appropriate when performance levels of derivative products are not too different, and customers' valuation and requirements for different market segments are not extremely diverse.

The factors that influence the decision to standardize and share a component or to go for a product-specific solution (in the sense of an *individualized component*) have received much attention in the academic literature. While Fisher et al. (1999) distinguish between components with *strong* and *weak* influence on quality, Davila and Wouters (2004) separate the components in *core* and *non-core* modules, and Toyota categorizes their parts into *aesthetic* and *functional* components (Fisher et al., 1999). Both studies conclude that the aesthetic parts are appropriate candidates to individualize. Consequently, the development team can focus on these components, as they are directly responsible for the products' perceived value. Moreover, imposing restrictions on the development team might inhibit their creativity that the NPD requires, especially at the beginning.

The degree of modularity can also be interpreted as a property of a product. An interesting question concerns the appropriate or optimal number of product variants a common technical base should be designed for, and how many module modifications are needed for a specific range of product variety. In other words, how high should the degree of modularity within a product family be? Chakravarty & Balakrishnan (2001) try to answer that question and develop a mathematical model to determine the optimal variance in order to maximize a firm's profits.

One of modularity's main benefits is the assembly of small, independently developed subsystems to a final product with extensive functionality (Baldwin & Clark, 1997). This characteristic (breaking down a complex product into smaller, individual modules) is a way to maintain *manageability* (Langlois, 2002). As a consequence, each subsystem can be processed individually. As mentioned earlier, the development of complex products like cars is not feasible in another way, as these kinds of products consist of many and still very complex subsystems.

This decomposing aspect of modularity (a complex product is divided up into smaller and simpler subsystems) allows a shift from radical to incremental innovation, which can accelerate further development in the next step. Therefore, a firm applying modularity can enhance the *innovation level* of its products, as new technology can be integrated faster. Developers can improve the product step by step via replacing technologically obsolete modules with new ones (without changing the remaining product). Only the internal content and performance of the replaced modules change. This allows a firm's products to remain technologically up to date in a cost-efficient way, which becomes even more important if a complex product entails technologies with deviating life cycles and if redesigning costs for integral products are high (Kamrad et al., 2013).

The decision whether it is a better idea to reuse a component for the product's next generation or to redesign/upgrade it, should be made against the backdrop of how the redesigned component can be priced (Wu et al., 2009). Balancing these opportunity costs (if the additional profits outweigh the redesign costs) of several component upgrades can be helpful when budget restrictions exist, but sometimes also strategic considerations force these decisions: If a component's functionality does not meet the current basic customer expectations or legal requirements anymore, a firm simply has to update or exchange the component. We found manifold terminology for this incremental "step-by-step" innovation. Garud and Kumaraswamy (1995) talk about *economies of substitution*, referring mainly to associated cost savings; Cebon et al. (2008) use the term *modular innovation* as one of four innovation types; and Ramachandran and Krishnan (2008) talk about *modular upgradeability*, referring to rapid sequential innovation in their study about software.

On the other hand, we can also think about difficulties in the context of modular innovation. Yet, negative cost effects of platform-based development have received far less research attention (Krishnan & Gupta, 2001; Persson & Åhlström, 2006). Miozzo and Grimshaw (2005) contradict the claim that modularity is beneficial for and accelerates the innovation process. Dealing with IT outsourcing in knowledge-intensive business services, they examine 13 IT outsourcing contracts and report difficulties concerning the cooperation between the firms and their suppliers. Though the study deals with the quite specific topic of IT services, it seems plausible that practical problems, like maintaining standardized interfaces or cooperation between firms in general, can be responsible for barriers in the innovation process.

Impact on sourcing, manufacturing, and logistics

Other areas that have received much research attention in the context of modular design, component commonality, and product platforms are sourcing, manufacturing, and logistics. Probably the most common argument for benefits of component commonality is economies of scale (Fisher et al., 1999). With larger quantities, the sourcing department can achieve better conditions in price negotiations with their suppliers—we refer to this effect as *purchase pooling*. This applies when a customer firm is able to purchase its desired quantity and quantity discounts are offered. Hu et al. (2013) contradict this widespread argumentation and base their study on powerful suppliers that can define price and quantity conditions. Developing a mathematical model, they conclude that firms can even harm themselves when pooling their purchases at a more aggregated level, as the powerful supplier can adapt the contract, benefit from the reduced demand variability, and extract profits from the buying firm.

Furthermore, modularity also impacts logistics and *inventory costs*. Researchers often report a positive effect on inventory system performance (Thomas & Warsing, 2009). Based on mathematical models and numerical simulations, a risk pooling effect can be identified, as it is easier to forecast demands on a generic than on a specific level. And, because modularity allows firms to use component variants in higher quantities, fewer components in total have to be kept in stock, i.e., lower inventory is needed and therefore, capital employed is reduced (Davila & Wouters, 2007; Hillier, 2002).

Another, but potentially unfavorable effect of modular components concerns higher *variable production costs* (compared to individualized components) (Fisher et al., 1999; Murthy & Blischke, 2000). This seems plausible if we talk about material costs: Modular parts need to fit in several end products that might have different requirements. Therefore, it might be more complex than an integral part that is specifically designed for just one end product. Or, a common component is used both in a low-quality version and in a high-end version of a product, and if the component has to meet the high-quality product's requirements, it will be over-specified (i.e., better than adequate) for some versions within the product family (Krishnan & Gupta, 2001; Ramdas et al., 2003). Fisher et al. (1999) develop an analytical model dealing with the key drivers of a component-sharing strategy. The model focuses on components with a weak influence on product quality. They test this model in an empirical study with data from six OEMs about automotive front brakes. They conclude that if components are downward compatible, manufacturing costs increase with the performance of the component, and economies of scale concerning production costs exist. Additionally, they observe a positive correlation between component and product variety. For example, a specific rotor is developed for every two additional platforms. As this is exactly the trend modularity wants to counteract, they relate this observation to individual teams' autonomy and the absence of a centrally coordinated component commonality policy.

Modularity also impacts *investments for manufacturing* processes. In many industries, specific machines and tools are needed to produce certain components. As fewer component variants have to be produced, also the investments in these production systems and tools may be less (Fisher et al., 1999).

Another, closely related impact of commonality refers directly to the manufacturing process, more specifically to the *number of set-ups*. As the total number of component variants decreases, the quantity of each produced component increases (if we assume a firm that applies a modular strategy will not produce a lower total volume of end products), and so the number of set-ups and related set-up costs in the production process decrease (Thonemann & Brandeau, 2000).

As already mentioned, some impacts are hard to quantify in monetary terms. The most common impact of modularity (besides costs) concerns increased flexibility or *agility* if modularity enables delaying the point of product differentiation, which means that prepackaged modules are held in stock until their final utilization is known (Christopher, 2000). Watanabe and Ane (2004) use simulation and find that a modular product architecture leads to an increasing manufacturing agility, which reduces the manufacturing lead time in a next step.

Another way to reduce costs is to *outsource* several production steps, e.g., if hourly rates of suppliers or in other countries are lower. Anderson and Parker (2002) deal with the make or buy decision in their analytical study, and they find a connection between the degree of modularity and outsourcing: increasing modularity leads to more outsourcing. Although modularity can be an enabler for cost savings through outsourcing, one should also consider difficulties in this context, which we already mention in an earlier section (Miozzo & Grimshaw, 2005).

Impact on marketing, sales, and distribution

We did not identify literature about the effects of modularity on costs and cost driver use in marketing, sales, or distribution. Nonetheless, modularity may impact the firm's image and the products' reliability, and so it is a significantly impacted area, mainly on the revenue side. We will discuss some implications and new challenges for the marketing activities and sales, because this is also an important part to get a holistic understanding of the topic.

If a modular strategy (increasing the number of derivative products for appropriate costs) is properly executed, *sales* volume, revenue, and market share will increase, because more market segments can be served (Nobeoka & Cusumano, 1997). Additionally, customers may be more satisfied with a customized product compared to a standardized mass product, which may lead to a greater willingness to pay and more buy decisions. Or, as in today's automotive industry, many markets are developing toward a personalized environment, so there is no choice but to offer customized products in order to stay competitive. "Today, we are witnessing customer-driven strategies instead of product-driven strategy" (Umit Kucuk & Krishnamurthy, 2007, p. 52).

In other words, the product differentiation decision is, at least in part, relocated from the firm to the customer. Or, you could also say that giving the customer the possibility to customize his/her product is a product differentiation feature per se.

Moreover, modularity influences *marketing research*. While the conventional marketing research process identifies consumer preferences to optimize a product's attributes according to a specific target segment, marketing research for modular products has to take the variances of these consumer preferences into account. So, it is less a task of identifying the specific needs a product has to satisfy in a particular market, but more about figuring out a whole range of several required product manifestations. In a next step, these are used to create a modular architecture that is able to serve the most profitable market segments. Additionally, the marketing department is required to position the firm via a relational marketing strategy—for example working out the benefits of the new product architecture for the customer, such as scalability, upgradeability, or improved serviceability (Sanchez, 1999).

As we mentioned before, the whole approach of modularity will only work in the long term if the derivative products, though they share common components, are well distinguishable for the customer. This has both *pricing and cannibalisation* impacts: If a premium-priced product variant seems similar in appearance and functionality, the customer has no reason to buy it and may choose the cheaper derivative. So, in order to realize premium prices, it makes sense not to share the components that have a direct impact on the product's quality from the customer's point of view, and therefore only share components the customer does not know or perceive as important (Fisher et al., 1999; Robertson & Ulrich, 1998).

Desai et al. (2001) also discuss the effect that commonality may hinder a firm to extract premium prices for the better product due to reduced differentiation. They develop an analytical model to examine the trade-off between manufacturing benefits of commonality for these marketing challenges. Additionally, they develop an index to operationalize the attractiveness of "making a component common" compared to other components. While there is a general agreement that different products should be well distinguishable in order to reduce cannibalisation, Subramanian et al. (2013) argue in a different way. Developing a mathematical model and illustrating its implementation with two Apple iPads, they conclude that the cannibalisation effect can also be beneficial for a firm when a third-party remanufacturer exists.

Kim and Chhajed (2000) argue in their study that a too noticeable application of commonality, such that a clear distinction of different products from a customer's point of view is not given anymore, impacts a product's utility in the eyes of the customer. They develop a mathematical model and examine how modularity and prices should be designed to reduce cannibalization and maximize profits when different product qualities are offered. As one result, they conclude that target segments' quality valuation is crucial when considering the usage of common components among segments. While most studies justify the commonality approach with cost savings, they reason that if a firm is able to price the valuation change, commonality can even be beneficial without these savings. Otherwise, if customers do not perceive any additional value, they will not necessarily pay price premiums for common components in their cheaper product variant (derived from the premium product) (Desai et al., 2001).

Besides the purchase price, the *quality* of a product and its components can be a key criterion for a customer's buying decision and willingness to pay. The key question is, if and how modularity affects product quality. We argue that generalized statements, such as that an increasing product quality and reliability always follows from a product platform strategy (Ben Mahmoud-Jouini & Lenfle, 2010), are not necessarily correct. Therefore, we want to discuss a quality trade-off.

On the one hand, due to a learning effect, the quality of a component applied in multiple products can be higher than a newly developed and individualized component. Additionally, if a company plans to utilize a component in more than one product, it might be willing to spend more money on development activities for this particular, shared component. This can also be a reason for a better quality compared to components developed for just a single product, where, just because of the lower total number of parts needed, less development budget is available. And, if different quality levels of products use the same component, the component might exceed the quality requirements for a range of the product family, except for the high-end product (Fisher et al., 1999).

On the other hand, a decreasing quality due to component commonality may occur if a component is not exactly designed and customized for the specific requirements of a single product. If the functional performance of a component is not only scalable, but also differs with respect to requirements, architecture, or other characteristics, the approach to replace several components by one shared component may lead to unfavorable quality effects because of several compromises. Ramdas and Randall (2008) study this quality trade-off of component commonality and define reliability as one dimension of quality. They conducted an empirical study and analyzed 693 observations from a data set of brake rotor failures from Ford. While they establish that the optimal technical fit of a component to a product's requirements improves quality, they also conclude that the experience effect is beneficial for quality (based on only one component in one company, which limits empirical generalizability). They reason that the relevance of this learning or experience effect decreases as a component is applied in more and more products over time (the marginal value of experience when going from one to two products is much larger than, for example, going from the tenth to the eleventh product also adopting that same component).

Another important impact of modularity that is also hard to quantify is increasing *flexibility*. Modularity entails the chance to react to technological changes, to deal with market uncertainty (Asan et al., 2008; Wouters et al., 2011), and it increases the number of market niches that can be occupied (Cebon et al., 2008), These strategic benefits might be hard to assess in cost savings, but they can be very valuable to a firm: If the marketing department detects a new market niche for a new derivate product, the development process needs not to start from the beginning. If modularity is implemented in an efficient and clever way, a platform and many components exist, and the new product can "help itself," so the new market can be served in a short period of time, and sales increase (compared to an integral strategy). Additionally, as requirements for a product differ from one market to another, fulfilling the different regional customer expectations is eased.

Ethiraj et al. (2008) examine the trade-off of modularity on *imitation* and innovation. As we already discussed the innovation benefits of this product architecture in one of the previous paragraphs, they conclude via simulation that the innovation gains of a complete modular design include the risk of imitation. They summarize that a nearly modular architecture outperforms both a fully modular approach (due to reduced imitation risk) and a non-modular architecture (due to enhanced innovation opportunities).

Impact on product use and maintenance

In this section, we discuss the effects of modularity after product development, when the product has already been sold to customers. We not only focus on the impacts for the firms, but also include the customer's perspective.

If you think about the one-to-one mapping from functions to components (Ulrich, 1995) we mentioned in the previous chapter, modularity eases the identification of a defective module if a certain functional performance is not given anymore. Instead of disassembling a whole integral product, damage diagnosis, as well as repair work or replacement, is accelerated. Therefore, modularity reduces *warranty costs*, as repairing or maintaining a product is facilitated (Murthy & Blischke, 2000). Additionally, due to the lower number of total components, service costs may decline (Robertson & Ulrich, 1998).

If we adopt the customer's perspective now, they can just exchange an obsolete module if a product is built up of independent functional units. Thus, the customer gets easier access to *upgrades*, which seems preferable from a customer's point of view, especially when a product's technology improves in a short period of time (Ramachandran & Krishnan, 2008). This might be a buying argument and therefore increase sales, as the upgradeability option extends the value of the customer's investment. On the other hand, this updateability might extend the period of use and reduce additional sales. Depending on a firm's sales strategy (e.g., if a firm focuses on revenues from product sales, or more on additional functions and updates), harmful impacts on sales seem possible too.

Ülkü et al. (2012) investigate consumers' reactions and valuation of modular products in three experimental studies. They report decision biases for modularly upgradable products. Counterintuitively, the research participants undervalued future savings of rapidly improving products through upgrades and overvalued upgrade savings of products with a long life cycle.

Impact on remanufacturing, recycling, and disposal

A firm's decision on which product architecture to apply has an influence even at the end of a product's life cycle, involving four different processes, remanufacturing, reuse, recycling, and disposal (Zhang & Gershenson, 2002), and briefly summarized as "retirement costs." In order to emphasize the importance of considering recycling and disposal aspects already in the development stage, Tseng et al. (2010) develop an algorithm to assess the costs and benefits of modularizing a product.

The cost-reducing impact of modularity in this last life-cycle stage is also hypothesized by Zhang and Gershenson (2002) (mainly because of the simplified update and decomposition characteristics). They examine the direct relationship between modularity and *retirement costs*. But, after analyzing 14 different products with varying degrees of modularity (captured by a modularity measure) and calculating the several retirement costs for these products, they could not find a statistically significant relationship between the degree of modularity and retirement costs.

In contrast, Abbey et al. (2013) argue that the easy-to-disassemble characteristic of modularity facilitates *remanufacturing* and reduces the separation time and cost at this stage. Maslennikova and Foley (2000) examined this issue during a case study at Xerox, selling printers, among other things. They found that the modular design of products enabled the company to implement an end-of-life take-back program. The company created 400 reprocessing and remanufacturing jobs, and it reused over 3.8 million components that fit into their quality criteria within one year. Not only did the company save the disposal costs, which many governments impose on these kinds of manufacturers; altogether, the net savings in one year were over US$80 million, also through reduced raw material purchases and energy savings.

Subramanian et al. (2013) deal with the topic of including remanufacturing considerations into component commonality decisions. They argue that profits can significantly increase when remanufacturing is considered right at the beginning of NPD projects. They criticize that many firms base their component commonality strategy only on manufacturing and sales, but they ignore the changes of cost reduction and cannibalisation effects when remanufacturing is also considered.

Replacing only a few broken or obsolete components can significantly *reduce waste*, in comparison to integral designed products where the whole product has to be disposed of (Kamrad et al., 2013). While for integral products, scrapping or material recycling is often the most adequate approach at this stage, modules offer the chance to be repaired, refurbished, or reused (Fernández & Kekäle, 2005). For this reason, modularity promotes the sustainability idea firms focus more on in recent years. The idea to offer consumers the possibility to renew only the defect part instead of discarding the complete product (Sharma et al., 2010) can also be valuable in the sense of a green image. Environmental-friendly manufacturing technology becomes more and more important, and firms spend large budgets on green marketing campaigns.

Cost allocation and modularity

The previous section implicitly addressed centralized decisions on modularity that consider a wide range of trade-offs for the entire organization. Two issues were not addressed: Can accounting systems provide information to support such decisions? And, what incentives do accounting systems provide to decentralized decision makers who are responsible for separate products, because of cost allocations? These issues are reviewed in this section.

Costing allocations for a centralized decision on modularity

Let's start with a simple example. Suppose that there are three products that if designed independently generate a profit of 310 monetary units. It is technically possible to design a common module and use this for two or even all three products. How can the accounting system provide information on the cost consequences of more modularity? We could not find many papers that explicitly address this issue, especially not in the accounting literature.

Park and Simpson (2005, 2008) use an ABC system to estimate the cost implications of design alternatives regarding which parts are based on the same common part. Although the paper is not always as clearly written as we would like from an accounting perspective, it is interesting to see how their ABC system includes detailed activities, including allocation of costs to those activities, to be able to estimate and compare the cost of parts when produced independently and also when produced as a common part.

Thyssen et al. (2006) discuss ABC and modularity based on a case study. Many costs that are common to a number of products will be, in ABC terminology, at the level of company-sustaining activities, product-line-sustaining activities, or module-sustaining activities. They argue that any allocation of such costs to cost objects for which these are common "(based on revenue, number of units, direct labor hours, etc.) is bound to be arbitrary insofar as there is no cause and effect relation between the costs and the objects. Instead, one should summate the contributions from all the relevant products and deduct the common cost as an aggregate figure" (Thyssen et al., 2006, p. 267). The latter recommendation is also common in German costing systems of the multistage contribution costing (Ewert & Wagenhofer, 2006; Kloock & Schiller, 1997).

Johnson and Kirchain (2010) also consider cost allocations of common components. First, they determine the costs of all product variants as if each variant were produced independently, so without the benefits of sharing. The "standalone" cost of a product variant is calculated by adding the costs of all components that are needed for the product. Then, the costs of all product variants are calculated with considering the benefits of sharing. The "shared cost" of a product variant is the sum of the costs of unique components and a slice of the shared costs for common components, whereby a product's cut of the shared costs is determined based on the production volume of that part that the product consumes relative to the total production volume of the part. So, in this study, the role of cost allocations is to have a more comprehensive calculation of the full cost of a product, including a share of common costs for the common components that are used for the product.

Cost allocations as incentives for decentralized decisions on modularity

Continuing the simple example with three products, suppose that if two of these use the common module, the profit from those two products is 300 and the profit from the third product is 40, so 340 from all three products together. If instead all three use the common module, costs decrease and the total profit is 400. How should the development costs and unit costs of the common module be allocated, such that it is attractive for the managers who are responsible for these products to adopt the common module?

More generally formulated, assuming that it is possible to decide on a modularity strategy that creates most advantages for the entire product portfolio (Ramdas et al., 2003), the question arises how to translate this into cost allocations for separate product-level decisions that will actually implement that chosen modularity strategy. Benefits for the entire portfolio, such as greater purchasing or manufacturing volumes and lower inventory holding costs for the entire organization (i.e., for all products together), do not necessarily make modularity attractive at the product level. For example, the development of a part just for one particular product may be relatively straightforward and inexpensive, but the development costs of a more broadly applicable part may be significantly higher. As another example, there could be a part that is exactly right for a particular product, but having to choose a part from the database of allowed parts may lead to overspecification and higher material costs, or it may result in performance degradation, negative customer reactions, and revenue losses. The system for the allocation of joint costs resulting from modularity to multiple products may or may not make it attractive to adopt modularity at the product level.

Yet, perhaps somewhat surprisingly, the issue of cost allocation and cost savings associated with modularity to products has not received that much explicit attention in the literature. Two related papers on remanufacturing illustrate this lacuna. The first study (Subramanian et al., 2013), also mentioned earlier in this chapter, addresses the question of the optimal component commonality decision for the entire organization when also considering remanufacturing of products. Examples are machine tools, consumer electronics, and tires. The second study (Toktay & Wei, 2011) explicitly considers that different divisions within the organization may undertake manufacturing and remanufacturing operations, and so incentives must be considered. The study analyzes the decisions of both divisions *on sales prices and production quantities*, and develops cost allocation mechanisms of the initial manufacturing cost between the two divisions to achieve that the decentralized decisions lead to the optimal result for the entire company. However, what is *not* addressed is the decentralized decision on *component commonality*: if the manufacturing division makes that product design decision, how can cost allocations be used to achieve that the decentralized component commonality decision also leads to the optimal result for the entire company?

Cost allocation may not be needed when the implementation of a chosen modularity strategy is implemented through action controls and/or performance measures that are not based on costs. To some extent, firms will probably use action controls to simply force the implementation of a chosen modularity strategy. For example, there could be a database with allowed parts, and there could be rules regarding modules that have to be incorporated into the product design (Davila & Wouters, 2004). Result controls may also directly focus on the implementation of a chosen modularity strategy by requiring progress on certain performance measures reflecting the level of modularity, which have been developed in various studies (Hölttä-Otto et al., 2012; Johnson & Kirchain, 2010; Thevenot & Simpson, 2006).

However, the interesting question concerns the "voluntary" adoption of a modularity strategy, simply because the common parts and modules enable the realization of target costs. Cost allocation for modularity is understood here as the allocation of the development costs of technology to products that use this common technology and the allocation of unit costs of modules to products that use these common modules (whereby module is meant to generally refer to parts, components, subassemblies, modules, or software—basically anything built into a product). In other words, what does a product pay for technology and modules that are used together with others, instead of just developing and buying on its own? How do these internal prices affect decision-making at the product level?

Israelsen and Jørgensen (2011) discuss this setting, drawing on Ramdas et al. (2003), and develop a model for the allocation of costs to products that use a common module. They present the example already introduced earlier: Suppose that three products can use a common module. If only two use this module, the profit from those two is 300 and the profit from the third product is 40. If instead all three use the common module, costs decrease and the total profit is 400. For the manager responsible for the third product to adopt the common module, the cost allocation system should result in a profit of at least 40 for that product. Their model does not consider revenue effects, and it requires cost allocations in such a way that none of the managers are less well-off (i.e., have higher costs for their own product). This implies that if the contributing projects are arranged in descending order of contributing profit, then at any given point, the marginal project incorporating the common module cannot have more profit increase allocated to it than the marginal profit increase of the portfolio of all participating projects.

The first rule they suggest is to *allocate the marginal profitability of a participating product to that particular project*. In the earlier example, the profit increase with the third product is 60, and that would be allocated to that third project. However, to achieve this end result for each product, the distinction between unit-level costs and development costs is considered. The overall profit increase is the result of lower unit-level costs and development costs, but at the product level, it may not work out that well. The unit cost of the common module is allocated to the products based on the number of units used by each product. Because of overspecification, that may lead to too high unit-level costs for some products, which can be corrected with a so-called lump sum credit. After this, the development costs are allocated to the products in such a way that the intended profit effects are achieved. They present a numerical example based on a case study of a company that develops high-tech, analytical instruments. In this example of six products that can all adopt a common module, the sixth product offers a marginal profit increase of 10,000 for the entire company if it also adopts the module. Just looking at this product, however, gives a different picture: when not taking the common module, the unit costs are 350,000 and the unique development costs are 100,000 (so 450,000 costs in total); when taking the common module, the unit costs increase to 472,500 in total. So, rather than allocating some of the development costs for the joint module to this product too, instead, a lump sum credit of 32,500 is "allocated" to this product, so that the costs are reduced to 440,000 and it enjoys its marginal profit increase of 10,000 that it contributes for the entire company. The paper also discusses various practical challenges with the proposed solution, drawing on the case study experiences.

Bhaskaran and Krishnan (2009) discuss a different but related context. The issue is again decentralized decision-making in the context of product development and the impact of financial incentives, but different firms are involved and different mechanisms than cost allocations are investigated. The starting point for this paper is that by working together on product development, the development costs are lower compared to the situation when the innovation would be done by a single firm. Beyond simple revenue sharing, these firms can decide on sharing of the development work and/or development investments if one firm conducts most of the development work. The paper investigates which cost- and effort-sharing mechanism is better, depending on a variety of conditions.

Modularity, implementation, and accountability

This review of the literature on modularity so far has, hopefully, made it clear that these cost management strategies involve a lot of incompleteness—as in calculations and performance measures that do not capture all the relevant dimensions of performance (Jordan & Messner, 2012). In practice, targets for manufacturing costs in the context of target costing and modularity are based on an endless number of assumptions about future sales prices, required features, and other product attributes, future costs and margins downstream in the supply chain, the firms' own margins and nonmanufacturing costs, breakdowns of overall manufacturing cost targets, etc. Having a manufacturing cost target for, say, the navigation system of a car of €87.34 looks incredibly "precise" and "objective" but is actually extremely arbitrary. Or, an organization may not break down cost targets to such a detailed level, thereby leaving much uncertainty for decision makers at that operational level (Jørgensen & Messner, 2010). Similarly, there are likely to be many issues with performance measures that are supposed to reflect the level of modularity, which were briefly mentioned above, or with performance measures in NPD more generally (Hertenstein & Platt, 2000). Moreover, the way in which costs of common modules are allocated (see the discussion in the "Cost allocation and modularity" section) is probably creating some strange incentives in many practical situations. Also, estimates of the costs of product designs that are still works in progress during the NPD project, for comparison with cost targets, will be flawed with uncertainty.

The point is this: accountability based on target costing and modularity can be very real—there might be all kinds of pressures, bad consequences, rewards, etc. connected to these targets—but those targets and supporting data will typically be highly arbitrary and artificial. Yet, it all looks terribly objective and factual. How does accountability come about? What role do incomplete performance measures, targets, and calculations have in NPD? When and how are people committed to work toward such soft but also hard targets? Several studies have looked at such issues in the context of NPD and the use of modularity.

Mouritsen et al. (2001, 2009) present several case studies on management accounting around NPD projects in technology companies. These studies demonstrate that we should not think about the usefulness of management accounting for NPD (only) in terms of how "accurate" those techniques are. "The primary quality of management accounting calculations in relation to innovation activities is hardly that they describe innovation activities and make them increasingly transparent" (Mouritsen et al., 2009, p. 747). In their LeanTech case, the company had outsourced a large part of its production processes. Having ABC information from its suppliers strongly influenced the company's development activities, in the sense that they wanted to use fewer different components to save adjustment time and costs.

Consequently, the range of components was reduced from 15,000 to 5,000 (Mouritsen et al., 2001, p. 234). Also, the large number of different intermediate products, such as printed circuit boards, used for assembling products was now seen as too costly. There was a push toward products that needed less physical adaptation, combined with the development of fewer modules but with more potential functionalities and software solutions for customer adaptation.

In this LeanTech case, costing information impacted product development, but not because the costing information would be "perfect." The calculations disregarded the additional costs due to the increasing average cost per unit on inventory, the risks and possible costs due to the increased waiting time for critical components, and the higher R&D costs because of increased complexity of technical development (Mouritsen et al., 2009). LeanTech and the other case companies made or considered particular extensions that could be claimed to make the existing calculations more complete. But that was not the crux. "Sales performance, contribution margin and ABC margin are powerful because they can motivate actions to be performed by innovators. This translation, rather than represent the innovation choices, creates a context for innovation activities to occur" (Mouritsen et al., 2009, p. 751). Management accounting calculations may be needed to make ideas visible and credible, and it can challenge managers to relate their ideas and concerns about innovation to other important considerations, such as strategic objectives, profitability of products, and operational constraints in their own organization or elsewhere in the value chain.

The research of Jørgensen and Messner (2009, 2010) focuses even more specifically on modularity. They report a case study on the introduction of a new product strategy in a medium-sized, family-owned Danish company. The study demonstrates the limitations of accounting calculations to analyze decisions and accountability. It suggests that the various models mentioned earlier are most often very difficult—if not impossible—to implement because of lack of clarity of the modular concept itself in a particular situation, the complexity of modeling the concept, and the lack of required data. We will summarize these two papers (Jørgensen & Messner, 2009, 2010) quite extensively, because this research is one of the few examples of research addressing accountability for modularity and costs in such depth, and it is thus particularly relevant for our review.

The initial decision in the case company (Jørgensen & Messner, 2009, 2010): The company they investigated wanted to achieve various strategic objectives through a modular product strategy, which involved investing in platform development from which technology and even physical modules could be reused. The study shows how different people had different ideas about what modularity would be and the effects it would have. For example, marketing people were thinking of modularization as something that would enable them to sell any customization the customer would want, mainly through software configuration. The service engineers from sales and marketing were concerned with what effect the proposed modular architecture would have on customers' cost of ownership. The manufacturing people wanted modules that were physically manageable, and hoped that modularization would enable faster production and separately testable modules. The quality manager wanted a design that would increase the number of instruments that pass the quality tests in the first attempt, etc.

Also, it becomes clear that these very diverse benefits (and costs) of modularity were difficult to calculate. Top management wanted to achieve higher efficiency in product development and greater flexibility in offering new products. Modularity intuitively seemed a good idea to achieve this. They were aware of the kinds of complex effects and trade-offs we have also reviewed earlier, but these could not be fully quantified.

Moreover, the calculation tool for evaluating the profitability of a new product was, principally, not geared to capture the effects of modularity, but rather to evaluate products separately. The company "used a spreadsheet model that required engineers or managers to fill in estimated unit costs in production, as well as material and labor costs for the development of the product" (Jørgensen & Messner, 2009, p. 113). Understandably, "the existing spreadsheet model was designed to handle only one product at a time, while in the case of modularity, there would be several products or product variants that had to be evaluated in tandem because they would share one or more modules" (Jørgensen & Messner, 2010, p. 193). "When modularity was introduced, the representational limits of the earlier mentioned calculation model became apparent" (Jørgensen & Messner, 2009, p. 118). Still, the CEO made the decision to go modular, because, as said earlier, intuitively it seemed a good idea, and many people also expected that they would learn much from the new project and then better understand the consequences.

Next, they present and discuss findings regarding the company's first two projects for developing modular products. The company's stage-gate system played an important role. A company manual specified the different stages, the responsibilities, the desired outputs, the required documentation, etc. Although this control system was quite detailed, it also explicitly stated the described processes that should be regarded as guidelines and could be adjusted to suit individual projects. This formalized control instrument was generally perceived as helpful in maintaining a certain level of efficiency.

Accountability at the gates: The evaluation process worked basically the same at the start of a new development project (i.e., the first gate) and at later gates. The calculation model that focused on the contribution margin ratio and payback ratio was revised based on new information obtained during the development project. Engineers and project managers had the opportunity to introduce add-on spreadsheets, and they could, to some extent, repair the calculation model with such technical solutions. An example is that the spreadsheet calculation model did not include indirect variable production costs, which the company's accounting enterprise resource planning (ERP) system actually added to the product cost based on the percentage of the direct variable costs. This could be corrected in the calculation model. Still, severe limitations remained, and managers in the case study mentioned that the implications of reuse, project lead time, and economies of scale were still not reflected in the calculation model.

So, accountability was *not* created through detailed cost and profitability targets and rigorous estimates of to what extent those were achieved. Instead, the management board focused on high-level targets and on coordination. Strategic objectives were not translated into numbers, but they were discussed together with financial arguments. Although strategic objectives such as quality, lead time, or production efficiency could not be fully quantified, the calculation model provided a starting point to talk about how design choices and trade-offs affected these strategic objectives. "The management board drew from their own practical expertise in order to 'see through' numbers that featured in the project reports" (Jørgensen & Messner, 2010, p. 202). "Strategic concerns were regarded as means to profitability that had to be balanced in a reasonable way" (p. 201). The management board focused its inquiry to emphasize that the integration of different concerns by different parties was important at any stage during the NPD project. They "used the meetings at the gate to ensure that there was local communication and coordination" (p. 202). These findings are related to how Mouritsen et al. (2009, p. 749) discuss their cases and suggest that financial numbers can influence NPD because "the calculation connects the innovation activity to other concerns."

Accountability at the stages (between the gates): Anticipation of the discussions with the board that project managers knew would take place at the gates also influenced how accountability was created between the gates (during the NPD stages). It made project managers think about how they could explain how their actions might impact overall profitability—even if such arguments could often not be translated into hard calculations. It made them consider how they could argue that their decisions supported strategic objectives, and it let them engage in horizontal information sharing so that they would be able to show a wider perspective. "The enforcement of financial accountability at the gates can be seen as a means to remind managers of the importance of accounting numbers—even if these are only imperfect representations of the decisions and practices in NPD" (Jørgensen & Messner, 2010, p. 202). These practices are understandable, but are not claimed to be optimal.

These studies convey a more realistic notion of accountability for modularity in NPD. While models in the literature depict optimal decisions for stylized settings (see above) and we can imagine a refined, "ideal" system with target costs and clear guidelines for the use of modularity (as described above), these empirical studies show that this may be illusory. "It was clearly impossible to decide upon every detail in advance" (Jørgensen & Messner, 2010, p. 195). The role of financial goals and calculations to create accountability for modularity can only be understood by seeing those goals and calculations in combination with other information and practices, such as focusing on high-level financial goals, discussing how calculations of financial goals are related to strategic goals that are not part of the calculation, and probing how actions have wider impact for various activities inside the company and for external parties. Financial goals and calculations can be a starting point, but managers will combine those with insights that are not compounded in financial models.

Conclusions

The purpose of this chapter was to provide an overview of our current understanding of modularity for cost management purposes based on various literatures. Our literature review shows that NPD and the use of modularity for cost management purposes are complex phenomena. Much more of the research reviewed here has been published in innovation and operations management than in the management accounting literature.

The purpose of modularity in the context of NPD and cost management is to coordinate design decisions across a portfolio of related products, in order to provide product variety in an efficient way. As such, it goes beyond target costing that focuses on the costs of products within the scope of a single NPD project. Within the overall idea of modularity, we mentioned three concepts. Component commonality has the perspective of existing components and concerns the use of these for products that are newly developed or redesigned. Modular design looks at the strategic design of a product family by defining building blocks and interfaces, such that individual components and modules can be used and replaced independently among different derivative products. Finally, a product platform is a basic architecture of the physical implementation of a functional design, which becomes the basis for a series of derivative products.

Our review of empirical research showed that there are several holistic case studies that are intended as inspirational and pragmatic illustrations of modularity. We also reviewed a large stream of literature that analyzes some of the impacts and trade-offs involved in using modularity for cost management purposes. Much of this research is not empirical and uses quantitative models that necessarily address rather stylized settings.

The two final topics identified in this literature review start to look at behavioral aspects. One is the design of allocation of costs that are shared across different products. How can these cost allocations provide incentives for product managers to adopt modularity and to accept more commonality across products, if that would be beneficial for the entire organization? The other topic is the question of how accountability for modularity comes about. One could image a refined system with accurate models that guide optimal decisions about modularity, detailed targets for costs and profitability of products and product groups, and accurate measurements of achieved modularity, costs, and profitability. However, the complexity of the decision models already suggests that such an approach may be naïve, and several empirical studies described more realistically how modularity was achieved.

Ideas for future research

One avenue for future research would be to conduct field research and investigate if and how quantitative models capture cost management issues around modularity in a real organization. Some research could focus on adjusting such models to much more complex settings, where decisions on products are not made simultaneously (so, there is a mix of "old," current, and future products) and that involves much more complicated products and many technical constraints. Quantitative models for such settings will likely be less comprehensive and elegant from a mathematical point of view but might, on the other hand, include more of the multifaceted aspects that are involved in many real-world situations.

Another topic for future research concerns cost allocations to influence decision-making at the level of target costing processes for individual NPD projects. On the one hand, this could investigate which modularity strategy the firm would provide and analyze cost allocations that stimulate behavioral congruence. But even more subtle: it is unlikely that the perfect and encompassing modularity strategy can be defined ex ante. Given an overall modularity strategy, it may still be optimal to sometimes allow exceptions. Cost allocations could provide the info and incentives to the responsible product managers for such decisions.

Decisions on modularity and cost allocations could also be explicitly embedded in a hierarchical planning process. The basic design of a hierarchical planning system includes the partitioning of the overall planning problem, and the linkage of the resulting subproblems (Hax, 2013). This means that the overall planning problem is decomposed, and first, some "hierarchical" or broader decisions are made, for example about the basic architecture of a product family in terms of shared systems, unique systems, and interfaces. These decisions create constraints for later and more detailed decisions, for example about specific modules to be developed. In a context of multiple products that are developed after each other and evolving information, such an approach might be useful.

Although not modularity per se, we believe that future research could also fruitfully investigate how firms deal with complexities of target costing systems. For example, how do they understand costs throughout the value chain? How do they set targets for initial development costs? How do they analyze trade-offs between initial development costs and later manufacturing costs? How do they analyze trade-offs between costs and other targets?

Perhaps one of the poorest understood topics is accountability when modularity is used for cost management purposes. There are huge complexities and uncertainties of modularity, so the supporting management accounting tools will only very incompletely be able to analyze trade-offs, provide targets, and measure results. Given these circumstances, we need to understand more realistically how modularity, cost management, and accountability work in practice, and what this means for management accounting and management accountants.

Notes

1 For example, Volkswagen, BMW, and Mercedes-Benz talk about their various platforms as a key strategy for managing costs. Wikipedia, *Volkswagen Group MQB platform*, http://en.wikipedia.org/wiki/Volkswagen_ Group_MQB_platform (accessed 11 January 2016). Herbert Diess, *R&D: Future-proofing the BMW group*, presentation dated March 20, 2013, downloaded from www.bmwgroup.com/e/0_0_www_bmwgroup_com/investor_relations/downloads/_pdf/BMW_Group_AIC2013_Presentation_R-D_Dr_Diess.pdf (accessed 11 January 2016). Autoevolution, *Mercedes-Benz will switch to just four car platforms*, www.autoevolution. com/news/mercedes-benz-will-switch-to-just-four-car-platforms-78508.html (accessed 11 January 2016).

2 Some examples of well-known papers on modularity that we already knew are Feitzinger & Lee (1997), Fisher et al. (1999), Fixson (2005), Labro (2004), and Ulrich (1995).

3 Examples of keywords used are modularity, modularization, module, modular design, delayed product differentiation and its abbreviation DPD, component commonality, part commonality, material commonality, component sharing, common component, shared component, product platform, and product family.

4 Note that the journals *Management Science* and *Decision Sciences* could also be considered as innovation and operations management journals, but these were already included in the Bonner et al. (2006) list.

5 For example, Unilever introduced the "Heartbrand" as a new symbol for their various existing ice cream brands around the world. The new logo replaced the previous design in most countries, but the local names (such as Wall's, Langnese, Frigo, Ola, Streets, and Algida) were carried on. However, packaging of products often does not have these local names on it, and consumers in different markets will "automatically" associate the Heartbrand logo on the product with their local brand name. Therefore, the same item can be sold in different markets. It is a very subtle form of creating more commonality of products across markets. See, for example, Wikipedia, *Wall's (ice cream)*, https://en.wikipedia.org/wiki/Wall%27s_(ice_cream) (accessed 11 January 2016); Louise Lucas and Barney Jopson, The complexities of simplifying, *Financial Times* (accessed 7 January 2016).

6 Bayou (1999) and Bayou & Reinstein (2003) are some of the earlier works that started to address the complexities of costing to support design decisions during NPD.

7 Beyond these costs, the company could also consider in its cost management efforts the costs its customers will incur when using the product and how these costs compare to competing products. This focus on "customer value" (Anderson et al., 2006; Wouters & Kirchberger, 2015) is beyond the scope of this chapter.

8 As a side remark, there are also many papers that introduce methods, models, or processes; how modularity can be developed and implemented; and illustrate this with a specific example (Martin & Ishii, 2002; Simpson et al., 2001; Suh et al., 2007). These examples are not based on empirical studies reporting findings from an actual application in an organization, but they are realistic, fictitious illustrations inspired by an earlier example reported in the literature or the authors' general knowledge. Some studies are based on actual cases, but without going into much detail of the field work—it's still about illustrating the model (Caux et al., 2006; Krishnan et al., 1999).

References

Abbey, J. D., Guide, V. D. R., & Souza, G. C. (2013). Delayed differentiation for multiple lifecycle products. *Production and Operations Management*, *22*(3), 588–602. doi:10.1111/j.1937-5956.2012.01370.x.

Anderson, E. G., & Parker, G. G. (2002). The effect of learning on the make/buy decision. *Production and Operations Management*, *11*(3), 313–339. doi:10.1111/j.1937-5956.2002.tb00189.x.

Anderson, J. C., Narus, J. A., & van Rossum, W. (2006). Customer value propositions in business markets. *Harvard Business Review*, *84*(3), 90–99, 149.

Anderson, S. W., & Dekker, H. C. (2009). Strategic cost management in supply chains, part 1: structural cost management. *Accounting Horizons*, *23*(2), 201–220. doi:10.2308/acch.2009.23.2.201.

Ansari, S., Bell, J., & Okano, H. (2006). Target Costing: Uncharted Research Territory. In C. S. Chapman, A. G. Hopwood, & M. D. Shields (Eds.), *Handbooks of Management Accounting Research* (Vol. 2, pp. 507–530). Oxford, United Kingdom. doi:10.1016/S1751-3243(06)02002-5.

Asan, U., Polat, S., & Sanchez, R. (2008). Scenario-driven modular design in managing market uncertainty. *International Journal of Technology Management*, *42*(4), 459. doi:10.1504/IJTM.2008.019386.

Baldwin, C. Y., & Clark, K. B. (1997). Managing in an age of modularity. *Harvard Business Review, 75*(5), 84–93.
Baldwin, C. Y., & Clark, K. B. (2000). *Design Rules: The Power of Modularity Volume 1*. Massachusetts: MIT Press Cambridge.
Bayou, M. E. (1999). Accounting for modular manufacturing: addressing new challenges. *Journal of Cost Management*, 13 (July/August), 11–20.
Bayou, M. E., & Reinstein, A. (2003). A management accounting taxonomy for the mass customization approach. In M. Epstein & M. A. Malina (Eds.), *Advances in Management Accounting* (pp. 169–189). Emerald Group Publishing Limited. doi:10.1016/S1474-7871(02)11007-0.
Bhaskaran, S. R., & Krishnan, V. (2009). Effort, revenue, and cost sharing mechanisms for collaborative new product development. *Management Science, 55*(7), 1152–1169. doi:10.1287/mnsc.1090.1010.
Bonner, S. E., Hesford, J. W., Van der Stede, W. A., & Young, S. M. (2006). The most influential journals in academic accounting. *Accounting, Organizations and Society, 31*(7), 663–685. doi:10.1016/j.aos.2005.06.003.
Campagnolo, D., & Camuffo, A. (2009). The concept of modularity in management studies: a literature review. *International Journal of Management Reviews, 12*, 259–283. doi:10.1111/j.1468-2370.2009.00260.x.
Caux, C., David, F., & Pierreval, H. (2006). Implementation of delayed differentiation in batch process industries: a standardization problem. *International Journal of Production Research, 44*(16), 3243–3255. doi:10.1080/00207540500521543.
Cebon, P., Hauptman, O., & Shekhar, C. (2008). Product modularity and the product life cycle: new dynamics in the interactions of product and process technologies. *International Journal of Technology Management, 42*(4), 365. doi:10.1504/IJTM.2008.019381.
Chakravarty, A. K., & Balakrishnan, N. (2001). Achieving product variety through optimal choice of module variations. *IIE Transactions, 33*(7), 587–598. doi:10.1080/07408170108936856.
Christopher, M. (2000). The agile supply chain. *Industrial Marketing Management, 29*(1), 37–44. doi:10.1016/S0019-8501(99)00110-8.
Davila, A., & Wouters, M. (2004). Designing cost-competitive technology products through cost management. *Accounting Horizons, 18*(1), 13–26. doi:10.2308/acch.2004.18.1.13.
Davila, A., & Wouters, M. J. F. (2007). An empirical test of inventory, service and cost benefits from a postponement strategy. *International Journal of Production Research, 45*(10), 2245–2267. doi:10.1080/00207540600725002.
Dekker, H. C., & Smidt, P. (2003). A survey of the adoption and use of target costing in Dutch firms. *International Journal of Production Economics, 84*(3), 293–305. doi:10.1016/S0925-5273(02)00450-4.
Desai, P., Kekre, S., Radhakrishnan, S., & Srinivasan, K. (2001). Product differentiation and commonality in design: balancing revenue and cost drivers. *Management Science, 47*(1), 37–51. doi:10.1287/mnsc.47.1.37.10672.
Duray, R., Ward, P. T., Milligan, G. W., & Berry, W. L. (2000). Approaches to mass customization: configurations and empirical validation. *Journal of Operations Management, 18*(6), 605–625. doi:10.1016/S0272-6963(00)00043-7.
Ethiraj, S. K., Levinthal, D., & Roy, R. R. (2008). The dual role of modularity: innovation and imitation. *Management Science, 54*(5), 939–955. doi:10.1287/mnsc.1070.0775.
Ewert, R., & Wagenhofer, A. (2006). Management accounting theory and practice in German-speaking countries. *Handbook of Management Accounting Research*, 2, 1035–1069. doi:10.1016/S1751-3243(06)02021-9.
Eynan, A., & Rosenblatt, M. J. (1996). Component commonality effects on inventory costs. *IIE Transactions, 28*(2), 93–104. doi:10.1080/07408179608966255.
Feitzinger, E., & Lee, H. L. (1997). Mass customization at Hewlett-Packard: the power of postponement. *Harvard Business Review, 75*(1), 116–121. doi:Article.
Fernández, I., & Kekäle, T. (2005). The influence of modularity and industry clockspeed on reverse logistics strategy: implications for the purchasing function. *Journal of Purchasing and Supply Management, 11*(4), 193–205. doi:10.1016/j.pursup.2006.01.005.
Fine, C. H. (2009). Clockspeed-based strategies for supply chain design. *Production and Operations Management, 9*(3), 213–221. doi:10.1111/j.1937-5956.2000.tb00134.x.
Fisher, M., Ramdas, K., & Ulrich, K. (1999). Component sharing in the management of product variety: a study of automotive braking systems. *Management Science, 45*(3), 297–315. doi:10.1287/mnsc.45.3.297.

Fixson, S. K. (2005). Product architecture assessment: a tool to link product, process, and supply chain design decisions. *Journal of Operations Management, 23*(3–4), 345–369. doi:10.1016/j.jom.2004.08.006.

Fixson, S. K. (2007). Modularity and commonality research: past developments and future opportunities. *Concurrent Engineering, 15*(2), 85–111. doi:10.1177/1063293X07078935.

Fixson, S. K., & Clark, J. P. (2002). On the Link between Modularity and Cost-a Methodology to Assess Cost Implications of Product Architecture Differences. In *IEEE International Engineering Management Conference* (Vol. 1, pp. 131–136). Cambridge, UK: IEEE. doi:10.1109/IEMC.2002.1038379.

Fredriksson, P. (2006). Mechanisms and rationales for the coordination of a modular assembly system. *International Journal of Operations & Production Management, 26*(4), 350–370. doi:10.1108/01443570610650530.

Fredriksson, P., & Gadde, L.-E. (2005). Flexibility and rigidity in customization and build-to-order production. *Industrial Marketing Management, 34*(7), 695–705. doi:10.1016/j.indmarman.2005.05.010.

Galvin, P. (1999). Product modularity, information structures and the diffusion of innovation. *International Journal of Technology Management, 17*(5), 467. doi:10.1504/IJTM.1999.002728.

Garg, A., & Tang, C. S. (1997). On postponement strategies for product families with multiple points of differentiation. *IIE Transactions, 29*(8), 641–650. doi:10.1080/07408179708966374.

Garud, R., & Kumaraswamy, A. (1995). Technological and organizational designs for realizing economies of substitution. *Strategic Management Journal, 16*(S1), 93–109. doi:10.1002/smj.4250160919.

Gershenson, J. K., Prasad, G. J., & Zhang, Y. (2003). Product modularity: definitions and benefits. *Journal of Engineering Design, 14*(3), 295–313. doi:10.1080/0954482031000091068.

Granlund, M., & Taipaleenmäki, J. (2005). Management control and controllership in new economy firms—a life cycle perspective. *Management Accounting Research, 16*(1), 21–57. doi:10.1016/j.mar.2004.09.003.

Halman, J. I. M., Hofer, A. P., & van Vuuren, W. (2003). Platform-driven development of product families: linking theory with practice. *Journal of Product Innovation Management, 20*(2), 149–162. doi:10.1111/1540-5885.2002007.

Hax, A. C. (2013). Hierarchical Production Planning. In *Encyclopedia of Operations Research and Management Science* (pp. 708–712). Retrieved from http://link.springer.com/referenceworkentry/10.1007/978-1-4419-1153-7_418.

Henke, J. W. (2000). Strategic selling in the age of modules and systems. *Industrial Marketing Management, 29*(3), 271–284. doi:10.1016/S0019-8501(99)00079-6.

Hertenstein, J. H., & Platt, M. B. (2000). Performance measures and management control in new product development. *Accounting Horizons, 14*(3), 303–323. doi:10.2308/acch.2000.14.3.303.

Hillier, M. S. (2002). Using commonality as backup safety stock. *European Journal of Operational Research, 136*(2), 353–365. doi:10.1016/S0377-2217(01)00027-3.

Hölttä-Otto, K., Chiriac, N. A., Lysy, D., & Suk Suh, E. (2012). Comparative analysis of coupling modularity metrics. *Journal of Engineering Design, 23*(10–11), 790–806. doi:10.1080/09544828.2012.701728.

Hu, B., Duenyas, I., & Beil, D. R. (2013). Does pooling purchases lead to higher profits? *Management Science, 59*(7), 1576–1593. doi:10.1287/mnsc.1120.1651.

Israelsen, P., & Jørgensen, B. (2011). Decentralizing decision making in modularization strategies: overcoming barriers from dysfunctional accounting systems. *International Journal of Production Economics, 131*(2), 453–462. doi:10.1016/j.ijpe.2010.12.020.

Jiao, J. (Roger), Simpson, T. W., & Siddique, Z. (2007). Product family design and platform-based product development: a state-of-the-art review. *Journal of Intelligent Manufacturing, 18*(1), 5–29. doi:10.1007/s10845-007-0003-2.

Johnson, M. D., & Kirchain, R. (2010). Developing and assessing commonality metrics for product families: a process-based cost-modeling approach. *IEEE Transactions on Engineering Management, 57*(4), 634–648. doi:10.1109/TEM.2009.2034642.

Jordan, S., & Messner, M. (2012). Enabling control and the problem of incomplete performance indicators. *Accounting, Organizations and Society, 37*(8), 544–564. doi:10.1016/j.aos.2012.08.002.

Jørgensen, B., & Messner, M. (2009). Management control in new product development: the dynamics of managing flexibility and efficiency. *Journal of Management Accounting Research, 21*(1), 99–124. doi:10.2308/jmar.2009.21.1.99.

Jørgensen, B., & Messner, M. (2010). Accounting and strategising: a case study from new product development. *Accounting, Organizations and Society, 35*(2), 184–204. doi:10.1016/j.aos.2009.04.001.

Kamrad, B., Schmidt, G. M., & Ulku, S. (2013). Analyzing product architecture under technological change: modular upgradeability tradeoffs. *IEEE Transactions on Engineering Management, 60*(2), 289–300. doi:10.1109/TEM.2012.2211362.

Kim, K., & Chhajed, D. (2000). Commonality in product design: cost saving, valuation change and cannibalisation. *European Journal of Operational Research, 125*(3), 602–621. doi:10.1016/S0377-2217(99)00271-4.

Kloock, J., & Schiller, U. (1997). Marginal costing: cost budgeting and cost variance analysis. *Management Accounting Research, 8*(3), 299–323. doi:10.1006/mare.1996.0048.

Krishnan, V., & Gupta, S. (2001). Appropriateness and impact of platform-based product development. *Management Science, 47*(1), 52–68. doi:10.1287/mnsc.47.1.52.10665.

Krishnan, V., Singh, R., & Tirupati, D. (1999). A model-based approach for planning and developing a family of technology-based products. *Manufacturing & Service Operations Management, 1*(2), 132–156. doi:10.1287/msom.1.2.132.

Labro, E. (2004). The cost effects of component commonality: a literature review through a management-accounting lens. *Manufacturing & Service Operations Management, 6*(4), 358–367. doi:10.1287/msom.1040.0047.

Langlois, R. N. (2002). Modularity in technology and organization. *Journal of Economic Behavior & Organization, 49*(1), 19–37. doi:10.1016/S0167-2681(02)00056-2.

Lau, A. K. W. (2011). Critical success factors in managing modular production design: six company case studies in Hong Kong, China, and Singapore. *Journal of Engineering and Technology Management, 28*(3), 168–183. doi:10.1016/j.jengtecman.2011.03.004.

Lehnerd, A., & Meyer, M. H. (1997). *The Power of Product Platforms - Building Value and Cost Leadership.* New York: Simon and Schuster.

Mahmoud-Jouini, S. B., & Lenfle, S. (2010). Platform re-use lessons from the automotive industry. *International Journal of Operations & Production Management, 30*(1), 98–124. Doi:0.1108/01443571011012398.

Martin, M. V, & Ishii, K. (2002). Design for variety: developing standardized and modularized product platform architectures. *Research in Engineering Design, 13*(4), 213–235. doi:10.1007/s00163-002-0020-2.

Maslennikova, I., & Foley, D. (2000). Xerox's approach to sustainability. *Interfaces, 30*(3), 226–233. doi:10.1287/inte.30.3.226.11666.

Mikkola, J. H. (2007). Management of product architecture modularity for mass customization: modeling and theoretical considerations. *IEEE Transactions on Engineering Management, 54*(1), 57–69. doi:10.1109/TEM.2006.889067.

Miozzo, M., & Grimshaw, D. (2005). Modularity and innovation in knowledge-intensive business services: IT outsourcing in Germany and the UK. *Research Policy, 34*(9), 1419–1439. doi:10.1016/j.respol.2005.06.005.

Mirchandani, P., & Mishrah, A. (2009). Component commonality: models with product-specific service constraints. *Production and Operations Management, 11*(2), 199–215. doi:10.1111/j.1937-5956.2002.tb00491.x.

Mouritsen, J., Hansen, A., & Hansen, C. Ø. (2001). Inter-organizational controls and organizational competencies: episodes around target cost management/functional analysis and open book accounting. *Management Accounting Research, 12*(2), 221–244. doi:10.1006/mare.2001.0160.

Mouritsen, J., Hansen, A., & Hansen, C. Ø. (2009). Short and long translations: management accounting calculations and innovation management. *Accounting, Organizations and Society, 34*(6–7), 738–754. doi:10.1016/j.aos.2009.01.006.

Muffatto, M., & Roveda, M. (2000). Developing product platforms: analysis of the development process. *Technovation, 20*(11), 617–630. doi:10.1016/S0166-4972(99)00178-9.

Murthy, D. N. P., & Blischke, W. R. (2000). Strategic warranty management: a life-cycle approach. *IEEE Transactions on Engineering Management, 47*(1), 40–54. doi:10.1109/17.820724.

Nobeoka, K., & Cusumano, M. A. (1997). Multiproject strategy and sales growth: the benefits of rapid design transfer in new product development. *Strategic Management Journal, 18*(3), 169–186. doi:10.1002/(SICI)1097-0266(199703)18:3<169::AID-SMJ863>3.0.CO;2-K.

Pandremenos, J., Paralikas, J., Salonitis, K., & Chryssolouris, G. (2009). Modularity concepts for the automotive industry: a critical review. *CIRP Journal of Manufacturing Science and Technology, 1*(3), 148–152. doi:10.1016/j.cirpj.2008.09.012.

Paralikas, J., Fysikopoulos, A., Pandremenos, J., & Chryssolouris, G. (2011). Product modularity and assembly systems: an automotive case study. *CIRP Annals - Manufacturing Technology, 60*(1), 165–168. doi:10.1016/j.cirp.2011.03.009.

Park, J., & Simpson, T. W. (2005). Development of a production cost estimation framework to support product family design. *International Journal of Production Research, 43*(4), 731–772. doi:10.1080/00207540512331311903.

Park, J., & Simpson, T. W. (2008). Toward an activity-based costing system for product families and product platforms in the early stages of development. *International Journal of Production Research, 46*(1), 99–130. doi:10.1080/00207540600825240.

Persson, M., & Åhlström, P. (2006). Managerial issues in modularising complex products. *Technovation, 26*(11), 1201–1209. doi:10.1016/j.technovation.2005.09.020.

Ramachandran, K., & Krishnan, V. (2008). Design architecture and introduction timing for rapidly improving industrial products. *Manufacturing & Service Operations Management, 10*(1), 149–171. doi:10.1287/msom.1060.0143.

Ramdas, K., Fisher, M., & Ulrich, K. (2003). Managing variety for assembled products: modeling component systems sharing. *Manufacturing & Service Operations Management, 5*(2), 142–156. doi:10.1287/msom.5.2.142.16073.

Ramdas, K., & Randall, T. (2008). Does component sharing help or hurt reliability? an empirical study in the automotive industry. *Management Science, 54*(5), 922–938. doi:10.1287/mnsc.1070.0791.

Ro, Y. K., Liker, J. K., & Fixson, S. K. (2007). Modularity as a strategy for supply chain coordination: the case of U.S. auto. *IEEE Transactions on Engineering Management, 54*(1), 172–189. doi:10.1109/TEM.2006.889075.

Robertson, D., & Ulrich, K. (1998). Planning for product platforms. *Sloan Managament Review, 39*(4), 19–31. Retrieved from http://www.ktulrich.com/uploads/6/1/7/1/6171812/platforms-smr.pdf.

Rosenau, M. D., & Rothberg, R. R. (2003). Book reviews. *Journal of Product Innovation Management, 14*(6), 526–534. doi:10.1111/1540-5885.1520197-i6.

Salvador, F. (2007). Toward a product system modularity construct: literature review and reconceptualization. *IEEE Transactions on Engineering Management, 54*(2), 219–240. doi:10.1109/TEM.2007.893996.

Sanchez, R. (1999). Modular architectures in the marketing process. *Journal of Marketing, 63*(Special Issue), 92. doi:10.2307/1252104.

Sanchez, R., & Mahoney, J. T. (1996). Modularity, flexibility, and knowledge management in product and organization design. *Strategic Management Journal, 17*(S2), 63–76. doi:10.1002/smj.4250171107.

Sanderson, S., & Uzumeri, M. (1995). Managing product families: the case of the Sony Walkman. *Research Policy, 24*(5), 761–782. doi:10.1016/0048-7333(94)00797-B.

Schilling, M. A. (2000). Toward a general modular systems theory and its application to interfirm product modularity. *Academy of Management Review, 25*(2), 312–334. doi:10.5465/AMR.2000.3312918.

Sharma, A., Iyer, G. R., Mehrotra, A., & Krishnan, R. (2010). Sustainability and business-to-business marketing: a framework and implications. *Industrial Marketing Management, 39*(2), 330–341. doi:10.1016/j.indmarman.2008.11.005.

Simpson, T. W., Maier, J. R., & Mistree, F. (2001). Product platform design: method and application. *Research in Engineering Design, 13*(1), 2–22. doi:10.1007/s001630100002.

Sköld, M., & Karlsson, C. (2012). Product platform replacements: challenges to managers. *International Journal of Operations & Production Management, 32*(6), 746–766. doi:10.1108/01443571211230952.

Stephan, M., Pfaffmann, E., & Sanchez, R. (2008). Modularity in cooperative product development: the case of the MCC "smart" car. *International Journal of Technology Management, 42*(4), 439. doi:10.1504/IJTM.2008.019385.

Subramanian, R., Ferguson, M. E., & Toktay, L. B. (2013). Remanufacturing and the component commonality decision. *Production and Operations Management, 22*(1), 36–53. doi:10.1111/j.1937-5956.2012.01350.x.

Suh, E. S., de Weck, O. L., & Chang, D. (2007). Flexible product platforms: framework and case study. *Research in Engineering Design, 18*(2), 67–89. doi:10.1007/s00163-007-0032-z.

Taipaleenmäki, J. (2014). Absence and variant modes of presence of management accounting in new product development – theoretical refinement and some empirical evidence. *European Accounting Review, 23*(2), 291–334. doi:10.1080/09638180.2013.811065.

Thevenot, H. J., & Simpson, T. W. (2006). Commonality indices for product family design: a detailed comparison. *Journal of Engineering Design, 17*(2), 99–119. doi:10.1080/09544820500275693.

Thomas, D. J., & Warsing, D. P. (2009). A periodic inventory model for stocking modular components. *Production and Operations Management, 16*(3), 343–359. doi:10.1111/j.1937-5956.2007.tb00263.x.

Thonemann, U. W., & Brandeau, M. L. (2000). Optimal commonality in component design. *Operations Research, 48*(1), 1–19. doi:10.1287/opre.48.1.1.12445.

Thyssen, J., Israelsen, P., & Jørgensen, B. (2006). Activity-based costing as a method for assessing the economics of modularization—a case study and beyond. *International Journal of Production Economics, 103*(1), 252–270. doi:10.1016/j.ijpe.2005.07.004.

Toktay, L. B., & Wei, D. (2011). Cost allocation in manufacturing-remanufacturing operations. *Production and Operations Management, 20*(6), 841–847. doi:10.1111/j.1937-5956.2011.01236.x.

Tseng, H.-E., Chang, C.-C., & Cheng, C.-J. (2010). Disassembly-oriented assessment methodology for product modularity. *International Journal of Production Research, 48*(14), 4297–4320. doi:10.1080/00207540902893433.

Ulaga, W., & Reinartz, W. (2011). Hybrid offerings: how manufacturing firms combine goods and services successfully. *Journal of Marketing, 75*(6), 5–23. doi:10.1509/jmkg.75.6.5.

Ülkü, S., Dimofte, C. V., & Schmidt, G. M. (2012). Consumer valuation of modularly upgradeable products. *Management Science, 58*(9), 1761–1776. doi:10.1287/mnsc.1120.1519.

Ulrich, K. (1995). The role of product architecture in the manufacturing firm. *Research Policy, 24*(3), 419–440. doi:10.1016/0048-7333(94)00775-3.

Umit Kucuk, S., & Krishnamurthy, S. (2007). An analysis of consumer power on the Internet. *Technovation, 27*(1–2), 47–56. doi:10.1016/j.technovation.2006.05.002.

Voss, C. A., & Hsuan, J. (2009). Service architecture and modularity. *Decision Sciences, 40*(3), 541–569. doi:10.1111/j.1540-5915.2009.00241.x.

Watanabe, C., & Ane, B. K. (2004). Constructing a virtuous cycle of manufacturing agility: concurrent roles of modularity in improving agility and reducing lead time. *Technovation, 24*(7), 573–583. doi:10.1016/S0166-4972(02)00118-9.

Wortmann, H., & Alblas, A. (2009). Product platform life cycles: a multiple case study. *International Journal of Technology Management, 48*(2), 188. doi:10.1504/IJTM.2009.024915.

Wouters, M. J. F., & Kirchberger, M. A. (2015). Customer value propositions as interorganizational management accounting to support customer collaboration. *Industrial Marketing Management, 46*, 54–67. doi:10.1016/j.indmarman.2015.01.005.

Wouters, M. J. F., & Morales, S. (2014). The Contemporary Art of Cost Management Methods during Product Development. In M. J. Epstein & J. Y. Lee (Eds.), *Advances in Management Accounting, Volume 24* (pp. 259–346). Emerald Group Publishing Limited. doi:10.1108/S1474–787120140000024008.

Wouters, M. J. F., Morales, S., Grollmuss, S., & Scheer, M. (2016). Methods for cost management during product development: a review and comparison of different literatures. *Advances in Management Accounting, In Press.*

Wouters, M. J. F., Workum, M., & Hissel, P. (2011). Assessing the product architecture decision about product features – a real options approach. *R&D Management, 41*(4), 393–409. doi:10.1111/j.1467-9310.2011.00652.x.

Wu, L., De Matta, R., & Lowe, T. J. (2009). Updating a modular product: how to set time to market and component quality. *IEEE Transactions on Engineering Management, 56*(2), 298–311. doi:10.1109/TEM.2008.2005065.

Zhang, Y., & Gershenson, J. K. (2002). Questioning the direct relationship between product modularity and retirement cost. *The Journal of Sustainable Product Design, 2*(1/2), 53–68. doi:10.1023/B:JSPD.0000016449.63718.43.

5

Composite measures in performance measurement

Paul Rouse and Julie Harrison

Effective performance evaluation typically requires measures that enable a multidimensional perspective to be provided. This comes at a cost which is the added complexity in synthesising multiple measures into a more tractable form. Typically, this is a single measure more commonly known as a composite measure that embodies multiple measures. This chapter examines both reflective and formative composite measures and describes various approaches to deriving a composite measure. While these approaches differ, they all require some system of weights and/or prices and include ratio analysis, total factor productivity (TFP), the Lee method and Data Envelopment Analysis (DEA).

What is a composite measure?

A composite measure is a single measure that comprises several measures and conceptually can be either *reflective* or *formative* (Bisbe, Batista-Foguet, & Chenhall, 2007; Edwards & Bagozzi, 2000). In the first type, the measures are reflective of the underlying or latent construct (Bollen & Lennox, 1991; MacCullum & Browne, 1993). For example, we might envisage that the accounting ability of a student (the construct) is reflected by their performance measured by quizzes, assignments, tests and final exams. The left half of Figure 5.1 depicts a reflective construct where the construct embodies the four measures: in our example, the student's accounting ability is reflected in the four assessment types. We might therefore expect these measures to be reasonably correlated as they attempt to capture the same underlying construct. Thus, we might disregard a measure that did not correlate well with the other measures. Furthermore, we might expect that manipulation of the measure per se does not improve the construct. Thus, the arrows in Figure 5.1 flow from the construct to the measures to show that causality flows from the construct to the measures. Continuing the student example, if the accounting ability of a student is high (low), then this should manifest itself in high (low) performance in their coursework and final exam.

By contrast, in the formative view, the measures define the construct (Bollen & Lennox, 1991; MacCullum & Browne, 1993). There is no latent or underlying construct that manifests itself in the measures. Instead, the measures constitute the construct. This is shown in the right half of Figure 5.1 where the causality flows from the measures to the construct.

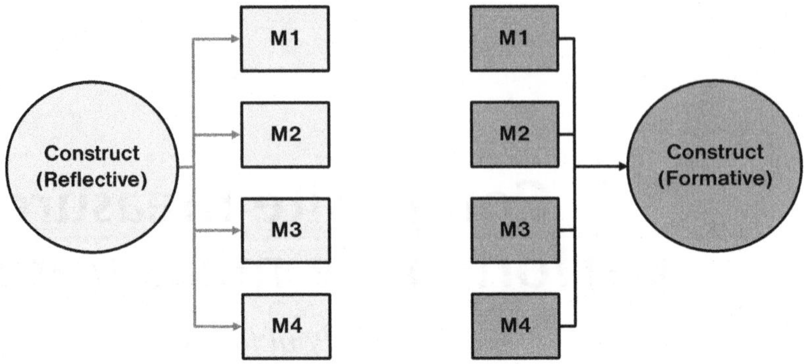

Figure 5.1 Reflective and formative composite measures

The balanced scorecard is a good example of a formative construct where four dimensions are used to define performance. Performance does not drive the measures; the measures determine what will be regarded as performance. The higher (lower) the measures, the higher (lower) the performance. In this concept, correlated measures are usually not desirable. Instead, measures that are different from each other, uncorrelated (or orthogonal in factor analysis terms), are preferred as they capture different aspects of performance, e.g. customer satisfaction, production efficiency, profitability and product innovation. We may hypothesise that good performance in these represents good performance overall, but the performance construct per se is unable to drive these aspects. Note that in order to obtain a composite measure, we will need some way of combining these measures, usually through prices or weights.

Jarvis, Mackenzie and Podsakoff (2003) provide guidelines to help decide whether a construct is reflective or formative:

> a construct should be modelled as having formative indicators if the following conditions prevail: (*a*) the indicators are viewed as defining characteristics of the construct, (*b*) changes in the indicators are expected to cause changes in the construct, (*c*) changes in the construct are not expected to cause changes in the indicators, (*d*) the indicators do not necessarily share a common theme, (*e*) eliminating an indicator may alter the conceptual domain of the construct, (*f*) a change in the value of one of the indicators is not necessarily expected to be associated with a change in all of the other indicators, and (*g*) the indicators are not expected to have the same antecedents and consequences. On the other hand, a construct should be modelled as having reflective indicators if the opposite is true.
>
> *(p. 203)*

The decision on whether a construct is reflective or formative may also be determined by the purpose of the measure. Is it to summarise several measures in order to better understand some desired construct such as "overall performance" (formative) or is it to better understand how well a particular construct performs such as "customer satisfaction" (reflective)?

Composite measures are familiar to most of us and can incorporate many different aspects of performance such as a technology achievement index of country performance (Cherchye,

Moesen, Rogge, & Van Puyenbroeck, 2007), school league tables,[1] Bhutan's Gross Happiness Index[2] and university rankings.[3] We shall discuss some of these later.

The general form of a composite index is as follows:

$$CI_j = \Sigma_{j,i} W_{j,i} M_{j,i}$$

where $W_{j,i}$ are weights to be assigned to measures $M_{j,i}$ for subjects (e.g. organisations) j and measures i. In general, weights sum to unity ($\Sigma_{j,i} W_{j,i} = 1$) and are bounded below at zero ($0 \leq W_{j,i} \leq 1$). There are several ways measures can be combined, which we illustrate next using the example data provided in Table 5.1.

University A has 41,000 students and an annual research income of $180,000. University B has 35,000 students and a research income of $200,000. Focusing solely on student numbers, one might conclude that University A has the best performance. However, University B might argue that its research income is higher, and therefore its performance is best. Therefore, we could construct a composite index in which we define performance in terms of numbers of students and research income, i.e. a formative approach. Let us consider some basic approaches to constructing this index.

1 Use equal weightings for both measures and simply calculate the mean of the raw numbers that appear in column 4 of Table 5.1. On this basis, the performance of University B (117.5) is higher than that of University A (110.5). But we have ignored the fact that the two measures are in different dimensions (numbers and dollars) when combining them. This is a questionable practice as the ranking of each university is contingent on the units of measurement. For example, conversion of the dollars into cents would place a higher weighting on research income.
2 Normalise the numbers in some way and calculate the mean average of these numbers. For example, normalise each measure using its distance from the minimum as a ratio of the range (note the superscript N denotes that the measure is normalised):

$$M_{j,i}^{N} = \frac{M_{j,i} - M_i^{\text{Min}}}{M_i^{\text{Max}} - M_i^{\text{Min}}}$$

Table 5.1 shows the range (maximum minus minimum) for each measure, and this is used to normalise the excess above the minimum for each measure. For example, calculation of this for the student numbers for University A would be (41−35)/6 = 1. Following this approach, Universities A and B would be ranked equally with a mean index of 0.5 as shown in column 4 of Table 5.2.

Table 5.1 Universities A and B illustrative data

	(2)	*(3)*	*(4)*
	Students (000's)	*Research income ($,000)*	*Mean of raw numbers*
University A	41	180	110.5
University B	35	200	117.5
Maximum	41	200	
Minimum	35	180	
Range	6	20	

Table 5.2 Basic approaches to composite measures for Table 5.1

	Normalise using range			*Distance to maximum*			*Weights on raw measures*		
	(2)	*(3)*	*(4)*	*(5)*	*(6)*	*(7)*	*(8)*	*(9)*	*(10)*
	Students	*Research income*	*Mean*	*Students*	*Research income*	*Mean*	*75:25*	*25:75*	*75:25 on distance measures*
University A	1	0	0.5	1.00	0.90	0.95	75.75	145.25	0.98
University B	0	1	0.5	0.85	1.00	0.93	76.25	158.75	0.89

3 Normalise the numbers using the distance to the maximum performance of each measure:

$$M_{j,i}^{N} = \frac{M_{j,i}}{M_{i}^{\text{Max}}}$$

For example, normalisation of the student numbers for University B would be 35/41 = 0.85 (rounded). Calculation of the mean for each shows that performance of University A is marginally higher than that of University B (see column 7 of Table 5.2).

4 Calculate the composite measure the same as 1 above, but use unequal weights placing 75% weighting on students and 25% on research income. Use of these weightings shows that University B is slightly better than University A as in column 8 of Table 5.2. In contrast, when placing 25% weighting on students and 75% on research income, performance of University B is considerably higher than that of University A as shown in column 9 of Table 5.2.

5 Use unequal weights of 75:25, combined with the distance to the maximum measures in columns 5 and 6 of Table 5.2, which produces a higher performance measure for University A than University B as shown in column 10 of Table 5.2.

These five approaches to calculating a composite measure for our example illustrate the flexibility of composite measures. In particular, they are able to incorporate a range of subjective judgements of the relative importance of individual measures. However, they also illustrate the sensitivity of the resulting measures to the method used to construct the index.

Why use a composite measure?

The different rankings provided by the five alternative approaches shown in Tables 5.1 and 5.2 reflect the units of measurement and weightings used, and show that performance can vary considerably when relying on a composite measure. This begs the question, why use a composite measure? There are several responses to this.

First, there are cognitive limitations to an individual's information processing abilities: "Because individuals have limited powers of understanding and can deal with only very small amounts of information at a time, they inevitably display limited rationality" (Emmanuel, Otley, & Merchant, 1998, p. 49). Thus, the reduction of multiple measures into a single composite measure assists in coping with complexity, though at the cost of limited rationality.

Second, not only are individuals unable to cope with more than a small, limited set of information, research cited by Macintosh (1985) shows that beyond a certain point, further information serves only to fossilise judgements due to overconfidence on the part of the expert judges. Fossilisation and overconfidence contribute to functional fixation manifested by a bias towards particular measures or perspectives. This is compounded by any increase in complexity manifested by a large number of measures often providing conflicting signals. This bias is contrary to the idea of an unbiased measurement or evaluation.

Hence, although the reduction of multiple measures into a single composite measure invariably loses some information, there is "value" in providing something tractable and conducive to human understanding provided that the process is transparent and acceptable to participants. Smith (1997) recommends a multivariate approach in this process which we interpret to include methods such as simple weighting systems to more sophisticated methods such as DEA.

Notwithstanding, there are issues that should be considered in this process. For example, the complexity of the method must be traded off against the user's capability to understand its application and results. Further, a method must not usurp managers' own beliefs as to the relative importance of areas of organisation performance. These need to be considered in establishing weighting systems. Nonetheless, a formal analysis compels management to take a more holistic view of performance through contemplating the appropriateness of the measures and their relative emphasis in the analysis. Formal weighting systems provide transparency and communicate managerial preferences across the organisation. It must be emphasised that weights are not necessarily "objective" or even "accurate"; they simply reflect perceived differences in importance amongst measures.

Composite measures using fixed weights

The most common approach to combining multiple measures of performance to construct a composite measure is to use fixed weights applied to each measure. An equal weighting of each measure is often the default approach adopted in many instances under the misguided belief that equal weights are unbiased. However, as shown in the example in Table 5.2, equal weights can introduce bias depending on the "true" relative importance of each measure. If fixed weights are to be used, then it is important that the selection of each measure consider both the relationship of the measure to performance, and the strength of the relationship relative to other selected measures. Ideally, fixed weights should reflect the desired balance of performance objectives or targeted performance. For example, consider the construction of a measure of performance for a group of primary schools. School managers are likely to consider desirable measures of performance to include student success in reading and mathematics. If these are the only two measures to be considered, is it also necessary to consider the relative importance of the two measures to overall performance? In this case, the target or desired outcome for students may be that schools should be performing equally well in terms of both dimensions of performance. In this example, the natural inclination to equally weight outcomes is likely to also reflect the desired outcomes.

As an alternative to equal weightings, composite measures can also be calculated using non-equal fixed weights. The advantage of non-equal weights is that they can be used to combine multiple measures that are not of equal importance. For example, a chain of restaurants might identify three important measures of performance as customer satisfaction (measured using a survey), revenue generation (measured using RevPASH, i.e. revenue per available seat hour), and sales growth. Management may consider that RevPASH is twice as important as the other two measures resulting in a composite measure calculated using a 25/50/25 fixed weighting of measures.

More formally, Lee (1992) described a method for calculating a composite performance measurement index that allows for non-equal weightings of measures and also provides a method for normalising measures that use different scales. This approach uses a matrix of performance measures that identifies the worst and best performance for each performance measure. Each measure is then normalised using a common scale (e.g. 0 to 10). For each measure, normal, best and worst performance results are identified and assigned to the common scale, with interpolations for the remaining levels. Management also determines, based on their experience or performance targets, the relative importance of the measures. This fixed weighting is used to calculate the composite performance measure, which comprises a weighted average of the individual measures' common-scale values.

This matrix of performance for the restaurant example is illustrated in Table 5.3. This matrix is used to calculate the overall performance scores for each restaurant based on its actual performance. Let us assume that management has agreed that the appropriate weights should be placed 25% on customer satisfaction, 50% on RevPASH and 25% on sales growth. For example, if one of the restaurants in the chain has a customer satisfaction of 90% (common scale = 8), a RevPASH of $42 (common scale = 6) and a sales growth of 10% (common scale = 10), its overall measure of performance would be 7.5 (25% of 8 plus 50% of 6 plus 25% of 10).

Although simple, this fixed weight method has some good features. First, it provides flexibility in the number of levels in the common scale, as well as in the pattern of possible results for each measure. It also allows for non-linear scales where improvements in measures become more difficult or easier as performance improves. Second, this approach allows for a separate consideration of the weights to be applied to individual measures from the scale (or value) applied to different levels of performance within each measure. Last, identifying reasonable estimates of normal, best and worst performance is not beyond the ability of most managers, making the method simple to apply and easily explained.

Problems may arise, however, where the number of levels of performance varies across different measures. For example, one measure may have only three possible results

Table 5.3 Fixed weight composite measure using a matrix of performance measures

Performance target	*Common scale*	*Customer satisfaction (%)*	*RevPASH*	*Sales growth (%)*
Best	10	100	$50	10
	9	95	$48	9
	8	90	$46	8
	7	85	$44	7
	6	80	$42	6
Normal	5	75	$40	5
	4	70	$38	4
	3	65	$36	3
	2	60	$34	2
	1	55	$32	1
Worst	0	<52	<$32	<1
Weighting		25%	50%	25%

corresponding to best, normal and worst, i.e. a categorical variable, in contrast to another measure whose results can span the entire performance scale, i.e. a continuous variable. Combining categorical and continuous measures can be problematic.

Composite measures in practice

League tables are a popular example of how composite measures are used in practice. Examples of league tables can be found in sports, education, health and business. They provide information on key measures for the teams or organisations being compared, with a composite measure used to provide rankings. The resulting rankings can be used to make national or international comparisons of relative performance. An example of a publicly available league table is the *Times Higher Education World University Rankings*.[4] This league table ranks world universities using 13 standardised performance measures combined to create a composite measure of performance. Measures are weighted so that the learning environment measures comprise 30% of composite measure, 30% of research output, 30% of research influence, 7.5% of international outlook and 2.5% of industry income. The stated purpose of educational rankings such as these is to assist potential students and employees to select schools or universities to attend or work for. The main problem with this approach is that the tables fail to take account of the context in which individual organisations operate. For example, when comparing school performance, poor relative performance may be the result of the location of the school, the socio-economic background of its students or other factors outside the control of school management. Further, schools that already struggle to attract students are likely to find that a low ranking can exacerbate this trend leading to a "death spiral" where fewer students mean less resources which causes lower rankings, and so on. For example, Harrison and Rouse (2014) describe the effect of competition on the performance of New Zealand schools when zoning was abolished. They found that average school performance was higher where schools were located in areas of high competition, but competition also widened the gap between the best and worst performing schools.

League tables are controversial, particularly in relation to their use in the public sector, given that they are often published widely by news outlets and used to identify the "best" and "worst" performing organisations. Further, their use in assessing and rewarding the performance of public-sector managers can lead to dysfunctional behaviour where the focus is placed on obtaining a good ranking, often at the expense of other organisation objectives that are not captured in the league table. Critics of league tables also point to the lack of context and statistical problems associated with the aggregation of different performance measures (Goldstein & Spiegelhalter, 1996). In particular, the method of constructing the rankings through the choice of measures and the method of weighting those measures can have a large impact on the performance rankings obtained.

One approach used to address the problem of lacking a context in league tables is the use of "value-added" composite measures, which seek to adjust outputs for the "quality" of inputs. For example, in the educational context, the "value-added" represents the improvement in educational achievement of a school's students rather than their absolute level of achievement (Hanushek, 1979). While this may address issues related to making comparisons of manager performance, it is less helpful if the purpose of the comparison is to help potential students or employees identify schools with the best absolute performance.

Another area in practice where composite measures are commonly found is the use of national rankings to measure relative performance of countries. Examples include simple economic indices calculated to measure relative economic performance, such as the Gross Domestic Product per capita, or more complex indices that attempt to adjust for differences in environmental variables. For example, measures have been developed to rank country performance in sporting events like the Olympics that are not based on a simple medal count, but instead adjust medal counts to reflect differences in country size, wealth and spending on national sports teams (Rogers, 2012; Zhang, Li, Meng, & Liu, 2009).

Composite measures are also used to measure qualitative dimensions of country performance, such as quality of life. An example of this type of composite measure is the Bhutan Gross National Happiness (GNH) index,[5] adopted by Bhutan as an alternative measure of country performance to more common economic measures such as the Gross Domestic Product per capita. This index uses key measures related to nine domains of human happiness: psychological well-being, health, time use, education, cultural diversity and resilience, good governance, community vitality, ecological diversity and resilience, and living standards. The index is constructed by defining a "sufficiency" cut-off level for each measure. If a person reaches that level, then any amount above the cut-off does not contribute to the individual's GNH score. This approach assumes, for example, that if income is greater than the sufficiency level, then an individual is no happier than someone who only earns income equal to that level. A person who achieves the sufficiency level for the weighted measures in six of the nine domains is defined as "happy". The GNH index for the country is calculated as one minus the percentage of people who are not "happy" multiplied by the average percentage of domains in which they lack sufficiency. This approach is designed to ensure that it provides policy incentives to increase individuals' happiness and also to address the insufficiency of those people who are not "happy", as defined.

Criticisms of fixed weight composite measures

The robustness of composite measures is dependent on the expertise of those involved in their construction in terms of selecting the right measures, identifying appropriate levels of performance and applying the optimal weightings to those measures. There is a trade-off between simplicity and objectivity. A common criticism of composite measures is that they rely on subjective assessments in their construction (Booysen, 2002). As a result, they can become measures of convenience where (1) individual measures contained within the composite are selected because of availability, rather than because they are related to the underlying performance construct the composite measure is seeking to capture; (2) weightings do not reflect the relative importance of individual measures to overall performance; and (3) they can reflect political processes, rather than business processes such that managers lobby to ensure that the performance measures used and the weightings adopted show their business in the best light.

Productivity analysis

Many of the criticisms of composite measures relate to the subjective nature of the construction process. This subjectivity can be reduced where performance is modelled using productivity analysis. This approach models the underlying production process (or production function) in terms of inputs and outputs of production. Performance is measured as the efficiency of conversion of inputs into outputs. Measures are included only where they relate to this production process and, critically, where increases in inputs are associated with increases in outputs (or at least non-negative changes in outputs), and vice versa.

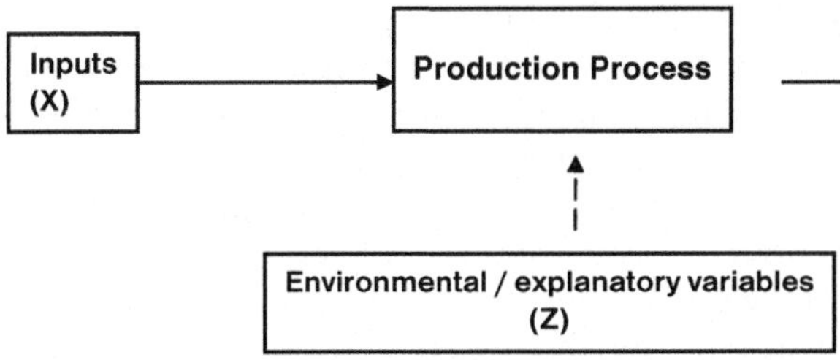

Figure 5.2 A production process consuming inputs to produce outputs

Let us explore an example, starting with Figure 5.2 depicting a production process that consumes inputs (X) to produce outputs (Y). Performance can relate to a firm, hospital, store, department, individual or even a period of time for a single organisation. These performance entities are referred to as decision-making units or DMUs. Not all DMUs face the same level playing field, and performance may be affected by environmental factors (Zs). For example, in dairy farming, inputs include cows, labour, feed, fertiliser and land, with a single output, milk. The productivity of a farm can be affected by environmental factors such as rainfall and soil quality.

Productivity is measured as the ratio of inputs to outputs or outputs to inputs. Partial productivity measures are frequently used in practice. These compare the quantity of outputs of production to an individual input and are used by managers to focus attention on key priorities. For example, in a dairy farm, a partial productivity measure would be litres of milk per cow, which the farmer would be interested in monitoring on a regular basis. To measure overall efficiency/performance, we need to include all outputs and inputs. Performance is then determined by comparing the measure of productivity to the best performance, in terms of either minimising input use or cost, maximising output production or revenue or maximising profit. Two main approaches can be used to calculate efficiency/performance. One approach is to use fixed weights and the other is to use "free" weights when combining inputs and outputs. We now discuss two techniques that illustrate these approaches: the TFP ratio and DEA.

Total factor productivity ratio (fixed weights)

TFP measures are productivity measures that use fixed weights determined using the prices of outputs and/or the costs of inputs (Coelli, Rao, O'Donnell, & Battese, 2005). The TFP ratio can be calculated as the quantity of outputs (y_r) produced multiplied by the price of each (p_r) output divided by the quantity of inputs (x_m) used multiplied by the cost of each input (w_m), as shown below:

$$\frac{\Sigma y_r p_r}{\Sigma x_m w_m} = \frac{y_1 p_1 + y_2 p_2 + \ldots + y_R p_R}{x_1 w_1 + x_2 w_2 + \ldots + x_M w_M}$$

where $r = 1, \ldots, R$ outputs and $m = 1, \ldots, M$ inputs.

This calculation requires knowing information about the individual quantities and prices for the inputs and outputs of all comparison groups. It may be possible to get this information if comparing within a single entity with multiple branches or comparing a single entity over time. However, obtaining this information for competitors is problematic.

In the case of temporal data, consideration must be given to the selection of the base (Coelli, Rao, O'Donnell, & Battese, 2005). For example, to obtain price index numbers, the Laspeyres index uses the base period quantities to weight the current and past period prices, whereas the Paasche index uses the current period quantities to weight the past and current period prices. To obtain quantity index numbers, the Laspeyres index uses the base period prices to weight the past and current period quantities, whereas the Paasche index uses the current period prices to weight the past and current period quantities.

We turn next to DEA in which the weights are "free" in the sense that they can vary across DMUs, which is very different from uniform systems of weights.

Data envelopment analysis (free weights)

Composite measures using fixed weights and productivity measures such as the TFP ratio tend to use common or uniform systems of weights whether it be prices or the weights themselves. Generally, the main problem with systems of uniform weights is obtaining agreement on appropriate weights. The importance and difficulty of this problem should not be underestimated. "[I]n any index of performance the decision as to what elements are to be included and what weights are to be attached to them is the essence of 'policy' making, because once these decisions are made the rest of the exercise is, in principle, essentially technical" (Williams, 1985, p. 9). Any system of weights is a communication of management priorities and a strategy that may not be acceptable to those whose performance is evaluated according to those priorities. Top-down imposition of weighting systems has a distinct Theory X connotation and flies in the face of notions such as organisational learning and empowerment. It may be appropriate when a "natural" weighting system exists, but in most practical situations, local perceptions and priorities differ from higher levels and from other local units. In these situations, a uniform system of weighting tends to frustrate learning and innovative activities at the level of individual units that are often better placed to pursue different strategic directions to match local conditions. In fact, this is usually the reason for the devolution of decision-making to local levels.

There are also situations where uniform weights are appropriate, most likely characterised by low task and environmental uncertainty. Situations of high task uncertainty with a dominant professional group culture would suggest large-scale resistance to the imposition of uniform weights for performance evaluation and measurement. For example, in New Zealand universities, there is often flexibility in the weights used to calculate final grades with some courses opting for a "double-chance" or "plussage" practice (Paxton & Wright, 2002). This approach calculates students' final grades as the higher of a combination of their coursework mark plus their final examination mark or 100% of their final examination. This allows both students who perform better at coursework and those who are better at taking exams to maximise their final grade.

DEA has the capacity to allow local policies and circumstances to be considered in performance evaluation (Charnes, Cooper, & Rhodes, 1978). It achieves this through a systematic search for weights, which will optimise performance for any individual unit. Thus, a set of weights is determined for each unit that presents that unit in its best possible light in contrast to the "top-down" approach that imposes a uniform set of weights on all units. In contrast to uniform systems of weights, in DEA, the weights are the unknown decision variables that are to be solved. This is done using linear programming methods, but the principles are fairly straightforward and are explained in the following.

Figure 5.3 shows a very simple example of six DMUs producing a single output (vertical axis) using a single input (horizontal axis). Rationally, we expect higher output levels with

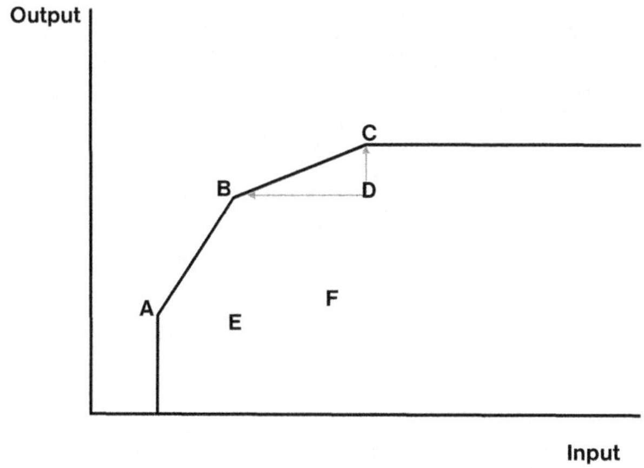

Figure 5.3 Single input–output process

higher input levels consumed, and we can see an upwards drift in the DMU input–output combinations as input increases. We can also see that some DMUs produce higher levels of output than other DMUs, or they produce the same level of output but use less input. These DMUs are shown connected by the solid lines. DMUs not on this line are considered to be dominated by the other DMUs and consequently deemed inefficient. Consider that DMU D consumes the same level of input as DMU C but produces a lower level of output. DMU D is said to be *dominated* by DMU C and is designated inefficient, with the amount of inefficiency shown by the vertical arrow from DMU D to DMU C.

Notice that this is an *output orientation* as inefficiency is measured in terms of the additional output required by DMU D given its current level of input. Alternatively, DMU B produces the same level of output as DMU D but does so using less input. The horizontal arrow from DMU D to DMU B shows the amount of inefficiency on an *input orientation*. It should be clear from Figure 5.3 and DMU D that inefficiency can be different depending on whether we adopt an input or an output orientation. We can identify an efficiency frontier of non-dominated DMUs being DMUs A, B and C that either produce the maximum output for their respective level of input or use the minimum input for their respective level of output.

Alternatively, we can consider a situation of two outputs and a single input as shown in Figure 5.4. The horizontal axis shows the ratio of output 1 to input, and the vertical axis shows the ratio of output 2 to input. There are eight DMUs in our example (numbered instead of letters to avoid confusion with the example in Figure 5.3). The efficiency frontier consists of those DMUs (1 through 5) that produce combinations of maximum outputs to input and are non-dominated by any other DMU. In contrast, DMUs 6, 7 and 8 lie below this frontier and are said to be dominated by the other five DMUs or combinations thereof.

Notice that some DMUs have a preference for either output 1 (DMUs 4, 5 and 8) or output 2 (DMUs 1, 2 and 6), while others are more "middle of the road" (DMUs 3 and 7). DEA allows flexibility in the weights to provide for these preferences, so that DMUs 1 and 5 are equally efficient, even though they clearly have different preferences for each output (e.g. if the DMUs were universities, output 1 could be teaching and output 2 could be research). The efficiency frontier corresponds to a production possibility frontier in economics, and movements along the efficient frontier represent changes in the marginal rates of substitution

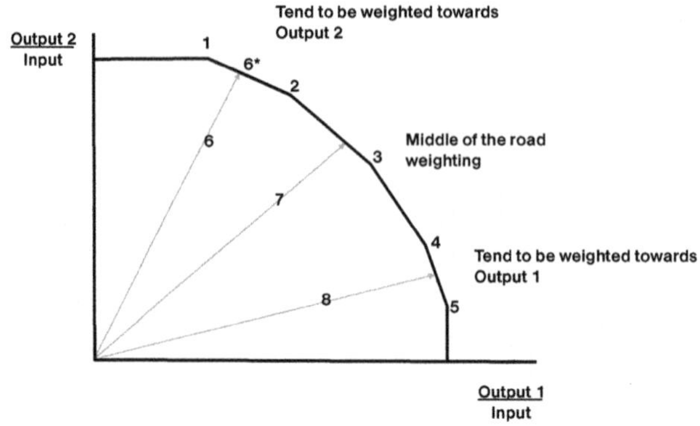

Figure 5.4 Two outputs and single input process

between the two outputs. For example, moving from DMU 3 to DMU 4 represents a trade-off of output 2 for output 1, and it can be seen that a relatively large amount of output 2 would need to be traded off for a smaller amount of output 1.

The inefficiency of dominated DMUs is measured by their distance to the frontier. For example, DMU6 is dominated by DMUs 1 and 2, and its inefficiency is measured by the distance to the frontier along the line emanating from the origin to its point of intersection with the line segment connecting 1 and 2, i.e. at point 6★. Looking at DMU 6, it appears to lie approximately three-quarters of the distance along this line from the origin. The following three key points should be noted:

- DMU 6's efficiency score is determined by its relative distance to the frontier, approximately 75%;
- the projected point at which the line from the origin passing through 6 intersects the frontier (6★) provides the targets for DMU6 to become efficient;
- the projection to the frontier preserves DMU 6's production mix of output 1 to output 2, e.g. DMU6 tends to prefer output 2 over output 1 as do DMUs 1 and 2.

Diseconomies relating to differences in size can be easily accommodated within the DEA models by adopting a variable returns to scale (VRS) model as opposed to constant returns to scale (CRS). Figure 5.5 uses Figure 5.3 to add a CRS frontier to the VRS frontier. Under CRS, an increase in inputs (say 10%) results in an equivalent increase in output (10%). Under VRS, an increase in input can result in a different increase in output. DMUs A and B lie in both the CRS and VRS frontiers, while DMU C lies only in the VRS frontier. Note that the VRS frontier consists of three parts: the vertical line from the horizontal axis to DMU A (increasing returns to scale), the line segment between A and B (CRS), and the right-hand segments of the VRS frontier between B and C and beyond (decreasing returns to scale).

Efficiency is still measured in terms of distance to the frontier, but now there are two possibilities. Note how DMU D is much more inefficient in an output orientation under CRS than VRS because the distance to the CRS frontier is much greater. Also note that DMU D's efficiency in an input orientation does not differ between CRS and VRS as it still projects onto B which is on the CRS part of the VRS frontier.

We next describe an application of DEA to illustrate its use in practical settings.

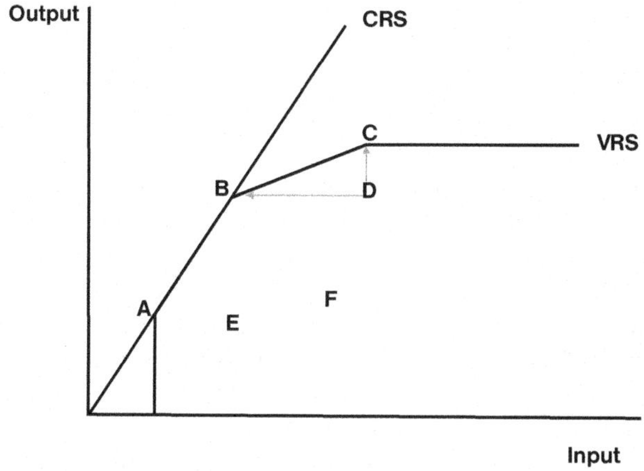

Figure 5.5 Constant and variable returns to scale

Application 1: Child immunisation activities in general practices[6]

In 2008, a study of immunisation activities of New Zealand (NZ) general practices (GPs) was carried out for the national District Health Board of NZ (DHBNZ). Twenty-four GPs agreed to participate in detailed time keeping and provision of information to identify the cost of immunisations provided. Data collection tools were developed with feedback from key stakeholder groups including general practitioners, practice managers and practice nurses, and pilot tested by three practices. These tools consisted of (1) a Financial and Total Practice Time Questionnaire (FTPTQ) that collected the total practice overheads and specific costs relating to immunisation and the total hours of work for all practice staff; (2) a questionnaire completed by the general practitioners to estimate their total immunisation time involvement over an average week; and (3) a manual log completed daily by practice nurses and administration staff involved in any of the tasks involved in immunisation service delivery. These manual logs were completed for a period of five days to assess the time spent by different practice staff. Finally, questionnaires covering the less common, monthly events were completed once by all staff involved in immunisation tasks.

An Activity-Based Costing (ABC) model was developed in which the main immunisation-related activities were identified and traced to vaccination events via measurement of both resources and activities. These activities and associated resources were classified into a four-level hierarchy:

Unit level: activities directly involved with the vaccination delivery, e.g. checking registration, vaccine preparation, obtaining informed consent, administering the vaccine, documentation, checking and routine follow-up.

Batch level: activities required to manage the service, e.g. waste removal costs specifically for sharps (needles), printing, postage and stationery incurred in making appointments and other correspondence concerning immunisations, vaccine ordering, audit procedures, generating routine immunisation appointments and reminders, and late immunisations.

Product sustaining level: activities to provide "resource capability", e.g. initial vaccination training, annual staff training and updates, CPR updates and cold chain accreditation, being the cost of demonstrating compliance with proper refrigeration requirements.

Facility level: practice-level costs/activities that are required to meet the infrastructure and/or organisation requirements to facilitate immunisation provision but are not directly traceable to immunisation activities per se, e.g. administration (rent, utilities, subscriptions, insurance and depreciation), the cost of support staff, including receptionists and practice managers, and those operating expenses not directly traceable to vaccinations such as consumables, after hours support, cleaning and laundry.

Figure 5.6 shows the DEA model (top half) and the CAM-I cross[7] ABC model (lower half). Note how the DEA model focuses on a process that consumes inputs to produce outputs. Compare the ABC model with its focus on an activity consuming resources to produce some product or service with DEA. The similarity is obvious, but there are differences. Generally, DEA uses fairly aggregated inputs and outputs, and the process is often at firm or branch level, i.e. the process contains activities. The ABC model deals with fairly specific activities, outputs and resources, and the activities can be at fairly micro levels. It should also be noted how the environmental factors in the DEA model can be linked to the cost drivers in the ABC model. Thus, understanding what factors influence performance in DEA scores can also help identify cost drivers in the ABC model.

The ABC model was used to provide more aggregated inputs for the DEA model as shown in Figure 5.6. The ABC model is shown in the lower half of the figure where resource

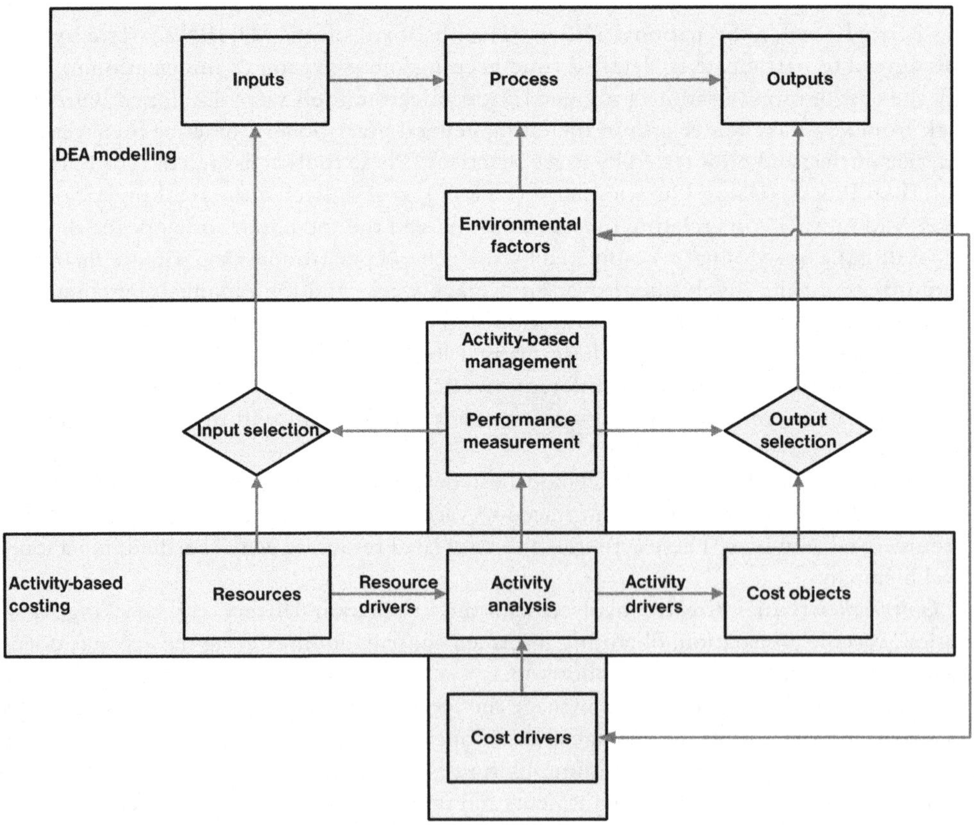

Figure 5.6 DEA and ABC interrelationships
Source: Rouse, Harrison and Turner (2010).

Table 5.4 DEA results for the 24 GP practices

	Constant returns to scale	*Variable returns to scale*		*Scale efficiency*	
DMU	*CRS*	*Input*	*Output*	*Input*	*Output*
Mean (%)	60	69	75	87	80
Median (%)	47	68	76	94	74
Std dev (%)	24	24	21	14	17
# efficient	3	5	5	4	3

drivers are used to identify consumption of resources by activities and activity drivers to identify consumption of activities by cost objects. The resources and cost objects are mapped onto the DEA model via the vertical arrows whereby inputs and outputs are selected from the resources and cost objects. Given that the ABC model is usually fairly detailed, the resources and cost objects typically need to be aggregated for use in the DEA model. The DEA model has 24 DMUs and two inputs (the unit-level primary activities aggregated by time and batch activities aggregated by cost) and a single output (number of vaccinations). Results of the DEA model are reported in Table 5.4.

Efficiency scores improve considerably under the assumption of VRS as opposed to CRS, and there is a higher level of efficiency when adopting an output as opposed to an input orientation. Approximately one-fifth (5 out of 24) of the practices are fully efficient (i.e. make up the efficient frontier) under VRS, and over half are 76% efficient or more. Scale efficiency is calculated by dividing the CRS scores by the VRS scores and shows that there are considerable differences in scale effects (87% for input and 80% for output orientations). This suggests that the practices vary in terms of size (which they do from 65 to 4,949 total vaccinations) and that the VRS model is probably a better fit than the CRS model.

As noted, the DEA inputs aggregated primary activities time and batch level costs from the ABC model. The detailed information from the ABC model in terms of resource drivers and disaggregated activities can be used to analyse the DEA results to identify environmental factors that influence efficiency scores, which in turn can provide insights into cost drivers shown by the arrows connecting the environmental factors box with the cost driver box in Figure 5.6. The details of each aggregated input are provided in Table 5.5 organised by quartile efficiency scores. Thus, in the top panel that reports the VRS output orientation results, there are four quartiles of GPs with mean efficiency scores of 48%, 66%, 86% and 100%, respectively. The corresponding mean times for each activity at unit level are shown across the columns for each row.

A "Y" is placed in the row below columns where there appears to be a trend.[8] For example, higher levels of efficiency are associated with lower times for vaccine preparation, informed consent, giving the vaccination, etc. Column 11 (number of registered patients) reveals increasing efficiency with larger practices with a weaker trend in column 12 (registered patients under the age of 5 years). There is an initial counter-intuitive trend in the deprivation index (higher scores indicate higher deprivation) where more inefficient practices are associated with lower levels of deprivation. The explanation for this is that practices in affluent areas take more time with clients who are more likely to seek in-depth information about benefits and risks of immunisation. In deprived areas, clients ask fewer questions and trust the health professional more, and so informed consent can often be briefer. Furthermore, in more deprived areas, there is the possibility of multiple vaccinations if larger families are all immunised in the same visit.

Table 5.5 DEA scores by quartiles across unit- and batch-level activities

(1)	*(2)*	*(3)*	*(4)*	*(5)*	*(6)*	*(7)*	*(8)*	*(9)*	*(10)*	*(11)*	*(12)*	*(13)*	*(14)*	*(15)*
DMUs in quartiles	*Average VRS output oriented efficiency*	*Registration check*	*Vaccine prep'*	*Obtaining informed consent*	*Giving vaccine*	*Documentation*	*Checking*	*Routine follow-up*	*Total minutes*	*Registered patients*	*Registered patients <5 years*	*Deprivation index*	*Local population*	
1	48%	3.6	5.7	5.3	6.6	3.5	5.1	1.0	30.8	3420	278	5	117	
2	66%	2.0	4.1	4.9	4.8	5.4	1.9	3.4	26.4	7745	770	6	110	
3	86%	2.2	2.2	4.3	3.6	3.8	2.4	2.4	20.9	7895	543	7	88	
4	100%	3.1	2.2	3.4	2.7	2.9	1.5	1.4	17.1	8700	680	8	66	
Trend			Y	Y	Y	Y	Y			Y	Y	Y	Y	
	Average CRS efficiency	*Claiming costs*	*GP time*	*Waste removal*	*Stationery*	*Vaccine ordering*	*Audit*	*Generate appoint's*	*Generate pre-appoint' reminders*	*Late immunisations*	*Check practice system*	*Organise Referrals*	*Adverse events*	*Late Immunisations Sub-total*
1	37%	$504	$2,469	$66	$363	$23	$3	$66	$25	$108	$63	$7	$7	$182
2	43%	$860	$3,768	$150	$768	$39	$8	$15	$22	$106	$55	$12	$9	$180
3	62%	$440	$1,071	$70	$1,065	$12	$7	$92	$4	$101	$26	$12	$8	$128
4	97%	$214	$329	$162	$803	$19	$7	$25	$4	$7	$11	$7	$4	$15
Trend		Y	Y						Y	Y	Y		Y	Y

Source: Adapted from Rouse, Harrison and Turner (2010).

The lower panel of Table 5.5 shows batch-level costs by activity. The CRS results are reported since batch-level costs are not volume driven but are more time related. The most noticeable trends are seen in the CRS results for claiming, GP time, reminders, and late immunisations. Late immunisations are regarded as a major nuisance by most practices, and column 15 shows a clear trend for the CRS results.

Informed by these analyses, we next examine one of the practices to see how DEA provides information for benchmarking which it can use to improve its performance. Selecting a DMU at random, DMU 8, and using the VRS input results, Table 5.6 provides typical DEA information for benchmarking.

DMU 8 is 67% efficient under VRS input orientation, and the actual value of its output (number of vaccinations) is 1,540 using inputs of primary activities (38,782 minutes) and batch-level costs ($4,923). Columns 3 and 4 report comparable figures for its benchmarking efficient peers, DMUs 11 and 22, and it should be immediately apparent that DMU 11 produces more vaccinations with lower inputs than DMU 8. The third row under columns 5 and 6 represents the proportions of DMUs 11 and 22 that are used to calculate the targets for DMU 8 in column 7. For example, 78.6% of DMU 11 vaccinations (1,717 × 0.786 = 1,349) plus 21.4% of DMU 22 vaccinations (891) equal 1,540, which is the number of vaccinations that DMU 8 is providing. The target inputs are calculated in a similar fashion, except now we can see that the target values are substantially less than DMU 8's actual values leading to a total input reduction required in order for DMU 8 to become efficient.

Using the ABC model detailed data for the three DMUs shown in Table 5.6, we can now provide some more directed advice as to where to look for improvements. Primary activities in minutes per vaccination for DMUs 8, 11 and 22 are provided in Table 5.7.

Table 5.6 Benchmarking and target performance improvements for DMU 8

(1)	*(2)*	*(3)*	*(4)*	*(5)*	*(6)*	*(7)*	*(8)*
	DMU	*Peer units*		*Peer units scaled*			
	8	*11*	*22*	*11*	*22*		
DMU 8: VRS input efficiency: 67%	*Actual*	*Actual*	*Actual*	*78.6%*	*21.4%*	*DMU 8 targets*	*Total input reduction*
Vaccinations	1,540	1,717	891	1,349	191	1,540	No change
Primary activities time	38,782	29,963	10,790	23,543	2,312	25,855	12,927
Batch-level costs	4,923	2,860	1,043	2,247	223	2,471	2,452

Source: Adapted from Rouse, Harrison and Turner (2010).

Table 5.7 Example of directed improvement advice

DMU	*Reg' check*	*Vaccine prep'*	*Informed consent*	*Giving vaccine*	*Documentation*	*Checking*	*Routine follow-up*	*Total min's*
8	1.0	3.0	7.5	6.6	4.5	1.1	1.5	25.2
11	1.1	1.5	7.7	1.3	3.0	1.1	1.7	17.5
22	1.8	1.5	2.3	1.8	2.0	1.6	1.1	12.1

Source: Adapted from Rouse, Harrison and Turner (2010).

It is apparent that preparation and administration of vaccine are the areas where DMU 8 should look to see why it takes so much longer than its peer DMUs. Examination of the batch-level costs (not reported here) shows that it spends $150 more than its peer DMUs on activities associated with late immunisations as well as substantially more on printing and stationery.

In summary, we can see that the DEA efficiency scores are composite measures that lend themselves easily to further analysis in order to identify underlying causes or drivers for poor performance. Their use in regression analysis should be readily apparent where there are sufficient degrees of freedom.

Conclusion

Composite measures enable managers to quickly assimilate the effect of multiple measures and gauge performance over time or across similar entities. However, this simplicity comes at a cost, which is the mechanism required to reduce multiple measures to a single measure. In this chapter, we have argued that these mechanisms need to be transparent and understandable to managers in order to avoid incorrect perceptions and inappropriate decisions. We have also highlighted the importance of understanding the nature of composite measures, be they reflective or formative, when designing composite measures. While this distinction has long been recognised in the literature (Bisbe, Batistia-Foguet, & Chenhall, 2007; Edwards & Bagozzi, 2000), it is less understood in practice, and we hypothesise that this might explain some criticisms of commonly used composite measures.

We have also summarised the main arguments for adopting composite measures and noted the advantages they have over multiple performance measures related to cognitive limitation, fossilisation and functional fixation (Emmanuel, Otley, & Merchant, 1998; Macintosh, 1985; Smith, 1997). However, composite measures have their own limitations, and we have illustrated how decisions regarding construction methods can result in very different performance rankings. Recognising the subjectivity of some of these decisions is key to assessing the robustness of composite measures. In this regard, we have concentrated on one key decision related to the use of fixed or flexible weighting systems to combine measures.

The choice of construction method will depend on data availability, timeliness and managerial appetite for complexity. We recommend DEA as a highly suitable method for situations with a reasonable number of entities where the number of input and output measures is not too great (e.g. less than 10) and the emphasis is placed on benchmarking and process improvement. We have shown, for example, how the ABC model and DEA can complement each other to provide considerable synergistic insights.

The increased use of composite measures and extension to aspects of daily life (e.g. the Gross Happiness Index) indicate that there is demand for such measures. We recommend that any such measure be accompanied by a careful explanation of how it is compiled and the rationale for the weighting systems employed.

Notes

1 For example, see www.best-schools.co.uk/uk-school-league-tables/, accessed 20 March 2017.
2 www.grossnationalhappiness.com/, accessed 20 March 2017.
3 For example, see www.topuniversities.com, accessed 20 March 2017.
4 www.timeshighereducation.co.uk/world-university-rankings/2015/world-ranking#/sort/0/direction/asc, accessed 20 March 2017.
5 See www.grossnationalhappiness.com/, accessed 20 March 2017.

6 For further information, see Rouse, Harrison and Turner (2010).
7 www.cam-i.org/docs/Toolkit_CAM-I_Cross.pdf, accessed 20 March 2017.
8 Regression results were not significant due to, we believe, the small number of GPs in our sample. While our interpretation of trends is not supported statistically, it proved of interest to those involved in the study and health specialists in this area.

References

Bisbe, J., Batista-Foguet, J.M., & Chenhall, R. (2007). Defining management accounting constructs: A methodological note on the risks of conceptual misspecification. *Accounting, Organizations, and Society 32*, 789–820.

Bollen, K. & Lennox, R. (1991). Conventional wisdom on measurement: A structural equation perspective. *Psychological Bulletin 110*(2), 305–314.

Booysen, F. (2002). An overview and evaluation of composite indices of development. *Social Indicators Research 59*, 115–151.

Charnes, A, Cooper, W.W., & Rhodes, E. (1978). Measuring the efficiency of decision making units. *European Journal of Operational Research 2*(6), 429–444.

Cherchye, L., Moesen, W., Rogge, N., & Van Puyenbroeck, T. (2007). An introduction to 'benefit of the doubt' composite indicators. *Social Indicators Research 82*, 111–114.

Coelli, T.J., Rao, D.S.P., O'Donnell, C.J., & Battese, G.E. (2005). *An Introduction to Efficiency and Productivity Analysis* (2nd ed.). New York: Springer.

Edwards, J.R. & Bagozzi, R.P. (2000). On the nature and direction of relationships between constructs and measures. *Psychological Methods 5*(2), 155–174.

Emmanuel, C., Otley, D., & Merchant, K. (1998). *Accounting for Management Control* (2nd ed.). London: International Thomson Business Press.

Goldstein, H. & Spiegelhalter, D. (1996). League tables and their limitations: Statistical issues in comparisons of institutional performance. *Journal of the Royal Statistical Society. Series A (Statistics in Society) 159*(3), 385–443.

Hanushek, E.A. (1979). Conceptual and empirical issues in the estimation of educational production functions. *Journal of Human Resources 14*(3), 351–388.

Harrison, J. & Rouse, A.P. (2014). Competition and public high school performance. *Socio-Economic Planning Sciences 48*(1), 10–19.

Jarvis, C.B., Mackenzie, S.B., & Podsakoff, P.M. (2003). A critical review of construct indicators and measurement model misspecification in marketing and consumer research. *Journal of Consumer Research 30*(3), 199–218.

Lee, J.Y. (1992). How to make financial and non-financial data add up. *Journal of Accountancy 174*(3), 62–66.

MacCullum, R.C. & Browne, M.W. (1993). The use of causal indicators in covariance structure models: Some practical issues. *Psychological Bulletin 114*(3), 533–541.

Macintosh, N.B. (1985). *The Social Software of Accounting and Information Systems*. New York: John Wiley & Sons.

Paxton, P. & Wright, C. (2002). The peer review process for the approval of new programmes in New Zealand universities: The experiences of one university. *Journal of Higher Education Policy and Management 24*(1), 101–116.

Rogers, S. (2012). Olympics 2012: The alternative medals table. *The Guardian (12 August 2012)*, retrieved from www.theguardian.com/sport/datablog/2012/jul/30/olympics-2012-alternative-medal-table (5 February 2016).

Rouse, P., Harrison, J., & Turner, N. (2010). Cost and performance: Complements for improvement. *Journal of Medical Systems 35*(5), 1063–1074.

Smith, M. (1997). Putting NFIs to work in a balanced scorecard environment. *Management Accounting (UK) 75*(3), 32–35.

Williams, A. (1985). *Performance Measurement in the Public Sector: Paving the Road to Hell, Arthur Young Lecture No. 7*. Glasgow: School of Accountancy, University of Glasgow.

Zhang, D., Li, X., Meng, W., & Liu, W. (2009). Measuring the performance of nations at the Olympic Games using DEA models with different preferences. *Journal of Operational Research Society 60*, 983–990.

6

External influences on metrics – regulation and industry benchmarks

Liz Warren and Karen Brickman

Introduction

The design of a Performance Management (PM) control system is a complex process. As argued by Franco-Santos *et al.* (2014), performance is both multi-dimensional and ambiguous, resulting in challenges for the designer. PM control system design involves establishing operational processes to be linked directly to the organisation's intended strategy. Designing a PM control system involves utilisation of Performance Measurement Systems (PMS), including benchmarking. However, there must be systems within the PMS to ensure targets/metrics or benchmarking processes are sufficiently flexible to accommodate change. To manage the complex processes within a PMS, the criticality of appropriate performance measurements for control systems, such as Total Quality Management (TQM), Six-Sigma and Just-In-Time (JIT), has long been recognised (Meybodi, 2015). In addition to appropriate measurements, it is noted that benchmarking can be used in many ways to achieve competitiveness, either to maintain continuous improvements or for process reengineering (Meybodi, 2015). Within the benchmarking literature, focus on the nature of the metrics has evolved over the three decades since research in this area emerged. While short-term targets were originally the common subjects of discussion when analysing financial and technical problems, these targets were frequently misaligned with the strategies of the organisation (Meybodi, 2015).

Companies invariably have strategies that provide two types of metrics/targets: those intended to help manage the internal operations of the organisation and those set to help achieve externally imposed targets. Arguably, there is a third type, i.e. intermediate cases, whereby companies design metrics to meet externally set targets, by measuring actions anticipated to achieve operational goals also. The combined approach to designing a good PM system reflects the complexity of the process involved.

The preceding Chapters 2 and 5 examined target setting in general and the manner in which multi-dimensional complexity can be analysed using composite measures, whereas this chapter presents a review of how the design of PMS can be shaped through regulation and benchmarking. It will also consider the industry benchmarks commonly adopted by organisations as components in their own PMS, within the target setting process, and will

Table 6.1 Summary of case studies presented in this chapter

Case	*Industry*	*Contextual factors impacting on the design of the PMS*	*Outcome*
1	Financial services: banking	Regulatory remuneration code changes and culture	An example of good practice that demonstrates how regulatory changes can be aimed at reducing excessive risk taking in settings where significant cultural changes have occurred, explaining the shaping of PMS in the form of a BSC
2	Utilities: retail electricity	Regulation on clear information	An example of how industry can comply with regulation without adjusting outcomes. Regulation shapes the design of metrics used within the PMS without achieving the behaviour sought
3	Financial services: banking	Industry benchmarking	An illustrative example that explains how companies can use data from other companies within the same industry to improve strategic outcomes
4	Utilities: electricity generation	Health and safety regulation and benchmarking	An example of good practice, providing evidence of how regulators can provide extremely useful information that the industry can use to create their own benchmarking systems
5	Utilities: electricity Distribution Network Operators	Regulatory data on reliability and availability	An illustrative example of how regulatory data can be used as a marketing tool in annual reports by industry reporting the same information to regulators and shareholders

explore some of the mandatory targets imposed via regulation. Additionally, this chapter will assess the theoretical impact of external data sources, while providing the reader with a variety of examples, in the form of case studies as illustrative examples;[1] Table 6.1 provides a summary of the cases presented herein.

Although the problems and unintended consequences of mis-designing metrics are not the main subject of this current chapter, they will appear towards the end of the chapter, and therefore, we will also touch on some of the general problems that arise.

PM design and control systems

Although the aim of this chapter is not to explain how and why organisations use PM systems for control or developmental reasons (for a good overview of this, see Chapter 2 and Ferreria and Otley (2009)), it is, however, important to first examine the context within which metrics are designed and used. Most of us are familiar with the sayings: 'what gets measured gets done' and 'you can't manage what you don't measure'. Crucially, this is not just important to the manager of an organisation but also has wider political, social and economic implications, because businesses form part of society.

The influence that wider society has on metrics can emerge in the form of laws, regulations, accounting standards and industry benchmarking, to name just a few. Regulators, politicians, consultants and independent lobbyists have the ability to influence the design of PMS, either directly or indirectly. This societal role is unremarkable, since studies exploring economic performance have often struggled to distinguish between the roles of ownership, competition, regulation and technological change (Adler, 2011; Parker, 2003). Therefore, we argue here that it is important to understand how external sources influence the nature and design of PMS, because, as argued by Adler (2011), there is a direct interplay between control systems and strategy formulation, with both external and internal factors. The PM process within organisations can involve many general processes, including "strategic planning, budgeting incentive compensation design and organizational structure" (Adler, 2011:251). However, the specific design and metrics used will be determined by the context.

Metrics can combine internal and external targets, and of course, these measures can be formal or informal, depending on how the PMS is designed. The design often relates to the size of the organisation and the industry it is a part of. Despite the nature of the metrics used, it is important to remember that whatever is being measured should facilitate learning (Canonico *et al.*, 2015; Franco-Santos *et al.*, 2014); otherwise, the process of measuring is futile. PMS should include a learning process and be flexible enough to allow change to prompt improvements; otherwise, the result is simply a PMS and not a PM control system. Although, unfortunately, in practice, this is often ignored becoming a box-ticking exercise to fulfill a duty of some sort.

Before discussing the influence of regulation and benchmarking on PM control systems, it is important for the reader to understand and clarify the difference between the two. Regulation is externally imposed upon an organisation, whereas benchmarking can be used both externally within an industry setting and internally within organisations. In addition, regulation is usually focused on outputs, i.e. results, whereas benchmarking offers a combination of results and processes that can impact results. When benchmarking is used within organisations and problems are identified, then managers have the ability to change those metrics to avoid further behavioural problems. However, if regulatory targets create problems whereby an organisation does not have the ability to change them, then the result is often dysfunctional behaviour on the part of the company, as will be discussed in the next section.

The role of regulation

Accountability is high among many private sector organisations. Indeed, stakeholders such as shareholders, the capital markets and regulators all require effective PM controls (Parker, 2003). Ferreira and Otley (2009:267) suggest that one of the key twelve questions organisations must address when considering their control systems is: "How have the PMSs altered in light of the change dynamics of the organization and its environment?" The majority of organisations working in regulated industries encounter both operating and regulatory risk, with regulation forming part of the external environment. When senior managers are considering the strategies (Adler, 2011) employed by their organisations, it is important that they also have access to detailed knowledge about the external environment (Parker, 2003), as it is a key factor in the successful design and operation of management control systems (Ferreira and Otley, 2009).

Regulation takes the form of rules, codes and directives intended to control activities carried out within various industry settings (Coglianese, 2012). Regulation has the force of law, but is not law; it is issued via governmental agencies, typically termed 'regulators', who operate at various levels. As Clarke (1994:340) explains, the law provides the enforcement model 'exclusionary targeting misconduct', while the regulatory model is arguably inclusionary, one 'that targets best practice'. Most PMS are predicated on the principle of seeking best practice to achieve a competitive advantage.

Although regulatory frameworks vary internationally, all the case studies/illustrative examples within this chapter relate to the UK setting. Therefore, a brief outline of the UK regulatory framework is provided below, before an explanation of how it can affect PMS.

The UK regulatory framework

The role of regulation within the UK rose to prominence in the early 1990s, when many of the utilities were subjected to the privatisation process (Warren, 2014; Warren and Burns, forthcoming). Regulations were introduced to counteract the supposed imperfections of competition (Crowther *et al.*, 2001); as Parker (2003) argued, at this time, regulation became a proxy for competition.

The key characteristics of the UK regulatory model were based on the Littlechild report of 1983; the foundations of which included independence, forward-looking incentive-based regulation, focus on consumers and their welfare, emphasis on competition, private ownership, strong legal and well-defined appeal rights and light-touch regulation (Stern, 2014). These foundations exerted a clear influence over organisations' PMS, because the targets set by the regulators were intended to have a strategic impact on the way the organisation operates. In addition, any incentives or sanctions provided by the regulators to encourage certain behaviours, such as environmental targets, or health and safety measures, also shaped organisations' internal metrics.

How can regulation influence metrics?

Parker (2003) argues that any company operating within a regulated industry must have in place structures and internal systems to support regulatory change. The PMS is an internal control system that should offer sufficient flexibility to change when the operating environment changes (Ferreira and Otley, 2009). As will be shown in Case study 1, following the financial crisis, the regulators had to be seen to make changes to address the perception that bankers were receiving excessive bonuses. Therefore, after the 2008 financial crisis, the role of regulation within the banking sector came to the forefront of debate, raising the question: what should regulators do to prevent its reoccurrence.

After the crisis, the International Monetary Fund (IMF) argued that three key areas must be improved: (1) incentives to provide loans to high-quality borrowers, (2) governance structures relating to the risk management of incentives and (3) the incentive structures of credit agencies (Nsouli, 208). In the UK, the second proposal, which was strongly favoured by Nsouli (2008), triggered numerous changes in the form of the implementation of new rules and policies. The bank considered in Case study 1, Barclays, addressed some of the issues highlighted by the regulators by creating new Balanced Scorecards (BSCs) for use within the PMS. In the case of Barclays, the PM system was sufficiently flexible to accommodate change, to learn from the mistakes highlighted by the regulators (Salz and Collins, 2013).

Case study 1 Regulation in the banking sector, the case of performance systems and excessive bonuses

Excessive bonuses in the financial services industry were seen to be one of the main causes of the 2008 financial crisis. Consequently, global regulators developed several remuneration codes of conduct for designing pay-per-performance systems, to ensure that the behaviour of employees under those systems aligns with the relationship between risk and return (Hartmann, 2012). The primary purpose of these codes was to mitigate employees' propensity to excessive risk taking.

In practical terms, this meant that post-crisis there was a change in how employees were assessed at year-end, and subsequently, how their bonuses were determined. Prior to these codes coming into effect, employees in revenue generating roles within the banking sector were predominantly assessed and awarded bonuses based on their financial performance, without much regard to *how* that financial performance was achieved. Today, the question of *how* financial performance is achieved has become a crucial part of the assessment and reward process. Additionally, non-financial performance measures, such as compliance with risk metrics and meeting training deadlines, have become increasingly important in the year-end review process. Another perceived failure of the pre-crisis incentive schemes was that they were too short-term orientated. Bonuses were paid based on deals made in the current year that could potentially turn to losses in subsequent years. The regulators' intention for the new remuneration codes was to overcome some of the shortcomings of the old systems. For example, in 2009, the UK Prudential Regulation Authority (PRA) implemented a remuneration code linking long-term incentives plans to performance and risk management, stating:

> The fundamental objectives of the remuneration policy are to sustain market confidence and promote financial stability through reducing the incentives for inappropriate risk taking by firms, and thereby to protect consumers. (PRA, 2013)

The remuneration code is applicable only to financial institutions; primarily the individuals in those institutions whose activities have a material impact on the firm's risk profile. The predominant features of the code are that a portion of relevant employees' remuneration is paid by deferred equity, and that their bonuses (both vested[2] and unvested[3]) are subject to clawback provisions. At least 40 per cent of an employee's bonus must be deferred for a period of 3 to 5 years. Additionally, there are two clawback provisions in operation: a malus clause and a clawback clause. The malus clause is a requirement for the employer to make "negative awards" when an employee has an unvested deferred bonus or a share incentive award, whereas the clawback clause is a requirement that the employee pays back an amount already received under a variable bonus or share incentive award following receipt of the cash or shares for a period of 7 years after payment. This can be enforced for employee misbehaviour, material error or a material risk management failure (taking into account when the material failure arose and the position of the employee at that time).

Here we take Barclays as an example. Barclays is a financial services firm with activities in retail banking, corporate banking, investment banking, and wealth and investment management. After the financial crisis, Barclays was hit with heavy penalties for various scandals, including mis-selling payment protection insurance, and foreign exchange and libor rigging scandals. In 2012, the board dismissed the then CEO, Bob Diamond, and appointed a new CEO, Anthony Jenkins, to bring about reform in response to these scandals. They also appointed a new Chairman, Sir David Walker, whose remit was to reform the culture at the bank. Working in partnership, Jenkins and Walker launched a programme called the 'transform project' to change the culture at Barclays and to make it the 'Go-To' bank. The first aspect they tackled as part of the transform programme was the bank's remuneration structure, which Walker referred to as formerly offering 'inappropriate incentivisation' (Skynews, 2012). Barclay's former remuneration structure rewarded staff for sales volumes, and Walker believed this played a crucial role in incentivising staff to mis-sell: "The inappropriate incentivisation is accountable for a lot of what has gone wrong. The problem that I think has been most serious is not so much levels of remuneration, but the gearing of remuneration to revenue" (Skynews, 2012). Walker also believed that shareholder pressure for quicker and greater returns was also part of the problem, stating: "They encouraged banks to lever up. The preoccupation with short-term revenues in the investment banks has been hugely damaging" (Skynews, 2012).

Pre-crisis, Barclays' philosophy with regard to remuneration was 'to use reward to drive a high-performance culture' (Barclays PLC Annual Report, 2006:126). Executive directors were awarded outstanding rewards for outstanding performance, and below median rewards for below median performance. Both qualitative and quantitative measures were used to assess performance, with quantitative assessment comprising the primary focus. Seventy-five per cent of the bonus award was paid in cash, with the remaining 25 per cent paid in deferred share awards.

To rectify the shortcomings of the former incentive structure, in 2013, Barclays introduced a BSC approach to performance reviews measuring both 'what' (i.e. revenues) people achieved and 'how' they achieved it. Barclays BSC measures performance against five key metrics: customer and client, colleague, citizenship, conduct and company (the 5Cs).

(*Continued*)

Employees had to align their objectives with the 5Cs of the BSC. They then received separate performance ratings in relation to 'what' and 'how'; that is, if an employee achieved the goals associated with the 'what', but in a manner not consistent with Barclays' culture, the 'how', then they were deemed to have failed to hit their target.

Bonus awards at Barclays are now based on an individual's performance rating, with the BSC playing the greatest role in determining the bonuses awarded. For very senior employees, who are entitled to Long-Term Incentive Plan awards (LTIPs), the BSC is used alongside other performance measures, which play a significant role in determining the size of the bonuses received. In 2014, annual bonus weightings were 50 per cent for meeting financial measures, 35 per cent for meeting BSC measures and 15 per cent for personal objectives. Employees also have to integrate risk and control objectives into their performance metrics. For example, traders are obliged to adhere to daily trading limits and cooperate with control functions, such as risk and product control. Evaluations relative to these control functions are now included in traders' performance reviews, and if they are deemed non-cooperative their bonuses and promotion prospects can be adversely affected.

Achievement of performance measures now also impacts LTIP awards. The LTIP already awarded can be reduced to zero under the clawback provisions, if an employee fails to meet any of the previously mentioned performance measures in a given year, or where there is evidence of misconduct, risk failure, or where a firm or business unit suffers a material downturn in its financial performance. Barclays also has the ability to clawback bonuses already paid to senior employees for a period of 7 years after payment, if there is evidence of serious individual misconduct and/or risk failure. For more junior staff members, there are no specific weightings balancing financial and non-financial measures. All these changes to the performance metrics set within Barclays, were influenced by changes demanded by the regulators.

Source: Unless otherwise stated, all data is taken from the 2014 Barclays Annual report.

Case study 1 provides evidence of how internal PM control systems can be influenced by external sources. Without regulatory intervention, it is highly unlikely that Barclays would have made such significant changes; moreover, the reputational risk would not have been as significant without the regulatory involvement.

Problems with regulation and performance metrics

Although regulation is intended to encourage best practice, and PM systems are intended to be flexible enough to incorporate this, it should be highlighted that not all regulation is seen by organisations as compatible with competitive business practices. A typical problem that regulators seek to protect consumers from is aggressive selling techniques, whereas increased sales targets are often part of a PM system (FCA, 2015). Therefore, the aims of the two parties may conflict. Although this chapter illustrates some examples of good practice; whereby regulation had a positive influence on the PM system, there are many examples where game playing has occurred. Although it appears that industry has engaged with the regulations, in reality one of the following three possibilities might have occurred:

1 Circumnavigation of the regulations, which can be achieved in a variety of ways.
2 Taking unpredicted actions to report desired outcomes, i.e. by misreporting actual results or taking undesirable actions to provide the 'right' result.
3 Deliberately ignoring the fact that their measures do not achieve the targets set, although they will justify their actions by arguing they have 'done the right thing'.

A classic case of regulation not working in the way that it was intended is described in Case study 2. When regulation is present, often applying policies and metrics to measure issues under scrutiny such as fair prices, organisations might work within the rules, but act in conflict with the regulator's original intention.

Case study 2, which is set within the privatised electricity industry, demonstrates how the regulator required simple, clear and fair information regarding pricing tariffs, so that consumers could make sensible choices to attain the best prices to match their circumstances. The suppliers within the industry indeed provided multiple tariffs; however, each company chose to present the information differently, making comparison very difficult for consumers. This, combined with aggressive sales tactics, resulted in the average consumer being overpowered by larger suppliers. This case demonstrates the ability of the industry to comply with regulatory policy, but in a way that allows them to continue with business as normal. Therefore, not all regulation will have a direct impact on PM systems or influence their design.

Case study 2 Great Britain's retail electricity market

The regulator Ofgem is responsible for a number of issues including emissions targets, security of supply (i.e. preventing blackouts) and maintaining competitive prices. Great Britain's energy market came under intense scrutiny during the period 2012–15 (CMA, 2015), with the general public expressing anger at the rising prices of 'necessity goods', such as gas and electricity. While emissions and security of supply remained stable between 2004 and 2014, prices did not. The price of electricity in the retail sector exceeded inflation for the 10-year period 2004–2014, such that in real terms prices had increased by 75% (CMA, 2015).

The regulator put a policy in place to govern prices and the market to provide simple, clear and understandable information for consumers to support their decision-making. The regulators carefully monitor prices, and ask suppliers to provide metrics on pricing through their Supply Market Indicator (SMI). However, although this is useful information, it does not create the behaviour that the regulators require in terms of making information easy for consumers to understand. Ofgem, who collect this data in the UK, must report all problems to the European Commission in accordance with annual reporting requirements under Directives 2009/72/EC (Electricity) and 2009/73/EC (Gas) (Ofgem, 2014b).

The background to the problem was that suppliers had produced a vast number of *tariffs* for consumers to select from, complicating consumer choice. Some of the big players also employed aggressive sales tactics, leading to problems within the industry, as noted by Ofgem in 2010. Despite regulatory policies relating to both clarity of information and the mis-selling of energy contracts, Great Britain continues to witness an increase in prices. Although the regulators issued sanctions:

> In May 2013 we penalised SSE £10.5 million for mis-selling. SSE had used misleading sales scripts providing inaccurate estimates and comparisons to customers and failed to adequately monitor its sales agents' activities. In December 2013 Scottish Power returned £8.5 million to customers after our investigation into mis-selling. It had failed to give customers accurate information about annual charges and about how much they would save if they switched supplier. (Ofgem, 2014b:7)

(*Continued*)

Despite these penalties Ofgem, continued to see problems in the industry. They introduced metrics regarding clear communication with the aim of offering more comprehensive information to consumers, as evidenced by significant changes in the information provided in bills for British consumers (Ofgem, 2014b). However, by 2014, Ofgem admitted that it was experiencing a problem with competition, indicating that this was impacting both clarity of information and pricing. As part of its response to this problem, suppliers were restricted to only using four sets of tariffs to simplify consumer information and to gain trust back within the market. The Competition and Markets Authority (CMA) was called in to investigate both the gas and electricity industry. Although originally clear metrics were introduced by the regulators, the companies within the industry chose to interpret them in a way that did not address the intended problem, as can be seen from the substantial fines issued by the regulators.

Source: All information from CMA (2015) and Ofgem (2014a) unless stated otherwise.

Case study 2 is a very good example of how regulation can influence metrics within organisations. However, it may not generate the behaviour the regulators were expecting; regulation can often create dysfunctional behaviour. Regulators often fall into the trap of incentivising organisations to do one thing, when in fact they are wanting to achieve something different (Kerr, 1995). Companies are complex and so are PM control systems; although, controlling behaviour to achieve organisational strategic outcomes can be achieved through these systems. However, control systems can also be manipulated to achieve targets set by external parties without influencing a company's operational priorities.

Thus far, in this chapter we have considered the influence of regulation on the metrics used within organisations, and observed the potential for problems when regulations seek to influence control systems; for example, when companies choose to game play within the rules. Not all regulatory change is straightforward. Indeed, Dassler *et al.* (2006:166) state that regulation is often "subject to information asymmetries that can lead to allocative and productive inefficiencies". When regulators find themselves lacking in information they often use benchmarking to resolve this deficit. Benchmarking can be used to track an organisation's performance against a comparable company.

The role of industry benchmarking

We have previously discussed the concepts of metrics and their role in the PM system. We will now consider how organisations can use metrics to compare themselves with their competitors. In an era of liberalisation, competition has prompted organisations to compete for both the best quality products and services and reduced costs (Kodali, 2008). Industry benchmarking is a process whereby organisations compare themselves with their competitors in terms of key performance or process related metrics. Maheshwari and Janssen (2013:83) extend this explanation by highlighting the difference between measuring and benchmarking; thus, "measuring is aimed at determining the performance based on some kind of criterion, whereas benchmarking is the activity to compare the resulting scores with some kind of norm". Arguably, benchmarking is a tool that management can use for "attaining or exceeding the performance goals by learning from best practices and understanding the processes by which they are achieved" (Kodali, 2008:258).

However, as argued by Deville (2009:251), "managers often do not have the best evaluation techniques at their disposal", especially when they are trying to utilise the PM system to remain competitive within their industry. Organisations seeking to improve or maintain their own competitive advantage often require data that is not publicly available; they have their own data sets, but not necessarily those of their competitors. Moreover, benchmarking can require a significant investment, in terms of both time and money.

Although large organisations can perform benchmarking exercises against departments or segments within their own organisation, allowing them to compete effectively within their industry, there needs to be some benchmarking against competitors, because it is a process that incorporates "evaluating best practice, assessing and comparing units fairly and classifying them" (Deville, 2009:258).

Hua and Lee (2014) observed that benchmarking evolved from the assessment of results-based metrics to the evaluation of capabilities. Analysing capabilities enabling organisations to achieve top performance can be a catalyst to improving performance. Therefore, for benchmarking to be successful it must be "integrated into organizational strategy and the process employs a wide range of performance measures that are consistent with organizational strategy" (Meybodi, 2015:2).

Which factors should be benchmarked?

Benchmarking takes many forms, and in the literature there is considerable debate over what the key elements of the process should include; for example cost, quality, delivery and customer service (Meybodi, 2015). Benchmarking literature has also recognised that the timing of the benchmarking is critical to the success of the tool (Kodali, 2008). For example, Anderson and McAdam (2004) argued that benchmarking was often used at the output stage of a process, known as the downstream process, resulting in lag benchmarks. The problem with lag benchmarks is that it is often then too late to instigate best practice to change anything. It is therefore suggested that 'lead benchmarking' is more appropriate; this lead benchmarking involves using key ratios from the upstream part of the organisation. The discussion of preferred benchmarking links back to Canonico *et al.*'s argument (2015); that is, the process of measuring targets must be part of the learning process. Meybodi (2015:1, citing Walsh (1993) and Kuebler (1993)) further argued that it should be an "effective means for learning and change because it exposes employees to new approaches, systems and procedures". By allowing employees to explore new ways of achieving best practice, a learning environment connecting organisational operations and strategies develops.

The learning process from benchmarking?

As commented on several times already PM control systems must have the room to facilitate learning. Hua and Lee (2014) found three stages to support learning within the benchmarking process:

1. Managers seek firms with superior performance and identify the relevant capabilities that drive the performance (the search stage).
2. Managers access capabilities distinctions between their own firm and benchmarking firms (the gap assessment stage).
3. Managers create and execute plans to close capability gaps identified in the second step (the capability improvement stage) (Hua and Lee, 2014:138).

Of course, the three stages, as described by Hua and Lee (2014), are not as easy as one might first assume. It is possible that companies do not know what their capabilities are, and may not have access to the external data required to execute a plan, or to close the gaps identified. In Case study 3, we will observe a situation in which the data required to perform effective benchmarking is not possible without the help of external parties.

Sometimes the information required to compare capabilities is highly commercially sensitive, requiring a third party to collate data and provide anonymous matrix tables to show comparative positions. Case study 3 exemplifies a situation in which the highly sensitive nature of the data required for metrics within the benchmarking process results in third parties being intermediate players. The banks discussed in Case study 3 needed to establish how successful they were compared with their competitors, in order to learn how to improve their own positions. However, they would not have been able to achieve this without external companies providing pertinent data. Benchmarking data is used within an organisation's own PMS to improve systems and processes, with the aim of improving their competitive position, in a rapidly changing environment.

Case study 3 Industry benchmarking in the financial services sector

Competitive industries, such as the financial services sector, rely on timely performance and management of information, to be able to react to environmental changes and compete effectively with their peer group. The banking sector has been subject to significant growth within the online segment of businesses, and so, for competitors to be successful they must evolve and adapt to trends in the market. A key trend relates to bank distribution channels. In the past 15 years, distribution channels have diversified, and customers can now select a number of options, such as visiting traditional branches, using ATMs, call centres, online banking and (within online banking) mobile banking.

Therefore, we ask: how do banks monitor and set targets that create effective PMS, which can provide control systems to ensure they remain competitive? As with other sectors, the answer is by using benchmarking. Typically, the data required is not publicly available, and so banks rely on external benchmarking companies to provide metrics. Benchmarking companies sell their services to competitors within an industry, retrieving data from individual organisations, checking that information and then reporting the metrics by creating a ranking system. This process is only effective if data remains anonymous. The resultant reports enable individual banks to correlate their performance with that of their peers, without knowing the names of the banks in each position. Those banks that receive these reports can assess their performance relative to that of their competitors and set their own metrics internally.

Benchmarking organisations also provide an invaluable control system to help identify improvements for organisations within the process, by collecting and synthesising comparable data. This is often not possible within the internal metrics designed without benchmarking aids, because all organisations have their own design systems, which do not make it easy to identify organisational improvements.

An external analysis of a peer group, such as the banking sector, can illustrate emerging trends, which can then be integrated into performance measurement systems and future strategies. The typical data sets that industry benchmarkers produce within the commercial banking sector aim to answer questions such as those listed below:

Market share and channel strategy

- Where do you rank in the market?
- How is your market share changing and what drives this performance?
- How does this affect your sales and servicing strategy?

Marketing efficiency

- How does your marketing strategy compare to those implemented by your competitors, in terms of size, distribution, and acquisition costs?
- How can you improve lead generation and conversion?
- How strong is your brand?

Customer journey

- How can you improve the usability of your mobile, online, and telephone processes?
- What are best practice conversion rates?

Sales value

- How does the value of your sales compare to that of your competitors?
- What opportunities are there to improve upselling, cross-product sales, customer retention and product usage?

Customer servicing

- How does the quality of your customer services compare to your competitors?
- How can you improve waiting times and abandonment rates whilst maintaining cost efficiency?
- How can you reduce the cost of servicing your customer base?

The data provided in answer to these questions offer key metrics, which can then inform the internal control systems of banks using these services.

Source: Information from: eBenchmarkers, www.ebenchmarkers.co.uk/benchmarks/.

Case study 3 clearly exemplifies how the external data sources provided by intermediary parties can help to influence the design of the metrics used with the commercial banks. Without these external data sets, the process of using comparative data is not possible. However, comparative data aids the learning process in more than one way; it can help to improve existing frameworks by identifying new capabilities, which may be required to improve competitiveness and which can help to improve the quality of any data used within internal PM control systems.

How regulation and benchmarking can work together

Earlier in this chapter, we briefly mentioned that regulators often use benchmarking to overcome the problem of information asymmetry. However, organisations often use regulatory data for benchmarking purposes within their own PMS, as can be seen in Case study 4. Health and safety is one of the key aspects mentioned by energy companies, because some of the jobs available are high risk. Therefore, Case study 4 represents a case in which the metrics reported to the regulator as part of a benchmarking process became target internal metrics. The benchmarking process by the regulator became a means to mitigate the risks associated with the operational aspects of the business. Case study 4 offers a good example of how influential external data sources affect the individual control systems within organisations, when incorporated into their PM control system.

Case study 4 Regulation and benchmarking, the case of Health and Safety in the electricity generation industry

Within Great Britain the Health and Safety Executive (HSE) is responsible for governing health and safety issues. The HSE's mission is to 'prevent death, injury and ill health in British workplaces through guidance, approved codes of practice and regulation' (HSE, 2015a). They have the force of law to help regulate all industries; this includes the use of the Health and Safety at Work Act 1974 and The Management of Health and Safety at Work Regulation 1999.

As part of the regulatory framework, there are mandatory reporting metrics, one of which is the Reporting of Injuries, Diseases and Dangerous Occurrences Regulations (RIDDOR) (HSE, 2015c). RIDDOR enforces a duty of care to all employers, to report any instances covered under this regulation, including any near misses. The issues covered under RIDDOR include death at work, specific injuries such as 10 per cent > burns, fractures, non-fatal injuries to non-workers, occupational diseases and gas incidents, among others.

If any of the instances named under the regulation occur, then a responsible person is required to report the incident to the HSE. In addition to the serious investigation this reporting might trigger, the statistics available can be used as metrics for public scrutiny. The serious nature of such incidents, and the presence of the data in the public domain, have influenced how organisations use this form of regulation internally.

One example of how the RIDDOR metrics have been translated into internal Key Performance Indicators (KPIs), leading to a benchmarking exercise can be seen within the electricity generation industry.

> Scottish Power realised that it was vulnerable to a catastrophic incident and that it did not have a structured approach to managing these risks or providing good information about the status on control systems. (HSE, 2011:1)

Therefore, Scottish Power analysed the data and guidance from the HSE, realising that it "highlighted gaps and recognised we needed good key performance indicators" (HSE, 2011:1).

While noting that the metrics used for RIDDOR would improve their own safety processes, which formed part of the larger PMS, they also recognised that they provided an excellent learning process, by using publicly available data as a benchmarking exercise with other industries.

> Our vision was one of business excellence in process safety and asset management. We wanted to learn from other sectors like chemical and major hazard industries.....through benchmarking leading companies. (HSE, 2011:1)

RIDDOR metrics formed part of Scottish Power's performance measurements systems, within major process safety incidents, thereby providing a good example of how regulation can influence the design of metrics within an internal control system, while also forming part of a benchmarking exercise within the same system.

Source: HSE, www.hse.gov.uk/comah/case-studies/case-study-scottish-power.pdf.

Case study 4 is an example of where an individual organisation chose to incorporate regulatory benchmarking data into their own PMS, because they perceived the value it would add to their own employees in the areas of health and safety. It was an example of how regulation and benchmarking can indirectly form part of a PMS.

Regulation, benchmarking, PM systems and formal reporting

As part of a control system, companies are often required to formally report their metrics to stakeholders (PWC, 2016) via annual reports, thereby having a direct influence on the PM system. The reporting that takes place is part of the corporate governance system, which forms part of the PM system. As can be seen in Case study 5, the regulators required formal reporting of metrics used within the wider PM systems in two forms: first, the regulatory reports on data provided in each company's own annual report, illustrating their performance in a benchmarking process for public scrutiny; and second, individual companies required to report the metrics in their own annual reports as part of a corporate governance system. It is hoped this formal reporting will influence behaviour and disseminate best practice throughout the industry as a whole.

Case study 5 Regulated customer satisfaction, the case of the Distribution Network Operators

Ofgem regulates the entire value chain within the gas and electricity sector within Great Britain. As part of their framework, they work with elements of the value chain that form natural monopolies within the electricity industry, such as the Distribution Network Operators (DNOs). Natural monopolies result in non-engagement with customer satisfaction, because there is no competition; however, the remit of the regulators is to protect customers and ensure they receive a good service, despite the lack of competition.

Therefore, in the case of the DNOs, Ofgem has created a customer satisfaction survey to provide transparency and avert adverse behaviour. As part of its survey process, they interview customers regarding three issues: supply interruptions, connections and general enquires. The data received from all DNOs are then made publicly available for anyone wishing to review the data. This creates a benchmarking exercise comparing all the DNOs across Great Britain.

(*Continued*)

Ofgem prepared an annual report for public scrutiny in 2010–11, from which an extract appears below (Table 6.2).

Table 6.2 DNO performance snapshot for 2010–11

Performance indicator	Reliability and availability	Customer satisfaction	Connections	Social responsibility
WPD West Midlands	⬤	○	◯	●
WPD East Midlands	⬤	○	◯	●
Electricity North West	⬤	○	◯	○
NPG Northeast	⬤	○	◯	●
NPG Yorkshire	⬤	○	◯	●
WPD South Wales	⬤	●	◯	●
WPD South West	⬤	●	◯	●
UKPN London Power	◯	○	◯	○

Source: Ofgem (2012).

The circles in the table denote a traffic light system, showing when a measurement system is used to indicate a company's position in the area being analysed. Therefore, green (darker shading) represents good performance, yellow (lighter shading) is neutral and red (not used in this example) means a penalty is actioned because they have not achieved what is required. The smaller circles indicate that this is a new area of analysis, which does not symbolise long-term performance.

In addition to their regulatory reporting on metrics, the individual DNOs now use such metrics as a basis for internal targets, and these are then published within their own annual reports.

Case study 5 also reveals how regulation can impact the design of a PM internal control system. The formal reporting of metrics is required, both by the regulatory body, and within their own annual reports to stakeholders.

Problems with benchmarking

Although benchmarking has provided many benefits as seen in case studies 3, 4 and 5, it is not without problems. Some of the greatest criticisms have been based on the 'shallow and incomplete' measures, of which users apparently have a limited understanding (Petrović *et al.*, 2012). Within internal control systems, and to aid PM management, it is imperative to use metrics that provide a bigger picture, if there are to be tangible improvements for the company.

Simply creating and using shallow metrics will not ensure a company works towards fulfilling its own strategies, nor will it automatically provide a competitive advantage.

Petrović *et al.* (2012) also argues that companies often engage in benchmarking, but then do not implement the operational processes required to engage in change, and as argued several times previously in this chapter, PM systems without the ability to educate and instigate change are worthless. There are also problems associated with the vagueness of those metrics set within benchmarking, as unsurprisingly, the focus is usually on one aspect of operations, resulting in companies paying too much attention to that one area. Focus on one area can mean they can fail to comprehend the bigger picture, thereby missing opportunities for innovation.

Conclusion

This chapter aimed to highlight that, although PM control systems are internal to organisations, they are affected by external bodies and data sources. The organisational context plays a significant role in the design of any PMS. PM target setting within organisations has clearly been heavily influenced by both regulation and benchmarking. However, the impact of external bodies/data sources is not necessarily beneficial. As Codagnone *et al.* (2015) have highlighted, the use of benchmarking has resulted in organisations becoming more alike, because they are all focusing on the same issues and of course the same may be true of the impact of regulation. This can inhibit innovation, and efficiency, and result in companies losing control of their own destinies.

The external environment has, and will continue to have, a significant impact on the way in which organisations operate and design their internal control systems, as can be seen in the case studies summarised in Table 6.1. It has been clearly identified within this chapter that companies are unable to ignore regulatory metrics. In some cases, industries have even found the metrics proposed by regulators useful, as illustrated in Case study 4, whereas in other cases, companies have played the game but continued to engage in behaviour that the regulator would consider far from ideal (Case study 2).

In terms of external data sources, regulation is not the only influencer. Organisations are now seeking best practice and one way in which they can achieve this is by engaging in a process of benchmarking; both in terms of the benchmarking results that they use and the key processes that produce results. Analysing the capabilities of those considered the best in their industry opens up opportunities for a learning process to take place.

The most important aspect of external data sources, when designing internal PM systems is to ensure that a system is flexible enough to withstand change. An inflexible control system would not successfully adapt at the rate regulation requires, nor would it accommodate the new capabilities identified in best practice within the industry, as recognised via benchmarking.

Acknowledgements

The authors thank Dr Carolyn Stringer and Professor David Otley for their insightful comments.

Notes

1 For ease, the case studies/illustrative examples will all be referred to as case studies from here.
2 A financial incentive where the employee is entitled to the full amount.
3 A financial incentive that has been awarded, but the employee is not yet entitled to the full amount.

References

Adler, R. (2011) Performance management and organizational strategy: How to design systems that meet the needs of confrontation strategy firms. *The British Accounting Review.* 43 (4), 251–263.

Anderson, K. and McAdam, R. (2004) A critique of benchmarking and performance measurement – Lead or lag. *Benchmarking: An International Journal.* 11 (5), 465–483.

Barclays (2006) 2006 Annual Report. Available at www.home.barclays/content/dam/barclayspublic/docs/InvestorRelations/AnnualReports/AR2006/2006-barclays-plc-annual-report.pdf (accessed 29 January 2015).

Barclays (2014) 2014 Annual Report. Available at www.home.barclays/content/dam/barclayspublic/docs/InvestorRelations/AnnualReports/AR2014/Barclays_PLC_Annual_Report_%202014.pdf.

Canonico, P., De Nito, E., Esposito, V., Martinez, M., Mercurio, L. and Iacono, M. (2015) The boundaries of a performance management system between learning and control. *Measuring Business Excellence.* 19 (3), 7–21.

Clarke, M. (1994) Regulation and enforcement. *Journal of Financial Crime.* 1 (4), 337–346.

CMA (2015) Energy market investigation: Summary of provisional findings report. www.gov.uk/cma-cases/energy-market-investigation (accessed 21 July 2015).

Coglianese, C. (2012) Measuring regulatory performance – Evaluating the impact of regulation and regulatory change. OCED. www.oecd.org/gov/regulatory-policy/1_coglianese%20web.pdf (accessed 21 July 2015).

Crowther, D., Cooper, S. and Carter, C. (2001) Regulation – The movie: A semiotic study of the periodic review of UK regulated industry. *Journal of Organisational Change.* 14 (3), 225–238.

Dassler, T., Parker, D. and Saal, D. (2006) Methods and trends of performance benchmarking in the UK utility regulation. *Utilities Policy.* 14, 166–174.

Deville, A. (2009) Branch banking network assessment using DEA: A benchmarking analysis – A note. *Management Accounting Research.* 20 (4), 252–261.

FCA (2015) GC15/1 Risks to customers from performance management at firms. www.fca.org.uk/news/guidance-consultations/gc15-1-risks-to-customers-from-performance-management-at-firms (accessed 21 July 2015).

Ferreira, A. and Otley, D. (2009) The design and use of performance management systems: An extended framework for analysis. *Management Accounting Research.* 20 (4), 263–282.

Franco-Santos, M., Rivera, P. and Bourne, M. (2014) *Performance Management in UK Higher Education Institutions: The need for a hybrid approach. Research and Development Series.* Cranfield: Cranfield University, School of Management, Series 3, Publication 8.1.

Hartmann, F. (2012). Can neuroscience inform management accountants? *Financial Management magazine* (Chartered Institute of Management Accountants). Available at www.fm-magazine.com/feature/depth/can-neuroscience-inform-management-accountants (accessed 12 May 2013).

HSE (2011) Case study: Scottish Power, power generation company gets to grips with process safety. www.hse.gov.uk/comah/case-studies/case-study-scottish-power.pdf (accessed 16 July 2015).

HSE (2015a) Inside HSE. www.hse.gov.uk/aboutus/insidehse.htm (accessed 16 July 2015).

HSE (2015c) Health and Safety Regulation...a short guide. www.hse.gov.uk/pubns/hsc13.pdf (accessed 16 July 2015).

Hua, N. and Lee, S. (2014) Benchmarking firm capabilities for sustained financial performance in the US restaurant industry. *International Journal of Hospitality management.* 36, 137–144.

Kerr, S. (1995) An academy classic. On the folly of rewarding A, while hoping for B. *Academy of Management Executive.* 9 (1), 77–14.

Kodali, G. (2008) Benchmarking and benchmarking models. *Benchmarking: An International Journal.* 15 (3), 257–291.

Maheshwari, D. and Jannsen, M. (2013) Measurement and benchmarking foundations: Providing support to organizations in their development and growth using dashboards. *Government Information Quarterly.* 30, S83–S93.

Meybodi, M. (2015) Consistency of strategic and tactical benchmarking performance measures: A perspective on managerial positions and organizational size. *Benchmarking: An International Journal.* 22 (6), 1019–1032.

Northern PowerGrid (2015) Annual stakeholder report 2015 – Northern PowerGrid. www.northernpowergrid.com/asset/1/document/1676.pdf (accessed 16 July 2015).

Nsouli, S. (2008) Lessons from the recent financial crisis and the role of the fund. IMF. www.imf.org/external/np/speeches/2008/062608.htm (accessed 13 March 2016).

Ofgem (2010) Electricity Distribution Price Control Customer Service Reporting – Regulatory instructions and guidance, version 2. www.ofgem.gov.uk/ofgem-publications/46557/customer-service-reporting-rigs-v2-final.pdf (accessed 16 July 2015).

Ofgem (2012) Electricity Distribution Annual Report. www.ofgem.gov.uk/ofgem-publications/46553/electricitydistributionannualreportfor201011.pdf (accessed 23 July 2015).

Ofgem (2014a) State of competition in the energy market assessment. www.ofgem.gov.uk/gas/retail-market/market-review-and-reform/state-competition-energy-market-assessment (accessed 21 July 2015).

Ofgem (2014b) 2014 Great Britain and Northern Ireland National Reports to the European Commission. www.ofgem.gov.uk/ofgem-publications/89147/nationalreport2014updated.pdf (accessed 23 July 2015).

Parker, D. (2003) Performance, risk and strategy in privatised, regulated industries. The UK Experience. *The International Journal of Public Sector Management*. 16 (1), 75–100.

Petrović, M., Bojković, N., Anić, I. and Petrović, D. (2012) Benchmarking the digital divide using multi-level outranking framework: Evidence from EBRD countries of operation. *Government Information Quarterly*. 29 (4), 597–607.

PRA (2013) Available at www.bankofengland.co.uk/pra/Pages/supervision/activities/aboutremuneration.aspx, accessed 29 January 2015.

PWC (2016) Reporting that satisfies regulators and stakeholders. www.pwc.co.uk/industries/financial-services/regulation/reporting-that-satisfies-regulators-and-stakeholders.html (accessed 21 March 2016).

Salz, A. and Collins, R. (2013) An independent review of Barclays Business Practices. A Salz review. online.wsj.com/public/resources/documents/SalzReview04032013.pdf (accessed 13 March 2016).

Skynews (2012). Barclays Boss: Banking Culture Has To Change. Available at http://news.sky.com/story/984178/barclays-boss-banking-culture-has-to-change (accessed 17 July 2014).

Stern, J. (2014) The British utility regulation model: Its recent history and future prospects. *Utilities Policy*. 31, 162–172.

Warren, L. (2014). Management control, regulation and investment uncertainty in the UK electricity generation industry. In Otley, D. and Soin, K. (eds), Management Control and Uncertainty. Basingstoke: Palgrave Macmillan, pp. 193–206.

Warren, L. and Burns, J. (Forthcoming) The role of the UK Management Accountant. In Goretzki, L. and Strauss, E. (eds), *The Role of the Management Accountant: Local Variations and Global Influences*. Routledge.

7

The cloud and management accounting and control

Martin Quinn and Erik Strauss

Introduction

A major driving factor of change to management accounting and management control has been the exponential developments in information technology in the past two decades or so (Sánchez-Rodríguez and Spraakman, 2012). Since the late 1990s, enterprise resources planning (ERP) systems have, for example, freed managers and accountants of much routine work. However, only more recently have we started to see the actual impact of ERP on the work of management accountants (e.g. Caglio, 2003; Dechow and Mouritsen, 2005; O'Mahony and Doran, 2008; Wagner *et al.*, 2011), moving their focus towards consulting and/or advising line managers (e.g. Goretzki *et al.*, 2013; Scapens and Jazayeri, 2003).

Concurrently, the advent of cloud computing technology has changed business and society in general, and might have a similar or even greater impact on accounting than ERP systems. While a novel research field for scholars of management accounting and control, cloud technology cannot but impact management accounting and management control systems. To understand the actual and potential impacts, the meaning of cloud computing should be clarified; no standard definition of cloud computing was apparent until 2011 (Grossman, 2009; Sultan, 2011; Voas and Zhang, 2009). The National Institute of Standards and Technology (NIST) provided an agreed definition as follows:

> Cloud computing is a model for enabling ubiquitous, convenient, on-demand network access to a shared pool of configurable computing resources (e.g., networks, servers, storage, applications, and services) that can be rapidly provisioned and released with minimal management effort or service provider interaction.
>
> *(NIST, 2011, p. 2)*

The NIST definition characterizes cloud computing via access that is in effect any time, any place and on any device, shared resources not owned by the user of those services (e.g. Google email services and storage), and elasticity as cloud services can be increased or decreased according to requirements.

Although the characteristics of cloud computing might be seen as primarily positive for management accounting and control, challenges might also arise that managers and accountants will be confronted with if they start to use cloud computing. Therefore, the aim of this chapter is to provide a short overview of the technological aspects of cloud computing, its advantages and challenges for managers and accountants and provide ideas for future research resulting from cloud computing's impact on management accounting and control.

To achieve this aim, the remainder of this chapter is presented as follows. Section "Cloud computing configurations, devices and reported advantages" outlines the various configurations of cloud computing, and provides some detail on cloud technology and devices and the advantages of the technology. This is followed by an outline of some general disadvantages and issues in Section "Issues with cloud technologies". Section "Cloud technology and management accounting and control systems" provides an overview and distinction of management accounting systems (MAS) and management control systems (MCS) as well as the advantages and risks of cloud computing for MAS and MCS. Section "Concluding remarks and future research opportunities" concludes with an outlook and future directions for further research.

Cloud computing configurations, devices and reported advantages

Before exploring some of the technical models of cloud computing, the NIST (2011) definition given above is detailed further. The NIST (2011) notes five essential characteristics of cloud computing as follows:

- On-demand self-service – a consumer of cloud computing resources can provision resources as needed and automatically without human interaction with a service provider.
- Broad network access – cloud computing resources are available over a network and accessed through standard mechanisms and devices (e.g. smartphones, tablets, laptops and workstations).
- Resource pooling – the cloud computing provider's resources are pooled and serve multiple consumers. Differing physical and virtual resources are dynamically assigned and reassigned according to consumer demand.
- Rapid elasticity – resources can be elastically provisioned and released, typically automatically. To the consumer, the resources may appear unlimited.
- Measured service – cloud systems automatically control and optimize resources using some metering capability (e.g. storage, processing, bandwidth and active user accounts). This allows resources to be monitored and controlled. It also provides a basis for cloud service providers to charge their customers.

Behind these five essential characteristics lie several configurations of cloud computing resources, which we explore below. These characteristics also suggest that several benefits are inherent to cloud computing in comparison to traditional technology resource configurations.

Cloud computing configurations

Cloud computing configurations can be distinguished according to deployment model and service model (NIST, 2011). A deployment model refers to the provisioning of the cloud computing infrastructure, and a service model refers to the technical capabilities of the deployment model. The deployment and service models need to be carefully considered. The model(s) adopted depends on what the organization wishes to achieve, affect how the cloud is to be used and raise varying control issues.

In general, there are three deployment models for cloud computing (NIST, 2011). One deployment model is *private cloud*. In the case of a private cloud, computing resources (e.g. networks, servers, data storage, software applications) are provided for the exclusive use of a single organization. The resources may be owned and managed by the organization, by an external provider or by a combination of both. Private cloud resources may be present on or off the organization's premises. A second deployment model is *public cloud*. In this method, computing resources are provided for open use by the general public, and typically the resources are on the premises of the cloud service provider. A third deployment model is a *hybrid cloud*. This is a mixture of the other two models. For example, access to some resources of a public cloud provider is restricted to use by a single organization. Research by Strauss *et al.* (2015) suggests that finance and accounting systems are more likely to adopt a private or hybrid cloud deployment. They also note the primary concern driving the deployment model is security.

With regard to service models, three typical configurations can be distinguished (NIST, 2011). First, Software-as-a-Service (SaaS) permits the user of the cloud service to run software applications on infrastructure in the cloud. In this model, any internet-enabled device can use the service. The user of SaaS has no control over the underlying infrastructure. Examples of SaaS are GoogleDocs and SAP Cloud Applications. In each example, the user runs the software over any internet device, but has no control over the hardware or networking capabilities. Second, Platform-as-a-Service (PaaS) permits the cloud user to develop or deploy applications using tools and infrastructure provided by the cloud service provider. Control over hardware infrastructure is unlikely, but control over some configuration is likely. For example, SAP HANA (a data analytics tool) is offered as a platform service (see http://hana.sap.com/platform.html). Finally, Infrastructure-as-a-Service (IaaS) is the provision of resources such as storage and other hardware in the cloud. In this model, the customer may run various operating systems and software applications, and has the most control over the use of the computing resources. An IaaS model may be useful to fast growing firms, or firms that have less capital to invest.

While the above three service models are commonly cited, it should be noted that they are not mutually exclusive. Organizations may adopt differing service models or deployment models depending on the nature of the information systems.[1]

Cloud devices

As noted previously, broad high-speed network access is one of the essential characteristics of cloud computing. Technological developments (i.e. network access) in devices used to access cloud computing resources have contributed to the growth in use of cloud resources. When we think of devices that can access cloud computing resources, we should consider any network-enabled device as capable of cloud access. Devices include personal and notebook computers, smartphones and tablets. The latter two devices, given their portability, reduced cost, ease of use and lack of storage/processing capability, have contributed substantially to the growth in cloud computing. In 2013, many developed countries had 75% smartphone penetration, with close to 100% of users accessing internet-based content on a daily basis (see http://think.withgoogle.com/mobileplanet/). The content accessed through apps (or applications) installed on these smart devices accounted for 50–75% of web access. Such apps could be anything from an email account to accessing a key organizational information system. This move towards mobile devices in recent years is set to continue and offers some specific advantages which are discussed now in the context of reported advantages of cloud computing. It also raises several concerns, which are outlined in section "Issues with cloud technologies".

Advantages of cloud technologies

The diffusion of cloud computing is the result of the advantages that it offers users. Marston *et al.* (2011) provide five advantages of cloud computing from a business perspective. First, it lowers the cost to smaller firms of resources – such as resource-intensive business analytics – that were previously available only to larger firms. This lower-cost computing also represents an opportunity to businesses in many developing economies that have been left behind in technology terms. Second, cloud computing provides immediate access to hardware resources with little or no capital investment. This implies a faster time to market in many businesses. This move to treating technology-related cost as an operational expense (as opposed to capital expenditure[2]) also reduces upfront capital costs of computing resources. Third, cloud computing can lower IT barriers to innovation – for example, the rapidly expanding apps development sector. Fourth, cloud computing allows an organization to scale services according to client demand. Resources can be scaled up or down dynamically, with minimal or no interaction with the service provider. Fifth, cloud computing has allowed the development of applications and delivery of services that were not previously possible.

In addition to the above advantages, another key advantage of cloud computing is device independence. For example, in a SaaS model, as the software is hosted in the cloud a user need only have an internet capable device to use the services. Indeed, the concept of Bring-Your-Own-Device (or BYOD) where employees use their own personal device has increased the reach of cloud computing (see, for example, Morrow, 2012). As mentioned in the previous section, the use of mobile devices in particular has increased. This supports time and location independence, which allows organizational members to seamlessly work with cloud-based services as they wish (Fernando *et al.*, 2013).

In the management accounting and control literature, there is little extant work on cloud computing. From a practitioner view, Strauss *et al.* (2015) report several advantages of cloud computing from the view of management accountants specifically. Their survey reports the two main advantages as time savings and more efficient business processes; but cost savings, improved systems scalability and more effective business processes were also noted.

Issues with cloud technologies

Although there are many reported advantages of cloud computing, it is not without issues which organizations need to consider. One of the greatest concerns reported by practitioners and information systems researchers is security, and we outline the key security issues first. Then, several other organizational and technical issues are detailed.

Strauss *et al.* (2015) reported security as the number one concern management accountants have towards cloud computing. From a technical perspective, cloud computing is "fraught with security risks" (Subashini and Kavitha, 2011, p. 1). For example, a public cloud is likely to have more security risks than a private cloud; or a SaaS model is more exposed to data transmission risks. Table 7.1 summarizes the security risks as reported by Subashini and

Table 7.1 Cloud security issues (SaaS model) – based on Subashini and Kavitha (2011)

Security risk	*Brief description*
Data security	Data are stored outside organization, and cloud providers are responsible for security.
Network security	Data flows over a network between cloud user and cloud provider. Such flows should be secured.
Data location	Data may be stored in another jurisdiction. This may raise issues of applicable data protection and similar legislation.
Data integrity and segregation	Data integrity is easier to enforce locally through database management. In a cloud computing environment, multi-tenancy poses issues of integrity and segregation of data.
Access, authentication and authorisation	Cloud service providers may have access to client data. User access is authenticated by the cloud provider, i.e. outside the client organization.
Data confidentiality	Depending on where the cloud provider is located, data may be more or less confidential based on local laws. For example, a cloud provider could be legally bound to report illegal activities to law enforcement or taxation authorities.
Application security	A technical area, which essentially involves ensuring that the application software uses good protocols and security measures to prevent breaches of security through a web browser.
Data breach	With more data stored in the cloud, breaches of security may affect many user organizations.
Availability and backup	Cloud services need to be available round-the-clock. Service providers must ensure backup infrastructure is available. Cloud users need to ensure their data are backed up in case of failure.
Sign-on process	The sign-on process needs to be secure and identities well managed. For example, should one user identity allow access to one or all cloud services used by an organization?

Kavitha (2011) for SaaS deployment models – arguably the most risky model. These risks can be managed or eliminated by information technology staff in an organization – but this is beyond the scope of this chapter. However, an appreciation of the risks is useful for those who design, implement and operate MCS that use cloud technologies. Furthermore, the risks might also result in additional costs – either for avoiding the risks or to make amends for potential security breaks.

As can be seen in Table 7.1, there are many security issues. These issues can be managed by information systems managers in larger organizations, but these may pose a greater challenge for smaller- and medium-sized organizations (Subashini and Kavitha, 2011). However, as noted by Strauss *et al.* (2015), cloud service providers can typically provide systems which are more secure than those normally within the remit of smaller- and medium-sized organizations. Nonetheless, security still remains a major concern of those adopting cloud computing (see, for example, Armbrust *et al.*, 2010; Marston *et al.*, 2011; Strauss *et al.*, 2015). Any service-level agreement[3] with cloud service providers should be examined by management to ensure issues such as those noted in Table 7.1 are reduced. Several of the issues identified above may also present as legal issues. For example, data protection legislation needs to be considered; are regulatory obligations adhered to? Are the cloud computing services subject to the laws of several legal jurisdictions? Will cloud service users seek an indemnity that any intellectual property used in the cloud does not infringe intellectual property rights and be protected? Termination of any service-level agreement needs to be carefully considered.

In summary, although the issues noted here are primarily technical, it is apparent that they also translate into real business issues which management needs to consider. As noted, anecdotal evidence suggests that data security remains a key concern. This, and the other issues mentioned, can be managed or reduced with adequate planning and preparation by the organization. Now that we have outlined the nature, advantages and issues around cloud computing, the remainder of this chapter examines interrelationships with and effects on MCS.

Cloud technology and management accounting and control systems

In this section, we will provide some thoughts on the influence of cloud technology on management accounting and control systems. After clarifying management accounting and control, we pay particular attention to the positive effects of the cloud. This is followed by a discussion of some potential risks of cloud technology for management accounting and control. As there is little extant literature on the subject matter in the management control/performance management or management accounting literature at present, we draw on some practitioner pieces and examples to provide some insights.

Management accounting and control

While management accounting provides managers with relevant information for decision-making, management control is the process by which managers ensure that employees carry out organizational goals (Merchant and van der Stede, 2011; Otley, 1999; Strauss and Zecher, 2013). Controls are necessary due to basic issues such as lack of direction, lack of motivation or personal limitations (e.g. Merchant and Van der Stede, 2011). Managers can use different kinds of MAS to make decisions and different MCS to ensure that the "behaviour and decisions of their employees are consistent with the organization's objectives and strategies" (Malmi and Brown, 2008, pp. 290–291). For example, managers can use planning, cybernetic controls (e.g. budgets or financial measurement systems), reward and compensation (e.g. incentive systems based on bonuses), administrative controls (e.g. organization structure or policies and procedures) and cultural controls (e.g. values, norms or symbols). The main difference between MAS and MCS is that MCS influences human behaviour, while MAS serves an information provision function for decision-making.

Traditionally, management accounting and control have been treated (and researched) as separate unconnected phenomena (Chenhall, 2003). Therefore, interdependencies and mutually constitutive relationships that might have an influence on the design and outcome of MAS and MCS had not been taken into consideration. However, recent studies emphasized the importance of conceptualizing management control as package (Malmi and Brown, 2008) or as system (Grabner and Moers, 2013), i.e. it should be understood as a set of multiple connected components that can influence each other (Strauss *et al.*, 2013). As the cloud is a technology that has the potential to digitally transform the entire organization, we draw upon these recent developments in management control research (e.g. Friis *et al.*, 2014) and interpret the effects of cloud technologies on management accounting and control as systems consisting of (potentially) mutually interdependent components influencing each other. While future research may reveal more detail, the limited research on cloud computing we note below has not treated management accounting and management control as separable, as the technology is adapted typically to all systems/sub-systems of a particular organizational function. For example, Strauss *et al.* (2015) note how customer service systems were more likely to be in the cloud. Taking this example, it is highly unlikely – and technically less feasible – to have some systems components in the cloud and some not. Thus, if and when accounting systems are migrated to a cloud configuration, it is highly likely that all accounting sub-systems will migrate – financial accounting, management accounting, management control and performance management systems.

How cloud technology can influence management accounting and control

Although we interpret MAS, as well as MCS, as systems of mutually interdependent components, we distinguish both kinds of systems to clearly show the influence of cloud technology on each. The main reason for our separation is that MAS have no influence on behaviour (e.g. Malmi and Brown, 2008) and focus more on information provision. As the cloud technology's influence on information provision is quite different from that on controlling behaviour, we analytically separate MAS and MCS here to be able to clearly show the effects of the cloud on both kinds of systems.

Management accounting systems

The basic purpose of MAS is to provide information to managers for decision-making (see, for example, Mouritsen, 1996). Accordingly, the performance of MAS will be evaluated by dimensions that have a direct positive link to decision-making. Typically, the time needed for information provision, the accuracy and relevance of data, and the costs of providing information are key dimensions used to evaluate MAS performance (e.g. Chenhall and Morris, 1986).

Due to the technological advances and issues mentioned in sections "Cloud computing configurations, devices and reported advantages" and "Issues with cloud technologies", it is apparent that cloud technologies can affect the performance of MAS in several ways. First, the cloud allows firms to use the calculative power of servers that are typically too expensive to maintain by themselves. If firms use, for example, the IaaS configuration, the cloud dramatically enhances the amount of data that can be analysed and provided as information for decision-making. Particularly, small- and medium-sized firms can benefit from increased calculative power for a relatively affordable cost. Furthermore, the accuracy of information may increase as firms do not need approximations or other heuristics due to this increased calculative power.

Second, the cloud offers firms the chance to use different kinds of tools that normally require large infrastructure investments (like servers) and, therefore, are typically the reserve of larger firms. If firms, for example, use the cloud in a SaaS configuration, they can run their MAS and add additional tools (for example, advanced reporting and analytical tools) as needed to the SaaS configuration in the cloud. The extended repertoire of tools is also accompanied by the effect that in a SaaS configuration, any internet-enabled device can be used to view and/or add relevant information for decision-making. The cloud transforms even basic smartphones into powerful information devices that can perform complex calculations. This transformation also has a side effect that managers and other users of accounting information need less accounting knowledge. For example, ad hoc adaptations by managers of discounted cash flow calculations can be done by directly adjusting system parameters on a smart device, as opposed to manual adjustment. There is thus little or no involvement of any accounting staff in such adaptations. Before the cloud, such adaptations were typically undertaken following consultation between the manager and the management accountant. Consequently, even more power is handed over to the system than when ERP systems were introduced (e.g. Baldvinsdottir *et al.*, 2010). Furthermore, lowering the barrier to access accounting information might foster the diffusion of an accounting perspective through the entire organization. Therefore, accounting information directly retrieved from the system might be more present in various situations (for example, when negotiating sales contracts real-time data of inventory could be checked at the customer site) but without financial experts explaining the possible meaning and pitfalls of the numbers. If this might be the case, the question arises what kind of role management accountants play in the future.

Third, the timeliness of information will increase as the cloud allows firms to draw on vast technical resources – this is particularly relevant for smaller- and medium-sized organizations as noted previously. Calculations that took hours/days to complete previously, are done now in seconds (e.g. Gates, 2008). Accordingly, if managers (or management accountants) need specific calculations, they can get "the information at the speed of thought". Furthermore, direct access to information via the cloud makes information demands independent of office hours and/or the schedules of traditional information providers like management accountants. Information for decision-making is accessible at any time. In addition, the increased use of mobile devices with the cloud results in new ways of using MAS. Before mobile devices and high-speed mobile networks, MAS had to be used via desktop PCs or mobile computers. Today, almost every mobile device can access MAS and MAS can be used more often outside and inside the firm. For example, salespeople can directly access cost accounting information if they negotiate potential discounts at clients' offices. Management accounting information is thus more prevalent outside the firm, where some business decisions are actually made.

Finally, all the above-mentioned influences are closely linked to cost. Cloud technology has the potential to substantially reduce costs of creating and maintaining MAS, with no or less operating expenditure than previous MAS. For example, a firm may no longer need to employ technical systems support or pay energy costs to run information systems (Strauss *et al.*, 2015; Marston *et al.*, 2011). As a consequence, the cloud may lead to an earlier introduction of MAS in start-up firms or to more extensive use in already established firms who were alienated previously for cost reasons.

In addition to these more technical influences on MAS, the cloud in combination with mobile devices has the potential to influence how management accounting information is displayed and consumed inside and outside firms. In the desktop era, management accounting information was (and still is to an extent) characterized by numbers resulting in job roles like "number cruncher" applied to management accountants (Byrne and Pierce, 2007). In the new era of mobile devices and cloud technology, new screen sizes and calculative power of new tools support vastly improved graphical illustration of management accounting information, i.e. whereas tables dominated before, figures and graphical outputs are increasingly common and more important. Consequently, MAS might be perceived as less numeric and easier to consume. This may reduce barriers to access and result in management accounting information being used by people who are less *au fait* with tables and numbers. Easier access to and presentation of accounting content can have a positive influence on the accuracy judgements that are based on these data (e.g. DeSanctis and Järvenpää, 1989). Whereas the development of figures and graphical outputs was often manual work for management accountants, cloud technology and new analytical tools (like, for example, SAP Simple Finance) automate their creation and may result in a more extensive use.

Management control systems

MCS aim to influence behaviour of human beings to ensure that their behaviour and decisions are in line with the organization's objectives and strategies. Therefore, the main tasks of MCS are to detect behaviour that is not in line, to avoid deviating behaviour and to support a change in behaviour if necessary (e.g. Anthony and Govindarajan, 2007; Simons, 1995). Cloud technology is influencing, and will continue to influence, each of these functions of a MCS as we will outline in the following examples.

The time required for correct and timely detection of deviating behaviour can be reduced with cloud technology, due to faster and better-connected devices. For example, budgets are immediately updated with new expenses, as in traditional systems. If budgets are exceeded, the user can be prompted that s/he has run out of money or the expenses even declined – the difference is this prompt can be sent to any device, anywhere and at any time. Result controls can also be updated faster, which leads to feedback that is more closely linked to the time of the performance, and thus more direct links between results and performance. Furthermore, cloud technology combined with mobile devices increases the pervasiveness of MCS in a firm, i.e. permanent control on a detailed level is now possible (and at a reasonable cost). This is best illustrated with some examples. As a first example, using GPS data from mobile devices in combination with current traffic information provided online, firms can control and optimize their fleet to optimize their fuel consumption. In turn, budget accuracy could be improved, customer satisfaction increased in the case of delivery services, or the fleet size optimized. Another example can be found in the home care sector. Providers in this industry now use apps that constantly monitor where home carers are and what they are doing (e.g. www.geopalsolutions.com/industries-and-customers/healthcare). This kind of app is typically based on standard tasks and records on a very detailed level – for example, it records when the home carer enters and leaves a home, and what s/he did. The detailed level of monitoring and resulting pervasiveness of management control portrayed in these examples is only possible as software hosted in the cloud has an effective unlimited capacity to store data.

With this unlimited capacity, many cloud-based tools permanently save changes to documents and other information, which makes it easy to identify failures and to correct them. In particular, if firms use cloud-based tools, many of these tools save information such as time, frequency, place or data displayed to the user. This information can be used as a control to determine if employees have based their decisions on the "right" information. In addition to failure detection, the calculative power of cloud-based tools makes it possible to detect conscious mistakes, i.e. fraud, as large data sets can be processed. This allows firms, for example, to check the time needed for every single invoice processed in the accounting department for the last 10 years. Any systematic differences detected may signal illegal activities.[4] Cloud technology not only reduces the time required to detect misalignment and increase the connectedness of different systems, but it may also predict behavioural misalignment. Predictive analysis is resource-intensive, but it can be efficiently and cost effectively realized using cloud technology. Even small firms or governmental organizations that are under pressure to save costs can use such analysis in the cloud. For example, many police forces are experimenting with predictive crime analyses (see, for example, www.forbes.com/sites/ellenhuet/2015/02/11/predpol-predictive-policing/).

Finally, cloud technology may result in less strict separation of diagnostic and interactive use of MCS (for interactive and diagnostic use, see, for example, Bisbe and Otley, 2004; Simons, 1995). Traditionally, diagnostic use of MCS means that MCS are used "on an exception basis to monitor and reward achievement of specified goals through the review of critical performance variables or key success factors" (Bisbe and Otley, 2004, p. 711). In contrast, interactive use of MCS can imply opportunity seeking and learning behaviour to adapt to competitive environments (Simons, 1995). Furthermore, interactive controls are characterized by a permanent personal involvement of top management in contrast to diagnostic controls. However, this separation between diagnostic and interactive uses may be less clear if firms use cloud technology. Due to the calculative power and anytime/anywhere access, cloud technologies can grant to a MCS, it may be difficult for employees to distinguish between diagnostic and interactive control. Accordingly, this may lead to perceived permanent control (as mentioned above), which in turn may have negative effects on performance.

Risks posed by cloud technology for management accounting and control

Although the cloud has many positive effects for MAS and MCS, there are some risks worthy of mention. The key risk is data security. If the entire management accounting and management control information is moved to a cloud configuration, the information is accessible from anywhere. Many firms perceive a loss of control over their data once it is stored outside the firm (Strauss *et al.*, 2015). In the same vein, a common argument against storing sensitive data in the cloud is that cloud servers are more often exposed to cyber-attacks than firms' internal servers (Subashini and Kavitha, 2011). Of course, this argument is (to a certain degree) correct, but the security investments and capabilities of cloud providers result in more secure systems than those internal to firms (Bourne, 2014). Accordingly, the expectation value of both options is similar. Furthermore, using mobile devices to access corporate databases bears a risk that such devices are more easily stolen or lost. Additionally, users of mobile devices are still not as sensitive to security issues as users of personal computers (Mylonas *et al.*, 2013), which increases security risks relative to personal computers. It should be noted that as the use of mobile devices increases, the number of cyber-attacks focusing on them is growing (Ruggiero and Foote, 2011).

Another risk, data protection, is closely linked to data security. As mentioned above, the cloud has the potential to extend the number of users of MAS and MCS. Such an extension means that not only traditional users such as managers or management accountants have access to data, but also other "new" users such as sales people. As a consequence, firms may have to review the access rights of their MCS – which are often based on traditional information demands and system structures like an ERP. This revision could be relatively challenging due to the extended number of tools that are used in the cloud. For example, if management cockpits with specific key performance indicators are used, it is necessary to guarantee that every user has the rights to access all data underlying those indicators. In addition to the sheer number of users, the user type may change from users that are familiar with accounting data to users that are not (that) familiar with accounting. As a consequence, the design and handling of MCS (and MAS) might be adjusted to a more diverse set of users, making the adjustment more challenging.

Furthermore, the anytime and anywhere accessibility is only one side of the story. Permanent access may result in expectations that everyone is accessing data all the time. Similar to email pushing to mobile devices, managers start to expect that not only all of their emails will be answered (due to mobile devices) but also all calculations and information provision tasks can be performed via mobile devices. This might lead to a growing conflation of private and professional life, which might reduce productivity, increase stress and reduce creativity. Some firms have already realized this risk and decided to stop the connection to email clients and cloud services for their employees at a certain time. For example, Volkswagen introduced a so-called "Blackberry break after quitting time" scheme, i.e. no emails and other data will be pushed to or are accessible via employees' mobile devices between certain hours. Conflating private and professional life may increase a perception of permanent supervision. It was noted above that the difference between diagnostic and interactive use of MCS might be distorted by the cloud. This, in turn, might lead to the perception that employees are permanently controlled by their supervisors, which is also fostered by the immediate update of all data stored in the cloud.

Finally, the increased speed of information provision may also cause faster decision-making. In general, decreasing the needed time for decision-making due to a reduced time for information gathering and processing is an advantage of cloud technology. However, the instantaneous update of information and the option of analysing data on a real-time basis may result in ad-hoc decisions being made too quickly. Today, reports are created that have a monthly or quarterly time focus. Managers are used to analysing numbers and graphs with these timeframes in mind. If the cloud changes the timeframe to a daily or real-time basis, this might cause misinterpretations by managers because they need some time to adjust their decision-making behaviour to it. For example, significant downturns on a quarterly basis might be indicators of serious problems, whereas volatile developments on a daily basis might be normal. If managers still have a quarterly time frame in mind, they might make wrong decisions or change too many organizational aspects. This kind of challenge was also present at the beginning of the ERP era when the introduction of real-time activity-based cost data bore the risk of not considering the change from actual to standard data (Cooper and Kaplan, 1998). However, management accountants were typically more present when such kind of data was interpreted and, thereby, able to secure the correct interpretation than in the new cloud era. In addition to unconscious misinterpretation of real-time data, the continuous update of information might induce that managers wait for potential changes of the numbers because this might change their decision. Assuming opportunistic behaviour, constantly changing information might provide chances for gaming behaviour, i.e. employees might wait for "the right information update" which justifies their preferred decision. This would lead to situations where opportunistic behaviour is less obvious and even backed by real-time information. Accordingly, the introduction and use of real-time information can also lead to a reduced effectiveness of management control.

Preliminary empirical insights on cloud technology influences on management accounting and control

Research on how cloud technology affects management accounting and control is still scarce due to the novelty of the technology. One of the few studies that already address this topic is Strauss *et al.* (2015). They used a mixed methods approach and conducted three interviews with technology experts (founder and managing director of a cloud storage solution provider and a technical expert; founder and managing director of a technology firm which uses and sells cloud technology solutions; sales manager with a leading provider of accounting software in the UK and Ireland) and surveyed controllers (management accountants) in Germany. A 76% response rate was achieved and respondents cover a broad industry spectrum including: consumer goods, engineering, chemicals, electronics, energy, metals, construction, media and public bodies.

The results of Strauss *et al.* (2015) show that only a few firms (25% of the sample) have moved their MAS and MCS to the cloud – which is still in line with Clinton and White (2012) who reported reservations on moving to the cloud. The key reasons for non-adoption of cloud technology were cited as data security and protection, and no efficiency gains expected. Firms that are already using the cloud cited easier system administration, cost efficiency and better system scalability as key advantages. After the introduction of cloud technology, the users reported a higher efficiency of business processes, time and cost savings as well as an improved scalability. With regard to the influence on the provision of information for decision-making and controlling employees' behaviour, Strauss *et al.* (2015) note that cloud-based systems are still primarily (73%) accessed using a corporate computer or laptop, with corporate smartphones and tablets being used one-third of the time. Although the cloud potentially offers flexibility with regard to time and place of using MAS and MCS, Strauss *et al.* (2015) found that most access happens within the business premises and within working hours, a trend common across all business areas. Their findings show that information from cloud-based systems is mainly presented in a mixed graphical/numeric format (84%), with the vast majority of it rated as detailed, timely and complete and is primarily in a standardized format (from ERP or similar standardized systems). Finally, they asked respondents for their overall perception of the decision-making process since their adoption of cloud-based technology. The majority of respondents (93%) agreed that cloud technology contributed positively to decision-making, with 32% suggesting that it has improved decision-making in comparison to previous systems. The reasons for the improvement were primarily seen in the creation of one shared database, reduction of redundant information and less information sharing via email.

Concluding remarks and future research opportunities

The previous sections of this chapter suggest that cloud technologies offer many advantages to businesses at present. There are of course disadvantages, centred mainly on security issues. However, it is reasonable to suggest that advantages such as reduced costs, scalable systems, portability and increased processing capability outweigh the security issues. As suggested in section "Issues with cloud technologies", security concerns can be managed by organizations. From the MAS and MCS view, it would seem without doubt that cloud technologies improve both by, for example, allowing firms to take advantage of processing or systems capabilities previously unaffordable or by increasing the pervasiveness of management control throughout an organization.

As noted previously, extant research in the management accounting and management control literature on cloud technologies is at present rather scarce. Given that we can almost take it for granted that the cloud will affect management control, it presents scholars with some excellent research opportunities, which we now suggest. While not intended as an exhaustive list, it does, we hope, encourage broad research using varying methodological approaches. Collaborations with researchers from the information systems stream may prove quite fruitful.

First, while the work of Strauss *et al.* (2015) reports that decision-making has improved post the adoption of cloud technologies, this exploratory research does not delve into the actual ways decision-making has changed. For example, future research might explore such questions as how has the decision-making process changed, why has it changed in this way, how were barriers to change overcome. It might also explore whether decision-making is more democratized. Second, the role of managers and management accountants in the cloud technology era could be explored. For example, how do managers interact with management accountants in a cloud technology environment? Do managers make more independent decisions? Do management accountants provide more or less advice to managers? Third, the role of management accounting itself is worthy of exploration. It has been hinted earlier that cloud technologies permit smaller firms to use management accounting tools and techniques that were previously the realm of larger firms. Does this happen, and if so what techniques are used? How are the technologies used and does the management accountant have a role to play? Another interesting research avenue may also be how management accounting is used throughout the organization, as cloud technologies have the ability to deliver systems and information to any device at any time. Fourth, as portrayed by some examples in section "Cloud technology and management accounting and control systems", cloud technologies can introduce controls in areas where accurate or workable controls were previously not possible. While such controls may be more task type controls, they ultimately direct organization members towards a desired behaviour and feed into MAS. For example, at the level of the individual, some apps – such as running or health apps – for use on smart devices seem to inspire the user with a strong level of motivation to achieve desired goals (i.e. fitness). Researchers could explore how such motivation can be transferred to meeting organizational goals using similar apps. The downside of such cloud-based control is the potential pervasiveness of control, and this may also be a fruitful area of research. Finally, many management control frameworks such as those of Malmi and Brown (2008), Ferreira and Otley (2009) and Simons (1995) are based on research prior to the cloud technology era. Given the effects the cloud is having, and is likely to have, on MCS and decision-making, elements of such frameworks may be worthy of new research. Taking Malmi and Brown (2008) as an example, they called for research on how elements of their MCS package interact. It is quite probable that cloud technologies may influence such interactions. Similarly, one question posed by Ferreira and Otley relates to "information flows, systems and networks" (2009, p. 268). Cloud technologies arguably improve information flows, allow better access to data and information in networks, and offer potentially better systems to many organizations.

To sum up, cloud technologies have already affected management control and management accounting systems. Future years are likely to see more and more services (such as MAS and MCS) move to a cloud environment, and indeed cloud services are considered to be the next utility service (see, for example, Buyya *et al.*, 2009). Thus, it is inevitable that cloud technologies will penetrate MAS and MCS to a greater extent. As management accounting and management control scholars, this presents a great research opportunity. We may have to gain some technical understanding – the basics of which we have outlined in this chapter – but the rewards in research terms are likely to be quite fruitful.

Notes

1 It should also be noted that practitioner literature cites further models, and that the service/deployment models will evolve over time; for example, Analytics-as-a-Service, Storage-as-a-Service and Monitoring-as-a-Service. Some practitioners even refer to XaaS or Anything-as-a-Service (see Accenture, 2012).

2 Practitioner literature refers to op-ex and cap-ex.
3 At present, service-level agreements are unique to each cloud provider. Some guidelines for users do exist – see, for example, European Commission (2014).
4 See www.sap.com/bin/sapcom/he_il/downloadasset.2013-09-sep-17-10.detect-prevent-and-deter-fraud-in-big-data-environments-pdf.html for more on this and additional fraud detection possibilities in a cloud computing environment.

References

Accenture, 2012. Where the Cloud Meets Reality: Scaling to Succeed in New Business Models, available at www.accenture.com/us-en/Pages/insight-cloud-meets-reality-scaling-succeed-new-business-models.aspx(accessed 15 March 2015).
Anthony, R. N., & Govindarajan, V. 2007. Management control systems (12th ed.). Boston: McGraw-Hill.
Armbrust, M., Fox, A., Griffith, R., Joseph, A.D., Katz, R., Konwinski, A., Lee, G., Patterson, D., Rabkin, A., Stoica, I., & Zaharia, M. 2010. Clearing the clouds away from the true potential and obstacles posed by this computing capability. *Communications of the ACM*, 53(4):50–58.
Baldvinsdottir, G., Burns, J., Nørreklit, H., & Scapens, R. 2010. Professional accounting media: Accountants handing over control to the system. *Qualitative Research in Accounting & Management*, 7(3):395–414.
Bisbe, J., & Otley, D. 2004. The effects of the interactive use of management control systems on product innovation. *Accounting, Organizations and Society*, 29(8):709–737.
Bourne, J. 2014. Look Closer to Home for the Biggest Cloud Security Issue, SME Execs Told. *Cloud Computing News*, available at www.cloudcomputing-news.net/news/2014/nov/27/look-closer-home-biggest-cloud-security-issue-sme-execs-told/(accessed 20 March 2015).
Buyya, R., Yeo, C. S., Venugopal, S., Broberg, J., & Brandic, I. 2009. Cloud computing and emerging IT platforms: Vision, hype, and reality for delivering computing as the 5th utility. *Future Generation Computer Systems*, 25(6):599–616.
Byrne, S., & Pierce, B. 2007. Towards a more comprehensive understanding of the roles of management accountants. *European Accounting Review*, 16(3):469–498.
Caglio, A. 2003. Enterprise resource planning systems and accountants: Towards hybridization? *European Accounting Review*, 12(1):123–153.
Chenhall, R. H. 2003. Management control systems design within its organizational context: Findings from contingency-based research and directions for the future. *Accounting, Organizations and Society*, 28(2):127–168.
Chenhall, R. H., & Morris, D. 1986.The impact of structure, environment, and interdependence on the perceived usefulness of management accounting systems. *Accounting Review*, 61(1):16–35.
Clinton, D., & White, L. R. 2012. The role of the management accountant: 2003–2012. *Management Accounting Quarterly*, 14(1):40–74.
Cooper, R., & Kaplan, R. S. 1998. The promise – and peril – of integrated cost systems. *Harvard Business Review*, 76(4):109–119.
Dechow, N., & Mouritsen, J. 2005. Enterprise resource planning systems, management control and the quest for integration. *Accounting, Organizations and Society*, 30(7–8):691–733.
DeSanctis, G., & Jarvenpaa, S. L. 1989. Graphical presentation of accounting data for financial forecasting: An experimental investigation. *Accounting, Organizations and Society*, 14(5–6):509–525.
European Commission. 2014. *Cloud Service Level Agreement Standardisation Guidelines*. Brussels, available at https://ec.europa.eu/digital-agenda/en/news/cloud-service-level-agreement-standardisation-guidelines (accessed 10 March 2015).
Fernando, N., Loke, S. W., & Rahayu, W. 2013. Mobile cloud computing: A survey. *Future Generation Computer Systems*, 29(1):84–106.
Ferreira, A., & Otley, D. 2009. The design and use of performance management systems: An extended framework for analysis. *Management Accounting Research*, *20*(4):263–282.
Friis, I. M., Hansen, A., & Vámosi, T. S. 2015. On the effectiveness of incentive pay: Exploring complementarities and substitution between management control system elements in a manufacturing firm. *European Accounting Review*, 24(2):241–276.
Gates, B. 2008. Business @ the Speed of Thought: Level 6, RLA. Harlow: Penguin.

Goretzki, L., Strauss, E., & Weber, J. 2013. An institutional perspective on the changes in management accountants' professional role. *Management Accounting Research*, 24(1):41–63.

Grabner, I., & Moers, F. 2013. Management control as a system or a package? Conceptual and empirical issues. *Accounting, Organizations and Society*, 38(6):407–419.

Grossman, R. 2009. The case for cloud computing. *IT Professional*, 11(2):23–27.

Huerta-Canepa, G., & Lee, D. 2010. A virtual cloud computing provider for mobile devices, ACM workshop on mobile cloud computing & services: *Social Networks and Beyond*, June 15, San Francisco, California, USA.

Malmi, T., & Brown, D. A. 2008. Management control systems as a package—Opportunities, challenges and research directions. *Management Accounting Research*, 19(4):287–300.

Marston, S., Li, Z., Bandyopadhyay, S., Zhang, J., & Ghalasi, A. 2011. Cloud computing – The business perspective.*Decision Support Systems*, 51:176–189.

Merchant, K. A., & Van der Stede, W. A. 2011. *Management Control Systems: Performance Measurement, Evaluation and Incentives*. Upper Saddle River, NJ: Prentice Hall.

Mouritsen, J. (1996). Five aspects of accounting departments' work. *Management Accounting Research*, 7(3):283–303.

Morrow, B. 2012. BYOD security challenges: Control and protect your most sensitive data. *Network Security*, 2012(12):4–8.

Mylonas, A., Kastania, A., & Gritzalis, D. 2013. Delegate the smartphone user? Security awareness in smartphone platforms. *Computers & Security*, 34:47–66.

NIST, 2011. The NIST Definition of Cloud Computing, Special Publication 800–145, National Institute of Standards and Technology, Gaithersburg, MD.

O'Mahony, A., & Doran, J. 2008. The changing role of management accountants; evidence from the implementation of ERP systems in large organizations. *International Journal of Business and Management*, 3(8):109–115.

Otley, D. 1999. Performance management: A framework for management control systems research. *Management Accounting Research*, 10(4):363–382.

Ruggiero, P., & Foote, J. 2011. Cyber Threats to Mobile Phones, US Cert, available at www.us-cert.gov/sites/default/files/publications/cyber_threats-to_mobile_phones.pdf (accessed 2 April 2015).

Sánchez-Rodríguez, C., & Spraakman, G. 2012. ERP systems and management accounting: A multiple case study. *Qualitative Research in Accounting & Management*, 9(4):398–414.

Scapens, R., Ezzamel, M., Burns, J., & Baldvinsdottir, G. 2003. *The Future Direction of UK Management Accounting Practice*. London: CIMA.

Scapens, R.W., & Jazayeri, M. 2003. ERP systems and management accounting change: Opportunities or impacts? A research note. *European Accounting Review*, 12 (1):201–233.

Simons, R. 1995. *Levers of Control*. Boston: Harvard Business School Press.

Strauss, E., Kristhandl, G., & Quinn, M. 2015. The effects of cloud technology on management accounting and decision making. *CIMA Research Executive Summary*, 10(6), available atwww.cimaglobal.com/Thought-leadership/Research-topics/Management-and-financial-accounting/The-effects-of-cloud-technology-on-management-accounting/ (accessed 11 February 2015).

Strauss, E., Nevries, P., & Weber, J. 2013. The development of MCS packages – Balancing constituents' demands. *Journal of Accounting and Organizational Change*, 9 (2):155–187.

Strauss, E., & Zecher, C. 2013. Management control systems: A review. *Journal of Management Control*, 23:233–268.

Subashini, S., & Kavitha, V. 2011. A survey on security issues in service delivery models of cloud computing. *Journal of Network and Computer Applications*, 34(1):1–11.

Sultan, N. A. 2011. Reaching for the "cloud": How SMEs can manage. *International Journal of Information Management*, 31(3):272–278.

Voas, J., & Zhang, J. 2009. Cloud computing: New wine or just a new bottle? *IT Professional*, 11(2):15–17.

Wagner, E., Moll, J., & Newell, S. 2011. Accounting logics, reconfiguration of ERP systems and the emergence of new accounting practices: A sociomaterial perspective. *Management Accounting Research*, 22(3):181–197.

8

Leveraging big data for organizational performance management and control

Damminda Alahakoon and Piyumini Wijenayake

Due to large-scale automation and computerization, business processes, as well as communication, within organizations generate and capture large volumes of data in electronic form. The rise of social media, Internet of Things (IOT), and popularity of multimedia have changed and revolutionized the way organizations function, products are manufactured and business is conducted. Such change has resulted in an overwhelming flow of data in both structured and unstructured formats creating what has been called the information age or the age of big data. Organizations that successfully extract maximum value from information and act on their insights have gained huge competitive advantage. The tools, technology and skills that enable organizations to harness the power of big data are referred to as business analytics. Forward-thinking business leaders will use big data as a management revolution, but there will be major challenges to face and resolve to achieve the status of a "big data-enabled organization". Management control and performance management systems need to adopt big data and data analytics for these to have an impact on organizational management. This chapter discusses the impact of big data on organizational performance management and control (PMC). The chapter will look into traditional management control systems (MCS) and performance management systems (PMS), and discuss how the age of big data will result in next generation MCS and PMS. A key factor in the new systems will be the integration of the ability to manage and use large volumes of diverse unstructured data. This will ensure that managers can access and measure, and hence know, radically more about their businesses from new information sources, and directly translate that knowledge into improved decision making and performance.

Performance management and control in the age of big data

Over the past few decades, the information technology systems assisting businesses in managing data have seen several paradigm changes. They have moved from decision support, to executive support, to online analytical processing, to business intelligence, to analytics and now to big data. The current big data phenomenon was made possible by the advancement of computing and digital storage capabilities which resulted in monitoring and storing data from a variety of digital streams – such as sensors, marketplace interactions and social information exchanges, etc. (Davenport, 2014).

It is essential to understand what constitutes big data in order to understand its effect on businesses. Even though initially characterized by the *volume* of data, the definition of big data is usually extended to 3Vs to include other characteristics including *velocity* – which identifies the high speeds at which the data are accumulated – and *variety* – which identifies the diverse formats and sources of data. Sometimes, this is further extended to additional Vs including veracity, value and variability (Chen, 2014). Recent surveys have shown a widespread belief that big data analytics offers value with half of the respondents saying that improvement of information and analytics was a top priority in their organizations (LaValle, 2011).

However, organizations' ability to harness the opportunities presented by big data is still in its infancy and requires new skills and a new management style (Dhar, 2014b). As with any new development, technology or concept, to be able to reap the benefits from big data, it is essential that various challenges and issues associated with integrating and adapting this technology are identified and addressed (Katal, 2013). Advanced analytics, made up of a suite of data mining, statistics, machine learning and artificial intelligence algorithms and tools in combination with data storage and management technologies provide the capability of reaping the benefits of big data. According to Mithas (2013), advanced analytics techniques can help organizations successfully handle complex decisions by providing new insights as well as create a virtuous cycle by generating a demand for better techniques, tools and approaches for leveraging big data and business analytics.

Over the years, companies have effectively used analytics to reap the benefits offered by data-driven decision making, and it has been demonstrated that companies that use analytics have achieved higher performance (Brynjolfsson, 2011). Data-driven decisions are better decisions, and the use of big data enables managers to decide on the basis of evidence rather than intuition. Since they are the enabling technologies and the environment, it can be said that big data and analytics technologies have the potential to revolutionize management and decision making (McAfee and Brynjolfsson, 2012). However, the traditional information management and analytics have solely been based on numbers and mostly focused on internal data. Big data differs notably in this regard where most of the data is externally generated and are in unstructured formats such as text. Organizations that adopt the necessary technical, cultural and managerial requirements to embrace big data technologies will be able to make real-time business decisions and thrive, while those that are unable to embrace and make use of this shift will find themselves at a competitive disadvantage.

The saying "you can't manage what you don't measure" has been attributed to both W. Edwards Deming and Peter Drucker. Because of big data, managers have better opportunities to measure, understand more about their businesses and use such knowledge for improved decision making and performance (McAfee and Brynjolfsson, 2012). To realize such improvements, PMS and MCS need to adapt to the new big data environment. PMS are traditionally used to capture and evaluate performance information, which enables the identification of key success factors for an organization (Schläfke, 2012). The new-generation PMS must understand the availability of more and diverse data and information both internal and external, and have the capability to link, relate and integrate such information into the processes identifying organizational success factors. MCS translate strategy into action and also monitor the impact on organizational performance from such actions. They must now have the capability, knowledge and tools to transform the new data-driven information and knowledge into organizational strategies, and also be able to monitor the effect of such new strategies.

The rest of this chapter is organized as follows. The next section describes the key features of big data and advanced analytics technologies. Then, we will look at the background and context for PMS and MCS and how data analytics could be integrated with these systems. The impact of analytics on performance management and control is discussed next, and an extension to maturity models in performance management systems is presented. The impact of big data analytics in PMS is then discussed. We then highlight the challenges with adopting big data technologies in organizations before concluding the chapter.

Big data and analytics

This section provides a brief introduction to the term big data with some background on how and why this is significant from a business and organizational perspective. The technologies and tools for harnessing the value of big data are presented, and key data analytics techniques are described.

The big data environment

Big data is a term used to capture the changes brought about by the explosion in the quantity and diversity of high-frequency digital data generated from an increasing number of diverse data sources (Ammu, 2013). It could also be thought of as the new data and information-intensive environment we live in sometimes called the information age.

Almost all activities now generate data, and George (2014) has categorized such data into three main categories as (a) public data, (b) private data and (c) exhaust. Public data is mostly collected by governments, governmental departments and local authorities, such as data relating to transportation, property and assets, energy use and health care. Private data refers to private information held by private firms, non-profit organizations and individuals, and include consumer transactions, radio-frequency identification tags (RFID) used by supply chains, movement of company goods and resources, web browsing and mobile phone usage. Data exhaust or ambient data is passively collected, such as internet searches and telephone hotlines. Although with limited value at the original data-collection point, these can be used to infer people's needs, desires and intentions. Another data source is community data such as consumer reviews on products. Voting buttons and Twitter feeds also contribute to the diversity and volume of big data and are versatile sources to distil meaning to infer patterns in social structure and self-quantification data. Data self-collected by individuals through the quantification of personal actions and behaviours such as through wristbands that monitor exercise and movement is becoming another significant source (George, 2014).

From a public benefit aspect, these data hold the potential for decision makers to track development progress, improve social protection, and understand where existing policies and programs require adjustment (Ammu, 2013). But manipulation and analysis of these data require the use of powerful computational techniques to unveil trends and patterns within and between these extremely large socioeconomic data sets. New insights derived from such value extraction can be used to complement the traditionally static official statistics, surveys and archival data sources (George, 2014). For private organizations, such data makes it possible to better understand their customers and stakeholders, adapting their internal processes, workflows and decision making, thus providing more customized services and products with better communication.

However, the term "big data" has misleadingly focused attention on the volume or the size of the data. It is important to understand the properties and characteristics that make up big data to realize that big data is much more than a large volume of data.

Properties of big data

A widely known definition of big data refers to the 3Vs, volume, velocity and variety, as the key properties.

Volume

Volume means that there is a growing quantity of data (Spiess, 2014). At present, data exists in petabytes and is expected to increase to zettabytes in the near future. The current social networking sites generate terabytes of data on a daily basis (Katal, 2013).

Velocity

Velocity refers to the speed of the data being generated from various sources. This characteristic is not only limited to the speed of incoming data but also speed at which the data flows (Katal, 2013). Speed of data creation has become even more important than the volume in situations where the ability to capture and learn near real-time from data is a crucial factor. Real-time or nearly real-time information makes it possible for an organization to be much more agile than its competitors (McAfee and Brynjolfsson, 2012).

Variety

Very diverse types of data are generated by organizations and individuals. It includes the traditional data but also the semi-structured and unstructured data such as messages, updates, images, readings from sensors, GPS signals, and also from sources such as web pages, web log files, social media sites, email, documents, cell phones, sensors, etc. All this data is diverse and multi-modal, made up of a mix of numeric, categorical, text, images and multimedia (Katal, 2013; McAfee and Brynjolfsson, 2012).

In addition to the 3Vs, further Vs – veracity, value and variability – have been added to expand the definition of big data.

Big data technology, analytics and tools

Due to the (above-mentioned) properties of big data, structured databases that stored the majority of corporate information until recently are ill suited to store and process big data. Traditional systems are also not sufficiently capable in performing the analytics on data constantly in motion (McAfee and Brynjolfsson, 2012).

At the same time, the steadily declining costs of all the elements of computing such as storage, memory, processing and bandwidth have resulted in previously expensive data-intensive approaches becoming quite viable and practical. As more and more business activity is digitized, new sources of information and ever-cheaper equipment combine to bring on a new era: where large amounts of digital information exist and are accessible on virtually any topic of interest to a business.

Today, many businesses are managed using operations support or business support systems (OSS/BSS) reliant on traditional database, data warehouse and business intelligence tool sets. These technologies are typically applied to the data in each organizational silo, and are configured to create reports and dashboards aimed at solving the business problems of the individual divisions. As the traditional tools are not scalable and cost effective for very large data sets, very often data is left unanalysed, and data from multiple organizational units not correlated. To address these limitations, technologies designed to handle data on a massive scale have emerged and are being called "big data technologies" (Spiess, 2014).

Unlike the structured data that can be handled repeatedly through a Rational Database Management System (RDBMS), semi-structured and unstructured data that make up a big percentage of big data may call for ad hoc and one-time extraction, parsing, processing, indexing and analytics requiring scalable and distributed environments. MapReduce has been hailed as a revolutionary new platform for such large-scale, massively parallel data access. Built on MapReduce, Hadoop provides a Java-based software framework for distributed processing of data-intensive transformation and analytics and the top three commercial database suppliers: Oracle, IBM and Microsoft, have all adopted Hadoop in their technology platforms (Chen, 2012). Hadoop- and MapReduce-based systems have become another viable option for big data analytics in addition to the commercial systems developed for RDBMS, column-based Database Management Systems (DBMS), in-memory DBMS and parallel DBMS (Chen, 2012). The open source Apache Hadoop has also gained significant traction as a big data technology including Chukwa for data collection, HBase for distributed data storage, Hive for data summarization and ad hoc querying, and Mahout for data mining. Data analytics tools and algorithms utilize these big data platforms to manage and handle the requirements of big data.

Data analytics refers to the business intelligence and analytics (BI&A) technologies that are founded upon data mining, machine learning and statistical analysis. Most of these techniques rely on the mature commercial technologies of relational DBMS, data warehousing, Extract Transform and Load (ETL), Online Analytical Processing (OLAP) and Business Process Management (BPM). Since the late 1980s, various data mining algorithms have been developed by researchers from the artificial intelligence, algorithm and database communities. Some of the most widely accepted and used data mining algorithms are C4.5, k-means, SVM (support vector machine), Apriori, EM (expectation maximization), PageRank, AdaBoost, kNN (k-nearest neighbours), Naïve Bayes and CART.

These algorithms cover classification, clustering, regression, association analysis and network analysis. Most of these popular data mining algorithms have been incorporated in commercial and open source data mining systems. Other advances such as neural networks for classification/prediction and clustering and genetic algorithms for optimization and machine learning have all contributed to data mining in diverse applications (Chen, 2012).

Techniques such as Bayesian networks, Hidden Markov models, support vector machines, reinforcement learning and ensemble models have been applied to data, text and web analytics applications. Other new data analytics techniques explore and leverage unique data characteristics, from sequential/temporal mining and spatial mining, to data mining for high-speed data streams and sensor data. Many of these methods are data-driven, relying on various anonymization techniques, while others are process-driven, defining how data can be accessed and used. The big data technologies and platforms such as MapReduce and Hadoop support the application of these algorithms on big data.

Data analytics in performance management and control

The term "intelligence" has been used in artificial intelligence by researchers since the 1950s. However, "business intelligence" or BI became a popular term in the business and IT communities only in the 1990s. In the late 2000s, "business analytics" was introduced to represent the key analytical component in BI (Davenport, 2014). More recently, the terms "big data" and "big data analytics" have been used to describe the aforementioned massive data sets and the analytical techniques used on them in applications (Russom, 2011).

According to Hal Varian, Chief Economist at Google and Emeritus Professor at the University of California, Berkeley, the opportunities associated with data and analysis in different organizations have generated a significant interest in BI&A. BI&A is often referred to as the techniques, technologies, systems, practices, methodologies and applications that analyse critical business data to help an enterprise better understand its business and market, and make timely business decisions. In addition to the underlying data processing and analytical technologies, BI&A includes business-centric practices and methodologies that can be applied to various high-impact applications such as e-commerce, market intelligence, e-government, healthcare and security (Russom, 2011).

Most of the literature on data analytics focuses on the application of analytics tools and techniques on various data sets. These highlight the data-related issues as well as the technology and algorithmic aspects in data analytics. Comparatively, very little has been published on how analytics could support management and decision making within an organization.

Organizations typically store their critical data arising from various transactions in relational databases. Such data is mostly structured data. However, there is a large amount of unstructured data generated from blogs, images, email, social media, scientific experiments, various surveys, etc. that contain useful information. Mining these kinds of data is becoming extremely useful for making intelligent business decisions (Dhar, 2014b).

PMS and MCS support management control and decision making in organizations. According to Ferreira and Otley (2009) introduced in chapter 2, an effective and complete PMS should:

- a Clarify the vision and mission of an organization and focus attention of managers and employees on this vision and mission,
- b Identify the key success factors and clarify how these can be brought to the notice of managers and employees,
- c Illustrate how the organizational structure affects PMC design and use,
- d Highlight processes and activities that are required for the implementation of organizational strategies and plans,
- e Identify the key performance measures,
- f Identify the appropriate performance targets for the key performance measures,
- g Identify the already existing performance evaluation processes,
- h Set the rewards for target achievement,
- i Highlight the information flows that can support the performance management.

A PMS is focused on the measuring of performance, but this alone does not provide a competitive edge to an organization (Schläfke, 2012). It is imperative that an organization understands the business dynamics and reviews strengths, weaknesses as well as opportunities and threats. A further important factor is to ensure that the right data is available and also the skills and capability to transform such data into appropriate information. As previously discussed, advanced analytics tools and techniques can be used to generate insights from diverse data sources. Therefore, by incorporating into PMS, these have the potential to extend the domain of performance management to provide an improved understanding of business dynamics and lead to better decision making. Use of analytics can extend performance management from purely focusing on financial performance drivers to the inclusion of non-financial data by bringing in techniques such as mathematics, statistics, econometrics, data mining, machine learning, information technology and tools for data gathering and analysis.

Schläfke (2012) has called such extensive use of analytical techniques within PMS performance management analytics (PMA). PMA involves the extensive use of data and analytical methods to understand relevant business dynamics, to effectively control key performance drivers and to actively increase organizational performance. In order to effectively incorporate business analytics, organizations must satisfy a number of key requirements such as availability of data, appropriate IT infrastructure and related skills including business data analysis skills. An analytical management system's value is extremely high in an organization that already has an advanced IT infrastructure such as an enterprise resource planning (ERP) system, data warehouse, data mining systems or well-established customer relationship management. Based on a model of applications of PMA proposed by Schläfke (2012), we propose a model for the key components of PMA as shown in Figure 8.1. In this model, PMA is considered as the intersection between (a) organizational business processes and information systems, (b) decision support systems and (c) analytical, data mining techniques and tools.

The design and implementation of an analytical PMS require a thorough understanding of the organization and its business model, its performance indicators, its key success factors, information and data sources. It is also very important to be clear about the techniques that alert management about data, transactions and events, therefore triggering

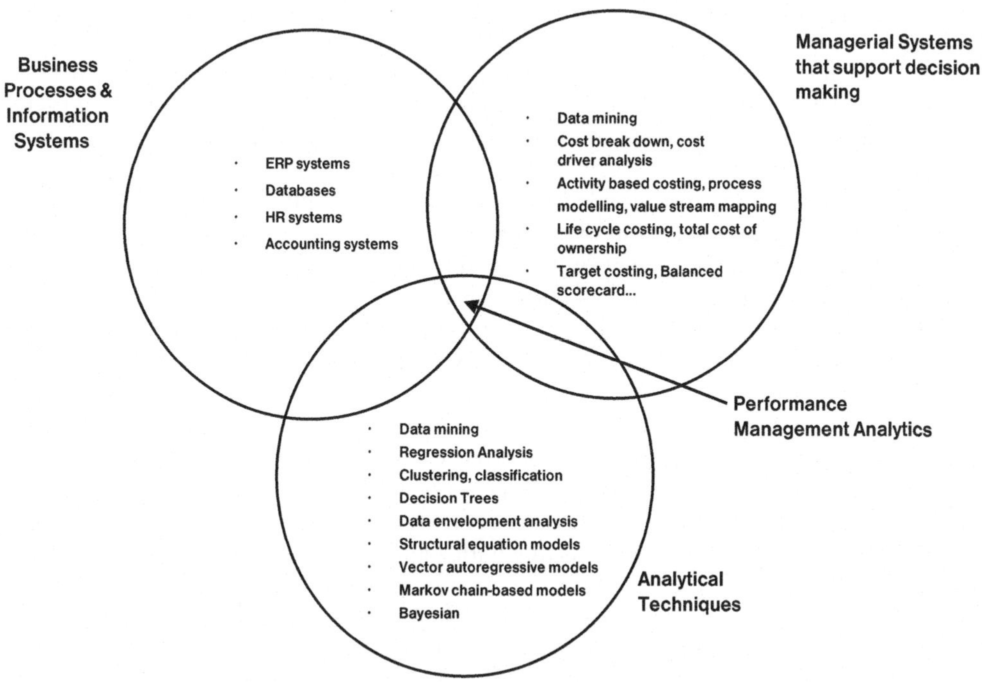

Figure 8.1 Key components of organizational performance management analytics

suitable actions. It is important to build such a system with a solid foundation such as a good theoretical framework.

Schläfke *et al.* (2012) have proposed a multi-layer performance management framework that will provide decision makers with additional information that could address the limitations of traditional PMS and enable the use of analytics. With the use of the four layers for capturing business drivers in inputs, processes, outputs and outcomes, coupling of performance drivers, identifying levers of control and designing such controls, and finally internal and external communication of the performance drivers, PMC is achieved. PMC systems thus gather and use information to evaluate the performance of multiple organizational resources such as human, physical, financial and also organization as a whole in terms of the organizational strategies. They will also include control systems such as tools for steering an organization towards its strategic objectives to realize competitive advantage.

Evolution and maturity of performance management and control systems

The information-rich big data environment has resulted in the generation of new types of data, different and diverse from the traditional data used in organizations. Since this non-traditional data accounts for 80 per cent of enterprise data and continues to grow rapidly, enterprises have realized the need for a strategy to combine both traditional and non-traditional data together to support the organizational PMC processes. As discussed in the previous section, the new discipline known as PMA has arisen in the attempt to cater to this need. However, these attempts are still in infancy in their path towards achieving PMA on an integrated enterprise wide data management platform (Dhar, 2014b). To appreciate the need and value of a PMA and its role in an organization, it is necessary to have a good understanding of the diverse types of data that contribute to the big data environments in organizations. These are considered as the information assets of an organization. It is also important to understand the organizational processes that generate and capture this data.

Organizations rely on a growing set of applications to communicate with and provide services/products to today's demanding consumer and business communities:

- They are collecting, storing and analysing more granular information about more products, people, and transactions than ever before.
- They rely on email, collaboration tools and mobile devices to communicate and conduct business with customers and business partners.
- They are creating, receiving and collecting machine and sensor-generated messages, sometimes at very high volumes, and are driving operations and business processes from that message data.

The growth in the number, size and importance of information assets is not limited to just large government agencies, large enterprises or internet web sites. A wide variety of organizations, ranging from small- and medium-sized businesses (SMBs) to large enterprises and government agencies, are dealing with a flood of data as they and their customers (Villars, 2011):

- Digitize business records and personal content (including the generation of ever-larger numbers of photos, movies, and medical images) driven by continued advancements in device features, resolution and processor power.

- Instrument devices (e.g. set-top boxes, game systems, smartphones, smart meters), buildings, cities and even entire regions to monitor changes in load, temperatures, locations, traffic patterns and behaviours.
- Address governance, privacy and regulatory compliance requirements that complicate the retention of business information.

To cater to this data-intensive environment, a new breed of analytics systems, as well as algorithms and tools, have evolved and been created. Figure 8.2 shows the evolution of the BI&A systems in organizations in the first column, the data types in column two and algorithms and techniques in column three.

Business intelligence in the past was mainly derived from database management-based structured data stores. Reporting and querying (such as SQL) enabled the retrieval of the required information and transforming into end user-requested formats. As described above, the past decade has evolved in to the big data environment with a flood of unstructured data as well as the wide use of mobile devices. To cater to the needs of this environment, new analytics tools and techniques have evolved such as text and web analytics and social media and network analytics.

A strategy to understand and also capture the impact of this change and evolution in the data-intensive environment on PMC is to observe the levels of maturity in such systems in organizations. Patas (2015) has discussed such maturity levels highlighting the levels of maturity reached based on IT-enabled capabilities. The different levels of maturity have been detailed from the perspectives of corporate planning and corporate reporting. Table 8.1 is based on and extends the maturity levels from Patas (2015).

The two new maturity levels are proposed to cater to the present and future of PMC systems. In the data-driven stage, the previous IT-enabled systems are extended and harnessed with advanced analytics techniques as well as the capabilities of handling unstructured and large internal and external data sources. For reporting, more derived insights rather than direct retrieved data and also much improved visualization capabilities are used. In the future level of maturity, the mobile environment and the wider usage and availability of IOT systems and data will be the key defining factor. This will generate and make available highly granular data, and the systems and algorithms will have to cater to these requirements.

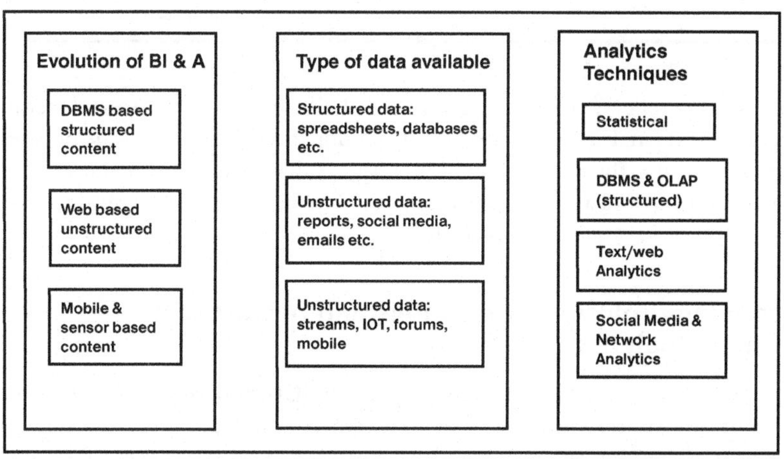

Figure 8.2 Evolution of analytics, types of data and techniques

Table 8.1 Evolution of corporate planning and reporting capabilities for management control systems

Maturity level descriptor	*Corporate planning capability*	*Corporate reporting capability*
Basic	Financially oriented and manually done using spreadsheets	Highly manual, paper-based reports oriented towards financial measures and external requirements
Guided	Supported by basic IT systems	Included reporting and analysis services for corporate and business units
Integrated	Well-organized, financially oriented planning systems	Well-designed, automated reporting with risk and compliance measures and advanced analytics
Strategy-driven	Supported by Advanced IT–for organizational vision and strategy	Reporting with emphasis on strategy measures, analysis and instruments
IT-advanced	Supported by modern IT for process optimization, planning integration and enhanced quality	Reporting utilizes modern IT-enabled systems with mobile devices and dashboards
Data-driven and big data(current and near future)	Supported by advanced analytics tools and technologies incorporating structured and unstructured data from internal as well as external environments	Further extending reporting capabilities in IT-advanced stage with insights derived from data using descriptive and predictive analytics. Better visualizations and visual analytics
Mobile, web-based and IOT era(next generation)	Ability to work with highly granular information, supported on web-based and mobile devices, and cloud-based technology and applications	Wide use of mobile and web-based systems, ability to drill down to highly granular levels due to availability of such detailed data. Personalized reporting and ability to link with wider external systems and data sources

The reporting also reflects these changes and will also have to cater to the technical needs of linking with external data sources for enriching internal data. It can be seen that the data-driven level is mostly an evolution due to the availability of new data and the advancement of data handling and analytics technologies. The next generation level is mainly due to the acceptance in society of the mobile life styles and also the advent of IOT.

New technology solutions for establishing performance management analytics

Figure 8.3 provides a summary of how organizational processes are generating different types of data from multiple sources. The first two columns are separated into three main rows catering for the key categories of processes within an organization – front, internal and back ends. The majority of the new data are considered as unstructured and require

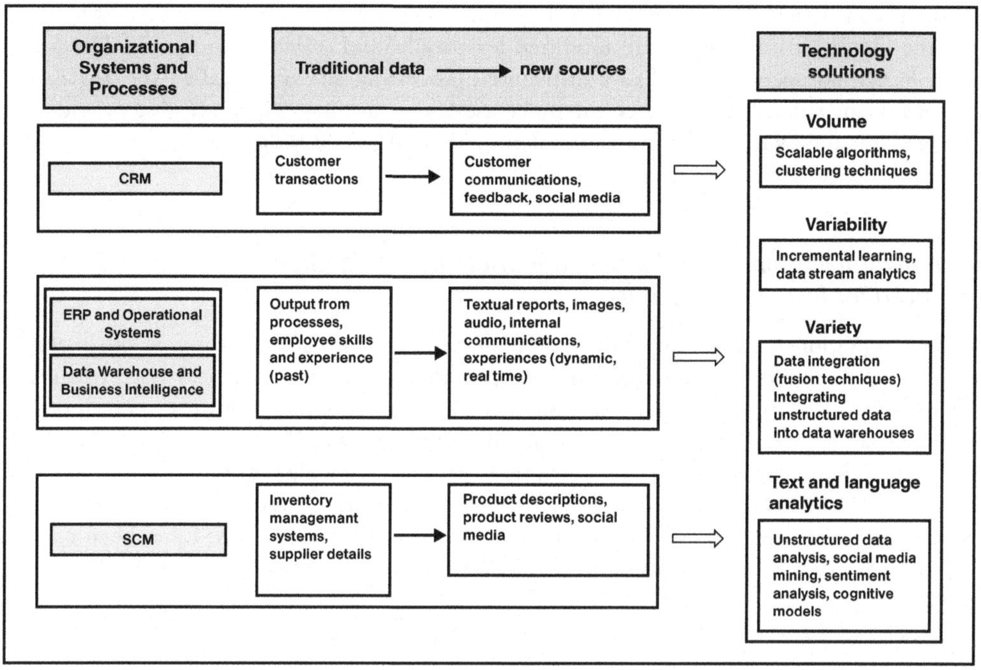

Figure 8.3 Organizational processes, traditional and new types of data and technology solutions for big data

more sophisticated processing and new technologies for analysis and insight generation. The new data are also mostly massive in volume, change frequently and generated from diverse sources, thus satisfying the 3Vs, volume, variability and variety. To address these requirements new algorithms are being researched and developed. The following section describes key technological developments providing an example case study of how one key technology is being enhanced and developed to cater to the new environment. The following key technologies are listed in Figure 8.3 as technology solutions for addressing the new requirements. Each technology solution is elaborated using an example based on a series of new algorithms being developed by the authors and their research colleagues. The foundation technology is the Growing Self Organizing Map (GSOM) (Kohonen, 1995) which is a structure adapting dynamic version of the popular Self Organizing Map (SOM) (Alahakoon, 2000) algorithm. The SOM is widely used and is a popular data clustering and visualization tool. The GSOM was an innovative extension of the SOM, which can dynamically adapt to changing data. Although the original GSOM has been adopted internationally for a range of applications, it does not cater to the needs of big data in its original form. Several new innovations are being carried out to enable the GSOM technology to be applied with big data.

Scalable algorithms and clustering techniques – to address large volumes

Although there are many popular and effective data mining algorithms and tools, many of them cannot be used with very large data volumes. A number of key research pathways are being followed to address this need. Several distributed computing platforms such as Apache

Hadoop and Apache Spark have been developed which can be utilized with existing data mining algorithms once they are modified for parallel and scalable processing. The original GSOM has been extended to a distributed processing algorithm called the distributed GSOM (Ganegedara, 2014), which can make use of the advantages in processing provided by the Hadoop and Spark platforms, thus enabling the SOM/GSOM technology to be applied with very large volumes of data.

Incremental learning and data stream analytics – to address the need for fast-changing data

A key limitation of most data mining and machine learning algorithms is the inability to adapt their models as data changes. The problem is even more critical with streams of data where it is difficult to train machine learning models which require several iterations over the same data. A new stream of machine learning research is focusing on the development of incremental learning and adaptive versions of the algorithms. A new version of incremental GSOM called Incremental Knowledge Aquiring Self-Learning (IKASL) (De Silva, 2010) has been successfully developed to cater to this need. IKASL has been used to capture patterns and events from streams of text, news feeds, tweets and smart electricity meter readings.

Data integration to address the need of managing variety in data

Patterns in data can occur across multiple data sets. Such data could be multi-source and multi-modal. Such data need to be integrated for the patterns to become visible, and as such, algorithms that cater to this need are being developed. The GSOM fusion algorithm (Fonseka, 2011) is the GSOM-based solution for this requirement. Inspired by the multi-sensory integration capabilities in the human brain, this technology has already been successfully trialled with text, image and numeric data.

Text and language analytics

This is one of the most important and essential requirements of the big data era. Massive volumes of text are being created from various sources with social media and the Internet being the biggest contributors. This data is very rich with information, but it is difficult for a machine to extract value from text due to the semantics and language characteristics of text. Social media with its own unique language and communication style further adds to the complexity. Many algorithms are being developed to address these requirements – catering to different aspects of the problem such as natural language processing (NLP)-based techniques to capture language constructs and grammar, fast processing and indexing techniques to address data sparsity aspects of text, and cognitive situation models to capture semantics and meaning in text. One of the GSOM solutions has addressed the sparsity and speed of processing problems of text with the introduction of the Fast GSOM algorithm (Alahakoon, 2000).

The different technologies described above are the key research focus pathways in addressing the needs of moving traditional data mining technology to the big data environment. The work is ongoing and will continue to be a high-priority research area.

Impact of big data and analytics on performance management control systems

According to McAfee and Brynjolfsson (2012), the use of big data and analytics is not only applicable to companies *born digital* such as Google and Amazon, but also has the potential to transform traditional businesses as well and provide competitive advantages. Due to analytics-enhanced PMC, managers now have the capacity to make better predictions and smarter decisions, and carry out more effective interventions based on data and information rather than intuition.

Big data and analytics can impact the PMC of an organization in diverse ways as discussed in Davenport (2013). For ease of presentation and understanding, we have grouped these under three main key categories as follows:

a impact on organizational systems and processes,
b impact in improving existing tasks and workflows,
c impact on organizational decision-making culture.

Impact on organizational systems and processes

There are several ways big data can have an impact on changing organizational systems and processes. By making information more accessible to stakeholders in a timely manner, the organization creates higher transparency generating high value. Using automated algorithms to support human decision making also impacts systems and processes. In some cases, decisions will not necessarily be automated but augmented by analysing huge, entire data sets using big data techniques and technologies rather than just smaller samples. New innovative business models, products and services are enabled due to big data. Insights gleaned from the use of products or services can be used for improvements for the innovation of new products.

Impact in improving existing tasks and workflows

Use of big data can substantially improve the time required to perform a computing task, or new product and service offerings, and reduce the cycle time for complex and large-scale analytical calculations (Davenport, 2013). Big data can also be a valuable tool for analysis of individual or team behaviour, using sensors or badges to track individuals as they work together, move around their workspace, or spend time interacting with others or allocated to specific tasks (George, 2014). Organizations can collect more accurate and detailed performance data (in real- or near real-time) on everything from product inventories to personnel sick days and use such data to analyse variability in performance and to understand its root causes can enable leaders to manage performance to higher levels (Manyika, 2011). Big data also allows organizations to create highly specific segmentations and to tailor products and services precisely to meet those needs. This approach is well known in marketing and risk management. Consumer goods and service companies that have regularly used segmentation for many years have begun to deploy ever more sophisticated big data techniques such as the real-time micro-segmentation of customers to target promotions and advertising (Manyika, 2011).

Creating a new culture of decision making

Managerial challenges are greater than the technical challenges when implementing a big data strategy (McAfee and Brynjolfsson, 2012). When there is a scarcity of data, data is expensive to obtain or is not available in digital form, it makes sense to let well-placed people make decisions, which they do based on experience they have built up and patterns and relationships they have observed and internalized. According to McAfee and Brynjolfsson (2012), executives interested in leading a big data transition should start with two simple techniques.

> *First, they can ask* "What do the data say?" and then "Where did the data come from?," "What kinds of analyses were conducted?," "How confident are we in the results?" *Second,decision makers can allow themselves to be overruled by the data*; a powerful indication of importance given to data.
>
> *(McAfee and Brynjolfsson, 2012, p. 66)*

This is an essential step in changing the culture towards a data-driven organization.

Big data adoption: challenges and solutions

As described in the previous sections, although big data brings about features to handle the complex requirements of today's organizations towards a data-driven PMC, there are still many challenges in adoption of big data at enterprise level (Russom, 2011). In this section, the key challenges for adoption of big data technologies and strategies to overcome them are discussed.

Management challenges for big data

Organizations will not reap the full benefits of a transition to using big data unless they are able to manage change effectively. Three key management challenges as per McAfee and Brynjolfsson (2012) are summarized below.

Leadership

Although companies will have more and better data with advanced analytics tools, this will not replace the need or the tasks to be carried out by the business leaders. Business leaders will still have to set the vision, observe and understand the market trends, use experience, intuition and creativity to come up with new offerings, and also address the needs of customers, employees and other stakeholders. The difference will be that they will have access to data from more and diverse sources as highlighted previously in Figure 8.3 and also have the knowledge and technologies to generate insights by manipulating these variety of data. Successful companies in the future will have forward thinking and big data savvy leaders who will champion the introduction and establishment of the new technologies into their organizations.

Skill management

As described above, the new era will result in a range of new technologies and tools being introduced into business day to day operations as well as managing and manipulating the new data sources. Although it is anticipated that some tasks – thus certain jobs – will become obsolete, a range of new jobs to cater to the new environment will arise. For example, the managers will be able to directly access and immerse themselves in the data for insight generation and analysis. This means that less staff will be required for providing technical and data support and report generation. But due to the needs of the fast-changing data environment, the models built may require faster updates or regeneration for changed situations – this will require more staff with these skills. It will also be necessary to maintain staff skill levels and continually update them with regular training programs (McAfee and Brynjolfsson, 2012; Villars, 2011).

Technology

The technology landscape is fast changing, with new algorithms, tools, vendors and methodologies being proposed and introduced almost daily. These technologies are quite affordable even to smaller organizations, and most of the software is now open source. To be competitive in this fast-changing environment, business organizations must make sure that regular reviews of the technologies are carried out and updates made. Since these technologies require highly specialized skills, it is also important to reskill staff or hire suitable new staff. Therefore, it is essential that strong focus with high-level support for keeping up with the technology is set up as a necessary component of a big data strategy (McAfee and Brynjolfsson, 2012).

Other big data challenges faced by organizations

Privacy and security

This is a vital issue with the high sensitivity of big data. It is now possible to link personal information of a person with large external data sets leading to the inference of new facts about that person. These kinds of facts could be confidential and the person might not want the data owner to know of them. However, user information is collected and analysed in order to add value to the business of organizations by building up the capacity to advise, guide and support, and this is done by creating insights into users' lives which they are unaware of (Katal, 2013).

Data access and sharing of information

In order to make precise, timely decisions, it is necessary that data be available in time, and in accurate and complete form. This makes data management and governance more complex as it requires data to be open and available to government agencies in a standardized manner. Thus, careful thought needs to be put into setting up the organizational data policy as this will lead to better decision making and higher productivity (Katal, 2013).

Quality of data

Having larger data sets available over longer periods of time for analysis will deliver superior and more accurate results. Using such data in decision making will definitely lead to better results. Business leaders will require more data storage, whereas IT leaders will consider all technical aspects before simply storing all the data. Big data focuses on quality capture for better results rather than maintaining very large, irrelevant, low-quality data. This further leads to various enquiries such as how to ensure which data is relevant, and how much data is enough for decision making and whether the stored data is accurate or not to draw conclusions from (Katal, 2013).

Development scalability and maintainability

The lack of many technologies that suit the big data scale such as Testing, Deployment and Administration tools, and Integrated Development Environments (IDEs) make the development and maintenance phase of big data slow and difficult. Big data teams require a range of skills ranging from application logic and data modelling to infrastructure administration proficiency. Thus, the availability of proper sets of tools in these areas could help enterprises develop and maintain big data more efficiently (Dhar, 2014b).

Reusability

The enormous volume, velocity and variety of big data could result in difficulty for humans to comprehend the total picture of the project or operation. This could result in the development of non-reusable solutions.

Thus for the adoption of big data, an integrated big data architecture, across structured and unstructured data sources, and a proper data model should be available.

Conclusion

In the last few years, big data technologies have gained considerable attention due to their potential to transform data mining and business analytics practices and the possibility for a wide range of highly effective decision-making tools and services. This chapter looked at big data mainly focusing on the impact on PMC systems. The concept of PMA was discussed and a model of the components of PMA developed. The chapter also discussed the evolution of MCS and the new analytics technologies and systems that have come up to fill the requirements of the new systems. The evolution of PMCs was investigated from a corporate planning capability aspect as well as reporting perspective. The current maturity model for PMCs was extended with new data-driven level and a future mobile and IOT environment-based level of maturity. The chapter then looked at the main impact of big data and analytics on PMC and finally presented the main challenges in the adoption of big data in organizations.

In conclusion, big data and analytics have not only made a significant impact on organizational PMC, but have been a key driver in the evolution of PMC systems. It is expected that this trend will continue and that the current data-driven level of maturity will move on to the next generation of mobile device and web-based systems that also work with much higher granularity of data. New algorithms, tools and technology will develop to support these requirements with advanced analytics and machine learning, extending into deep learning and cognitive computing-based highly intelligent algorithms.

References

Alahakoon, D., Halgamuge, S. K., and Srinivasan, B. (2000). Dynamic Self-Organizing Maps with Controlled Growth for Knowledge Discovery. *IEEE Transactions on Neural Networks*, *11*(3), 601–614.

Ammu, N. and Irfanuddin, M. (2013). Big Data Challenges. *International Journal of Advanced Trends in Computer Science and Engineering*, *2*, 613–615.

Apache Spark. (n.d.). Retrieved from Apache Software Foundation: http://spark.apache.org/.

Brynjolfsson, E., Hitt, L. M., and Kim, H. H. (2011). Strength in Numbers: How Does Data-Driven Decisionmaking Affect Firm Performance? *Social Science Research Network (SSRN 1819486)*. Retrieved from http://papers.ssrn.com/sol3/Papers.cfm?abstract_id=1819486.

Chen, C. L. P. and Zhang, C-Y. (2014). Data-Intensive Applications, Challenges, Techniques and Technologies: A Survey on Big Data. *Information Sciences, 275*, 314–347. Retrieved from http://dx.doi.org/10.1016/j.ins.2014.01.015.

Chen, H., Chiang, R. H. L., and Storey, V. C. (2012, December). Business Intelligence and Analytics: From Big Data to Big Impact. *MIS Quarterly: Management Information Systems, 36*, 1165–1188.

Davenport, T. H. (2014). *Big Data at Work: Dispelling the Myths, Uncovering the Opportunities*. Boston, MA: Harvard Business Review Press, 21–25.

Davenport, T. H. and Dyche, J. (2013). *Big Data in Big Companies*. SAS International Institute for Analytics, Maggio.

De Silva, D. (2010). *A cognitive approach to autonomous incremental learning*. Thesis, Monash University, Faculty of Information Technology. Clayton School of IT, Melbourne.

Dhar, V., Jarke, M., and Laartz, J. (2014, May). Big Data. *Business & Information Systems Engineering*, pp. 257–259.

Dhar, S. and Mazumder, S. (2014). Challenges and Best Practices for Enterprise Adoption of Big Data Technologies. *Journal of Information Technology Management, XXV*, 38–44.

Ferreira, A. and Otley, D. T. (2009). The Design and Use of Performance Management Systems: An Extended Framework for Analysis. *Management Accounting Research, 20*(4), 263–282.

Fonseka, A., Alahakoon, D., and Rajapakse, J. (2011). A Dynamic Unsupervised Laterally Connected Neural Network Architecture for Integrative Pattern Discovery. *International Conference on Neural Information Processing*, pp. 761–770. Berlin: Springer.

Ganegedara K. M., T. V. (2014). *Exploratory data analysis using scalable self-organising maps*. thesis, Monash University, Faculty of Information Technology. Clayton School of IT, Melbourne.

George, G., and Hass, M. (2014, April). Big Data and Management. *Academy of Management Journal, 57*, 321–326.

Katal, A., Wazid, M., and Goudar, R. H. (2013). Big Data: Issues, Challenges, Tools and Good Practices. *2013 Sixth International Conference on Contemporary Computing (IC3)* (pp. 404–409). Red Hook, NY: IEEE.

Kohonen, T. (1995). *Self-Organizing Maps*. Berlin, Germany: Springer Verlag.

LaValle, S., Lesser, E., Shockley, R., Hopkins, M. S., and Kruschwitz, N. (2011). Big Data, Analytics and the Path from Insights to Value. *MIT Sloan Management Review, 52*(2), 21.

Manyika, J., Chui, M., Brown, B., Bughin, J., Dobbs, R., Roxburgh, C., and Byers, A. H. (2011). Big Data: The Next Frontier for Innovation, Competition, and Productivity. McKinsey Global Institute.

McAfee, A. and Brynjolfsson, E. (2012, October). Big Data: The Management Revolution. *Harvard Business Review*, 59–68.

Mithas, S., Ramasubbu, N., and Sambamurthy, V. (2011, March). How Information Management Capability Influences Firm Performance. *MIS Quarterly, 35*, 237–256.

Russom, P. (2011). *Big Data Analytics*. TDWI Best Practices Report.

Schlafke, M., Silvi, R., and Moller, K. (2012). A Framework for Business Analytics in Performance Management. *International Journal of Productivity and Performance Management, 62*(1), 110–122.

Spiess, J., T'Joens, Y., Dragnea, R., Spencer, P., and Philippart, L. (2014). Using Big Data to Improve Customer Experience and Business Performance. *Bell Labs Technical Journal, 18*, 3–17.

Villars, R. L., Olofson, C. W., and Eastwood, M. (2011). *Big Data: What It Is and Why You Should Care*. IDC Information and Data.

What Is Apache Hadoop? (n.d.). Retrieved from Apache Hadoop: http://hadoop.apache.org/.

Part II
People and management control

9

The role of the finance professional in performance management and control

Pascal Nevries and Rick Payne

Introduction

> In the long run, the division of functions will probably depend on the capacity of the professions providing personnel for {controller} departments. If so, the future organizational patterns will be much influenced by what the industrial accounting profession makes of itself. If it can attract men of superior competence and broad training, these are likely to lead to larger responsibilities for the profession.
>
> *(Simon et al., 1954, p. 10)*

Finance professionals[1] play a pivotal role in managing performance in many companies. Activities span a wide array from cash management to developing strategy. Finance professionals work at every hierarchical level (starting from the CFO, who usually sits on the board, to business analyst) and, apart from working in the finance department, are often embedded in other functions while maintaining a reporting line to the CFO (e.g. marketing controllers). Through highly specialised know-how, control of the firm's financial database and managerial influence, finance professionals can be crucial to the design and outcomes of a firm's performance management system (PMS). The precise role of finance professionals and finance departments in any particular organisation will depend on numerous factors (ICAEW, 2011) including culture (organisational and national, Granlund and Lukka, 1998a; Ahrens and Chapman, 2000), organisational politics (Ahrens and Chapman, 2000), industry sector, technology (Granlund and Malmi, 2002) and market conditions (Gerstner and Anderson, 1976).

In this chapter, we will highlight the core activities regarding the finance professional's contribution to performance management and examine what characterises successful finance departments. We will not consider specific finance knowledge covered in finance and accounting textbooks, such as the Capital Asset Pricing Model, but focus on the people working in the finance department. Our review of the role of the finance professional in performance management and control is informed by a review of the academic management accounting literature, practitioner surveys, numerous individual and group discussions with finance professionals, and personal experience. We searched academic databases for terms relating to the personnel (e.g. "business partnering", "controller", "financial controller",

"CFO", "activities", "roles") and their contribution to performance management (e.g. "performance", "management", "success"). From the resulting papers that explicitly discussed the role of the finance professional in performance management, we followed up relevant citations. More details and a complementary analysis of practitioner surveys (and a broader academic literature review) are available in the ICAEW report "The Finance Function: A Framework for Analysis" (2011), and we have not generally cited individual surveys in this chapter. However, we found few empirical specifics on the performance management activities undertaken and what drives their success. Thus, when our arguments extend beyond the scope of academic publications, we also draw on practitioner surveys, our discussions with finance professionals and our own experience.

We will round off this chapter by discussing whether there has been an increase in the influence of finance departments, finance career paths and also briefly consider the challenging times that lie ahead for finance professionals.

Ferreira and Otley's extended framework for analysing performance management systems

Ferreira and Otley's (2009) extended framework for analysing PMS provides a useful basis for scoping and analysing the role of finance professionals in performance management and control. The framework sets out 12 aspects of PMS (see Figure 9.1) in an attempt to provide

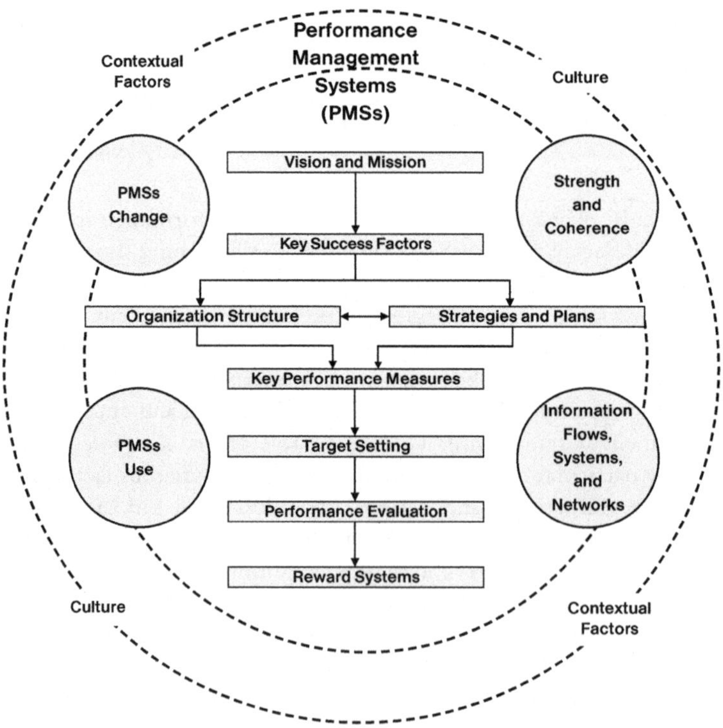

Figure 9.1 The design and use of performance management systems: an extended framework for analysis

Source: Used with permission and modified from Ferreira, A. and Otley, D. 'The design and use of performance management systems: an extended framework for analysis' (2009, p. 268).

a comprehensive overview. We use the framework as it was intended, i.e. as "a descriptive tool that may be used to amass evidence" (p. 266). To the best of our knowledge, the framework has not previously been used to provide a structure for analysing the role of the finance professional in performance management. We believe the elements of the framework are reasonably self-explanatory at a summary level, but we will go into more detail on some areas as we analyse the role of the finance professional. Given the breadth of activities and range of people involved in performance management and control, we focus our discussion on where finance professionals have the potential to play a particular role because of their training, experience and position in the organisation.

From strategy to performance: the contribution of finance professionals

Vision and mission

> If you want to build a ship, don't drum up people to collect wood and don't assign them tasks and work, but rather teach them to long for the endless immensity of the sea.
>
> *(Antoine de Saint-Exupéry)*

Some argue that achieving superior performance begins with setting ambitions and goals (Wilson, 1992). The most abstract and general manifestations of goals are usually vision and mission. The vision encapsulates the position the firm aims to achieve in the far future, while the mission dissects how the firm views itself in an ideal state, including its purpose and, sometimes, its values (Stone, 1996). As Ferreira and Otley put it, "Vision and mission statements are landmarks that guide the process of deciding what to change and what to preserve in strategies and activities in the face of changing environments (Collins and Porras, 1996)" (Ferreira and Otley, 2009, p. 268). Ferrari and, as a more down-to-earth example, St. John's Ambulance, express the following vision and mission statements.

> Ferrari, Italian Excellence that makes the world dream.
>
> *(Ferrari vision, 2016)*

> We build cars, symbols of Italian excellence the world over, and we do so to win on both road and track. Unique creations that fuel the Prancing Horse legend and generate a "World of Dreams and Emotions".
>
> *(Ferrari mission statement, 2016)*

> Everyone who needs it should receive first aid from those around them. No one should suffer for the lack of trained first aiders.
>
> *(St. John's Ambulance vision, 2016)*

> "Our mission is to:
>
> - provide an effective and efficient charitable first aid service to local communities
> - provide training and products to satisfy first aid and related health and safety needs for all of society
> - encourage personal development for people of all ages, through training and by volunteering within our organisation."
>
> *(St. John's Ambulance mission statement)*

Finance professionals contribute to the firm's vision and mission in at least three ways. First, they help to create a vision and mission (Weber *et al.*, 2007). Many companies do not have explicit vision and mission statements, sometimes by conscious choice, but also because of neglect as the issues of day-to-day operations take precedence. Finance professionals help overcome this inertia through organising strategic planning processes (Burns and Baldvinsdottir, 2005) with an awareness that vision and mission help frame an appropriate strategy. They therefore push and promote the engagement to create vision and mission statements, even though the content may not finally be decided by finance professionals (alone). However, finance professionals may be well placed to influence vision and mission because their role in pulling together and analysing information from across the organisation means they see the big picture.

While by their nature vision and mission should be designed to last, finance professionals are similarly well placed to identify when the vision and mission are becoming disconnected from strategy. This brings us to the second contribution finance professionals can make through their relative neutrality and objectivity fostered by their training and position in the organisation (Friedman and Lyne, 1997; Weber and Schaeffer, 2008). Thereby they can help ensure that the necessarily fuzzy, creative and often emotional process is tempered by rationality and produces a vision and mission grounded in reality and tailored to the company.

Third, vision and mission unfold their full potential only if communication ensures that employees develop a level of understanding sufficient to guide decision making and action. For instance, Ferrari employees "live the company" and know its vision and mission by heart (not something seen in many organisations!). It helps that the finance department engages at all hierarchical levels and across all organisational units where, as we shall see, they advise on decisions, set financial policies, analyse management information and communicate performance. As a result, finance professionals can help to communicate and cascade a firm's vision and mission such that it is reflected in the daily activities of employees. A good example is the budgeting process, which finance professionals control and which helps to manifest abstract strategic thinking in daily activities.

Key success factors

When it comes to identifying key success factors, the finance professional's training and experience in business and financial modelling support the identification of cause and effect relationships (i.e. the underlying drivers of performance). Perhaps the most prominent, systematic approach to identifying key success factors and their impact on performance is the use of strategy maps and balanced scorecards as developed by Kaplan and Norton (2004). Based on such structures, the role finance professionals play in managing key success factors will depend on the key success factors under consideration. For example, in ensuring that an organisation has an appropriate capital structure and available funding, the finance professional's role will be critical. They will take a lead in analysing the organisation's cost of capital and the availability and pricing of different funding sources; they will negotiate with providers and seek to ensure good-quality investor relations (ICAEW, 2011). On the other hand, a critical success factor of recruiting and retaining creative staff would be the domain of HR and line management. Clearly, however, finance will influence how much can be invested in any particular success factor.

Organisation structure and strategies and plans

Finance professionals, apart from the CFO, are unlikely to have a significant role in designing organisational structures, such as reporting lines, job descriptions and the degree of decentralisation. However, on accounting, controls and regulation they do have some influence. This can be seen in considerations of appropriate profit and cost centre structures, ensuring appropriate segregation of duties, setting levels of delegated spending authorities and deciding on the most appropriate legal ownership structures. These all have a part to play in facilitating organisational performance and maintaining control.

Strategising and planning are one of the key contributions finance professionals make to PMS – not least because they are often responsible for managing the strategic planning process (Weber *et al.*, 2007). When organisations conceptualise a new strategy, finance professionals will both contribute ideas and test and quantify the ideas of others. Their toolbox facilitates the analysis, substantiation, rationalisation and funnelling down of the multitude of strategic options which the creative processes of strategy formulation should generate (Weber *et al.*, 2007). For example, a controller would be expected to have highly developed skills in the use of scenario analyses, sensitivity analyses, simulation modelling, competitor analysis, Porter's Five Forces, gap analysis, SWOT analysis and Ansoff's matrix, among others (Guilding *et al.*, 2000; Langfield-Smith, 2008; Weber and Schaeffer, 2008). In using the appropriate tools effectively, finance professionals are well placed to consolidate the results of these analyses into a presentation of the organisation's structure, strategic position, its operating environment and ideas for exploiting opportunities and overcoming threats. Studies show a substantial involvement of the finance function in all these activities, especially regarding organisation of the strategy process and conducting the relevant analyses (Langfield-Smith, 1997; Nevries *et al.*, 2007; Weber *et al.*, 2007). Senior finance professionals who sit on executive management teams or strategic steering committees will also influence the decision on which strategy to pursue (Burns and Baldvinsdottir, 2005). It is also worth noting that Zoni and Merchant (2007) found that the formalisation of strategic planning and budgeting processes is associated with increased involvement of controllers in decision making.

While line managers are responsible for implementing the strategy, finance professionals play a number of roles. First, finance professionals extend their analytical support to more operational levels through, for example, financial forecasting and cost analysis. Second, they are often called on to negotiate between competing demands for resources between organisational units, particularly when bottom-up budgets do not match top-down strategic and financial aspirations. It is worth noting that budgets provide an interesting reference point for deciding whether espoused strategies are supported by real resource allocations – new initiatives are much more difficult to pursue if the resources are not already in the budget (Parker and Kyj, 2006; Weber *et al.*, 2007; Weber and Schaeffer, 2008). Third, the logistical challenge in large organisations of managing a complex planning and budgeting process, which often goes through numerous iterations, should not be underestimated.

Key performance measures and target setting

Key performance measures and targets play an integral part in focusing managerial attention, analysing and evaluating performance, and thereby allocating incentives as part of the variable pay in reward systems (Ferreira and Otley, 2009). As mentioned above, finance professionals play an important role in deciding what to measure and which measures are most important for managing performance and monitoring strategy. Measures will include lead and lag indicators, and may be financial or non-financial. Even with respect to financial outcomes, the choice of measures is not easy – for example, should listed firms focus on total shareholder return, Economic Value Added (EVA™) or earnings per share? Non-financial measures may also be influenced by finance professionals and they are often responsible for comprehensive measurement systems, such as the balanced scorecard (Kaplan and Norton, 1992). Finance professionals should be aware of the pros and cons of different measures and decide on what measures are most appropriate in different circumstances. Once appropriate measures have been decided upon, finance professionals play a key role in communicating these measures, be it through reporting, establishing self-service information systems, or ongoing interactions and meetings with managers.

Finance professionals influence the derivation of appropriate targets, especially financial ones, through the analysis of previous performance and forecasting. This analysis helps set the boundaries of minimum, achievable and stretch targets. The experienced finance professional will seek to ensure that distinctions are made between budgets, designed to allocate resources and control expenditure, and targets, which are designed to motivate high performance. Moreover, finance professionals will also challenge managers who overstate projected costs and understate projected revenues in order to ensure targets are met while bearing in mind that such behaviours can be seen as a means of managing risk in uncertain environments (Elmassri and Harris, 2011).

Performance evaluation and controlling strategy

Performance evaluation, which is at its most visible in formal appraisal systems, is usually conducted by line managers based on a process managed by human resource departments (see chapter 15). The role of the finance department is limited to the influence that the strategy process has on the setting of individual objectives and the use of performance information produced by the finance department. This information will be used more intensively where objectives are based on financial measures and achievement is judged on formulaic calculations rather than subjective evaluations.

Controlling strategy includes such activities as results controls, premise control and strategic monitoring (Schreyoegg and Steinmann, 1987). Ex post results controls built around feedback from analysing where actual performance deviates from planned performance provide an essential means of deciding whether the current strategy is working or needs to be changed. However, such feedback may not be timely enough and restrict an organisation's ability to take corrective action. Therefore, performance evaluation also needs to include monitoring progress on strategic milestones and using more proactive approaches such as strategic surveillance and premise control (Schreyoegg and Steinmann, 1987). Strategic surveillance involves the constant monitoring of internal and external threats to the strategy. Premise controls are more specific and designed to identify and continuously check the validity of the most important premises on which plans and strategies are built, for example assumptions about oil prices, exchange rates and pricing policies of competitors. In Germany, controllers are given full responsibility for carrying out these tasks, both as part of the strategic planning process and during strategy implementation (Weber *et al.*, 2007). Where this is the case and line managers do not carry any responsibility, successful performance evaluation and strategic control hinge on the capacity, motivation and competence of finance professionals. This is a concern because studies show a desire for more performance evaluation and strategic control (Weber *et al.*, 2007). When asked for reasons about shortcomings, practitioners mention limited capacity and the prioritisation of other (more operational) activities that are mandatory and failures are more easily discovered. As a result, paradoxically, strategic activities that can have higher value are drowned out by lower-value activities.

Reward systems

The role of the finance professionals in designing reward systems seems limited, with no specific mentions in practitioner surveys of finance's role (ICAEW, 2011). The discussion above shows finance's key role in managing areas, such as performance measurement, upon which reward systems are based. The specific design of the reward system such as salary structures and the split between fixed and variable pay is likely to be the responsibility of human resource departments. However, the reward system will need to be affordable, and therefore, finance can have significant influence on the overall level of salary and bonus awards. It is interesting to note that while the design of incentive systems is a major research area for management accounting academics, there is little research on the role that management accountants play in the design process.

Four intertwined characteristics of PMS

Ferreira and Otley (2009) identify four general aspects that characterise PMS and are intertwined with the processes described above – PMS information flows, systems and networks, PMS strength and the coherence between its elements, PMS use and PMS change. Finance professionals will play an important role in each of these interrelated aspects of performance management and control.

Finance departments control substantial parts of organisational information systems, including one of the most important sources of performance management information – the general ledger and its sub-ledgers. These substantiate broader information systems such as enterprise resource planning systems (where finance may also have significant influence, Goretzki *et al.*, 2013) and functional systems such as human resource systems and customer relationship management systems. As we have seen, the recording of actual performance is an essential part of monitoring whether a strategy is working, forecasting future performance and calculating reward. The complexity of calculating actual performance should not be underestimated as it entails the use of complex rules, for example on when revenue should be recognised, and assumptions and estimates, such as whether debts will be repaid. Management reporting, budgeting and planning processes also generate significant information flows and are often the most visible finance processes for other managers.

Importantly, information system integration has been shown to improve the effectiveness of finance departments in their strategic and performance management roles (Chang *et al.*, 2014). Thus, the coherence of performance management and control systems is home turf of management accountants and controllers. Their role in consolidating and analysing information across multiple departments and divisions will highlight inconsistencies in how performance is managed. They will also be in a strong position to tell whether key performance measures are aligned with strategy.

The way in which PMS are used is clearly fundamental, although the term "use" still needs further development (Ferreira and Otley, 2009). The intensity of use is one aspect, and this will in part depend on the success of finance departments in their performance management role. For example, there is some evidence to suggest that finance professionals place a higher value on the reports they produce and the analytical techniques they use compared to line managers (Pierce and O'Dea, 2003). The communication skills of finance professionals and constructing a customer-oriented PMS will help make PMS an integral part of managers' day-to-day work routines. Skills and customer orientation will feature prominently in the next section where we discuss drivers that separate successful from less successful finance departments.

PMS change for a number of reasons, including reacting to changing environments (Chenhall, 2003), organisational structures (Gosselin, 1997) and strategies (Langfield-Smith, 1997). By being quick to react and redesigning PMS, finance professionals can help ensure organisations adapt more quickly to new circumstances (Baines and Langfield-Smith, 2003). Better finance departments are particularly proactive and establish early warning systems that aim to provide information about developments and trends with respect to customers, competitors and the external environment, i.e. strategic surveillance as discussed earlier. Finance professionals, especially controllers, may establish a system across the organisation, and globally if necessary, where designated experts regularly report on business relevant trends (Weber *et al.*, 2007). Experts can be both internal (e.g. the head of technology in an Indonesian subsidiary) and external (e.g. leading academics with industry knowledge). Finance professionals at headquarters consolidate the independent information and whenever one topic or trend emerges that is common to a substantial portion of the experts involved, a task force will start analysing its relevance (Weber *et al.*, 2007).

Culture and context

Ferreira and Otley (2009) recognise the impact of culture and contextual factors on PMS, and the role of finance professionals will also be impacted. While a discussion of culture is beyond the scope of this chapter, it is important to note that finance departments will both be influenced by organisational culture and play a part in shaping it (Lambert and Sponem, 2012). For example, finance may introduce a detailed, bureaucratic budgeting process because it fits the organisational culture and thereby further entrench a bureaucratic culture or, conversely, seek to lead a move away from bureaucracy by taking a more informal, high-level approach which may result in greater resistance because it will challenge existing norms and beliefs.

The importance of operational controls

Anthony (1965) developed a three-level classification of control — strategic planning, management control and operational control. Using the Ferreira and Otley (2009) framework has focused our discussion at the strategic planning and management control levels. However, the importance of the finance professional's role in operational control, the process of assuring that specific tasks are carried out effectively and efficiently, should not be underestimated. Failures in very basic controls, e.g. in credit monitoring, safeguarding assets and working capital management can very quickly lead an organisation into difficulties. When such failures contribute to cash shortages, financial misstatements and fraud the result can be catastrophic, as many corporate scandals have proven. Finance professionals will be responsible for ensuring appropriate controls are in place to prevent such occurrences and should stand up to any attempts at management override.

Drivers of successful finance departments

Earlier, we discussed the areas of performance management that finance professionals are most likely to be involved with and the likely nature of that involvement. However, the intensity of involvement and the chances that finance professionals and finance departments make a positive contribution to organisational performance depend on their effectiveness. The factors that drive their effectiveness are discussed below.[2]

Individual knowledge, skills, attitudes and attributes

> Senior practitioners displayed idiomatic competence, integrating diverse experiences into flexible yet recognizable articulations of practice.
>
> *(Ahrens and Chapman, 2000, p. 496)*

Over the years, numerous practitioner surveys have tried to identify the most important personal attributes of successful finance professionals working in business, usually by asking finance professionals to rank a predefined, and sometimes long, list of attributes, e.g. Siegel *et al.* (1996) and Hays (2014, 2015). It is difficult to systematically combine the knowledge from these surveys as the results depend on the particular way questions are phrased, the breadth of the categories used and the use of overlapping categories (e.g. listening skills and interpersonal skills). For our purposes, we have been guided by the surveys but have focused on those attributes that seem to be most relevant to performance management. We have also excluded from our discussion general areas, such as leadership and management, which, while important, apply to all those involved in performance management.

Technical skills

Technical finance skills are regarded as a given for finance professionals. Their training is rooted in the generation and use of accounting information for analytical and decision-making purposes. This includes deciding on the appropriate accounting treatment of sometimes complex business transactions. Inappropriate treatment will provide misleading performance information and faulty decisions. Even basic errors such as failure to accrue for costs incurred or capitalising operational costs can inflate actual performance and result in the continued investment in loss making products and services.

As we have seen earlier, a range of strategic and financial tools and techniques will also be at the disposal of a successful finance professional. This enables them to choose the right tool for the job. For example, costing techniques include standard costing, activity-based costing and target costing each with its own advantages and disadvantages.

Analytical skills

In the information era, with the buzz/hype around big data and analytics, analytical skills seem to be in high demand (Davenport and Patil, 2012). Analytical skills go beyond technical skills and include the ability to identify and structure performance problems and challenges, take a range of perspectives in assessing problems, apply various tools and techniques in order to highlight possible solutions based on the best evidence available and combine this with organisational knowledge to recommend courses of action (ICAEW, 2014). Effective finance professionals will have highly developed analytical skills obtained through both classroom learning and experience of carrying out various forms of analyses throughout their careers. Particular strengths should lie in taking an objective and holistic view of the organisation and connecting strategic and operational variables with financial performance. However, finance professionals have been faulted for underplaying the importance of qualitative variables (such as customer satisfaction) and hidden internal costs (such as wasted management time when clerical support staff are made redundant).

Communication and influencing skills

Excellent analysis counts for little unless it is communicated effectively, and the importance of communication skills features highly in practitioner surveys (e.g. ICAEW/Robert Half, 2011). And, while effective communication is relevant to all disciplines involved in performance management, successful finance professionals face specific challenges. Rightly or wrongly, accountants have been criticised for lacking communication skills (Siriwardane and Durden, 2014). If this stereotype persists in the minds of other managers, finance professionals may have to work doubly hard to overcome this bias.

In addition, the communication of financial information, which is often based on accounting concepts others find difficult to grasp, requires particular skills. These include the ability to know what technical assumptions are decision-relevant and to explain necessary accounting concepts without using technical jargon. It is often a difficult judgement call to know how much detail to provide, particularly as different users of financial information will have different preferences and needs. For example, an experiment by Hirsch, Seubert and Sohn (2015) found that "managers perform poorly when only provided with tables, and they achieve the overall best score when provided with both tables and graphs, whereas students perform similarly in both conditions". Sometimes, what seem like small details can have a major effect, such as the interest rate assumptions used in a discounted cash flow analysis for an investment decision.

Clearly, the communication skills required may be oral or written, but it is worth noting that finance professionals should be particularly adept in developing financial tables and presenting information visually such that the information is understood as easily and quickly as possible. Participating in decision making and driving effective performance management processes also require well-developed influencing skills. For example, many performance management processes, such as budgeting, are fraught with politics and the pursuit of individual interests. As a result, finance professionals need to use their influencing skills to tease out information that managers may prefer to keep to themselves, gain acceptance of stretching targets and ensure that organisational objectives take precedence over parochial ones.

Business understanding and commercial acumen

Business understanding is essential if finance professionals are to make the most of the other skills and attributes we have discussed (Scapens *et al.*, 2003).The way in which the business works (or could be made to work) provides the context for the selection, implementation and use of performance management processes, financial tools and analytical outputs. Moreover, it is difficult to see how others will be influenced by finance if they do not ground their arguments and proposals in the realities of business circumstances, internal and external.

The related attribute of commercial acumen is also identified as highly important for successful finance professionals (Hays, 2014, 2015). The term is interpreted broadly to mean focusing on business objectives, such as profitability, rather than dogmatically sticking to bureaucratic processes. It should be borne in mind that managers sometime accuse finance departments of not being commercial because finance has vetoed a manager's project or investment proposal. This ignores the fact that the finance professional's role in "saying no" to financially damaging initiatives is an important part of being commercial. Furthermore, we should not underestimate the power of contributing to performance management informed by commercial acumen on the increased demand it creates from managers to involve finance professionals even more intensively (Friedman and Lyne, 1997).

Backbone and integrity

Wielding influence in performance management requires backbone. New strategies, demanding targets and innovative ideas are all likely to generate resistance. Backbone, the ongoing ability to continue to stand up and argue for one's views despite opposition from powerful others, is an important part of overcoming such resistance. For example, Lambert and Pezet (2010) show how finance professionals had to overcome stress and stand firm in order to maintain their influence.

Such backbone can be particularly important when ethical issues are at stake and finance professionals need to act with integrity. For example, finance professionals can find themselves pressured to report results in ways that present a misleadingly favourable view of the performance of the managers they work with. Sometimes, a fine line needs to be found as best illustrated by the following quote:

> If (the manager) tells me that "Yes, we've understood it, we know that it's financial suicide, but there are other goals that play a role, so let's do it!" – then I may go along sometimes. But what I cannot do is bow my head and say: "Okay, guys, I'll do the calculations and give you what you want."
>
> *(CFO quoted by Weber and Nevries, 2011, p. 28)*

It will be interesting to see how the Volkswagen (and other car manufacturers identified since) emissions scandal plays out and the degree to which PMS drove unethical behaviour and how many people knew about the manipulation of data but did not have the backbone to deal with the issue before it became public.

It is worth noting that accountants who are members of professional bodies are bound by ethical codes set by their institutions and generally follow the International Federation of Accountants' *Code of Ethics for Professional Accountants*™ (IFAC, 2015). These set out guidelines and requirements in relation to integrity, objectivity, professional competence and due care, confidentiality and professional behaviour. Such guidelines are important and helpful, but acting with integrity also requires sound ethical reasoning and the courage to act (ICAEW, 2007).

The above discussion highlights the challenge for finance professionals in developing a broad range of skills and a depth of business understanding in order to contribute to performance management. Moreover, this is not a one-off exercise – technical and specialist skills need to be kept up to date in the face of changing accounting rules and new financial techniques. Maintaining an understanding of the business and the drivers of performance requires ongoing commitment in the face of changing markets and technological developments.

Relational drivers

While the above drivers of successful finance departments focus on the individual attributes of finance department team members, other drivers relate to the way in which finance departments and other departments work together.

Trust

Working effectively with other managers on performance management requires mutual trust (Granlund and Lukka, 1998a; Burns and Baldvinsdottir, 2005). Trust can be viewed as perceived credibility or the firm belief in the reliability or ability of someone. It contributes to success in part because trust reduces perceived risk and the need to check information for oneself, and thereby leads to smoother processes and decisions taken more rapidly with greater confidence.

There are two defining elements of trust that characterise the relationship between managers and finance staff – trust in an individual's competence and trust in an individual's integrity. We have discussed above some of the skills and attributes that will be necessary for managers to trust in a finance professional's competence. This includes a technical element of trust that finance professionals have the proper knowledge of tools and techniques. For example, if a manager has to make a decision between two investment alternatives, he or she needs to rely on the finance person to apply the correct methods of calculating firm values, discount rates, etc.

Building trust in one's integrity is more complex. Important factors include fulfilling promises, being honest and acting in accordance with moral expectations (ICAEW, 2007). However, finance professionals can find themselves in difficult positions that make it difficult to be trusted by all relevant stakeholders in performance management. For example, embedded controllers can be accused of being "head office spies" by business divisions and "too close to the business" by head office.

Trust is built over the long term but can be destroyed quickly (e.g. Child, 2001). In other words, managers begin to trust finance professionals when they repeatedly receive accurate reports, delivery on commitments and honest answers to questions. As trust grows, managers will ask for greater input to performance management issues from finance teams that can increase trust still further (Lambert and Sponem, 2012). However, one slip can quickly undermine a relationship.

Collaboration and customer orientation

Collaboration refers to two or more organisational units or people working together to produce an outcome. Such working together on joint goals makes for more intense learning than a service relationship, where finance departments may simply provide reports and information. More specifically, a high level of collaboration provides the finance department with insights into specific internal customer needs, and provides the means to adapt and deliver customised services.

Studies have demonstrated that collaboration within finance, i.e. between controllership departments, management accounting service providers and internal audit, and with other functions such as strategy departments, has a positive impact on the service quality of the finance department (see Birl, 2007; Knollmann, 2007). Team working is seen by operational managers as an important means of improving the quality and relevance of financial information and also reducing the perception gap where finance professionals place a higher value on the information they provide and the techniques they use compared to their internal customers (Pierce and O'Dea, 2003). The collaboration necessary to introduce activity-based techniques, such as activity-based costing, and the resulting improvement in management information has been shown to improve relations between management accountants and operational managers, and increase the influence of accountants in decision making (Friedman and Lyne, 1997).

Collaboration between finance professionals and managers is more likely if finance demonstrates customer orientation (Weber and Nevries, 2011). Marketing research has shed many lights on the importance of customer orientation, both for the supplier to ensure future demand and for the customer to gain optimally designed products. As an internal supplier, finance departments can apply this research in supporting managers in their performance management objectives. For example, it is important for finance staff to understand the preferences and personalities of their customers. Why? Because different personalities, different levels of expertise, and different viewpoints and motivations mean that each manager perceives finance products and services differently. A report containing detailed financial tables and calculations may appeal to a number-driven type of person but not to a manager who prefers concise and written interpretation. More specifically, Cardinaels (2008) showed experimentally that those with a low level of cost accounting knowledge made better decisions when presented with graphs rather than tables and that conversely those with a high level of cost accounting knowledge made worse decisions using graphs.

Taken together, the levels of trust, collaboration and customer orientation are important factors in determining the success of finance departments. Where they are sub-optimal, finance's attempts to improve performance can be misguided (Nor-Aziah and Scapens, 2007). However, when in place, they can ultimately lead to finance departments achieving what Weber and Nevries (2011) call "The Next Level" of co-creating services. We will highlight this potential in the conclusion and outlook section.

Are finance professionals in control of their role in performance management?

Our discussion so far shows that skilled finance professionals should be able to make a significant contribution to performance management. However, for this contribution to materialise such skills need to be combined with a desire and commitment to making the most of them. For example, Burns and Baldvinsdottir (2005) highlight the importance of individual proactivity in the case of a financial manager who gained significant organisational influence over strategy and performance management, and Goretzki *et al.* (2013) show how a new CFO played an important role in driving a broader business involvement of finance professionals as they moved to a business partnering approach.

This need for proactivity shows that the involvement of finance professionals in performance management is by no means a given and we need to consider the organisational environment in which they work. For example, Wolf *et al.* (2015) show that management expectations play a key role in determining the involvement of controllers in business decisions. Borrowing the term munificence from the characterisation of external markets (Dess and Beard, 1984) and applying it internally are a helpful approach. For our purposes, internal munificence describes an organisation's internal market and the extent of generosity and support given by the organisation as a whole to the finance department. In situations of low internal munificence, the finance department's activities may be constrained and make it difficult for finance to serve its internal customers effectively. For example, finance departments will find it difficult to garner the necessary investment in people, systems and processes in order to contribute effectively to performance management (Byrne and Pierce, 2007). Indeed, finance departments may find themselves supplanted by internal competitors and so called "shadow accountants" (Shank, 2006) or outsourced service providers (Bhimani and Willcocks, 2014). Furthermore, managers may actively resist finance involvement because it entails giving up power. For example, Ezzamel and Burns (2005) discuss the failure of finance managers to strengthen their influence when buyers and merchandisers successfully resisted the introduction of stricter controls and EVA™. Conversely, high internal munificence facilitates the growth and development of finance departments such that they can contribute more to performance management.

Has the role of the finance professional in performance management increased over time?

Many commentators continue to claim that the influence of finance professionals in areas of performance management, such as strategy, has increased (e.g. Wolf *et al.*, 2015). However, the empirical evidence is scant. We are not aware of any large-scale surveys taken at two points in time that would support the argument. There is some support for the claim from longitudinal case studies. Järvenpää (2007) studied a large Finnish-based division of a large global group between 1995 and 2001, and found that a wide range of cultural and other interventions supported an increase in the business orientation of the finance department. Similarly, Goretzki, Strauss and Weber (2013) examined how controllers in an international manufacturing firm, headquartered in Germany, gained legitimacy as business partners over a 17-year period. At a UK manufacturing arm of a global network in the pharmaceuticals industry, from the mid to late 1990s, Burns and Baldvinsdottir (2005) witnessed the development of "hybrid accountants", who combined technical accounting roles with involvement in strategic and operational decision making.

Although other studies point to significant involvement of finance professionals in performance management, the methodologies only show the role at a point in time and cannot demonstrate change, although Vaivio and Kokko (2006) make a case for no longer being able to fully identify the "bean counter" role in Finland, while earlier Granlund and Lukka (1997) had done so. Particularly interesting is Lambert and Pezet's (2011) study in a French car parts manufacturer in that it identifies a case where the influence of finance professionals may be too great. Based on survey research, Graham, Davey-Evans and Toon (2012) argue that "the role of the financial controller has not transformed in recent years, but has instead enlarged, incorporating more 'forward looking elements' concerned with the management of the whole business" (p. 71). As well as being a point in time, some of the studies are very old (e.g. Simon *et al.*, 1954; Gerstner and Anderson 1976; Sathe 1983) indicating that the role of finance professionals in PMS has been established for some time and change is more about how such influence is wielded. Our interpretation of the evidence is that there is no identifiable trend of accounting professionals increasing their influence in performance management. Rather, it seems that some companies make more extensive use of finance professionals in performance management depending on the factors discussed in the section above.

Career paths of finance professionals including country differences

> The perfect finance person has mastered the technical, they're strong on the interpersonal, they have worked in different countries and done operational roles and seen finance from the other side of the fence.
>
> *(Andy Halford, former CFO of Vodafone, EY, 2010)*

Career paths matter because the experience that finance professionals develop over the course of their careers significantly impacts the degree to which they can contribute to performance management and control. The career paths to the top finance job in organisations, i.e. CFO or Finance Director, vary significantly, particularly when we compare different countries. The main lesson for those wanting to recruit finance professionals to help with performance management is to avoid stereotyping because finance professionals bring a broad skill set (see above). Below we consider some typical career paths.

While a first degree is not a requirement for a successful finance career, most CFOs of large companies today have been to university (the Hays, 2014 survey in Australia and New Zealand shows a figure of 99 per cent and the Hays, 2015 survey in the UK shows a figure of 66 per cent). This may or may not mean a degree in finance, accounting or commerce. In the USA, nearly all states require a significant number of accounting credits at university level to enter a Certified Public Accountant (CPA) programme. The focus of UK professional qualifications is more about studying while working with no specific degree requirements. In Germany (and other Continental European countries), aspiring finance professionals tend to select a specialised university major in financial accounting, finance or management accounting/controlling depending on the type of role they are aiming for. Thus, for all specialisations within the finance department, a university degree is expected (Ahrens and Chapman, 2000); professional qualifications such as chartered or certified accountancy represent a niche market. It is also worth noting that while some professional accounting bodies such as the Association of Chartered Certified Accountants (ACCA), American Institute of Certified Public Accountants (AICPA) and the Institute of Chartered Accountants in England and Wales (ICAEW) are broadly based and support their members throughout their varied careers, others, such as the Compaignie Nationale des Commissaires aux Comptes (CNCC) in France, focus on auditing only.

One of the key differences in early career paths is that between initially joining an accounting practice as opposed to the finance department of an organisation. In the UK and commonwealth countries, many finance professionals start off as auditors before moving into business (Hays, 2014, 2015) – this can be immediately after qualifying through to making it to partner and then moving directly into a CFO role. The advantages of an audit training include seeing the operations of many businesses, analysing business processes and developing project management skills. Those moving straight into a finance department develop an early understanding of the finance needs of line managers and an in-depth understanding of a particular business.

The next major difference is whether finance professionals build a career within the finance department or spend time working in different functions or general management roles. Finance departments offer a wide range of possibilities some of which are shown in a typical finance career track below (Figure 9.2). The finance career track continues to dominate in most countries (EY, 2010; Hays, 2014, 2015; Spencer Stuart, 2015). As well as specifically performance management-oriented roles, experience gained in investor relations, treasury and corporate finance (including mergers and acquisitions) would all be particularly relevant.

Experience in general management, strategy and operations is not uncommon for Group CFOs, and some see this as growing in importance (EY, 2011; Spencer Stuart, 2015). Gaining a different perspective on business through an operational role is likely to be highly valuable in contributing to performance management and empathising with line managers. Other factors to consider in how well finance professionals can contribute to performance management include international experience and industry knowledge. Surveys show quite a variation between countries, with 37 per cent of UK CFOs having worked outside their home country (Hays, 2015), 50 per cent of USA Fortune 100 CFO external hires (Russell Reynolds, 2012) and 57 per cent of Australia/New Zealand CFOs (Hays, 2014). The majority of organisations look for in-depth industry knowledge (Russell Reynolds, 2012), but others may see the benefit of bringing in new ideas from a different sector – with maybe the tech sector being in particular vogue at the moment.

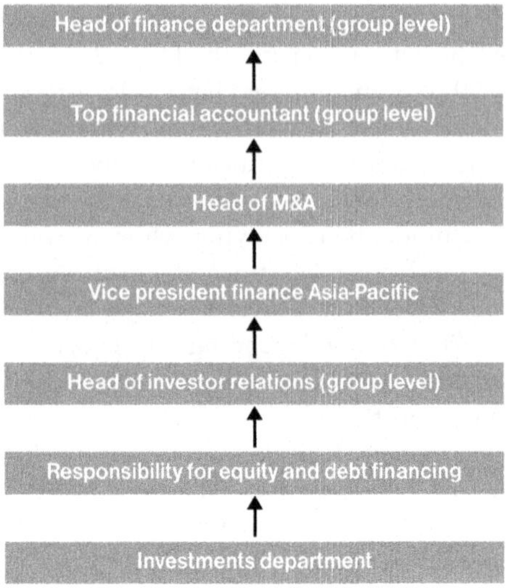

Figure 9.2 Typical career path in the finance function
Source: Adapted from Weber and Nevries 2011, p. 41.

Conclusion and outlook

This chapter has shed light on the multitude of important impacts finance professionals have on performance management and control. We built on the performance management control framework outlined by Ferreira and Otley (2009) to analyse the breadth of influence that goes beyond reporting and analysis to include commercial and strategic decision making. In many companies, they manage the strategy process and draw on strengths such as finance knowledge, relative objectivity and down to earth rationality. To help our understanding of how an optimal contribution can be made, we outlined the most substantial drivers of creating a strong and successful finance department. Only skilled, willing finance professionals who engage in collaborative and customer-oriented services will have the chance to develop their full potential in helping to manage and control performance in companies.

The finance profession and accounting has been adept at drawing on other bodies of expertise (Miller, 1998) and adopting new technologies (ICAEW, 2013) in order to adapt to change. This will need to continue if finance professionals are to maintain and develop their role in performance management and control. For example, Kaplan has argued that for finance professionals to take advantage of advances in analytics they will "require extensive training in modelling, multivariate statistics and econometrics" (Sharman, 2008, p. 20). It will be interesting to see whether so-called data scientists challenge the position of finance professionals as leading analysts in organisations. Furthermore, even though the claims around artificial intelligence, robotics and automation may be inflated, especially in the short term, they do suggest that the jobs of many knowledge workers could be under threat (Frey and Osborne, 2013; Susskind and Susskind, 2015).

One response to such threats would place still further emphasis on the importance of communication skills, collaboration and customer orientation that we have already highlighted.

In this line of thinking, Weber and Nevries (2011) adapted insights from marketing research to develop an approach that enables finance professionals to co-create services (see Vargo and Lusch, 2004) with their internal customers. When co-creating services, finance professionals work closely with managers and organisational silos are broken down. Here, we are talking of collaboration at a deep level, with finance professionals and managers trusting each other enough to truly open up and address previously undiscussable issues and barriers to performance and thereby learn from previous failures and overcome personal shortcomings. This can be extremely challenging, particularly when there are significant pressures for individuals to be perceived as high performing. However, with the increasing automation of complex tasks in individual domains, competitive advantage will more and more depend on effective collaboration and co-creation across domains (Tett, 2015).

Further research

Ferreira and Otley's (2009) framework has been highly cited (592 citations according to Google scholar, June 2017) and used extensively to look at performance management processes. It could be used for further empirical research on the roles of finance professionals. For example, international, longitudinal surveys of the time spent by finance professionals on each element of the framework would provide much better evidence on whether and how the role of the finance professionals in organisations is changing. Also, as previously highlighted, the extensive research by management accounting scholars on incentives could valuably be extended to look at the role of finance professionals in the design of reward systems.

More importantly, more research is required on the impact that finance professionals and finance departments as a whole have on organisational performance and in particular how specific approaches improve or damage performance. Establishing meaningful cause and effect relationships between particular variables and organisational performance is extremely challenging; however, we believe that building such a knowledge base is important for those managing organisations and those involved in educating finance professionals.

Notes

1 The term finance professional covers a broad spectrum of job titles and activities and thus can be understood in various ways. In this chapter, we view finance professionals as employees who hold a position in the finance department, where the position may be described as management accountant, financial analyst, financial reporting, corporate planner, controller, business analyst or decision support. See Weber and Nevries (2011) for a more extensive list and description of job titles and activities. While we refer to Chief Financial Officers (CFOs), this is not in their role as members of the executive team and often the board where they inevitably play a role in all aspects of running a business. Not included is personnel specialising in tax or audit.

2 We build our reasoning on the few extant academic publications, our own empirical research and experiences in the field.

References

Ahrens, T. and Chapman, C. S. (2000).Occupational identity of management accountants in Britain and Germany. *European Accounting Review*, 9(4), 477–498.

Anthony, R. N. (1965). *Planning and Control Systems: A Framework for Analysis*. Boston, MA: Division of Research, Graduate School of Business Administration, Harvard University.

Baines, A. and Langfield-Smith, K. (2003). Antecedents to management accounting change: a structural equation approach. *Accounting, Organizations and Society*, 28, 675–698.

Bhimani, A. and Willcocks, L. (2014). Digitisation, 'Big Data' and the transformation of accounting information. *Accounting and Business Research*, 44(4), 469–490.

Birl, H. (2007). *Kooperation von Controllerbereich und Innenrevision: Messung, Auswirkungen, Determinanten* (Vol. 24). Wiesbaden: Springer.

Burns, J. and Baldvinsdottir, G. (2005).An institutional perspective of accountants' new roles – the interplay of contradictions and praxis. *European Accounting Review*, 14(4), 725–757.

Byrne, S. and Pierce, B. (2007).Towards a more comprehensive understanding of the roles of management accountants. *European Accounting Review*, 16(3), 469–498.

Cardinaels, E. (2008). The interplay between cost accounting knowledge and presentation formats in cost-based decision-making. *Accounting, Organizations and Society*, 33(6), 582–602.

Chang, H., Ittner, C. D. and Paz, M. T. (2014). The multiple roles of the finance organization: determinants, effectiveness, and the moderating influence of information system integration. *Journal of Management Accounting Research*, 26(2), 1–32.

Chenhall, R. (2003). Management control systems design within its organizational context: findings from contingency-based research and directions for the future. *Accounting, Organizations and Society*, 28, 127–168.

Child, J. (2001). Trust—the fundamental bond in global collaboration. *Organizational Dynamics*,29(4), 274–288.

Collins, J.C. and Porras, J.I. (1996). Building your company's vision. *Harvard Business Review*, 74, 65–77.

Davenport, T. H.and Patil, D. J. (2012). Data scientist: the sexiest job of the 21st century. *Harvard Business Review*, 90(10), 70–76.

Dess, G. G. and Beard, D. W. (1984). Dimensions of organizational task uncertainty.*Administrative Science Quarterly*, 29, 52–73.

Elmassri, M. and Harris, E. (2011). Rethinking budgetary slack as budget risk management. *Journal of Applied Accounting Research*, 12(3), 278–293.

EY. (2010).*The DNA of the CFO, a Study of What Makes a Chief Financial Officer*, EY.

EY. (2011). *Finance Forte: The Future of Finance Leadership*, EY.

Ezzamel, M. and Burns, J. (2005). Professional competition, economic value added and management control strategies. *Organization Studies*, 26(5), 755–777.

Ferrari vision and mission statement. (2016). Accessed March 8, 2016 from http://corporate.ferrari.com/en/about-us/ferrari-dna.

Ferreira, A. and Otley, D. (2009).The design and use of performance management systems: an extended framework for analysis. *Management Accounting Research*,20(4), 263–282.

Frey, C. B. and Osborne, M. A. (2013). The future of employment: how susceptible are jobs to computerisation. Accessed April 8, 2016 from www.oxfordmartin.ox.ac.uk/downloads/academic/The_Future_of_Employment.pdf.

Friedman, A. L. and Lyne, S. R. (1997).Activity-based techniques and the death of the beancounter. *The European Accounting Review*, 6(1), 19–44.

Gerstner Jr., L. V. and Anderson, M. H. (September 1976). The chief financial officer as activist. *Harvard Business Review*, 54(5), 100–106.

Goretzki, L., Strauss, E. and Weber, J. (2013).An institutional perspective on the changes in management accountants' professional role. *Management Accounting Research*, 24(1), 41–63.

Gosselin, M. (1997). The effect of strategy and organizational structure on the adoption and implementation of activity-based costing. *Accounting, Organization and Society*, 22, 105–122.

Graham, A., Davey-Evans, D. and Toon, I. (2012).The developing role of the financial controller: evidence from the UK. *Journal of Applied Accounting Research*, 13(1), 71–88.

Granlund, M. and Lukka, K. (1997). From Bean-Counters to Change Agents: The Finnish Management Accounting Culture in Transition. *The Finnish Journal of Business Economics*, pp. 213–255.

Granlund, M. and Lukka, K. (1998a). It's a small world of management accounting practise. *Journal of Management Accounting Research*, 10, 153–179.

Granlund, M. and Lukka, K. (1998b). Towards increasing business orientation: Finnish management accountants in a changing cultural context. *Management Accounting Research*, 9, 185–211.

Granlund, M. and Malmi, T. (2002). Moderate impact of ERPS on management accounting: a lag or permanent outcome? *Management Accounting Research*, 13(3), 299–321.

Guilding, C., Cravens, K. S. and Tayles, M. (2000). An international comparison of strategic management accounting practices. *Management Accounting Research*, 11, 113–135.

Hays. (2014). *DNA of a CFO*. Australia.

Hays. (2015). *DNA of a Finance Director.* UK.
Hirsch, B., Seubert, A. and Sohn, M. (2015). Visualisation of data in management accounting reports: how supplementary graphs improve every-day management judgments. *Journal of Applied Accounting Research*, 16(2), 221–239.
ICAEW. (2007) *Reporting with Integrity.* London: ICAEW.
ICAEW. (2011). *The Finance Function: A Framework for Analysis.* London: ICAEW.
ICAEW. (2013). *Finance in the Broadest Sense.* London: ICAEW.
ICAEW. (2014). *Finance Business Partnering: a guide.* London: ICAEW.
ICAEW/Robert Half. (2011). *Career Benchmarking Survey 2011: Business.* London: ICAEW.
IFAC. (2015). *Handbook of the Code of Ethics for Professional Accountants.* New York: IFAC.
Järvenpää, M. (2007). Making business partners: a case study on how management accounting culture was changed. *European Accounting Review*, 16(1), 99–142.
Kaplan, R. S. and Norton, D. P. (1992). The balanced scorecard: measures that drive performance. *Harvard Business Review*, 70, 71–79.
Kaplan, R. S., and Norton, D. P. (2004). *Strategy Maps: Converting Intangible Assets into Tangible Outcomes.* Boston:Harvard Business Press.
Knollmann, R. (2007). *Kooperation von Controllerbereich und Strategieabteilung: Messung, Wirkungen, Determinanten* (Vol. 26). Wiesbaden: Springer.
Lambert, L. and Pezet, E. (2011). The making of the management accountant – becoming the producer of truthful knowledge. *Accounting, Organizations and Society*, 36(1), 10–30.
Lambert, C. and Sponem, S. (2012). Roles, authority and involvement of the management accounting function: a multiple case-study perspective. *European Accounting Review*, 21(3), 565–589.
Langfield-Smith, K. (1997). Management control systems and strategy: a critical review. *Accounting, Organizations and Society*, 22, 207–232.
Langfield-Smith, K. (2008).Strategic management accounting: how far have we come in 25 years? *Accounting, Auditing & Accountability Journal*, 21, 204–228.
Miller, P. (December 1998). The margins of accounting. *European Accounting Review*, 7(4), 605–621.
Nevries, P., Kornetzki, T. and Weide, G. (2007). Characteristics of the Strategic Planning Process and the Relevance of Management Accounting: Evidence from German DAX30 Companies, working paper, WHU – Otto Beisheim School of Management.
Nor-Aziah, A. K. and Scapens, R. W. (2007). Corporation and accounting change. The role of accounting and accountants in a Malaysian public utility. *Management Accounting Research*, 18, 209–247.
Parker, R. and Kyj, L. (2006). Vertical information sharing in the budgeting process. *Accounting, Organizations and Society*, 31, 27–45.
Pierce, B. and O'Dea, T. (2003). Management accounting information and the needs of managers. Perceptions of managers and accountants compared. *The British Accounting Review*, 35, 257–290.
Russell Reynolds Associates. (2012). Where Do CFOs Come from? New York: Russell Reynolds Associates.
Sathe, V. (Winter 1983). The controller's role in management. *Organizational Dynamics*, 11(3), 31–48.
Scapens, R. W., Ezzamel, M., Burns, J. and Baldvinsdottir, G. (2003). *The Future Direction of UK Management Accounting Practice.* London: Elsevier/CIMA.
Schreyoegg, G. and Steinmann, H. (1987). Strategic control: a new perspective. *Academy of Management Review*, 12, 91–103.
Shank, J. K. (2006). 'Strategic cost management: upsizing, downsizing, and right (?) sizing'. pp. 355–379 in Bhimani, A. ed. (2006). *Contemporary Issues in Management Accounting.* Oxford: Oxford University Press.
Sharman, P. (2008). Meet Bob Kaplan, *Strategic Finance*, March pp. 19–20.
Siegel, G. (1996). *The Practice Analysis of Management Accounting.* Montvale, NJ: Institute of Management Accountants.
Simon, H. A., Kozmetsky, G., Guetzkov, H. and Tyndall, G. (1954). *Centralization Vs. Decentralization in Organizing the Controller's Department: A Research Study and Report.* New York: Controllership Foundation, Inc.
Siriwardane, H. and Durden, C. (2014). The communication skills of accountants: what we know and the gaps in our knowledge. *Accounting Education*. 23(2), 119–134.
Spencer Stuart. (2015).*CFO Route to the Top 2015*, London: Spencer Stuart.
St. John's Ambulance vision and mission. (2016). Accessed March 15, 2016 from www.sja.org.uk/sja/what-we-do/vision—mission-and-values.aspx.

Stone, R.A. (1996). Mission statements revisited. *SAM Advanced Management Journal*, 61(1), 31–37.

Susskind, R. and Susskind, D. (2015). *The Future of the Professions: How Technology Will Transform the Work of Human Experts*. Oxford: Oxford University Press.

Tett, G. (2015). *The Silo Effect: The Peril of Expertise and the Promise of Breaking Down Barriers*. London: Little Brown.

Vaivio, J. and Kokko, T. (2006). Counting big: re-examining the concept of the bean counter controller, business. *Aikakauskirja LTA*, 49–74.

Vargo, S. L. and Lusch, R. F. (2004). Evolving to a new dominant logic for marketing. *Journal of Marketing*, 68(1), 1–17.

Weber, J. and Nevries, P. (2011).*Drivers of Successful Controllership: Activities, People, and Connecting with Management*. New York: Business Expert Press.

Weber, J., Nevries, P., Christoph, I., Pfennig, C., Rambusch, R. and Spatz, A. (2007). *Controlling und Strategie*, Advanced Controlling Series, Weinheim: Wiley.

Weber, J. and Schaeffer, U. (2008). Introduction to Controlling, Stuttgart: Schäffer-Poeschel.

Wilson, I. (1992): Realizing the power of strategic vision. *Long Range Planning*, 5, 18–28.

Wolf, S., Weißenberger, B. E., Wehner, M. C. and Kabst, R. (2015). Controllers as business partners in managerial decision-making: attitude, subjective norm, and internal improvements. *Journal of Accounting & Organizational Change*, 11(1), 24–46.

Zoni, L. and Merchant, K. A. (2007). Controller investment in management: an empirical study in large Italian corporations. *Journal of Accounting and Organizational Change*, 3(1), 29–43.

10

The role of strategic planning

A case study in UK higher education

Elaine Harris and Mark Ellul

Introduction

This chapter provides a reflective account of the changing role of the planning department in the performance management and control (PMC) of a relatively small UK university. We define PMC as a set of management practices formulated to achieve an organisation's strategic goals and shape its strategic direction. While responsibility for performance measurement has generally been seen as that of the finance function of an organisation (ICAEW, 2009), the widespread use of balanced scorecards (Kaplan and Norton, 1996) and competitor analysis (Porter, 1990) has expanded the need for more non-financial data. In some sectors such as Higher Education (HE), the strategic planning team is being tasked with addressing this need (Lerner, 1999), though research on this aspect of PMC is limited (see Seneviratne and Hoque's Chapter 24 in this volume). What we explore in this chapter through an illustrative case study is the role of planning in relation to other parties and how that has changed over a 5-year period.

Both of the authors were employed in the case organisation during the period of the study (2010–2015), during which the title, role and responsibilities of the Director of Planning (DOP) changed, so it can be seen both as a longitudinal case study and as participatory action research. The methodology is based on a combination of documentary analysis and a series of loosely structured conversations between the authors around the themes of strategic planning and decision-making processes, organisational structure and the implementation of key performance indicators (KPIs). It differs from many other management control case studies as it places the spotlight on the role of the planning department and on the DOP.

This case is the result of participation in action research based on Elden and Levin's (1991) co-generative learning model, with the dual outcomes of a new shared understanding to enhance organisational learning as well as the production of an academic output. Rather than presenting a hierarchical organisation chart to show the position of strategic planning, an actor network is presented that places strategic planning in the centre of a web of professional relationships. However, we do not claim to have used actor network theory as we have not interviewed other actors in the organisation. The role analysis has been based on Sharrock's (2012) adaptation of Quinn *et al.*'s (2007) eight management roles in a mixed economy university setting, based on four Australian universities. This provides a somewhat structural and technical analysis, which is followed by an analysis of the strategic planning process using Ferreira and Otley's (2009) framework (see Figure 9.1, page 160).

The main aim of the chapter is to present an insight into the changing role of strategic planning in an HE setting during a period of unprecedented change, through the eyes of two of the actors involved in the organisation. Following this introduction, the chapter is structured in four substantive sections. First, the case study context and research methodology set the scene for the case study. The analysis is then organised into three sections providing a mapping of professional relationships in the actor network, an analysis of the principal activities and responsibilities (the management roles), and the answers to eight questions on PMC based on Ferreira and Otley's (2009) framework (see Figure 9.1). Conclusions are drawn about the changing role of planning in the delivery of the institution's goals. Due to the particular role of literature in an action research study, as an integral part of the learning and as a means of making sense of the action, it is interwoven with the analysis of professional practice.

Case study context and research methodology

The case organisation is a relatively small university situated in a beautiful parkland campus in London with a long history (175 years) at the forefront of early years' education. It has retained the ethos that came from its four constituent colleges, having strong links with churches (Catholic, Church of England, Methodist and Ecumenical) and a concern for the social and spiritual well-being of its students through its evolution into a modern university (Watson, 2010).

The case study begins in 2010, when both of the authors were appointed to newly defined senior management roles (following a restructuring of the university into ten academic units and a centralised administration). This chapter explores the changing role of the centralised planning team from the dual perspectives of its leader and a member of the Business School professoriate, captured through a series of recorded one-to-one discussions and email exchanges. These personal reflections have been analysed together with relevant documentary evidence such as job descriptions and specifications, the strategic plan (2014–2019), progress reports and KPIs. No other members of the university were interviewed or directly involved in this action research project, but the account presented here has been shared with and verified for factual accuracy by the relevant Pro Vice-Chancellor (PVC) and Director of Finance (DOF).

Meetings lasted a little over 60 minutes, and the themes that provided a focus for discussions were as follows:

- changes in the job role from the Head to DOP,
- role of the planning team and relationships with significant groups of actors,
- development of the university strategic plan and a set of corporate KPIs,
- monitoring operational performance through departmental KPIs,
- performance management and the changing HE environment.

Analysis of the records of these meetings and the documents specified above took place between the meetings, and the content (i.e. tables and figures) was shared and confirmed as the project progressed. Drafts of the chapter were considered by the authors and reviewed over a period of 12 months, then shared with the PVC and DOF to whom the DOP reports for comment and verification of factual content. Academic literature cited in the chapter was also shared and discussed either in the meetings or in email exchanges to support the analysis.

The work was guided by principles of action research (McNiff and Whitehead, 2002; Harris, 2008; Coghlan and Brannick, 2010). We adopted McNiff and Whitehead's (2002, p. 15) definition of action research as "a particular way of researching your own learning". The study aimed to analyse changes in PMC practice over the 5 years from the personal perspective of two organisational members for the purpose of professional development and continuous improvement. Linking theory and practice in this analysis enabled suggestions for future action and possible changes to benefit the organisation as well as contributing to the wider academic community (Harris, 2008, p. 17).

Doing action research in your own organisation presents certain advantages, not least in terms of access to relevant, contextual, informal and sometimes confidential or privileged data, but also presents challenges in terms of authenticity, disclosure and lack of anonymity (Coghlan and Brannick, 2010, pp. 123–124). No confidential data are presented here, as the focus of this research is on the process of performance management and on changing management practice of the DOP rather than on an evaluation of the organisational performance itself. We made a decision to co-author the account of our shared sense-making. We decided not to interview others to avoid complex issues of anonymity.

As part of the new centralised administration of the university in 2010, the planning team technically sat within the finance function, with the Head of Planning (as the job title was) reporting to the DOF. The purpose of the Head of Planning role was defined in 2010 as to

> "Lead a team dedicated to providing services supporting the delivery of the University's strategic objectives". This included "supporting the senior team in developing the University's new Strategic Plan and monitoring performance against targets". It went on to specify "The Head of Planning will be responsible for leading and managing the Planning Team within the Finance department".

The title, grade of post and role changed in 2014 to Director of Planning, reporting to the PVC and DOF, whose responsibility included oversight of estates, library and learning services as well as the finance and planning functions. Since January 2014, the number of staff had expanded from 4 to 11 and was positioned alongside the finance function, with a newly appointed Head of Finance leading the adjacent department, both reporting to the same PVC and DOF.

The role still covered planning, analysis and data provision, supporting decision making and risk management, but had been extended to cover student target setting, statutory returns, management of the timetabling department, the workload planning model, responsibility for student surveys (e.g. module evaluations and first destinations), policy analysis and "contribution to the governance and leadership of the University". Part of the purpose of the role has been redefined as follows:

> To align strategic planning across academic and professional service departments; leading on target setting, monitoring, and assessment of departmental and institutional performance and provide a focal point within the University for support of initiatives and projects.

Mapping professional relationships

The new strategic planning role had expanded the areas and level of responsibility, essentially from a data management role to a senior management role, having interaction with a greater variety of internal and external parties, which made relationship management a key skill. Figure 10.1 shows the position of strategic planning within an actor network. The nature of each relationship is analysed below, taking each group in turn anti-clockwise. The size of the "bubbles" in the diagram represents the relative importance and frequency of the interactions between the DOP and others.

The actor network is defined here as the web of institutional relationships between the strategic planning team and the groups of actors they engage with in their professional practice. Most groups are also organisational members, including functional teams such as finance. Of the twelve groups, including the planning team, nine are internal and three stretch beyond organisational boundaries to planners in other HE institutions (competitors), non-executive members of the governing body and government agencies. The nature of interactions between the DOP and the groups identified is explained below. The DOP (co-author) was placed in the centre, and the Director of the Business School (lead author) was one of ten heads of academic departments.

Senior management team

The group called the Financial Strategy Group (FSG) comprised the Vice-Chancellor (VC), PVC and DOF, Deputy Vice-Chancellor (DVC) and the Registrar, met weekly to consider the whole management agenda, not just financial matters, to which the DOP was asked to report periodically and on an ad hoc basis. The contact with members of this group

Figure 10.1 Position of SP in the actor network

(individually and as a group) was of great importance, so took priority over almost everything else. This reflected the turbulence in the HE environment and the greater appetite for information shown by the particular post-holders, especially the DVC (in post from 2012) in making decisions related to the academic portfolio, the curriculum and recruitment activities. The physical location of members of the DOP's team close to members of the senior management team was critical to good working relationships.

Academic departments

There was not much formal contact beyond the monthly meetings of Senate (the highest-level academic committee comprising the VC, provosts, registrar, heads of academic and service departments and elected staff and student representatives). However, the DOP had almost daily contact with academic leaders at various levels on a less formal basis. This increased after the DOP took over responsibility for timetabling and workload planning.

Academic support departments (Registry, library, IT student services, etc.)

The planning function worked with Registry and Admissions in order to submit statutory returns. The Academic Registrar remained the owner of student data, but the planning team was responsible for pulling the data together to submit to statutory (government) bodies. The planning team worked closely with the data owners to ensure that all data represented the most accurate picture of activities. The need for accurate data was emphasised by the linkage between the statutory returns made and funding and the usage of data to create metrics that formed the university's Key Information Set (KIS), its "league table positions" and will be used in new initiatives like the Teaching Excellence Framework (TEF). The planning unit also supported other service departments by disseminating key information such as student numbers and survey results in order to improve the level of service offered to students. The DOP team also worked closely with IT to ensure that the systems were kept up to date and fit for purpose to ensure the provision of accurate information in an accessible format.

Estates

This function had responsibility for timetabling in 2010. The timetabling team moved from estates into the planning department in 2014. It was (and to some extent still is) an area of high staff sensitivity throughout the university. The process was becoming more effective from a management control perspective, as it became integrated with student numbers planning and staff workload planning. It may not have been so popular with academic heads who perhaps felt a loss of autonomy in terms of staff activity management, but that had started prior to the move (with a new workload policy being devised and negotiated with the unions). The planning team became responsible for producing the room utilisation returns to Higher Education Statistics Agency (HESA), so interaction with estates was mainly to input to the estates management report and to deal with extra-curricular room allocations handled by the conferencing and events team.

Finance

There was regular interaction between these two "sister" departments, again with the planning team providing student forecast and registration numbers to allow finance to make the link with student loan data and update revenue forecasts and cash flows. They also worked together on the "What if? scenarios" to support strategic decision making.

Human resources

The main interaction was to compile the annual staff return to HESA. The accuracy of staff numbers and classifications (e.g. support staff, academic staff, subject areas, qualifications) impacted on both internal and published measures such as staff student ratios (SSR) that in turn impacted on league table positions. The DOP sat on the phase one project group to design a new human resources (HR) information system, so the level of interaction was higher during that time. Another ad hoc link with HR was over staff union matters such as the academic staff workload policy and information, the responsibility for which the DOP took on (from a timetabling management perspective). The planning unit worked with HR on annual reports in relation to equality and diversity data related to staff. In addition, the planning team worked closely with HR, providing data collection and analysis expertise in developing staff surveys.

Marketing communications and recruitment

The frequency of interaction between the DOP and the heads of these two marketing functions was at least weekly, almost daily, mainly on the subject of student numbers in relation to applications and enrolments identifying areas of strength and weakness, especially at key times in the annual cycle, reporting actual against target student numbers. As this was driving the main revenue stream, it was the single most critical KPI the university had. They worked together to produce and interpret trend analysis and benchmarking data. In addition, the units worked together to identify new markets and areas of recruitment.

Students

In 2014, the annual Destination of Leavers in Higher Education (DLHE) survey was brought in-house to be handled by the planning team after a period of time in which it had been outsourced. The new planning role also included responsibility for collecting and analysing module evaluation forms that students were asked to complete towards the end of each module. Other student surveys included an applicant survey to discover why an applicant decided to come to the university (or not), a new entrants survey conducted in the first year to see how students were settling in and a graduate survey to find out what graduates were doing ahead of the official DLHE survey which was conducted 6 months after graduation. This helped academic and service departments to gauge student satisfaction and make improvements that may have had an impact on the National Student Survey (NSS) conducted by Ipsos Mori halfway through year 3 (that appeared in the league tables and will be a key metric in the TEF).

Competitors

The direct interaction with competitors (as opposed to via HESA) was mainly through attendance at the National Planners group, where representatives of other universities met quarterly to discuss responses to government initiatives and new regulations as well as through informal networks of former colleagues. As a result of the many changes to policy in the sector, Higher Education Institutions (HEIs) found themselves unsure of what was happening or what was expected of them; therefore, informal links with others in the sector provided reassurance and insight. This networking helped to build up a number of personal contacts who could be contacted for advice, e.g. "how are you handling the x initiative at your university?" Universities compete in home and overseas markets for students but generally talked to competitors more in the HE sector than managers might in other industries. They also collaborated, for example, on solving information systems problems. It was possible to use the planners meetings to gauge how well an institution was doing vis-à-vis its competitors by how much information was given and how much was taken. Over the 5 years, the DOP felt he had moved from being a "taker" to being a "giver", e.g. by making presentations on using HESA statistics.

Board of governors (university council and its committees)

The DOP was required to attend both an annual council meeting to present the university performance against KPIs and also sub-group meetings such as the audit committee or finance and general purposes committee (FGPC) on an ad hoc basis, e.g. on risk management. He also had quite regular informal conversations with the chair of FGPC concerning matters such as student numbers. In addition to this, the DOP provided data analysis and ad hoc reports to the governors. Reports included analysis of student satisfaction, student achievement (academic outcomes) and success (employment).

Government bodies (e.g. HEFCE, HESA and NCTL)

The Higher Education Funding Council of England (HEFCE) and the National Council for Teaching and Leadership (NCTL) are government agencies responsible for the regulation and funding of universities. Together with HESA, they call for statistics from universities in the form of statutory returns, for example on student numbers (recruitment and retention). Compliance with this requirement was essential for the university to retain its status as a university and entitlement to government funding. In return, these three bodies provide the university with national statistics and competitor information, including sector league tables to inform its strategic planning. While the main interaction was annual, the nature of this relationship and the accuracy of the data provided were considered to be crucial to the future of the institution.

The nature and emphasis of this relationship had shifted over the past 5 years from one of data accuracy and compliance (giving information) to one of enhancing the institution's position in terms of funding and reputation. Benchmarking (using information received) was used to take actions to ensure that the university could be portrayed in the best light in future league tables while retaining the integrity of accurate data. While the senior team would not have regarded the university as being totally driven by league tables in what it did, many of the key measures used in league tables marry with key objectives and assisted with their wish to improve the position of the university in the published league tables that may have influenced student choice.

Government was also considered in this study as a policy-making body. This would not necessarily have featured in the diagram so much in 2010 in relation to the planning role as it was then defined, but related to the responsibility in the new job role to "lead on the interpretation of and provide guidance and recommendations on policy relating to Higher Education". The responsibility for co-ordinating responses to government white papers and consultations became that of the new Director of Communications (DOC) within the VC's office, but the setting of fees within the new government funding policy required the modelling of alternative fee levels and likely student numbers to support decision making on this key issue to forecast the impact on revenues. This work obviously also overlapped with the work of the finance function.

Management role analysis

In this section, we analyse the role of the DOP using Quinn *et al.*'s (2007) framework. The framework was developed for eight general management roles: Director, Producer, Co-ordinator, Monitor, Facilitator, Mentor, Innovator and Broker. Sharrock (2012, p. 333) positioned two roles into each of four quadrants in a two-by-two matrix using the dimensions of inward or outward looking and flexibility versus stability. On the inward looking side of the matrix, he paired the Mentor and Facilitator roles together as seeking flexibility, labelled *Professional Community* and the Monitor and co-ordinator roles as seeking stability, labelled *System Integrity*. On the outward looking side, he paired Innovator and Broker roles as seeking flexibility, labelled *Creative* Engagement and the Director and Producer roles as seeking stability, labelled *Sustainable* Enterprise. He then added six indicative tasks to each of the eight roles for university management. In Table 10.1, we have used Sharrock's university-specific framework to analyse the role of strategic planning in university PMC by taking extracts from the DOP job specification and matching illustrative activities and university performance measures to the indicative tasks identified by Sharrock (2012, pp. 333–335).

Table 10.1 Quinn's management role analysis

Quinn's management roles and indicative tasks	*Extracts from DOP job specification*	*Illustrative activity/relevant university performance measures*
Director Highlight the risks and opportunities faced by the enterprise	• Ensure that risks spanning the university are identified from the operational and strategic planning process and managed effectively.	Through managing the risk management process for the university. Providing an annual report to Audit Committee of our assessment of institutional risks. Through analysis of data and provision of high-quality management information to inform staff and senior management of our relative performance in a range of performance measures.
Producer Use everyone's time, talent and energy efficiently	• To ensure that all departments, academic and professional services are fully supported to manage their respective areas effectively and efficiently, taking account of financial constraints.	Robust information systems have been developed to allow staff to help themselves to a range of data to answer queries efficiently and effectively. More streamlined approaches to business and operational planning have been produced with an emphasis on data-led metrics.

Quinn's management roles and indicative tasks	*Extracts from DOP job specification*	*Illustrative activity/relevant university performance measures*
Co-ordinator Use effective systems to keep programmes on track	• Lead the design, establishment and delivery of internal strategic and operational plans, providing information, advice and consultancy support to departments.	Measurement of inputs, outputs, progress: • entry qualifications and tariff, • student satisfaction, • retention (programme completion), • achievement (degree classification), • destination (employment).
Effectively combine the contributions of different work units	• Leading the timetabling team to ensure that an effective timetable is delivered to students in an efficient timeframe to maximise student and staff satisfaction.	Collate staffing, teaching and room requirements and allocate physical resources across the university: • space utilisation, • student satisfaction, • staff satisfaction.
Make sure that all contributors know what to do, by when	• Work with staff throughout the university to develop strategy that will effectively assist in enhancing performance across the university including alerting the university to new strategic opportunities. • Promote good practice throughout the university in all areas of planning, such as the value of target setting, benchmarking, monitoring and review of performance against KPIs, ensuring that this practice is embedded within every area of university operation.	Communicate timetable and process for annual planning cycle. Build relationships with key contributors across the university and communicate effectively deadlines for activities and workflows.
Keep all contributors clear on their budget limits	• Support the PVC and DOF and Head of Finance in developing and maintaining, an integrated budget and strategic planning cycle and associated processes and be a lead contributor on establishing the university's approach to future planning. • To be responsible for setting and monitoring of achievable annual intake targets to meet university academic and financial objectives and external controls and policies. • Provide detailed monitoring, forecasting and advice on student recruitment including the clearing process.	Target student number setting and monitoring: • target, forecast and actual FTE students by programme, mode, fee category and department; • feed target data into the university budgetary forecast model; • provide contributors with timely management information.

(*Continued*)

Quinn's management roles and indicative tasks	*Extracts from DOP job specification*	*Illustrative activity/relevant university performance measures*
Communicate changes to targets and schedules as needed	• Devise and champion a professional approach to strategic and operational planning which will successfully inform the future direction of the university.	Strategic, operational and business planning: • provide key information sources alongside templates for plans to be completed in, • use data to prioritise areas of improvement within a range of metrics to be addressed within plans, • maintain feedback loop with key contributors to maintain a schedule of work and activities.
Resolve conflicting priorities between different work units	• To ensure that rooms are available for corporate events to maximise the university's non-regulated income while having minimum impact on the teaching timetable.	Resolving clashes within the teaching timetable and between teaching and events.
Monitor Keep stakeholders reliably informed and up to date	• To provide strategic direction for the provision of all management Information, analysis and statutory returns, including HESA, NCTL and HEFCE data submissions. • Drive strategy through the provision and analysis of insightful data in a range of formats to meet target audience needs including the FSG, Senate, University Council and all other university committees.	Providing statistics and annual returns to external/funding agencies. Providing regular data analysis for internal stakeholders.
Follows relevant policies and procedures	• Interpret and advise on the policies, rules and initiatives of funding bodies and other appropriate bodies to ensure that the university is in the best position to respond to these and remain compliant with them.	Interprets information coming from central government and government agencies and provides advice and guidance to senior management on how best to respond, thus steering the university.
Tracks performance with suitable measures	• Monitor the achievement of university objectives and provide comprehensive reports to FSG, Council and other university committees and senior staff as appropriate. • Develop and manage analyses of externally produced indicators (e.g. HESA PIs, league tables, NSS) and produce internal briefings on our relative performance in the sector.	Provides analysis of KPIs by subject area and department against sector averages: • SSR, • student satisfaction, • spend on IT/library resources per student, • research assessment, • student achievement, • student continuation.

Quinn's management roles and indicative tasks	*Extracts from DOP job specification*	*Illustrative activity/relevant university performance measures*
Judges quality against suitable standards	• Develop and manage analyses to inform recruitment and retention strategies and support continuous review and refinement of the university's academic portfolio, including competitor and benchmark analysis. • Conduct primary market and opinion research, including the student satisfaction surveys and provide analysis and advice based on this. • To be responsible for the annual completion of university-wide evaluation of all modules undertaken by students. In conjunction with LTEU, develop the questions asked, the use of the data and dissemination of the results.	Measurement and analysis of performance against sector averages and key competitors. Student satisfaction surveys at module, programme and department levels. Measurement and analysis of performance against sector averages and key competitors.
Produces financial reporting that is timely and accurate	• To interrogate, analyse and provide an in-depth review/ audit of all of the university's statutory returns and sign off all information that is submitted to our statutory customers.	To be the first part of the financial reporting process. Feeding in student number targets into the university financial models. To review and compare financial performance indicators (FPIs) to key competitors and the sector.
Produces activity reporting that is timely and accurate	• Develop and manage a predictive model for student number target setting, including financial implications, to inform business planning scenarios and resource allocation. • To contribute to strategic direction for student data quality and those activities whereby this is monitored, and strategic assurance that student data are utilised internally and externally to maximum accuracy, timeliness and institutional advantage.	Predicting and reporting student recruitment (weekly then daily during clearing): • variances between targets and forecast. Through working with data owners in compiling statutory returns.
Facilitator Encourage people to collaborate a lot	• Ensure that the departments engage with all functions of the university to provide advice and support on-going strategic developments.	To facilitate cross-departmental working through joining up a number of university functions. To work with all departments, support and academic supporting their aims and objectives.

(Continued)

Quinn's management roles and indicative tasks	*Extracts from DOP job specification*	*Illustrative activity/relevant university performance measures*
Mentor Encourage individuals to learn and develop their careers	• Support the professional development of all team members.	Openly participate in work shadowing, mentoring and development of staff. Encouraging staff to learn and grow in their roles. Encourage staff to be involved in local, regional and national levels and to promote training and development opportunities.
Innovator Adopts up-to-date work methods and makes best use of new technologies	• Build a multi-perspective approach to horizon scanning and use established networks of contacts within the HE sector and beyond ensure that the university benefits from innovative thinking from within HE and other sectors/industries.	Work closely with internal and external (to the university) colleagues on local, regional and national stages to stay up to date with the most up-to-date working practices. To maintain good working relationships with government and government agencies to gauge and test good practice.
Broker Gain access to the meetings where key decisions are made and tap external resources	• Represent the university at a range of local, national and international initiatives, for example working and development groups.	To sit on local, regional and national, working groups, committees and development groups, both internal and external to the university. To assist government and government agencies in setting policy through working groups and consultations. To assist third parties such as Ipsos Mori in developing key initiatives such as the NSS.

While there were elements of the DOP role and strategic planning activities in each of Quinn's (2007) eight management roles, it was the co-ordinator and monitor roles where there was the greatest emphasis and a larger number of illustrative activities. The emphasis of the DOP role on Sharrock's (2012) *System Integrity* quadrant (monitor and co-ordinator) was unsurprising. While we agreed that generally the role of the DOP was about making sure that the statistical information used by the university to support its planning and control activities was accurate, complete and fit for purpose, it was not always intended to seek stability, where, for example, the benchmarking data pointed to a need for change to ensure the university maintained or improved its competitive position. Also, given the competitive landscape in HE, the monitoring role had a more external or outward looking focus, for example monitoring the university's position in the national and international league tables.

So, while we found Sharrock's (2012) indicative tasks useful to aid our analysis (in column 3 of Table 10.1), we did not find the matrix dimensions so applicable. For this reason, we stuck to Quinn *et al.*'s eight roles (in column 1 of Table 10.1). With the focus of this book on PMC, we have identified specific measures used in the case of the university (and many others) to monitor inputs, outputs and progress, for example entry qualifications (tariff) and degree classifications achieved by students, which could be combined to measure progress in terms of added value (though added value is not included in league tables as such).

The monitor role for strategic planning teams in HE was two-way, in that internal data were collected to report to both senior management in the university and external agencies, for example the main funding bodies, but then the analysis compiled by external agencies from across the sector accessed by the university was a crucial part of the market intelligence informing the university's strategic plans. One of the most crucial and newest areas of responsibility for the DOP was leading the timetabling team, allocating physical resources and co-ordinating this with staff resources (the responsibility of the academic departments). The responsibility for space utilisation used to be with the estates team, but there were issues with the co-ordination with student number planning and academic staff workload planning. The authors of this chapter were both instrumental in the decision to move this responsibility across to the strategic planning team. The move had not solved all of the issues to everyone's satisfaction (see below), but progress had been made. It gave the DOP role a higher profile within the university than it had previously and freed up the estates team to manage the huge campus development programme that started in 2014/2015.

The Innovator and Broker roles were possibly more relevant for the DOP at this university as he had greater profile in the sector networks and higher-level access to key policy makers and external agencies in the UK than other similar post-holders may have had. The raising of the job specification to a higher grade afforded the post-holder to place more importance upon the director and producer roles. With the planning team working alongside the finance team, both the DOP and DOF roles were clearly becoming more strategic as the university faced the growing challenges of a HE sector that was expected by government to become more financially self-sustaining. In terms of a critique of Quinn *et al.* (2007), we found that the eight roles lack sufficient emphasis on risk and feel risk management could be justified as the ninth role. In the next section, we analyse ways in which the DOP interacted with other actors in setting strategic goals and identifying action plans and KPIs to deliver the university's strategy.

Strategic planning and performance management practice

We adopted and adapted the set of eight functional questions from the Ferreira and Otley (2009) framework (see Figure 9.1), introduced by Dugdale in Chapter 2 of this volume (pp. 17–18), as our analysis framework for exploring PMC practice. We replaced the sixth question on target performance (so as not to disclose confidential information) with one about the current topics of debate on PMC in the organisation. As our focus of enquiry was on the role of strategic planning in PMC, these eight questions seemed highly relevant.

What is the vision and mission and how is it communicated?

The time frame of a strategic plan in a UK university has normally been 5 years (Lerner, 1999), but after an especially turbulent time in HE during the 2011–2014 cycle, where the funding model changed significantly and the uncertainties of market forces began to sink in, the university developed a new mission statement communicated in the 2014–2019 strategic plan (the following text is quoted from that document):

We support all of our students, whatever their background, to reach their full potential. We provide a personal learning experience, helping our students grow as individuals and to be responsible citizens and leaders.

We ensure our students become the sort of graduate most valued by employers: a confident, critical thinker, adaptable, open to new ideas, able to work well with people from all walks of life, and with first-class communication skills.

We are focussing on creating new knowledge and ideas that help us to understand our world and make it a better place and we ensure our research informs our teaching.

What are the organisation's key success factors?

A set of longer-term goals for 2025 was developed with two overarching aims:

- to develop successful alumni,
- to create and disseminate world-class knowledge and ideas.

The organisation's key success factors articulated in a set of eight 2025 goals covered:

1. international reputation,
2. research quality ranking,
3. student satisfaction,
4. the university rated highly as an employer by staff,
5. citizenship and place of students/graduates in society,
6. graduate employability,
7. campus environment,
8. quality of partnerships with other institutions and organisations.

What strategies and plans are adopted and what processes/activities ensure its success?

The 2014–2019 strategic plan (see below) was developed by following a process that matched well with the ten steps recommended by Lerner (1999, p. 7–8) in the strategic planning primer for HE, namely:

1. vision/mission,
2. environmental scan (i.e. strengths, weaknesses, opportunities and threats (SWOT), market forces, labour market, etc.),
3. gap analysis (between desired future and current state),
4. benchmarking (reference point from selected sample across the sector),
5. strategic issues (fundamental to achieving desired state),
6. strategic programming (goals, plans, actions/tactics),
7. emergent strategies (Mintzberg, 1994: 23–25),
8. evaluation of strategy (KPIs, monitoring),
9. review,
10. strategic thinking (embedding strategies).

In terms of a critique of Lerner's process, there was no mention of strategic facilitation, which the authors felt was part of the DOP's professional role.

What is the organisation structure and how does it affect the strategy and control?

The university had a relatively flat organisational structure, appropriate to its size and cost base. While we did not feel the presentation of a traditional organisation chart to be especially helpful here, we placed more emphasis on the actor network (mapped out in Figure 10.1). Suffice to say that there was no elaborate matrix structure or hierarchical faculty structure, but ten subject-based academic departments and a similar number of non-academic departments covering academic support (registry, library, IT and learning services, students services, etc.), estates, finance, HR and marketing. The process outlined above was initiated by the top team lead by the VC, working closely with the director of communications and DOP. When it came to step 6, the board of governors, provosts (DVC plus three deputy provosts) and departmental heads were consulted and Senate formally approved the plans.

The strategic planning process, and more specifically the annual operating plans, had moved from being a more bottom-up process pre-2014 to a more top-down process post-2014, in part due to a more challenging HE environment. There was a change of emphasis as the bottom-up process had proved too difficult to integrate, with 20 or so disparate departmental plans based on uncoordinated assumptions. It could be argued that while departments liked to have some input to the former operating plans, the plans had very little impact on the day-to-day management of departments or on actual performance, especially where so many agents (such as academics and students) seemed to have and exercise the "ability to do otherwise" (Giddens, 1979, p. 56). The top-down approach to planning may have resulted in a more coherent plan, but there were other mechanisms (for example strict budgetary control) employed to control the activities of individuals and departments (see below).

What KPIs are derived from objectives and strategy?

The strategic plan 2014–2019 had an action plan and associated KPIs in each of seven areas. Rather than listing them directly from the strategic plan, they are summarised and organised into a form of balanced scorecard (Kaplan and Norton, 1992) in Figure 10.2, as this gives a picture of the "balance" (or not) between them.

Financial	Customer
• **Financial sustainability (2 measures: EBITDA & liquidity)**	• **Student recruitment (3 measures: new subjects, market share & entry tariff)** • **Student satisfaction & retention (4 measures)** • **Graduate employability (6 measures)**
Learning & Growth	**Operating environment (replacing Internal Business Process)**
• **Staff profile & satisfaction (2 measures)** • **Knowledge creation (2 research measures: REF & funding)**	• **Campus enhancement (4 measures: 2 based on NSS & 2 campus awards)**

Figure 10.2 Balanced scorecard with 23 KPIs

There were 13 KPIs (57 per cent out of a total of 23) within the "customer" quadrant that were all about the students, that drive revenue in what Sharrock (2012) calls a mixed economy university (focused on both teaching and research). There were only two KPIs in the "financial" quadrant, but it was the student recruitment targets that impacted the most on revenue. It was the four campus-based KPIs in the quadrant typically labelled "internal business process", but labelled operating environment here that required heavy amounts of financial investment. What appeared to be missing here were measures of productivity of the main resource (academic staff time), so this is explored more below.

There may only have been four KPIs in the "learning and growth" quadrant, but the two research-based KPIs carried an exceptional amount of weight as they determined staff recruitment decisions and reward policies. If one were to expect (as management accounting text books tend to portray) a balanced scorecard to have more or less an equal number of KPIs in each of the four quadrants, it could be interpreted that our analysis shows an "unbalanced scorecard", with a range from 2 (financial) to 13 (customer) KPIs. However, we note that KPIs may not be equally weighted, for example maintaining a satisfactory earnings before interest, tax, depreciation and amortisation (EBITDA), liquidity and research excellence record were of crucial importance.

Also, the quality of the campus (our operating environment) was seen as a strong competitive factor as it has tended to attract students who have had considerable choice (around 150 HE institutions nationally, with some 20 within close proximity) and was seen as a vital investment for long-term sustainability. Even though the market for on-line or off-campus education was expanding, so many institutions wish to have a physical presence in the nation's capital city, that the demand for shared space was expected to fill any gaps that could possibly arise from recruiting fewer campus-based students. Hence, campus enhancement was seen as a relatively low-risk activity. We therefore suggest that the apparent imbalance is justified and that the term "balanced scorecard" is potentially unhelpful. The alternative term "dashboard" may be more appropriate to this case study.

What are the current topics of debate in terms of performance management and control?

The current topics of debate among academics and university management in the university (and the HE sector generally in the UK) in terms of PMC broadly fitted under the following four headings:

- Research Excellence Framework (REF) – how could changes in the rules and process recommended by the Stern (2016) report impact on PMC.
- Teaching Excellence Framework (TEF) – new process to be implemented in 2016/2017 that places greater emphasis on measures such as the NSS scores.
- Britain's proposed exit from the European Union (EU) – impact on research funding if as was expected the EU funding accessed up until exit is cut off.
- Staff recruitment, motivation, retention and individual workloads, rewards and penalties (see below) – impacted by changes in the HE environment above.

Chapter 27 in this volume written by Broadbent deals with the impact on our research of the most recent REF and Chapter 13 by Carter deals with this and workload issues, essentially arguing that the time spent by academics on research outside normal contract hours has not been measured. There was much dissatisfaction with seeing students as customers and the NSS as a flawed measure of teaching quality (see, for example, Bennett and Kane, 2014; Lenton, 2015). These debates will no doubt continue.

How is individual and group performance evaluated and with what consequences?

The ten academic departments each had a distinct set of programmes and projects, so it was relatively straightforward to set targets/KPIs derived from the university set, covering the "customer" and "learning and growth" areas, mainly based on student data (recruitment, entry tariff, retention, achievement, satisfaction, etc.) and research performance (number of publications rated from 1★ to 4★). The KPIs for the non-academic departments were obviously related to the functional areas concerned. Departmental performance was also monitored by budget variance reports, where targets were set for non-fee income such as research contract income and revenue generated from collaborative partnerships.

Individual academic staff performance was monitored annually through a performance review process, based on self-evaluation and management evaluation against agreed objectives. The objectives may have been partly suggested by individuals and partly by management to align to departmental and university priorities. There was interim monitoring based on module evaluations (student surveys), but that was not strictly attributed to individuals in the case of team-taught modules, though module conveners were held responsible for the results for their modules, both student satisfaction and achievement. The consequences for individual members of staff are dealt with in the next section. For the department, the consequences could have included a strategic review involving more scrutiny and the possible addition or closure of programmes, financial rewards or penalties in terms of increases or decreases in discretionary elements of the following year's budget, and more or less challenging target KPIs set for the next year.

What rewards and penalties follow from meeting (or not) performance targets?

There was no performance-based pay structure as such, so little opportunity for individuals to earn financial rewards for meeting objectives. However, there was a structured pay scale with an annual opportunity for those lower on the scale to apply for promotion, for example from senior lecturer positions to reader or principal lecturer positions. It was also possible for any academic staff member who was not a professor to apply at any time for promotion to professorial level. That could leave a majority of staff with little intrinsic reward for good performance. However, there was also a form of reward that was time allocation within the workload for the following year, where meeting research output targets resulted in 30–40 per cent of time being given as a research allowance. Equally if such targets were not met for 2 consecutive years, the research allowances previously given may have been taken away. It could be argued that this had greater consequence as it would have been very difficult to regain this allowance once lost. The penalty for poor research performance was therefore to be given a higher teaching load.

Poor teaching performance in an annual review normally resulted in an improvement plan at the individual level, e.g. staff training, or at the module level. If no improvement was made or the issues were more severe, it could lead to disciplinary action being taken. This could lead to written warnings and ultimately loss of position or renegotiation of the employment contract. However, this was a very time-consuming and slow process, so such decisions were not taken lightly. Evidence could be difficult to establish or justify where predominantly team performance was measured. Often, the outcome of poor performance in one role may have resulted in the allocation of (and retraining for) a different role or the restructuring of a failing part of the organisation. This situation applied across the sector, which involved working closely with union representatives and was not seen as particularly satisfactory by employees, unions or management.

In terms of the conceptual model Broadbent and Laughlin (2009) developed to build on the Ferreira and Otley (2009) framework (see Figure 9.1), the additional questions they suggested were not explicitly used in our conversations and analysis, but their models of rationality were considered in drawing the conclusions presented in the final section of this chapter.

Concluding comments

Our main aim in this chapter was to provide an insight into PMC in a university setting from a DOP role perspective and to examine how that role has evolved and how it relates to other business functions, in particular finance. The case study presented here should be interpreted in the context of the size (small) and history (merger of four colleges). We conclude that planning has developed strategically as a distinct role in PMC in this case (and in the HE sector more generally), which is both separated from the finance professional role (as a contrast to Nevries and Payne's Chapter 9) and operates alongside the finance function.

From our analysis of performance management practice in the case organisation, the design of the performance management system could be seen as following more of an instrumental rationality than a communicative rationality, using Broadbent and Laughlin's (2009) model. We argue that this transactional approach to PMC is also likely to be taken in many other HEIs in the UK given where they are in the development of strategic planning in HE and the extent of government regulation imposed on the sector. However, our analysis of the professional relationships above does show signs of a more communicative rationality at play, and a more relational approach could therefore be developed. It is clear that interviews with more organisational members would be required in order to make full use of Broadbent and Laughlin's model, which was beyond the scope of our project.

For the purposes of our participatory action research project, the Ferriera and Otley (2009) framework (see Figure 9.1) served us well. It was found to be helpful to the authors in understanding the significance of the changes made by the university. Broadbent and Laughlin's (2009) model could be employed more fully if a further case study were to be conducted. Alternative approaches to a further study might also be to use actor network theory (Callon, 1986) or strong structuration theory (Stones, 2005). A further study could usefully include more analysis of risk management practice and processes to deal with complexity and uncertainty in strategic decision making.

The case study adopted a very relational model of enquiry, but the choice of analysis frameworks and the process of sense-making resulted in a more structural and technical analysis. More critical insights could be uncovered at the departmental level and in the involvement of more colleagues in the organisation. However, the focus here on the functional aspects of strategic planning offers an insight into PMC in the context of a university that could illuminate the pathways to a deeper understanding of PMC in the HE arena.

References

Bennet, R. and Kane, S. (2014). "Students' interpretations of the meanings of questionnaire items in the National Student Survey", *Quality in Higher Education*, Vol. 20, No. 2, pp. 129–164.

Broadbent, J. and Laughlin, R. (2009). "Performance management systems: a conceptual model", *Management Accounting Research*, Vol. 20, No. 4, pp. 283–295.

Callon, M. (1986). "Some elements of a sociology of translation: domestication of the scallops and the fishermen of St. Brieuc Bay" in Law, J. (ed.) *Power, Action, and Belief: A New Sociology of Knowledge.* London: Routledge, pp. 196–233.

Coghlan, D. and Brannick, T. (2010). *Doing Action Research in Your Own Organization*, 3rd ed. London: Sage.

Elden, M. and Levin, M. (1991). "Cogenerative learning: bringing participation into action research" in Whyte, W. F. (ed.) *Participatory Action Research.* Newbury Park, CA: Sage, pp. 128–142.

Ferreira, A. and Otley, D. A. (2009). "The design and use of management control systems: an extended framework for analysis", *Management Accounting Research*, Vol. 20, pp. 263–282.

Giddens, A. (1979). *Central Problems in Social Theory*, London: Macmillan.

Harris, E. (2008). "Action research" in Thorpe, R. and Holt, R. (eds.) *The Sage Dictionary of Qualitative Management Research*, London: Sage.

ICAEW. (2009). *Finance's Role in the Organisation*, London: ICAEW Finance and Management Faculty.

Kaplan, R. S. and Norton, D. P. (1992). "The balanced scorecard: measures that drive performance", *Harvard Business Review*, Vol. 69, No. 1, pp. 71–79.

Kaplan, R. S. and Norton, D. P. (1996). *The Balanced Scorecard*, Boston, MA: Harvard Business School Press.

Lenton, P. (2015). "Determining student satisfaction: an economic analysis of the National Student Survey", *Economics of Education Review*, Vol. 47, pp. 118–127.

Lerner, A. L. (1999). *A Strategic Planning Primer for Higher Education*, California: California State University, Northridge.

McNiff, J. and Whitehead, J. (2002). *Action Research: Principles and Practice*, 2nd ed. London: RoutledgeFalmer.

Mintzberg, H. (1994). *The Rise and Fall of Strategic Planning*, London: Prentice Hall.

Porter, M. (1990). *The Competitive Advantage of Nations*, New York, NY: Free Press.

Quinn, R., Thompson, S., McGrath, M. and St. Clair, L. (2007). *Becoming a Master Manager: a competing values approach*, Hoboken, NJ: John Wiley.

Sharrock, G. (2012). "Four management agendas for Australian universities", *Journal of Higher Education Policy and Management*, Vol. 34, No. 3, pp. 323–337.

Stern, N. (2016) "Building on success and learning from experience: an independent review of the research excellence framework", UK government Department for Business, Energy and Industrial Strategy, accessed 8 August 2016 at www.gov.uk/government/uploads/system/uploads/attachment_data/file/541338/ind-16-9-ref-stern-review.pdf

Stones, R. (2005). *Structuration Theory*, Basingstoke: Palgrave.

Watson, N. (2010). *The Story of Roehampton University*, London: Third Millennium Publishing.

11

Managing ambiguity

Changes in the role of the chief risk officer in the UK's financial services sector

Anette Mikes and Maria Zhivitskaya

In the wake of the 2007–2009 financial crisis, continuing corporate debacles, and ongoing corporate governance calls for the appointment of chief risk officers (CROs) and risk management committees, it is important to understand what role risk officers do or may play. The signals are mixed. The compliance imperative requires banks and insurers to implement a firm-wide risk management framework complete with analytical models for measuring and controlling quantifiable risks, while corporate-governance guidelines advocate a 'business partner' role. How are senior risk officers to strike a balance?

According to the practitioner literature on risk management, a CRO should focus on developing fruitful interactions between risk managers and the organisation's managerial and executive layers (Economist Intelligence Unit Limited, 2010), for example by adopting the role of 'strategic business advisor' (KPMG, 2011: 27).

Indeed, the rising visibility of enterprise risk management (ERM) places demands on the risk manager to operate as a partner to business decision makers – proactively assessing and communicating uncertainty – rather than as a reactive control agent (Power, 2007). But do risk managers live up to such lofty expectations? The academic literature on ERM has recently produced a string of studies to uncover risk management *in situ*, as an organisational and social practice (Mikes, 2009, 2011; Arena *et al.*, 2010; Hall *et al.*, 2015; Kaplan and Mikes, 2016). These shed light on the political conflict that risk management practices face during their implementation as they confront pre-existing control mechanisms. For example, in Arena *et al.*'s (2010) three comparative case studies of ERM implementation in non-financial firms, there is a continuous and evolving interaction between pre-established management practices and ERM. The risk function that emerges from the process in each case is unique to its organisation. Thus, there is an important distinction between what risk managers might do and what they actually do inside organisations.

Other studies of the financial services sector have found both patterns and variation in the roles and practices of risk management functions (Mikes, 2008, 2009, 2011; Zhivitskaya, 2015).

This chapter focuses on the evolution of the roles of the CRO in the UK financial services sector. We ask the following questions:

- What underlying pressures have brought about the growth and development of risk management in financial services?
- What roles have risks managers come to serve in financial organisations?

We argue that the increasing take-up and formalisation of risk management is attributable less to its maturity and proven worth than to the increasing regulatory and corporate-governance expectations placed on risk professionals. In this context, we see not only an expectations gap opening around the role(s) of the CRO, but also significant ambiguity.

Methodological notes

Both of us have been conducting field research on risk management in the financial services industry. Although we carried out our research projects independently during 2007–2015, we crossed paths regularly and informally compared notes, discussing any complementary or conflicting findings. In the end, we found it fruitful to integrate our findings on risk management into a framework that combines a micro-focus – what risk managers actually do – with a macro-focus – what external forces make them do it.

What follows is an overview of our key findings in three categories: the external origins of internal risk management practices; the roles of the risk function; and toolmaking, alliances and the politics of risk management.

The external origins of internal risk management practices

Bank regulators have long been creating incentives for the sector to adopt ERM. Corporate-governance trendsetters, such as COSO (2004) and the Turnbull Committee (1999, revised in 2005), advocated ERM as a process that would ensure the successful implementation of strategies by any organisation (and, in fact, targeted mainly non-financial companies). Power (2007) proposed that it was the rise of the shareholder value imperative, closely related to recent corporate-governance trends, which paved the road for ERM in financial institutions. In any case, the financial crisis of 2007–2009 brought a major re-evaluation of the expectations for risk management, increasing the responsibility of both risk managers and their board-level masters in the context of an ongoing shake-up of corporate governance in banking.[1]

In particular, the Walker committee (2009), having investigated governance in the UK banking industry, focused its attention on risk management and specifically on the contribution of risk committees. Walker's review indicated the emergent importance of risk oversight and board risk committees, using the word 'oversight' 61 times in 174 pages. The review developed new expectations both of CROs and of directors overseeing risk managers.

Walker suggested, for example, that a risk committee should be created in order to advise the board on the firm's current risk exposures and its risk strategy. In order to do that, a dedicated non-executive director (NED) is needed 'to focus on high-level risk issues in addition to and separately from the executive risk committee process' (Walker, 2009: 12). One of the report's most fundamental contributions was to stir into action those major financial institutions that did not have board risk committees. Indeed, separate board risk and audit committees became the norm and, by 2015, all of the UK's ten largest banks had risk committees, compared to only two in 2008 (PricewaterhouseCoopers, 2016).

Walker's suggestion also made the separation of risk oversight from risk management explicit since non-executives, who oversee from above, by definition cannot be managing. Thus, 'risk oversight is defined as the board's supervision of the risk management framework and risk management process. Risk management is distinct from risk oversight, as it is a responsibility of a company's management team' (International Corporate Governance Network, 2010).

Walker further recommended that risk committees should be supported by a CRO 'with clear enterprise-wide authority and independence' (Walker, 2009: 12). This observation appears to have influenced how risk oversight is carried out in practice because it suggested that non-executives should be more directly involved in the risk management process, thus bringing non-executive directors (NEDs) closer to the business and giving them more responsibility for business processes. Indeed, a number of organisations (such as HSBC and Lloyds in banking, and Prudential and Zurich in insurance) have gone further and put the CRO on the board, increasing the visible power of that role.

Walker also noted that 'ideally, corporate governance and regulation of a financial entity should be mutually reinforcing' (Walker, 2009: 25). By suggesting that regulators and corporate governance should support each other, this observation brings regulators closer to the business process itself as they oversee the internal overseers more tightly. The Financial Services Authority (FSA), the UK's financial watchdog at the time, responded by promising more thorough oversight of the 'quality and effectiveness of firms' corporate governance structures' (Financial Services Authority, 2010: 9).

It is notable that it was in the aftermath of the Walker review that the FSA reoriented its discourse from risk-based regulation to risk oversight and more in-depth firm-level corporate governance. As Spira and Page observe, the FSA and legislators have refocused on internal control issues as a not-so-unusual policy response to crises and have begun emphasising the board's monitoring role (Spira and Page, 2010).

Walker's recommendations also enhanced the importance of the role of the CRO within the organisation: 'Alongside an internal reporting line to the CEO or CFO, the CRO should report to the board risk committee, with direct access to the chairman of the committee in the event of need' (Walker, 2009: 19). In response, the FSA (2010) mentioned 'oversight' in three out of ten points for the description of the CRO's role and six out of seven points in the description of the board risk committee. This demonstrates not only an increased regulatory interest in corporate governance, but also the active inclusion of the CRO in the practices of board-level risk oversight.

In April 2013, FSA was split into the Prudential Regulation Authority (PRA) and the Financial Conduct Authority (FCA). Banks, insurers and major investment firms are thus now dual-regulated. In July 2014, the PRA issued a consultation paper, 'Strengthening accountability in banking: a new regulatory framework for individuals', as a part of the response to the Parliamentary Commission on Banking Standards. The 'Strengthening accountability in banking' policy also manifests itself through the PRA's requirement that boards be responsible for 'risk appetite' and 'risk culture' – two new 'objects' of governance.

In the following section, we review the evolution of the roles of the risk management function and highlight the increasing expectations that surround risk management and the CRO as they get involved in executive-level risk oversight.

The roles of the risk function

Drawing on fieldwork carried out before, during and in the aftermath of the financial crisis, Mikes (2008, 2009, 2011) presented evidence of systematic variation in risk management practices in the financial services industry and developed the concept of calculative cultures to explain these differences. These longitudinal field studies give us a sense of the emerging roles that risk managers play in organisational control and the political challenges of doing so.

For example, according to an early survey of risk management practices in the UK banking sector (Mikes, 2008), by the time of the financial crisis, risk managers had diverse roles. The particular amalgam of these roles characterised a given organisation's risk management function. The following four roles were prevalent:

- *Compliance champion.* The risk function was focused on complying with pressing stakeholder requirements, keeping up with new regulations, and building and safeguarding the risk management framework, which determined what risks must be addressed and by whom. Senior risk officers in this role oversaw the development of risk measurement tools for each risk type in the framework and provided assurance to senior management that adequate controls and processes were in place.
- *Modelling expert.* The risk function was focused on highly sophisticated risk modelling and on delivering the most advanced measurement and compliance options from the regulatory menu. Senior risk officers spearheaded the implementation of firm-wide risk models that could give an aggregate view of a firm's financial risks, focusing on quantifiable market and credit risks.
- *Strategic advisor.* Senior risk officers gained board-level visibility and influence largely due to their command of business knowledge and their experience of what could go wrong. Their role was to bring judgement into high-level risk decisions, challenge the assumptions underlying business plans, and use traditional risk controls and lending constraints to alter the risk profile of particular businesses.
- *Strategic controller.* The risk function, having built sophisticated firm-wide risk models offering an aggregate view of the financial risks, enabled the company to operate a formal risk-adjusted performance management system. Senior risk officers presided over the close integration of risk and performance measurement, and ensured that risk-adjusted metrics were reliable and relied on. They advised top management on the absolute and relative risk-return performance of various businesses and influenced how capital and investments were committed.

The compliance champion role was ingrained in the mandate of all risk functions, both then and now. The modelling expert role has also been encouraged by regulators, today more than ever. Banks with high modelling propensity had (even before the financial crisis) developed their own internal rating models in the credit risk area and the so-called 'advanced measurement approach' to operational risks. Banks with lower modelling propensity implemented simpler risk measurement models, choosing between the prescribed 'basic' or 'standardised' approaches. But other risk-modelling practices appeared to remain optional: some banks took portfolio-level initiatives, such as active credit-portfolio management; others did not. Some linked their risk exposure measurement to fair value accounting; some did not.

The taxonomy distinguishes two parallel strategies that may confer higher strategic significance on the risk function, suggesting that the role of 'business partnering' can take either the form of 'strategic advisor' or the form of 'strategic controller'. Both roles assume high path dependency: the requisite resources and capabilities can only be obtained over time. The strategic advisor role requires an intimate knowledge of the business and what can go wrong; that is, it requires experience, attainable only through long service and a course of successes, losses and crises. The strategic controller role assumes the sophisticated risk-modelling capability foundational to risk-based performance management. However, any initiative to define what 'good performance' means in a given organisation is inherently political. Risk teams with highly advanced models and analytical talent need executive support to succeed in the world of organisational politics. That is, risk-adjusted performance measures will not work by themselves; they must be made to work. Senior risk officers with exceptional political flair and communication skills will find it easier to make risk numbers count in planning, performance management and board decisions (Mikes, 2011), but the absorption of risk-adjusted metrics, such as economic capital, into mainstream reporting, target-setting and statutory capital means that risk numbers now 'count' more readily than in the past.

Toolmaking, alliances and the politics of risk management

Research carried out at two major banks in London between 2006 and 2011 – that is, before, during and after the financial crisis – made it possible to observe how risk managers of equal ability and potential to exert influence come to have greater or lesser influence on their organisations' decision makers (Hall *et al.*, 2015). While one of the risk management groups in the study was deeply engaged in critical work throughout the company by 2011, the other was divided into two loosely connected groups specialising in distinct areas of organisational life and was largely absent from critical decision making outside these areas. How did these two executives and their teams achieve such disparate outcomes? The study identified critical competencies – toolmaking being a central one – that risk managers (and, for that matter, other types of functional executive) can develop in order to increase their chances of widespread and lasting impact. Toolmaking is the process of creating, configuring and reconfiguring tools. Risk managers who do this by incorporating not only their own expertise, but also their users' suggestions, become more influential than those who deploy tools that only they can understand. Thus, increasing the influence of risk managers involves an analysis not only of their interpersonal connections with other managers, but also of whether (and how) they construct, deploy and reconfigure tools.

It has been common in the financial services sector to lament the unreasonableness of regulators' demand for relevant yet independent risk management functions (Hall *et al.*, 2015; Stulz, 2015). But NEDs, who constitute the risk committees that the CROs are supposed to support, grapple with the same tension.

As CROs are increasingly expected to build linkages to – and ally themselves with – NEDs, it is helpful to review briefly their shared challenges and how NEDs' responsibilities shape the roles of risk managers.

In their pioneering study of the roles of NEDs, Roberts *et al.* (2005) suggested three linked sets of characteristics that NEDs should embrace: 'engaged but non-executive', 'challenging but supportive' and 'independent but involved'. This taxonomy is helpful up to a point, as balancing these inherent tensions is a defining feature of oversight, but fieldwork conducted 9 years later suggests that NEDs find it difficult to do (Zhivitskaya, 2015). The variety of the interviewees' descriptions of what it means to be a successful NED demonstrates that the intrinsic nature of the role can be quite ambiguous and is changing (Zhivitskaya, 2015), as summarised in Table 11.1.

Table 11.1 The changing role of NEDs

Category	*Traditional views*	*Emerging views*
Primary role	Friend of management	Policing management (quasi-regulator)
Interactions with management team	Only with CEO	Web of interactions with several executives
Relationship with regulators	Informal liaison with regulators	Formal interviews with regulators as part of 'close and continuous' supervision
Formal role in risk oversight	Risk is a latent concern	Risk is a formal concern discussed in a separate risk committee
Interactions with CRO	Informally motivate and encourage the CRO	Monitor, evaluate and challenge the CRO
Accountability to stakeholders	Accountable to main board	Accountable to board and accountable directly to regulators and shareholders
Scope of attention	Broad business scope (breadth, rather than depth)	Request deeper dives and undertake thematic work (both breadth and depth of attention are important)
Involvement with management team	Arm's-length oversight	More directive; active guidance of management team (e.g. remuneration)
Information-gathering methods and flows	Board reports	Board reports; external validation and check by mobilising informal contacts with management team, including CRO

NEDs display an identifiable sense of dependency on the CRO, since information flowing to the risk committee comes primarily from within the risk organisation. Therefore, it is not surprising that NEDs emphasise the need for a close link with the CRO, based on mutual respect and trust. Non-executives also tend to be particularly conscious of the danger of being kept in the dark about problems and disputes within management; they see the CRO as their 'eyes and ears' within the company structure.

CROs thus have multiple (and potentially conflicting) accountabilities. First, they are accountable to their executive management, whom they may aspire to serve as relevant and involved advisors or performance controllers. Second, they are accountable to their NEDs, who rely on them as trusted advisors ('eyes and ears') and want them to form an independent view of the business and the trustworthiness of the executive management team. Third, they are accountable to regulators, whose demands for transparency they must meet by building the relevant modelling and reporting infrastructure.

Discussion: the expectations gap

As discussed above, risk managers seem to be riding a favourable tide, both in and outside financial services, with regulators, standard setters and professional associations advocating their value. Thus, the conditions for the healthy growth of the risk management industry seem remarkably favourable. It is therefore something of a puzzle why dissatisfaction with risk management practices is so evident in recent surveys (KPMG, 2013; RIMS and Advisen, 2013). Risk managers vary widely in their satisfaction with their own progress (RIMS and Advisen, 2013), while a survey of C-suite executives found fewer than half convinced that their organisation has an effective risk management program (KPMG, 2013).

When managerial activity is specifically directed at solving a pressing problem (in this case, making the risks more visible and the firm more able to manage them), one can imagine several causes of disappointment. One is that the underlying problem is growing: the environment is (or is generally perceived to be) changing, with risks becoming more numerous, diverse and complex. Another issue arises from how risk management practices arose and, as a discipline, became overloaded with unreasonable hopes and ambitions. We see both of these issues as prevalent.

On the one hand, risk management is always playing catch-up. This view has recently been voiced by consultants who point to the 'capability gaps' opening up between 'increasing risks' on the demand side and 'existing risk management programs' on the supply side (PricewaterhouseCoopers, 2015). Critical academic studies have highlighted the supply-side growth of the risk management industry, which is drawing a seemingly inexhaustible roster of concerns into a fluid 'new class of managerial objects, namely non-existent yet possible events' (Power, 2013: 530). Under regulatory pressure, seemingly understood (if not always successfully controlled) organisational phenomena are recast into risks (non-existent yet possible events). Power (2013) illustrated this with the transformation of fraud-detection practices into fraud-risk management, indicating the increasing perimeter of concern entertained by executives in conjunction with their 'responsibilisation' for such risk. Meanwhile, new risks, such as cyber-terrorism and cyber-security, enter 'top risk agendas' (in a 2015 PricewaterhouseCoopers survey, data security and piracy risks were the second highest concern). This suggests that risk management practices will always be playing catch-up and that no amount of financial regulation can prevent future disasters.

On the other hand, risk managers in the financial services sector are being overloaded with high hopes that need to be reined in or at least critically evaluated. The highest hope is that 'mature' risk management practices drive superior financial performance. Yet this assertion awaits empirical scrutiny, and in the meantime, we have to question it as an automatic presumption on which practitioners and consultants often rely. The expectations and claims made about risk management are either too general to be meaningful, such as 'integration and coordination across risk, control and compliance functions' (Ernst & Young, 2012) or merely pretentions, such as 'cultivating a risk intelligent culture' (Deloitte, 2012). The consequence is that a certain universalism is spreading in the practitioner risk management literature, obscuring a potentially rich and varied map of practices that are nevertheless taking root.

The field studies we have reviewed suggest that the success of risk managers is contingent on their ability to forge connections with influential colleagues (such as NEDs) and to keep creating and improving tools that convey and share their own (and others') expertise. But further understanding of the political and situational enablers of risk management practices requires continuing fieldwork.

Although our chapter focuses on the UK financial services sector specifically – this is the context in which we have the accumulation of field evidence to present the evolution of the CRO role – we see the need for extending fieldwork beyond financial services, as did Arena *et al.* (2010). We must keep studying the various risk management practices emerging in the trenches before we jump into conclusions about the roles or consequences of risk management. A more nuanced, descriptive, field-based contingency research agenda (as advocated by Mikes and Kaplan, 2015) will uncover a fascinating diversity of context-specific practices and, in due course, help us understand the need for the variation we see. We can lament this ambiguity and lack of closure and indeed, many consultants, corporate-governance advocates and standard setters have invested heavily in promoting universalistic prescriptions for the roles and practices of risk management and of the CRO. But in fact, diversity is our key to moving ahead in the great endeavour to 'tame uncertainty'.

Note

1 This is epitomised by the assessment of the UK Parliamentary Commission: 'The corporate governance of large banks was characterised by the creation of Potemkin villages to give the appearance of effective control and oversight, without the reality' (UK Parliament, 2013).

References

Arena, M., Arnaboldi, M., & Azzone, G. (2010) The organizational dynamics of enterprise risk management. *Accounting Organization and Society*, 35, 659–675.

COSO (2004) The Committee of Sponsoring Organizations of the Treadway Commission: Enterprise Risk Management – Integrated Framework.

Deloitte (2012) Cultivating a Risk Intelligent Culture: Understand, measure, strengthen, and report. London: Deloitte Touche.

Economist Intelligence Unit Limited (2010) Risk Management in the Front Line.

Ernst & Young (2012) Turning Risk into Results.

Financial Services Authority (2010) Consultation Paper: Effective corporate governance: Significant influence controlled functions and the Walker review.

Hall, M., Mikes, A., & Millo, Y. (2015) How do risk managers become influential? A field study of toolmaking in two financial institutions. *Management Accounting Research*, 26, 3–32.

The International Corporate Governance Network (2010) ICGN Corporate Risk Oversight Guidelines.

Kaplan, R. S., & Mikes, A. (2016) Risk management—The revealing hand. *Journal of Applied Corporate Finance* 28 (1): 8–18.

KPMG (2011) Risk Management: A Driver of Enterprise Value in the Emerging Environment. Amstelveen: KPMG International.

KPMG (2013) Developing a strong risk appetite program. Amstelveen: KPMG International.

Mikes, A. (2008) Chief risk officers at crunch time: Compliance champions or business partners? *Journal of Risk Management in Financial Institutions* 2 (1): 7–25.

Mikes, A. (2009) Risk management and calculative cultures. *Management Accounting Research* 20 (1): 18–40.

Mikes, A. (2011) From counting risk to making risk count: Boundary-work in risk management. *Accounting, Organizations and Society* 36 (4–5): 226–245.

Mikes, A. and Kaplan, R. S. (2015) When one size doesn't fit all: Evolving directions in the research and practice of enterprise risk management. *Journal of Applied Corporate Finance.* 27 (1): 37–41.

Power, M. (2007) *Organized Uncertainty: Organizing a World of Risk Management.* Oxford: Oxford University Press.

Power, M. (2013): The apparatus of fraud risk. *Accounting, Organizations and Society*, 38, 525–543.

PricewaterhouseCoopers (2015) Risk in Review – Decoding Uncertainty, Delivering Value.

PricewaterhouseCoopers (2016) Board governance: Higher expectations, but better practices?

RIMS and Advisen (2013) Enterprise Risk Management Survey.

Roberts, J., McNulty, T., & Stiles, P. (2005). Beyond agency conceptions of the work of the non-executive director: Creating accountability in the boardroom. *British Journal of Management*, 16(s1), S5–S26.

Spira, L. F., & Page, M. (2010) Regulation by disclosure: The case of internal control. *Journal of Management & Governance,* 14(4), 409–433.

Stulz, R. (2015) Risk-taking and risk management by banks. *Journal of Applied Corporate Finance*, 27(1), 8–19.

Turnbull (2005) Internal Control: Revised Guidance for Directors on the Combined Code, Financial Reporting Council.

UK Parliament (2013) Parliamentary Commission on Banking Standards Final Report.

Walker, D. (2009) Review of Corporate Governance in UK Banks and other Financial Industry Entities.

Zhivitskaya, M. (2015) The practice of risk oversight since the global financial crisis: Closing the stable door? PhD thesis, The London School of Economics and Political Science (LSE).

12

Behavioural issues in performance-management practices

Current status and future research

Xuan Thuy Mai and Zahirul Hoque

Introduction

Performance management is an important element of an organisation's management-control processes and has been a focus of management-accounting research for more than two decades. This chapter presents a review of behavioural issues associated with organisational performance-management practices. This review covers the period from 1992 to 2015, contributing to the literature on performance-management systems (PMS) in a number of ways. First, it provides the most current review of PMS behavioural research. Second, it extends prior reviews by assessing the behavioural causes and consequences of PMS. Finally, it assists PMS researchers to identify areas for further research.

This chapter first introduces PMS in the behavioural context. It then discusses the principal theories used to explore behavioural issues related to PMS. Subsequently, it explores methodological issues relating to PMS research and then discusses the consequences and causes of PMS in different stages of its application in organisations. The final section provides the conclusion and identifies areas for future research.

What is PMS?

A PMS is defined as a system of defining, controlling and managing the achievement of performance at the societal, organisational and individual levels (Broadbent and Laughlin, 2009). This definition is adopted from the theoretical framework of PMS introduced by Ferreira and Otley (2009). This framework (see Figure 9.1) includes 12 questions that must be addressed in developing PMS. The core ideas of the performance-management framework are as follows: (1) vision and mission, (2) key success factors, (3) organisational structure, (4) strategies and plan, (5) key performance measures, (6) target setting, (7) performance evaluation, (8) reward systems, (9) information flows and supporting network, (10) uses of PMS, (11) PMS changes and (12) strength and coherence of PMS. This framework focuses on the continuous management and control of the performance cycle, which begins with organisational vision and mission; ends with reward systems and considers PMS changes, supporting information systems and links between PMS components. However, given the concern of the accounting profession with 'identifying, measuring, processing and reporting' business information for decision-making purposes, PMS research in the discipline of accounting often pays more attention to the performance-measurement component of performance management. This is sometimes considered a 'reduction of performance management to performance measurement' (Broadbent and Laughlin, 2009). Nevertheless, one of the principal purposes of performance measurement is to manage performance, and in line with the popular quotation 'what gets measured gets done', performance measurement has become an inevitable part of any performance-management process within an organisation. It should also be noted that Bourne and Neely's (2003) definition of PMS includes most elements of the performance-management process specified by Ferreira and Otley (2009). This chapter considers PMS a system of defining, measuring and controlling performance at the individual, organisational and societal levels. This chapter focuses on understanding the behavioural issues associated with performance-measurement and performance-management processes. Therefore, it will discuss behavioural research on the adoption, development, application and uses of PMS as a performance-management tool.

In the 1980s, accounting-based performance measures were criticised for being financially based, short term and locally or departmentally focused (Johnson and Kaplan, 1987). The most intense criticism focused on how traditional accounting-based performance measures encouraged dysfunctional behaviours of both managers and employees. Following such criticism, research on performance measurement and PMS was completed in an attempt to develop new PMS to minimise problems caused by traditional performance measurement and assist performance-management processes. As a result, tools such as the performance-measurement matrix (Keegan *et al.*, 1989), balanced scorecard (Kaplan and Norton, 1992) and the performance prism (Neely *et al.*, 2002) were introduced. Such tools created a platform from which to examine PMS at the conceptual and empirical levels. At the conceptual level, some researchers have provided conceptual frameworks to guide organisations in the process of developing their own PMS (Broadbent and Laughlin, 2009; Ferreira and Otley, 2009; Otley, 1999). Other researchers have questioned the reliability of the assumptions underlying PMS frameworks (Norreklit, 2000, 2003). At the empirical level, considerable research has explored how different PMS have been adopted and implemented in organisations (Davis and Albright, 2004; Hussain and Hoque, 2002). Some studies have examined the implementation of PMS and identified conditions for the success or failure of applying PMS (Beard, 2009; Scapens and Robert, 1993).

One branch of PMS research focuses on the examination of the human behaviour associated with the application of PMS (Chang, 2006; Hall, 2008; Yang and Modell, 2013). This behavioural research addresses the questions of whether modern PMS can help reduce dysfunctional behaviours in managers and employees. Behavioural research is not a new area in the management-accounting literature as the first research examining behavioural consequences of budgeting was Argyris (1952) and since then, there have been several attempts to review behavioural issues in this area. For example, Dunk's (2001) review focuses on the behavioural consequences of budgeting practices, and Luft and Shields (2009) examine the psychological models used to explain behavioural aspects in management accounting. More recently, Franco-Santos *et al.* (2012) review the consequences of contemporary PMS and include a section on the behavioural consequences of applying PMS in the private sector, and Kidwell and Lowensohn (2011) review behavioural-accounting research in government agencies (i.e. the public-sector context). However, since the 1990s, there has been no specialised review that focuses exclusively on behavioural issues associated with PMS.

While behavioural issues in PMS have been examined considerably in various contexts, in management-accounting textbooks used for undergraduate and postgraduate accounting courses, behavioural issues in PMS do not receive adequate attention. The authors conducted a survey of 21 management-accounting textbooks and revealed that only one book devoted a chapter and three others devoted more than one page to behavioural issues related to PMS (see Appendix 12.1).

Review approach

The present review searched for behavioural research of PMS in 25 accounting journals and 50 business and management journals (see Appendix 12.2). These journals are highly ranked by the Australian Business Dean Council (ABDC), Australian Research Council (ARC) and the Association of Business Schools (ABS). Reviewing a large number of journals is expected to minimise the problem of bias, while still allowing control for research quality. The keywords used to search for literature were 'performance measurement', 'performance management', 'performance control', 'performance evaluation', 'key performance indicators' and 'the balanced scorecard'. Although this review focuses only on behavioural research relating to PMS, keywords relating to 'behaviour' were not used because the broad nature of behaviour means that using keywords could limit the yield of the search results, resulting in interesting articles being missed. For each journal, keywords were used to search for literature. The abstract of each search result was read to determine whether the article explicitly examined behavioural issues relating to PMS. Behaviours were considered to include motivational, cognitive or social behaviour at the individual or group level, as well as general behaviours at the organisational level. As this review only focuses on empirical research, analytical behavioural research relating to PMS was excluded.

One hundred and eighteen relevant articles were sourced: 80 per cent of which were published in 17 accounting journals, and 20 per cent of which were published in 11 business and management journals (see Appendix 12.3). Most of these articles originated from developed countries such as the United Kingdom (UK), the United States (US) and Australia, and only few of them from developing countries (see Appendix 12.4). It is also interesting to note that most behavioural research of PMS was conducted in the private sector (see Appendix 12.5) and focused on either the individual level or the organisational level, with little attention paid to the intragroup or interorganisational levels (Appendix 12.6). The 118 articles provide rich evidence for different behaviours that appear as causes or consequences of PMS application. The principal focus of this chapter is on analysing different human behaviours associated with PMS across the phases of adoption, development, implementation and uses. However, before examining behavioural issues related to PMS, it is worth providing an understanding of the theoretical bases and methodologies used in these studies to allow for greater understanding and judgement of the results presented in this chapter.

Psychological theories in PMS behavioural research

A great deal of behavioural research in PMS is supported by psychological theories. This review found that of the 118 articles examined, 42 did not employ any theory, and of the remaining 76 papers, 49 used psychology theories. That is, approximately, 41 per cent of the articles used psychological theory to support the research on behavioural issues related to PMS. Given that the principal purpose of psychology is to examine the human mind and behaviour (Gross, 2005), the predominance of the use of psychological theory in behavioural research of PMS is not unexpected. The use of theory in this area has a great effect on the research results because it influences how researchers interpret behaviours and relationships between behaviours and PMS elements. Table 12.1 presents the psychological theories that are used in PMS behavioural research. The psychological theories used in PMS research can be grouped into the areas of motivational, cognitive and social psychological theory (Binberg *et al.*, 2007).

Table 12.1 Psychology theories used in behavioural research in PMS

Psychology theories	*Studies*
Cognitive theories	
Cognitive bias theories (actor-observer bias, correspondent bias, ambiguity tolerance theory, effort bias)	Wong-on-wing *et al.* (2007), Liedtka *et al.* (2008), Libby *et al.* (2004), Bol and Smith (2011)
Cognitive limitation and information processing theories	Kaplan *et al.* (2012), Ghosh and Lusch (2000), Ghosh (2005), Lipe and Salterio (2000), Lipe and Salterio (2002), Banker *et al.* (2004), Robert *et al.* (2004), Dilla and Steinbart (2005), Kaplan and Wisner (2009), Cardinaels and Van Veen-Dirks (2010), Kelly (2010), Grafton *et al.* (2010)
Melioration theory	Farrell *et al.* (2012)
Motivation theories	
Expectancy theory	Decoene and Bruggemen (2006)
Theories of trust	Chenhall and Langfield-Smith (2003)
Attribute theory	Choi *et al.* (2012), Schiff and Hoffman (1996), Hartman and Slapnica (2009), Xu and Tuttle (2005), Wong-on-wing *et al.* (2007)
Goal setting theory	Cheng *et al.* (2007), Webb (2004), Verbeeten (2008), Marginson *et al.* (2014)
Organisational-justice theory	Lau and Sholihin (2005), Sholihin and Pike (2009), Lau *et al.* (2008), Lau and Moser (2008), Hartman and Slapnica (2009), Burney *et al.* (2009)
Social-psychology theories	
Role theory	Burney and Widener (2007), Lau (2011), Burkert *et al.* (2011), Hall (2008)
Impression management theory	Webb *et al.* (2010), Lau and Martin-Sardesai (2012)
Social identity theory	Du *et al.* (2012), Antonsen (2014)
Social comparison theory	Xu and Tuttle (2005), Cianci *et al.* (2013)

Notes: The table only lists theories that were used by two or more studies. Some other theories, which were used in single studies, are not listed in this table.

Motivational theories propose that human beings are motivated by different sources and they perform better if they are motivated. Based on such theories, researchers have tested whether design and implementation of PMS motivate people, and therefore improve performance. It is claimed that several characteristics and processes of PMS such as goal setting or fair performance-measurement and performance-evaluation processes improve performance through their motivational effect. In particular, goal theory suggests that appropriate goal setting can improve performance and effort (Cheng *et al.*, 2007), or can induce managers' impress management and goal-setting behaviour (Webb *et al.*, 2010). Further, according to role theory, the diagnostic and interactive use of performance measures increases managerial role clarity and psychological empowerment, which increase their performance (Marginson *et al.*, 2014). Alternatively, organisational-justice theory explains how the fairness of performance measures and evaluation processes influences behaviour through factors such as perceived fairness and work motivation (Hartmann and Slapničar, 2012; Lau and Sholihin, 2005).

Cognitive-psychology theories claim that human beings cannot make perfectly rational decisions due to their limited capability to process information. Researchers use cognitive theories to understand how different PMS characteristics influence the decision making of managers and employees. Examples of cognitive behaviours are managers' decision-making quality (Kaplan and Wisner, 2009; Lipe and Salterio, 2002), the relative weight of measures (Cardinaels and Van Veen-Dirks, 2010), decision making relating to the structure of the combination of financial and non-financial measures (Lipe and Salterio, 2000), the experience of managers in using PMS (Dilla and Steinbart, 2005; Libby *et al.*, 2004) and employees' decisions relating to effort allocation (Farrell *et al.*, 2012).

Social-psychology theories are concerned with how social factors influence human behaviour. PMS behavioural researchers used these theories to explain the influence of different social factors such as social identity, social interaction and relationship or personal perceptions on various PMS-related behaviours such as setting targets for performance measures, weighting measures in performance evaluation or using measures in decision making. For example, using social identity theory, Du *et al.* (2012) found that if subordinates and superiors have similar political connection to government and come from the same geographical location, subordinates tend to be rated more favourably. This is explained as people who have the same social identity tend to have more frequent social interaction, leading to higher level of trust and stronger sense of loyalty (Du *et al.*, 2012).

Far fewer institutional theories than psychological theories were used in the articles reviewed. However, such theories were found to be the second most used for behavioural research relating to PMS (nine articles). The research reviewed used these theories to examine organisational-level behavioural issues in the process of PMS adoption and implementation. For example, the theory of new institutional sociology (NIS) (DiMaggio and Powell, 2000; Meyer and Rowan, 1977) helps to explain how PMS adoption is influenced by different external and internal factors (Hussain and Hoque, 2002). It is also used to explain the issue of decoupling between formal PMS and actual PMS practice caused by conflicting interests and social pressure among decision makers (Modell, 2001). Other theories found to be used by few studies were economics theories such as agency theory, the resource-based view and sociological theories such as Latour's (1987) Actor Network Theory (ANT) or Giddens's (1984) Structuration Theory (ST) (Table 12.2).

Table 12.2 Economic theories, Institutional theories, Sociology theories and other theories used in behavioural research in PMS

Theories	*Studies*
Economic theories	
Economic theories	Li *et al.* (2013), Woods (2012), Widener (2006)
Agency theory	Dossi and Patelli (2010), Moers (2005), Ittner *et al.* (2003a), Azofra *et al.* (2003), Surysekar (2003), Du *et al.* (2013), Perego and Hartman (2009), Decoene and Bruggeman (2006), Verbeeten (2008), Grafton *et al.* (2010), Widener (2006)
Resources-based view	Widener (2006), Speckbacher and Wentges (2012), Gates and Langevin (2009), Grafton *et al.* (2010)
Contingency theory	Ittner *et al.* (2003b), Gates and Langevin (2009), Perego and Hartman (2009)
Institutional theories	
Institutional theory (OIE)	Artz *et al.* (2012), Chang (2006), Yang and Modell (2013), Conrad and Uslu (2010)
New institutional sociology (NIS)	Hussain and Hoque (2002), Kasperkaya (2008), Rautianen (2009), Malmi (2001), Modell and Weisel (2008)

Notes: The table only lists theories that were used by two or more studies. Some other theories, which were used in single studies, are not listed in this table.

Methodological issues in behavioural PMS research

Table 12.3 represents the frequency distribution of articles grouped according to the data collection methods used in the research reviewed. The most widely used data collection methods in the reviewed articles were survey (35.59 per cent), case study (23.73 per cent) and experiment (23.73 per cent). Survey was the most popular method because it appears to be easier to approach participants to conduct surveys, rather than inviting participants to be involved in an experiment or asking them to conduct an interview. The comparative ease of using the survey method may be because participants prefer their identity not to be disclosed

Table 12.3 Frequency distribution of behavioural research in PMS by data collection techniques

	Year				*Sector*		
	1990–2000	*2001–2010*	*2011–2015*	*Total*	*Private*	*Public*	*Total (%)*
Case study/field study	3	22	3	28	17	11	23.73%
Survey	1	27	14	42	34	8	35.59%
Experiment	3	15	10	28	27	1	23.73%
Mixed methods	0	4	1	5	5	0	4.24%
Action research	0	4	2	6	5	1	5.08%
Archival	1	3	4	8	7	1	6.78%
Other (literature review)	0	1	0	1	1	0	0.85%
Total	8	76	34	118	96	22	100.00%

Notes: Most experiments used students as participants but the experiment settings referred to private sector circumstance. Mixed methods include studies employed more than one techniques to collect data (e.g. survey and interview).

when revealing their behavioural issues. The case study method was another widely used approach to collect data. Using the case study method can help researchers to collect a wider range of data, but gaining access to the field can be challenging. Researchers using the case study method often gain access to the field through personal relationships or the endorsement of an organisation. However, the use of such connections may pose a problem to the researcher's neutrality and position of objectivity when exploring the phenomenon under research. The experiment method was also found to be a popular methodology used in psychologically based studies, which often used university students as participants. Using this method with university students involves some limitations. For example, university students may not possess certain skills or the necessary experience and accumulated professional knowledge to perform certain decision-making tasks (Birnberg, 2011). In addition, the behaviour of university students in experimental settings might not reflect a real-life situation in which other conditions may influence their actions. Other methods used in the reviewed research include archival (in which secondary data are collected through secondary sources of information such as company documents, meeting minutes and books); action research (in which researchers participate in the field processes and activities) and mixed methods (in which researchers use a combination of survey and archival methods, survey and interview methods or archival and interview methods). It is worth noting that for research into behavioural issues relating to PMS in the public sector, the most popular method was found to be the case study method.

In the data analysis, 70 per cent of the articles reviewed used quantitative data analysis. Such analysis includes regression, correlation analysis, analysis of variance (ANOVA), multivariate analysis of variance (MANOVA), descriptive analysis, partial least squares (PLS) and structural equation modelling (SEM) path analysis. Thirty per cent of the articles reviewed used qualitative data analysis, including interview quotations, content analysis, archival analysis, participation and observation of PMS practice.

Relationship between methodology and theory selection

Chua (1986) argues that there is a relationship between the use of theory and methodology in conducting research because these choices originate from the researcher's worldview. Many accounting researchers have either a positivist view or a constructivist worldview. Mainstream positivist accounting researchers often construct predicted statements about the relationship between research objects and then test their predictions. To achieve the research objective, data are often obtained in a large-scale survey or through experimental or archival data. These data sets are then processed by statistical software to test predetermined claims. In contrast, constructivist accounting researchers assume that human beings and the world are interdependent: human behaviour creates the social environment of the world in which we live, and human behaviour is then influenced by the social environment of the world in which we live. The world is understood subjectively through individuals' perceptive lenses. As a result, to understand a phenomenon, it is essential to examine it in the context in which it arises. Constructivist researchers often go deeply into the field to seek understanding of the entire process embodied by the researched phenomenon. As a result, the methods of qualitative case study, participatory study or longitudinal study are often adopted and results are interpreted by researchers using their chosen theoretical frameworks.

Table 12.4 demonstrates that the selection of theory applied in behavioural research related to PMS relates to the methodology adopted to conduct the research. This review found that most studies that used psychological and economic theories also employed quantitative methodology. These studies tested the relationship between PMS issue(s) and behaviour(s)

Table 12.4 Cross distribution of behavioural research in PMS by data collection method and data analysis method

	Case/field study	*Survey*	*Experiment*	*Mixed methods*	*Action research*	*Archival*	*Other (literature review)*	*Total*
Qualitative								
Interview quotes	4	0	0	0	0	0	0	4
Participation/observation	3	0	0	0	3	0	0	6
Comparative analysis	2	0	0	0	0	0	0	2
Narrative description	7	0	0	0	0	0	0	7
Qualitative coding	7	0	0	2	1	0	0	10
Social network analysis	0	0	0	0	1	0	0	1
Holistic analysis	1	0	0	0	0	0	0	1
NE	3	0	0	1	0	0	1	5
Total qualitative	27	0	0	3	5	0	1	36
Quantitative								
Regression/ANOVA/MANO-VA/correlation/*t*-test, Chi-square test	0	14	26	2	1	7	0	50
Descriptive analysis	1	4	0	0	0	1	0	6
PLS/SEM/path analysis	0	24	1	0	0	0	0	25
Planned comparison test	0	0	1	0	0	0	0	1
Total quantitative	1	42	28	2	1	8	0	82
Total	28	42	28	5	6	8	1	118

by using the experimental or survey methods to collect data. The collected data were then analysed by employing regression/hypothesis testing, ANOVA/MANOVA or PLS/SEM. In contrast, studies that employed qualitative research (which accounted for less than 30 percent of all the articles reviewed) principally applied the theories of old institutional economics (OIE), NIS, ANT or ST to explain the behaviours associated with the process of adoption, development, implementation and usage of performance measures. With these theories, data were most commonly collected from archival research, in-depth interviews, participation diaries and observation notes. These types of data were principally analysed using qualitative coding, and content or interview quotation analysis.

This demonstrates that behavioural research tends to be positivist rather than constructivist. A great deal of positivist research employs theories of psychology to support hypothesis construction. Psychology is a science relating to human behaviour. It considers human behaviour as an object that can be studied independently. This underlying assumption is coincident with the functionalist worldview. The positivist approach assumes that human behaviour is an object that exists objectively and independently, and can have relationships with other objects (e.g. PMS), which also exist objectively and independently. The relationship between objects can be observed and reliably tested if the number of observations is sufficient. Most research (60 per cent) in the present review takes this approach to studying behavioural issues related to PMS. The studies were found to employ quantitative testing of hypotheses that were built around claims from psychological theories related to human

Table 12.5 Theories and research methodologies

Theories	*Methodology* Qualitative	Quantitative	Mixed	Total
NE (literature)	20	22	0	42
Psychology-based theories	3	45	2	50
Economic theories	3	16	0	19
Institutional theories	8	1	0	9
Sociology theories	4	0	0	4
Organisational theories	0	2	0	2
Total	38	86	2	126

Notes: The number of papers is more than 118 because in terms of theories, some papers used more than one theory. These papers are included in different theory categories. Mixed methodology refers to study that combined both quantitative and qualitative data analysis.

behaviour. Based on these claims, the researchers build testable statements or predictions about the relationship between human behaviour and features of PMS, then collecting survey or archival data and processing these data using econometric models and computer software. Confirmation or rejection of a null hypothesis with a certain percentage of confidence is the basis for the conclusions drawn from such studies. However, it is noted that a rejection of a predicted relationship does not mean the relationship does not exist. It simply means the evidence is not sufficient to confirm the relationship.

In contrast, a smaller number of studies using institutional theories such as ANT or ST are constructivist. These studies examine the process of adoption, development or implementation of PMS and the human behaviours that arise from these processes. Such studies principally use sociologically based theories. In sociology, human behaviour is studied through its relationship to society. That is, human behaviour and social practice are considered to be born within each other, rather than to be two separate objects that exist independently. Therefore, to understand the processes through which behaviour and PMS practices originate, researchers must follow and explore them within organisational contexts. Consequently, such research uses methods such as case studies, participatory action studies, observational and longitudinal studies. These methodologies are also widely used for research in the areas of social science. Data collected from interviews, observation or participatory notes are interpreted in light of the theories chosen by the researchers. As a result, this approach provides a rich and deep understanding of the phenomenon. Nevertheless, these studies are often criticised for being subjective because the results are influenced by the researchers' interpretative scheme.

These two different approaches to PMS behavioural research present results that are different in nature. While the results of positivist studies in this area focus on confirming or rejecting a predicted relationship between PMS elements and behaviours, the results of constructivist studies provide insightful explanations of how some behaviours occur. While the results are different, they provide complementary information. Readers of such research must examine the results of both approaches with appreciation and caution, considering the methodologies and theories the research uses (Table 12.5).

Behavioural issues associated with PMS

This review groups behavioural research into four stages of PMS, including (1) adoption, (2) design and development process, (3) implementation process and (4) the use of PMS.

In each PMS stage, human behaviours as consequences and causes of different PMS issues are discussed. This approach is expected to benefit practice and research. In particular, practitioners can gain knowledge of possible behaviours relating to PMS application stages, enabling them to take appropriate steps to minimise undesirable behaviours and promote desirable behaviours. For researchers, this approach provides a comprehensive review to assist in identifying opportunities for further behavioural research related to PMS.

Adoption of PMS – internal demand or external pressure

A great deal of research has focused on understanding the behavioural consequences of PMS adoption. It has been found that organisations can adopt PMS to respond to external pressure for compliance with external regulation and legislation or to meet an internal demand for efficiency. Chang (2006) reports that when PMS adoption follows a request or requirement from government, managers distort the organisation's priorities and manipulate performance information to seek legitimacy and protect their self-interest. This occurs because when a PMS is designed at the top level, it is meant to serve objectives that are principally strategic, which might conflict with the priority of efficient operation at the local level. When there is a conflict of interest among various stakeholders, to protect their self-interest, managers must make decisions that favour the more powerful constituents. In another study, Yang and Modell (2013) found that one problem of organisations importing an external PMS is that it creates conflicting perceptions in relation to performance, which encourage the conflict-balancing behaviour of managers. A recent conceptualisation of PMS focuses on merit-based performance as a replacement for moral-based performance. This shift in the concept of performance required managers to balance the new and old concepts of performance and adapt to the changing power relationship. In Yang and Modell's (2013) study, the participant manager demonstrated a deep interest in the reform, inducing this manager to exert great effort to balance the conflicting performance concepts and create a smoother transition.

Managers' interests have also been found to contribute to the voluntary adoption of PMS. For example, in a study of 177 firms, Widener (2006) found that labour-intensive firms that employ hierarchical pay structure tend to use a combination of financial and non-financial performance measurements in their PMS. It was found that the managers use both types of performance measurements in performance evaluation to reduce the perception of pay inequity among employee groups. However, this performance-measurement strategy was found to be employed only by managers who exhibited a high level of impression management. Lau and Martin-Sardesai (2012) found that employees' concern for fairness in the workplace and managers' desire to manage their image of being fair led to managers adopting PMS that integrates financial and non-financial performance measures. In both cases of Widener (2006) and Lau and Martin-Sardesai (2012), comprehensive PMS was adopted to increase managers' image of being fair in performance evaluation. Researchers have also found a connection between managers' focus on strategic objectives and their decision to adopt a PMS (Fleming *et al.*, 2009; Perego and Hartmann, 2009). In particular, when managers perceive uncertainty about one aspect of a firm's strategy, they tend to adopt a PMS dimension to help them manage that particular aspect. For example, managers concerned about their environmental strategies adopt a PMS that systematically reports environmental-performance measures (Perego and Hartmann, 2009). Similarly, if managers are more interested in growth strategies, they tend to adopt a more balanced or integrated PMS (Fleming *et al.*, 2009).

PMS design and development – multidimensional performance measures and participatory development processes

In the phase of PMS design and development, typical behaviours are associated with performance-measure design and development processes. The design of a PMS typically involves constructing performance measures and target setting at different levels in organisations. Researchers have examined behaviours influenced by strategically linked performance measures and have found that if performance measures are connected to strategies, then managerial strategic focus, judgement and decision making can be improved (Cheng and Humphreys, 2012; Chenhall *et al.*, 2013; Gates and Langevin, 2010; Sandtroms and Toivanen, 2002; Woods and Grubnic, 2008). Additionally, strategically linked PMS helps to communicate strategies to employees, which improves their awareness of strategies, consequently promoting their involvement and motivation, and reducing their resistance to change (Papalexandris *et al.*, 2004). However, if causal links between strategic objectives and performance measures are inaccurate and perceived to be subjectively determined, confusion and tension among managers may arise (Papalexandris *et al.*, 2004).

Another aspect of PMS design is the structure of financial and non-financial measures. As Webb *et al.* (2010) found, employees' concern for fairness and managers' negativity bias affected comprehensive PMS design. This is because when there is a threat of bias in performance evaluation, managers try to minimise potential unfairness by including financial and non-financial multidimensional performance measures. This strategy was perceived by managers to provide more comprehensive information for performance evaluation.

Setting targets for performance measures creates many behavioural issues among managers and employees. In many decentralised organisations, setting performance targets is delegated to departmental managers or even individual employees. However, Rhodes *et al.* (2008) found that in a culture dominated by the values of conflict avoidance, saving face, maintaining harmony and congenial relationships, employees tend to set targets or select measures that are easily achieved and managed. For example, Indonesians have a strong cultural tendency for conflict avoidance and saving face. In this culture, people are afraid that if they set high targets and cannot achieve them, they will lose face (Rhodes *et al.*, 2008). Webb *et al.* (2010) found that when employees were allowed to select their own goals, the employees' intention to manage impression influenced their selection of goals. In Webb *et al.* (2010), managers created a 'goal menu' from which employees could select goals, and it was found that employees select their goals according to their past performance to make sure they maintain an impression of a good performer. For example, if they had performed well in a previous period and wanted to maintain the impression of good performer, they would set high-level goals. Conversely, if they had performed badly, they would select a 'safer', low-level goal. This tendency may negatively affect the goal of participative PMS design.

Participation in PMS development has been reported to be associated with favourable and unfavourable behaviours. Research has found that the participative PMS development process improves managers' learning and mental-model similarity (Capelo and Dias, 2009). Participative PMS development has also been found to enhance managers' and employees' perceived capability and attitude towards taking initiative to improve their performance (Groen *et al.*, 2012), as well as their motivation, involvement and cooperation (Decoene and Bruggeman, 2006; Papalexandris *et al.*, 2004). However, during the participation process, conflict between top- and middle-level managers in relation to performance-measurement priorities and purposes or causal links between strategic objectives and performance measures might occur, consequently creating tension between managers in different levels (Malina and

Selto, 2001; Marginson, 2002). Further, Kruis and Widener (2014) found that managers' involvement in PMS design contributed to PMS success only if there was a high level of information asymmetry and a low interdependence between managers and employees. They found that if the contrary situation, the influence of managers in PMS design increased failure. At the intraorganisational level, the inclusion and participation in the development of non-financial performance measures was found to improve learning and dialogue between headquarters and subsidiaries (Dossi and Patelli, 2010).

Implementation – managers' determination and employees' support

Manager and employee behaviours have been found to be critical to the success or failure of PMS implementation. It was proven that it is important for managers to have determination and capacity, as well as to have employees' support to achieve success in PMS implementation (Tung *et al.*, 2011). It has been found that continuous and consistent support from top management (Bourne, 2005; Toulson and Dewe, 2004; Tung *et al.*, 2011) and managers' ability to balance multiple conceptions of performance measurement and the interests of multiconstituents within the organisation (Yang and Modell, 2013) greatly contribute to the success of PMS implementation. In addition, Umashev and Willett (2008) found that leadership style and employee empowerment influence PMS implementation success or failure. In particular, weak leadership and inadequate training were found to lead to ineffective communication of PMS, in turn increasing confusion about the operation of PMS (Umashev and Willett, 2008). Further, a lack of employee empowerment due to a rigid management hierarchy was found to reduce employee involvement and participation in PMS implementation, thus decreasing their sense of responsibility. All these conditions were found to lead to the failure of PMS implementation. In addition, in a complex situation in which many organisations were involved in the development and implementation process of a single PMS, managers' inability to resolve controversy among various actors led to the failure of PMS (Arnaboldi and Azzone, 2010). This occurred because the PMS never became a final system but remained a quasi-object that continuously changed to meet individual actors' needs.

Employee support is another factor that has been found to be important to successful PMS implementation. It has been found that tension and conflict among employees (Masquefa, 2008; Rautiainen, 2010), employee resistance to PMS implementation and low expertise and commitment level (Cavalluzzo and Ittner, 2004; Siverbo and Johansson, 2006) lead to unsuccessful PMS implementation. In contrast, employees' perceived ease of use of performance measures and participation in PMS implementation have been found to increase their intention to use measures, consequently influencing their actual use of measures (Dyball *et al.*, 2011).

A good relationship between employees and managers is said to increase the chance of successful PMS implementation. For example, trusting relationships among colleagues in the workplace were found to reduce resistance to new PMS and help to gain employee acceptance of new PMS (Masquefa, 2008). Effective communication between managers and employees relating to the strategic objectives of performance measures was found to help employees allocate their efforts and improve performance in desired areas (Farrell *et al.*, 2012). In contrast, ineffective communication or one-way reporting in the implementation process negatively affected employees' acceptance, perception and use of PMS (Malina and Selto, 2001). In addition, distance between and isolation of worker groups was found to lead to unsuccessful PMS implementation (Conrad and Uslu, 2011). In general, successful PMS implementation has been found to lead to increased motivation, involvement and teamwork among employees (Abdel-Maksoud *et al.*, 2010; Azofra *et al.*, 2003; Papalexandris *et al.*, 2004), while unsuccessful PMS implementation has been found to lead to loss of employees' motivation and enthusiasm (Kasperkaya, 2008).

Use of PMS

The use of performance measures is claimed to create many favourable behaviours. Researchers have found that the general use of PMS can contribute to greater employee effort through clear assignment of responsibility and improved worker involvement (Azofra *et al.*, 2003). It has also been found that the general use of PMS can contribute to improved manager decision making and learning, as well as self-monitoring ability because the use of performance measures focuses managers' attention on important performance areas (Artz *et al.*, 2012; Bisbe and Malagueño, 2012; Hall, 2011; Tuomela, 2005; Wiersma, 2009). Further, the use of comprehensive performance measures and strategically linked performance measures has been reported to lead to better managerial performance through its effect of improving role understanding (Burney and Widener, 2007; Hall, 2008) and increasing job satisfaction (Yeung and Berman, 1997). The use of comprehensive performance measures increases role understanding by providing greater information about roles and responsibility, as well as the firm's expectations. This leads to managers achieving greater satisfaction through higher job performance by achieving the firm's expectations. The use of PMS in general is also claimed to contribute to changing citizenship behaviour (Burney *et al.*, 2009) and corporate culture (Bititci *et al.*, 2006; Jazayeri and Scapens, 2008; Ukko *et al.*, 2007).

As part of the performance-management process, performance measures are commonly used to evaluate employee performance. The decision making of managers is the most widely researched behaviour in relation to performance evaluation. The topics that have been researched in this area include managers' choice of performance measures, weights assigned to measures and the interpretation of measures in performance evaluation. Many studies have found that managers' subjective judgements (Kaplan *et al.*, 2012; Upton and Arrington, 2012; Woods, 2012) greatly affect their choice of measures used for performance evaluation. In particular, Kaplan *et al.* (2012) found that between strategically linked measures and non-strategically linked measures, managers tend to give more weight to measures that demonstrate negative performance. Kaplan *et al.* (2012) termed this behaviour the 'negative judgement bias', which means the tendency to weigh the measures linked to negative performance more heavily than the ones linked to positive performance. In a lab study using white American graduate students at a US southeastern university, Upton and Arrington (2012) found that racial bias embedded in managers' implicit attitudes also leads to managers choosing measures that unfavourably evaluate African-American workers. It is also possible that managers use objective performance measures in a subjective manner, which might lead them to downgrade high performance when it is unexpected because of low performance in the past, or conversely, to upgrade unexpected low performance based on high performance in the past. As found by Lau and Sholihin (2005), a behavioural effect of using performance measures in evaluation is an improvement in job satisfaction. However, this job satisfaction effect occurs indirectly through improved managers' perceived fairness and interpersonal trust. Lau and Sholihin (2005) found that the relative importance of non-financial measures in evaluation did not have a better effect on job satisfaction than financial measures. This result challenges the perception that the use of combined financial and non-financial measures for performance evaluation can improve fairness more effectively than the use of pure financial measures.

Other researchers have reported that the way that performance measurement is used for performance evaluation creates many behavioural consequences for employees. In particular, the subjective use of objective performance measures for evaluation purposes was found to lead to conflict and tension among employees (Ross, 1994), as well as stress, pressure and anxiety (Ter Bogt and Scapens, 2012). This is because employees experience confusion when objective measures are subjectively used by evaluators to measure performance. Kunz (2015) found that using objective measures could improve employee motivation. However, this effect only occurs when employees have low intrinsic motivation. Where employees have high intrinsic motivation, combined objective and subjective measures in evaluation have demonstrated a more positive effect on employees' motivation. Conversely, the use of multiple performance measures for evaluation purposes can lead to goal conflict and negatively influence role understanding (Cheng *et al.*, 2007) and employee commitment (Lau and Oger, 2012; Sholihin and Pike, 2009).

The use of performance measures for compensation has been found to influence the way managers exert their efforts in job performance. For example, Surysekar (2003) found that if the firm greatly reduced the weight of the measure 'meeting the target output' in the compensation mechanism, employees decreased their total effort allocated to achieving the target output. This effect remained even when this weight adjustment was accompanied by an increase in weight of the measure 'output that meets quality standard' (Surysekar, 2003). In contrast, the combined use of strategic and non-strategic measures in a bonus plan leads to an increase in managers' efforts to achieve strategically linked measures and diminishes managers' self-enhancement behaviours (Cianci *et al.*, 2013). Specifically, when strategic measures are used in an incentive scheme, managers plan to allocate more hours to work on them. However, if comprehensive measures are used in an incentive plan, managers plan to allocate fewer total work hours. Chenhall and Langfield-Smith (2003) found that the use of performance measures in a gain-sharing system improves organisational trust and employee cooperation, but inhibits personal trust when used in combination with team-based structural-performance measures.

It was found that the use of subjective measures in an incentive plan led to desirable and undesirable behaviours. Subjective performance measures used in an incentive contract were found to increase employees' willingness to share knowledge with co-workers and pursue extra role behaviours more than they do in a formula-based incentive system (Cheng and Coyte, 2014). This is because in a more flexibly weighted incentive scheme, there is an opportunity for desirable but informal performance aspects to be considered when determining the weight of an incentive. Thus, such a scheme motivates employees to share knowledge and help their colleagues. Conversely, Ittner *et al.* (2003a) report that subjective multiperformance measures used in a bonus plan allow managers to exhibit favouritism behaviour in their measures for performance evaluation, for example, placing greater weight on financial measures, non-predictive measures or changing the performance-evaluation period.

The evidence seems to suggest that it is misleading to state that PMS creates behavioural changes because the behaviours associated with PMS often stem from the way people are involved in the system, rather than from the system itself. There is a great deal of evidence to confirm that the success or failure of a system is mainly connected to how people interact with the system. The PMS itself may be well designed and developed but without the cooperation of people involved, it is difficult for a PMS to achieve its original purpose. Through quantitative behavioural research, the relationships between behaviours and different PMS aspects are confirmed or rejected. In the meantime, qualitative behavioural research offers rich explanations for these relationships. Therefore, future PMS behavioural research should continue to focus on exploring the relationship between the use of PMS and human behaviour. At the same time, it also needs more understanding of how and why people are involved in the PMS in the way they are.

Future behavioural research of PMS

This review reveals some potential opportunities for future research. One possibility is to examine the interrelationship between behaviours and PMS issues instead of focusing on the one-way relationship between them. It is worth noting that current research on behavioural PMS often examines human behaviour from one perspective either as a cause or consequence of PMS adoption, development, implementation and uses. While some research explores behavioural causes and consequences in the same study, it does not examine one type of behaviour from the perspective of cause and consequence. This review has revealed that most behaviours, including general human behaviours and work-related behaviours, are studied as both a cause and a consequence but have not been included in the same study or linked to the same PMS issue. For example, Masquefa (2008) and Rautiainen (2010) claim that tension and conflict affect the PMS implementation process, while a series of studies have claimed that PMS implementation causes conflict and tension (Ahn, 2001; Marginson *et al.*, 2014; Papalexandris *et al.*, 2004). Such results would suggest an interrelationship between conflict and tension and PMS implementation. Therefore, it would be interesting for future research to explore the interrelationships between behaviours and PMS by examining one behaviour as both a cause and consequence of a PMS issue.

Another possibility is to explore the process of PMS becoming practice, and the behavioural issues associated with this process. Future research may focus on the role of human social interaction in the PMS production and reproduction process. To achieve such studies, researchers should view accounting practice as a result of human behaviour, where practice is produced and reproduced through actors' processes of social interaction. In daily activities, PMS is implemented and used by all actors in an organisation, and individuals interpret PMS by their own perceptions and react to the system accordingly. In such a process, PMS can also influence individuals' existing perceptions and change them. These changes are then reflected in the individuals using the tool, which ultimately changes the tool itself. This process occurs in a continuous flow of daily human activities. Current studies mainly focus on how the PMS implementation process occurs and what kinds of behaviours have been observed. Very limited effort has been devoted to understanding how the interaction process of actors in the system can form, maintain or change PMS practices and behaviours. As many studies (e.g. Arnaboldi and Azzone, 2010; Dossi and Patelli, 2010; Modell, 2003; Modell and Wiesel, 2008; Yang and Modell, 2013) have noted, through interaction between actors, including inside and outside organisations, the system and practices form, maintain and change. The present review also notes the limited use of popular sociology theories such as ANT or ST in understanding the interaction processes of different actors in PMS application. Therefore, a promising opportunity for future studies is to employ ANT or ST or any other sociology theories to explore why and how interaction between actors brings about the establishment and evolution of PMS.

Conclusion

This chapter has reviewed past studies on behavioural issues in performance-management practices. Accounting journals seem to be more likely than other business and management journals to publish PMS behavioural research. In addition, the majority of PMS behavioural research has been conducted in developed countries, and only a few studies have been conducted in developing countries. Researchers seem to have focused on private-sector organisations such as those in the manufacturing and service industries, rather than on those in the public sector such as governmental organisations and public-service organisations. Research topics range from quantitative testing of relationships between different behaviours and PMS issues to qualitative examination of the PMS application process and its associated behaviours. The present review has demonstrated that the way people are involved in the use of PMS often leads to other behavioural issues, which are often mistakenly considered behavioural consequences of PMS.

A wide range of theories was used to examine behavioural issues of PMS. Psychological theories and economic theories were popularly used to confirm or reject the relationship between behaviours and PMS issues. While theories such as neo-institutional theory and OIE and sociology theories (i.e. ST, ANT and social network theory) are not as widely used as other theories, they add interesting and valuable perspectives on PMS behavioural research. These theories help explain behaviours in the processes by which PMS institutes changes and is embedded into organisational daily practices. However, these theories have not addressed the issues of how the interaction among actors leads to the evolution of PMS, despite all the theories agreeing that interaction among actors leads to changes of organisational practices. Therefore, future research may seek alternative theories that can provide an explanation for the processes by which interactions among actors within outside organisations influence the way performance-measurement practices are formed and transformed.

This review has demonstrated that quantitative data collection and data analysis methods were employed far more often than qualitative data collection and data analysis methods. The difference in methodology adoption is principally attributed to the research questions of interest. Quantitative methods are popular options for studies examining the relationship between human behaviours and PMS. Qualitative research was employed by studies that investigated behaviours in the PMS application process. However, a limitation of qualitative studies is the poor discussion relating to the process by which the data were coded or interpreted. Such studies provided inadequate detail to explain steps they employed to extract meaning from the data collected. This weakness resulted in a reduction in the validity and reliability of the findings presented. Thus, in future qualitative studies, researchers should focus on clearly explaining the steps taken to extract meaning from interviews, participation notes and observation. Such explanation would add greater understanding for readers, as well as credibility for research findings.

This review has several limitations. It was completed using journals that are ranked high in the fields of accounting, business and management to ensure the quality of the research reviewed. Although there were many journals included in this review, this selection process may have led to valuable and interesting research published in other journals being overlooked. This selection process may also have led to bias in the results. For example, highly ranked accounting journals are known for their preference for mainstream accounting research that employs quantitative methodologies (Malmi, 2010), while it is important to consider research from all research paradigms (Deegan, 2016). Second, due to limitations of space, not all the research results are reported in this chapter. This chapter selectively discussed the most interesting and important results. This may have led to interesting findings being excluded. Future research may extend the review to include research from a wider variety of journals and provide a broader view on all behavioural issues.

Appendix 12.1 Coverage of behavioural issues of PMS in MA textbook

Authors	*Year*	*Title*	*Chapter on performance measurement and management*	*Human behavioural aspect of PMS*	*No of pages (total accumulation)*
Atrill and McLaney	2009	*Management Accounting for Decision Makers*	Yes	No	
Barfield, Raibon and Kinney	2005	*Cost Accounting – Tradition and Innovations*	Yes (PMS and BSC)	Yes	2 pages
Bhimani, Hongren, Datar and Foster	2008	*Management and Cost Accounting*	Yes	Yes	1 page
Coombs, Hoobs and Jenkins	2005	*Management Accounting: Principles and Application*	Yes (Performance measurement system)	Yes	12 lines
Crosson and Needles	2010	*Managerial Accounting*	Yes	No	
Davis and Davis	2014	*Managerial Accounting*	Yes	No	
Edmonds, Tsay and Olds	2011	*Fundamental Managerial Accounting Concepts*	Yes (Performance evaluation and Financial statement Analysis)	No	
Garrison, Noreen, and Brewer	2010	*Introduction to Managerial Accounting*	Financial Statement Analysis, BSC	No	
Hansen, Mowen and Guan	2009	*Cost Management – Accounting & Control*	Yes (BSC)	Yes	2 pages
Hilton and Platt	2014	*Managerial Accounting – Creating value in a dynamic business environment*	Yes	Yes	1 page (in a section about ethics)
Hoque	2005	*Handbook of Cost and Management Accounting*	Yes	Yes	A chapter
Horgren, Datar and Rajan	2012	*Cost Accounting – A managerial emphasis*	Yes (BSC)	No	
Horgren, Harrison and Oliver	2012	*Financial and Managerial Accounting*	Yes (BSC)	No	
Lanen, Anderson and Maher	2011	*Fundamentals of Cost Accounting*	Yes	Yes	1/2 page
Kinney and Raibon	2011	*Cost Accounting – Foundation and Evolution*	Yes	Yes	3 pages

(Continued)

Authors	*Year*	*Title*	*Chapter on performance measurement and management*	*Human behavioural aspect of PMS*	*No of pages (total accumulation)*
Langfield-Smith, Thorne, Smith and Hilton	2014	*Management Accounting – Information for creating and managing value*	Yes	Yes	1 page
Rich, Jones, Heitger, Mowen and Hansen	2010	*Cornerstones of Financial & Managerial Accounting*	Yes (BSC)	No	
Warren, Reeve and Duchac	2009	*Managerial Accounting*	Yes	No	
Weetman	2009	*Financial and Managerial Accounting – An Introduction*	Yes (BSC)	Yes	14 lines (1/4 page)
Weygant, Kimmel and Kieso	2012	*Managerial Accounting – Tools for business decision making*	Yes	No	
Wild and Shaw	2010	*Managerial Accounting*	Yes	No	

Appendix 12.2 List of journals under review

ABBR	*Accounting Journals*	*ABBR*	*Business and Management Journals*
MAR	*Management Accounting Research*	AMP	*Academy of Management Journal*
AOS	*Accounting, Organizations and Society*	AJM	*Academy of Management Learning and Education*
BRIA	*Behavioral Research in Accounting*	BJM	*Academy of Management Perspectives*
TAR	*The Accounting Review*	CMR	*Academy of Management Review*
BAR	*British Accounting Review*	HBR	*Administrative Science Quarterly*
JMAR	*Journal of Management Accounting Research*	HR	*Australian Journal of Management*
ADIC	*Advance in Accounting*	HRMJ	*British Journal of Management*
CPA	*Critical Perspectives on Accounting*	HRMR	*California Management Review*
ABR	*Accounting and Business Research*	I&M	*Decision Sciences*
CAR	*Contemporary Accounting Research*	IJHRM	*European Journal of Information Systems*
JAPP	*Journal of Accounting and Public Policy*	IJOPM	*Harvard Business Review*
A&F	*Accounting and Finance*	JAP	*Human Relations*
AAAJ	*Accounting Auditing and Accountability Journal*	JBR	*Human Resource Management*
ABACUS	*Abacus: A Journal of Accounting, Finance and Business Studies*	JWB	*Human Resource Management Journal*
EAR	*The European Accounting Review*	LRP	*Human Resource Management Review*
TIJA	*The International Journal of Accounting*	MIR	*Information and Management*
AH	*Accounting Horizons*	MISQE	*International Journal of Human Resource Management*
API	*Accounting and the Public Interest*	MITSMR	*International Journal of Operations and Production Management*
FAM	*Financial Accountability and Management*	OMEGA	*International Journal of Production Economics*
IIAEd	*Issues in Accounting Education*	ORL	*International Journal of Production Research*
JAAF	*JAAF – Journal of Accounting Auditing and Finance*	SMJ	*Journal of Applied Psychology*
JAE	*Journal of Accounting and Economics*	SO	*Journal of Business*
JAL	*Journal of Accounting Literature*	SCM	*Journal of Business Research*
JAR	*Journal of Accounting Research*	SDR	*Journal of Business Venturing*
RAS	*Review of Accounting Studies*	IJPR	*Journal of International Business Studies*
JCAE	*Journal of Contemporary Accounting and Economics*	AMJ	*Journal of Management*
JPPAFM	*Journal of Public Budgeting, Accounting and Financial Management*	AMLE	*Journal of Management Information Systems*

(Continued)

ABBR	Accounting Journals	ABBR	Business and Management Journals
RGNPA	*Research in Governmental and Non-Profit Accounting*	AMR	*Journal of Management Studies*
FTA	*Foundations and Trends in Accounting*	ASQ	*Journal of Operations Management*
		DS	*Journal of Organizational Behavior*
		EJIS	*Journal of Product Innovation Management*
		HRM	*Journal of World Business*
		JB	*Leadership Quarterly*
		JBV	*Long Range Planning*
		JIBS	*Management International Review*
		JM	*Management Science*
		JMIS	*MIS Quarterly*
		JMS	*MIS Quarterly Executive: A Research Journal Dedicated to Improving Practice*
		JOM	*MIT Sloan Management Review*
		JOB	*OMEGA International Journal of Management Science*
		JPIM	*Operations Research*
		LQ	*Operations Research Letters*
		MS	*Organization Science*
		MISQ	*Organization Studies*
		OR	*Organizational Behavior and Human Decision Processes*
		OS	*R & D Management*
		OST	*Research in Organizational Behavior*
		OBHDP	*Strategic Management Journal*
		ROB	*Strategic Organization*
		IJPE	*Supply Chain Management: An International Journal*
		R&DM	*System Dynamics Review*

Appendix 12.3 Distribution of behavioural research in PMS by journals

		No of articles in private sector				*No of articles in public sector*				
ABBR	*Accounting Journals*	*1990–2000*	*2001–2010*	*2011–2015*	*Total*	*1990–2000*	*2001–2010*	*2011–2015*	*Total*	*Total*
MAR	*Management Accounting Research*	0	9	9	18	1	2	0	3	21
AOS	*Accounting, Organizations and Society*	2	9	4	15	0	1	0	1	16
BRIA	*Behavioral Research in Accounting*	1	8	2	11	0	0	0	0	11
TAR	*The Accounting Review*	1	4	3	8	0	0	1	1	9
BAR	*British Accounting Review*	0	4	1	5	0	0	0	0	5
AAAJ	*Accounting Auditing and Accountability Journal*	0	1	0	1	0	3	1	4	5
FAM	*Financial Accountability and Management*	0	0	0	0	0	4	1	5	5
JMAR	*Journal of Management Accounting Research*	0	3	1	4	0	0	0	0	4
ADIC	*Advance in Accounting*	0	0	3	3	0	0	0	0	3
CPA	*Critical Perspectives on Accounting*	0	1	1	2	0	1	0	1	3
ABR	*Accounting and Business Research*	1	1	0	2	0	1	0	1	3
ABACUS	*Abacus: A Journal of Accounting, Finance and Business Studies*	0	1	0	1	0	2	0	2	3
CAR	*Contemporary Accounting Research*	0	2	0	2	0	0	0	0	2
EAR	*The European Accounting Review*	0	0	1	1	0	0	1	1	2
JAPP	*Journal of Accounting and Public Policy*	0	0	1	1	0	0	0	0	1
A&F	*Accounting and Finance*	0	1	0	1	0	0	0	0	1
TIJA	*The International Journal of Accounting*	0	1	0	1	0	0	0	0	1
	Total articles (accounting journals)	5	45	26	76	1	14	4	19	95
Business and Management Journals										
LRP	*Long Range Planning*	1	6	0	7	0	0	0	0	7
IJOPM	*International Journal of Operation and Production Management*	0	2	2	4	0	0	0	0	4
HRM	*Human Resource Management*	1	0	0	1	0	1	0	1	2

(Continued)

		No of articles in private sector				No of articles in public sector				
ABBR	*Accounting Journals*	*1990–2000*	*2001–2010*	*2011–2015*	*Total*	*1990–2000*	*2001–2010*	*2011–2015*	*Total*	*Total*
IJHRM	*International Journal of Human Resource Management*	0	1	0	1	0	0	1	1	2
IJPE	*International Journal of Production Economics*	0	2	0	2	0	0	0	0	2
HRMJ	*Human Resource Management Journal*	0	0	0	0	0	1	0	1	1
JOPM	*Journal of Operations Management*	0	1	0	1	0	0	0	0	1
R&DM	*Research and Development Management*	0	1	0	1	0	0	0	0	1
SJM	*Scandinavian Journal of Management*	0	0	1	1	0	0	0	0	1
SDR	*System Dynamics Review*	0	1	0	1	0	0	0	0	1
SMJ	*Strategic Management Journal*	0	1	0	1	0	0	0	0	1
	Total articles published in B&M journals	2	15	3	20	0	2	1	3	23
	Total articles under review	7	60	29	96	1	16	5	22	118

Appendix 12.4 Frequency distribution of behavioural research in PMS by geographical location

	Year				*Sector*		
Countries	*1990–2000*	*2001–2010*	*2011–2015*	*Total*	*Private*	*Public*	*Total (%)*
US	3	22	10	35	33	2	29.66
Australia	2	7	6	15	11	4	12.71
UK	2	8	0	10	7	3	8.47
Netherlands	0	6	1	7	6	1	5.93
Finland	0	6	0	6	5	1	5.08
China	0	2	2	4	2	2	3.39
Portugal	0	1	1	2	2	0	1.69
Spain	0	2	1	3	2	1	2.54
Canada	1	2	0	3	3	0	2.54
Germany	0	1	3	4	4	0	3.39
France	0	2	1	3	3	0	2.54
Sweden	0	2	0	2	0	2	1.69
Italia	0	2	0	2	1	1	1.69
Indonesia	0	2	0	2	1	1	1.69
Belgium	0	1	1	2	2	0	1.69
Slovenia	0	1	1	2	2	0	1.69
Norway	0	0	1	1	1	0	0.85
Others (multiple locations)	0	9	6	15	11	4	12.71
Total	8	76	34	118	96	22	100.00

Appendix 12.5 Frequency distribution of behavioural research in PMS by research settings

	Year				
Sector	*1990–2000*	*2001–2010*	*2011–2015*	*Total*	*Total (%)*
Private sector					
Manufacturing (including maritime)	2	25	5	32	27.12
Services (including telecom)	0	5	2	7	5.93
Banking/financial services	0	6	5	11	9.32
Retail	2	2	0	4	3.39
Various industries (more than one industry)	1	8	9	18	15.25
NA (experiment without explicit industry)	2	13	9	24	20.34
Total private sector	5	46	21	96	81.36
Public sector					
Local government/municipal units	1	5	0	6	5.08
Government departments/state agencies	0	2	1	3	2.54
Healthcare	0	3	1	4	3.39
Higher education	0	1	1	2	1.69
Others (including HR organisations, state-owned enterprises, state banks, various public industries)	0	6	1	7	5.93
Total public sector	1	17	4	22	18.64
Total	8	76	34	118	100.00

Appendix 12.6 Frequency distribution of behavioural research in PMS by level of analysis

	Year				*Sector*		
	1990–2000	*2001–2010*	*2011–2015*	*Total*	*Private*	*Public*	*Total (%)*
Individual level	4	28	22	54	51	3	45.76
Intra-individual/team/business unit/department/division level	0	4	0	4	4	0	3.39
Organisational level	3	39	10	52	35	17	44.07
Interorganisational level	0	2	0	2	2	0	1.69
More than one level	1	3	2	6	4	2	5.08
Total	8	76	34	118	96	22	100.00

References

Abdel-Maksoud, A., Cerbioni, F., Ricceri, F. & Velayutham, S. 2010. Employee morale, non-financial performance measures, deployment of innovative managerial practices and shop-floor involvement in Italian manufacturing firms. *The British Accounting Review*, 42, 36–55.

Ahn, H. 2001. Applying the BSC concept—An experience report. *Long Range Planning*, 34, 441–461.

Antonsen, Y. 2014. The downside of the balanced scorecard: A case study from Norway. *Scandinavian Journal of Management*, 30(1), 40–50.

Argyris, C. 1952. *The Impact of Budgets on People*. New York, The Controllership Foundation.

Arnaboldi, M. & Azzone, G. 2010. Constructing performance measurement in the public sector. *Critical Perspectives on Accounting*, 21, 266–282.

Artz, M., Homburg, C. & Rajab, T. 2012. Performance-measurement system design and functional strategic decision influence: The role of performance-measure properties. *Accounting, Organizations and Society*, 37, 445–460.

Azofra, V. N., Prieto, B. & Santidrián, A. 2003. The usefulness of a performance measurement system in the daily life of an organisation: A note on a case study. *The British Accounting Review*, 35, 367–384.

Banker, R. D., Chang, H. & Pizzini, M. J. 2004. The BSC – Judgmental effects of performance measure linked to strategy. *The Accounting Review*, 79(1), 1–23.

Beard, D. F. 2009. Successful application of balanced scorecard in higher education. *Journal of Education for Business*, 84, 275–282.

Birnberg, J. G. 2011. A proposed framework for behavioral accounting research. *Behavioral Research in Accounting*, 23, 1–43.

Binberg, J. G., Luft, J. & Shields, M. D. 2007. Psychology theory in management accounting research. *In:* Chapman, C. S., Hopwood, A. G. & Shields, M. D. (eds.) *Handbook of Management Accounting Research*. The Netherlands, Elsevier, pp. 113–135.

Bisbe, J. & Malagueño, R. 2012. Using strategic performance measurement systems for strategy formulation: Does it work in dynamic environments? *Management Accounting Research*, 23, 296–311.

Bititci, U. S., Mendibil, K., Nudurupati, S., Garengo, P. & Turner, T. 2006. Dynamics of performance measurement and organisational culture. *International Journal of Operations & Production Management*, 26, 1325–1350.

Bol, J. C. & Smith, S. D. 2011. Spillover effects in subjective performance evaluation: Bias and the asymmetric influence of controllability. *The Accounting Review*, 86(4), 1213–1230.

Bourne, M. 2005. Researching performance measurement system implementation: The dynamics of success and failure. *Production Planning & Control*, 16, 101–113.

Bourne, M. & Neely, A. 2003. Implementing performance measurement system: A literature review. *International Journal of Business Performance Management*, 5, 1–24.

Broadbent, J. & Laughlin, R. 2009. Performance management systems: A conceptual model. *Management Accounting Research*, 20, 283–295.

Burkert, M., Fischer, F. M. & Schäffer, U. 2011. Application of the controllability principle and managerial performance: The role of role perceptions. *Management Accounting Research*, 22(3), 143–159.

Burney, L. & Widener, S. K. 2007. Strategic performance measurement systems, job-relevant information, and managerial behavioral responses—Role stress and performance. *Behavioral Research in Accounting*, 19, 43–69.

Burney, L. L., Henle, C. A. & Widener, S. K. 2009. A path model examining the relations among strategic performance measurement system characteristics, organizational justice, and extra- and in-role performance. *Accounting, Organizations and Society*, 34, 305–321.

Capelo, C. & Dias, J. F. 2009. A system dynamics-based simulation experiment for testing mental model and performance effects of using the balanced scorecard. *System Dynamics Review*, 25, 1–34.

Cardinaels, E. & Van Veen-Dirks, P. M. G. 2010. Financial versus non-financial information: The impact of information organization and presentation in a balanced scorecard. *Accounting, Organizations and Society*, 35, 565–578.

Cavalluzzo, K. S. & Ittner, C. D. 2004. Implementing performance measurement innovations: Evidence from government. *Accounting, Organizations and Society*, 29, 243–267.

Chang, L.-C. 2006. Managerial responses to externally imposed performance measurement in the NHS: An institutional theory perspective. *Financial Accountability and Management*, 22, 63–85.

Cheng, M. M. & Coyte, R. 2014. The effects of incentive subjectivity and strategy communication on knowledge-sharing and extra-role behaviours. *Management Accounting Research*, 25, 119–130.

Cheng, M. M. & Humphreys, K. A. 2012. The differential improvement effects of the strategy map and scorecard perspectives on managers' strategic judgments. *The Accounting Review*, 87, 899–924.

Cheng, M. M., Luckett, P. F. & Mahama, H. 2007. Effect of perceived conflict among multiple performance goals and goal difficulty on task performance. *Accounting & Finance*, 47, 221–242.

Chenhall, R. H. & Langfield-Smith, K. 2003. Performance measurement and reward systems, trust, and strategic change. *Journal of Management Accounting Research*, 15, 117–143.

Chenhall, R. H., Hall, M. & Smith, D. 2013. Performance measurement, modes of evaluation and the development of compromising accounts. *Accounting, Organizations and Society*, 38, 268–287.

Choi, J., Hecht, G. W. & Tayler, W. B. 2012. Lost in translation: The effects of incentive compensation on strategy surrogation. *The Accounting Review*, 87(4), 1135–1163.

Chua, W. F. 1986. Radical development in Accounting thought. *The Accounting Review* 61(4), 601–632.

Cianci, A. M., Kaplan, S. E. & Samuels, J. A. 2013. The moderating effects of the incentive system and performance measure on managers' and their superiors' expectations about the manager's effort. *Behavioral Research in Accounting*, 25, 115–134.

Conrad, L. & Uslu, P. G. 2011. Investigation of the impact of 'Payment by Results' on performance measurement and management in NHS Trusts. *Management Accounting Research*, 22, 46–55.

Davis, S. & Albright, T. 2004. An investigation of the effect of BSC implementation of financial performance. *Management Accounting Research*, 15, 135–153.

Decoene, V. & Bruggeman, W. 2006. Strategic alignment and middle level managers' motivation in a balanced scorecard setting. *International Journal of Operations and Production Management*, 26, 429–448.

Deegan, C. 2016. So, who really is a 'noted author' within the accounting literature? A reflection on Benson et al. (2015). *Accounting, Auditing & Accountability Journal*, 29, 483–490.

Dilla, W. N. & Steinbart, P. J. 2005. Relative weighting of common and unique balanced scorecard measures by knowledgeable decision makers. *Behavioral Research in Accounting*, 17, 43–53.

DiMaggio, P. J. & Powell, W. W. 2000. The iron cage revisited: Institutional isomorphism and collective rationality in organisational fields. *Advances in Strategic Management*, 17, 143–166.

Dossi, A. & Patelli, L. 2010. You learn from what you measure: Financial and non-financial performance measures in multinational companies. *Long Range Planning*, 43, 498–526.

Du, F., Tang, G. & Young, S. M. 2012. Influence activities and favoritism in subjective performance evaluation: Evidence from Chinese state-owned enterprises. *The Accounting Review*, 87, 1555–1588.

Du, Y., Deloof, M. & Jorissen, A. 2013. Headquarters-subsidiary interdependencies and the design of performance evaluation and reward systems in multinational enterprises. *European Accounting Review*, 22(2), 391–424.

Dunk, A. S. 2001. Behavioral research in management accounting: The past, present and future. *Advances in Accounting Behavioral Research*, 4, 25–45.

Dyball, M. C., Cummings, L. & Yu, H. 2011. Adoption of the concept of a balanced scorecard within NSW Health: An exploration of staff attitudes. *Financial Accountability and Management*, 27, 335–361.

Farrell, A. M., Kadous, K. & Towry, K. L. 2012. Does the communication of causal linkages improve employee effort allocations and firm performance? An experimental investigation. *Journal of Management Accounting Research*, 24, 77–102.

Ferreira, A. & Otley, D. 2009. The design and use of performance management systems: An extended framework for analysis. *Management Accounting Research*, 20, 263–282.

Fleming, D. M., Chow, C. W. & Chen, G. 2009. Strategy, performance-measurement systems, and performance: A study of Chinese firms. *The International Journal of Accounting*, 44, 256–278.

Franco-Santos, M., Lucianetti, L. & Bourne, M. 2012. Contemporary performance measurement systems: A review of their consequences and a framework for research. *Management Accounting Research*, 23, 79–119.

Gates, S. & Langevin, P. 2010. Human capital measures, strategy, and performance: HR managers' perceptions. *Accounting, Auditing & Accountability Journal*, 23, 111–132.

Ghosh, D. 2005. Alternative measures of managers' performance, controllability, and the outcome effect. *Behavioral Research in Accounting*, 17, 55–70.

Ghosh, D. & Lusch, R. F. 2000. Outcome effect, controllability and performance evaluation of managers: Some field evidence from multi-outlet businesses. *Accounting, Organisation and Society, 25*, 411–425.

Giddens, A. 1984. *The Constitution of Society: Outline of Structuration Theory*. UK, Polity Press.

Grafton, J., Lillis, A. M. & Widener, S. K. 2010. The role of performance measurement and evaluation in building organizational capabilities and performance. *Accounting, Organizations and Society*, 35(7), 689–706.

Groen, B. A. C., Wouters, M. J. F. & Wilderom, C. P. M. 2012. Why do employees take more initiatives to improve their performance after co-developing performance measures? A field study. *Management Accounting Research*, 23, 120–141.

Gross, R. 2005. *Psychology: The Science of Mind and Behaviour*. Dubai, Hodder Arnold.

Hall, M. 2008. The effect of comprehensive performance measurement systems on role clarity, psychological empowerment and managerial performance. *Accounting, Organizations and Society*, 33, 141–163.

Hall, M. 2011. Do comprehensive performance measurement systems help or hinder managers' mental model development? *Management Accounting Research*, 22, 68–83.

Hartmann, F. & Slapničar, S. 2012. The perceived fairness of performance evaluation: The role of uncertainty. *Management Accounting Research*, 23, 17–33.

Hussain, M. M. & Hoque, Z. 2002. Understanding nonfinancial performance measures practice in Japanese banks: A new institutional sociology Perspective. *Accounting, Auditing & Accountability Journal*, 15, 162–183.

Ittner, C. D., Larcker, D. F. & Meyer, M. W. 2003a. Subjectivity and the weighting of performance measures: Evidence from a balanced scorecard. *The Accounting Review*, 78, 725–758.

Ittner, C. D., Larcker, D. F. & Randall, T. 2003b. Performance implications of strategic performance measurement in financial services firms. *Accounting, Organizations and Society*, 28(7–8), 715–741.

Jazayeri, M. & Scapens, R. W. 2008. The business values scorecard within BAE systems: The evolution of a performance measurement system. *The British Accounting Review*, 40, 48–70.

Johnson, H. T. & Kaplan, R. S. 1987. *Relevance Lost: The Rise and Fall of Management Accounting*. Boston, MA, Harvard Business School Press.

Kaplan, R. S. & Norton, D. P. 1992. The balanced scorecard: Measures that drive performance. *Harvard Business Review*, 70, 71–79.

Kaplan, S. E., Petersen, M. J. & Samuels, J. A. 2012. An examination of the effect of positive and negative performance on the relative weighting of strategically and non-strategically linked balanced scorecard measures. *Behavioral Research in Accounting*, 24, 133–151.

Kaplan, S. E. & Wisner, P. S. 2009. The judgemental effect of managerial communications and a fifth balanced scorecard category on performance measurement. *Behavioral Research in Accounting*, 21, 37–56.

Kasperkaya, Y. 2008. Implementing the balanced scorecard: A comparative study of two Spanish city councils—An institutional perspective. *Financial Accountability and Management*, 24, 363–384.

Keegan, D. P., Eiler, R. G. & Jones, C. R. 1989. Are your performance measures obsolete? *Management Accounting*, 70(12), 45–50.

Kelly, K. 2010. Accuracy of relative weights on multiple leading performance measures: Effects on managerial performance and knowledge*. *Contemporary Accounting Research*, 27(2), 577–608.

Kidwell, L. A. & Lowensohn, S. 2011. A review and assessment of behavioral accounting research in government. *Journal of Accounting Literature*, 30, 41–67.

Kruis, A.-M. & Widener, S. K. 2014. Managerial influence in performance measurement system design: A recipe for failure? *Behavioral Research in Accounting*, 26, 1–34.

Kunz, J. 2015. Objectivity and subjectivity in performance evaluation and autonomous motivation: An exploratory study. *Management Accounting Research*, 27, 27–46.

Latour, B. 1987. *Science in Action: How to Follow Scientists and Engineers through Society*. Cambridge, MA: Harvard University Press.

Lau, C. M. 2011. Nonfinancial and financial performance measures: How do they affect employee role clarity and performance? *Advances in Accounting*, 27(2), 286–293.

Lau, C. M. & Martin-Sardesai, A. V. 2012. The role of organisational concern for workplace fairness in the choice of a performance measurement system. *The British Accounting Review*, 44, 157–172.

Lau, C. M. & Moser, A. 2008. Behavioral effect of nonfinancial performance measure: The role of procedural fairness. *Behavioral Research in Accounting*, 20(2), 55–71.

Lau, C. M. & Oger, B. 2012. Behavioral effects of fairness in performance measurement and evaluation systems: Empirical evidence from France. *Advances in Accounting*, 28, 323–332.

Lau, C. M. & Sholihin, M. 2005. Financial and nonfinancial performance measures: How do they affect job satisfaction? *The British Accounting Review*, 37, 389–413.

Lau, C. M., Wong, K. M. & Eggleton, I. R. C. 2008. Fairness of performance evaluation procedures and job satisfaction: The role of outcome based and non-outcome based effects. *Accounting and Business Research*, 38(2), 121–135.

Li, W., Alam, P. & Meonske, N. 2013. Performance measure properties and efficacy of incentive contracts: perceptions of U. S. employees. *The International Journal of Human Resource Management*, 24(17), 3378–3392.

Libby, T., Salterio, S. E. & Webb, A. 2004. The balanced scorecard: The effects of assurance and process accountability on managerial judgment. *The Accounting Review*, 74, 1074–1095.

Liedtka, S. L., Church, B. K. & Ray, M. R. 2008. Performance variability, ambiguity intolerance, and balanced scorecard-based performance. *Behavioral Research in Accounting*, 20(2), 73–88.

Lipe, M. G. & Salterio, S. E. 2000. The balanced scorecard: Judgmental effects of common and unique performance measures. *The Accounting Review*, 75, 283–298.

Lipe, M. G. & Salterio, S. E. 2002. A note on the judgmental effects of the balanced scorecard's information organization. *Accounting, Organisation and Society*, 27, 531–540.

Luft, J. & Shields, M. D. 2009. Psychology models of management accounting. *Foundations and Trends in Accounting*, 4, 199–345.

Malina, M. A. & Selto, F. H. 2001. Communicating and controlling strategy: An empirical study of the effectiveness of the balanced scorecard. *Journal of Management Accounting Research*, 13, 47–90.

Malmi, T. 2010. Reflections on paradigms in action in accounting research. *Management Accounting Research*, 21, 121–123.

Marginson, D. E. W. 2002. Management control systems and their effects on strategy formation at middle-management levels: evidence from a UK organization. *Strategic Management Journal*, 23, 1019–1031.

Marginson, D., McAulay, L., Roush, M. & Van Zijl, T. 2014. Examining a positive psychological role for performance measures. *Management Accounting Research*, 25, 63–75.

Masquefa, B. 2008. Top management adoption of a locally driven performance measurement and evaluation system: A social network perspective. *Management Accounting Research*, 19, 182–207.s

Meyer, J. W. & Rowan, B. 1977. Institutionalized organizations: Formal structure as myth and ceremony. *American Journal of Sociology*, 83, 340–363.

Modell, S. 2001. Performance measurement and institutional processes: A study of managerial responses to public sector reform. *Management Accounting Research*, 12, 437–464.

Modell, S. 2003. Goals versus institutions: The development of performance measurement in the Swedish university sector. *Management Accounting Research*, 14, 333–359.

Modell, S. & Wiesel, F. 2008. Marketization and performance measurement in Swedish central government: A comparative institutionalist study. *Abacus*, 44, 251–283.

Moers, F. 2005. Discretion and bias in performance evaluation: the impact of diversity and subjectivity. *Accounting, Organizations and Society*, 30(1), 67–80.

Neely, A. D., Adams, C. & Kennerley, M. 2002. *The Performance Prism: The Scorecard for Measuring and Managing Business Success*. London, FT Prentice Hall.

Norreklit, H. 2000. The balance on the balanced scorecard—A critical analysis of some of its assumption. *Management Accounting Research*, 11, 65–88.

Norreklit, H. 2003. The balanced scorecard: What is the score?—A rhetorical analysis of the balanced scorecard. *Accounting, Organisation and Society*, 28, 591–619.

Otley, D. 1999. Performance management: A framework for management control systems research. *Management Accounting Research*, 10, 363–382.

Papalexandris, A., Ioannou, G. & Prastacos, G. P. 2004. Implementing the balanced scorecard in Greece: A software firm's experience. *Long Range Planning*, 37, 351–366.

Perego, P. & Hartmann, F. 2009. Aligning performance measurement systems with strategy: The case of environmental strategy. *Abacus*, 45, 397–428.

Rautiainen, A. 2010. Contending legitimations: Performance measurement coupling and decoupling in two Finnish cities. *Accounting, Auditing & Accountability Journal*, 23, 373–391.

Rhodes, J., Walsh, P. & Lok, P. 2008. Convergence and divergence issues in strategic management—Indonesia's experience with the balanced scorecard in HR management. *The International Journal of Human Resource Management*, 19, 1170–1185.

Robert, M. L., Albright, T. L. & Hibbets, A. R. 2004. Debiasing balanced scorecard evaluations. *Behavioral Research in Accounting*, 16, 75–88.

Ross, A. 1994. Trust as a moderator of the effect of performance evaluation style on job-related tension: A research note. *Accounting, Organisation and Society*, 19, 629–635.

Sandtroms, J. & Toivanen, J. 2002. The problem of managing product development engineers: Can the balanced scorecard be an answer? *International Journal of Production Economics*, 78, 79–90.

Scapens, R. W. & Robert, J. 1993. Accounting and control: A case study of resistance to accounting change. *Management Accounting Research*, 4, 1–32.

Schiff, A. D. & Hoffman, L. R. 1996. An exploration of the use of financial and nonfinancial measures of performance by executives in a service organisation. *Behavioral Research in Accounting*, 8, 134–153.

Sholihin, M. & Pike, R. 2009. Fairness in performance evaluation and behavioral consequences. *Accounting and Business Research*, 39, 397–413.

Siverbo, S. & Johansson, T. 2006. Relative performance measurement in Swedish local government. *Financial Accountability and Management*, 22, 271–290.

Speckbacher, G. & Wentges, P. 2012. The impact of family control on the use of performance measures in strategic target setting and incentive compensation: A research note. *Management Accounting Research*, 23(1), 34–46.

Surysekar, K. 2003. A note on the interaction effects of non-financial measures of performance. *Management Accounting Research*, 14, 409–417.

Ter Bogt, H. J. & Scapens, R. W. 2012. Performance management in universities: Effects of the transition to more quantitative measurement systems. *European Accounting Review*, 1–47.

Toulson, P. K. & Dewe, P. 2004. HR accounting as measurement tool. *Human Resource Management Journal*, 14, 75–90.

Tung, A., Baird, K. & Schoch, H. P. 2011. Factors influencing the effectiveness of performance measurement systems. *International Journal of Operation and Production Management*, 31, 1287–1310.

Tuomela, T.-S. 2005. The interplay of different levers of control: A case study of introducing a new performance measurement system. *Management Accounting Research*, 16, 293–320.

Ukko, J., Tenhunen, J. & Rantanen, H. 2007. Performance measurement impacts on management and leadership: Perspectives of management and employees. *International Journal of Production Economics*, 110, 39–51.

Umashev, C. & Willett, R. 2008. Challenges to implementing strategic performance measurement systems in multi-objective organizations: The case of a large local government authority. *Abacus*, 44, 377–398.

Upton, D. R. & Arrington, C. E. 2012. Implicit racial prejudice against African-Americans in balanced scorecard performance evaluations. *Critical Perspectives on Accounting*, 23, 281–297.

Verbeeten, F. H. M. 2008. Performance management practices in public sector organizations: Impact on performance. *Accounting, Auditing & Accountability Journal*, 21(3), 427–454.

Webb, A., Jeffrey, S. A. & Schulz, A. 2010. Factors affecting goal difficulty and performance when employees select their own performance goals: Evidence from the field. *Journal of Management Accounting Research*, 22, 209–232.

Webb, R. A. 2004. Managers' commitment to the goals contained in a strategic performance measurement system. *Contemporary Accounting Research*, 21(4), 925–958.

Widener, S. K. 2006. Human capital, pay structure, and the use of performance measures in bonus compensation. *Management Accounting Research*, 17, 198–221.

Wiersma, E. 2009. For which purposes do managers use balanced scorecards? *Management Accounting Research*, 20, 239–251.

Wong-on-Wing, B., Guo, L., Li, W. & Yang, D. 2007. Reducing conflict in balanced scorecard evaluations. *Accounting, Organisation and Society*, 32, 363–377.

Woods, A. 2012. Subjective adjustments to objective performance measures: The influence of prior performance. *Accounting, Organizations and Society*, 37, 403–425.

Woods, M. & Grubnic, S. 2008. Linking comprehensive performance assessment to the balanced scorecard: Evidence from Hertfordshire City Council. *Financial Accountability and Management*, 24, 343–361.

Xu, Y. & Tuttle, B. M. 2005. The role of social influence in using accounting performance information to evaluate subordinates: A causal attribution approach. *Behavioral Research in Accounting*, 17, 191–210.

Yang, C. L. & Modell, S. 2013. Power and performance: Institutional embeddedness and performance management in a Chinese local government organisation. *Accounting, Auditing & Accountability Journal*, 26, 101–132.

Yeung, A. K. & Berman, B. 1997. Adding value through human resources: Reorienting human resource measurement to drive business performance. *Human Resource Management Journal*, 36, 321–335.

13

Accounting for the immaterial

The challenge for management accounting

David Carter

With an historic base in the material, particularly with roots in the industrial revolution and in drawing upon the influences of Fordist production and Taylor's scientific management, management accounting tends to focus on production, control and measurement (Frezatti *et al.*, 2014). In this sense, traditional management accounting tools and technologies, including cost, budgets and variances, provide a foundation for controlling material production (Chapman, 1998). Management accounting, in this context, is highly effective, and equally, there has been evidence of a degree of flexibility within these foundational technologies, such as developing and applying the techniques to different environments including service and merchandising (Puxty, 1993). However, the base tools and technologies do structure and constrain organisations in a certain cultural way (Morgan, 1988).

As advanced capitalist economies have developed, there has been a 'genuflection' to immaterial forms of value creation (Spence & Carter, 2011). In this sense, 'ideas' are crucial to the new economy as access to immaterial production is the driver of 'new wealth' (Hardt & Negri, 2000, 2005). There is an essential role for management accounting, particularly with respect to information and decision-making, but a challenge with how management accounting approaches the immaterial is that the tools and techniques of management accounting focus on the tangible, measurable and controllable. Thus, oftentimes, knowledge workers are asked to meet arbitrary, numeric-based targets that reflect a translation of management accounting into the factory to account for ideas. This is fundamentally a trade-off between trust and control. As such, the question is whether extending the ambit of management accounting to the immaterial is by logical design.

This chapter identifies the key challenges that the immaterial provides for management accounting. This is done by examining two case studies in higher education research management and by examining billing practices at professional firms (such as accountants and lawyers). This allows an opportunity to critique current practice, as well as considering options for identifying new approaches to managing the immaterial.

Introduction

The purpose of this chapter is to explore a set of rival, evaluative conceptions pertinent to management accounting and perhaps, accounting more generally. In particular, the focus of this work is to interrogate the conception of value that underpins traditional accounting measurement. In that, the chapter is a political intervention. It illustrates the impact of a transfer of the value construct from traditional material management accounting to the emergence of an immaterial-based capital. Thus, as the value within accounting is focused on a traditional materialism, this impacts on the construction, employment and use of management accounting tools and techniques. I will endeavour to illustrate how the limits of the 'traditional' construct of value are constraining and potentially disrespectful to immaterial labour (research in management accounting and accounting more generally illustrates the disrespectful nature of accounting to material labour).

In order to progress this argument, this chapter proceeds as follows: the first section examines three assumptions with respect to management accounting, concerning the service function of management accounting to management, the illogic of counting and the consequent excess, and the relationship of this chapter to existing work on immaterial labour in accounting. Immaterial labour stands in contrast to industrial, material labour, as it focuses on the creation of the immaterial, such as knowledge, information or communication (Hardt & Negri, 2005). Immaterial labour includes creative or intellectual labour, such as the services provided by the professionals such as lawyers or where an artist produces an artwork, and it includes affective labour, where the labour produces an 'affect' such as with a carer caring for an elderly patient in a care facility. The second section examines two issues concerning current management accounting literature with respect to control and discipline and existing research relevant to the issues of immaterial labour. The third section theorises issues pertinent to the problem of control with immaterial labour and its implications on accounting, and the fourth section reflects on two examples of immaterial labour, as illustrative of the challenges and illogic of applying management accounting tools and techniques to immaterial labour. These examples include (a) 6-minute units in professional practice and the emergence of value-based billing, and (b) current performance practices concerning research outputs in universities. The chapter concludes by reflecting on the idea that immaterial labour, by its constitution, is an excess and that it attempts to control and capture the value of immaterial labour through management accounting techniques, and thus is a failing technology. In fact, the chapter argues that for the purposes of the effective use of immaterial labour, trust, simply, is the most appropriate management answer. There is no need for accounting control, because if immaterial labour operates for the organisation and produces immaterial outputs, the incentives are already aligned for the expropriation of the immaterial output by capital. The organisation claims the immaterial benefit, and by dint of the employment contract, the immaterial labourer is materially rewarded (through a salary or similar).

Unpacking some assumptions

I want to make a couple of assumptions clear from the beginning of this exercise with respect to two positions concerning management accounting which then requires some reflection on immaterial labour more generally. The first assumption concerns the purpose of management accounting. Arnold and Hope (1983, p. 3) remind us that 'Management accounting is concerned with the provision of information to those responsible for managing businesses and other economic organisations to help them in making decisions about the future of the organisation and in controlling the implementation of the decisions they make'. This simple definition illustrates that management accounting is supposed to be accounting for management (and other internal users), and in that capacity, management accounting is not a simple reporting mechanism, but rather, operates within the organisation in a multi-faceted, multi-dimensional manner. Equally, in this, management accounting serves a broad range of interests within the organisation including management, employees and managers and is both a translation of strategy, mission and objectives, but also, management accounting is transformative in how it communicates strategy, mission and objectives. In a simple sense, if accounting is the language of business, then management accounting is the language of doing business internally. As an evaluative exercise, then, there is merit in evaluating the effectiveness of how management accounting communicates information to management (and in the context of this chapter, how effective management accounting is in communicating information to management and other users concerning immaterial labour). Management accounting is *par excellence*, in relation to control, concerning the management of material labour. This chapter will hold, though, that by focusing on the material outputs of immaterial labour, the consequent management accounting information is partial, one-sided and unhelpful.

Take Morgan's (1988, p. 483) illustration of the impact of introducing accounting control techniques into a hospital. In that sense, the doctors and nurses employ a variety of immaterial activities in the act of health care, including diagnosis, problem solving, treatment, caring, empathy and skill. This is a good example of a form of immaterial activity that combines intellectual and creative labour, service labour and affective labour, with a focus on material corporeal outputs. Morgan (1988, p. 483) argues:

> For example, in hospitals introducing systems that make patients or departments profit or cost centres, nurses and other staff often end up as extensions of the new financial systems, recording and allocating their time and use of materials much more rigorously than under more traditional systems of management (Davis, 1986). In the process, the nurses' relations with patients on the one hand and doctors on the other, change, as an orientation to control costs, or 'stay within budget', intrudes on decisions that used to be dominated by considerations of health care. The process seems to be particularly evident in relation to the more qualitative aspects of nursing, especially in nonlife-threatening situations. Under the requirement of 'meeting budget' the whole work orientation of nursing staff can change towards an administrative rather than patient-oriented focus. Financial controls can make hospitals more efficient. But they can also make them less humane.

However, the mythology that these mechanisms allude to is that new public management techniques and management accounting have immaterial labour under control. While efficiency of patient throughput, in relation to maternity care or post-surgery, may result in immediate cost reductions, this is not a proxy for control over the immaterial. This is simply control of the process once the immaterial component of the labour process has determined a suitable outcome. It certainly may have impact on 'humanity', and the work practice orientation of immaterial labour most certainly has an administrative focus, but it imposes obligations regarding the material components of the work. What might be posited is that management is comfortable in that this constitutes a proxy for control over immaterial production, but efficient throughput (as a material exercise) does not render decisions, empathy, or a smile controlled or controllable. Administrative efficiency does not produce faster immaterial products, and in this sense, the argument is that immaterial labour is an excess.

The second assumption pertinent to this chapter, from a sociological perspective, concerns the limits of measurement. This chapter holds that Cameron (1963, p. 92) is correct in saying '[n]ot everything that can be counted, counts. And not everything that counts can be counted'. This is a relevant quote for this chapter, because, as a polemic, it challenges the limits of the reified system of material measurement embodied in management control systems. For example, consider the role of targets in a retail service environment for an employee. Internal to the logic of such a target is a form of target setting, but these targets constitute a logic of broader control. It is not only an attempt to control the employee by communicating an objective of the organisation, but it also extends a pretence of control to factors external to the organisation. For example, satisfying a sales target, as a form of performance evaluation, is little within the individual employee's control, as issues such as the current state of the economy, the weather, disposable income, fashion trends, inflation and interest rates are all outside the ambit of influence of the employee (Morgan, 1988; Hines, 1989). In effect, an employee can provide exemplary service, but the actual sale event must be triggered by the purchaser. As Baker and Bettner (1997, p. 293) comment, '[a]ccounting's capacity to create and control social reality translates into empowerment for those who use it ... accounting is not a static reflection of economic activity, but rather is a highly partisan activity'. This is a problem for management accounting as it illustrates the limits of trying to control the immaterial by trying to count the immaterial and the consequent impact of that reductionist activity. I will do this by reflecting on two short examples: the 6-minute model for time-recording in professional organisations such as law and accountancy firms, and the management control systems with respect to academics and their productivity for the purposes of quality evaluation, such as the Research Excellence Framework (in the UK) and the Excellence in Research Assessment (in Australia) (and its many variants across the academic world). In a sense, the question at play is whether management accounting can and whether management accounting should attempt to measure immaterial production, for two reasons: (a) Does such a system constitute measurement of immaterial labour or is it a crude attempt at control? (b) Are there consequent impacts on immaterial labour that suggest that such management techniques might be counter-productive?

This chapter is concerned with accounting for immaterial labour, and in that sense, the chapter is not about knowledge management or accounting for knowledge per se. In recognising the continued research on intellectual capital accounting (ICA), I maintain the position elucidated in a paper published with Spence in 2011 (Spence & Carter, 2011, p. 313):

> Labour circumvents management accounting controls and financial accounting does not really know what it is trying to measure. It is these failures which explain the emergence of ICA, itself a manifestation of capital's belated recognition of the immaterial and the importance of the social factory. Through ICA one can discern a will-to-expropriation of the General Intellect which is deeply unsettling. Similar problematics arise in intellectual capital reporting as with management accounting and financial accounting. The movement to intellectual capital reporting invokes an irrationality due to the arbitrariness over what, how, when and why to measure the immaterial. Further, this move towards recasting the organisational boundaries to is indicative of an attempt to find new sources of value and to expropriate hitherto unmeasured, unmanaged and unmediated areas of social life.

Finally, it is necessary to account for one further caveat. In essence, in Spence and Carter (2011), we argued that accounting, as a form of calculative rationality, seeks to control and discipline labour. Nothing here constitutes a shift from the general politics of that paper. The chapter continues to hold that the value of 'social life' is in excess and should remain in excess of capital. That is, accounting technologies, as the language of capital, continue to seek to expropriate from the 'biens communs':

> This paper has delineated the general will-to-measure, control and discipline which underlie accounting technologies. It has traced the move from traditional rational calculative practices – as embodied in MA and FA – through to the emergence of a more qualitative, rational calculative practice as embodied in technologies such as the balanced scorecard but, more specifically, reporting on IC. As regards to MA and FA, we have questioned the rationality applied to these technologies. Accounting reifies the objective, the technical, the rational, the numeric and the calculative but once one scratches the surface of accounting technologies, their inherent irrationality and arbitrariness is exposed... Despite pretence of rationality and objectivity, accounting is incomplete in these regards because accountants construct boundaries around these. However, this is not a choice made by accountants (Hines, 1988); their rationality is bounded by the underlying philosophical foundations of accounting itself, which prevent them from conceiving of a way to capture anything but a partial representation of the General Intellect.
>
> *(Spence & Carter, 2011, p. 313)*

This is part of a broader politics, particularly as capital needs access to immaterial labour in the generation of new capital. In part, it illustrates the current approach to management accounting as a chronically failing technology by illustrating the excess, but in light of this polemic, it is an attempt to see a way forward for management accounting; not in the sense of enhancing productivity, but in the sense of making management accounting more useful. Labour will continue to be in excess of measurement, and capital continues to 'purchase' social life through the factory without walls (Hardt & Negri, 2000), but there may be a way of enhancing the interface (perhaps by reducing the tension) between labour and capital. This work, then, is both complementary to the 2011 publication and an extension of that work.

Immaterial labour and accounting

There is a growing literature on the challenge of post-Fordist economies and the emergence of immaterial labour (in the accounting context, see, Harney, 2006; Adkins, 2009; Spence & Carter, 2011; Böhm & Land, 2012; Mäkelä, 2013; Cooper, 2015). However, it is important to clarify what is signified by the concept of 'immaterial' and what it signifies in a politics of labour. Immaterial labour is a particular term of the autonomist Marxists, and it constitutes an opposition to materialism and material labour. There are similar ideas in relation to Foucault's (2008) work on the bio-political. To understand the immaterial, it is a relational concept to a set of competing signifiers, such as Fordist, material labour and the providence of Taylorist scientific management. Cooper and Taylor (2000, p. 4) argue:

> Scientific Management played and continues to play a central role in shaping the capitalist work process ... Taylorism took capitalist control to an entirely new level by asserting that an absolute necessity for adequate management is the dictation to the worker of the precise manner in which work is to be performed. Taylor insisted that management could only be a limited and frustrated undertaking so long as workers were left with any discretion in the implementation of their work. To totally alleviate management's

> frustration, Taylor developed a revolutionary division of labour. Taylor's basic concern was that workers should produce 'a fair day's work', meaning all the work which workers could do without injury to their health, at a pace that could be sustained through their working lifetime...

Traditional material capital invoked a focus on Fordist production through increasing specialisation and a resulting division of labour: material production was the application of the body to produce material outputs (Cockburn, 1987; Burris, 1993). The calculative, rational practices of management accounting, then, reflect this Fordist, Taylorist foundation. De Angelis and Harvie (2009, p. 6) suggest:

> Against this, we argue that the war over measure continues at the point of immaterial, self-organised and cooperative production. Capital is indeed pervasive, and its means of measurement often appear distant and elusive. But they nevertheless contribute to the constitution of the norms and modes of production – the *how?*, *how much?*, *how long?* and *how many?* that delimit our social doing. While thinkers such as Hardt and Negri are celebrating the impossibility of measuring immaterial production, the heirs of Frederick Taylor and Dickens' Gradgrind are attempting to do just that. An army of economists, statisticians, management-scientists and consultants, information-specialists, accountants, bureaucrats, political strategists and others is engaged in a struggle to commensurate heterogeneous concrete human activities on the basis of equal quantities of human labour in the abstract, that is, to link work and value. Far from the law of value being redundant, as Negri and Hardt have suggested, it is increasingly assuming the form of a struggle over measure, even in the realm of immaterial production.

However, this differs in a post-Fordist economy, where knowledge is important and production is still 'grounded in the body' (Spence & Carter, 2011, p. 305). However, the value of 'immaterial' labour is the driver of future capital (see, e.g., Böhm *et al.*, 2008; Jones & Murtola, 2012; Harney & Dunne, 2013). But as Harney (2005) and Bryer (2006) argue, such immaterial labour is harder to control and measure, as immaterial production and labour are internal to the employee (see Hochschild, 1983, for a detailed account of the production of immaterial effects, in the sense of control through managing smiles and affective relationships). Land and Taylor (2010, pp. 399–400) argue that '...value production has moved outside the workplace to subsume the whole of society and life itself ... all acts of social production, even life itself, become potentially value-productive forms of labour'.

In this sense, Hardt and Negri (2005, p. 108) identify different conceptualisations of labour in a post-Fordist economy. Traditional Fordist production is material production, and therefore, it concentrates on employers extracting productive value from employees. This is the traditional role of management accounting (Puxty, 1993). Hardt and Negri (2009, pp. 131–134), in relation to immaterial production, suggest that there are three forms of immaterial labour, as alluded to above: (a) advanced industrial production work that requires aspects of the immaterial due to technological advancement in production; (b) intellectual, creative labour; and (c) affective labour. Given the implications of a knowledge economy, or more specifically, the implications of immaterial production, there seems a lacuna between the tools and techniques of accounting and the current demands of management and employees concerning information useful in the management of labour.

Thus, in a knowledge economy and the service functions of many advanced capitalist economies, the nature of labour is different:

> Industrial labour has given way to 'immaterial labour', being labour which creates immaterial products such as knowledge, information, communications or relationships (Hardt and Negri, 2005). This is often conceived of through constructs such as cognitive labour, intellectual labour or service work, each of which refers to labour that is primarily intellectual or linguistic, involving problem solving, symbolic or analytical tasks and linguistic expression. Affective labour is a further dimension of immaterial labour, being labour that produces affects such as feelings of well-being, comfort or excitement. Some jobs solely aim to deliver this, although such affects are increasingly elements of the way in which all work is completed. Hardt (1999) argues that the relational aspects of affective labour produce social networks and forms of community which signal the breaking down of the division between economy and culture.
>
> ...
>
> This is not to say that material labour has disappeared from view. On the contrary, material labour still dominates quantitatively. It is primarily immaterial products that are produced. The process of producing these products remains grounded in the body. The corporeality of immaterial labour is not necessarily less than in material labour. The point, however, is that all forms of labour increasingly genuflect to the immaterial. Thus, immaterial labour exercises a qualitative hegemony on all forms of labour.
>
> *(Spence & Carter, 2011, p. 305)*

This presents challenges to traditional accounting, and especially to management accounting. Harney (2005, p. 579) argues that traditional accounting tools and techniques shape the measurable and controllable, and thus, immaterial labour generates '[a] crisis of measurement brought on by the growing dominance of what Marx named the General Intellect is a profound challenge not only to management but specifically to its *recording-machine*, accounting [emphasis in original]'. Given this foundation, and given the 'genuflection' to immaterial labour, immaterial production and immaterial capital, it is important to determine what the foundation is of management accounting and why this creates a 'crisis of measurement'.

The foundations of management accounting as material capital

Management accounting tends to focus on production, control and measurement. Frezatti *et al.* (2014, p. 427) suggest that 'management accounting artefacts support, facilitate, enable, and constrain' management accounting (Hines, 1988, Morgan, 1988; Puxty, 1993; Chapman, 1998). However, the focus of traditional management accounting tools and technologies, including cost, budgets and variances, provides a foundation for controlling material production (Chapman, 1998). Management accounting, in this context, is highly effective, and equally, there has been evidence of a degree of flexibility within these foundational technologies, such as developing and applying the techniques to different environments including service and merchandising (Puxty, 1993). However, the base tools and technologies do structure and constrain organisations in a certain cultural way (Morgan, 1988). Puxty (1993, p. 4) introduces the classic materialist conception of management accounting:

> Management accounting is a set of social practices that delineate the space within which the activity of the workforce might be made visible and susceptible to rational calculation … [It] is an instrument within an enterprise that facilitates the exploitation of, and extraction of surplus value from, its employees by the capitalist interests that, through management control the accounting system.

Frezatti *et al.* (2014, p. 430) argue that management accounting gives a partial, stylised representation of any phenomenon it attempts to represent. As Morgan (1988, p. 480) states,

> … accountants try to represent organisations and their activities in terms of numbers. This is metaphorical. And like all use of metaphor, it gives but a partial and incomplete representation of the reality to which the numbers relate. The numerical view … ignores those aspects of organisational reality that are not quantifiable in this way.

This suggests that the form of valorisation in management accounting is contestable and contingent. This allows Bryer (2006, p. 553) to argue that management accounting imposes a particular method of valorisation with respect to accountability:

> … accounting is the most important control system because it allows capital to 'control' labour in both common meanings of the word – to dominate and to regulate … accounting shapes workers' behaviour in capital's interest, not that it directly determines their thoughts'.

Consequently, there is evidence of this, for example, in Armstrong (2006) where accounting operates as a form of discipline, and thus, restricts creativity as it encourages time-based or activity-based production (against standards and budgets, for example).

This alludes to the foundation of management accounting in a materialist conception of production, understood as a form of political economy. There is considerable debate in management accounting concerning the role of management accounting as a technology of control over labour and the range of technologies applied to control productive, material labour in better ways. Such control mechanisms may not have been the genesis of management accounting for some researchers (see Johnson & Kaplan, 1987; Loft, 1995). However, much critical work in accounting has identified the routes of labour control in the critique of the underpinning logic of neo-classical economic rationalism (see, for example, Hopper & Armstrong, 1991; Uddin & Hopper, 2001; Harney, 2005; Bryer, 2006). In accounting, labour process theorists such as Hopper (1990) and Armstrong (2002) suggest that management accounting techniques reproduce class structure and conflict in the extraction of surplus value. Alawattage and Wickramasinghe (2008, p. 297) argue that 'control systems are argued to be the means of domination through which one party (mainly capital) disciplines and governs the other (mainly labour). Control systems are not only political but also historical'. Spence and Carter (2011, p. 308) in drawing on Bryer (2006, p. 589) suggest that 'Labour Process Theorists might be criticised for idealising management control strategies which, in reality, are haphazard and give way to strategies of "responsible autonomy". Rather, capitalism controls labour via the imposition of a regime of accountability for the circulation of capital'. This viewpoint is not held universally. For example, Emmanuel *et al.* (1990, p. 98) recognise, at best, that accounting plays a supplementary role in controlling labour, as 'it cannot be overemphasised that accounting is just one technique that is available to assist in the control process, not the totality of that process'. However, Spence and Carter (2011) and Bryer (2006, p. 552) reject this separation:

> Accounting is not the only technique of management control, and it does not reflect or allow us to understand and control all aspects of an organisation's reality. Nevertheless, accounting is the 'totality' of the control process because it provides an objective framework within which all other control systems and realities are subsidiary and subservient.

After a broad sweep of literature concerning political economy, management accounting and control, Alawattage and Wickramasinghe (2008, p. 298) agree:

> Thus, it is established, though with different theoretical explanations, that management accounting techniques do play a constitutive and a transformative role in labour control. In critical accounting literature, the development of management accounting techniques in the West, one way or the other, has been attributed to the quest for better methods in disciplining labour.

However, this focus has traditionally been on material political economy and material production. Control, in the multi-variant forms, has not, as Harney (2006) and Bryer (2005) suggest, taken account of the rise of the genuflection to immaterial labour. New management techniques have emerged, as a response, by attempting to institute a more holistic approach to information, such as the Balanced Scorecard (with increased qualitative measures of performance), flexibility budgeting and responsibility accounting. Elmassri *et al.* (2016, p. 152), in the context of Strategic Investment Decision-Making, argue that

> Recent SID research signals a shift ... to a conceptual focus that reflects the impact of different influences upon SIDM, including risk assessment, politics, culture and social issues. Some strategic management accounting literature on making strategic decisions also suggests that the organisation's increasing tendency to emphasise non-financial considerations illustrates the potential mediating impact of strategic considerations.

Spence and Carter (2011, p. 308) consider this 'reinvention' and argue:

> MA has tried to reinvent itself, moving from its traditional position of stifling innovation to one which innovation is enabled. Mouritsen *et al.* (2009) suggest that MA provides a context within which innovation can occur. However, they also show how MA simultaneously fails to make innovation transparent...Thus, even if we interpret the [Balanced Scorecard] as an attack by capital, an attempt to more effectively control immaterial labour for the sake of accumulation (Hopper, 1990), it does not fully succeed in transferring knowledge from labour to capital. The immaterial thus remains 'in excess' of capital's attempts to define and control it.

It is in the context of 'immaterial labour' that a 'crisis of measurement' emerged. Traditional accounting techniques do not apply well to the immaterial. This congenital failure, for De Angelis and Harvie (2009, p. 15), constitutes a struggle over measure:

> We suggest that it is productive to understand these practices in terms of struggle over *measure*. This is useful because it helps us both understand what is happening within higher education in its own terms, and also to link developments in this sector to processes of measure elsewhere in the economy and society. By struggle over measure, we mean to retrieve an old preoccupation embedded in classical Marxism's categories of value. For us, the capitalist production of value that Marx discusses in *Capital* is a

> category of struggle. Moreover, this struggle includes a struggle over measure(s): the daily struggle over the *what, how, how much, why* and *who* of social production. This struggle goes on in any sphere of social production in which capital seeks to valorise itself vis-à-vis the self-valorising practices and desires of the producers (whether 'material' or 'immaterial') …

One of the substantive problems for management accounting and a response to 'the crisis of measurement' is that much of management accounting is based on time. Time is an effective control mechanism, with respect to material labour. It accords with hourly wages, production standards (x per minute, per hour) and it is an effective mechanism for control (material production is best expressed in the typical 8-hour working day). This is a preoccupation with measurement, and time is one of the prime measures and is the source of a fundamental control mechanism for management accounting according to Nandhakumar and Jones (2001, p. 194):

> Time in accounting is predominantly conceptualised in terms of measurable clock time (Ezzamel & Robson, 1995; Loft, 1990) which enables precise timing of activities and thereby their coordination across a particular place. Thompson (1967) has argued that this clock-time is an important feature of capitalism, necessary for the control of the labour process. Through standards, budgets and plans, accounting therefore seeks to mobilise cost and effort in temporal terms and to manage time as a scarce resource. In this way, accounting is seen as providing a neutral, objective and calculable domain that would allow organisations to be governed (Miller & O'Leary, 1993). In order to enable management control, accounting practice typically treats organisational work as decomposable into discrete activities, the duration and measurement of which are capable of precise definition and measurement, and which may therefore be reliably estimated.

However, this does not translate effectively to immaterial production. We see these attempts, but they are far from convincing: sell a certain amount per hour; serve a certain number of customers per hour; allocate 15 minutes of activity to care for an elderly person; throughputs in hospital and other health care; allocate activity on a 6-minute basis or produce a certain number of academic research outputs in a year. The problem is that this is a mere illusion of control. Each of these measures reifies the material element of the work (sales, customers, care, linking time to output, papers, etc.), and thus, this constitutes a congenital failure to address the immaterial element of the labour process. However, these become a proxy for control and a valorisation process of 'what, how, how much, why and who of social production' (De Angelis & Harvie, 2009, p. 15).

Furthermore, there is significant literature in accounting concerning the impact of the focus on control within management accounting on trust and dysfunctional behaviour (see, for example, Dermer & Lucas, 1986; Merchant *et al.*, 2003; Alvesson & Kärreman, 2004; Berry *et al.*, 2005). Researchers, in effect, simply accept the problems concerning 'control' and thus, try to solve these problems: Hopper and Powell (1985, p. 435) argue that 'the awareness of "behavioural dysfunctions" merely spurred on their endeavours to refine measurements to rectify such aberrations'. Equally, the literature accepts that the function of organisations is to control labour. Puxty (1993) illustrates the impact of functionalist and determinist assumptions concerning labour. In particular, the assumption often applied to labour is that they are 'rational, utility maximisers' and consequently, as they respond in a deterministic manner to financial and other incentives, they can be 'directed' (Ouchi, 1979; Puxty & Chua, 1989;

Speklé, 2001). Thus, this means that management accounting does little to deal with dysfunction, but rather the control of labour is a means to financial ends, as 'management control processes ... are concerned with the cognition and application of, ideally, substantively rational choice models for enterprise control' (Puxty & Chua, 1989, p. 134). However, this is, in its own way, a limited view of the organisation:

> The question of rationality-irrationality is itself invalid. It is the wrong question – that is, such a dichotomy is the wrong metric. Rationality is in the eye of the beholder, and the rationality of any act is not structurally intrinsic to that act but inheres only in the perception of the observer which may to a greater or lesser extent be grounded in the norms of society. Thus, if we claim that actions within organisations are in some way 'irrational' we are merely stating that they do not conform to the norms of society as we perceive them.
>
> *(Puxty & Chua, 1989, pp. 134–135)*

Consequently, there is a potential problem with trust in management accounting, partly due to the simplistic and potentially disrespectful approach to labour (Chua, 1986). Baldvinsdottir (2009) discusses how trust might be institutionalised through management accounting. Baldvinsdottir (2009) points to the establishment of trust as the routines and stability of management accounting can promote trust, especially through the use of such information in a sensitive and ethical manner. However, Baldvinsdottir (2009, p. 58) concludes by identifying three sources of distrust in management accounting:

> To conclude, this paper has presented three different symptoms of distrust have been identified: (1) distrust between the evaluator and the evaluated; (2) distrust of the management accounting figures; and (3) distrust of the management accountant. The first symptom occurs either when the employees distrust the performance evaluation made by the management or when the management distrusts the employees' performance. The treatment suggested in these situations is the mobilization of the management accountant's diplomacy. For the second symptom, distrust of the management accounting figures, the treatments suggested are: a) the mobilization of the management accountant's instrumental competence, i.e., 'correcting' the figures; or b) changing the basis for the evaluations. Finally, for the third symptom, distrust of the management accountant, the treatments suggested are: a) the identification and mobilization of the carrier of trust; or b) replace the management accountant.

As such, it constitutes a fundamental challenge to management accounting and immaterial labour, because the effective exchange is one of expropriation, which contains within it, the potential for conflict and distrust. Lazzarato (2004) argues that immaterial labour should be understood as 'invention', and this is developed through the Microsoft critique, where 'Gates became the richest man on earth in a couple of decades by appropriating the rent received from allowing millions of intellectual workers to participate in that particular form of the "General Intellect" he successfully privatised and still controls' (Žižek, 2009, p. 146). For Lazzarato (2004, pp. 142–143), '...invention ... is the result of the collaboration and coordination of a multitude of agents whose ideas are "rarely glorious, in general anonymous... of infinitesimal innovations brought by each little man to the common endeavour"'. In that sense, immaterial labour is complex and is therefore a 'non-place with respect to capital' (Negri & Hardt, 1999, p. 82). As a consequence, in relation to immaterial labour, Spence and Carter (2011, p. 308) argue that management accounting thwarts both the creative and aesthetic dimensions of production (essentially the main sources of value), and thus is a failing technology:

> Thus, MA might be characterised as a congenitally failing technology. Although it seeks to discipline labour for the sake of accumulation, it is never fully successful in this regard. This is not to say that MA is not implicated in exploitation because of overhead allocation problems. Measurement of labour is increasingly difficult to locate yet remains important as what has historically kept worker self-activity at bay (Harney, 2006). MA still provides sense and order. However, it is important to point out that accounting's power is not monolithic.

If management accounting is 'congenitally failing', there is a need to reflect on why immaterial labour poses difficulties. The previous discussion has alluded to why immaterial labour is an excess, but there are two aspects in particular of immaterial labour, that cause immaterial labour to be problematic for management.

The immaterial in immaterial labour

Immaterial labour conceptually questions the classical approaches to understanding work, in the materialist conception of work. In principle, all immaterial labour involves a corporeal element. As Hardt and Negri (2005, pp. 145–146) suggest, '[m]aterial production – the production, for example, of cars, televisions, clothing, and food – creates the means of social life ... Immaterial production, by contrast, including the production of ideas, images, knowledges, communication, cooperation, and affective relations, tends to create not the means of social life but social life itself'. Thus, the application of a skillset is a component of immaterial labour: for example, in relation to creative or intellectual labour, the skills are of an informational, problem-solving, entrepreneurial nature; for affective labour, the skills are fundamentally human in the ability to read, understand and respond to a situation with emotional, cultural and social intelligence; and for the advanced industrial immaterial labour, the more manual orientation requires the use of creativity and 'thinking outside the box'. The nature of immaterial labour takes us outside the factory walls, to a factory of ideas without walls: this is the 'factory of the mind' (Hardt & Negri, 2000, p. 293). Thus, given this 'excess', management accounting and management more generally attempt to exert controls over this 'factory of the mind', including attempts to manage the skillset and productive capacity, in managing social relations and social cooperation (Lazzarato, 2004; De Angelis & Harvey, 2009).

By its very nature, though, immaterial production is about the 'new'. Each act of immaterial labour is a new immaterial product: the academic paper, the new 'fashion' trend, the generation of a feeling to inclusion or the legal opinion to a problem. In effect, each new immaterial product is about establishing 'tomorrow', and in a capital sense, it is about consumers and markets. Each new immaterial product communicates a new possibility (a new way of knowing), and therefore, it envisages a renegotiation for capital of consumption. Thus, the essence of the immaterial product is that as ideas generate future capital, the immaterial product is produced socially and not through capital (Lazzarato, 2004). What management accounting is trying to do is capture the social aspect and turn it into capital (in a valorised form). This is a significant departure from Taylorism and equally from traditional material management accounting. This is the first challenge for management accounting, as the tools and techniques of current management accounting are not flexible enough to deal with the social side of immaterial labour – accounting valorises the capital side.

The second problem for management accounting concerns control and relates to the immaterial labour cycle. The fundamental challenge to management accounting and, more particularly, the logic of control inherent to management accounting systems is that the labour cycle to immaterial production differs to the traditional production cycle facilitated through a focus on time in material labour. The effective challenge is that there is a relevant and radical autonomy within immaterial production. Despite its corporeal form, immaterial labour is a direct challenge to the classical understanding of the work place and work, itself. More concerning for capital systems is that the 'use value' of immaterial production (its current and future capital values) is autonomous. The goal, of course, is to turn the immaterial product into a tradeable commodity in the form of a service, a new material product or a combination of both. It is about new ways of doing, of knowing and new ways of 'being', in the deeper ontological sense: but they are internal to the being. Hardt and Negri (2005) take this further to suggest that the valuable sense of immaterial production is actually social life itself. Immaterial production is addressed to the social and draws from the social. For example, in the immaterial components of affective labour, the production of a smile, a tender touch or a production of associated humanity, is addressed to a social problem (pain, comfort, inclusion), but is also produced through drawing on the social (to understand, read and respond to the situation in a socially appropriate, recognised and constructed manner). The problem for management accounting systems is that there is no methodology available to understand this interaction. Accounting values through appropriation of the 'value' of the output (the service or the affect) and then proceeds to normalise and standardise the time value of the output. However, that is a fundamental misunderstanding of the process of immaterial production (Harney, 2006). It is not time-bound, but it is socially bound. The immaterial labour is facilitated by the ability to access the social, address a response to the social and thus draw from the social. Accounting expropriates the value of these moments, but in the creation of new capital futures, accounting does not value the idea, but its material value as a future (the ultimate fair value, so to speak). This expropriation actually divorces the material output from its immaterial innovation, and thus, capital is not 'innovative', unless one recognises expropriation as a form of innovation. The management control process seeks to control innovation through controlling organisational processes (such as time, targets and expectations), but it is a failing technology, as immaterial production is an excess outside of control.

Thus, in sum, we have two fundamental problems at hand for management accounting: (a) the tools and techniques of current management accounting are not flexible enough to deal with the social side of immaterial labour and thus, management accounting valorises the capital side of immaterial labour, and (b) immaterial production constitutes a challenge to the logic of control inherent to management accounting systems as there is a relevant and radical autonomy within immaterial production. To illustrate the challenges with this, these problems are illustrated through the following two case studies. The first short case study concerns 6-minute units and the valorisation of the capital aspects of creative, intellectual labour of professions including lawyers and accountants. The second short case study concerns the performance measurement of academic research and the challenge of autonomy.

Six-minute units: making every minute count

As the chapter has illustrated, management accounting operates as a control technology. Professional firms, such as law firms and accountancy firms, tend to operate a disciplining technology by requiring their professionals to account for their time on the basis of 6-minute units and to charge these units of activity to client cost centres. Brown and Lewis (2011, p. 880) discuss this control component as follows:

> The time/billing routine was thus a normalizing technique that subjugated lawyers by rendering them subject to processes of comparison and correction, and as such was equivalent to other recognized disciplinary techniques such as dress codes and timetables. It was a means of measuring labour and binding them to a system with which they came to define their organizational reality and their own identities (cf. Covaleski *et al.* 1998: 302; Grey 1994): to be a productive lawyer (and law firm) meant engaging effectively in the time/billing routine. Concomitantly, this activity made them recordable, visible, and calculable and allowed comparisons of an individual's documented achievements against organizational norms. Time-related routines led to processes of normalization which produced hierarchies of differentiation through quantitative measurements by which the firm hoped to change people's behaviours. Billable hour and fee recovery targets (hourly, daily, weekly, monthly) were kinds of quasi-contracts, to be 'enforced' if an individual departed from established norms. This was a continuous process of fabrication through which individuals were disciplined and selves objectified and transformed into manageable and self-managing subjects.

This section reflects my own professional experience. During my time in a law firm, the 6-minute process presented a form of ethical dilemma. I remember worrying at the end of a week if I had not accounted for my time and who should be charged for particular activities and for how much. A favourite category in my firm was thinking time and research time. Both of these constitute broad categories and were essential to the production of legal outputs, and they are effectively immaterial categories of labour. However, they are not real: it is artificial, as I do not think in 6-minute timeslots. Equally, the categories are processes for allocating time created artificialities. For example, developing a legal opinion surely should involve thinking (I am fairly sure my clients expected that), but drafting had a separate code to research and thinking time. I also reflect on my frustration at the difference between my charge out rate (on an hourly basis) and the salary that I was earning (worse still was when I would calculate my salary by the number of hours worked).

However, Brown and Lewis (2011) illustrate the key points of this chapter in relation to the control components of management accounting. Six-minute units operated as a form of 'normalisation', as each lawyer was expected to achieve a target of 1,300 billable hours. As Brown and Lewis (2011, p. 880) illustrate, this is a form of normalisation, because '…lawyers talked about their selves in terms specified by the firm's protocols, [which] constitute[s] a system of avowal in which they were discursively constructed, their failings highlighted, improvements specified and forces for normalization enjoined'. Despite immaterial production being 'new', the 6-minute units help immaterial professionals to be made 'comparable' to other professionals within the same space, as it creates a form of comparative performance measurement (Brown & Lewis, 2011, p. 874). Brown and Lewis (2011) suggest that this is a mechanism for controlling immaterial labour and rendering it measurable. A good lawyer is a productive lawyer, and a good lawyer is a good 6-minute recorder. Thus, a mechanism tied to billing becomes a mechanism for scrutiny and control, and attempts to reduce immaterial productivity to the visible and calculable. In effect, this produced the 'governed'. Targets, expectations, comparisons and organisational trends are all aspects of the performance management and thus control.

In relation to our first challenge (the valorisation of the capital side), this is an example par excellence. Each part of the professional process from problematisation to design to production is about producing the 'novel' and the 'new'. Each iteration, each scenario or each client constitutes a new 'social', and in that sense, each immaterial output communicates a new way of knowing, which requires the 'social'. The immaterial product is produced socially for the social. However, the 6-minute process reduces the activity solely to a process of capital valorisation and applies the simple time/billing/client dichotomy.

In response, there has been a recent shift to remove 6-minute units, which are perceived as antiquated. The increased adoption of 'value-based' billing is a new method, and the advantage of this approach is bringing cost certainty for clients, thus mirroring the move in accounting to activity-based measurement. The basic logic of this move is that for customers, particularly in the professional fields of law and accounting, this gives a degree of cost certainty. LexisNexis (2013) reports, in relation to legal billing, that value-based billing

> 'aligns the lawyers' incentives with the clients' interests, so both are focused on achieving the desired results, not how many hours it takes to get there ... for establishing value... you would: (1) articulate to the firm what value you place on the different types of work they perform; (2) determine whether the firm can provide services for a fee consistent with that value; (3) set the fee for the work and discuss the project scope; (4) expect the firm to request a retainer that is either a portion or the full cost of the project; (5) meet with the firm; (6) ensure that the firm is focused on delivering high-quality services.

Value-based billing might remove the preoccupation with accounting for 6-minute units in the daily professional life, and while this might remove elements of the surveillance and control, this is no panacea. This is for two reasons. First, in applying the logic of Brown and Lewis (2011), the normalising and comparative components of the billing process continue, as there is still a focus on the material outputs of immaterial labour. There is still a focus on billing for the organisation and on making money, and fee recovery targets are likely to still persist. Time may be removed as the direct comparator, but there is still a time component to the value calculation. Second, this approach does nothing to consider the problem of the excess in terms of the social. The value-based approach continues to reify the economic value of the immaterial production. Thus, as long as this valorisation process continues, the role of management accounting is to continue to control and the 'crisis of measurement' continues. In light of this congenital failure, the next short case study concerns the 'radical' autonomy of academics or academia and the limits of the performance evaluation techniques applied.

The immaterialism of academic labour: material control

Most academics understand the challenge and the regimes of material control applied to research outputs. The influence of new public management and the broader ideological influence of liberal market reforms resulted in a significant number of measures, citation indices and ranking exercises in relation to academic research activities. In effect, the immaterial exercise of idea creation, research development and article production, through performance evaluation exercises, has been reduced to a form of metric or measurement. While each university and each rankings exercise will emphasise that quality is the central condition of any department or any national research exercise, it is clear that there are quantity components in-built into the exercises.

It is important to note that this is not a critique, per se, of a quality focus on research, but it is a critique of the crudeness of quantity and measures being associated with the exercise. Crudely, each researching academic (including lecturers, assistant professors, professors and variants) at a university has an associated performance expectation concerning research outcomes in a period of time. For example, in the UK, each academic is effectively expected to present at least four 'quality' outputs in a 6-year research excellence framework (REF) period. Most Australasian universities expect at least four outputs in every 3-year cycle. These numbers and time frames are purely arbitrary, and despite this arbitrariness, they are instituted, and in that sense, they are very (materially) real. De Angelis and Harvie (2009, p. 18) argue:

> But these norms are also real – or material – in the sense that they help shape the form of academic labour in both its educational and research contexts. They do so by counter-posing the measures of capital, which privilege the meeting of abstractly defined targets (whether these indicate financial viability or consistency with government policies), to the immanent measures of immaterial labourers, who instead privilege the intellectual and relational content of their work...Conversely, an 'efficient' lecturer is one who uses the pittance of his or her research allowance and produces 'measurable output' – one article in a 'good' refereed journal each year – without asking for more time off teaching. It goes without saying that, unless such a lecturer is able to beat norms elsewhere, and recuperate time in this way, then they will be forced to extend their own working day and week. In this way, a quantitative definition of socially necessary labour-time for the labour of a lecturer emerges as the result of an ongoing process of norm-definition.

The challenges with these time-based, quantity metrics are threefold. The first problem is that, given the publication cycle, the time frame in reference is really a measure of historical immaterial production, rather than current immaterial production. It is, of course, one of the challenges of different disciplinary journal traditions, but there is a marked difference between sciences and technology and business and economics.

> There were striking differences between disciplines with business/economics having around twice the total delay submission to publication compared to chemistry.
>
> *(Björk & Solomon, 2013, p. 920)*

The average total time to publication for a chemistry paper from being received by a journal to publication in that journal was 9 months. The equivalent for a paper in business and economics, from reception to publication, was 17.7 months (Björk & Solomon, 2013). Thus, some of the outputs counted in a particular frame of reference relate to work completed in a previous cycle. More so, this does not take account of the immaterial production itself. The 17.7-month average lead time to publication only counts once the article has been received by the journal. This says nothing of the actual immaterial production (the actual research) and whether the paper is conferenced. Actual publication time from idea construction, research, writing, submission, response to review and hopefully acceptance can be many years. Thus, time to publication is not within the control of the researcher.

This alludes to the second key point, which relates to the challenge of research more generally. Publication, itself, is not a neutral process. I remember my first ever round of research assessment at a former university, where the metric was four outputs during a period, but the overall assessment was an assessment of quality. A senior professor submitted a paper published in a working paper series as one of his outputs, which was intriguing as this professor had published in some of the leading journals in the relevant field. On inquiring why this choice was made, the professor in question stated that it was the best research work that they had produced. It was not published, in the traditional sense of a book or journal output, but it was published in the recognised working paper format. The challenge with journal production is multi-faceted, but journals have particular foci that are of interest to them, and the peer review process is both fascinating and complex. A simple reflection on the intensity and passion evident at many conferences, research seminars and workshops is illustrative of the challenges in the peer review process. Academics, by their nature, and potentially more so in the social sciences, are fiercely protective of their academic contributions. The tenure wars in the United States concerning feminist legal scholars or the significant intellectual debate with respect to positivism in accounting are illustrative of the politics of research. Arguably, it is a crucial difference between the materialism of material production and the materialism of immaterial production. In the immaterial space, the academic controls the generation of draft research to the extent of submission to a journal, but this same academic researcher has little control over whether that research output is actually published and in what form.

Finally, given work intensification and different working models (including on-line learning and distance education), the requirements for research work extend the time that the academic is at work. As De Angelis and Harvie (2009, p. 18) argue, these performance requirements require the academic to extend their working day, working week and working time. The nature of immaterial labour is that the corporeal components (the mind) are always present, but time is scarce. De Angelis and Harvie (2009, p. 6) argue that

> Academic work possesses all the basic characteristics of immaterial labour. It is a form of directly social work, in which the form of social cooperation is crucial in defining the 'output'; moreover, it is a form of doing that is necessarily grounded on relational awareness. It is labour that produces affects. Academic work is also a context for the production of ideas, in the form of research-papers, books, conference presentations, lectures and so forth. Moreover, this production is 'bio-political' and can occur at any time: we have both experienced waking up in the middle of the night with the solution to a problem intractable during our formal working day, or reached insights that will find their way into a paper whilst playing with a child.

As a consequence of the 'bio-political', the impact of performance intensification and performance control, as well as the combined impacts of journal agendas, publication lead times, and the politics and process of research outputs, constitutes an effective gifting of social and private life to the university. It is easy to account for efficiency with the benefit of hindsight, and it is easy to be instrumental, but each immaterial output is new, novel and was produced exactly as it was produced, and consequently, this polemic is illustrative of the limits of management, as we have few insights, given the autonomy of immaterial labour.

The idea that this chapter illustrates is that the radical autonomy of immaterial labour eludes capture in the management accounting performance evaluation techniques applied in academic publishing. We have seen an increase in 'production' of research following the introduction of measurement expectations and indices. However, at what cost? If the institution of new public management in universities resulted in work intensification and work moving outside of the university, then this is not efficiency: arguably it is not an increase in productivity (on a time scale, per se). However, it is simply an expropriation of social and private life for capital gain, given that the university is progressively understood as a business. The radical autonomy of immaterial labour is not controlled through material measures, and the arbitrariness and partiality of material measures are further evidence of the congenital failure of management accounting technologies in this capacity. Thus, it is not control of the immaterial process (which is an excess); this is a crude surveillance technology, which presents the opportunity for some concluding comments.

Concluding comments: a new approach for immaterial labour

Each attempt at instituting control of immaterial labour is failing and will fail. The chapter presented examples from retail, care, universities, professional firms and others to illustrate that each measure for material control of immaterial labour (in illustrating the crisis of measurement) is arbitrary, partial and congenitally failing. The chapter suggested two challenges for control with respect to immaterial labour, including the (first-order) social component of immaterial production and the radical autonomy of immaterial labourers. The examples of the 6-minute units and the academic research output expectations illustrate the limits of management accounting as they reify the economic component of the output and attempt to control the material component of immaterial production (but do nothing to affect the immaterial component). This is a crisis and struggle over measurement, and this is unhelpful for management for which management accounting is supposed to be providing information. However, in the examples I have discussed, management accounting provides a faux illusion of control.

I posit a different approach. I suggest we return to a fundamental logic of trust. Why? So far, the argument would suggest that with respect to immaterial labour, *the best management accounting approach is in fact no management accounting approach*. The traditional arguments concerning control may not apply to accounting for the immaterial. All the organisational incentives exist already without the need to apply accounting systems that, potentially, are disrespectful to the human condition itself. If Puxty (1993) is correct, in that management accounting delineates a space for control and for making the extraction of surplus value visible, then this does not apply to immaterial labour and may in fact be counter-productive and counter-intuitive. Such arbitrary and limited surveillance devices may be counter-productive to the immaterial activity: lawyers worry about 6-minute units; academics complain about work intensification and the arbitrariness of measured outputs. Moreover, the fundamental mis-logic here is that control mechanisms produce discord and distrust with immaterial labour. The performance evaluation of management control with respect to immaterial labour extends only to the material components of immaterial production as rational and calculative.

The chapter has illustrated how the immaterial components are an excess; hence, two issues arise. First, the 6-minute unit analysis indicates a form of gaming and artificiality as lawyers negotiated the game. This illustrates that while immaterial labour is being disciplined to follow the routine, it does not accord with disciplining of the immaterial activity. Immaterial production is outside the scope of control, as 6-minute units do not make immaterial production happen more effectively, efficiently or faster. Second (and it is an area that needs more study), there has been an increase in academic publications in the material quantitative era of metrics and research assessment exercises. Perhaps the new public management reform afforded greater attention to publication practice, but that does not necessarily accord with control. My fear is that the arbitrary performance evaluation mechanism of x publications per year or per time period has effectively purchased time in the form of social and private life. While the combination of management accounting and Taylorist scientific management focused on the productive targets such as x number of material outputs per hour, the logic was a control logic in aligning the interest of the employee with the organisation. However, the key issue here was time was also controlled. The employee worked 8 hours (or some variation). This is not the case with the logic of performance evaluation with respect to immaterial labour. Time, as Nandhakumar and Jones (2001) illustrate, is a problematic device. In that capacity, Harney (2006), Bryer (2005), De Angelis and Harvie (2009), and Spence and Carter (2011) all suggest that immaterial labour is outside of control and time is different. The hypothesis is that the management accounting performance targets have purchased time in the form of social and private life. This, as Hardt and Negri (2005) suggest, is expropriation from the 'biens communs', but also is not control or discipline in the classic sense of management accounting. This extends the scope of management accounting as a mechanism of constraining and capturing immaterial time outside of the workplace. The fundamental problem is that ideas happen when they happen: anywhere, anytime (De Angelis & Harvie, 2009, p. 6).

Thus, in relation to Baldvinsdottir (2009) and the production of distrust, this management accounting imposition is problematic. By extending influence into social and private life, in a crude attempt at control, it produces distrust in at least two ways:

a Distrust of the Evaluator: Immaterial labour is aware that the targets, standards, performance measures and other metrics that focus on the material outputs of immaterial production are arbitrary. This contains within it the possibility for creating distrust between immaterial labour and management. For example, management suggesting that a performance evaluation target has not been satisfied involves a critique of some elements outside the control of immaterial labour.

b Distrust of the Figures: The material figures are not necessarily within the control of the immaterial labour. As we suggested, meeting a sales target is a matter of luck associated with a whole range of different socio-economic factors. Equally, in relation to research output, this is outside the ambit of control of the academic as the process is political and complex. Thus, the figures are questionable. Baldvinsdottir (2009) suggests 'correcting' the figures, but it is not possible with immaterial production. Any material component of control misrecognises the excess. The chapter suggests that simple trust is a solution, with no formal management control.

The material attempts at control of immaterial labour are counter-intuitive in two ways. First, capital cannot extract surplus value in the same way that it extracts surplus from material labour. Material labour is exploited in the manner by which their material outputs produce profit margins for the organisation over and above the time-value reward for the labourer. Thus, in applying Fordist and Taylorist logic, the role of management accounting is to facilitate this extraction of surplus by standardising production targets (as expected material outputs per hour), setting expected production and targets (through budgets), minimising the costs associated with each material output (in relation to costs of input, including labour cost and overhead costs) and then to control for any variances (see the literature on costing studies and labour process theory). Second, immaterial labour is different to material labour. As Spence and Carter (2011, p. 313) argue, 'Within this context, measuring labour's contribution to value creation in terms of the money value of socially necessary labour time as do traditional political economy theorists in the accounting literature or in terms of hours worked... only produce the most impoverished of calculations. Immaterial labour is so *hors mesure* that any attempt to measure or represent it fails to make any sense philosophically' [emphasis in original]. As Harney (2006, p. 936) suggests, there is a disconnect between accounting and labour, as 'we are indeed witnessing a crisis in accounting, but at a more profound level than we have dared to contemplate'.

Thus, trust. The role of a good accountant should be critically evaluative of their own craft. Management accounting is excellent at providing information in certain contexts, but in relation to immaterial labour, it is congenitally failing. We (management accounting scholars and practitioners) should recognise this limit and recognise when our tools and techniques are not working in the way that we suggest they are. Given that the immaterial is outside of measure control, we can continue to force counter-productive and counter-intuitive measures, or we can say enough is enough. If our role is to provide management with relevant information for decision-making, we are not able to do that. Thus, we should rely on trust, not by instituting new measures but simply by recognising that no new control mechanisms are required. All of the management concerns are aligned: we should simply manage that. If an academic publishes a quality article, that serves to develop both their career and the reputation of the university. If a creative guru creates a new wonder technology, as Lazzarato (2004) suggests, this is the culmination of generations of ingenuity, and this material product was produced socially and it creates new futures. This will benefit the capital organisation (with new potential capital) and the individual receives reward (including prestige, promotion and money). As stated, not everything that counts can be counted (Cameron, 1963). I take this further, not everything that *counts should be counted.*

References

Adkins, L. (2009), Feminism after measure. *Feminist Theory*, 10(3), pp. 323–339.

Alawattage, C. & Wickramasinghe, D. (2008), Appearance of accounting in a political hegemony. *Critical Perspectives on Accounting*, 19(3), pp. 293–339.

Alvesson, M. & Kärreman, D. (2004), Interfaces of control. Technocratic and socio-ideological control in a global management consultancy firm. *Accounting, Organizations and Society*, 29(3–4), pp. 423–444.

Armstrong, P. (2002), The costs of activity-based management. *Accounting, Organizations and Society*, 27(1), pp. 99–120.

Armstrong, P. (2006), Ideology and the grammar of idealism: The Caterpillar controversy revisited. *Critical Perspectives on Accounting*, 17(5), pp. 529–548.

Arnold, J. & Hope, T. (1983), *Accounting for Management Decisions*. New York: Prentice Hall.

Baker, C.R. & Bettner, M.S. (1997), Interpretive and critical research in accounting: A commentary on its absence from mainstream accounting research. *Critical Perspectives on Accounting*, 8(4), pp. 293–310.

Baldvinsdottir, G.H. (2009), Management accounting and the institutionalization of trust. *Problems and Perspectives in Management*, 7(2), pp. 53–60.

Berry, A.J., Broadbent, J. & Otley, D.T. (eds). (2005), *Management Control: Theories, Issues and Performance* (2nd ed.). Hampshire: Palgrave Macmillan.

Björk, B. C. & Solomon, D. (2013), The publishing delay in scholarly peer-reviewed journals. *Journal of Informetrics*, 7(4), pp. 914–923.

Böhm, S. & Land, C. (2012), The new 'hidden abode': Reflections on value and labour in the new economy. *The Sociological Review*, 60(2), pp. 217–240.

Böhm, S., Spicer, A. & Fleming, P. (2008), Infra-political dimensions of resistance to international business: A Neo-Gramscian approach. *Scandinavian Journal of Management*, 24(3), pp. 169–182.

Brown, A.D. & Lewis, M.A. (2011), Identities, discipline and routines. *Organization Studies*, 32(7), pp. 871–895.

Bryer, R.A. (2005), A Marxist accounting history of the British industrial revolution: A review of evidence and suggestions for research. *Accounting, Organizations and Society*, 30(1), pp. 25–65.

Bryer, R. (2006), Accounting and control of the labour process. *Critical Perspectives on Accounting*, 17(5), pp. 551–598.

Burris, H.B. (1993), *Technocracy at Work*. Albany: State University of New York Press.

Cameron, W.B. (1963), *Informal Sociology: A Casual Introduction to Sociological Thinking* (Vol. 21). New York: Random House.

Chapman, C.S. (1998), Accountants in organisational networks. *Accounting, Organizations and Society*, 23(8), pp. 737–766.

Chua, W.F. (1986), Radical developments in accounting thought. *The Accounting Review*, 61(4), pp. 601–632.

Cockburn, C. (1987), Restructuring technology, restructuring gender. In *American Sociological Association Meeting*, Chicago.

Cooper, C. (2015), Accounting for the fictitious: A Marxist contribution to understanding accounting's roles in the financial crisis. *Critical Perspectives on Accounting*, 30, pp. 63–82.

Cooper, C. & Taylor, P. (2000), From Taylorism to Ms Taylor: The transformation of the accounting craft. *Accounting, Organizations and Society*, 25(6), pp. 555–578.

De Angelis, M. & Harvie, D. (2009), 'Cognitive capitalism' and the rat-race: How capital measures immaterial labour in British Universities. *Historical Materialism*, 17(3), pp. 3–30.

Dermer, J.D. & Lucas, R.G. (1986), The illusion of managerial control. *Accounting, Organizations and Society*, 11(6), pp. 471–482.

Elmassri, M.M., Harris, E.P. & Carter, D.B. (2016), Accounting for strategic investment decision-making under extreme uncertainty. *The British Accounting Review*, 48(2), pp. 151–168.

Emmanuel, C., Otley, D. & Merchant, K.A. (1990), *Accounting for Management Control* (2nd ed.). London: Chapman & Hall.

Foucault, M. (2008), *The Birth of Biopolitics*, G. Burchell (transl.). New York: Palgrave.

Frezatti, F., Carter, D.B. & Barroso, M.F.G. (2014). Accounting without accounting: Informational proxies and the construction of organisational discourses. *Accounting, Auditing & Accountability Journal*, 27(3), pp. 426–464.

Hardt, M. & Negri, A. (2000), *Empire*. Cambridge, MA: Harvard University Press.

Hardt, M. & Negri, A. (2005), *Multitude: War and Democracy in the Age of Empire*. New York: Penguin Press.

Hardt, M. & Negri, A. (2009), *Commonwealth*. London: Belknap Press of Harvard University Press.

Harney, S. (2005), Why is management a cliché? *Critical Perspectives on Accounting*, 16(5), pp. 579–591.

Harney, S. (2006), Management and self-activity: Accounting for the crisis in profit-taking. *Critical Perspectives on Accounting*, 17(7), pp. 935–946.

Harney, S. & Dunne, S. (2013), More than nothing? Accounting, business, and management studies, and the research audit. *Critical Perspectives on Accounting*, 24(4–5), pp. 338–349.

Hines, R.D. (1988), Financial accounting: In communicating reality, we construct reality. *Accounting, Organizations and Society*, 13(3), pp. 251–261.

Hines, R.D. (1989), Financial accounting knowledge, conceptual framework projects and the social construction of the accounting profession. *Accounting, Auditing & Accountability Journal*, 2(2), pp. 72–92.

Hochschild, A.R. (1983), *The Managed Heart*. Berkeley: The University of California Press.

Hopper, T. (1990), Social transformation and management accounting: Finding relevance in history, in Gustafson, C. & Hassel, L., (eds.), *Accounting and Organizational Action*. Turku: Abo Academy Press, pp. 111–148.

Hopper, T. & Armstrong, P. (1991), Cost accounting, controlling labour and the rise of conglomerates. *Accounting, Organizations and Society*, 16(5–6), pp. 405–438.

Hopper, T. & Powell, A. (1985), Making sense of research into the organizational and social aspects of management accounting: A review of its underlying assumptions. *Journal of Management Studies*, 22(5), pp. 429–465.

Johnson, H.T. & Kaplan, R.S. (1987), The rise and fall of management accounting. *IEEE Engineering Management Review*, 3(15), 36–44.

Jones, C. & Murtola, A.M. (2012), Entrepreneurship and expropriation. *Organization*, 19(5), pp. 635–655.

Land, C. & Taylor, S. (2010), Surf's up: Work, life, balance and brand in a new age capitalist organization. *Sociology*, 44(3), pp. 395–413.

Lazzarato, M. (2004), From capital-labour to capital-life. *Ephemera*, 4(3), pp. 187–208.

LexisNexis. (2013), Value-based billing: The alternative to alternative fee arrangements. Available from www.lexisnexis.com/communities/corporatecounselnewsletter/b/newsletter/archive/2013/03/02/value-based-billing-the-alternative-to-alternative-fee-arrangements.aspx#sthash.IKCm38hc.dpuf.

Loft, A. (1995), *The History of Management Accounting: Relevance Found*. New York: Prentice Hall.

Mäkelä, H. (2013), On the ideological role of employee reporting. *Critical Perspectives on Accounting*, 24(4), pp. 360–378.

Merchant, K.A., Van der Stede, W.A. & Zheng, L. (2003), Disciplinary constraints on the advancement of knowledge: The case of organizational incentive systems. *Accounting, Organizations and Society*, 28(2–3), pp. 251–286.

Morgan, G. (1988), Accounting as reality construction: Towards a new epistemology for accounting practice. *Accounting Organizations and Society*, 13(5), pp. 477–485.

Nandhakumar, J. & Jones, M. (2001), Accounting for time: managing time in project-based teamworking. *Accounting, Organizations and Society*, 26(3), pp. 193–214.

Negri, A. & Hardt, M. (1999), Value and affect. *Boundary 2*, 26(2), pp. 77–88.

Ouchi, W.G. (1979), A conceptual framework for the design of organizational control mechanisms, in Emmanuel, C., Otley, D. & Merchant, D. (eds.) *Readings in Accounting for Management Control*. London: Thomson, pp. 63–82.

Puxty, T. & Chua, W.F. (1989), Ideology, rationality and the management control process, in Chua, W.F., Lowe, T. & Puxty, T. (eds.) *Critical Perspectives in Management Control*. London: Palgrave Macmillan, pp. 115–139.

Puxty, A. (1993), *The Social and Organizational Content of Management Accounting*. London: Academic Press Paperback.

Speklé, R.F. (2001), Explaining management control structure variety: A transaction cost economics perspective. *Accounting, Organizations and Society*, 26(4–5), pp. 419–441.

Spence, C. & Carter, D. (2011), Accounting for the General Intellect: Immaterial labour and the social factory. *Critical Perspectives on Accounting*, 22(3), pp. 304–315.

Uddin, S. & Hopper, T. (2001), A Bangladesh soap opera: Privatisation, accounting, and regimes of control in a less developed country. *Accounting, Organizations and Society*, 26(7–8), pp. 643–672.

Žižek, S. (2009), *First as Tragedy, Then as Farce*. London: Verso.

14

The (ir)relevance of performance measurement to performance management?

Lin Fitzgerald, Rhoda Brown, Ian Herbert, Ruth King and Laurie McAulay

Introduction, literature review and research questions

Common threads from influential performance management frameworks suggest that strategy defines the measures that drive organisational performance; the combined effects of targets and rewards motivate individual behaviour, and information flows from this process enable learning and adaptability, thus contributing to current and future performance (Fitzgerald and Moon, 1996; Otley, 1999, 2003; Kaplan and Norton, 2008). Empirical studies have provided some support for these frameworks (see Ferreira and Otley, 2009, for a review), and each stage in this process has received considerable elaboration, including studies of the formation of deliberative strategy as a top-down process, communicated by strategy maps (Kaplan and Norton, 2008); the development of performance metrics providing goal-driven motivation (Simons, 2005); the design of rewards to provide incentives (Simons, 1995; Kaplan and Norton, 2008); and the use of information flows for diagnostic, interactive, feedback and feed-forward control (Grafton, Lillis and Widener, 2010; Kaplan, 2010).

Despite the intuitive and compelling nature of the "strategy–performance measurement–information flow–rewards" model, other authors have challenged the concept of a top-down framework with performance measurement at its centre. In particular, the set of practices that Kaplan and Norton refer to as "strategic alignment" (Kaplan and Norton, 2006, 2008) occupy disputed ground. While the early iterations of balanced scorecard models (Fitzgerald *et al.*, 1991; Lynch and Cross, 1991; Kaplan and Norton, 1992) might have implied that the route to controlling organisational performance lay through devising tight measures and key performance indicators (KPIs), there has been a growing recognition that effective control and effective performance are more about finding a way of working through people and encouraging commitment and constructive behaviour. Merchant and Van der Stede (2003) describe this type of performance management as "results control", and their insight is that such controls "influence actions because they cause employees to be concerned about the *consequences* of the actions they take. The organisation does not dictate to employees what actions they should take; instead employees are *empowered* to take those actions they believe will best produce the desired results" (Merchant and Van der Stede, 2003). This notion can be related back to the influential analysis provided by Ouchi (1980), who identified three mechanisms that mediate transactions, in particular employment transactions, between individuals. In Ouchi's world, there are two critical elements that determine the most efficient mechanism of intermediation: first, the degree of ambiguity in the measurement of an individual's performance, and second, the degree of congruence between the goals of the organisation and of the individual employee. In circumstances where performance can be measured uniquely and with some degree of accuracy and where goal congruence is high, the most efficient mechanism is likely to be market transactions or exchanges. A market mechanism will fail, however, in the event of bounded rationality or opportunistic behaviour by individuals, arising from an uncertain or complex environment or in other cases when the market is not believed to be efficient. These circumstances can be overcome, to an extent by the second transaction mechanism, a bureaucracy. In the bureaucracy, much of the uncertainty and complexity facing the individual is overcome by the organisation appointing managers to allocate and direct day-to-day work activities, and the probability of opportunistic behaviour is reduced by systems of surveillance and monitoring of performance. The environment in which the bureaucratic organisational form ceases to be efficient is one where it becomes impossible to evaluate the value added to the organisation by an individual, for example where the tasks performed are unique, where the tasks of different individuals are completely integrated or where there is a high degree of goal incongruence. In these circumstances, organisations can come to rely on socialisation as the principal mechanism of control, and Ouchi refers to this final mechanism as that of the "clan" (after the definition of Durkheim, 1933). This mechanism is less about control of the organisation by market discipline, or hierarchy and rational evaluation, and more about managing people's behaviour through shared beliefs and values.

The traditional, top-down, "control and feedback" approach to performance management could be viewed as sitting within the bureaucracy arm of Ouchi's analysis, where strategies are fed down the organisation and translated into strategy maps and performance measures down to the level of the individual. This kind of top-down control system might imply more reliance on the diagnostic use of performance indicators (Simons, 1995, 2005), and the potential dysfunctional consequences of such systems have been long established (see, for example, Dearden (1969) on the use of Return on Investment (ROI) measures and Keller (1989) on budget slack in General Motors). Whereas in relation to environments where decisions are less routine and where there is a high level of uncertainty, writers return to the idea of softer measures and less direct controls. Simons (1995) terms these types of controls "interactive", Merchant and Van der Stede (2003) refer to "cultural controls" and "personnel controls", Henri (2006) refers to "flexibility values" and Ouchi (1980, see above) to the "clan" mechanism. The elements these analyses have in common are their focus on managing through people and achieving control by securing the commitment of employees through some process of aligning individual and organisational goals.

Within this context, organisations with shared service centres (SSCs) are particularly interesting cases to study, for a number of reasons. First, the SSC is becoming an increasingly popular way for organisations to manage their administrative functions. In many instances, the initial driving force behind the creation of SSCs is one of efficiency and cost reduction or, at least, the constraint of costs within contractual limits (via service-level agreements). Most of these costs, since they arise from generic service activities (such as the finance function, payroll or IT services), have, in the past, been considered mainly in terms of the classic internal resource allocation problems of transfer pricing or overhead allocation. In this context, the difficulties involved in measuring the performance of workers in support service roles are well known. The SSC model attempts to address these issues by imposing the discipline of external markets, where this is possible, on the service functions. This becomes a more complex task as

SSCs' processes move up the added value chain from transactional services to include analysis and reporting functions. Given their central roles in the control of organisations, improving efficiency and re-engineering business processes to bring them closer to a market environment, SSCs present a fertile ground for investigation of the practices of performance management. The role of the SSC in such organisations lies at the heart of the complicated and disputed process of "strategic alignment", for it is here that the top-level strategies are transformed into performance measures and targets, and here that the results control can be effected.

In addition, the structure of organisations with SSCs may be somewhat different from other organisations. The creation of a quasi-autonomous segment in the centre of the organisation has the potential to cut across the traditional hierarchy. The process of drawing together different service functions and encouraging them to pin their performance measures to external referents is likely to result in channels of communication and reporting that run horizontally across the organisation, or at least the shared service part of it, rather than from top to bottom. The structure of the SSC creates the potential to disrupt the traditional power structure of the bureaucracy, and this has been argued by some to be significant enough to justify the SSC model as new organisational form. It is possible that this flattened structure might render the performance management system more amenable to interactive and behavioural controls. Finally, the achievement in SSCs of cost reduction via task standardisation leads to new problems of management. Many of the roles in SSCs involve very repetitive activities, and the advances in Enterprise Resource Planning (ERP) systems have resulted in the deskilling of previously more varied clerical jobs, such as human resource or accounts payable functions. The point about SSCs is often to render individual tasks more similar, to combine them and achieve efficiency by increasing volume. Therefore, while the relatively unskilled, routine tasks lend themselves well to "diagnostic control" (Simons, 1995) systems, the main problem in such environments becomes one of how to motivate employees to maintain the consistency and the volume and how to avoid dysfunctional behaviour.

The management of performance in this context is thus, in Ouchi's terms, likely to be less about bureaucratic mechanisms and more about clan mechanisms. Our starting point for investigation is thus how, in this context, the traditional, diagnostic type of control mechanism is used. Therefore, our research question is: "how is performance managed in Shared Service Centres"?

Research methods and the case company

The findings presented here derive from the analysis of a single case organisation, Network Rail. The case is one of five organisations, studied as part of a larger research investigation into performance management in SSCs (see Fitzgerald *et al.*, 2012). The data collected for the case study included 13 semi-structured interviews with personnel from the Network Rail SSC, lasting on average 60–90 minutes and conducted with either two or three interviewers. The interviews were transcribed and analysed using NVIVO software. Other sources of case information include publicly available websites, published annual reports and unpublished corporate documentation. Once written up, the case study was sent to senior representatives from the Network Rail SSC for validation of the detailed information.

The case company: Network Rail

The predecessor of Network Rail, Railtrack plc, was created in 1994 as part of the railway privatisation programme under the Thatcher government. The company was sold in 2002 to

Network Rail (NWR), which is a company limited by guarantee. NWR owns the tracks, signalling equipment, tunnels, bridges and level crossings for the UK railway network and 2,500 railway stations, although NWR only manages a handful of these directly, most of them being managed by the train-operating companies, who are NWR's main customers. Ticket sales and the pricing of fares on trains are also the preserve of the train-operating companies, and NWR is not directly involved in these activities. The company has 35,000 employees, and it spends £14 million per day on operating, maintaining and regenerating the rail network. Total revenue was £5,712 million in 2011, of which £5,408 million arose from franchised track access and grant income (Network Rail, 2011). Franchised track access income is invoiced to train-operating companies on the basis of agreements finalised with the Department for Transport. Network Rail is regulated by the Office of Rail Regulation (ORR) and is subject to detailed operating requirements that are set out in "Control Period Delivery Plans", each of which covers a period of 5 years. The relevant issue for our period of study (number 4) covers a 5-year period from 2009 to 2014. There are also periodic governmental reviews, including the most recent "Report of the Rail Value for Money Study" commissioned by the Department for Transport (2011) and ORR, from an independent committee chaired by Sir Ray McNulty.

Creation of the financial shared service centre (FSS)

Network Rail identified a programme of cost reduction measures in 2004 as a result of external pressures (The Hackett Group, 2011). One of the cost reduction measures adopted was to centralise part of the company's finance operations, which were spread across more than 20 locations, into a financial shared services (FSS) centre located on one site in Manchester. The introduction of FSS facilitated a process of centralisation and standardisation. Efficiency is achieved by moving appropriate transactional accounting away from business units and into FSS, where processes are rationalised through changed technological and manual processes. The transactional processing centres are on an Enterprise Resource Planning system, Oracle.

The overarching strategy of FSS appears to be to support Network Rail's efficiency objective by providing a low-cost and reliable portfolio of services that "meets and exceeds customer expectations". This strategy involves the selection of an appropriate portfolio of services (accounts receivable, accounts payable, central accounting services, national accounts and business improvements) and the development of structures to align the objectives of the FSS and Network Rail.

Strategic alignment

Structures and systems developed within FSS to assist in the delivery of its strategy are summarised and communicated to staff on the *World Class Board* and supported by *Signal Stations*. These provide visual representations of performance indicators and are placed prominently within the open plan layout in which FSS operates. The *World Class Board* comprises a circular diagrammatic representation of strategy and operations. A *Signal Station* for each of the FSS teams is located adjacent to the areas in which the team works.

Visual management: the World Class Board

There are six interlinked elements on the *World Class Board*, laid out in a circle: the vision, the operating model, projects, benchmarks, funding targets and visitors' letters, and the circle is closed by four words summarising company values: "Determination", "Teamwork", "Respect" and "Pride". The corporate vision on the *World Class Board* is summarised in three clear statements at the company, finance division and FSS levels (Figure 14.1): "to provide a safe, reliable and efficient railway that is fit for the 21st century"; "to be universally perceived as a valued business partner"; and "to be a world class service provider".

The most pervasive statement of company belief system and values, running through the interviews and evident in the physical observation of corporate communication, is the concept of the "4Cs" operating model, which was devised by the Head of FSS. The "4Cs" concept operates as a mantra to support strategic focus and engagement throughout the FSS. Processes and projects are justified and measured against the 4Cs. Innovations and changes are made in the name of the 4Cs, and the term is frequently evoked by employees to express pride in both the organisation and the senior management. "4Cs" is an acronym for Compliance, Cycle Time, Customer Service and Cash. The mantra of the 4Cs provides a common vocabulary, which was frequently evident during interviews, and is considered to be "a simple, accessible and tangible concept" (FSS manager). It thus provides a framework for consideration of both financial and non-financial performance measures, and functions in two major ways. First, it translates NWR strategy into ideas that can be assimilated and applied at all levels of the organisation down to ground-level operations, and second, it operates as a shared, sacrosanct, symbolic code that encapsulates the organisational belief system and values.

There are four benchmarking processes within FSS, one internal to NWR and three external: "Q12", Investors in People, European Foundation for Quality Management (EFQM) and Hackett. These processes serve the purpose within the FSS of referencing the external market place and acknowledging the role of market discipline in improving process

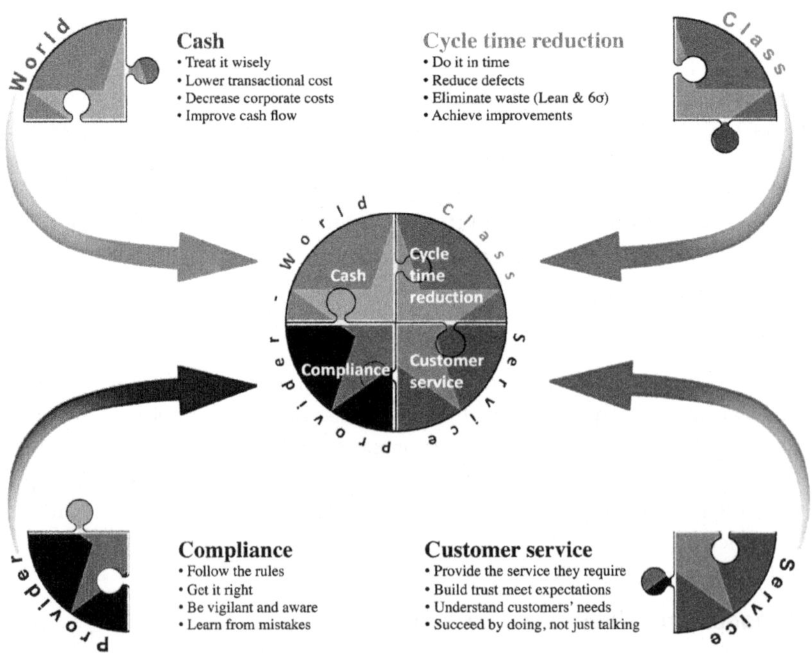

Figure 14.1 The 4Cs operating model

efficiency. The motivation for these measures derives from a desire "to measure where we're up to" because "we really need to measure ourselves to know where we really are" (FSS manager). Each of these four areas is described on the *World Class Board* where the current standing of the FSS is summarised.

- "Q12" is an employee engagement survey that is administered throughout NWR. FSS scores more highly than the Network Rail average on sixteen out of the seventeen items and achieves an overall average in excess of 4 on a 1 to 5 scale.
- "Investors in People" represents a major investment for FSS. Bronze status was achieved in February 2011 and through a process of strategic engagement, meetings and interviews with every member of FSS staff, silver status was achieved in September 2011.
- EFQM is a quality and process improvement model based on the idea that outcomes of quality management are achieved through a number of "enablers". The *World Class Board* summarises its general approach.
- Hackett provides "benchmarking information that compares the company's spending on its support services to that of similar organizations" (Kaplan and Norton, 2006: 120). Network Rail is classed as "world class" following the most recent Hackett analysis. Hackett thereby provides a measure of FSS' global competitiveness compared to other service centres.

The link is made back to the overall strategic objectives of NWR by a section on the *World Class Board* detailing the requirements to meet the terms of the latest round of government funding in the "Control Period 4 Planning Requirements". "Key messages" from Network Rail's Chief Executive Officer are also presented, alongside statements supporting the commitment of FSS to its customers. The top right-hand corner of the *World Class Board* is devoted to letters from recent visitors to FSS that provide either supportive messages that reinforce FSS' status as a world-class provider of services or messages spelling out specific impacts of FSS on other organisations.

Signal stations

The *World Class Board* is supported by *Signal Stations* that provide summaries of objectives and projects together with descriptions of achievement for each service team within FSS. The *Signal Stations* are 3 ft high display stands, with four faces each split into three sections, which can be rotated by hand and moved around the floor on castors. They provide written, numerical and pictorial depictions of the work of each functional area.

Figure 14.2 shows part of the *Signal Station* for the billing team within Accounts Receivable. The board is personalised through a photograph of members of the team; and the train, designed by a member of the team, in the bottom right-hand corner. Other *Signal Stations* included more fanciful artwork including one with a fleet of flying saucers moving through space and one with a graph/map where the markers were small steam trains. The top right-hand corner shows the overall assessment for the team, with a "green light" indicating an overall good performance. Two graphs on the left-hand side present two major KPIs: "Train error counts" (errors that are corrected manually or automatically for the Track Access Billing System that provides information from which train-operating companies are invoiced) and Track Access Billing System Availability. A block on the right-hand side gives a further KPI in the form of details of train- and freight-operating companies that have committed to supporting an Accounts Receivable initiative, on-train metering, which allows electricity

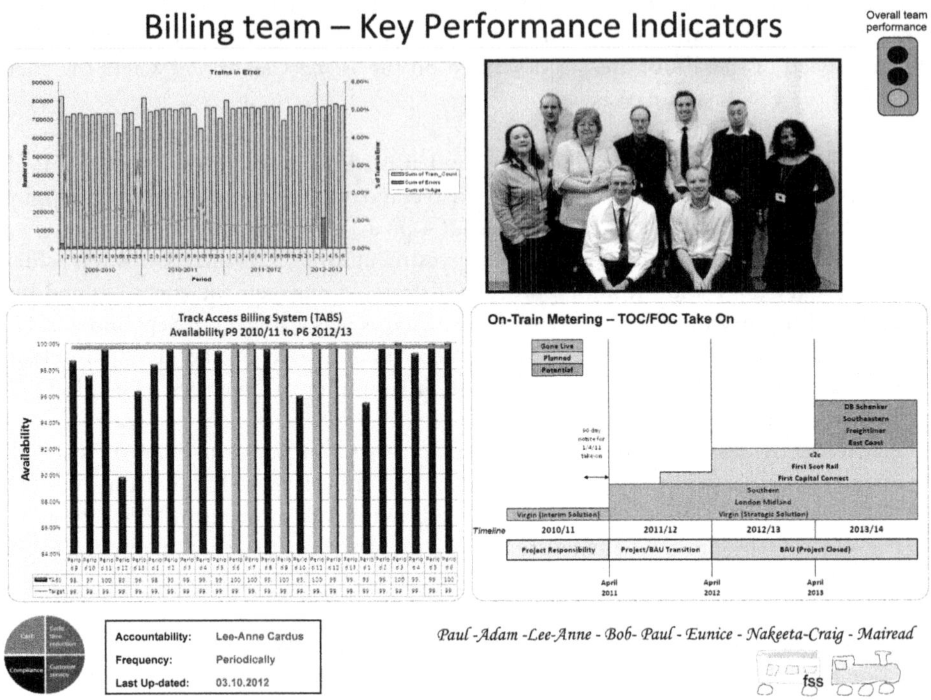

Figure 14.2 Performance measures from the billing team signal station

usage to be charged on an actual basis. The circle in the bottom left-hand corner is a diagrammatic representation of the "4Cs".

The *Signal Station* for each team records an analysis of their performance categorised according to the "4Cs" framework. The "cash" dimension of performance is measured in terms of £s saved per year. For instance, the National Accounts team saved £300,000 by introducing a new pension accounting system and £8,000 through a "Headcount Reporting Mechanism". The "cycle time" dimension is measured in terms of hours saved per period. For example, the National Accounting team saved 135 hours per period through the "removal of excess processing time" and 1 hour per period by introducing a "new cheque printing solution". The "customer service" and "compliance" dimensions are both measured according to the impact of specific projects. The measure is categorical and denominated in terms of "high", "medium" or "low". For instance, the "new cheque printing solution" is assessed as achieving a high impact on external customers. For "compliance", the development of a Track Access Billing Reference Manual by National Accounting has been assessed as achieving a high impact on people and processes.

Beyond the World Class Board *and* Signal Stations

FSS applies a range of ready-made business management strategies. Most notable among these are "Six Sigma" and "Lean". The motivation for adopting a wide range of management practices is explained by the Head of FSS in the following terms:

> Instead of focusing on getting an EFQM score [or] getting Investors in People – I've gone past that now – we're developing a high performing model around the 4Cs. If we focus on a high performing model, [EFQM and Investors in People] are going to happen. In one sense, we don't need them ... However, it's important for the staff to think "Yes, [we]'re world-class". [We] need some trinkets. [We] need some celebrations...

Legitimacy is provided through initiatives that focus on EFQM, Investors in People and the Hackett range of measures. These external standards provide benefits through reputational markers of success ("trinkets" and "trophies"). The emphasis, however, is in on "the team", the individuals who comprise FSS. "The team" provides the capability to achieve world-class standards ("they're going to win everything we need to win").

There are hundreds of performance measures and KPIs in evidence in the FSS across all the functional areas of NWR. In this regard, "KPI" is a misleading term because there are so many performance indicators, with little attempt to define "key" in the strict sense of the focused set of measures that define strategy in the way indicated by Kaplan and Norton's (2008) description of the Balanced Scorecard. Instead, the role of performance measures within FSS appears to be currently focused on signalling the need for investigation and subsequent action. Additionally, performance management addresses "how did people do that, not just what they did" (FSS manager). As a consequence, performance management is "more to do with motivation and attitude and the way people approach things rather than what they actually do". Performance management therefore involves the engagement of staff throughout FSS. This staff engagement is promoted through the *World Class Board* and *Signal Stations*, which serve a number of purposes. To quote managers within FSS, they "give identity and pride to the team", provide "an important tracker for how we're doing against project [deadlines] and KPIs", "concentrate people's minds on what we're aiming to achieve and how far we've gone" and provide a "display to people who [visit] to show achievements". *Signal Stations* in particular supply "more immediate visibility to the teams as to how well they're doing and what they're going to be doing in the future" (FSS manager). Given their visibility, they allow performance and process achievements to be discussed with outsiders and between teams, thus providing potential for all members of FSS to engage with each other's work. *Signal Stations* are personalised and "the teams own" them, leading to increased "interest" that "engenders a team spirit" (FSS manager). A final theme within interviews was the extent to which the *World Class Board* and *Signal Stations* counteract the tendency for staff within FSS to be self-critical. While reflexivity supports the aim of continuous improvement, visual representations of achievement are important to morale. One manager expressed this point as follows:

> "We tend sometimes [to] be over-critical of ourselves and not really recognise what we've actually achieved. Olympic athletes probably criticise themselves for not going a bit faster. The fact that they're faster than most people in the world doesn't seem to cross their mind at times. And so what you need to do I suppose sometimes is to remind people of what we have achieved."

Discussion and conclusions

Kaplan and Norton (2006, 2008) propose a traditional view of strategy as a top-down process where organisational objectives cascade down the organisation and influence transactional operations. This process can be seen at work within NWR and FSS. The corporate aims and objectives, as determined by NWR's board of directors and influenced by external forces including the ORR and the McNulty Review, are communicated down through the organisation. Business units within Network Rail deliver safety, reliability, efficiency, innovation and sustainability, supported directly by FSS through initiatives such as the on-train metering system and indirectly by freeing business units from transactional processing. Most notably, FSS contributes to the strategic aim of efficiency by reducing costs through the standardisation of processes. A top-down model, however, does not fully describe the process of strategic alignment within NWR. The most marked departure is the innovative nature of some of the FSS practices, including change management initiatives that have impacts across NWR. It might be said that FSS drives NWR strategic implementation with regard to innovation through the bottom-up exercise of influence that comes with the deployment of standardised and/or novel processes that must be "sold" to the business units. Innovation in terms of continuous improvement and standardisation was described by one of the managers as "winning hearts and minds". A shared service centre is uniquely placed in an organisation because, as noted earlier, its structure opens up new channels of communication, horizontally, across the organisation. The management of an SSC involves closer scrutiny of external market conditions and competitors than might otherwise be the case, and this, combined with its position in the administrative heart of the organisation, provides the potential for SSC lead initiatives to cut through the normal hierarchical process of directing and reporting in organisations.

While top-down influence is evident in the FSS performance review system and in initiatives originating from the Head of FSS, including the "4Cs", the mechanism by which strategies are translated into operational practices is far less straightforward than a model such as Kaplan and Norton's (2006, 2008) process of strategic alignment might suggest. Part of the strategy of FSS involves the engagement of individuals at all levels, and so initiatives are sold upwards to the senior management team in the bottom-up exercise of influence. Figure 14.2 illustrates the circulation of influence within the top-down and bottom-up implementation of strategy which defines performance management for FSS. In this model, the management of people and the management of processes are as important as managing by traditional measures of performance such as KPIs. The inter-relationships between each of the three boxes describe a dynamic and recursive set of relationships that contrast with Kaplan and Norton's (2006, 2008) linear, one-directional model.

Performance measurement is clearly important within FSS. Nevertheless, it is possible to argue that processes are at least as important as performance measures. For instance, while FSS is a world-class service provider by Hackett measures, such as the cost per £ billion turnover or the cost per employee, performance measures do not necessarily indicate the processes that are necessary to achieve world class. Determining the processes that are necessary to achieve world-class performance goes beyond the ability of performance measures to signal the existence and availability of appropriate processes (Figure 14.3).

A process orientation is emphasised within FSS through the need for continuous improvement. It is the role of the Business Improvement team, in particular, to support the four service delivery areas in sustaining continuous improvement through a range of initiatives. These include not only Lean Management and Six Sigma but also Investors in People. Performance management within FSS thereby relies upon continuous improvement and demands, "a change in mind-set and a change in the way you work" (FSS manager). A "change in mind-set" requires the engagement of staff throughout FSS that goes beyond performance measurement.

The effectiveness of traditional models such as the Balanced Score Card (Kaplan and Norton, 1992), Levers of Control (Simons, 1995) and strategy maps (Kaplan & Norton, 2006) is

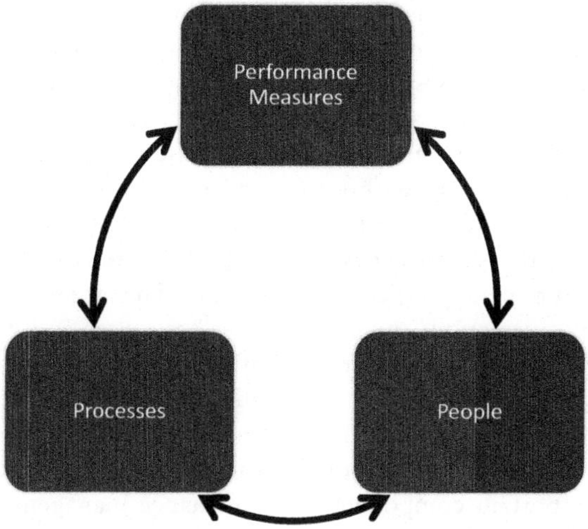

Figure 14.3 Performance management as a set of relationships between performance measures, people and processes

usually defined in terms of whether they make a measurable difference to the performance of an organisation. In FSS, it appears that managing employees' beliefs and organisational identity via the "4Cs" mantra is more important than traditional performance measures. The Head of FSS describes his operation as "a hundred people who are just a machine of delivery". In this environment, where the tasks are very standardised and the people performing them cannot innovate or personalise them at the transactional level, the management problem becomes one of re-humanising the workforce and keeping them engaged.

The Head of FSS describes the "4Cs" model as follows:

> [I]t's about behaviour and it's about actually everything we do; and that's translated into real delivery. McNulty says, "We want a centralised and functional organisation to go to a decentralised organisation". I'm saying, "It doesn't make any difference to what we do because at the end of the day, do you want me to save you money? do you want me to do it quicker? do you want me to make you feel good as a customer? ... The 4Cs model is beyond shared services. It's about any service proposition. No matter what you do as an organisation, I'll fit in [as a service provider]; because why wouldn't you want those 4 things from me as a provider?"

Returning to Ouchi's (1980) analysis of the mechanisms by which people and organisations transact, we see in FSS an environment with a high degree of task standardisation but also high levels of ambiguity in the measurement of what an individual's performance in FSS contributes to the overall value of NWR and thus, potentially, a low degree of congruence between the goals of the organisation and the individual employee. In this situation, the most effective form of transacting is via Ouchi's "clan" mechanism. The "4Cs" model is a device to signify belonging to the FSS clan.

In summary, if we conceive performance management within FSS as a top-down strategic process consistent with Kaplan and Norton (2006, 2008), then we have a partial description of the achievements of this shared service centre. FSS measures performance across the six areas that epitomise the service sector: competitiveness, financial performance, quality of service, flexibility, resource utilisation and innovation (Fitzgerald *et al.*, 1991). Through leadership and human resource management, FSS defines necessary dimensions of performance, establishes targets and uses performance measures to inform rewards based upon achievement. These are the necessary ingredients of effective performance management (Fitzgerald and Moon, 1996; Fitzgerald, 2007). Yet while FSS conforms to traditional concepts of performance management within the services industry, performance management within FSS is more than specifying performance dimensions, target setting and rewarding. This traditional framework is a partial description that captures a unidirectional relationship *from* performance measurement *to* processes and people. The larger picture provided by FSS is defined by complex interactions involving people, processes and performance measures within both top-down and bottom-up lines of influence that depend upon the engagement of staff at all levels. FSS' achievement is to link all three boxes in Figure 14.3, within relationships that are bi-directional, giving rise to dynamic and recursive relationships.

In relation to the research question, posed earlier, about whether performance measurements are the most important component of performance management in SCCs, the evidence from NWR indicates that the answer may be that the traditional means of achieving control through reporting of performance measures and consequential actions may not be paramount. It is possible to achieve control and manage performance through other means. The FSS reports hundreds of KPIs, and the role these measures play in the process of strategic alignment is not at all clear. What is clear is the significance of the alignment of belief systems and organisational identities achieved with the "4Cs" mantra. Weick (1995) reports a story, attributed to a Nobel Prize winner, that makes the point, "any map will do". The point is that maps do not necessarily need to possess representational faithfulness; they need to secure strategic commitment and action, as in the case of travel maps detailing underground stations. Consistent with the argument that "any map will do", it may not matter exactly what is measured and reported as long as those measuring and reporting identify sufficiently with their clan and believe that they all share the same experience, the same values and the same sense of achievement.

Acknowledgements

Funding from CIMA's General Charitable Trust for the project reported in Fitzgerald *et al.* (2012) is gratefully acknowledged. The authors also thank our Research Associate, Rosamund Chester Buxton, for her work on the CIMA project.

References

Dearden, J. (1969). The case against ROI control. *Harvard Business Review*, 47(3), 124–135.

Department for Transport. (2011). Realising the Potential of GB Rail: Final Independent Report of the Rail Value for Money Study: Detailed Report. UK: Department for Transport. Retrieved November 11, 2011, from http://assets.dft.gov.uk/publications/report-of-the-rail-vfm-study/realising-the-potential-of-gb-rail.pdf.

Durkheim, E. (1933). *The Division of Labor in Society*. G. Simpson (Trans.). New York: Free Press.

Ferreira, A. & Otley, D. (2009). The design and use of performance management systems: An extended framework for analysis. *Management Accounting Research*, 20, 263–282.

Fitzgerald, L. (2007). Performance Measurement. In T. Hopper, D. Northcott, & R. Scapens, (Eds.), *Issues in Management Accounting* (3rd ed.) (pp. 223–241). Harlow: Prentice Hall.

Fitzgerald, L. & Moon, P. (1996). *Performance Measurement in Service Industries: Making it Work*. London: The Chartered Institute of Management Accountants.

Fitzgerald, L., Johnston, R., Brignall, S., Silvestro, R. & Voss, C. (1991). *Performance Measures in Service Businesses*. London: The Chartered Institute of Management Accountants.

Fitzgerald, L., Brown, R., Chester-Buxton, R., Herbert, I., King, R. & MacAuley, L. (2012). *Relevance Regained? Performance Management in Shared Service Centres*. London: The Chartered Institute of Management Accountants.

Grafton, J., Lillis, A.M. & Widener, S.K. (2010). The role of performance measurement and evaluation in building organizational capabilities and performance. *Accounting, Organizations and Society*, 35, 689–706.

The Hackett Group. (2011). Creation of Word-Class Finance Shared Services Center in Under 18 Months Possible with Proven Best Practices. In The Hackett Group, Global Business Services Process Perspective Case Study (pp. 1–7). The Hackett Group.

Henri, J-F. (2006). Management control systems and strategy: a resource-based perspective. Accounting, *Organizations and Society*, 31, 529–558.

Kaplan, R.S. (2010). Conceptual Foundations of the Balanced Scorecard. Harvard Business School Working Paper, 10–074.

Kaplan, R.S. & Norton, D.P. (1992) The Balanced Scorecard – Measures that Drive Performance. *Harvard Business Review*, (January-February).

Kaplan, R.S. & Norton, D.P. (2006). *Alignment: Using the Balanced Scorecard to Create Corporate Synergies*. Boston: Harvard Business School Press.

Kaplan, R.S. & Norton, D.P. (2008). *The Execution Premium: Linking Strategy to Operations for Competitive Advantage*. Boston: Harvard Business School Press.

Keller, M. (1989). *Rude Awakening: The Rise, Fall, and Struggle for Recovery of General Motors*. New York: William Morrow & Co.

Lynch R.L. & Cross K.F. (1991). *Measure Up! Yardsticks for Continuous Improvements*. Cambridge USA: Blackwell.

Merchant, K.A. & Van der Stede, W. (2003). *Management Control Systems: Performance Measurement, Evaluation and Incentives*. Harlow, UK: FT Prentice Hall.

Network Rail Website. Accessed November 11, 2011, from www.networkrail.co.uk.

Office of Rail Regulation. (2008). Promoting safety and value in Britain's railways: our strategy for 2009–14. Office of Rail Regulation. Retrieved November 11, 2011, from www.rail-reg.gov.uk/upload/pdf/388.pdf.

Otley, D. (1999). Performance management: a framework for management control systems research. *Management Accounting Research*, 10, 363–382.

Otley, D. (2003). Management control and performance management: whence and wither? *British Accounting Review*, 35, 309–326.

Ouchi, W.G. (1980). Markets, bureaucracies and clans. *Adminstrative Science Quarterly*, 25, 129–141

Simons, R. (1995). *Levers of Control: How Managers Use Innovative Control Systems to Drive Strategic Renewal*. Boston: Harvard Business School Press.

Simons, R. (2005). *Levers of Organization Design: How Managers Use Accountability Systems for Greater Performance and Commitment*. Boston: Harvard Business School Press.

Weick, K.E. (1995). *Sensemaking in Organizations*. Thousand Oaks, CA: Sage Publications.

15
Leadership and control

Craig Marsh

Introduction

Experience and research suggests that the narrative of the strong organisational leader who is able to manipulate directly the behaviour of employees is alive and well. An important part of the toolkit of the organisational leader is the performance management system. HR Best Practice dictates that performance appraisal directs and controls behaviour in a way that is consistent with the company's strategic goals; employees are rated according to their contribution to their subset of those goals, and are often encouraged, through competencies or value-laden feedback mechanisms, to align their behaviour, and even their thoughts, to the leader's will. This chapter will present case material that further explores the achievements and limitations of such organisational structures of control. We will argue that the role of operational, or first-line, as opposed to executive, leadership in any system of behavioural control is still largely undervalued, and that organisations tend to neglect the importance of questions of morality, fairness and justice in ensuring that performance management systems actually have the effect they are intended to have.

Literature review

Over a generation or so of theorising on 'Human Resource Management' (HRM), considerable attention has been given to defining the impact on organisational performance. The 'evidence' for the impact of HRM practices on company performance derived from a largely empirical research paradigm which claimed to have demonstrated a link between models of HRM and company performance, for example (Delaney and Huselid, 1996; Delery and Doty, 1996; Huselid *et al.*, 1997; Huselid, 1998; Huselid *et al.*, 2003). Partly because of these definitive empirical claims of impact, and catalysed by the effects of globalisation, what was initially a North American conceptualisation spread round the world (Brewster *et al.*, 2004; Sparrow *et al.*, 2004). Previously named 'Personnel' departments become re-branded 'Human Resources' (HR), and companies based in cultures as diverse as France, Japan and India adopted what rapidly became universally recognised HR 'best practices' (Delbridge *et al.*, 2000; Scullion, 2000).

Performance management has been regarded for several years now as one such core HRM 'best practice' (Osterman, 1994; Pfeffer, 1994; Pfeffer, 1998). Den Hartog *et al.* (2004) define it, thus making clear the relevance of an integrated approach to performance:

> Performance management has come to signify more than a list of singular practices aimed at measuring and adapting employee performance. Rather, it is seen as an integrated process in which managers work with their employees to set expectations, measure and review results, and reward performance, in order to improve employee performance, with the ultimate aim of positively affecting organisational success.
>
> *(p. 556)*

For almost as long as the theorising on HRM, there has also been a parallel strand of critical writing falling essentially into two camps. First, the so-called 'rhetoric versus reality' debate, which argued that what is said in theory about HRM bears little resemblance to practice (Legge, 1995; Sparrow and Marchington, 1998). Second, some commentators placed HRM, and specifically performance management, in the category of a technique of disciplinary power; they saw parallels between Foucault's (1979) account of the association of power with disciplinary techniques of knowledge of detail, and subsequent objectivising of the individual, and techniques of personnel psychology which underlie HRM (Deetz, 1992; Townley, 1993; Newton, 1994). Newton and Findlay (1998) summed up this argument by placing performance appraisal directly in the 'contested terrain of control, and thus ... at the heart of the management of the employment relationship' (p. 142).

In the intervening years since the 'contested terrain' of HRM was defined, it is remarkable how little is still known of the effects of such techniques of performance management on the individual employee (Farndale and Kelliher, 2013). This has been a space often referred to in the literature on HR over the years as the 'black box' of the HR/organisation performance relationship (Legge, 2000). One reason for this relative dearth of information is the limited amount of research directed at understanding HRM implementation (Watson, 2004; Guest, 2011). Boselie *et al.* (2005) argued that most studies of the impact of HRM practice orient towards the 'macro' or 'managerialist' perspective, with a dearth of studies of the role of the immediate line manager or supervisor 'in the enactment process' (p. 74). They recommended research oriented increasingly towards 'micro' analyses that seeks to understand in much greater depth 'employees' actual experiences of HRM (ibid., p. 82).

It has also become increasingly recognised that the role of the first-line manager is crucial in successful implementation of HR practices (Hales, 2005; Nehles *et al.*, 2006) or 'unlocking the black box' (Hutchinson and Purcell, 2003) as these practices are increasingly delegated to line managers to implement in the modern organisation (Purcell and Hutchinson, 2007).

One such technique implemented under the banner of HR 'best practice' is performance appraisal, one in which first-line managers have a central role to play, and which is a constant source of dissatisfaction among managers and employees, despite its widespread use (Elicker *et al.*, 2006; Dusterhoff *et al.*, 2014).

Employees' perceptions of fairness and procedural justice play a key role in employee outcomes considered crucial to organisation success, such as decision making (Goksoy and Alayoglu, 2013), satisfaction (Kuvaas, 2006), commitment and engagement (Cheng, 2014), and organisational citizenship behaviours (Thurston and McNall, 2010). The immediate supervisor of the employee is a key actor in the success of the process of performance appraisal, and a critical influence on employee perceptions of fairness and justice (Purcell and Hutchinson, 2007; Byrne *et al.*, 2012; Sumelius *et al.*, 2014).

The practical problems

As a practitioner, both in HR roles and as a senior executive, I have had direct experience of the systematic (macro) and local (micro) implementation of performance management systems. In recognition of the recent comments in the literature of a dearth of evidence of employees' actual experience of techniques of appraisal, I will discuss a recent case. It is arguable that many of the features of the system illustrated in this case are variable from one process to another and from one organisation to the next. My thesis, however, is that these differences are but insignificant variations around two elements found in the majority of performance management systems and which largely dictate individual and organisational outcomes from such systems. Those are the general rating of individual performance and the link, either directly or indirectly, to pay.

Let us consider some of the consequences of running performance schemes for a workforce whose main currency, and value added to their organisation, is the deployment of their knowledge. Fairly typical of such schemes is a general – usually annual – performance-rating scale, which serves the purpose of allowing the organisation to place its people into categories differentiated by levels of performance. At its origin – as most of such schemes have their source – is the General Electric (GE) vitality curve, devised in the 1960s as a way of identifying the top 10 per cent and bottom 10 per cent performers, mainly. In most organisations, this, or some variation of it, is now used for two main purposes: to allocate a sliding scale of performance pay according to the rating, and to identify different groups of 'talent' so specific actions can be taken for each group.

The rating is generally obtained from a performance appraisal process and allocated by the employee's immediate line manager. Some oversight is applied, either by the next manager in the hierarchy or by a functional manager attached to the employee who has responsibility for their long-term development; and in some organisations, there may be an element of '360' – that is, performance information gathered on the individual from a wider group of people who are in regular contact with him or her and who can, it is felt, give a view on the individual's work.

Such are the bones of most schemes of performance management these days; they are widespread, they all tend to function in broadly the same way, and they are propagated by HR professionals who consider such structures to be 'best practice' and are therefore enshrined in accrediting bodies' training materials. I am probably on safe ground when I say they rely on a foundation of rationality and objectivity; that is, on the principle that an individual's performance can be evaluated, rated and categorised accurately and without bias (Halpern, 2015). Remove that foundation – or recognise that decision making, especially decision making related to individual performance – is fundamentally irrational, and the entire edifice crumbles. For that reason, HR professionals devise ever more sophisticated frameworks – criteria, rubrics, competence frameworks and the like – for analysing performance against objective criteria and to ensure that a given rating has the same value wherever it is applied.

So, let us now consider what actually happens when such schemes are put into practice, with particular attention to the decision making of the first line manager. Before doing so, I would posit a working assumption: that is, unless a performance management system possessing the two elements I described above – a system of performance rating, and a link to pay (indirect or direct) – actually results in individuals being motivated to perform better, then they are unlikely to deliver any kind of performance improvement, either at individual or at organisational level.

With that assumption in mind, here are some questions that any such scheme perforce must be able to answer.

1 Can an entire year's performance be accurately summarised in one rating? Even if the performance period is less than 1 year (month, quarter, etc.), the question remains valid.
2 Can a manager objectively and rationally evaluate an employee's performance in one rating?
3 Can an effective structure for performance management be devised which does not require performance ratings or performance rated pay?
4 Can a performance-rating scheme, and its attendant performance-related pay, ever be considered fair by employees? (Do you want engaged employees?)
5 Can a scheme containing performance ratings and performance-related pay actually motivate employees to perform better?
6 Can the need to rate individual performance accurately ever be reconciled with the company's need to place limits on its budget for annual salary increases?

Case analysis

Let us consider these questions through Cathy's case, a first-line manager, who has eight employees doing some form of work requiring the use of their brains rather than their muscles. Like 90 per cent of managers, she's done quite an effective job over the year keeping them on track, maintaining a good working relationship with them, and meeting with them regularly one to one to review their performance against their annual objectives, and do some coaching where needed. The unit is well regarded; on the whole, it has done what the company expects of it, and Cathy is considered an effective manager. She has had no turnover of staff, bar one who left the area, resigned, and was replaced 3 months ago by a new arrival to the team. Now, it is time for Cathy to complete their annual performance appraisals.

The first mantra of appraisals that we all know and love is that of 'no surprises', and Cathy is fully indoctrinated in good HR practice. She has maintained good records of face-to-face discussions over the year and shared these with her team; and so, she believes that she can summarise their performance pretty well on the (lengthy) online form HR provides for the purpose, and there won't be too much in there they don't already know. Step one, however, is for the employees to evaluate their own performance, so she invites them to do so and gives them a couple of weeks to fill in the appropriate section. Now, they will, of course, have in their minds when they're completing the form, the fact that Cathy will need to give them a performance rating of 1–5 (1 being substantially underperforming, 5 being outstanding), and that this rating will impact their salary increase for next year.

So inevitably, despite the detailed competencies, objectives (agreed at the end of the last performance cycle) and rating descriptions, they tend to write up a good story of their year. They don't even necessarily do this consciously; but the incentive, built into the process, is to describe their performance in a relatively good light. Assisting them in orienting it in this way is the fact that the objectives they agreed with Cathy 12 months ago have evolved. In some cases, they agreed new ones with their manager; but the nature of their work, as well as the rapidly changing business environment, means that there is always daylight between what was written down and what they've actually done. This gives them room for manoeuvre and a great deal of subjective opinion on how they describe their performance. One or two, who know they've not done as well as they should, are even able to cast performance issues in a better light, with the benefit of hindsight, because of this room for manoeuvre.

Cathy, meanwhile, is incentivised quite differently by the performance management system. To start with, she knows that no matter how well her team has performed over the year, she is expected by HR to return a set of ratings that roughly match a normal distribution curve. Whether that expectation is formalised (in the shape of a specific policy) or not, HR departments of necessity have a limited overall budget to manage to for the periodic performance-related increase in pay. At the highest level of analysis, the employee as an economic entity and member of a valid statistical population will demonstrate levels of performance rating matching a normal distribution curve, and budgets are calculated accordingly. If we were to engage in some archaeology of knowledge, the GE vitality curve would undoubtedly raise its head again as the original source of this type of thinking.

In this particular case, Cathy's HR group haven't set a formal requirement for her ratings to map to any such curve, but she knows from experience that when she submits her team's reviews, any rating set for her eight employees that looks particularly 'abnormal' – especially skewed too far to the right, or in other words, rated 'too highly' – will be returned to her for reassessment. No matter what justification is offered for how well her group is performing, when ratings are aggregated the company simply can't afford to have every department over-egg the ratings pudding; otherwise, the amount budgeted for the increase will be blown. So that rating managers get this message, and to attempt to minimise debates over ratings at source, each one is allocated their own budget to spend for the increase. This year, the company's allocated increase is 3 per cent on basic salary; so in Cathy's case, she has 3 per cent of her team's basic salaries to play with. She cannot exceed this amount, whatever the overall level of performance of her team.

This competing set of dynamics (the 'top-down' and the 'bottom-up') lands squarely on the desk of the first-line manager to resolve. No matter how good a job he or she has done to manage performance expectations over the year, there is always a circle to be squared. So, how does this play out in Cathy's case? This is how. First, she collects and reviews the eight self-assessments from her team with sufficient time to go back to each one of her employees and 'renegotiate' the performance rating that she will recommend to her boss and HR. The alternative is that she submits a different rating, and the employee finds out the difference when the company writes to them in about 6 weeks to advise them formally of this year's performance increase. She would much rather they find out now what they will actually get, to the extent that is possible, though she is forbidden by company rules from actually telling them what the amount is going to be until they receive their letter, as final budget decisions on allocated amounts are only made once all ratings have been aggregated. So, her room for manoeuvre is limited to making sure that they know what ratings she will submit to the company, and why.

She needs to do this with varying degrees of impact for every one of her eight team members. One is relatively easy; Matt, who joined 3 months ago, is excluded from the performance increase automatically, because he joined too recently to be included. He's young, enthusiastic and ambitious; he's already made quite an impact on the wider department with his fresh approach and new ideas; and his self-evaluation is actually somewhat conservative. He's not been here long enough to learn how to play the system, and in any case, he knows he won't get an increase this year. In his performance review with Cathy, he is perfectly happy with his new role, she encourages him appropriately, and the discussion ends well.

The other team members, however, are more problematic. All seven have given themselves an 'exceeds' rating, a '4' (on the scale of 1–5), bar one, Julie, who has scored herself '5' (the top mark). Now, Cathy has a very good team; she is generally recognised as a supportive, fair and effective team manager; and her team's performance reflects well on her leadership skill. Her own performance review (and rating) is in large part determined by her capability as a first-line supervisor. In a (of course entirely imaginary) world with no need to give a rating, and therefore no link to performance pay, the performance review cycle would be the culmination of her year's work as a good supervisor, where she discusses and agrees with each of her team members a balanced and accurate written evaluation of their performance, identifying areas of development, praising particular achievements, and discussing plans for the following year.

But this is the real world. Instead, she's faced with the task of orienting each of her discussions into what is essentially a negotiation over what rating they should get, with each employee quoting evidence to support their case, and with Cathy having to justify why they are 'only' going to get a satisfactory rating of 3. This game happens every year, with minor adjustments here and there to the same basic process; and instead of it being a celebration of the team's success, it becomes an entirely unsatisfactory battle of wits, the result of which is very few people emerge satisfied, let alone 'engaged'.

One brief explanatory point here, about the 'satisfactory' rating. Cathy's company has a five-point rating scheme, which allows for the 'middle' rating. Some schemes are deliberately designed, with say six or four ratings, to avoid this middle point, because of course professionals in the field have understood that it's an easy option for managers 'just' to give the middle rating. Regardless of the scheme, however, any rating structure has an inbuilt competing performance dynamic. The PR campaign around any such scheme will always identify the rating which means (a) that you're 'performing your job effectively' and (b) that you should be very happy to receive such a rating.

This narrative is rarely borne out in reality. In the same rhetoric, the company also encourages 'high performance standards' and ensures that only a small group is given the top one or two ratings and the commensurate salary increase. Companies in the knowledge sector recruit, by and large, high-performing people; they set their expectations high with their performance rhetoric and incentive schemes; and then they expect the majority (back to the 'distribution curve') to be happy and engaged when they receive the equivalent, however it's referred to, of a 'satisfactory' rating (otherwise known as 'good', 'effective' or 'at the required level' depending on the organisation). Managers have a far greater capacity to deceive themselves than their employees. Everyone knows this is happening, and yet companies continue to create such systems that perpetuate the myth of 'high performance management'.

Back to Cathy, because the process isn't over yet, by any means, even after she manages to minimise the damage to levels of motivation she's managed to create in her team throughout the year. Her only saving grace during the discussions is that her team members have been through this several times already; they know the game, she knows the game and they know she knows. They just have to play it for a while, and limit the damage, before they can return to their normal business of doing their best for the organisation. They all also appreciate the opportunity to have a good, all-encompassing, well-managed, one-to-one discussion about how they're getting on, if they can move beyond the inevitable and largely pointless rating negotiation.

Let us review briefly here one of the remaining seven performance discussions she has with her team, to illustrate the nature of these. One individual in particular, Jeremy, has been struggling in recent months due to a particularly challenging personal crisis, and has taken several short breaks while he attempted to resolve it. As a highly valued member of the team and, to this date, a trusted and very competent performer, both Cathy and his colleagues have rallied round over the period to support him by taking on extra work when necessary, covering his priority tasks when he has been absent, and ensuring that he received as much personal support as possible. Jeremy, in return, has clearly done his best to continue his responsibilities when he could, and has at the time of the review largely returned to normal duties.

By objective measure, however, against the detailed criteria laid out for Cathy's rating evaluation, and almost inevitably, his work performance has suffered. His rating is the lowest of the team, and he is the one person who most warrants a '2' ('below average'). Is that the 'right' decision? Jeremy has rated himself a '3'; he has argued that his effort to maintain his usual levels of performance during the time of his personal difficulties has been even greater than it was under normal circumstances, while recognising that some of his tasks were not completed or were completed poorly. Cathy also understands that given his still-fragile psychological state, a 'below average' rating at this particular moment may put back his recovery.

Returning briefly to the imaginary world without ratings, Cathy's difficulty is removed instantly, because Jeremy's otherwise honest self-evaluation would lead to a straightforward (and quick) review of performance with common agreement already established on the review period covered, allowing the majority of the meeting to concentrate on a constructive, future-oriented coaching session.

She decides the right thing to do for him at this moment in his employment is to rate him a '3', and she duly submits this to the review committee for approval. That decision means that no members of her team have received a '1' or '2' rating. Practically, it is almost unheard of for anyone in the company to receive a '1' in any case; custom and practice simply militates against such a poor rating, and by and large any individual susceptible to receiving one will likely have been managed out well before reaching that point. But she expects scrutiny on her judgement over the lack of '2' ratings. Two members of her team have received a '4', which she realises will also attract attention; but she feels reasonably confident that she can justify those with their exceptional performance over the period, which has been noted already by many of her senior colleagues.

Her final task – at least at this first stage of the review process – is to balance her budget for the projected increase. With five '3' and two '4' ratings (Matt's salary increase had already been excluded, as a new employee), she has to reduce the proposed increase for her effective ('3') performers in order to give an extra amount to her two 'above average' ('4') employees, even though she knows that this will result in a lower increase for her effective performers, possibly in contrast to their peers in other teams, especially the larger teams, whose managers were able to match more closely the distribution curve of ratings used to establish the budget in the first place – simply because they have a more statistically valid size of population to work with.

Cathy now attends a meeting incorporating her colleagues in the business unit, their HR business partner, and her direct boss, the purpose of which is to review, one by one, the employees in her team and justify the ratings she has given to them, so as to ensure a consistent approach across the department. In some years, this 'levelling' meeting follows the performance review discussions with employees; this year, it is after. Naturally enough, the meeting concentrates on ratings, because it's the common currency of performance, and like any organisation using them, the underlying principle is that employees can learn to give that currency the same value everywhere. Her fellow supervisors follow the same process.

Relative to previous years, this meeting runs reasonably well for Cathy, in any case. One of her colleagues has a much harder time justifying his ratings to his fellow managers, as he seems to them to have awarded more '4's than is warranted by the contribution of his team to the organisation. Around a third of the meeting is taken up by a discussion on the rating of one particular employee of his, who has her rating reduced from '4' to '3' as a result (Cathy's boss makes the decision); secretly, Cathy is relieved that this left very little time to cover her group, so she emerged from the meeting with her ratings proposal intact. She also knows that she's not 'out of the woods' yet, because her proposals will receive further scrutiny as they travel up to the CEO and VP of HR, but at each stage the ratings are consolidated into a wider organisational group. So, assuming the company makes its budget for this year's performance increase, she knows it's very unlikely she'll be asked to make further changes.

Essentially, that means she and the team now have to wait for HR to produce the formal letters giving them their increase; although she can be reasonably sure that there will be no changes to the rating given, it's entirely possible that the amount of increase she has allocated will change, according to the ratings profile of the rest of her department. So, her employees cannot, or at least should not, find out about her performance decisions until this final letter is issued as confirmation. The remaining consolidation process, and the final decision of the CEO, takes around 4 weeks from the 'levelling' meeting run by her boss, and about 2 months from the time her team filled in their self-evaluation form.

In calendar terms, the letters arrive at about the middle of March, for a review period finishing in December. Naturally, it would be illogical to discuss next year's performance objectives until the letters have been issued, and Cathy can run the final performance discussion with her teams, advising them of their increase, their final rating, and signing off on last year's process, all of which is done by the end of that month (March); she combines those discussions with agreement on their next year's objectives (which of course began in January).

In this entire edifice of performance, this monument to man as a rational being, the second biggest flaw in the structure – and one which is as yet apparently unquestioned by the company – is that it takes 3 months of the year to reach its conclusion. Managers like Cathy, who try to make it work, understand this flaw and work out informal objectives with them at the start of the performance period, rather than when 25 per cent of it has already passed; this on the understanding that when they're formally written down and agreed in late March they may look quite different in some cases. How she accounts for this 3-month period in the formal reporting of the employee's performance, so that it doesn't unfairly affect rating decisions the following year, depends entirely on the individual's situation; 2 years ago, for example, she had one of her team working most of his time on a large project, which was cancelled in March. She then had to engineer that individual's objectives to make sure that his performance in the first quarter wasn't entirely expunged from the record. That was a 'worst case', but this kind of 'fiddling of the system' to make it work is endemic. And, let us remind ourselves that it is entirely down to the requirement to give individual ratings, which is in turn entirely due to the link to performance pay.

In the paragraph above, I said the 'second biggest flaw'. Towards the end of March, employees receive their formal letters informing them of their increase in basic pay, which is the ultimate goal of this performance structure. In this rational approach to control of individual performance, let us consider the hypothesis on which it is constructed, that is, that individuals are motivated to higher levels of future performance by linking their historical performance to their pay. Prove that hypothesis to be wrong, and the structure I have described loses its raison d'etre.

Let us then return to Cathy's situation. The result of 3 months' work of evaluation, discussion and renegotiation is that her team of eight receive increases on their basic pay from zero (Matt, the new guy) through to 2.75 per cent. The effective range of increase for effective performers ('3' rating or above) is 1.25 per cent.

I won't attempt to go into any detail about how those increases are received by Cathy's team – or any other's in the company, for that matter; let us simply say that it was 'varied'. Rather, I would invite the reader to consider the possibility that the pay increase they receive has, at best, no impact on their motivation to perform in the following year, and at worst, it has a destructive impact. Systems of organisational control, like the case I have described, are founded on the principle that people make rational decisions based on calculated considerations of economic benefit, and that any other type of decision is 'irrational'. I received a pay increase of 1.75 per cent, because I was considered by the organisation to have been an effective performer last year signalled to me by my '3' rating, and I am therefore going to calculate that next year I will try even harder, so that I increase the possibility of receiving a '4' rating next year, and thereby receive a performance increase of 2.25 per cent instead. Not only is this flawed, it's actually bizarre that organisations construct mechanisms based on the belief that people actually do make this calculation.

In fact, as David Halpern has eloquently and convincingly shown in his recent book on the Government's Behavioural Insights Team (the 'Nudge Unit') (Halpern, 2015), 'irrational' is a term that 'fails to capture the remarkable performance of people nearly all the time' (p. 5). One example from his book serves to illustrate the point. People have a very strong aversion to loss, an insight that will often override more rational calculations. Whereas standard systems of performance-related pay have no impact, one experiment in the education field has found that 'telling teachers at the beginning of the year what their bonus would be, but that it would be cut at the end of the year if their pupils failed to reach a certain standard, did lead to a boost in performance' (p. 285).

There is no question that it would be possible to identify and improve specific details of the performance structure I have described. There is, for instance, the issue of 'direct' or 'indirect' links between pay and performance much beloved of HR business meetings. The purpose of presenting the case is not, however, to conduct such an analysis of what may or may not be changed in this organisation's approach. Rather, it is to highlight the similarities with the majority of performance management techniques that have, at their base, the assumption that individual performance can be controlled – and improved – through a single objective measure of effectiveness and the concomitant link to performance pay, directly or indirectly. Modifying elements of such techniques around the edges will not change this flawed assumption lying at their heart.

The persistence of common themes of employee performance appraisal is undoubtedly one of the best examples of valuing large-scale 'rational' and 'objective' mechanisms of control over individual perceptions of fairness and distributive justice, which have far more impact on individual motivation to succeed. The result is a substantial loss of value – both time and money – and the disengagement of large swathes of the working population. Those common themes are the persistence with structures of employee ratings, and the concomitant link to performance-related pay. Other than in certain specific types of work – notably sales, where it can be argued that there is a direct 'line of sight' between the performance level expected and a variable structure of financial incentive – it isn't too much of a generalisation to say that these techniques of control simply don't work.

As Dusterhoff *et al.* (2014) put it recently, 'The performance appraisal process is increasingly seen as a key link between employee behaviour and an organization's strategic objectives. Unfortunately, performance reviews often fail to change how people work, and dissatisfaction with the appraisal process has been associated with general job dissatisfaction, lower organizational commitment, and increased intentions to quit. Recent research has identified a number of factors related to reactions to performance appraisals in general and appraisal satisfaction in particular. Beyond the appraisal outcome itself, researchers have found that appraisal reactions are affected by perceptions of fairness and the relationship between the supervisor and the employee' (p. 265).

Even in sales organisations, the links between performance delivered and incentive paid require extremely well-thought-out, not to say highly complex, mechanisms to ensure that there are limited unintended consequences of the incentive scheme, especially in service organisations – and these days, most organisations have some element of service – when it is notoriously difficult to quantify the required level of performance. Does the company attach the incentive to the immediate sale, regardless of the long-term value – or otherwise – placed on the satisfaction of the customer acquired? Or, does the scheme take into account the real value to the organisation of the sale, that is, the acquisition of a returning customer?

A moment's thought of the complications arising from such a question indicates the need for great care in devising such schemes, even without the need to refer to some perhaps now apocryphal examples of where such incentives have achieved precisely the opposite effect, namely the destruction rather than creation of value to the organisation. Such schemes are 'wide open' to gaming by sales staff. In my present business, private education, the US Government uncovered – and legislated against – the widespread practice of incentivising staff to sell degree courses to individuals who simply could not afford to pay for them or who were ill equipped to complete their course, thus incurring huge debts via federal loan schemes.

My own company was notably exonerated from such practices, but I have still witnessed the internal struggle – still continuing – to find an effective mechanism of incentivising those who enrol students onto their degree programmes in ways that avoid the payment of a sales bonus for the acquisition of a student who clearly meets selection criteria on paper, but who has a high risk of leaving the course before the end of their programme because they are otherwise ill equipped to complete their studies. It is possible – and many schemes have been tried – but the temptation offered by the sales bonus to make a short-term acquisition at the expense of long-term value always remains, unless it is highly regulated. Such risks are of course exacerbated by the quarterly or annual review of financial performance that is a common feature of most companies these days, itself a structure that militates against the recognition of the long-term value of a customer acquired through a sale.

And that is in a sales unit. What of the rest of the organisation where – for the vast majority of us – there is no such link – line of sight – between what we do for the company, and what we receive as incentive pay? It is, of course, quite logical that any organisation should wish to ensure that its workforce is aligned with, and working towards, its performance goals. A brief reflection on the opposite situation illustrates that an orientation to continuous performance improvement is a desirable goal. Consider the organisation that is unable to make any differentiation between those employees who are conscientious, attentive, engaged, perform at a high level and willing to learn; and those who are not. The company can take no action in either case; it must treat both types of employee in precisely the same way, and for those who 'underperform', they have no ability to remove them from their jobs unless they perform a criminal act. Although this example perfectly describes many public-sector organisations in different parts of the world today, it is unlikely to be a model that anyone who is interested in the creation of value would be keen to pursue.

There is, I should say, nothing wrong with organisational efforts to control and improve individual performance. Is it possible to devise a structure that removes this flaw? Halpern's example from education described above certainly shows the way and illustrates how using a different assumption about modifying behaviour, using, rather than eliminating, irrationality, could work.

I will describe a concrete case of an alternative structure that also moves some way to removing this flaw.

Practical 'quasi' experiment

For the last 5 years, I have been running a business unit split conventionally into a number of departments, whose heads reported to me. The formal performance management mechanism of half of those department heads, and the people who worked for them, looked very similar to the case I have described above. For reasons largely out of my control, the other half was not directly employed by the organisation, but worked for me through an agency contract, even though – to all intents and purposes – these people were fulfilling similar responsibilities and roles to the people who were directly controlled. Managing these department heads, and the people who worked for them, through an agency or external contract relationship had, on the one hand, clear legal restrictions on what I could do to implement performance management control measures with them. On the other hand, serendipitously, it also offered the opportunity, as a scholar practitioner, to operate two quite different mechanisms of performance control over very similar populations over an extended period. Not a random control trial exactly, but certainly an interesting opportunity to compare and contrast the results.

The critical difference was that with my agency group, I had no requirement to link, and indeed was legally prevented from linking, their pay (or more accurately, their 'fee') to performance; this also obviated the need to assign an overall performance rating to them. As contractors, the formal process of managing their performance was relatively straightforward: they had their responsibilities specified through the agreement we had with them to provide a service to the organisation, and the annual renewal of that agreement signified to them that they had delivered that service adequately over the previous 12 months. In theory, that was the only formal structure I had to use. HR systems of control of performance such as the case I have described in detail above are by definition restricted to those who are fully employed by the company. Given the preponderance of agency and contract staff in the modern organisation, this restriction places one obvious limit on their impact, but it is not my main point here.

On the face of it, one would understandably assume that half of my business unit who benefited from the full suite of tools of performance measurement, control and incentivisation – not to mention the relative security theoretically entailed by being directly employed – would result in a higher-performing group. The use of agency staff is controversial, and morally questionable. Much of what is written about their impact is critical; they are often used as an illustration of the fragmentation of work (Thompson, 2011), the instrumentalisation of the working relationship, and the reduction in security of employment; for the last reason especially, 'zero-based contracts' were a political football kicked around during the recent UK election campaign.

I will return briefly to these controversies later, not least the moral issue. For the moment, however, I will remain with the performance question.

At best, there was no difference, over time, in the relative performance of the two groups; at worst, the agency group delivered far more continuous performance, and performance improvement, over the 5 years, than the fully employed group.

I cannot, I should say here, present a statistical analysis to support that assertion. What I can do is point to some salient indicators that have led me to this conclusion. External validation is one. The performance of the agency group was under constant observation from partner organisations and clients, as their work involved direct contact with both, so there was no question of hiding their work from scrutiny. In no single case, in the 5 years, was there an issue of performance raised by client or partner that originated from their status as agency staff. Indeed in the case of our clients, they were at all times unaware of the nature of the relationship my people had with our organisation.

A second indicator derives from the flesh I put on the bones of the legal requirement to renew their contracts (or not) every year, as such a system was clearly woefully inadequate for the kind of service-related performance I required from this group. For front-line staff – and there were around 500 of them – I was able to devise, collect and measure very detailed information – at the transactional level – about how well they were performing, which provided me with a regularly updated dashboard of service-level indicators. These measures were used by their supervisors – also agency staff – to review their performance regularly, provide coaching and guidance where needed, and furnish accurate information to support decisions on contract renewal. Needless to say, there was no requirement for supervisors to engage in the kinds of contortions required of Cathy, as I described above, to come up with a rating.

At the business unit level, I was able to adjust measures and allocate resources according to the trends revealed by the dashboard.

At the department head level (my direct reports), and their supervisor teams, I instigated a system of weekly one-to-one discussions that managers recorded and sent out to the individual, which ensured that we had a continuous conversation about their work, and notes which captured discussions to minimise ambiguity and provide evidence of them if needed. My interaction with those agency department heads and supervisors was as frequent as it was with any of my directly employed team. To all intents and purposes, and for daily business, their employment status was irrelevant. Their annual contract renewal was automatic and based on an informal 'how are you doing' type discussion – essentially a chance to review the year, and look forward to the next one. I kept their fees under close scrutiny, but ensured that they received a market, not performance, related increase to those fees every year which was commensurate with whatever inflation-based increase was being offered to our employees.

'Scores' of department performance staffed by agency people – measured by customer and partner retention and satisfaction through my dashboard – moved steadily upward over those 5 years.

However, the third set, and I believe most important, indicators of the relatively successful performance of the 'agency' group derived from measures of engagement, productivity and length of service, all of which are more commonly thought to be applicable to a fully employed population, not a contracting one. In all of these measures, the contracting group actually performed as well or better than the employees.

From the outset, I was aware of the significant risk of the contracting group behaving in a way akin to mercenaries, with no particular connection or allegiance to our organisation, and coming and going as they saw fit. A significant proportion were able to work for other organisations at the same time as our own, as many were part time, and to compound the risk the group were entirely remotely based and spread around the world.

Within the legal constraints of their contracting arrangement, I found room to create methods to maximise their engagement with us, as well as their levels of performance, as follows. The principle was simple – when working for us, we would try and ensure that they were fully engaged with us. This was a pragmatic as well as a principled judgement, because we believed it would be better for our business. They were recruited to high standards and given all relevant training and development for their role. They were included in our regular organisation structures. And, they were provided with a support network including a social community, resources for self-actualisation, and conferences and meetings to give them opportunity to participate in organisation business.

They were still not, however, employees, and they were excluded from all of the traditional benefits enjoyed by people of that status in our organisation, as well as not being subject to the regular performance management system I illustrated in Cathy's case above. Contractually and legally we treated them as we were obliged to – as agency staff.

Conclusions

What this quasi 'experiment' in performance management highlights therefore is that effective performance can be achieved without recourse to mechanisms of control founded in performance ratings and performance-related pay, which, despite their widespread use, remain ineffective and unpopular. The result is that, at the level of operational leadership, two distinct and competing organisational narratives meet, and conflict. One is the 'engagement' narrative, which traces its origins back through a generation of management writing, and proposes that organisations are more successful if they create an environment in which their people are motivated, committed and engaged in their work, because then they will strive to do better each day. This is the affect, the appeal to the heart, and has led over 25 years to an industry of writing and consulting on 'leadership', and a revolution in HR towards values-based systems of performance management.

References

Boselie, P., Dietz, G. & Boon, C. 2005. Commonalities and contradictions in HRM and performance research. *Human Resource Management Journal*, 15, 67–94.

Brewster, C., Mayrhofer, W. & Morley, M. (eds.) 2004. *Human Resource Management in Europe: Evidence of Convergence?*, Oxford: Elsevier.

Byrne, Z. S., Pitts, V. E., Wilson, C. M. & Steiner, Z. J. 2012. Trusting the fair supervisor: the role of supervisory support in performance appraisals. *Human Resource Management Journal*, 22, 129–147.

Cheng, S. Y. 2014. The mediating role of organizational justice on the relationship between administrative performance appraisal practices and organizational commitment. *International Journal of Human Resource Management*, 25, 1131–1148.

Deetz, S. 1992. Disciplinary power in the modern corporation. *In:* Alvesson, M. & Willmott, H. (eds.) *Critical Management Studies*. London: Sage. pp. 21–45.

Delaney, J. T. & Huselid, M. 1996. The impact of human resource management practices on perceptions on organizational performance. *Academy of Management Journal*, 39, 949.

Delbridge, R., Lowe, J. & Oliver, N. 2000. Worker autonomy in lean teams; evidence from the world automotive components industry. *In:* Proctor, S. & Mueller, F. (eds.) *Teamworking*. London: Macmillan. pp. 125–142.

Delery, J. & Doty, H. 1996. Modes of theorising in SHRM: tests of universalistic, contingency and configurational performance predictions. *Academy of Management Journal*, 39, 821.

Den Hartog, D. N., Boselie, P. & Paauwe, J. 2004. Performance management: a model and research agenda. *Applied Psychology: An International Review*, 53, 556–569.

Dusterhoff, C., Cunningham, J. & Macgregor, J. 2014. The effects of performance rating, leader-member exchange, perceived utility, and organizational justice on performance appraisal satisfaction: applying a moral judgment perspective. *Journal of Business Ethics*, 119(2), 265–273.

Elicker, J. D., Levy, P. E. & Hall, R. J. 2006. The role of leader-member exchange in the performance appraisal process. *Journal of Management*, 32, 531–551.

Farndale, E. & Kelliher, C. 2013. Implementing performance appraisal: exploring the employee experience. *Human Resource Management*, 52, 879–897.

Foucault, M. (ed.) 1979. *Discipline and Punish*, Harmondsworth: Penguin.

Goksoy, A. & Alayoglu, N. 2013. The impact of perception of performance appraisal and distributive justice fairness on employees' ethical decision making in paternalist organizational culture. *Performance Improvement Quarterly*, 26, 57–79.

Guest, D. E. 2011. Human resource management and performance: still searching for some answers. *Human Resource Management Journal*, 21, 3–13.

Hales, C. 2005. Management: continuity and change in the role of first-line manager. *Journal of Management Studies*, 42, 471–506.

Halpern, D. 2015. *Inside the Nudge Unit: How Small Changes Can Make a Big Difference*, London: WH Allen.

Huselid, M. 1998. The impact of HRM practices on turnover, productivity, and corporate financial performance. *In:* Mabey, C., Salaman, G. & Storey, J. (eds.) *SHRM: A Reader (Open University).* Sage.

Huselid, M., Becker, B. & Ulrich, D. (eds.) 2003. *The HR Scorecard*, Boston, MA: HBS.

Huselid, M., Jackson, S. & Schuler, R. 1997. Technical and strategic HRM effectiveness as determinants of firm performance. *Academy of Management Journal*, 40, 171–188.

Hutchinson, S. & Purcell, J. (eds.) 2003. *Bringing Policies to Life: The vital role of front line managers in people management*, London: CIPD.

Kuvaas, B. 2006. Performance appraisal satisfaction and employee outcomes: mediating and moderating roles of work motivation. *International Journal of Human Resource Management*, 17, 504–522.

Legge, K. (ed.) 1995. *HRM: Rhetorics and Realities*, London: Macmillan.

Legge, K. 2000. Silver bullet or spent round? Assessing the meaning of the 'High commitment Mgt'/ performance relationship. *In:* Storey, J. (ed.) *HRM: A Critical Text.* London: Thomson.

Nehles, A. C., Van Riemsdijk, M., Kok, I. & Looise, J. K. 2006. Implementing Human Resource Management Successfully: A First-Line Management Challenge. Mering: Rainer Hampp Verlag.

Newton, T. 1994. Discourse and agency: the example of personnel psychology and assessment centres. *Organization Studies*, 15, 879–902.

Newton, T. & Findlay, P. 1998. Playing God? The performance of appraisal. *In:* Mabey, C., Salaman, G. & Storey, J. (eds.) *SHRM: A Reader (Open University).* Sage.

Osterman, P. 1994. How common is workplace transformation and who adopts it? *Industrial and Labor Relations Review*, 47, 173–88.

Pfeffer, J. (ed.) 1994. *Competitive Advantage through People: Unleashing the Power of the Workforce*, Boston: Harvard Business School Press.

Pfeffer, J. (ed.) 1998. *The Human Equation: Building Profits by Putting People First*, Boston, MA: Harvard.

Purcell, J. & Hutchinson, S. 2007. Front-line managers as agents in the HRM-performance causal chain: theory, analysis and evidence. *Human Resource Management Journal*, 17, 3–20.

Scullion, H. 2000. International HRM. *In*: Storey, J. (ed.) *HRM: A Critical Text.* London: Thomson.

Sparrow, P., Brewster, C. & Harris, H. (eds.) 2004. *Globalizing Human Resource Management*, London: Routledge.

Sparrow, P. & Marchington, M. (eds.) 1998. *HRM The New Agenda*, Harlow: Pearson.

Sumelius, J., Björkman, I., Ehrnrooth, M., Mäkelä, K. & Smale, A. 2014. What determines employee perceptions of HRM process features? The case of performance appraisal in MNC subsidiaries. *Human Resource Management*, 53, 569–592.

Thompson, P. 2011. The trouble with HRM. *Human Resource Management Journal*, 21, 355–367.

Thurston, P. W. & Mcnall, L. 2010. Justice perceptions of performance appraisal practices. *Journal of Managerial Psychology*, 25, 201–228.

Townley, B. 1993. Foucault, power/knowledge, and its relevance for HRM. *Academy of Management Review*, 18, 518–45.

Watson, T. 2004. HRM and critical social science analysis. *Journal of Management Studies*, 41, 447–467.

Part III

Performance Management and Control in different contexts

16

Theorising management accounting practices in less developed countries

Chandana Alawattage, Danture Wickramasinghe and Shazhad Uddin

Introduction

The last two decades have witnessed a growth in research on accounting in less developed countries (LDCs). In particular, critical accounting scholarship in the area of management accounting in LDCs, though still in its infancy (Hopper and Bui, 2015), has become an important field of research. Recently, LDCs have become interesting research sites in which to explore various management accounting dynamics associated with globalisation and neoliberal reforms, the diffusion of management accounting technologies and the development of the management accounting profession and education (Hopper *et al.*, 2009).

Given the politically and culturally rich idiosyncratic contexts of LDCs, a wide array of methodo-philosophical approaches has been deployed with different strategies for access, ethnographic encounters and theoretical sensitisation. Not surprisingly, LDCs' management accounting research has so far provided an interesting and diverse range of insights into how management accounting has been implicated within and outwith formal organisational settings. Many social theories including orthodox Marxism, neo- and post-Marxism, Weber's interpretive sociology, Bourdieu's reflexive sociology, actor-network theory and various versions of institutional theory have been used to shed light on diverse understanding of management accounting practices. In this chapter, we aim to explore the particular theoretical trajectory that critical accounting research has taken to understand the political and cultural peculiarities of management accounting practices in LDCs, and potential paths for future investigation. Here, our primary attention is on the 'theorisation project'.

This chapter has three parts. In the following section, we present the theoretical underpinnings of early management accounting studies, which were prescriptive in nature and firmly rooted in the normative/functionalist paradigm. In the subsequent section, we present the conceptual framework used to capture the critical theorisation project of management accounting studies in LDCs, noting three major themes. First, in line with the neo-Marxist beginnings of Western critical accounting research, we explore how accounting researchers from LDCs adopted similar perspectives to explain the political-economic roles of accounting, while locating these within the historical and political idiosyncrasies of colonial and postcolonial LDCs. This neo-Marxist theorisation of the connection between accounting and political reforms in LDCs is discussed in section 'Theorising the political and historical connection: accounting and political reforms in LDCs'. Second, life beyond formal organisational settings is an important aspect of LDCs: the informal, the convivial, the cultural and the civic have always been defining parameters in the operation of accounting and other calculative practices. Accordingly, we see the development of a theorisation project that concentrates on how accounting reshapes and reproduces social structures and processes beyond formal organisational settings in LDCs. This is discussed in section 'Theorising the civic connection: accounting beyond organisations'. Third, the political and economic interests of Western institutions have resulted in the transfer of Western management accounting technologies such as activity-based costing (ABC), balanced scorecards (BSC) and enterprise resource planning (ERP) to commercial and non-commercial organisational settings in LDCs. Drawing on social theories, researchers have demonstrated the cultural-political complications of knowledge transfer to LDCs. We discuss this aspect of theorisation in section 'Theorising epistemic connection: the appearance of new management accounting'. The final section summarises the chapter, with a note on potential directions for future critical accounting research on LDCs.

Prescriptive management accounting: normative and functionalist perspectives

LDCs began to attract the attention of accounting researchers in the 1970s. However, much of this early research was largely normative, concentrated on possibilities for exporting Western management accounting technologies to organisations in LDCs and the 'practical' issues of 'implementing' such technologies (e.g. Enthoven, 1973, 1977). Western technologies were assumed to be universally applicable, in that necessary conditions were established for their implementation through appropriate management consulting and other advisory services. Thus, they were, and still are, in mainstream accounting circles, driven by the managerial ethos and the 'business' of selling Western management accounting technologies to their non-Western counterparts. Therefore, the fundamental focus of these early studies was to understand how such management accounting tools could effectively and efficiently be implemented in LDCs and how the cultural-political idiosyncrasies could be mitigated through appropriate processes of consultation, education, planning and monetary (and other) incentives (see Enthoven, 1973, 1977). These studies still dominate the stream of accounting and management research in LDCs. Institutions such as consulting/accountancy firms, development agencies and business schools continue to be the main proponents of such studies. Nevertheless, for these early (and ongoing) research studies, LDCs were not unique sites for understanding or exploring their idiosyncrasies and how such idiosyncrasies impact on management accounting practices, but sites awaiting convergence with the West.

Though less 'critical', the 1980s and 1990s witnessed the differentiation of LDCs as distinct cultural sites for accounting research. This initiative stemmed from the influence of Hofstede (1980b, 1991) on management and accounting research. His work provided an attractive analytical framework for accounting researchers to explain how and why accounting technologies are implicated differently in different national contexts. Hofstede's cultural dimensions became analytical criteria for differentiation between West and East, and developed and underdeveloped.

The popularisation of these cross-cultural analyses of accounting and management control practices (e.g. Hofstede, 1980a, 1981; Olve *et al.*, 1988; Hofstede, 1990; Singh, 1990; Harrison, 1992; Pratt and Beaulieu, 1992; Chow *et al.*, 1994; Sondergaard, 1994) was indeed a natural extension of the epistemic trajectory, especially the behavioural accounting project initiated by Hopwood (1974, 1976) and others (e.g. Gambling, 1976b,a; Marques, 1976; Tomassini, 1976) as a critique of the mainstream neoclassical, economics-based, normative/managerial analysis of accounting. Epistemically, this was when systems theory and contingency theory (vis-à-vis the neoclassical economic framework of agency theory) became a popular theoretical framework among accounting researchers with regard to accounting and management control systems. Initially, contingency variables such as environment, strategy, structure, technology and size became the bases upon which differences in the variability and outcomes of management and accounting control systems could be explained across different organisational settings. Hofstede's contribution indeed provided a taxonomy through which culture could be introduced as an additional variable into this contingency theory-based analytical trajectory to explain such management control system variability. This was interesting for accounting research on LDCs because this cultural taxonomy (rather than other contingency variables) provided an analytical basis for differences in management control systems across national boundaries to be conceptualised and tested. Thus, East and West, developed and underdeveloped, began to appear in accounting research as differentiating site specifications on the basis of cultural characterisations (see Baydoun and Willett, 1995). Culture became a 'variable' in explaining management control system variability between West and East, developed and underdeveloped.

However, contingency theory-centric cultural studies have been subject to severe criticism, especially by critical accounting studies. Within the epistemic parameters of contingency theory, culture is conceived only as a taxonomical characteristic rather than an underlying force, institution or process of collective human action, framed within a rather positivistic survey-type 'testing' of differences and associations. This has been seen as an unhelpful conception of culture that is unable to capture the cultural politics underlying the historical evolution of accounting and control systems in LDCs. This is discussed further below.

Critical accounting scholarship: conceptual framework

A central theme in critical accounting scholarship is the location of accounting within wider political structures, processes, institutions and discourses. Critical theorists see accounting simultaneously as a product and a constitutive element of such wider political dynamics; there is a dialectical connection between accounting and its institutional political context. While accounting evolves with the dynamics of capitalism and modernity, it also contributes to capitalistic development by providing the necessary technological, organisational and micro-political means (see Hoskin and Macve, 1986, 1988; Johnson and Kaplan, 1987; Hopper and Armstrong, 1991). Embedded in such macro and micro processes, we see three distinct elements that shape and reshape academic endeavours in the theorisation of management accounting practices in LDCs (see Figure 16.1).

First are the cultural-political circumstances of LDCs and their influence on management accounting practices. Second are the accounting practices that researchers may encounter during their ethnographic (and other) fieldwork, comprising the content and focus onto which the context is projected. Third are 'fashionable' developments in critical accounting research circles in terms of the particular theoretical frameworks and methodological approaches embraced by Western researchers. These relate to the 'academic self' of the researchers and the 'epistemic baggage' that they 'extract' in researching accounting in LDCs.[1] When these three elements converge, we see how critical accounting research on LDCs

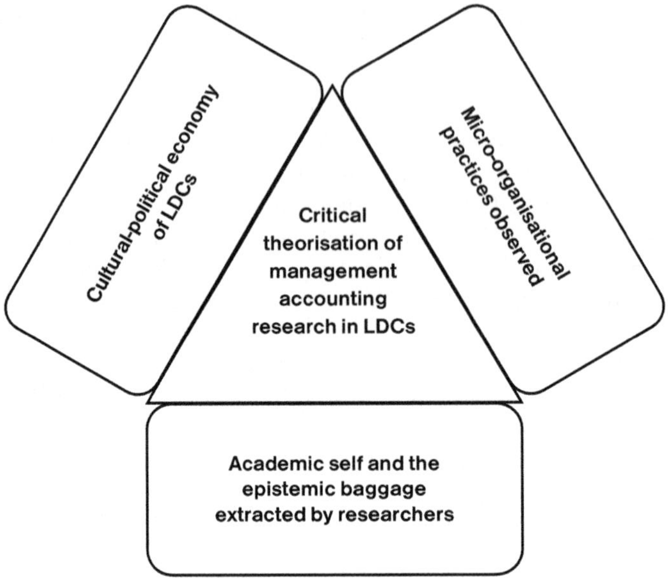

Figure 16.1 Elements in theorising accounting in LDCs

has evolved: by addressing cultural-political and economic issues emanating from different macro-political economic policy and development regimes, by bringing different ethnographic and other forms of field data to micro-organisational practices of accounting, and by using different epistemic tools to sensitise the connection between these macro-political dynamics and micro-organisational practices. Three distinct theoretical projects that can be discerned within the critical scholarship are discussed below.

Theorising the political and historical connection: accounting and political reforms in LDCs

Not until the early 1990s, when Professor Trevor Hopper and his colleagues at the University of Manchester began to supervise a group of PhD students from LDCs, did accounting research on LDCs start to receive 'critical' attention. This was an interesting time, in both the epistemic and the political-economic sense. During this period, LDCs were experiencing a political-economic transition from embryonic socialism and state capitalism to market capitalism. Marking the rise of free market capitalism and the demise of socialism, structural adjustment programmes such as privatisation and new public management were well under way, with a view to establishing a new political-economic order within LDCs.

In this macro-political economic scenario, most large economic enterprises in LDCs were being sold off or had gone through a privatisation process. It was these economic enterprises into which the Manchester PhDs went to do their ethnographic (and other) fieldwork. These ethnographic encounters in accounting were interesting because they provided opportunities to observe how accounting practices were implicated within a wider political-economic transformation of nation states. These researchers found from their micro-organisational data that accounting and management control systems were politicised and operated within particular political rationales idiosyncratic to LDCs. These findings were markedly different from normative/functionalist management accounting studies of LDCs.

Understanding of accounting and management control as a political-economic-cultural phenomenon cannot be attributed wholly to the empirical data collected by these researchers, although they played a critical role. In order to grasp the political sensitivity of such data and their connection to the macro context, an appropriate theoretical mindset was also necessary. The particular epistemic trajectory of Western accounting scholarship at that time, especially the revival of neo-Marxist analysis in the famous labour process debate and the emergence of new institutional sociology, indeed provided this 'epistemic baggage' to connect the micro-organisational practices that they observed with the macro-political changes.

The exposure of PhD researchers on LDCs from Manchester and other places to this academic debate at that time provided the necessary conditions to create a group of 'epistemic selves' who would eagerly engage in the project of exploring postcolonial political rationales of accounting and management control. In this sense, the beginning of the critical political theorisation of accounting and management control practices in LDCs was the result of a particular condition whereby the incidental overlapping of the three elements mentioned in Figure 16.1 provided the necessary impetus to theorise the political connection by locating accounting within the politico-historical processes of postcolonial states.

The beginning of this political theorisation[2] was marked by Hoque and Hopper's (1994) study of management control in a Bangladeshi jute mill (Hoque and Hopper, 1994; see also Hoque and Hopper, 1997). Triangulating fieldwork data with a survey and other secondary data, and taking an interpretive methodological approach, this study revealed how operational control, especially budgetary control, operated at the level of practice and why systems of control worked in the ways they appeared to do. Hoque and Hopper (1994, p. 25) argued that

> the formal design of accounting and accountability systems, which on the surface were textbook models of rational resource allocation and hierarchical accountability, had been reduced to ritualistic and institutionalized roles within the mills with the gaining of external legitimacy being their primary purpose. Such policies, coupled to political interventions, rendered the accounting and accountability systems ineffective for managers involved in operational decisions and control.

The outcome of this was that managers found their way into social, personal and political controls, including the mobilisation of trade union political patronage, to cope with the uncertainty created by friction between the official legitimating interface of accounting and shop-floor operational realities. This made control in the mill a cultural-political phenomenon rather than the computational strategy of rational decision-making processes. However, these findings were not fundamentally different from what had been observed in Western counterparts by other new institutional sociologists, especially regarding public-sector corporations (Berry *et al.*, 1985; Hopper *et al.*, 1986; Ansari and Euske, 1987; Covaleski and Dirsmith, 1988; Ouibrahim and Scapens, 1989; Ansari and Bell, 1991; Jones and Sefiane, 1992; Covaleski *et al.*, 1993).

This cultural-political nature and the peculiar connection of state and party politics with control at the point of production were investigated by a stream of subsequent studies. Hoque and Hopper's (1994) work recognised the cultural-political sensitivity of accounting in LDCs but limited its analysis to processes of institutional legitimation and ritualisation, ignoring the way in which state and trade union politics make their way into the politics of production. Uddin and Hopper's (2001) contribution was to take political analysis a step further, bringing state and production politics together. With the theoretical ambition of developing a 'political economy of accounting' in LDCs, they examined a much broader set of issues pertaining to the political connection of accounting and control: the role of accounting in manufacturing consent and coercion at the point of production; the way in which state politics involving political parties, classes, trade unions and external financial institutions interact with labour resistance at the point of production to transform controls, including accounting; and the possibility of modelling the historical transformation of accounting in enterprises in LDCs, especially ex-British colonies. These issues were addressed first through a political definition of 'regimes of control', for which theoretical insight was derived from Burawoy's (1979, 1985) neo-Marxist notions of hegemonic and despotic regimes (see also Gramsci *et al.*, 1971), and second through examination of political mechanisms, such as internal labour markets, internal state and gaming behaviour, by which consent (and coercion) is reproduced at the point of production. The data drawn from an intensive case study of a soap-manufacturing company in Bangladesh revealed not only a historical trajectory in the evolution of control regimes from colonial despotism to market despotism through political hegemony, but also the particular and historically specific role played by accounting under each regime of control. Hoque and Hopper's theory was that such control regimes are the product of the infusion of state politics with the politics of production, and that the role assumed by accounting under each of these distinct control regimes is driven by the necessity of (re)producing either the coercion or consent necessitated and conditioned by the political dynamics of the time.

This line of theorisation is important because it helps us to understand the way in which accounting and management control, though similar in technical terms, have differed in historical and political terms in LDCs. Two main themes are important in this respect. First is the way in which strong political states (though imperfect and inefficient in terms of Western democratic and market economy ideals) penetrate into organisational regimes of control. Crony capitalism, paternalism and patronage politics have been identified not only as structural parameters through which political state interference takes place in LDCs, but also as salient features that differentiate the politics of production in LDCs from their developed counterparts. Several empirical case studies have demonstrated specific ways in which such political processes and structures have played a part in reshaping management accounting.

Wickramasinghe *et al.* (2004), for example, reported how Japanese attempts to restructure the management control system and install a 'new work culture' in privatised Sri Lankan Telecom were imperfect and reverted to the 'old inefficient formal' bureaucracy through 'regulatory capture' by political forces operating within and beyond the company walls, especially trade unions affiliated with party politics. Alawattage and Wickramasinghe (2008) provided another Sri Lankan example, from the privatised plantation sector, of how management control systems are constituted neither by prototypical accounting practices nor by formal management control systems, but by a historically specific system of ethnic politics, an ethnicised trade union movement associated with the political and cultural rights of a particular minority ethnic category enslaved within Sri Lankan plantations by British imperialism. As in the Bangladeshi cases studied by Hopper and his colleagues (Hoque and Hopper, 1994; Uddin and Hopper, 2001), in these Sri Lankan cases, we see the decoupled, ritualised, ceremonial and legitimating role of accounting within a highly politicised regulatory environment. Operational and strategic decisions are framed largely within political hegemonies – strong state patronage apparatuses and fractionalised party politics that penetrate into day-to-day operational matters. All these studies make a salient point about the way in which management accounting and control systems operate in LDCs: these changes are not simply organisational, but their roots are also cultural-political and historical.

The second theme is that postcolonial developments in organisational forms and control systems seem to be associated with three distinct historical phases. First is the nationalisation phase, constituting postcolonial nation-building projects often brought about through the nationalisation of colonial enterprises, resulting in state-owned, centralised and large bureaucracies, often with nationalistic political (and even military) leaderships that allow political ideologies of nationalism and ethnic politics to override the economic rationales of management control systems. In accounting research on LDCs, this post-independence political trajectory has been often theorised as the *historical context* of current modes of management control systems, using history as a key explanatory device in theorising management control systems in LDCs.

Second is the neoliberal political transformation phase directed at the privatisation and modernisation of large state-owned enterprises with a neoliberal market economic rationale. In accounting research, developments in this phase have been often conceptualised as *political processes of transformation*. As summarised in this section, much of this theorisation endeavour draws on empirical data from the early 1990s and 2000s on political processes of structural transformation in LDCs.

Third is the organisational learning phase, in which the state politics of transforming large corporate entities in LDCs seem to play a less crucial role in the national political or development agenda. Instead, the political agenda of development has now turned to rural development projects such as microfinance, where NGOs play a significant role. Hence, accountability structures and processes of microfinance and NGOs have become more appealing accounting themes. In the case of large corporate entities, with much less involvement of state politics, the transformational dynamics of management accounting have now become more or less a matter of organisational learning within global epistemic networks diffusing Western management accounting technologies and knowledge, such as BSC, ABC and ERP. Two distinct theoretical endeavours seem to have emerged in management accounting research on LDCs dealing with these new phases of economic development and organisational learning. First, we see theoretical projects concentrating on management accounting practices with civic connections, microfinance and wider stakeholder participation. Second, management accounting researchers on LDCs are deploying social theories to understand the global diffusion of management accounting technologies and epistemic connections. Both of these theoretical endeavours are presented below.

Theorising the civic connection: accounting beyond organisations

Over the past decade, the economic logic of development based on structural transformational politics (such as privatisation and state budget reforms) has been reinventing itself as a social or civic logic of development. Policy discourses based on the notion of 'social capital' as a driver of development (and as an obstacle to tackling it positively) have become popular among international development funding agencies such as the World Bank, IMF, OECD and Asian Bank (see Putnam *et al.*, 1994; Dasgupta and Serageldin, 2001). The institutional implications of this policy reorientation are significant. First, civil society development is considered to be a crucial element in social development, such as the enhancement of grassroots democracy, racial, ethnic and gender discrimination, the elimination of corruption and social entrepreneurship (Dasgupta and Serageldin, 2001). Second, under the development bandwagon of empowering civil society, NGOs have become some of the most important institutional and accountability vehicles for making a viable political connection between economy, polity and civil society. Third, microfinance is seen as an important mode of development finance for the achievement of wider development goals. The World Bank, Asian Bank and many other international development agencies, as well as national governments, have recognised microfinance as a central pillar in their rural development strategies.

Taken together, these policy reorientations have reconstructed rural social spaces, such as villages, as 'developmental spaces' to be organised and managed through various technologies of governance and accountability, including accounting (see Alawattage *et al.*, 2014). This evolutionary trajectory of the political economy of LDCs is interesting for accounting scholars because accountability is no longer a phenomenon to be understood as enacted through formal channels of organisational relationships; instead, 'micro-accountabilities' (Alawattage *et al.*, 2015), which hold individuals convivially accountable to each other in their local settings, must be recognised as a central tool of social governance under neoliberalism, and as a strong means of integrating LDC societies into the global neoliberal economy.

As Figure 16.1 indicates, the shifting cultural-political circumstances of LDCs and micro-organisational practices are driving critical accounting scholars to new theoretical frontiers. Alawattage *et al.* (2015), for example, provide a Foucauldian biopolitical analysis of commercial microfinance, illustrating how accounting technologies are being used as biopolitical tools to govern populations in ways that extend economic production beyond the factory into the lives of individuals and every part of the global economy.

'Neoliberal biopolitics' (Foucault, 2010; Munro, 2012) represents an extension of economic rationalism into areas of life that have not previously been considered in economic terms. In the case of microfinance, this is evident in the biopolitical processes of reorganising so-called 'poor women' (who were traditionally considered as a pathological category of, *inter alia*, the 'welfare dependent', 'budget burdened' and 'un-bankable') into a set of 'self-help groups'. This new recognition transforms them into 'bankable', 'poor enterprising clients', capable of investing regular savings in a microfinance institution. These savings go a long way to proving first their creditworthiness, and then their capacity to borrow and repay microcredit (although at a very high interest rate averaging around 24 per cent per annum, a rate three times the typical commercial credit rate available to wealthy business people).

This 'bankability' of the 'poor women' is constructed through a set of micro-disciplinary practices, which Alawattage *et al.* (2015), drawing on Foucault, call 'centripetal processes of neoliberal biopolitics'. In a Foucauldian sense, these centripetal forces of biopolitics operate not just on the anatomo-politics of the body but also on the micro-relations through which the body is disciplined, controlled and secured. Alawattage *et al.* (2015) find that, of the four centripetal forces of neoliberal biopolitics, entrepreneurship and financial self-discipline operate as psychoanalytic conditions of the exercise of biopolitical power over the body, while the other two – small group accountability and micro-banking – are its relational and institutional apparatuses.

Such disciplinary apparatuses alone cannot explain the growth and *modus operandi* of neoliberal governmentality. Centrifugal forces of biopolitics are required to organise populations and connect individuals to the economy, and extend neoliberal governance to the perimeter of what Hardt and Negri (2000) refer to as 'empire'. Alawattage *et al.* (2015) identify empirically four such centrifugal forces that connect individual bodies, as objectified bodies of neoliberal development discourses, to the global economy: biopolitical poverty calculations, corporatisation of the village, animation of microfinance projects, and assembly of biopolitical accounts. A key effect of these centrifugal and centripetal forces of neoliberal biopolitics is the 'immaterialisation of labour', which is indeed a salient feature of postmodern capitalism or empire (see Hardt and Negri, 2000; Munro, 2012).

Hence, Alawattage *et al.* (2015) observe that 'poor women' spend much of their time in communicative activities within microfinance groups, in symbolic activities for producing knowledge that makes their own lives visible to the centre, and in affective work that fosters convivial relationships of care within the groups. These are a set of well-structured activities (through microfinance programming and training of individuals and groups) driving towards the construction of the 'financial discipline' of making savings and repaying loans and interest. In this way, microfinance displaces and distributes the primary functions of capital: the management of production and bearing of risk. As such, in a microfinance regime, capital no longer purchases labour and transforms it into labour power within disciplinary spaces such as factories. Instead, capital distributes the job of raising and managing capital to labourers, in the guise of entrepreneurship, so that poor villagers who would otherwise sell their labour to capital in the context of material labour for a fixed wage now bear the financial risk of their own labour. For this privilege, they pay comparatively much higher interest to their microfinance banks; capital is thus able to earn a return on a risk that it neither bears nor manages (see Alawattage *et al.*, 2015, p. 39). Thus, in the neoliberal capitalism evolving in LDCs, emerging structures and processes of micro-accountability can be seen, which manage the circulation of surplus value rather than managing its material production.

An interesting observation made by accounting research dealing with the 'civic connection' is the way in which civil society, microfinance and NGOs overlap in articulating new modes of accountability, and their complexities and paradoxes. Different notions of accountability have entered the academic and managerial policy debate as a key element in empowering civil society. In exploring the central role, evolutionary trajectories, complexities and paradoxes of accountability, the research has reached a somewhat common normative ground that organisational 'formal or hierarchical accountabilities' are necessary but insufficient conditions. Social forms of accountability, through which NGOs are made accountable to grassroots civil society members, and through which such civil society members' views and opinions are actively integrated into civil society development programmes (rather than just being Western superimpositions), are indeed understood as central to a meaningful developmental regime in LDCs.

The empowerment of civil society as a strategic pillar of development demands the ontological and epistemological supremacy of civil society in accountability terms: elements of civil society (such as poor women, communities, villagers and recipients of the services of the development state) are to be recognised as a dominating force towards which accounts must be directed, and their epistemic capacities enhanced to engage in such accountability processes and practices (see Gray *et al.*, 2006; Unerman and O'Dwyer, 2006; Lehman, 2007; O'Dwyer and Unerman, 2007, 2008; O'Sullivan and O'Dwyer, 2009). This is now emerging as 'social' or 'bottom-up' forms of accountability, which are increasingly being discussed in the NGO literature (see O'Dwyer, 2005; O'Dwyer and Unerman, 2007; O'Dwyer and Boomsma, 2015). Hence, development accounting should be understood in terms of changes taking place in accountability structures, practices and relations that connect global development capital with various civic spaces on the peripheries.

However, empirical observations regarding ways in which accountability structures grow in LDCs paint a less positive picture. While there have been some positive developments and genuine attempts to develop social forms of NGO accountability (see O'Dwyer, 2005; O'Dwyer and Unerman, 2008; O'Sullivan and O'Dwyer, 2009), the overarching structural tendency is for hierarchical functional forms of accountability dominated by large international donor agencies to colonise these social forms. Dixon *et al.*'s (2006, 2007) Zambian case studies provide a good example in this regard. Their empirical data reveal how the

Zambian microfinance industry is moving towards a crisis because the intended bottom-up, trust-based, social form of developmental accountability is being progressively supplanted by a functional form of accountability which increasingly creates social interactions based on a lack of trust and confidence, thereby weakening any moral obligation to go beyond merely superficial rule compliance.

Nevertheless, initially, and especially at the inception of microfinance as a set of grassroots financing strategies for the poor and NGOs as organisations *of* and *for* civil society, such accountability took a more social form, mostly in the form of 'social movements' emanating from the grassroots politics of democracy, anti-colonial independence, poverty alleviation and development. Most southern NGOs were evolutionary outcomes of such socio-political movements, which were initially anti-(post)colonial and driven towards identification of a 'domestic' and 'indigenous' mode of development, a mode of development that would integrate the aspirations and capabilities of grassroots communities. A classic example is the initial development of microfinance in Bangladesh as a social movement, which emanated from the grassroots as an indigenous solution to the inherent incapacity of the mainstream banking sector to cater for the needs of the poorest (see Sinclair and Korten, 2012).

Similarly, Alawattage *et al.*'s (2014) case study of Sri Lanka's largest and oldest NGO, Sarvodaya, provides a good example of how such social forms of accountability have been colonised by the recent development of functional forms aiming primarily to meet the accountability demands of international donors. In its early phases, during the mid-1950s, against the backdrop of the postcolonial politics of constructing an independent nation, Sarvodaya emerged, similarly to the Ghandian movement in India, as an indigenous social movement to mobilise the rural masses, based on (a) the traditional Buddhist concept of *shramadana* (free giving of collective labour), and (b) the traditional social structures and rituals associated with pre-colonial agricultural labour sharing. In this social form, accountability was based on the archaic village rituals of *pawul hamuwa* (the ritualistic gathering of families in the village temple to discuss their development needs and activities). The organisational and communicative apparatuses were indeed participatory and grassroots; and development initiatives indeed emanated from local people, enabling them to claim ownership of such programmes. The initial success of this initiative as an indigenous model of civil society development attracted the attention of global development financiers as an exemplary model of 'village-based development', resulting in a massive injection of foreign aid and assistance to this social movement and turning it into a massive 'organisation'.

However, partly due to the inherent incapacity of its initial organising paradigm of 'domestic order of worth' (see Boltanski and Thévenot, 2006) to cope with the ever-expanding geographical, financial and activity domains, and partly due to the economic and political dynamics of a nation and global development state in which neoliberal political ideologies became the dominating organising principles, this social movement was soon transformed into what Alawattage *et al.* call 'a conglomerate of NGOs', mainly providing microfinance-based development assistance to so-called 'poor enterprising clients'. This NGO model reveals a rather functional, corporate-type accountability structure, tracing the way in which foreign development capital is deployed. The villagers who, when it was a social movement, were active designers of the development of their own villages have now been transformed into 'recipients of international development assistance'.

In summary, what has been experienced during the recent past is an interesting but paradoxical development of accountability in relation to the rapid growth of microfinance, NGOs and other civil society development programmes. The normative intention of such development initiatives has often been identified as the construction of a more democratic, participative, social form of accountability structure to facilitate an inclusive and participatory mode of development. However, despite such noble aspirations, the empirical and historical trajectories appear rather contradictory and paradoxical, leading to the coexistence of social and functional forms, but with a clear tendency for the latter to colonise the former and supplant the trust-based community mode of participatory accountability with more top-down, rule-based accountability, particularly to meet the information needs of large international donors. Social and convivial forms of accountability structures, processes and practices seem to be surviving, but only insofar as they can contribute to the accumulative necessities of global capital. Despite the development aspirations attributed to microfinance and NGOs as civil society-based development strategies, and despite some clear positive contributions to the advancement of LDCs, they have been largely neoliberal modes of 'fracking the bottom of the pyramid' (cf. Prahalad, 2006).

Theorising epistemic connection: the appearance of new management accounting

In recent times, LDCs have imported new management accounting ideas as a result of colonial legacies, compounded by neo-colonial relations. Relatively recently, these uncritical transfers of management accounting knowledge have become the subject of inquiry for critical accounting scholars. As Figure 16.1 indicates, armed with critical epistemic tools, researchers began to question the applicability of Western management accounting tools under alien conditions. This is discussed below.

The notion of epistemic connection, in the context of our task, originates from the word 'episteme' coined by Foucault (Foucault and Sheridan, 1972), meaning a total set of relations that unites a set of discursive practices, giving rise to changes in existing epistemological figures, sciences and possibly formalised systems. The role of actors is to problematise what is now and mobilise what is better by availing themselves of the political power of their epistemic centres, such as universities, consultancy networks, professional associations, and government and extra-government agencies. This is reflected in recent management accounting initiatives. For instance, building on his Harvard connections, Robert Kaplan has become a leading epistemological figure as a result of his (and his colleagues') articulation of the new ideas of ABC and BSC. The epistemic connections have been identified and critiqued by critical accounting scholars. Jones and Dugdale (2002) have argued that ABC has become a 'bandwagon' representing a modernistic phase of cost management and related calculative practices. Hopper and Major (2007) have found that ABC projects have been handled by epistemic communities, making projects possible at organisational levels. Similarly, as Qu and Cooper (2011) have observed, BSC has been globally diffused and popularised due to the power of global networks. Hence, an episteme is not just an idea forming an epistemology but also a set of discursive practices that gives rise to the popularisation of certain ideas in a given context.

Thus, it is unsurprising that local firms in LDCs have succumbed to the powerful Western ideas of new management accounting technologies, despite the contexts in which they operate. On the one hand, a 'colonial mentality' gives rise to a struggle over whether traditional values and meanings should be substituted by new ideas. On the other hand, neo-/postcolonial tendencies that enable isomorphic power in the diffusion and popularisation of new ideas appear to be an imaginable position for local firms to hybridise existing practices or replace old practices with new ideas. These tensions have been studied and theorised in some LDC studies, although much work remains to be done.

Cost reforms in a Sri Lankan hospital are an example of epistemic connections, as evidenced in Wickramasinghe's (2015) work. Within a broader epistemic programme of neoliberalisation of LDC states, and in the name of evidenced-based management (a form of NPM project designed for LDC healthcare systems), a new cost accounting system was introduced to Sri Lanka. The epistemic community, including the World Bank, World Health Organization (WHO), Japan International Cooperative Agency (JAICA) and Asian Development Bank (ADB), used the 'absence of Western cost accounting' in a Sri Lankan hospital as an opportunity to introduce a new cost accounting system in a selected hospital as a pilot project. Wickramasinghe (2015) draws on works by Deleuze (Deleuze, 1995; Deleuze and Guattari, 1987) and Bauman (2001) to theorise how old cost confinements are being broken down, and to illustrate ways in which management accounting is now 'getting off the ground' to infuse policy guidance into the decision-making arena in the provincial healthcare system in Sri Lanka.

Similarly, Wickramasinghe *et al.* (2007) studied a Sri Lankan case of implementing and using BSC in a local firm manufacturing electrical appliances, which they called Alpha. They found that this use of BSC was linked to an epistemic connection materialised through the son of the owner, who picked up the idea from his higher education in the USA. This was coupled with a local diffusion programme led by CIMA. However, the Alpha case points to a failure, in that the practice lasted only a few years because the engineers who took ownership and leadership of the implementation of BSC were criticised for their inadvertent ignorance of accountants, who often wanted to 'do something' about budgeting in place of BSC. Consequently, the owner realised that this 'professional rivalry' had to end, and 'financial' eventualities became more significant than the non-financial perspectives introduced by BSC. As a result, after 3 years of operating BSC in an ERP environment, the owner-managers decided to abandon the practice.

This has some theoretical implications, as Wickramasinghe *et al.* (2007) have articulated. First, it is a manifestation of the power of epistemic connection between the global and the local. On the one hand, the idea of BSC was linked with global players, who often seek to diffuse, popularise and institutionalise an idea. On the other hand, local professional bodies and their allies 'wanted something from the West' to maintain their 'colonial' psyches in the context of postcolonial experiments. These two simultaneous forces made BSC ideas inspiring and inevitable. Such rhetoric introduced a new organisational language for the managers to use and enforce on others at grassroots levels. However, in consequence, this rhetoric encountered a set of organisational complexities manifested as 'professional rivalry' between engineers and accountants. This was not a sudden, sporadic and atypical instance. Two competing logics born out of Sri Lankan socio-cultural circumstances gave rise to this so-called failure.

ERP has also made important progress around the world, inspiring managers to reconfigure their organisations. This resulted from the agenda of ERP proponents in the West (Nolan, 1979), who insisted that ERP could enhance organisational integration and performance so that accounting became just a cog in the overall ERP-led organisational configuration (see Dechow and Mouritsen, 2005; Dechow *et al.*, 2006). However, critical accounting researchers have conducted a number of studies in Western research sites to explore how ERP actually works in such contexts (Quattrone and Hopper, 2001; Scapens and Jazayeri, 2003; Dechow and Mouritsen, 2005; Dechow *et al.*, 2006), which has stimulated LDC researchers to explore how LDC contexts produce different practices with unintended consequences. To illustrate this phenomenon, we have picked two important pieces of work by Jack and Kholeif (2008), who have embarked on a theoretical agenda drawing on Stones' (2005) strong structuration theory (SST), and by How and Alawattage (2012), who have triangulated actor-network theory with a cultural economic analysis.

Jack and Kholeif (2008) studied an Egyptian case to examine how management accountants were implicated in an ERP system. The ERP project was funded by the European Union (EU) to establish and practise ERP-led accounting and other management processes in the Industrial Modernization Centre (IMC) in Egypt. Although this initiative initially faced some resistance from the established bureaucracy, through the EU's involvement and the use of an influential vendor organisation traditionalism was somehow replaced by the new ERP system. In order to discuss this transformational attempt and its social and organisational consequences, Jack and Kholeif drew on Stones' (2005) SST. SST encourages researchers to explore particular agents and structures, where individual agents are situated in a web of position-practice relations. Jack and Kholeif claim that, despite the power of a fashionable system like ERP, it was difficult to establish sustainable structures because of the inevitability of conflicting dispositions and conjecturally specific understandings of the roles of different groups, especially management accountants. In short, management accountants were not prepared to accommodate the new organisational ethos and resulting accounting practices as their prevailing structures were not amenable to such a move. This does not mean that this difficulty is an issue only within LDCs, as studies in the West have also emphasised this aspect (Granlund and Malmi, 2002; Scapens and Jazayeri, 2003); however, what is salient in this case is that, because of this structural constraint, not only was poverty reduction an arduous task, but the constraint itself was also an attribute of underdevelopment. Without a radical change in such constraining structures, development remains unattainable.

How and Alawattage's (2012) work corroborates the above argument with evidence from a Malaysian case. They studied a Malaysian firm in which the managers were inspired by a customised ERP/SAP project, which ostensibly redefined their form of accounting. They focused on the question of the paradox between political imperfections and the legitimation of accounting changes through a SAP/ERP platform. They found that management accounting was decoupled from the daily operations of the firm, but the new system was well represented at head office ceremonies involving reporting and associated manifestations of SAP/ERP legitimation and signification. Interestingly, the outcomes were not characterised as a set of failures because the issues were camouflaged by so-called legitimation of the use of the SAP/ERP mantra.

How and Alawattage used actor-network theory eclectically by triangulating the ideas of neo-institutionalism and political economy. A process of sociological translation problematised the old use of accounting without SAP/ERP, promoted interest in the use of the new SAP/ERP-based accounting, and achieved some mobilisation and enactment in the use of the new system. At the same time, this process of translation was driven by an environment of isomorphism that legitimised the institutionalisation of the boundary object of SAP/ERP in the alien context of Malaysia. However, the prevalence of inevitable political and economic 'imperfections' in the Malaysian context created a political economy that decoupled the system from operations while being legitimised by the state.

Both ERP cases point to the significance of epistemic connection through which new management accounting ideas are propagated, imposed and legitimised. The needs of LDCs, now defined in terms of development, poverty reduction, change, empowerment and the like, were all tackled through this epistemic connection. However, external hopes are invariably subject to mundane realities manifested in both structural conditions and agential resistance. Accounting changes and their embedded development aims should be researched with such theoretical insights in mind.

Conclusion

Our aim has not been to undertake a state-of-the-art review of accounting research in LDCs. Rather, this chapter has focused on the theorisation project of LDC management accounting scholars, drawing mainly (but not wholly) on the authors' personal endeavours at theorisation. We have attempted here to articulate when we started our journey, what has been done so far and where we are going. Table 16.1 provides a summary of the theorisation trajectory over the last three decades. In particular, the table shows what has been explored and how the management accounting issues have been theorised.

First, the management accounting agenda emerged through identifying LDC accounting as a distinct realm of research, but this recognition was limited to identifying the destination of Western management accounting technologies. Inspired by neoclassical economic analyses, contingency theorisation and an extension of Hofstedian cultural analysis, as illustrated in Table 16.1, the researchers underappreciated the influence of the local context and focused mainly on the issues of making Western management accounting amenable to local practitioners and policy makers. As a result, relationships between accounting and the wider context in which it operates remained unproblematic and, in turn, unexamined. The theorisation project did not expand from simple modelling based on neoclassical economics, contingency theory and its extensions into the 'cultural factor'.

Second, as the agenda of critical/interpretive research developed in the late 1980s and early 1990s, Hopper *et al.* (2009) revealed that the LDC context was no longer a given phenomenon. Rather, the underlying ramifications and accompanying issues became the centre of attention for researchers who migrated to Western research centres, especially in the UK.

Table 16.1 Theoretical trajectories of management accounting practices

Theorisation of management accounting	*Theoretical frameworks drawn on*	*Key findings/conclusions*
Prescriptive management accounting	Neoclassical economics, contingency theory and Hofstedian analyses of culture	Accounting in LDCs unproblematic – it is just a matter of 'technology transfer' and its adaptation to a different cultural context
Theorising the political connection	Development sociology; political economy	Coexistence of feudal and capitalist modes of production has changed the meaning and practices of accounting, creating issues in the execution of neoliberal reform programmes
Theorising epistemic connection	Eclectic use of post-structural/postmodern analysis of organisational sociology coupled with structuration theory, ANT and neo-institutionalism	While the accounting change agenda is inspired by the global function of idea developments, local ramifications come to reconstitute these changes, their meaning, and sustainability
Theorising civic connection	Post-Foucauldian and post-structural theory of development/underdevelopment	There has been a reconstruction of rural social spaces (e.g. villages) as 'developmental spaces' to be organised and managed through various technologies of governance and accountability, including accounting

These researchers began to read beyond accounting to unveil the underlying social, cultural and political issues that constitute the nature of accounting in action in LDC organisations. As seen in Table 16.1, this gave rise to the 'political connection' that shapes the nature of LDC accounting practices, especially the issue of the articulation of a non-capitalist mode of production in relation to the dominant capitalist mode. Such attempts resulted in the use of cultural-political economy as a leading theoretical framework.

Third, the theorisation project of LDC researchers entered into the new realm partly because the research space began to change as a result of significant changes in the political-economic trajectory of LDCs. The logic of development began to include a social or civic logic of development in its vocabularies. The new development discourse called on management accounting technologies to organise and manage the 'development space' (see Alawattage *et al.*, 2014). As summarised earlier, this evolutionary trajectory of the political economy of LDCs required the establishment of 'micro-accountabilities' (Alawattage *et al.*, 2015) as a central tool of social governance under neoliberalism and a strong mode of integrating LDC societies into the global neoliberal economy.

Inspired by post-Foucauldian readings, the researchers began to examine how neoliberalism is shaping and reshaping the lives of the poor in LDC societies, and how such efforts are producing new markets in which accounting has a vital role to play beyond the organisational ontology. In particular, they see how traditional convivial relations are being used to create markets and a space to change unprecedented regimes of calculative practices. In doing so, they observe how globalisation of the neoliberal ethos has been coupled with accounting technologies and has been reproduced in very local contexts.

Fourth, the transfer of Western management accounting knowledge has received new momentum with the force of globalisation, structural adjustment programmes and the free roaming of consultancy firms in LDCs (Ashraf and Uddin, 2013). Thus, the researchers have begun to deploy various social theories with an understanding of epistemic connections and management accounting knowledge transfer projects. The resulting eclectic approaches, coupled with structuration theory, actor-network theory and variants of institutional theory, have generated further research revealing how epistemic connections materialise at local sites in LDCs. The researchers have found that, despite ambitions to adopt new management accounting ideas in LDC organisational settings, the perennial issue of the prevalence of colonial/neo-colonial hybridity has hampered implementation, produced unintended consequences, and has sometimes led managers to abandon their ideas altogether (Ashraf and Uddin, 2016). Such findings have made theoretical contributions, in that the structuration of accounting into better practices is far from satisfactory due to agential issues resulting from LDC idiosyncrasies.

Finally, we do not claim to have comprehensively covered all theorisation attempts to enhance understanding of management accounting practices in LDCs. This chapter merely highlights the area to which the researchers have so far contributed theoretically, especially within critical accounting traditions. We also do not claim or suggest theoretical closure. Instead, we call for further theorisation of each of the areas highlighted in Table 16.1. In extending, expanding and continuing LDC management accounting research, future researchers should examine how they might contribute to this agenda.

Notes

1 It should be noted that, paradoxically and ironically, much accounting research *on* LDCs is carried out not *for* LDCs audiences 'out there' but for a set of institutionalised audiences 'in here' in the West. Hence, LDC research has tended to manifest 'postcolonial practice' in the West. However, as has been the case regarding most epistemic developments in postcolonial spaces out there in the

peripheries, such 'activities' in the West do have an epistemic influence within LDCs, the West being an epistemic reference point for academics in LDCs.

2 It is easy to see how the neo-Marxist and new-institutionalist tendencies of the critical management accounting project in the late 1980s and the 1990s in the UK, especially Berry *et al.*'s (1985) National Coal Board case study, have provided the epistemic underpinning for this beginning.

References

Alawattage, C., and D. Wickramasinghe. 2008. Appearance of accounting in a political hegemony. *Critical Perspectives on Accounting* 19 (3):293–339.

Alawattage, C., C. Graham, and D. Wickramasinghe. 2015. Microaccountability and biopolitics: Microfinance in a Sri Lankan village. In *Interdisciplinary Perspectives on Accounting Conference*. Stockholm, Sweden, 1–48.

Alawattage, C., D. Wickramasinghe, and A. Tennakoon. 2014. Performing civil society. In *Performance Management in Nonprofit Organizations: Global Perspectives*, edited by Z. Hoque and L. Parker. London: Routledge, 394–418.

Ansari, S. L., and J. Bell. 1991. Symbolism, collectivism and rationality in organisational control. *Accounting, Auditing & Accountability Journal* 4 (2).

Ansari, S., and K. J. Euske. 1987. Rational, rationalizing, and reifying uses of accounting data in organizations. *Accounting, Organizations and Society* 12 (6):549–570.

Ashraf, J. and S. N. Uddin. 2013. A consulting giant; a disgruntled client: A 'Failed' attempt to change management controls in a public sector organization. *Financial Accountability and Management* 29: 186–205.

Ashraf, J. and S. N. Uddin. 2016. Regressive consequences of management accounting and control reforms: A case from a less developed country. *Critical Perspectives on Accounting*. Forthcoming.

Bauman, Z. 2001. *The Individualized Society*. London: Wiley.

Baydoun, N., and R. Willett. 1995. Cultural relevance of western accounting systems to developing countries. *Abacus* 31 (1):67–92.

Berry, A. J., T. Capps, D. Cooper, P. Ferguson, T. Hopper, and E. A. Lowe. 1985. Management control in an area of the NCB: Rationales of accounting practices in a public enterprise. *Accounting, Organizations and Society* 10 (1):3–28.

Boltanski, L., and L. Thévenot. 2006. *On Justification: Economies of Worth*. Princeton, NJ: Princeton University Press.

Burawoy, M. 1979. *Manufacturing Consent: Changes in the Labor Process Under Monopoly Capitalism*. Chicago: University of Chicago Press.

———. 1985. *The Politics of Production: Factory Regimes Under Capitalism and Socialism*: London: Verso.

Chow, C. W., Y. Kato, and M. D. Shields. 1994. National culture and the preference for management controls: An exploratory study of the firm—Labor market interface. *Accounting, Organizations and Society* 19 (4–5):381–400.

Covaleski, M. A., and M. W. Dirsmith. 1988. The use of budgetary symbols in the political arena: An historically informed field study. *Accounting, Organizations and Society* 13 (1):1–24.

Covaleski, M. A., M. W. Dirsmith, and J. E. Michelman. 1993. An institutional theory perspective on the DRG framework, case-mix accounting systems and health-care organizations. *Accounting, Organizations and Society* 18 (1):65–80.

Dasgupta, P., and I. Serageldin. 2001. *Social Capital: A Multifaceted Perspective*: Washington, D.C.: World Bank.

Dechow, N., and J. Mouritsen. 2005. Enterprise resource planning systems, management control and the quest for integration. *Accounting, Organizations and Society* 30 (7–8):691–733.

Dechow, N., M. Granlund, and J. Mouritsen. 2006. Management control of the complex organization: Relationships between management accounting and information technology. In *Handbooks of Management Accounting Research*, edited by A. G. H. Christopher, S. Chapman and D. S. Michael: Elsevier, 625–640.

Deleuze, G. 1995. *Negotiations, 1972–1990*. New York and Chichester, UK: Columbia University Press.

Deleuze, G., and F. L. Guattari. 1987. *A Thousand Plateaus: Capitalism and Schizophrenia*. Minneapolis: University of Minnesota Press.

Dixon, R., J. Ritchie, and J. Siwale. 2006. Microfinance: Accountability from the grassroots. *Accounting, Auditing & Accountability Journal* 19 (3):405–427.

———. 2007. Loan officers and loan 'delinquency' in Microfinance: A Zambian case. *Accounting Forum* 31 (1):47–71.

Enthoven, A. J. H. 1973. *Accountancy and Economic Development Policy.* Amsterdam; London: North-Holland Publishing Co.

———. 1977. *Accounting Systems in Third World Economies.* Amsterdam; Oxford: North-Holland Publishing Co.

Foucault, M. 2010. *The Birth of Biopolitics: Lectures at the Collège de France, 1978—1979.* New York: Picador.

Foucault, M., and A. Sheridan. 1972. *The Archaeology of Knowledge.* London: Tavistock Publications.

Gambling, T. 1976a. Human resource accounting: Past, present and future: Edwin H. Caplan and Stephen Landekich (New York: National Association of Accountants, 1975). *Accounting, Organizations and Society* 1 (2–3):281–279.

———. 1976b. Systems dynamics and human resource accounting. *Accounting, Organizations and Society* 1 (2–3):167–174.

Gramsci, A., Q. Hoare, and G. Nowell-Smith. 1971. *Selections from the Prison Notebooks of Antonio Gramsci.* London: Lawrence and Wishart.

Granlund, M., and T. Malmi. 2002. Moderate impact of ERPS on management accounting: a lag or permanent outcome? *Management Accounting Research* 13 (3):299–321.

Gray, R., J. Bebbington, and D. Collison. 2006. NGOs, civil society and accountability: making the people accountable to capital. *Accounting, Auditing & Accountability Journal* 19 (3):319–348.

Hardt, M., and A. Negri. 2000. *Empire.* Cambridge, MA.; London: Harvard University Press.

Harrison, G. L. 1992. The cross-cultural generalizability of the relation between participation, budget emphasis and job related attitudes. *Accounting, Organizations and Society* 17 (1):1–15.

Hofstede, G. 1980a. Angola coffee — or the confrontation of an organization with changing values in its environment. *Organization Studies* 1 (1):21–40.

Hofstede, G. 1980b. *Culture's Consequences: International Differences in Work-Related Values.* Beverly Hills: Sage Publications.

———. 1981. Management control of public and not-for-profit activities. *Accounting, Organizations and Society* 6 (3):193–211.

———. 1990. A reply and comment on Joginder P. Singh: 'Managerial culture and work-related values in India'. *Organization Studies* 11 (1):103–106.

———. 1991. *Cultures and Organizations: Software of the Mind.* London: McGraw-Hill.

Hopper, T., and P. Armstrong. 1991. Cost accounting, controlling labour and the rise of conglomerates. *Accounting, Organizations and Society* 16 (5–6):405–438.

Hopper, T., and B. Bui. 2015. Has Management Accounting Research been critical? *Management Accounting Research* In Press, Corrected Proof: 1–21.

Hopper, T., and M. Major. 2007. Extending institutional analysis through theoretical triangulation: Regulation and activity-based costing in Portuguese telecommunications. *European Accounting Review* 16 (1):59–97.

Hopper, T., D. J. Cooper, T. Lowe, T. Capps, and J. Mouritsen. 1986. Management control and worker resistance in the National Coal Board: Financial controls in the labour process. In *Managing the labour process*, edited by D. Knights and H. Willmott. Aldershot: Gower, 109–141.

Hopper, T., M. Tsamenyi, S. Uddin, and D. Wickramasinghe. 2009. Management accounting in less developed countries: What is known and needs knowing. *Accounting, Auditing & Accountability Journal* 22 (3):469–514.

Hopwood, A. G. 1974. *Accounting and Human Behaviour.* 1st American ed. Englewood Cliffs, N.J.: Prentice-Hall, 1976.

Hopwood, A. G. E. 1976. *Human Resource Accounting.* [S.l.]: Pergamon.

Hoque, Z., and T. Hopper. 1994. Rationality, accounting and politics: A case study of management control in a Bangladeshi jute mill. *Management Accounting Research* 5 (1):5–30.

———. 1997. Political and industrial relations turbulence, competition and budgeting in the nationalised jute mills of Bangladesh. *Accounting and Business Research* 27 (2):125–143.

Hoskin, K. W., and R. H. Macve. 1986. Accounting and the examination: A genealogy of disciplinary power. *Accounting, Organizations and Society* 11 (2):105–136.

———. 1988. The genesis of accountability: The west point connections. *Accounting, Organizations and Society* 13 (1):37–73.

How, S.-M., and C. Alawattage. 2012. Accounting decoupled: A case study of accounting regime change in a Malaysian company. *Critical Perspectives on Accounting* 23 (6):403–419.

Jack, L., and A. Kholeif. 2008. Enterprise resource planning and a contest to limit the role of management accountants: A strong structuration perspective. *Accounting Forum* 32 (1):30–45.

Johnson, H. T., and R. S. Kaplan. 1987. *Relevance Lost: The Rise and Fall of Management Accounting.* Boston, MA.: Harvard Business School Press.

Jones, T. C., and D. Dugdale. 2002. The ABC bandwagon and the juggernaut of modernity. *Accounting, Organizations and Society* 27 (1–2):121–163.

Jones, C. S., and S. Sefiane. 1992. The use of accounting data in operational decision making in Algeria. *Accounting, Auditing & Accountability Journal* 5 (4).

Lehman, G. 2007. The accountability of NGOs in civil society and its public spheres. *Critical Perspectives on Accounting* 18 (6):645–669.

Marques, E. 1976. Human resource accounting: Some questions and reflections. *Accounting, Organizations and Society* 1 (2–3):175–178.

Munro, I. 2012. The management of circulations: Biopolitical variations after Foucault. *International Journal of Management Reviews* 14 (3):345–362.

Nolan, R. 1979. Managing the crises in data processing. *Harvard Business Review* 57 (2):115–126.

O'Dwyer, B. 2005. The construction of a social account: A case study in an overseas aid agency. *Accounting, Organizations and Society* 30 (3):279–296.

O'Dwyer, B., and R. Boomsma. 2015. The co-construction of NGO accountability. *Accounting, Auditing & Accountability Journal* 28 (1):36–68.

O'Dwyer, B., and J. Unerman. 2007. From functional to social accountability. *Accounting, Auditing & Accountability Journal* 20 (3):446.

———. 2008. The paradox of greater NGO accountability: A case study of Amnesty Ireland. *Accounting, Organizations and Society* 33 (7–8):801–824.

Olve, N.-G., A. Westelius, and A.-S. Westelius. 1988. Managers' attitudes—a comparison between Sweden and China. *Scandinavian Journal of Management* 4 (1–2):63–75.

O'Sullivan, N., and B. O'Dwyer. 2009. Stakeholder perspectives on a financial sector legitimation process: The case of NGOs and the Equator Principles. *Accounting, Auditing & Accountability Journal* 22 (4):553–587.

Ouibrahim, N., and R. Scapens. 1989. Accounting and financial control in a socialist enterprise: A case study from Algeria. *Accounting, Auditing & Accountability Journal* 2 (2).

Prahalad, C. K. 2006. *The Fortune at the Bottom of the Pyramid.* Upper Saddle River, N.J.: Wharton School Pub.

Pratt, J., and P. Beaulieu. 1992. Organizational culture in public accounting: Size, technology, rank, and functional area. *Accounting, Organizations and Society* 17 (7):667–684.

Putnam, R. D., R. Leonardi, and R. Y. Nanetti. 1994. *Making Democracy Work: Civic Traditions in Modern Italy.* Princeton: Princeton University Press.

Qu, S. Q., and D. J. Cooper. 2011. The role of inscriptions in producing a balanced scorecard. *Accounting, Organizations and Society* 36 (6):344–362.

Quattrone, P., and T. Hopper. 2001. What does organizational change mean? Speculations on a taken for granted category. *Management Accounting Research* 12 (4):403–435.

Scapens, R. W., and M. Jazayeri. 2003. ERP systems and management accounting change: Opportunities or impacts? A research note. *European Accounting Review* 12 (1):201–233.

Sinclair, H., and D. C. Korten. 2012. *Confessions of a Microfinance Heretic: How Microlending Lost Its Way and Betrayed the Poor.* Berrett-Koehler Publishers.

Singh, J. P. 1990. Managerial culture and work-related values in India. *Organization Studies* 11 (1):075–101.

Sondergaard, M. 1994. Research note: Hofstede's consequences: A study of reviews, citations and replications. *Organization Studies* 15 (3):447–456.

Stones, R. 2005. *Structuration Theory.* London: Palgrave Macmillan.

Tomassini, L. A. 1976. Behavioral research on human resource accounting: A contingency framework. *Accounting, Organizations and Society* 1 (2–3):239–250.

Uddin, S., and T. Hopper. 2001. A Bangladesh soap opera: Privatisation, accounting, and regimes of control in a less developed country. *Accounting, Organizations and Society* 26 (7–8):643–672.

Unerman, J., and B. O'Dwyer. 2006. Theorising accountability for NGO advocacy. *Accounting, Auditing & Accountability Journal* 19 (3):349–376.

Wickramasinghe, D. 2015. Getting management accounting off the ground: post-colonial neoliberalism in healthcare budgets. *Accounting and Business Research* 45 (3):323–355.

Wickramasinghe, D., T. Gooneratne, and J. A. S. K. Jayakody. 2007. Interest lost: The rise and fall of a balanced scorecard project in Sri Lanka. In *Envisioning a New Accountability* 13:237–271.

Wickramasinghe, D., T. Hopper, and C. Rathnasiri. 2004. Japanese cost management meets Sri Lankan politics: Disappearance and reappearance of bureaucratic management controls in a privatised utility. *Accounting, Auditing & Accountability Journal* 17 (1):85–120.

17

Performance measurement and supply chain management

Tony Mancini, Maria Argyropoulou and Rachel Argyropoulou

Measuring the performance of any business process has attracted the interest of academics and practitioners in their attempt to evaluate 'how a business works' (Argyris, 1977) and to find ways of improving decision making. There have been many definitions of what performance means, and many performance measurement (PM) frameworks have been recommended reflecting the various perspectives in the academic community as well as changing needs in the business world. Perhaps the most common definition was given by Neely *et al.* (1995), who defined PM as the 'process of quantifying effectiveness and efficiency of action' offering researchers and practitioners a way to approach the complex reality of performance into 'a sequence of limited symbols than can be conveyed, in a meaningful manner under similar circumstances' (Lebas, 1995), enabling interested parties to monitor performance and diagnose problems (Waggoner *et al.*, 1999). The most frequently used measures are financial and evaluate the financial performance by reporting costs, income and profits or the economic state of an organisation.

The dependence on the sole use of financial measures received much criticism in the literature mainly because they rely on historic data and cannot provide insight for future performance as in the case of Enron (Richard *et al.*, 2009). Managers responded by seeking different approaches for the measurement of the business processes and turned to non-financial performance indicators (PI) to quantify and control performance related to various stakeholders such as customers, employees and the society (Argyropoulou, 2013). New measures of qualitative and quantitative nature, as well as frameworks, were introduced, tested and implemented by firms in their attempt to capture the most important variables that should be used to manage the multiple dimensions of business performance. The literature provides us with different PM frameworks which, according to De Toni and Tonchia (2001, pp. 50–51), can be split into five typologies: (1) *internal that measure a firm's processes or external* that aim at capturing the 'performance perceived by external stakeholders such as customers, shareholders and suppliers'; (2) *value chain* measures that are focusing on the measurement of the value added in various organisational processes; (3) *hierarchical or vertical* measures that use cost and non-cost performance on different levels of aggregation, until they ultimately become financial; (4) '*frustrum*' models that measure the performance at the operational/low level without the scope of translating them into financial measures; and (5) *balanced* models that consider performance measures from various perspectives.

Argyropoulou (2013) provided a short description of the PM frameworks that fall under the above typologies. The Strategic Measurement and Reporting Technique (SMART) model introduced by Lynch and Cross (1991), known also as the Performance Pyramid framework, classifies performance in four different hierarchical levels that are interlinked, however, to promote aligned goals and translate the strategic financial objectives into operational PIs (Kald and Nilson, 2000). The results and determinants matrix by Fitzgerald *et al.* (1991) provides two main categories of measures: those related to financial results and those that determine the results and are not financial such as quality, flexibility, resource utilisation and innovation. The Business Excellence model introduced by the European Foundation of Quality Management (1993) was based on the same approach: enablers and results. The enablers would be: people, policies and resources and the results would be people again, society and customers. Despite, however, its popularity for all Total Quality Management practices, researchers found it difficult to operationalise the concepts and establish the variables for further academic research (Neely *et al.*, 2000). Brown (1996) argued that companies should control all different stages of business processes and proposed the macro process framework that distinguishes between the inputs, the processes, the outputs and the outcomes.

Realising the need for the use of financial and non-financial metrics for a more balanced method of PM, Kaplan and Norton introduced the balanced scorecard (BSC) in 1992 to address 'a serious deficiency in traditional management systems: their inability to link a company's long-term strategy with short-term action' (Kaplan and Norton, 1996). The BSC received criticism in the literature for its simplicity and inability to include all stakeholders (such as suppliers) (see Hoque and James, 2000). Moreover, for some authors (e.g. Jensen, 2001), it is rather difficult for all measures to improve simultaneously that limits its robustness and comprehensiveness. Nonetheless, since its introduction, the BSC has been widely used by companies wishing to translate strategy into a set of metrics which promoted the framework as a strategic management tool.

Supply chain performance measures

The use of PM by supply chain managers is an integral part of the strategic decision-making process, but the identification of metrics is not easy due to the various stakeholders across the supply chain channel, which entails politics as well as information asymmetry (Gunasekaran and Kobu, 2007). For the purposes of this study, metrics evaluate the success of supply chain strategies 'without which a clear direction for improvement and realization of goals would be highly difficult' (Gunasekaran *et al.*, 2001, p. 72). The field of PM in supply chain management is not new. The Supply Chain Operations Reference (SCOR) model developed by the Supply Chain Council (SCC) in 1996 has been widely used by practitioners from various industries as it integrates process measurement and benchmarking strategies into a holistic framework that aligns business goals across the supply chain (Li *et al.*, 2011). The model links the key supply chain processes (plan, source, make, deliver, return and enable) that capture the scope of any supply chain and provide managers with a set of metrics for the monitoring, control and improvement of complex processes.

During a 3-day executive seminar co-sponsored by the Council of Logistics Management in 1996, the Council of Logistics Management introduced the Global Supply Chain Framework (GSCF), which included eight processes for the management of customer relationship, customer service, demand, order fulfilment, manufacturing flow, supplier relationship, product development and returns. Both frameworks were used in the industry, each one revealing strengths and weaknesses that were reported in the pertinent literature. The GSCF is based mainly on cross-functional involvement as it encompasses all aspects of the business, placing an emphasis on marketing as well as research and development that entails top management involvement. This strategic scope limited the use of GSCF to companies with a strong market orientation. Smaller companies or companies with difficulty in improving various business processes at the same time turned to the SCOR framework that focused mainly on core supply chain areas such as purchasing, logistics, and manufacturing (Lambert *et al.*, 2005). According to the authors, these are the two important supply chain frameworks that represented different ways of measuring performance and that managers have the discretion of using the one that suits best their channels' unique needs. In the past three decades, following the introduction of the SCOR and GSCG, there have been many studies that focused on the type of measures used in the industry and their effectiveness. Companies started using different approaches to measure their supply chain performance due to the diversity of each chain's members and pursuit of different goals. Severe competition and rapid change have made some observers maintain that competition is evolving from an emphasis on firm battles between supply chains (Connelly *et al.*, 2013).

Globalisation and expansion of outsourcing have resulted in transforming the supply chain structure to a network form, stressing international competition (Barrientos *et al.*, 2016). The increased challenges of globalisation coupled with sustainability and green concerns advocated new metrics that would take into account environmental regulations as well as the socio-environmental benefits of circular supply chains (Hsu *et al.*, 2013). The implementation of advanced Information Systems such as CPFR software (Collaboration, Planning, Forecasting Replenishment) and the effectiveness of the information produced (Argyropoulou *et al.*, 2015) added complexity to the PM problem in modern supply chains.

The design, implementation and use of specific performance measures are not a one-off decision, and a 'right supply chain strategy' cannot be generalised as argued by Gopal and Thakkar (2012). Following a thorough review on the pertinent literature from 2000 to 2011, the authors concluded that performance achievement in modern supply chains cannot be captured in one framework as there is a never-ending effort to maintain a contemporary PM system (p. 535). This seems to be in alignment with the review findings from Akyuz and Erkan (2010) that encourage future research in PM in the new supply chain using the SCOR and BSC models as well as new frameworks that include 'development of

Figure 17.1 Distribution of reviewed papers by publishing year

partnership, collaboration, agility, flexibility, information productivity and business excellence metrics' (p. 5153). In view of the above analysis, the remainder of this chapter presents the findings from a literature review conducted on the most recent papers published in the last 7 years (Figure 17.1)

Reviewing the recent literature on supply chain performance

The pertinent literature on supply chain performance was extracted from Scopus®. This database is considered the widest and most updated for social studies. The search engine allows for multiple options such as author, affiliation, topic and year of publication that help users focus on their research questions using a number of criteria that suit their study best. For the purposes of this chapter, the search criteria included key words such as supply chain AND performance frameworks, supply chain AND performance measures in the title and abstract. To retrieve the most recent research papers, the search criteria allowed for publications of the last 6 years meaning 2010 to 2016.

These search criteria produced an outcome of 357 papers. When, however, these were further limited to peer-reviewed journal papers (book chapters and conference papers were not included), the number was reduced to 34. All 34 papers were carefully examined, and seven articles were eliminated as their purpose and findings would not contribute to this particular study. To justify the scope of this research, the review of the selected papers was based on the following criteria:

- use of existing models such as the BSC and SCOR,
- use of other than BSC and SCOR frameworks,
- related literature review papers,
- general issues and trends in the field of supply chain performance.

Table 17.1 shows the distribution of the articles with regard to the publishing journals. The distribution of papers with regard to their topic is illustrated in Figure 17.2.

Table 17.1 Distribution of articles with regard to journals

Journal name	*No. of articles*
International Journal of Production Research	7
International Journal of Productivity and Performance Management	5
Production Planning & Control	2
International Journal of Production Economics	4
Applied Mathematical Modelling	1
Baltic Journal of Management	1
Computers & Industrial Engineering	1
European Journal of Operational Research	1
Expert Systems with Applications	1
Facilities	1
Industrial Management & Data Systems	1
Journal of Intelligent Manufacturing	1
Optimization	1
Total	27

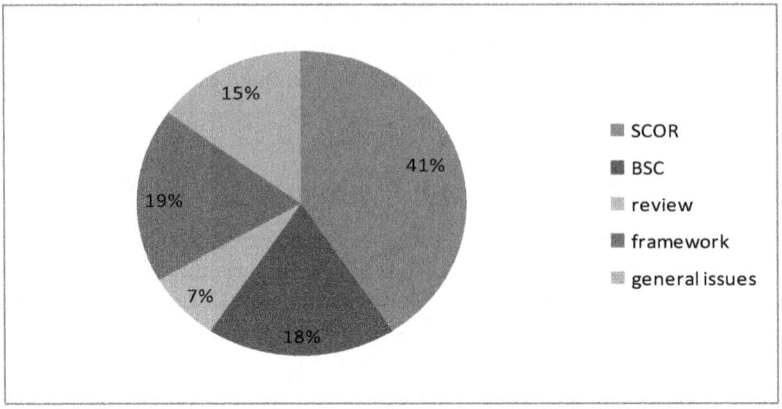

Figure 17.2 Distribution of articles with respect to their topic

SCOR and BSC in the recent supply chain performance literature

Akyuz and Erkan (2010, p. 5153) highlighted the importance of both frameworks in modern supply chains explaining the importance of balance between short- and long-term objectives and the involvement of various stakeholders as in the case of multinationals. Both frameworks are discussed in the remaining of this section.

Being a hierarchical model with three process levels, SCOR has always motivated academics to decompose problems into simpler sets of criteria (see Huan *et al.*, 2004; Xu *et al.*, 2008). The majority of the research papers are still using mathematical techniques such as the Analytical Hierarchy Process (AHP) to form an objective function to optimise supply chain processes (Li *et al.*, 2011). This was further supported by a recent review (Subramanian and Ramanathan, 2012) in which the authors found that the AHP method has been widely used to address problems related to managing the supply chain.

Kocaoğlu *et al.* (2013) used the values of metrics from previously developed scenarios and combined AHP with TOPSIS to present how the SCOR Model Level 1 metrics can provide a flexible use of ranked criteria for the measurement of supply chain performance. Advocating the use of AHP method, Elgazzar *et al.* (2012) linked supply chain processes to the overall financial performance of a firm. The AHP method has been, however, criticised by other academics who expressed concerns as to the application of one single model for (a) the needs of supply chain partners operating at different levels of maturity (Estampe *et al.*, 2013) and (b) the representation of unique contextual-geographic realities in global supply chains (Cai *et al.*, 2009). To address the limitations inherent in studies using the AHP, Sellitto *et al.* (2015) developed a multivariate structure model organised in a 4 × 4 matrix, containing the SCOR processes (source, make, deliver, return, but not plan), and performance attributes such as reliability, responsiveness, agility, cost and assets. The innovative model was tested successfully in a set of companies that compose part of a footwear supply chain in Brazil which, according to the authors, was characterised by 'high and low levels of maturity and information availability' (Sellitto *et al.*, 2015, p. 4919).

The AHP method and the reliance on the perception of a group of managers in a single case constitute, however, a major limitation for other academics who chose other theories and mathematical approaches to identify the appropriate supply performance measures. The Level 1 and Level 2 SCOR metrics were used by Ganga and Carpinetti (2011), who applied the fuzzy logic to predict causal relationships in the supply chain performance, whereas Bai and Sarkis (2012) applied the Rough-set theory (Pawlak, 1982) to shorten the list of the SCOR criteria determining a core set of external supply chain performance measures to internal performance expectations and outcomes.

Our review of the recent literature (2010–2016) revealed limited empirical research that explores how the SCOR metrics are affecting overall supply chain performance. The most important field study research focused on a survey of 232 Chinese companies with ISO 9000 certifications. Li *et al.* (2011) argued that each decision area (plan, source, make, deliver, return) has a positive impact on both 'customer-facing supply chain quality performance and internal-facing firm level business performance' (p. 33). Wang *et al.* (2010) used the case study approach to discuss the limitations of SCOR when implementing BPR. The study revealed the inability of the model to measure performance in multi-echelon supply chains. The authors proposed a mapping technique based on Causes/Effects, the SCOR Standard, and Mutual Solution (CESM) that can be useful in multinational supply chain projects. Persson (2011) tested new developments in the SCOR template in a Swedish multinational (Alfa Laval). His simulation experiment focused on different supply chain structures, and although the usefulness of SCOR was confirmed, it was found difficult to adopt it in all instances (p. 294). The simulation modelling based on SCOR was also discussed in a subsequent research by Long (2014) who provided agent building blocks to integrate the highly standardised SCOR processes and argued in favour of the possibility for configuring complex supply chain networks and for examining different what-if scenarios.

Contrary to the use of SCOR in the Operations Research and adoption of modelling approaches, the use of the BSC attracted business researchers who used 'four dimensions' metrics to construct measuring instruments for survey or case study research. The BSC was ranked as the most common approach (Piotrowicz and Cuthbertson, 2015), although this specific research revealed that keeping a balanced approach between financial and non-financial metrics is not always an important concern. The key factor to measure the supply chain performance is how the different BSC perspectives are coordinated towards the achievement of strategic goals (Bryceson and Slaughter, 2010). This caveat motivated a recent research by Shafiee *et al.* (2014) who used various BSC metrics and the Data Envelopment Analysis model (DEA) to calculate the efficiency score of supply chain performance in 22 Iranian food supply chains, and the results showed a striking focus on the customer perspective which is in full agreement with the findings from a research on the food industry as reported by Bigliardi and Bottani (2010).

This finding was further supported by Callado and Jack (2015), who conducted a survey involving 121 supply chain members in various SM roles in the Brazilian agribusiness. The authors explored the use of 49 PIs corresponding to the four perspectives of the BSC. The main objective of the research was to identify which metrics are related to four specific supply chain roles: retailers, distributors, producers and suppliers. Although the BSC was found to have produced all necessary metrics for the purpose of the research, the analysis of the findings revealed that different members in the supply chain use different sets of performance criteria with the exception of the immediate customer's satisfaction metrics which are equally significant for all members in the supply chain. The customer-related criteria had been found to carry the highest weight in supply chain performance in another research by Najmi and Makui (2012).

Realising the importance of performance metrics interdependencies, Najmi and Makui (2012) developed a conceptual model that was based on the BSC and SCOR metrics. Using the AHP and the Decision Making Trial and Evaluation Laboratory (DEMATEL) method, the authors proposed a four-level framework. Level 1 metrics included the strategic BSC perspectives enriched with the environmental concerns, whereas Level 2 included the SCOR attributes. These were further decomposed into Level 3 and Level 4 criteria. The model was tested using the case study methodology in the automotive industry operating in Tehran, which is characterised by tough competition and strong customer focus.

Development of other frameworks in the supply chain performance field

In the context of supply chain measures, there have been several other studies that used different approaches for the construction of frameworks and identification of metrics to optimise processes and improve performance. El-Baz (2011) proposed a framework that contained measures from different departments and evaluated their relative importance using the Analytic Hierarchy Process (AHP). The framework was tested in a manufacturing company and provided an evaluation of the performance of various departments in the case organisation. The expansion of the service industries affected a new stream of research that used service organisations for the validation of frameworks. Cho *et al.* (2012) took a number of metrics related to demand, customer and supplier relationship management, as well as capacity and resource management, service performance, information and technology management processes and evaluated them using AHP in a hotel supply chain. The lacuna in the service supply chain measurement field motivated Lega *et al.* (2012) who introduced and tested a framework to assess the supply chain performance in the public healthcare sector.

Moreira and Tjahjono (2016) developed a conceptual framework that uses measures from the exiting literature for ex ante decision making at an operational level. The authors applied their framework to a case company and reported how the components of the framework were analysed. Despite the limitations related to the case study research, the proposed framework can help academics and practitioners aiming at satisfying fluctuating customer demand.

Considering the main difficulties when developing a PM system in the context of a collaborative supply chain, Papakiriakopoulos and Pramatari (2010) proposed a set of performance measures to be maintained by the collaborative platform. Using two case organisations in Greece, the authors argued that companies' operation in networks should synchronise their business processes before the design and implementation of a new PM system. They also concluded that it is very difficult to define one framework for different members in the supply chain even if the channel is coordinated by IT platforms.

Following a different approach based on the content, context, process framework (CCP), Cuthbertson and Piotrowicz (2011) came up with the same conclusions as they argued that SCPM should be viewed as 'system tailored to specific supply chain requirements' (p. 583). Motivated by the same research objectives, Azevedo *et al.* (2013) proposed a set of measures that would be used by all members in a supply chain. By adopting the interpretive structural modelling (ISM) approach and the practical experience of five experts in the automotive industry, the study identified the contextual relationships among the suggested measures (inventory level, operational costs, lead time, business wastage, environmental costs, delivery time, customer satisfaction and C2C cycle). The conclusions, however, were based on one Portuguese automotive supply chain, and the findings cannot be generalised and, thus, become applicable to other industries in other countries.

Sustainable supply chains

Sustainability is not a new concept. It was first introduced at the United Nations Conference on Environment and Development in 1992[1] due to rising concerns over the deterioration of the global environment due to malpractices related to the use of resources, social justice and community development (Veleva and Ellenbecker, 2001). Although applying the principles of sustainable production received worldwide acceptance as an idea, industries are still challenged to produce sustainable goods and services and, at the same time, achieve economic growth by fully complying with the societal development and environmental conservation principles and approaches (Tseng *et al.*, 2009). Perhaps the best definition for sustainable supply chains is 'the managing of resources to ensure profitability whilst still caring for the social well-being and impact on the environment' (Hassini *et al.*, 2012), which is actually a shorter version of a previous definition by Seuring and Müller (2008, p. 1700) who isolated the economic, environmental and social dimensions of sustainability.

With that definition in mind, a previous review on the performance metrics revealed a need for research on the appropriate frameworks due to the incompatibilities between the traditional measures and the various as well as complex needs of sustainable supply chains (Lehtinen and Ahola, 2010). For the authors, the current measures could not be used in multinationals and extended enterprises facing pressures from the global economy. This is because the involvement of different players results in major difficulties on what and when to measure especially when using environmental indicators (Hervani *et al.*, 2005). This argument is still acknowledged by all researchers exploring this topic, as there is a general lack of agreement by academics and practitioners on how to measure social goals that are difficult to quantify.

One more challenge in the measurement of sustainability are the trade-offs that are inherent in the management of supply chains. For example, producing eco-design products might be very costly for many organisations that need to increase their economic indicators for sustainable growth. To this end, Hahn *et al.* (2015) proposed a framework that would release the tension when pursuing conflicting goals and is based on the integrative view of sustainability which in simple words implies integration of all sustainability principles without a priori emphasis on any achievement (p. 297). These arguments received the attention of other researchers (see Schaltegger and Burritt, 2014) who supported transparency for flexible and innovative sustainable supply chains. There have been various other papers on the topic of sustainable supply chain measures. Using fuzzy multi-attribute utility theory (MAUT), Erol *et al.* (2011) developed a framework that was tested using data from a grocery retailer in Turkey. Their work might help decision makers identify the criteria and opportunities for the improvement of supply chains.

As expected, the SCOR model had been tested as a practical decision support tool for environmental assessment (Bai *et al.*, 2012). The authors adopted the sourcing function of the SCOR model by using the grey based neighbourhood rough-set methodology and introduced a seven-step methodology that sheds some useful insights to the field from a sustainable supply chain perspective (p. 91). The main limitation of this study is that the methodology and framework are conceptual and the practicality needs to be tested in real-life situations where complete data can be available for all suppliers of an extended supply chain. Xiao *et al.* (2012) used the SCOR model as a basis to propose a new logistics operation reference model that includes reverse logistics. In a very recent literature review paper, Ntabe *et al.* (2015) found a trend in the adoption of the GreenSCOR for environmental assessment. However, our review indicated a rather limited interest in the use of the model in sustainable supply chains.

Hassini *et al.* (2012) proposed another framework that was tested in a Canadian utility operating in a regulated energy market. The case organisation developed a PM system consisting of sustainability PIs following an iterative and rigorous process of designing, implementing and refinement of the metrics. The study confirmed the complexity of the measurement problem that lies in the unique needs of the various players as the chosen metrics did not receive unanimous acceptance.

Contrary to previous research approaches, Samuel *et al.* (2013) did not try to develop a new framework. The authors used the five-tier framework already recommended by the Lowell Centre for Sustainable Production (LCSP)[2] as well as the Global Reporting Initiative (GRI) indicators[3] to measure the sustainability of the practices adopted by a petrochemical industry in Malaysia. The findings from the case study confirmed the usefulness of the measures and the compliance from the company in implementing the appropriate principles towards sustainability.

Hansen and Schaltegger (2014) proposed the Sustainable Balanced Score Card (SBSC) with three dimensions of sustainability performance with all the limitations of work that is conceptual in nature. Following a thorough review of the literature, Tajbakhsh and Hassini (2015) proposed a seven-dimension sustainable set of metrics to break down the complex problem of sustainability into manageable approaches for academics and practitioners pursuing different goals in extended supply chains. Our review of the papers, focusing mainly on the last 6 years, showed an increased interest in the adoption of sustainability practices for modern supply chains operating in a multinational environment, due to environmental concerns, global competition, green practices and pressures from various stakeholders including the government (Hassini *et al.*, 2012). A previous extensive academic research produced a total of 2,555 unique metrics (Ahi and Searcy, 2015) that do not seem to be helping researchers and practitioners find a manageable framework and, currently, existing recommendations lay the foundation for future work that will simplify this measurement process.

Conclusions and recommendations

This study has been conducted with a view to exploring the recent developments in the field of supply chain performance measurement focusing on published research during the last 6 years. Keeping the importance of a balanced approach in mind and the use of non-financial measures for the evaluation of supply chain performance, the study summarised the most important business frameworks aiming at the identification of the metrics that have or are being implemented by the managers of global supply chains. In our attempt to delve into this topic further, a literature review of the recent publications has been conducted. The methodology started with a rather broad base of publications that were further scrutinised for their relevance to and focus on this specific work.

Twenty-seven papers were carefully reviewed, helping us to find out which frameworks are being used in the new supply chain era as well as the methodologies and approaches followed by academics when trying to introduce new metrics or test existing ones. Our findings reveal that the BSC model still lies at the heart of modern supply chain PM systems.

As far as the SCOR model is concerned, the review revealed limited empirical research as most of the recent publications place an emphasis on mathematical techniques such as the AHP to form an objective function that optimises supply chain processes (see Li *et al.*, 2011).

The BSC, on the other hand, has attracted the interest of academic and industry research as the combination of financial and non-financial measures for a balanced collection of measures is being emphasised to involve the multiple stakeholders, especially in extended enterprises operating with global supply chains. Notwithstanding the worldwide acceptance of the BSC, the analysis of the findings reveals that there are several caveats when implementing it as different members of the supply chain value differently the four BSC perspectives with the exception of the immediate downstream customer's satisfaction related measures. Interestingly, Cuthbertson and Piotrowicz (2011) came up with the same conclusions, arguing that SCPM should be viewed as 'system tailored to specific supply chain requirements' (p. 583).

Supporting the idea of novel measures instead of the existing frameworks, Azevedo *et al.* (2013) adopted the ISM approach to suggest measures that can be used by all members in the automotive supply chain. Another stream of research focused on new metrics for the service sector. The findings from Cho *et al.* (2012) and Moreira and Tjahjono (2016) can help academics and practitioners with an interest in the hotel and healthcare industry.

The research interest in sustainable supply chain PM is steadily increasing as a response to growing concerns related to the need of simultaneously addressing the three dimensions of sustainability (economy, society and environment). The inherent trade-offs in sustainable supply chains can become even more challenging in companies operating in an international environment where societal values are difficult to comprehend before trying to quantify them. We would say that the recent analysis by Hahn *et al.* (2015) might help companies align conflicting goals but the question for the one best framework still remains open. We would tend to agree with Beske-Janssen *et al.* (2015, p. 675) who advocate for the use of GRI that is well received by practitioners and can lead future research into corporate practice. There is a need for empirical research involving global enterprises and multinationals for the development of new frameworks or expansion of existing ones that can integrate measures with the changing social and environmental concerns. Concluding this chapter, it should be mentioned that companies with multiple stakeholders cannot implement a uniform measurement system, and this is because different members in a supply chain pursue different goals and are reluctant to share information with their supply chain partners (Jüttner, 2005). Advanced ERP versions enable external collaboration, data sharing and global access to operational data. The Advanced Planning Optimizer (APO) model[4] introduced by SAP can allow planning along a multi-echelon supply chain. Various complex variables are factored in and the model works very well in multinationals but when attempting to share information outside the company's boundaries it faces the same problems and behaves as a single echelon application.

E-supply chain solutions that can be maintained by a collaborative platform might support the alignment of measures which, however, must be determined and synchronised prior to any PM system implementation. Chen and Wang (2016) used a case study approach and a logistics and transport data exchange platform, and demonstrated ways to enhance the integrative functions of a platform-based supply chain PM system.

Notes

1 United Nations Conference on Environment and Development, Rio de Janeiro, Brazil. Agenda 21: Programme of Action for Sustainable Development. New York: United Nations, 1992.
2 http://www.sustainableproduction.org/.
3 https://www.globalreporting.org/Pages/default.aspx.
4 http://searchsap.techtarget.com/definition/Advanced-Planner-and-Optimizer.

References

Ahi, P., & Searcy, C. (2015) 'An analysis of metrics used to measure performance in green and sustainable supply chains' *Journal of Cleaner Production*, 86, pp. 360–377.

Akyuz, G.A. & Erkan, T.E. (2010) 'Supply chain performance measurement: a literature review' *International Journal of Production Research*, 48(17), pp. 5137–5155.

Argyris, C. (1997) 'Organizational learning and management information systems', *Accounting, Organizations and Society*, 2(2), pp. 113–123.

Argyropoulou, M. (2013) 'Information system's effectiveness and organisational performance', PhD Thesis, Brunel University.

Argyropoulou, M., Reid, I., Michaelides, R. & Ioannou, G. (2015) 'Supply chain information systems and organisational performance in economic turbulent times. In: *IEEM2015 International conference on Industrial Engineering and Engineering Management*, 6th–9th December 2015, Singapore (In Press).

Azevedo, S., Carvalho, H. & Cruz-Machado, V. (2013) 'Using interpretive structural modelling to identify and rank performance measures', *Baltic Journal of Management*, 8(2) pp. 208–230.

Bai, C. & Sarkis, J. (2012) 'Supply-chain performance measurement system management using neighbourhood rough sets', *International Journal of Production Research*, 50(9), pp. 2484–2500.

Bai, C., Sarkis, J., Wei, X. & Koh, L. (2012) 'Evaluating ecological sustainable performance measures for supply chain management', *Supply Chain Management: An International Journal*, 17(1), pp. 78–92.

Barrientos, S., Gereffi, G. & Pickles, J. (2016) Editorial 'New dynamics of upgrading in global value chains: shifting terrain for suppliers and workers in the global south', *Environment and Planning A*, 48(7), pp. 1214–1219.

Beske-Janssen, P., Johnson, M.P. & Schaltegger, S. (2015) '20 years of performance measurement in sustainable supply chain management – what has been achieved?', *Supply Chain Management: An International Journal*, 20(6), pp. 664–680.

Bigliardi, B. & Bottani, E. (2010) 'Performance measurement in the food supply chain: a balanced scorecard approach', *Facilities*, 28(5/6), pp. 249–260.

Brown, M.G. (1996) *Keeping Score: Using the Right Metrics to Drive World-Class Performance*, Quality Resources: New York.

Bryceson, K.P & Slaughter, G. (2010) 'Alignment of performance metrics in a multi-enterprise Agribusiness', *International Journal of Productivity and Performance Management*, 59(4) pp. 25–350.

Cai, J., Liu, X., Xiao, Z. & Liu, J. (2009) 'Improving supply chain performance management: a systematic approach to analyzing iterative KPI accomplishment', *Decision Support Systems*, 46(2), pp. 512–521.

Callado, A.A.C. & Jack, L. (2015) 'Balanced scorecard metrics and specific supply chain roles', *International Journal of Productivity and Performance Management*, 64(2), pp. 288–300.

Cheng, M.C.B & Wang, J.J. (2016) 'An integrative approach in measuring hub-port supply chain performance: potential contributions of a logistics and transport data exchange platform', *Case Studies on Transport Policy*, 4(2), pp. 150–160.

Cho, D.W., Lee, Y.H., Ahn, S.H. & Hwang, M.K (2012) 'A framework for measuring the performance of service supply chain management Soft Computing for Management Systems', *Computers & Industrial Engineering*, 62, pp. 801–818.

Connelly, B.L., Ketchen, D.J. & Hult, G.T.M. (2013) 'Global supply chain management: toward a theoretically driven research agenda', *Global Strategy Journal*, 3(3), pp. 227–243.

Cuthbertson, R. & Piotrowicz, W. (2011) 'Performance measurement systems in supply chains', *International Journal of Productivity and Performance Management*, 60(6), pp. 583–602.

De Toni, A. & Tonchia, S. (2001) 'Performance measurement systems models, characteristics, and measures', *International Journal of Operations and Production Management*, 21(1–2), pp. 46–70.

El-Baz, M.A. (2011) 'Fuzzy performance measurement of a supply chain in manufacturing companies', *Expert Systems with Applications*, 38, pp. 6681–6688.

Elgazzar, S., Nicoleta, T., Hubbard, N. & Leach, D.L. (2012) 'Linking supply chain processes' performance to a company's financial strategic objectives', *European Journal of Operational Research*, 223(1), pp. 276–289.

Erol, I., Sencer, S. & Sari, R. (2011) 'A new fuzzy multi-criteria framework for measuring sustainability performance of a supply chain', *Ecological Economics*, 70(6), pp. 1088–1100.

Estampe, D., Lamouri, S., Paris, J.L. & Brahim-Djelloul, S. (2013) 'A framework for analysing supply chain performance evaluation models', *International Journal of Production Economics*, 142, pp. 247–258.

Fitzgerald, L., Johnston, R., Brignall, T.J., Silvestro, R. & Voss, C. (1991) *Performance Measurement in Service Businesses*, The Chartered Institute of Management Accountants: London.

Ganga, G.M.D. & Carpinetti, L.C.R. (2011) 'A fuzzy logic approach to supply chain performance management', *International Journal of Production Economics*, 134(1), pp. 177–187.

Gopal, P.R.C. & Thakkar, J. (2012) 'A review on supply chain performance measures and metrics: 2000–2011', *International Journal of Productivity and Performance Management*, 61(5), pp. 518–547.

Gunasekaran, A. & Kobu, B. (2007) 'Performance measures and metrics in logistics and supply chain management: a review of recent literature (1995–2004) for research and applications', *International Journal of Production Research,* 45(12), pp. 2819–2840.

Gunasekaran, A., Patel, C. & Tirtiroglu, E. (2001) 'Performance measures and metrics in a supply chain environment', *International Journal of Operations & Production Management,* 21(1/2), pp. 71–87.

Hahn, T., Pinkse, J., Preuss, L. & Figge, F. (2015) 'Tensions in corporate sustainability: towards an integrative framework', *Journal of Business Ethics,* 127(2), pp. 297–316.

Hansen, E.G. & Schaltegger, S. (2014) 'The sustainability balanced scorecard: a systematic review of architectures', *Journal of Business Ethics,* 4(1), pp. 1–29.

Hassini, E., Surti, C. & Searcy, C. (2012) 'A literature review and a case study of sustainable supply chains with a focus on metrics', *International Journal of Production Economics,* 140(1), pp. 69–82.

Hervani, A.A., Helms, M.M. & Sarkis, J. (2005) 'Performance measurement for green supply chain management', *Benchmarking: An International Journal,* 12(4), pp. 330–353.

Hoque, Z. & James, W. (2000) 'Linking balanced scorecard measures to size and market factors: impact on al performance', *Journal of Management Accounting Research,* 12, pp. 1–17.

Hsu, C.C., Tan, K.C., Zailani, S. & Jayaraman, V. (2013) 'Supply chain drivers that foster the development of green initiatives in an emerging economy', *International Journal of Operations & Production Management,* 33(6), pp. 656–688.

Huan, S.H., Sheoran, S.K., & Wang, G. (2004) 'A review and analysis of Supply Chain Operations Reference (SCOR) model', *Supply Chain Management: An International Journal,* 9(1), pp. 23–29.

Jensen, M.C. (2001) 'Value maximisation, shareholder theory and the corporate objective function', *European Financial Management,* 7(3), pp. 297–317.

Jüttner, U. (2005) 'Supply chain risk management', *The International Journal of Logistics Management,* 16(1), pp. 120–141.

Kald, M. & Nilsson, F. (2000) 'Performance measurement at Nordic companies', *European management Journal,* 18(1), pp. 113–127.

Kaplan, R.S. & Norton, D.P. (1992) 'The balanced scorecard-measure that drive performance', *Harvard Business Review,* 70(1), pp. 71–79.

Kaplan, R.S. & Norton D.P. (1996) 'Translating strategy into action: the balanced scorecard', *Harvard Business Review,* 69(1), pp. 131–138.

Kocaoğlu, B., Gülsün, B. & Tanyaş, M. (2013) 'A SCOR based approach for measuring a benchmarkable supply chain performance', *Journal of Intelligent Manufacturing,* 24(1), pp. 113–132.

Lambert, D.M., Garcı́a-Dastugue, S.J., & Croxton, K.L. (2005) 'An evaluation of process-oriented supply chain management framework', *Journal of Business Logistics,* 26(1), pp. 25–52.

Lebas, M.J. (1995) 'Performance measurement and performance measurement', *International Journal of Production Economics,* 41(1/3), pp. 23–35.

Lega, F., Marsilio, M. & Villa, S. (2012) 'An evaluation framework for measuring supply chain performance in the public healthcare sector: evidence from the Italian NHS', *Production Planning & Control,* 24(10–11), pp. 931–947.

Lehtinen, J. and Ahola, T. (2010) 'Is performance measurement suitable for an extended enterprise?', *International Journal of Operations & Production Management,* 30(2), pp. 181–204.

Li, L., Su, Q. & Chen, X. (2011) 'Ensuring supply chain quality performance through applying the SCOR model', *International Journal of Production Research,* 49(1), pp. 33–57.

Long, Q. (2014) 'Distributed supply chain network modelling and simulation: integration of agent-based distributed simulation and improved SCOR model' *International Journal of Production Research,* 52(23), pp. 6899–6917.

Lynch, R.L. & Cross, K.F. (1991) *Measure Up – The Essential Guide to Measuring Business Performance,* Mandarin: London.

Moreira, M. & Tjahjonoa, B. (2016) 'Applying performance measures to support decision-making in supply chain operations: a case of beverage industry', *International Journal of Production Research,* 54(8), pp. 2345–2365.

Najmi, A. & Makui, A. (2012) 'A conceptual model for measuring supply chain's performance', *Production Planning & Control,* 23(9), pp. 694–706.

Neely, A., Bourne, M. & Kennerley, M. (2000) 'Performance measurement system design: developing g and testing a process-based approach', *International Journal of Operations and Production Management,* 20(10), pp. 1119–1145.

Neely, A., Gregory, M. & Platts, K. (1995) 'Performance measurement system design: a literature review and research agenda', *International Journal of Operations and Production Management*, 15(4), pp. 80–116.

Ntabe, E.N., LeBel, L., Munson, A.D. & Santa-Eulalia, L.A. (2015) 'A systematic literature review of the supply chain operations reference (SCOR) model application with special attention to environmental issues', *International Journal of Production Economics*, 169(C), pp. 310–332.

Papakiriakopoulos, D. & Pramatari, K. (2010) 'Collaborative performance measurement in supply chain', *Industrial Management & Data Systems*, 110(9), pp. 1297–1318.

Pawlak, Z. (1982) 'Rough sets', *International Journal of Computer and Information Sciences*, 11(5), pp. 341–356.

Persson, F. (2011) 'SCOR template—a simulation based dynamic supply chain analysis tool', *International Journal of Production Economics*, 131(1), pp. 288–294.

Piotrowicz, W. & Cuthbertson, R. (2015) 'Performance measurement and metrics in supply chains: an exploratory study', *International Journal of Productivity and Performance Management*, 64(8), pp. 1068–1091.

Richard, P.J., Devinney, T.M., Yip, G.S. & Johnson, G. (2009) 'Measuring organisational performance: towards methodological best practice', *Journal of Management*, 35(3), pp. 718–804.

Samuel, V.B., Agamuthu, P. & Hashim, M.A. (2013) 'Indicators for assessment of sustainable production: a case study of the petrochemical industry in Malaysia', *Ecological Indicators*, 24, pp. 392–402.

Schaltegger, S. & Burritt, R. (2005) 'Corporate sustainability', in Folmer, H. and Tietenberg, T. (Eds), *The International Yearbook of Environmental and Resource Economics 2005/2006*, A Survey of Current Issues, Edward Elgar, Cheltenham, pp. 185–222.

Sellitto, M.A., Pereira, G.M., Borchardt, M., da Silva, R.I.V. & Vegas, C.V. (2015) 'A SCOR-based model for supply chain performance measurement: application in the footwear industry', *International Journal of Production Research*, 53(16), pp. 4917–4926.

Seuring, S. & Müller, M. (2008) 'From a literature review to a conceptual framework for sustainable supply chain management', *Journal of Cleaner Production*, 16(15), pp. 1699–1710.

Shafiee, M., Lotfi, F.H. & Saleh, H. (2014) 'Supply chain performance evaluation with data envelopmentanalysis and balanced scorecard approach', *Applied Mathematical Modelling*, 38, pp. 5092–5112.

Subramanian, N., & R. Ramanathan, R. (2012) 'A review of applications of analytic hierarchy process in operations management', *International Journal of Production Economics*, 138, pp. 215–241.

Tajbakhsh, A. & Hassini, E. (2015) 'Performance measurement of sustainable supply chains: a review and research questions', *International Journal of Productivity and Performance Management*, 64(6), pp. 744–783.

Tseng, M.L., Divinagracia, L. & Divinagracia, R. (2009) 'Evaluating firm's sustainable production indicators in uncertainty', *Computers and Industrial Engineering*, 57, pp. 1393–1403.

Veleva, V. & Ellenbecker, M. (2001) 'Indicators of sustainable production: framework and methodology', *Journal of Cleaner Production*, 9, pp. 519–549.

Waggoner, D.W., Neely, A.D. & Kennerley, P. (1999) 'The forces that shape organisational performance measurement systems: an interdisciplinary review'. *International Journal of Production Economics,* 60–61, 53–60.

Wang, W.Y.C., Chan, H.K. & Pauleen, D.J. (2010) 'Aligning business process reengineering in implementing global supply chain systems by the SCOR model', *International Journal of Production Research*, 48(19), pp. 5647–5669.

Xiao, R., Cai, Z. & Zhang, X. (2012) An optimisation approach to risk decision-making of closed-loop logistics based on SCOR model, *Optimisation*, 61(10), pp. 1221–1251.

Xu, W.X., Xu, L., Liu, X.M. & Jones, J.D. (2008) 'A new approach to decision-making with key constraint and its application in enterprise information systems', *Enterprise Information Systems*, 2(3), 287–308.

18

AirAsia

Towards a 'new world' carrier strategy and implications for performance management system design

Ralph Adler, Carolyn Stringer, Paul Shantapriyan and Georgia Birch

Introduction

This chapter explores the changes occurring in the adopted strategies of airlines and the implications of new strategic orientations on the design of organisational performance management systems. The contingency theory literature recognises the impact of different strategic positions (e.g. Porter's low-cost and differentiation strategies) on performance management system design (Anthony and Govindarajan, 2007). However, there has been little attention given to performance management design for organisations adopting a hybrid cost leadership/differentiation strategy (Adler, 2011; Ferreira and Otley, 2009; Ozdemir and Mecikoglu, 2016).

Airline competition continues to intensify, primarily as a result of further growth in the number of carriers adopting a low-cost strategy (LCS). When faced with a highly competitive environment, an organisation's ability to survive and succeed largely depends on how fully the organisation can understand its customers' needs and how quickly it can respond to changes in these needs (Sweeney, 1998). The needs of airline passengers are shifting. Air travellers are now looking for carriers that can offer the complete combination of high-quality service, on-time plane arrivals and low fares (Dostaler and Flouris, 2004). To align with this new customer mandate (Dell'Era and Verganti, 2010), airlines are beginning to realise that they must move beyond the pursuit of one of Porter's generic strategies (e.g. low cost) and begin adopting a hybrid cost leadership/differentiation strategy, what airline experts are calling the 'new world' carrier (Dell'Era and Verganti, 2010; Dostaler and Flouris 2004; Virgin Australia, 2011).

The purpose of this chapter is twofold. First, it examines the features of a successful LCS airline and how airline carriers are moving towards adopting a hybrid strategy, called the 'new world' carrier. The second purpose is to examine the implications of changing to a hybrid strategy for the design of performance management systems. The performance management literature recognises that successful companies typically have a good 'fit' between strategy and performance management system design (Adler, 2011; Anthony and Govindarajan, 2007; Ferreira and Otley, 2009).

We use AirAsia as an illustrative case as it is one of the industry's fastest-growing and most successful low-cost carriers, and it operates in an industry characterised by intense competition and rapidly evolving customer perceptions about what constitutes value. We find that AirAsia's successful LCS is underpinned by a variety of unique business activities and performance management processes. Together with the generic operational practices of low-cost carriers (e.g. standardised fleet), their unique position is maintained through its employee-centred human resource practices, a supportive organisational culture, and the clear and consistent communication of its brand. Current changes in the expectations of airline passengers, however, are likely to require AirAsia to become a 'new world' carrier. We find that it is well positioned to do so, and its performance management systems are already similar to what we would expect from companies following a hybrid strategy.

The next section of the chapter examines the implications of strategy on the design of performance management systems. We then discuss the LCS model, including reasons for its growth and common mistakes made when implementing it. The next section provides a detailed discussion of AirAsia, primarily focusing on the linked set of business activities and performance management processes and systems that serve to underpin its LCS. Then, we examine the factors associated with and characteristics of the newly emerging hybrid model ('new world' carrier), and the implications of adopting a 'new world' carrier strategy for AirAsia's performance management system design. The conclusion is offered in the final section.

Performance management

Performance management is the holistic framework that connects strategy formulation evaluation and implementation to an organisation's culture, structure, operating systems and human resource practices (Adler, 2011). Performance management is broader than the traditional focus on management control systems. Anthony and Govindarajan (2007, p. 6) state that 'management control is the process *by which managers influence other members of the organization to implement the organization's strategies*'. However, the term management control is declining partly because of the negative connotations around 'control' and partly because separating the link between strategy, management control and operations has become untenable in the modern environment (Ferreira and Otley, 2009; Otley, 2012).

Ferreira and Otley's (2009) seminal paper develops a performance management framework that includes a holistic range of performance management processes (e.g. vision and mission, strategy, structure, measures, target setting, performance evaluation, reward systems, information flows). More recently, Adler (2011) builds on Ferreira and Otley (2009) by focusing more on the context in which the performance management processes operate. Adler includes the external environment (e.g. global economy, national environment) and internal environment (e.g. leadership, life cycle stage), organisational context (e.g. organisational culture), organisational structure, human resource practices (e.g. selection, training), as well as the operating systems and procedures (which were the focus of Ferreira and Otley's 2009 framework (see Figure 9.1, p. 160)).

There is no universally applicable design for performance management systems. Managers can make strategic choices about where to position their organisations, and contingency theory research predicts that certain types of performance management system design is more suited to different strategies (Chenhall, 2007). Contingency theory research has examined the link between strategy and performance management design (see Langfield-Smith, 1997, 2007 for reviews), and this is a central tenet of the balanced scorecard (Kaplan and Norton,

2008). What is increasingly apparent from contingency theory research is that strategy is a key contingency variable that impacts on the design of an organisation's performance management system (Langfield-Smith, 1997, 2007; Otley, 1999). There is also research that shows that a good 'fit' between strategy and performance management processes leads to higher organisational performance (Govindarajan, 1988; Govindarajan and Gupta, 1985). Further, Langfield-Smith (1997) finds that there is a level of consistency between the performance management characteristics of organisations following low-cost and defender strategies.

Low-cost strategic positions 'fit' with performance management systems where there is a conservative culture, centralised organisational structure, formalised and financially based strategic planning, specialised and formalised work procedures, more emphasis on financial data, cost efficiency, tight budget control and output control. In terms of human resource practices, individual evaluations emphasise performance to budget targets, incentive systems that are formulaic and financially focused, and training and employee development focusing on specialisation, task efficiency and cost control (Adler, 2011; Anthony and Govindarajan, 2007).

Adler (2011, p. 261) also examines how performance management systems would be different if an organisation was to follow a hybrid strategy (what is called becoming a 'new world' carrier in the airline industry). He argues that for 'new world' carriers, a good performance management design would include a collaborative culture, a lean and flat organisational structure, team work, collective responsibility, interactive strategic planning, hybrid customer-orientated and tight control budgeting systems. In terms of human resource practices, performance evaluations and rewards are group based, with the emphasis on empowering employees and training them to be multi-skilled.

Airlines: low-cost strategy

It is difficult to overstate the velocity of change that is sweeping the global economy (Sweeney, 1998). Sweeney (1998, p. 672) argues that 'Businesses must contend with emerging competitive threats not only from traditional rivals but from start-up companies and diversifying giants in other industries as well'. The airline industry is no exception, and, if anything, faces a harsher and more intensely competitive environment than many other industries. Since deregulation, the US airline industry has lost $60 billion over the last 32 years (Borenstein, 2011).

The airline market is commonly divided into full-service carriers (FSCs) and LCSs. The LCS market has expanded exponentially since its inception in the 1970s. European LCS passenger numbers have increased from 8 million in 1998 to 59 million in 2005 (Binggeli and Pompeo, 2005). In the US, LCSs now account for approximately 30 per cent of the domestic airline market (de Wit and Zuidberg, 2012).

Two reasons are commonly given for the success of the LCS model. First, LCSs have succeeded not only because they have wrested market share from the FSCs, but also because they have managed to stimulate new, additional customer demand (Barrett, 2004). People who were unable to afford air travel in the past can now do so. The second reason LCSs have succeeded is due to their effective management of costs. With a ruthless focus on costs, LCSs have sought to squeeze every last drop of avoidable cost out of the system. They have chosen, for example, to operate out of remote, less costly airports. Furthermore, they use point-to-point flights, which eliminate the activity of moving passengers' bags between connecting flights and, in the process, achieve greater airplane utilisations through quicker turnaround times (i.e. the amount of time between when a plane arrives and next departs).

The rise of the LCS has not gone unchallenged. FSCs have responded to the competitive threat of LCSs in three main ways: establishing their own LCS subsidiaries, using their political influence to restrict LCSs' operations (e.g. airport landing rights) and engaging in price wars. These responses have reduced the growth opportunities of LCSs and, on occasion, have served to bankrupt LCSs. As an example, in 1994, Air New Zealand created Freedom Air as its subsidiary to counteract the competitive threat of the then fledgling LCS, Kiwi Air. Freedom Air engaged Kiwi Air in a price-based war of attrition, to which the latter eventually succumbed. Freedom Air won because it could draw upon the large capital reserves of its parent, something Kiwi Air could not do.

One of the most common reasons for LCS failure is trying to copy the Southwest Airlines model, which has traditionally been seen as the LCS gold standard, without fully understanding the complexities and subtleties of the model's linkages. Airlines that superficially copy the Southwest business model often only focus on the operational factors, for example, flying one type of aircraft, using secondary airports and unbundling services. What is overlooked is how Southwest effectively combines these operational factors (Porter, 1996). A good fit between strategy and its performance management processes lies at the heart of Southwest's success, including its unique culture, communication techniques and organisational practices (Gittell, 2004).

AirAsia

The story of a highly successful LCS

A particularly successful low-cost carrier is AirAsia Berhad, more commonly known simply as AirAsia. AirAsia was founded in 1993 as a Malaysian-based, low-cost domestic airline, with the dream of making flying possible for everyone (AirAsia, 2010a). This goal is pursued by providing services at a price that is simply lower than any competitor's price by ensuring high efficiency and maintaining simplicity (AirAsia, 2014). AirAsia's cost leadership strategy is based largely on the Southwest Airlines model, with some slight modifications to fit better the local flavour of Asia (AirAsia, 2010a). Similar to other successful LCSs, AirAsia operates a standardised fleet of aircraft; ensures high aircraft utilisation; uses secondary, low-cost airports; and flies point to point. Where AirAsia differs from its rivals is that its cheap fares are complemented by courteous service. Together, the cheap fares and courteous service translate into high customer satisfaction (O'Connell and Williams, 2005). Skytrax, a UK-based airline research company, named AirAsia the best low-cost airline for 2007, 2009, 2010, 2011, 2012, 2013, 2014 and 2015 (World Airline Awards, 2015). Additionally, AirAsia won the award for the airline with the lowest operating cost in 2010; its costs being 3.5US¢/seat/km (Ahmad, 2010).

Prior to AirAsia's start-up, there were few LCSs operating in the Asian market. There was a commonly expressed belief that the low-cost model adopted in Europe and the US could not be replicated in Asia. The argument was based on there being a lack of secondary airports, greater distances between the relatively few airports that did exist and regulatory restrictions that prevented access to international markets (O'Connell and Williams, 2005). While several Asian LCSs eventually did appear – including Citilink in Indonesia and JAL Express, Air Do, and Skymark in Japan–none '... significantly impact[ed] their respective markets' (O'Connell and Williams, 2005, p. 260).

AirAsia has proved itself the notable exception to the perceived impediments to LCS success in Asia. From its very beginning, AirAsia learned to develop creative solutions to various market and regulatory constraints. As one example, when the Thailand government relaxed its regulations of airlines' international activities as a way to develop and promote tourism in Thailand, AirAsia pounced (Francis *et al.*, 2006). By registering in Thailand, it avoided its home country's regulations on international air travel and was able to begin international flights.

Today, AirAsia offers domestic and international flights to over 400 destinations, covering 25 countries. Its growth has undoubtedly been helped by a benign environment, including a large population base, a rising middle class with increasing leisure time and disposable income, and a lack of cost-competitive substitute transportation options (Goldman, 1997). The geography of the Asian continent further supports the necessity of air transportation. There simply is no other viable and efficient mode of transport.

AirAsia's success is evident in the data presented in Tables 18.1 and 18.2. The data show that AirAsia was impacted by the 2008 global financial crisis, but has since rebounded. For the year ending 2008, AirAsia had a RM 96.5 million loss. This loss can largely be attributed to the global financial crisis. AirAsia has since recovered due to a number of factors, including tight revenue management that has seen increases in the number of passengers over the period of 2008–2012. Unit passenger revenue has grown from RM 197 to RM 227. There has also been tight cost control where the cost/ask in US cents from fuel hovers around 2.20. For example, in 2010, the cost/ask (from fuel) was 2.24, and in 2012, the cost was 2.17.

AirAsia has continuously expanded the number of its planes and flights. It ordered 225 Airbus planes in late 2007. This asset expansion resulted in AirAsia's debt doubling from the 6-month end in 2007 to the year ended in 2008. Since 2010, AirAsia has had improved performance, which has come from its successful pursuit of a hybrid strategy supported by aggressive revenue management, increased operational cost management and tight load factor control.

Performance management

The implementation of AirAsia's strategy is underpinned by a variety of unique business activities and performance management processes and systems. Most prominent are its treatment of employees, its culture and the manner in which AirAsia is branded and marketed to the public. Each of these factors is discussed below.

Table 18.1 Assessment of AirAsia's financial performance

	2006	*2007 (ending 30th June)*	*2007 (6 months ending December)*	*2008*	*2009*	*2010*	*2011*	*2012*
NP/Equity	0.084	0.300	0.203	–0.309	0.193	0.292	0.234	0.212
NP/Pretax Profit	0.765	1.791	1.538	0.571	0.814	0.966	1.095	0.416
Pretax Profit/EBIT	1.192	0.997	1.329	2.472	0.682	1.030	0.428	1.093
EBIT/Sales	0.112	0.174	0.190	–0.133	0.291	0.270	0.404	0.376
Sales/Assets	0.358	0.335	0.170	0.277	0.275	0.298	0.445	0.393
Assets/Equity	2.292	2.876	3.072	5.926	4.349	3.636	2.777	3.147
ROI	0.037	0.104	0.066	–0.052	0.044	0.080	0.084	0.067
EPS	0.038	0.211	0.180	–0.209	0.184	0.383	0.307	0.308
P/E	45.12	9.34	8.41	–7.65	4.74	3.55	8.51	11.73

Table 18.2 Operational performance measures for AirAsia

	2008	*2009*	*2010*	*2011*	*2012*
Passengers Carried	14,253,244	11,808,058	17,986,558	17,986,558	19,678,576
Capacity	19,016,280	15,660,228	20,616,120	22,474,620	24,751,800
Seat Load Factor (%)	75	75.4	78	80	80
ASK (million)	21,977	18,717	24,362	26,074	28,379
RPK (million)	15,432	13,485	18,499	21,037	22,731
Average Fare (RM)	168.2	204	177	176	187
Ancillary Income per Pax (RM)	29.1	20	44	45	40
Unit Passenger Revenue (RM)	197.3	224	221	221	227
Rev/ASK (sen)	13.54	15	16.21	17.16	17.6
Rev/ASK (US cents)	3.84	4.43	5.61	5.6	5.72
Cost/ASK (sen)	10.41	12.8	11.83	13.54	13.56
Cost/ASK (US cents)	2.95	3.84	3.87	4.11	4.4
Cost/ASK-ex fuel (sen)	6.15	5.38	6.86	5.99	6.69
Cost/ASK-ex fuel (US cents)	1.74	1.61	2.24	2.21	2.17
Aircraft (end of period)	48	44	53	57	64
Average Stage Length (km)	1,166	1,207	1,184	1,162	1,148
Number of Flights	105,646	89,118	114,534	124,853	137,510
Fuel Consumed (barrels)	3,779,698	3,254,201	4,106,672	4,290,284	4,685,895
Average Fuel Price (US$/barrel)	70.4	128	96	131	135

Note: Key performance measures for airlines include revenue per passenger km/miles (RPK) and available seat km/miles (ASK).

Source: Information is from AirAsia's Annual Reports and AIRASIA BERHAD's quarterly reports for December 2011 and 2012, www.airasia.com/my/en/about-us/ir-quarterly-reports.page# (Accessed 14 January 2014).

First, AirAsia has a genuine understanding of the value of its human resources. It recognises that its people are what have made it the successful airline it is. Although AirAsia is a low-cost airline, it does all it can to ensure high employee satisfaction and morale. The philosophy of the airline is to attract the best people, train them and retain them (AirAsia, 2010b). To help achieve this philosophy, a corporate culture department was established in 2004. At AirAsia, it is believed that 'every aspect of the business model must be simplified so that its whole philosophy, vision and objectives … are understood by all stakeholders' (AirAsia, 2010b).

Promoting employee empowerment is a centrepiece of AirAsia's human resource practice. The company operates a flat hierarchy and uses an open office layout, both of which are intended to enhance employee empowerment and reduce cultural or social barriers (Ahmad, 2010). Ideas that are proposed by anyone can be implemented, face-to-face meetings are encouraged, and all managers have blogs and Twitter accounts to share their experiences. Everyone at AirAsia addresses one another on a first-name basis, and senior management commonly dress casually in an effort to minimise the perceived power distance between themselves and other employees (AirAsia, 2010c).

The second pillar underpinning AirAsia's unique strategy is its culture. The culture is characterised by innovation, openness, youthfulness, an audacious sense of fun and a never-say-die attitude (Ahmad, 2010). As such, this culture is supportive of and conditioned by the airline's commitment to simplified work structures, transparent performance management practices and employee empowerment.

Tony Fernandes, AirAsia's chief executive officer (CEO), helps to create and shape the airline's culture. He believes that the airline's vision must be clear and concise, its work practices simplified and streamlined, and its employees valued and respected (AirAsia, 2010c). He demands transparency in decision making and encourages loyalty. Furthermore, he is always willing to make himself accessible to the media and the investor community (Airlinetrends, 2012).

The third pillar underpinning AirAsia's unique strategy comprises the manner in which the airline is branded and marketed. Consistent with its 'fun and trendy' image, AirAsia leverages the Internet for further developing and communicating its brand. Like most organisations, AirAsia maintains a Facebook page. However, unlike its counterparts, it more fully embraces this social networking tool, regularly updating its Facebook page. As a further testament to its hip communication style, AirAsia is recognised as the world's best airline for replying to tweets, responding to more than 40 per cent of the tweets it receives.

In terms of AirAsia's brand communication, the aim of the airline is to attract the widest publicity to create maximum awareness from around the world (Lim *et al.*, 2009). AirAsia sponsors three global sports icons: Manchester United, Queens Park Rangers and William's Formula 1 racing team. As a result of these sponsorships, the AirAsia name is displayed to millions of viewers around the world. Through AirAsia's numerous acts of generosity, the airline has been coined the 'people's airline'. For example, it raised US$128 million for UNICEF in 2010; it created the 'Donate loose change campaign' for needy heart patients; and it is famously known for its free-seats campaign, whereby it offers 1 million free seats on flights across its extensive network (AirAsia, 2010b). Ultimately, AirAsia has set the benchmark for corporate social responsibility very high.

In summary, to allow AirAsia to cement its position as the 'people's airline', the sources of competitive advantage are through the combination of generic LCS operational practices (e.g. standardised fleet and high aircraft utilisation) and performance management processes, including employee-centred human resource practices, a supportive organisational culture, and the clear and consistent communication of its brand. These points are further elaborated in Table 18.3.

Table 18.3 Sources of competitive advantage

Sources of competitive advantage	*Explanation*
1 generic LCS operational practices; a limited passenger service; b short-haul, point-to-point routes often through secondary airports; c standardised fleet of aircraft; d high aircraft utilisation.	• Enables AirAsia to cut costs and offer its travel service at a price that is lower than competitors. • Flying out of secondary airports keeps the airline's expenses down, as take-off and landing fees are cheaper. • AirAsia only uses one type of airplane, the Airbus A320. This keeps maintenance costs down and increases the efficiency of operations. • Increases AirAsia's efficiency and lowers costs.

(Continued)

Sources of competitive advantage	*Explanation*
2 Human resource practices a productive, skilful and empowered employees; b senior managers strong in strategy formulation and implementation; c influential personal networks.	• Philosophy is to attract the best, train them and retain them. There is a great sense of empowerment in AirAsia. A flat hierarchy helps break down psychological and cultural barriers, and the open office layout encourages fluid interactions. • They have taken proven strategies by other low-cost carriers and implemented these: – Ryanair's operational strategy, – Southwest's people strategy, – EasyJets' branding strategy. • Strong links to government and airline industry leaders: – Thaksin Shinawatra, the former Thai prime minister, holds a 50 per cent stake in Thai AirAsia. This has helped to open up and capture a sizeable market in Thailand; – strong working relationship with Airbus enabled the airline to get a sizeable discount for the aircraft purchased.
3 Culture a focused mission, b simple, lean operations, c bold and aggressive.	• AirAsia's entire strategic focus is concerned with low cost. Having such a clear mission has enabled the business to grow rapidly and gives it clear insight into where it will be positioned in the future; it has also enabled the airline to target a niche market. • CEO Tony Fernandes believes that every aspect of the business must be simplified so that its philosophy, vision, mission and objectives can be understood by stakeholders (AirAsia, 2010b). • Expanding into new markets. • Increasing the number of flights. • Purchase of new aircraft. • Vision of becoming the people's airline, as measured by market results and its reputation as a good, fun and generous employer.
4 Marketing and branding a employee buy-in and commitment; b good implementation plan.	• Senior management has successfully managed to develop a brand-based culture that is supported and embraced at all levels of the organisation. • AirAsia is an astute user of social media and the Internet.

'New world' carrier strategy?

'New world' carrier

AirAsia's likely future challenge will come from being able to meet customer demands for an air service that combines the features of both the LCS and FSC models, what industry experts are calling the 'new world' carrier. Instead of the industry's current two distinct markets model – the LCS and FSC – it is predicted that airlines will need to learn how to fuse elements of the cost leadership and differentiation strategies (Dostaler and Flouris, 2004).

Cooper (1995), who uses the automobile industry as his primary example, recounts how the survival zone of auto producers collapsed in the mid-1980s. Cooper describes how in the 1960s auto producers could choose among a variety of unique strategies, with each strategy implying different trade-offs between cost and quality. By the mid-1980s, however, the industry's viable competitive space collapsed, allowing no choice other than the pursuit of a singular strategy of head-to-head competition (what Cooper terms a confrontation strategy).[1] A confrontation strategy permits no trade-offs between cost and quality. Rather, it imposes on producers high minimum thresholds for both low cost and high quality. Firms that are unable to meet these minimum thresholds become uncompetitive and lose market share. Figure 18.1 is a generalised illustration of Cooper's ideas.

The black dots in the lower right-hand corner of Figure 18.1 represent customer demand. Prior to the collapsing of the survival zone, the customer demand was spread across what this illustration shows as five producers. One producer was the cost leader, and the other four were pursuing some form of differentiation. The migration of customer demand to the low-cost and high-quality region, due to such factors as increased choice through globalised competition and ever-rising customer expectations, means that the five producers must migrate too (as indicated by the five arrows) or face the loss of their markets. Upon migrating to this new region of customer demand, producers will find themselves squeezed together in a highly diminished competitive space, one that no longer permits the exclusive pursuit of cost leadership or some form of differentiation. Instead of navigating the spacious strategic blue oceans that Kim and Mauborgne (2005) speak about, producers will find themselves eye to eye and toe to toe in a confrontation strategy with their rivals.

Common signs of an approaching survival-zone collapse are mature product/service life cycles, high intra-industry competition (and sometimes even extra-industry competition via the presence of substitute products/services) and high customer power. These signs were all

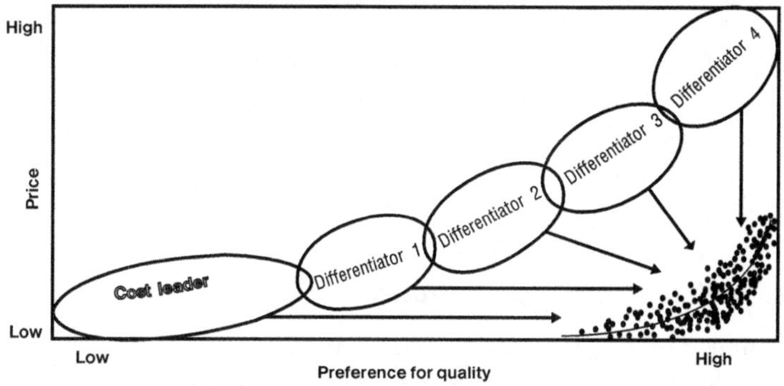

Figure 18.1 Emergence of a confrontation strategy due to the collapsing of an industry's competitive space

present in the automobile industry before its survival-zone collapse. These signs have also been present for many years in the electronics, whiteware and banking industries, with all three industries being characterised by significant competitive confrontation (Adler, 2011).

The airline industry appears to be exhibiting signs of survival-zone collapse. Air travel is a well-established service that industry experts are increasingly referring to as a commodity service (Lawson, 2005). Competition is perceived as very high. Industry experts have argued that deregulation and the advent of the LCS have ushered in high levels of competition and even hyper-competition in some regional markets (Adler, 2011). The power wielded by airline passengers is deemed to be substantial. Customers commonly use the Internet to search out the lowest possible fares, while at the same time expecting high-quality service from whichever airline they choose to fly. This means that revenue management, operational cost management and capacity management become pivotal (Rouse *et al.*, 2010).

AirAsia has encountered evidence of these signs of survival-zone collapse in its Indonesian market. In particular, it has discovered that the preferences of its Indonesian passengers are quite different from what its LCS model provides. Its lack of extra passenger services and its reluctance to take passengers with heavy baggage have deterred significant numbers of Indonesian people from flying with AirAsia (Ong and Tan, 2010).

AirAsia has taken steps towards evolving its strategy to meet this changing environment. An important agent in driving this change is the company's CEO (Ocasio and Joseph, 2008). AirAsia is now introducing full-service elements to cater for the differing and changing demands of customers. Part of this change is occurring because budget travellers no longer dominate the passengers flying with AirAsia; the airline is now attracting corporate and government business travellers (Ahmad, 2010). To meet this changing demand, AirAsia X was launched in 2007 to provide high-frequency and point-to-point routes to the long-haul business market (AirAsia, 2010b). More recently, AirAsia entered into a strategic alliance with the FSC Malaysian Airways. This collaboration could accelerate AirAsia's evolution towards a hybrid strategy, especially if the operating characteristics of the two airlines become more aligned.

Other low-cost carriers have also taken steps to switch to hybrid strategies. After operating for several years as a low-cost carrier, a change in customer expectations prompted Virgin Australia to improve its services and become a 'new world' carrier (Virgin Australia, 2011). Management made the decision to shift the strategic direction of the airline in order to compete more effectively with Qantas in the business travel market. This decision may be very fortuitous for Virgin Australia, as Qantas's reputation has been seriously eroded by various recent safety problems (ABC News Australia, 2011).

Southwest Airlines is another airline that has moved towards a hybrid strategy. Southwest has maintained its low fares and only charges for value-added items. It does not charge customers for changing their flight plans, checking bags, making seat selections, choosing curbside check-ins, or making telephone reservations or for fluctuations in fuel prices (Gittell, 2004). Southwest Airlines has a strong focus on customer and employee satisfaction, and has introduced loyalty programmes.

The preferred path to a 'new world' strategy

In theory, attainment of this 'new world' carrier status can occur in one of two ways: airlines can begin as an FSC and incorporate the further features of the LCS, or airlines can begin as an LCS and incorporate the further features of the FSC. In practice, however, the preferred path may be limited to the latter approach. Sweeney's (1993) work has indicated that the successful attainment of a hybrid strategy begins by mastering the activities behind cost leadership. Once achieved, the firm's business practices evolve to include a quality focus. In the final evolutionary stage, the firm adds product/service customisation to its previously learned mix of low cost and high quality. At this point, the firm, or in this particular case the airline, will have earned the nomenclature of 'new world' carrier.

As previously noted, several FSCs have added LCS subsidiaries to their organisational structures. In other words, these FSCs have adopted a twin structure with twin strategies as opposed to an integrated structure with an all-encompassing hybrid strategy. Singapore Airlines is a classic case in point. It created a separate organisation, Scoot, in 2011 to counteract the challenge from LCSs entering its key markets. However, a twin structure and strategy is not always successful.

Continental Airways provides an instructive example of what can go wrong when an FSC adopts a twin structure, twin strategy approach. In 1993, the airline created an LCS subsidiary called Continental Lite. Within 2 years, Continental Airlines abruptly ended what it had originally trumpeted as an industry-leading innovation. Its then CEO, Gordon M. Bethune, lamented, 'It was an awfully expensive experiment', with losses topping US$140 million (Bryant, 1995).

The 'airline-within-an-airline' model Continental Airlines tried to pursue lacked strategic coherence. Instead, it produced a number of strategic compromises. For example, Continental Airlines recognised that travel agents were a necessary part of its FSC market, but an expensive burden on its LCS market. Needing to simultaneously slash *and* retain the travel-agent commissions, it chose a compromise strategy of reducing the commissions. In a similar manner, Continental Airlines could not afford to offer the same frequent-flier benefits to both its LCS and FSC fliers, so it compromised by offering reduced rewards. These actions pleased no one. Customers became dissatisfied and travel agents unmotivated. Porter (1996) summed up the situation as a classic case of being 'stuck in the middle'.

Air New Zealand represents the closest example of an FSC that has adopted elements of the LCS. The airline is increasingly incorporating elements of the LCS model into its traditional FSC business model. This response is largely due to what Air New Zealand CEO Rob Fife contended was the only viable way to compete in a market experiencing abnormally high levels of competition and still struggling to rebound from the 2001 industry downturn that followed the terrorist attacks in New York City (Adler, 2011; Owen, 2011). More and more, Air New Zealand is focusing on reducing its costs and its prices. But unlike the 'new world' carrier, which is capable of achieving both low costs and high service, Air New Zealand appears content to sacrifice various services (e.g. free checked baggage, free in-flight meals and entertainment) in its quest to offer low fares. In other words, Air New Zealand seems to be undergoing a transformation from an FSC to an LCS.

According to Sweeney (1998, 1993), it is not surprising to find FSCs unable to successfully pursue a hybrid strategy. Sweeney has argued that the only truly successful pathway to adopting a hybrid strategy is to begin by mastering the activities behind cost leadership. Once this has been achieved, the firm then progresses to include a quality focus. When the firm has successfully learned to provide a low-cost, high-quality product/service, and is able to do so without sacrificing cost for quality (Porter's admonishment about being stuck in the middle), the firm is ready to progress to the final stage of including the provision of product/service customisation. In this final stage, the firm has successfully adopted a hybrid strategy and evolved to what Sweeney calls a world-class organisation.

Based on Sweeney's argument, LCSs, and especially AirAsia, since it is widely perceived as best in its class for achieving low costs (Ahmad, 2010), are well placed for attaining the 'new world' carrier nomenclature. Presently, these airlines have succeeded in providing low fares by eliminating wasteful activities and designing business processes, practices and systems of the highest efficiency. The next challenge for the LCSs is to include value-adding services, and to do so without increasing the cost structure. While far from easy, Sweeney (1993) shows that a subset of the 12 case firms he studied were capable of achieving this outcome through both hard work and a willingness to encourage and reward creativity. In fact, Sweeney (1993) explicitly describes a firm's attainment of world-class organisational status as passing from the stages of the efficient caretaker through to the creative innovator.

'New world' strategy and performance management

How would the change to a hybrid 'new world' carrier strategy impact on AirAsia? As a low-cost carrier, contingency theory would expect AirAsia's performance management system to be similar to other low-cost organisations in having a conservative organisational culture, centralised organisational, operating systems that have specialised processes, simple coordinating mechanisms, strategic planning that is financially based around budget targets, formula-driven incentive payments, training focused around efficiency, and cost control (Adler, 2011; Anthony and Govindarajan, 2007). In contrast, AirAsia's performance management system is quite different from a typical LCS.

We find that AirAsia is already moving towards a performance management system similar to other organisations adopting a hybrid strategy such as the 'new world' carrier. AirAsia is well placed to move towards being a 'new world' carrier, as the performance management system already has a unique culture that values team work, innovation, fun and openness. It has a flat structure where employees at all levels are empowered to make decisions and to share ideas that can be implemented. Air Asia also has a strong sense of collective responsibility, as well as a focus on keeping costs low. These elements of performance management are consistent with performance management design for organisations adopting a hybrid (cost leadership/differentiation) strategy. This is consistent with Adler's (2011) findings that organisations following a hybrid strategy have performance management system designs that include a collaborative organisational culture, a lean and flat organisational structure, team-based work procedures, a sense of collective responsibility, interactive planning systems, team-based incentives, and human resource systems that encourage empowerment and multi-skilling.

AirAsia's CEO seems to be already leading the way towards providing full-service elements to the airline's offerings. This will need to translate into a change in culture that embraces both low cost and providing more customer service. This will require hybrid systems that are customer focused and provide tight cost control. The main challenge for AirAsia will be getting the right balance between keeping costs low, while at the same time providing additional customer services.

Conclusion

The LCS model has been instrumental in pushing down airfares and opening up new markets. Many LCSs have greatly profited; others have struggled and even failed. As struggling and failed airlines have often belatedly learned, success in the LCS market demands more than the mere adoption of the core, generic elements of the LCS model, that is, limited passenger service, short-haul, point-to-point routes often through secondary airports, standardised fleet of aircraft and high aircraft utilisation. LCS success additionally demands the design and implementation of business activities and performance management processes and systems that strategically link together and create competitive advantage.

AirAsia is an example of a particularly successful LCS. It has complemented its adoption of the generic LCS model with employee-centred human resource practices, a supportive organisational culture, and the clear and consistent communication of its brand. Together, these practices have enabled the airline to develop into the best low-cost carrier in the world and cement its position as the people's airline. The AirAsia case provides practical insights into the way AirAsia's performance management practices align to support its LCS strategy.

Changing customer expectations, however, appear to be sweeping across the airline industry. Passengers are increasingly demanding that airlines provide both low-cost fares and high levels of passenger service, particularly in Asia. To align with this new customer mandate, airlines may find that they need to move beyond the pursuit of one of Porter's generic strategies to the adoption of a hybrid cost leadership/differentiation strategy (what Cooper (1995) calls a confrontation strategy). The industry has already named this hybrid strategic approach the 'new world' carrier. In theory, attainment of this 'new world' carrier status can occur in one of two ways: airlines can begin as an FSC and incorporate the further features of the LCS, or airlines can begin as an LCS and incorporate the further features of the FSC.

We find that AirAsia's performance management system is already well on the way to developing the type of performance management system that fits with adopting a hybrid strategy. Getting the right balance between keeping costs low and providing additional customer services will undoubtedly prove challenging. However, the airlines that successfully meet this challenge will find that they not only achieve financial reward in the medium term but, and even more importantly, that they are in a better position to accomplish the fundamental objective of every business: improving the chances of their very survival.

The usual limitations of case study research apply. Further research could usefully explore how airlines like AirAsia might successfully move to the hybrid strategy. In addition, this research might examine how these airlines might achieve the right 'fit' between the 'new world' carrier strategy and the design of the performance management system, as they strive to excel simultaneously at low-cost and high-quality service.

Note

1 A hybrid strategy is when organisations can choose their strategy, whereas a confrontation strategy is when there is no possibility for differentiation and organisations are competing in the same space.

References

ABC News Australia (2011). www.abc.net.au/news/2011-10-29/qantas-locking-out-staff/3608250 (Accessed 10 January 2014).

Adler, R.W. (2011). 'Performance management and organizational strategy: How to design systems that meet the needs of confrontation strategy firms', *The British Accounting Review, 43*(4), 251–263.

Ahmad, R. (2010). 'AirAsia: Indeed the sky's the limit!', *Asian Journal of Management Cases,* 7(7), 7–31.

AirAsia (2010a). *Welcome to AirAsia.* Retrieved from www.airasia.com/my/en/corporate/irstrategy.page (Accessed 3 August 2012).

AirAsia (2010b). *Welcome to AirAsia.* Retrieved from www.airasia.com/my/en/corporate/iraboutairasia.page (Accessed 3 August 2012).

AirAsia (2010c). *Welcome to AirAsia.* Retrieved from www.airasia.com/my/en/corporate/careers_10reasons.page? (Accessed 3 August 2012).

AirAsia (2014). www.airasia.com/au/en/about-us/corporate-profile.page (Accessed 14 January 2014).

Airlinetrends. www.airlinetrends.com (Accessed 3 August, 2012).

Anthony, R.N., and Govindarajan, V. (2007). *Management Control Systems*, McGraw-Hill Irwin: New York.

Barrett, S. (2004). 'How do the demands of airport services differ between full-service carriers and low-cost carriers?' *Journal of Air Transport Management, 10*(1), 33–39.

Binggeli, U. and Pompeo, L. (2005) 'The battle for Europe's low-fare flyers', *The McKinsey Quarterly, 8*(1), 1–7.

Borenstein, S. (2011). 'On the persistent financial losses of U.S. Airlines: A preliminary Exploration', Working Paper, National Bureau of Economic Research.

Bowden, S. (2003). 'Kiwi International Airlines: Judo strategy and its limits', *Journal of the Australian and New Zealand Academy of Management, 9*(2), 1–7.

Bryant, A. (1995). 'Company reports: Continental is dropping "lite" service', *New York Times*, April 14.

Chenhall, R.H. (2007). 'Theorizing contingencies in management control systems research'. In: Chapman, C.S., Hopwood, A.G., Shields, M.D. (Eds.), *Handbook of Management Accounting Research*, vol. 1. Elsevier, Oxford, UK, 163–205.

Cooper, R. (1995). *When Lean Organizations Collide: Competing through Confrontation*. Harvard Business School Press, Cambridge.

Dell'Era, C. and Verganti, R. (2010). 'Collaborative strategies in design-intensive industries: knowledge diversity and innovation', *Long Range Planning, 43*(1), 123–141.

de Wit, J. and Zuidberg, J. (2012). 'The growth limits of the low-cost carrier model', *Journal of Air Transport Management, 21*, 17–23.

Dostaler, I. and Flouris, T. (2004) 'Business strategy and competition for the future of the airline industry', *Aerlines Magazine, e-zine edition, 28*, 1–3.

Ferreira, A. and Otley, D. (2009). 'The design and use of performance management systems: An extended framework for analysis', *Management Accounting Research, 20*(4), 263–282.

Francis, G., Humphreys, I., Ison, S., and Aicken, M. (2006). 'Where next for low-cost airlines? A spatial and temporal comparative study', *Journal of Transport Geography, 14*(2), 83–94.

Gilbert, D., Child, D., and Bennett, M. (2001). 'A qualitative study of the current practices of no frills airlines operating in the UK', *Journal of Vacation Marketing, 7*(4), 302–315.

Gittell, J. (2004). 'The Southwest Airlines Way: Using the power of relationships to achieve high performance', *Industrial and Labor Relations Review, 57*(3), 90–101.

Goldman, S. (1997). 'Asia airlines: Cycle what cycle?' *The Asian Regulatory Environment, 17*, 8–15.

Govindarajan, V. (1988). 'Approach to strategy implementation at the business-unit level: integrating administrative mechanisms with strategy', *Academy of Management Journal, 31*, 828–853.

Govindarajan, V. and Gupta, A.K. (1985). 'Linking control systems to business unit strategy: impact on performance', *Accounting, Organizations & Society, 10*(1), 51–66.

Kaplan, R.S. and Norton, D.P. (2008). 'Mastering the management system', *Harvard Business Review, 86*, 63–77.

Kim, W.C. and Mauborgne, R. (2005). *Blue Ocean Strategy: How to Create Uncontested Market Space and Make the Competition Irrelevant*. Harvard Business School Press, Cambridge.

Langfield-Smith, K. (1997). 'Management control systems and strategy: A critical review', *Accounting Organizations & Society, 22*(2), 207–232.

Langfield-Smith, K. (2007). 'A review of quantitative research in management control systems and strategy'. In: Chapman, C.S., Hopwood, A.G., Shields, M.D. (Eds.), *Handbook of Management Accounting Research*, vol. 2. Elsevier, Oxford, UK, pp. 753–784.

Lawson, T. (2005). 'When being the lowest cost is not enough: Building a successful low-fare airline model in Asia', *Journal of Air Transport Management, 24*, 119–132.

Lim, K., Mohamed, R., Ariffen, A., and Guan, G. (2009). 'Branding an Airline: A case study of AirAsia', *Malaysian Journal of Media Studies, 11*(1), 35–48.

Ocasio, W. and Joseph, J. (2008). 'Rise and fall – or transformation?: The evolution of strategic planning at the General Electric Company, 1940–2006', *Long Range Planning, 41*(3), 248–272.

O'Connell, J. and Williams, G. (2005). 'Passengers' perceptions of low-cost airlines and full-service carriers: A case study involving Ryanair, Aer Lingus, AirAsia and Malaysian Airlines', *Journal of Air Transport Management, 11*(4), 259–272.

Ong, W. and Tan, A. (2010). 'A note on the determinants of airline choice: The case of AirAsia and Malaysian Airlines', *Journal of Air Transport Management, 16*, 209–212.

Otley, D. (2012). 'Performance management under conditions of uncertainty: Some valedictory reflections', *Pacific Accounting Review, 24*(3), 247–261.

Owen, P. (2011). 'Flying high', *Engineering Insight, 12*(1), 20–22.
Ozdemir, E.D. and Mecikoglu, S. (2016). 'A case study on performance implications of hybrid strategy in Automotive Supplier Industry', *International Business Research, 9*(6), 31–43.
Porter, M. (1996). 'What is strategy?', *Harvard Business Review,* 61–78.
Quiggen, J. (1997). 'Evaluating airline deregulation in Australia', *The Australian Economic Review, 30*(1), 45–56.
Rivkan, J. (1997). 'Reproducing knowledge: Replication without imitation at moderate complexity', *Organisation Science, 12*(3), 274–294.
Rouse, P., Maguire, W., and Harrison, J. (2010), *Revenue Management in Service Organisations.* Business Expert Press, New York.
Sweeney, D. (1998). 'Global market trends in the networked era', *Long Range Planning, 31(*5), 672–683.
Sweeney, M. (1993). 'Strategic manufacturing management: Restructuring wasteful production to world class', *Journal of General Management, 18*(3), 57–76.
Sydney Morning Herald. (2010). www.smh.com.au/travel/travel-news/survival-in-the-skies-20101210–18sa0.html (accessed 14 November 2013).
Virgin Australia. (2011). Retrieved from www.virginaustralia.com/nz/en/about-us/company-overview/virgin-australia-history/ (Accessed 3 August 2012).
World Airline Awards. (2015). www.worldairlineawards.com/Awards/a_z_airline_winners.html (Accessed 4 May 2016).

19

Comparative insights into management control practices in two Sri Lankan banks in the public and private sectors

Tharusha Gooneratne and Zahirul Hoque

Introduction

The past several decades have seen an elevated interest in the design and operation of management control systems (MCS) in organizations in both the public and private sectors. Initial insights into management control date back to the pioneering work of Robert Anthony, whose classic definition was, 'management control is the process by which managers ensure that resources are obtained and used effectively and efficiently in the achievement of the organization's objectives' (Anthony, 1965, p. 27). Over the years, the notion of 'management control' has attracted a wide range of connotations and progressed amid the plethora of definitions. From a technical point of view, MCS are seen as analytical and calculative processes used to make decisions and achieve organizational objectives, which are focused on accounting-based controls such as budgeting (Otley, 1994, 1999). From a more contemporary sense, management control encapsulates not only formal, financially quantifiable information for managerial decision making; instead, it embraces broad-scope information with the emphasis on the entire organization and the longer term (Chenhall, 2003). Seen in this light, MCS are socially constructed phenomena within the particular context in which they operate, while being subject to wider social, economic and political pressures (Berry *et al.*, 1985). Such a view captures the interdisciplinary nature of management control and echoes that MCS cannot be seen purely as technically rational activities divorced from broad societal relationships or from the actions of actors and other forces. The current chapter shares such sentiments.

Quite apart from the above, a review of past MCS studies reveals that a relatively large body of research views management control from the eyes of the manufacturing sector (Abernethy & Lillis, 1995; Hoque & James, 2000), and that research confined to service organizations is rather limited (Chenhall, 2003; Lowry, 1990; Modell, 1996). In recent years, the service sector, especially the banking industry, has long been considered as an important vehicle for sustainable economic growth in developed and developing countries. This chapter seeks to contribute to the body of knowledge on MCS research drawing empirical evidence from the Sri Lankan banking arena. Even though the significance of banking operations is acknowledged, and control practices have become a central issue in the research agenda in management accounting, there are many unasked, unexplored or under-explored research questions in relation to the banking industry. Little is known about how management control is translated into practice in public- and private-sector commercial banks, and whether control practices in public-sector banks differ from those in the private sector. We aim to fill in this apparent gap in prior research using two commercial banks in Sri Lanka.

The open economic regime operating in Sri Lanka since 1977 enabled the private sector to play a more dynamic role in the economy as a whole, and in the sphere of commercial banking in particular. As for the commercial banking arena, the neo-liberalized era witnessed the entry of a number of foreign banks and domestic private banks to the industry. To keep up with this emerging competitive environment, state-owned banks focused on commercially oriented and customer-focused banking business, in addition to their customary social and development banking services geared towards local businesses and the rural community. Commercial banks occupy a predominant place in the Sri Lankan financial system (Dassanayake, 2000), and within the composition of the financial services sub-sector licensed commercial banks (LCBs) form the largest component. For a relatively small nation of 20 million people, Sri Lanka has a high number of LCBs, and the contemporary Sri Lankan banking industry represents an arena in which both public- and private-sector players are brought into a single competitive footing. One may claim that 'the industry is over-banked', although there is significant concentration. Among the 22 LCBs, only the six largest (two public and the 'big four' private) banks have established their presence across the entire nation, with most of the other banks operating only within the more economically prosperous areas.

The rest of the chapter is structured as follows. First, 'Status Quo of Management Control Research in the Banking Sector' provides a glimpse of the status quo of management control research in the banking sector by highlighting the insights from prior research and identifying gaps in extant literature. Then, 'Methodology' presents the methodology, while a comparative analysis capitalizing on field study evidence is offered in 'Towards a Comparative Analysis'. Finally, 'Research Implications and Conclusions' depicts the research implications, conclusions and contributions along with lessons and insights for practicing managers and corporate strategists of banks and other organizations.

Status quo of management control research in the banking sector

The current body of literature has seen the publication of several studies of management control in the banking arena. The works of Berry *et al.* (1991), Cobb *et al.* (1995), Helliar *et al.* (2002), Hussain and Hoque (2002), Norris (2002) and Soin *et al.* (2002) are significant here.[1] Despite the issues explored and the differing settings, they share the commonality of foregrounding control issues of banks.

In terms of topics, despite the focus on ABC (e.g. Innes & Mitchell, 1997; Norris, 2002; Soin *et al.*, 2002), surprisingly few prior attempts have been centred on the balanced scorecard (BSC) (see Aranda and Arellano, 2010; Braam & Nijssen, 2004; and Davis & Albright, 2004 for some exceptions). Further, notwithstanding the existence of several studies using multiple cases (McNamara & Mong, 2005, which encompasses two banks/a mobile telecommunication company; Hussain & Hoque, 2002 on four Japanese banks; Berry *et al.*, 1991, and Norris 2002 founded on the UK context), there is limited discussion of management accounting in banks involving a public- and private-sector comparison. Given the contextual differences, much could be added by focusing on this area. While a limited number of in-depth case studies exist, previous work has been set at a single level (e.g. branch, departmental or organizational). Contextually, the countries of origin of prior studies are diverse, primarily from the UK, with US, Italy, Finland, Sweden, Japan and Brazil, among others.

While such endeavours are worthy of respect, further research issues await to be explored within management accounting scholarship. For instance, the translation of management control into practice in public- and private-sector banks has not been the focus of prior attempts. Drawing empirical evidence from two comparative case studies (one of the two state-owned banks and one of the 'big four' private-sector banks) cascaded down to the Sri Lankan context for illustrative purposes, this chapter sheds light on how public- and private-sector commercial banks designed, operated and used formal MCS to manage their day-to-day operations. Although operating in the same industry, encountering a similar competitive landscape, there are inherent differences between the public and private sectors, and the working environments of the two banks are deemed to be different. Such differences are thought to have ramifications for MCS as well.

Methodology

This chapter delves into the dynamics of the formal control systems in place in the two banks, how key members in the institutional and organizational fields shape the design and operation of their control practices, to what extent the information generated by control systems meets the needs of external constituents and organizational managers at various hierarchical levels, and to what extent the institutional differences between the two distinct sectors, public and private, produce differences in MCS. These deliberations are explored using the Sri Lankan banking context for illustration, and leaning primarily on the theoretical templates of actor-network theory (ANT), supplemented by new institutional sociology (NIS). ANT[2] is used to explore how the design and operation of MCS are shaped by actions of key actors and the relational networks formed therein, while the NIS perspective is used to understand how various isomorphic pressures drive organizations to implement and use a particular control system (DiMaggio & Powell, 1983; in accounting research, see e.g. Carpenter & Feroz, 1992, 2001; Covaleski & Dirsmith, 1986, 1988a, b, 1991; Shapiro & Matson, 2008). By drawing insights from the theories of ANT and NIS, which complement each other (see Hoque *et al.*, 2013), this chapter shows how the dual facets, internal actor-networks (micro) and external institutional influences such as government regulation, mimic forces and normative pressures (macro) are intertwined in the formation, operation and use of MCS.

Data collection was conducted in two phases: (i) a pilot study and (ii) a main study. An interview guide (see Appendix 19.1) was formulated with some open-ended questions covering broad areas of interest such as historical and background knowledge of the two banks, their processes, and nature of their MCS. This was used in the pilot study. As the study progressed in the main stage, these interview questions were continually refined to capture emerging issues at the two sites. What emerged from the pilot study interview data was that in Bank Alpha budgeting remained the solitary means of management control, and that Bank Omega had moved through several phases of management control. Accordingly, during the main phase in Bank Alpha, questions were aimed at uncovering budgetary control practices, and in Bank Omega, the interviews mainly revolved around identifying the rationale for changing forms of management control.

The data were mainly gathered via in-depth interviews with people drawn from diverse portfolios (including accounting, marketing, human resources and operations) as well as different hierarchical levels in the corporate ladder (such as senior management, regional/area managers, branch managers and functional managers) across different locations (at head office, regional/area offices, branches). Across the pilot and the main studies, 31 interviews at Bank Alpha and 30 interviews at Bank Omega were conducted. Complementary to these interviews, several officials in external institutions related to banking such as the Central Bank of Sri Lanka (CBSL) and the Institute of Bankers of Sri Lanka (IBSL) were also contacted. As emerged from these interviews, their influence on management control of commercial banks is marginal. Nevertheless, these discussions facilitated obtaining important information regarding the nature of the industry, regulation, policy issues, competition among commercial banks and insights into comparison of public versus private.

Interview data were supplemented by perusal of various documents. This ranged from annual reports and web pages of the two banks and press releases to an array of internal documents, such as monthly management accounts, internal memos, office instruction circulars, budget procedures, variance analysis reports, board papers, annual budget, corporate plan, branch performance report, expenditure report and BSC reports. Further, libraries of the CBSL and IBSL were visited and an analysis of related documents, banking magazines, journals and books was carried out.

The next section offers a comparative analysis capitalizing on evidence from the two banks.

Towards a comparative analysis

The focal point of this section is to tease out the similarities and differences in control practices in terms of design and operation issues, their uses, as well as mapping out the present focus and future route to MCS in the two banks.[3] It sheds light on questions such as

- How has the contextual variance between public and private influenced control practices?
- To what extent do organizational actors in different stratus of management and external institutional forces influence control practices?
- Does traditional budgetary control gain a prominent foothold in organizational planning, controlling and decision making processes?
- Does budgetary control give way to more contemporary strategic performance measurement systems such as the BSC, or do traditional budgeting practices become interwoven with contemporary techniques?

The selection of these two banks is justifiable given their significant presence in the commercial banking industry of Sri Lanka, as two of the six largest players. They operate under common traditions and concerns, within the same regulated banking environment in Sri Lanka, encountering a similar competitive landscape. Nevertheless, there are inherent differences in the organizational and institutional environments, as one (Bank Alpha) is in the public sector, while the other (Bank Omega) is in the private sector.[4] As a state-owned bank, Bank Alpha confronts the task of balancing the multiple aims of maintaining profitability, serving the community and contributing to national economic development. As a private-sector bank, Bank Omega is driven primarily by the profit motive (maximizing shareholders' wealth), although it also contributes to the national economic development via paying taxes and generating employment. A salient feature that distinguishes the two cases is therefore their ownership structure. Contrasts are also evident in the areas of human resources, trade union influences, decision making and customers' perceptions. Given such differences, how MCS function in public- and private-sector banks within their broader social and institutional environments is the focus of this section.

A snapshot view of the comparative findings that emerged through data collected via 67 in-depth interviews (with various managers across different strata of the two banks and key informants from external institutions pertinent to the banking industry) and documentary analysis is shown in Table 19.1 and discussed in turn.

Control mechanisms deployed

Table 19.1 depicts the similarities and differences between the control mechanisms of the two banks. Bank Alpha shows how a budgeting system could encounter gradual improvements, whereas Bank Omega portrays how management control could be a cyclical process, moving through budgeting and BSC, undergoing a series of distinct phases.

In the early stages, Bank Alpha was attuned to comparing its performance against the prior year on an ad hoc basis, with a view to improving the previous year's results. With the accelerated competition in the 1980s, however, the bank was under pressure to improve its efficiencies, towards which goal an important response was the launch of the budgetary control system. Since then, it has progressed with incremental improvements in design, operation and uses, due to the efforts of members of the finance and planning division. Budgets add to the regime of command and control culture, and constrain freedom and autonomy, which is typical in the public sector, and evidently in Alpha.

Bank Omega originally set its sights on management control through traditional budgeting (phase one in Table 19.1). After recognizing the pitfalls of this financial performance-based MCS (budgeting system), it later shifted to a BSC in the belief that it would yield benefits, as demonstrated in numerous studies.[5] The receptiveness of key personnel to new techniques became a further compelling reason. The BSC was the main control mechanism during phase two. It evolved under the patronage of the ex-MD and the expertise of a renowned foreign consultant in the business of the BSC. For the ex-MD, the BSC project was seen as a sound choice for producing better performance management, and engagement of a major international consultant was paramount in bonding others towards it. The implementation of a new management technique is a costly exercise (McCunn, 1998; Rigby, 2001), requiring top management support and generous resources (Hoque, 2003; Kasurinen, 2002), and the ex-MD was willing to make this investment.

Budgetary control coexisted during phase two, although became secondary to the BSC, and served as an aid to it. This also shows that while some organizations (such as Alpha) may opt for a single control mechanism (such as budgeting), others (such as Omega) may deploy multiple means (such as budgeting and BSC). In the event there are multiple control systems, it is important that there is coherence between the BSC and other systems (such as budgetary control) and that the messages conveyed are consistent. Although hailed as a masterpiece with the blessing of the ex-MD, the reign of the BSC was short lived. For a control system such as BSC to be tenable, the underpinning actor-network needs a certain level of take-up where apathy, resistance and dissent are overcome, and various interests of actors intersect (Latour, 1996). In Bank Omega, this occurred only in the short term. In the long term, the organization moved back to budgeting, given its members' resistance to the BSC and as desired by new entrants to top management. That step heralded phase three of management control. This sequence reinforces the contention that controls introduced for rational economic purposes can evolve into very different purposes, accompanying various issues

Table 19.1 Comparative findings of management control in Bank Alpha and Bank Omega

				Design and operation of management control				
Bank	*Phase*	*Period*	*Control mechanisms in place*	*Key internal actors*	*Key external forces*	*Use of management control information*	*Current status*	*Future direction*
Bank Alpha	No clear phases or periods of MCS, control mechanisms progressed through gradual improvements		Budgetary control	DGM–Finance and Planning, AGM–Budget and Strategic Planning, Manager–Budgetary Control	Coercive pressures (compliance with state policy), normative influences (ICASL, local universities)	Budgets used for external legitimacy and for internal management control at the top management level (partial use diagnostically and interactively)	Dominance of traditional budgeting	Refinements to budgetary control and a possible shift to BSC
Bank Omega	Phase One	Inception to 2003	Budgetary control	Manager–Finance	Normative influences (local universities)	Ad hoc use of budgets for internal management control (partial use diagnostically)	Dominance of traditional budgeting	Refinements to budgetary control and a possible shift to the BSC
	Phase Two	2004 to 2008	Mainly BSC, secondarily Budgetary control	Former MD, Strategic Planner, foreign consultant	Normative influences (BSC diffusion programs, academic and professional bodies)	Mainly BSC used for internal management control (partial use diagnostically and interactively)		
	Phase Three	2009 to date	Budgetary control	CFO, Manager–Finance, Manager–Planning	Mimic behaviour (ex-employer of CFO)	Budgeting used for internal control (partial use diagnostically and interactively)		

(Wickramasinghe *et al.*, 2004), and that conflicting interests and values can lay technologies open to challenge and transformation. Hence, no solution (for example a control system) becomes permanent, as some prominent managers can exert influence more effectively than others at various periods. Design and operation of control systems in the two banks are the focus of the next section.

Design and operation issues

Important differences were found in the areas of design and operation of MCS in the two banks. As a state-owned enterprise (SOE), Bank Alpha typically used formal systems and procedures, which were extended to the accounting arena for budget designs. Although such a formal structure existed on paper, actual practice did not fully resemble it. Budget preparation deadlines were not rigorously enforced, and not all managers enthusiastically contributed towards the budgetary process. Apart from this, its budget design was subject to coercive isomorphic pressures from the owner/government, due to external legitimacy concerns (DiMaggio & Powell, 1983).

In sharp contrast, as typical to the private sector, Bank Omega exhibited fewer restrictions and its board of directors was at liberty to make its own decisions, including in accounting-related matters. In the absence of specified procedures supported by documentary evidence, its MCS design featured changing forms across time, as desired by powerful actors such as the former MD and the current CFO. Under the previous management, the MD (himself an accountant) had been instrumental in forming control practices in the bank. Not only did he initiate the BSC, it took shape as he intended. On the other hand, the budgetary control system prevalent from 2009 mirrored the aspirations of the CFO.

Of further interest, the case data exhibited how academic and professional backgrounds of key actors in finance and planning areas were instrumental in shaping MCS in the two banks. In Bank Alpha, the advocates of budgeting such as DGM–Finance and Planning, AGM–Budget and Strategic Planning and Manager–Budgetary Control were chartered accountants, members of the Institute of Chartered Accountants of Sri Lanka (ICASL), and/or holders of accounting/business degrees from local universities. The CFO and the Manager–Finance of Omega, also promoters of budgeting, were business graduates from local universities. This was at variance with the background of the champions of its BSC project, the ex-MD and the ex-Strategic Planner. While the former possessed the Chartered Institute of Management Accountants (CIMA) and ICASL qualifications, the latter held multidisciplinary skills with qualifications in marketing, banking, MBA, in addition to a local university degree. This raised the following questions: are the management faculties of *local* universities and the main *local* professional accounting body (ICASL) diffusing the same message that budgeting should predominate? In contrast, did the CIMA qualification of the ex-MD, and the multidisciplinary skills of the ex-Strategic Planner motivate them to look beyond budgeting? The situation also showed how normative influences from academic and professional institutions can become intertwined with actors' deliberations, as academic and professional backgrounds of key organization members were instrumental in shaping management control into their various forms in the two banks.

The budgeting system held different degrees of importance for different managers of Alpha, as the two groups, members of finance and planning and the branch/area managers, had opposing priorities. In the eyes of the former, it was of utmost importance. As the coordinators of the process, the overall responsibility for budgets was vested in their hands. They exhibited a deep-seated interest, as coming up with a 'good' budget was a medium to demonstrate their worth and to shine among peers. For the latter, smooth running of the branch/area took precedence over budgets. Although accustomed to the term 'budget', they did not necessarily share positive sentiments nor did they extend full efforts towards the budgetary process. Exacerbating this situation was their lack of budgeting expertise, as many had secured their positions through seniority (experience) rather than academic merit. While branch managers lacked deep understanding to formulate a good budget, area managers had inadequate knowledge to perform a proper review of it. Notwithstanding the availability of local information at the branch level, it is debatable to what extent such insights were reflected in the budget. The reality was that the branch managers created *something* in the name of *budget* ritualistically because they *had to do so* and forwarded it to their superiors (area managers), which got passed on to the next level without any value addition. Although budget results are suggested as a better basis for evaluating performance than past results, over three decades ago Wildavsky (1979) remarked that the largest determining factor of the size and content of a year's budget is the previous year. Similarly, budgeting at the branch and area levels turned out to be constructed incrementally, proceeding from a historical base.

The low interest of the branch/area managers also does not come as a surprise as although they were expected to give input, the budget ultimately imposed was that desired by the head office (finance and planning). This at times turned out to be wholly different from that initiated at the local level, as the centralized 'top-down' budgeting system handed power to the finance and planning division to *cut and chop resource allocations* as well as to *enhance budget targets*. While claims were made that the head office 'always increases targets', certain others were of the view that the head office 'simply does not accept the branch budget'. A few others maintained that rather than being mutually agreed the budget targets were imposed in an autocratic fashion with branches not consulted in the process. Such negative sentiments, although not shared by all, were expressed rather strongly by some. Conceptually, although the structure was in place, thorough engagement of various managers was not visible in Bank Alpha. Faced with such a scenario, observed practice was that the budgeting tasks were vested in the hands of accountants in the head office. This was nevertheless interpreted by some as 'control' rather than 'coordination' of the budget.

Differences existed between the words of accounting and non-accounting managers regarding the 'control role' of the finance and planning division. In contrast to the view of certain branch managers, members of finance and planning described their grounds for altering the budget 'as coordinators of the process', in recognition of the need to fall in line with government expectations and management pressure for higher achievement. Despite such rationales, the head office 'coordinated' or 'controlled' budget attracted minimum attention from branch/area managers as well as from functional heads, who interpreted that it was in the 'powerful hands of finance and planning people'. Nevertheless, across the bank budgeting was accepted as a fact of life and a taken-for-granted course of action.

In Bank Omega, a BSC operated under the previous management. Various managers were brought into the BSC system through compulsion rather than any convincing logic, and it was not powerful enough to bind these various actors to launch a successful scorecard for long-term sustainability. If the underlying actor-network holds, the technologies (in this instance the BSC technology) would continue across time and space (Latour, 1987). However, Bank Omega's BSC found little resonance beyond the early network. Instead, a budgeting network is currently taking shape, led by the new CFO; time will tell its fate. Tensions between these networks were manifested in the words of various managers.

Literature has indicated that the design and operation of accounting systems carry implications for ensuing power relations among managers (Abernethy & Vagnoni, 2004;

Christiansen & Skærbæk, 1997; Hopper & Major, 2007), as became evident through the budgeting and BSC systems in the case banks. The disparity in the constitution of the finance and planning function is noteworthy here. In Bank Alpha, the economic research division was engaged in the macro-economic analysis connected to the preparation of the corporate plan and the budget. Management control and therefore the design and operation of budgets were handled by the finance and planning division, more specifically unified in the hands of a budgetary control unit within it. The tasks carried out by the economic research division and the finance and planning division were dissimilar and non-overlapping, and that mitigates any avenues for power struggles.

On the other hand, within Bank Omega in the initial stages (late 1980s to early 1990s), management control had a low priority. Later on (in 1996), while the (current) Manager–Finance was put in charge of management control, he instigated enhancements to control mechanisms (budgeting), learned from his accounting studies at a local university. Nevertheless, the introduction of the BSC in phase two not only brought in new calculable spaces, but it also altered the existing power relations of actors. While the BSC became a main concern for the management, especially for the ex-MD, as its facilitator the Strategic Planner gained supremacy vis-à-vis the Manager–Finance. During this era, the two divisions, strategic planning and finance, were in command of budgeting at various times, as directed by the management. Therefore, issues cropped up relating to 'who does what' at different occasions in time. The finance and planning function scattered across several divisions leading to overlapping tasks and role ambiguity was at the heart of such (implicit) struggles. In phase three not only was the BSC abandoned, but also the ex-Strategic Planner was moved off the finance and planning arena; a *new* planning department was established and budgeting was assigned to the finance division, although temporarily. These structural changes created a tacit form of power struggle between the ex-Strategic Planner and the *new* Manager–Planning, as well as between the ex-Strategic Planner and the Manager–Finance.

Organizational control systems, such as budgeting and BSC, are implemented by managers who occupied significant positions in organizations, and negotiated their interests to build alliances to support their beliefs. Only a budgeting network existed in Bank Alpha. Both a budgeting and BSC network were seen in Bank Omega, instigated from different agendas of different managers, who strove to tie other actors to relational networks of support. Whereas the budgeting network survived, the BSC network was obstructed by other managers who did not buy into that idea, as the solidification of a MCS such as budgeting or BSC is linked to the ways in which an organization's insiders avoid controversy and conflict, and draw support from key others. Bank Omega's BSC episode reflected a problem in bringing various managers on board and the ensuing silent struggle between its advocates in strategic planning at one end, and branch, regional managers and departmental heads at the other. For the former, BSC was a way to expand their empire and proclaim their worth; for the latter, the key concern was the business of banking, and plausibly the BSC was met with a low level of acceptance. Strategic planning operated in a separate territory with its own distinct identity, promulgating slogans such as *beyond budgeting* and *strategy focused organization*. Between these territories, rivalries existed, as evident in their body language.

Control systems get transformed as desired by powerful managers (the former MD and the current CFO), who maintained their version of what was apt in terms of management control (BSC and budgeting, respectively). The enthusiasm of the ex-MD gave rise to the BSC; his disappearance and the appearance of a CFO who displayed faint interest in the BSC contributed to its subsequent fall. This gave way to a budgeting system borrowed from the ex-employer of the CFO, exhibiting strong mimicry behaviour. Sustainability of a particular

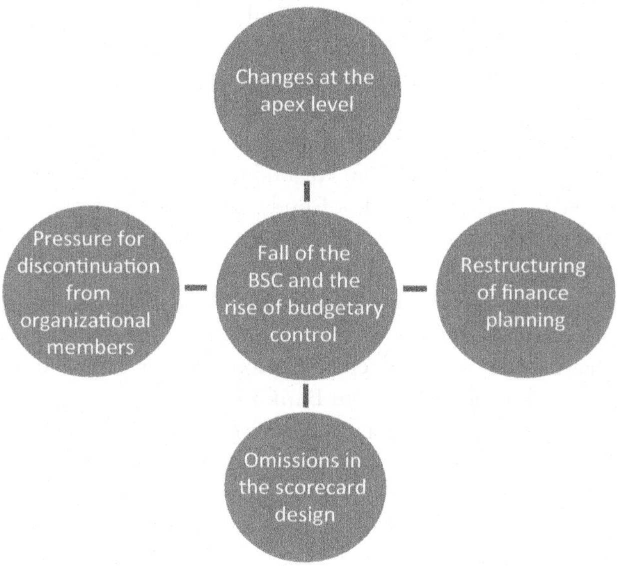

Figure 19.1 **Observed reasons behind the fall of the Balanced Scorecard and the rise of budgetary control**

MCS would depend on the efforts and power of the proponents of the various MCS. In Bank Omega, apart from the advocates of the BSC, other managers constituted a force in the opposite direction for its discontinuation, and proposing budgetary control, which became more powerful over time. To revitalize management control in the bank and to move forward, it was recognized that a department by the name of planning was needed. With the backdrop of strained relationships, to regain organizational-wide acceptance, the finance and planning function was restructured. In the restructure, a manager aligned to the thinking of the CFO was brought in and the Strategic Planner was moved off the territory of finance and planning. Four dimensions have emerged as critical to understanding the demise of the scorecard and the rise of budgeting, as presented in Figure 19.1.

To sum up, amid its inability to reconcile the viewpoints of diverse managers and technical flaws in the design, the BSC network in Bank Omega was not sustained. Exacerbating this, it did not accommodate the interest of the dominant new entrant, the CFO, who provided an alternative advocating the current budgeting system, which was more powerful than that of promoters of the BSC. It was also more appealing to the interests of the majority of branch/regional and functional managers, who were unconvinced about the merits of the BSC and hence dissociated from the BSC network. The BSC thus represents a project in decline and has come to resemble 'a utopia in the etymological sense, like an idea that has no place to land' (Latour, 1996, p. 120).

Use of management control information

From the standpoint of use, management control information is used by organizations to legitimize their existence via conformity to institutional rules and norms, and internally as a tool for organizational managers. Budgetary control system of Bank Alpha serves these dual roles; First, as typical to a large SOE, it created budget numbers to satisfy external legitimacy requirements (of the government) and meet societal expectations (as a SOE) by portraying a positive public image to outside constituents (DiMaggio & Powell, 1983; Meyer & Rowan, 1977). As depicted in Figure 19.2, not only is Bank Alpha required to provide information for the national budget, once it is prepared, it needs to fall in line with government's development initiatives, make allocations for social responsibility activities and offer concessions to the economy, which have ramifications for budgeting. Prior public-sector literature has highlighted this external legitimacy role of budgets (Ansari & Euske, 1987; Covaleski & Dirsmith, 1983, 1988a, 1991).

Second, the budgeting system serves strategic planning and controlling decisions of managers at the apex level through gradual improvements initiated by the finance and planning division, by way of regular budgetary reports and management forums. Meyer and Rowan (1977) suggested that coexistence of efficiency and institutional pressures could give rise to possible contradictions. Yet, field data from Bank Alpha have shown that its budgeting system served to legitimize the organization to its external constituents, while serving the quest for internal decision making at the top management level. This signals the significant use of budgetary control information, beyond a symbol of external legitimacy.

Paradoxically, despite their extensive use as an internal decision-making tool at the top management level, budgets became a less attractive tool at the practice level, as area/branch managers and functional heads of Bank Alpha did not actively participate in the budgeting network. In their minds, budgeting was of little use in everyday banking operations. Any use made of budgetary figures appeared to be of passive and ritualistic nature, to abide by top management (head office) directions by filling in routine budget reports, while they relied on experience and gut feeling in decision making at the local level.

A different scenario was observed in Bank Omega. As a private-sector entity, it had no statutory obligation to submit regulatory information to the state; its management control data generated through budgets, and the BSC was hardly used for external legitimacy, although it was extensively used internally.

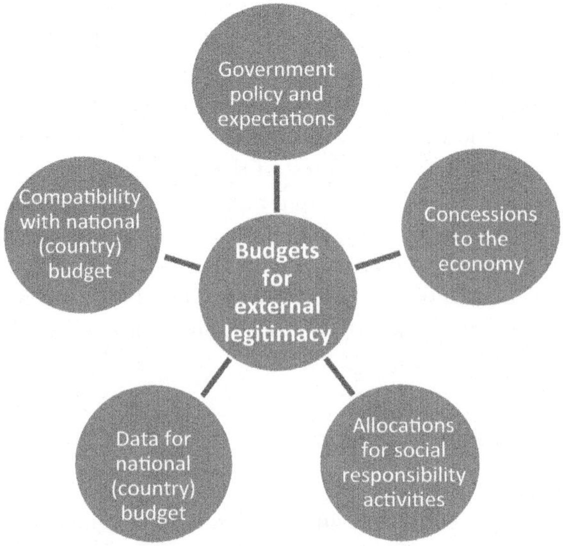

Figure 19.2 Budgets for external legitimacy: Bank Alpha

In terms of internal use, the uses of MCS are twofold: diagnostic and interactive (Simons, 2000). In Banks Alpha and Omega in their glory days, the MCS exhibited some form of these dual uses for the senior management, through various management control reports and performance review presentations. In Bank Alpha, while the monthly and quarterly budgetary control reports served diagnostic control purposes, the quarterly budget review presentation was of an interactive nature. In Bank Omega, the ad hoc budget reports generated in the early days were geared towards diagnostic use. In the second phase, the monthly performance monitoring via the BSC by the Strategic Planner mirrored connections to diagnostic orientation, while the BSC presentations to corporate management featured some ties to interactive use. In the latest scenario, the monthly and quarterly budget reports represented a degree of diagnostic use, and the extensive quarterly budget forum was to an extent of an interactive nature.

The field evidence indicated that the use of MCS was, however, fragmented in both banks. MCS was not linked to individual performance, nor were promotions correlated to target achievements; hence, there was a lack of penalty for under-achievement, which diminished the diagnostic use of MCS. Further, the two banks did not endorse that management control data became a means for continual challenge and debate, as at the MCS presentations managers simply accepted the wisdom of the top management and the finance division rather than questioning them. This diminished use of MCS interactively. Seen in this light in both banks, MCS had not reached the level of a complete diagnostic and interactive method.

Prior research has noted that the use of management control ranges from mostly diagnostic to a combination of diagnostic and interactive (Henri, 2006). Likewise, Bank Alpha initially used budgeting as a diagnostic control tool for top management and over time also as an interactive control tool through the quarterly review presentations. In Bank Omega, the ad hoc budget reports in phase one, where actual results were measured, compared with budgets, and corrective action was prescribed, represented solely diagnostic use. The subsequent use of control information for managerial decision making through the BSC and budgeting in phases two and three, respectively, resembled a combination of diagnostic and interactive uses. Complementary use of these dual levers of control such as observed in the two case banks has been advanced by a number of past researchers (Henri, 2006; Tuomela, 2005; Widener, 2007). For Henri (2006), diagnostic and interactive uses of management control represent complementary and nested functions, which need to be used jointly to manage inherent organizational tension between the freedom to innovate and predictable goal achievement. In a Finnish case study, Tuomela (2005) reported on the diagnostic and interactive use of the BSC. Widener (2007), who drew survey data from 122 CFOs, highlighted the need to use performance measurement systems both diagnostically and interactively to realize their full benefits. Diagnostic control systems facilitate the efficient use of management attention, while interactive systems consume management attention (Widener, 2007). In the two banks under study, while the monthly budget/variance reports to the board provided a snapshot view of performance, and became a means to track, review and support the achievement of predetermined goals, the quarterly presentation was time-consuming, given its focus towards discussion between managers. The findings presented here also correspond to the views of Henri, who claimed that these twin uses work simultaneously, but for different purposes.

Striking similarities in the uses of MCS are also visible in these two cases as follows: (a) there was an interplay between the uses of MCS information from an internal front, both diagnostically and interactively; (b) MCS use began as a diagnostic tool and later developed to both a diagnostic and an interactive tool; and (c) such use had limits.

To recap, the foregoing comparative analysis suggests that the procedural nature of the public-sector bank prompted laid down procedures for budget designs, whereas the absence of strict procedures meant that control systems in the private-sector bank were designed and operated as desired by its top management. The diverse use of management control information in the two sites was again partly attributable to the differences in the institutional settings, such as the dual use, external and internal in the former, compared to only internal use in the latter. It is also worthwhile to note here that the circumstances that led to such differences in MCS, apart from contextual variances between public and private, were also due to the deliberations of powerful organizational members and the alliances formed.

Current focus and future agenda

Although the differences form the main stream of this comparative analysis, there are also visible commonalities amid these differences. The current status in both banks resembles the dominance of budgeting, while their future directions rest on refinements to budgetary control and a possible shift to the BSC, as turned to next.

Reinforcing the sentiment that 'although sometimes criticized as being 'past its sell-by date', budgetary control systems still provide a unique contribution to the assessment of overall performance at the aggregate level' (Otley, 2006, p. 305), budgetary control occupies centre stage in both banks. Yet the events and conditions that led to this scenario in the two cases differ. In the absence of contemporary techniques, such as BSC being implemented in its entire history, budgetary control in Bank Alpha evolved through incremental improvements over a period of around three decades under the coordination and control of the finance and planning division. In Bank Omega, budgeting regained ascendancy following an unsuccessful BSC episode, and given the ideology of the new and powerful actor, the CFO. As a champion of budgeting, his pathway to success, to be in line with the bank's more successful competitor, his former employer, lay in a *simple* budgeting system.

All in all, one of the most intriguing themes to emerge through this comparative analysis is that budgetary control plays a pivotal role in the organizational landscape. This leads one to reflect on why it is so persistent. At this juncture, it's appropriate to quote from Wildavsky:

> Every criticism of traditional budgeting is undoubtedly correct. It is incremental rather than comprehensive; it fragments decisions, usually making them piecemeal; it is heavily historical, looking backward more than forward; it is indifferent about objective. Why, then has traditional budgeting lasted so long? My answer is: because it has the virtues of its own defects.
>
> *(Wildavsky, 1986, p. 327)*

In common with Wildavsky (1986), Bank Alpha attributed merits such as simplicity, easiness, controllability and flexibility to the continuity of traditional budgeting. Similar justifications favouring budgeting were offered by those opposing the BSC and proposing budgeting in Bank Omega. This analysis reinforces the contention that the answer to the question 'is the annual budget really dead?' (Ekholm & Wallin, 2000) is negative.

Despite the above, amid criticisms about budgeting as an 'unnecessary evil' (Wallander, 1999), and calls for 'beyond budgeting' (Hope & Fraser, 2000), two trends have emerged: (1) incremental improvements to budgeting, and (2) the use of alternative techniques such as the BSC. Interestingly, in parallel with such sentiments, further enhancements towards better budgeting, and a probable move to the BSC, were on the future agenda of both banks. The discussion to follow sheds light on this.

Apart from the current powerful presence of budgetary control, the desire to continue with it in the future was echoed by members at the apex level of the case banks, who stated that they intended to continue with budgetary control, albeit with potential refinements. For instance, both banks were working their way towards introducing an individual performance-based reward system. Nevertheless, respecting such efforts, it is claimed that none of better budgeting approaches provides a complete solution (Neely *et al.*, 2003), and arguably the BSC has 'something to offer' (Otley, 1994). In a similar vein, encouraged by the recent successful completion of its computerization project, several senior members of Bank Alpha pronounced their receptiveness towards new control tools such as the BSC. At Bank Omega, although the BSC has currently been shelved, some senior officials expressed interest in reintroducing it in the future.

A common ground is thus visible with the two banks contemplating a possible shift to the BSC in the future. Perhaps it is premature to pass judgment on this, and it remains to be seen whether it will materialize. It nevertheless lends support to previous research that has suggested that organizations need to augment the budget process with other approaches (Libby & Lindsay, 2010), and it reflects the growing receptiveness to movements such as beyond budgeting (Neely *et al.*, 2003). If this happened, for Bank Alpha, it would be perceived as a move towards a *better and a balanced* mode of control. For Bank Omega, it ought to be a *better BSC, a development over its former version*. Arguably, management control is a cyclical process moving through various modes of control. This seems justifiable as long as the lapses in previous phases are ironed out in the spirit of continuous improvement and better control is achieved. The cyclical nature is especially evident within the backdrop of today's severe competition and rapidly changing business environment, where a given state of a practice, including MCS, cannot be taken as optimal. It also reinforces that accounting is not a static phenomenon (see Hopwood, 1987).

The preceding comparative analysis offers extensions, complementary and conflicting insights into MCS in the two banks. BSC was claimed as a development (extension) over budgeting, and management control in Bank Omega extended a step further to the BSC. Complementarity was evident as the status quo in both banks demonstrated dominance of budgeting, and the future direction rests on further improvements to budgets and a probable move to the BSC. Differences occurred to the extent that Bank Alpha exhibited solely budgetary control, whereas Bank Omega featured dual modes of control, budgeting and BSC. Thus, beneath the facade of diversity, there was also an element of unity between the MCS in these two comparative cases.

Research implications and conclusions

This comparative analysis carries academic merit as well as practical relevance. Next, we turn to the important research implications it offers to literature, practice and future research, while ending with concluding remarks.

Implications to theory and literature

Theoretically, this research is inserted within two streams of literature, principally ANT with additional insights drawn from NIS. By combining actors' engagement with broader institutional concerns, the research illustrates how these dual theories together offer wider insights into the dynamics of management control in the banking setting. As the main theoretical lens of the study, ANT was useful in providing explanations of how powerful actors and the relational networks formed therein shaped control mechanisms (see Alcouffe *et al.*, 2008; Sandhu *et al.*, 2008 among others). However, ANT needed extension to incorporate the external institutional pressures (such as coercive, mimic and normative) that influence MCS. In this regard, NIS was instrumental (DiMaggio & Powell, 1983). For Bank Alpha, a SOE, coercive influences from the government became significant in budget design, and budgetary control information was significant as an external legitimacy device. In Bank Omega, the BSC project was subjected to normative advice from consultants and professional associations, and the current budgetary system exhibited mimetic behaviour on the part of the CFO to copy his ex-employer bank. Therefore, the design, operation and use of MCS in the case banks were not solely attributable to actions of actors; instead, an array of external institutional forces also became relevant. This chapter thus forms a possible dialogue between ANT and NIS, and shows that the two theories complement each other (also see Hoque *et al.*, 2013), and how integration of actors' deliberations with external institutional pressures is tenable.

This chapter, while specifically located within the budgeting and BSC literature, contributes to management accounting scholarship in a number of ways. It enhances understanding of the functioning of budgeting and BSC in business organizations. The level of concern about budgeting in practice suggests its potential for continual scholarly research. Although organizational budgeting practices have been extensively studied over the past several decades (e.g. Christiansen & Skærbæk, 1997; Hoque & Hopper, 1994; Tsamenyi *et al.*, 2002), what makes this study noteworthy is that it provides empirical evidence as to the predominance of budgeting, despite the presence of new MCS. This is important in the contemporary corporate arena that is bombarded with fashionable management techniques such as the BSC.

As for the BSC, prior studies have focused mainly on its technical properties (see Malmi, 2001; Nørreklit, 2000), and several have adopted large-scale, survey-based methods (see Hoque & James, 2000; Speckbacher *et al.*, 2003). In contrast, this chapter has shown how meanings attached to the BSC and the form it takes are the result of the interplay between heterogeneous actors, networks formed and external institutional forces within particular contexts. Such a contextually rich explanation of the research phenomenon has theoretical value (Vaivio, 2007). In terms of use, this chapter extends the results of past researchers on the dual use of MCS, diagnostically and interactively in tandem (Henri, 2006; Tuomela, 2005; Widener, 2007).

Practical implications

To articulate the differences in control practices and to derive lessons therefrom, although this study has garnered evidence from two Sri Lankan banks, of which the precise circumstances are unique, the similarities and differences observed in the design, operation and use of control systems carry wider practical implications. At the level of practice, this research thus provides a number of pointers as to how control systems can be developed and practised through mechanisms such as budgeting and BSC, and establishes some lessons which are likely to be relevant to practicing managers and corporate strategists of not only banks but also of other organizations.

Despite its high profile in academic and professional circles, the BSC was not sustained at Bank Omega. The field encounters portrayed how the BSC, which was at one point perceived as a *useful technology*, later became a *problematic technology*. Organizations often embrace Western management techniques such as the BSC, backed by powerful internal actors and the facilitation of reputed external consultants. Similarly, the top management of the bank approached the technique of BSC in the belief that it could be successfully implemented if sufficient effort was mobilized and if the *correct* path was followed. This view, however, proved illusory, and the story of the BSC of Bank Omega was essentially a tale of failure. This has direct practical relevance. It illustrates that in the absence of effective change management, techniques like BSC will not be sustained, and that concepts proposed in practitioner-oriented normative literature, although seemingly attractive, can be problematic when striving to make them operable and can turn into unpredictable pathways. There is often a gulf between the theoretical merits and practical implementation experiences of such techniques (Hope & Fraser, 2000), and the theoretical merits are not always realized in practice. The case of Bank Omega has rediscovered this. Despite the initial enthusiasm, the BSC was not implemented in a way that was desirable or aligned to the expectations of branch/regional and functional managers within the particular setting of the bank. The BSC has been withdrawn, and the bank has now bounced back to a budgetary control system. Hope and Fraser argued that most scorecards collide rather than connect with the budgetary system; arguably this was so in Bank Omega. Possibly as a result of such collision, the BSC departed and budgeting was sustained. If there was a real connection, both devices could have prevailed in the long term.

This chapter confirms some known behavioural consequences of implementing new tools, and reminds practicing managers that adequate planning *beyond the technical* is needed to reduce dysfunctional effects, such as non-cooperative behaviour and resistance to change. It suggests that rather than being fascinated by new tools, attention needs to be on the *mode of implementation* as suited to the idiosyncrasies of the organizational context as implementation of new techniques gets transformed into different forms in different contexts.

There is also a prevalent view that it is impossible to predict the value of the BSC before its implementation (Ahn, 2001), and that no simple delineation exists of the achievement or failure of such a program. Like any other new technology, the BSC needs to be assessed for its capabilities in each scenario (Andon *et al.*, 2005), and once embarked upon, its actual implementation and use tend to be a balancing act between different conflicting interests and dilemmas (Johanson *et al.*, 2006). The BSC may attract unease and doubt, and is unlikely to be imported in ready-made textbook form. Rather than imposing the orthodox BSC model, it needs to be made to work in a particular context. The shift from traditional (budgeting) to contemporary (BSC) modes of management control in Bank Omega was planned to enhance organizational effectiveness. However, the BSC project became problematic in the particular context of Bank Omega. If Western management techniques are to be infused into a local setting, it is necessary to examine their suitability, as they may lack universal validity across different cultures. Uncritical acceptance of such concepts may contradict deeply embedded viewpoints of the local social system (Nanayakkara, 1992, 1997), and the original BSC framework might therefore need to be amended during implementation to suit local conditions. This is a lesson for organizations embarking on such projects, across the world.

Implications for future research

This study could be extended along several dimensions. First, it would have been preferable to have more cases, and potential researchers might be inspired to do so. While this research drew from the Sri Lankan context for illustrative purposes, it opens up concomitant scope for future researchers to explore how these findings could be replicated in other settings (see Vaivio, 2007) in the realm of banking and beyond. Second, although the insights afforded by the two cases suggested that implementation of MCS is a cyclical process, as this study was limited by time constraints, the on-going negotiations and bargaining could not be observed over time. Extending the study chronologically would provide scope for future research to cast further light on this cyclical process. Third, evidence presented here has highlighted how budgeting practices become intertwined with contemporary techniques such as BSC, and how budgetary control maintains a prominent foothold in organizations. Future researchers are thus encouraged to look at the interplay between budgeting and BSC in banks as well as other organizations. This would deepen understanding of the functioning of single versus multiple forms of management control. Fourth, the analysis in this chapter was focused primarily at the organizational level, i.e. how control was exercised in two banks. Extending the line of inquiry of Bank Omega, the diffusion of BSC as a global technology at a broader level, and in Sri Lanka in particular, warrants investigation from future researchers.

Concluding remarks

Recapitulating the deliberations from the foregoing sections, the following conclusions are postulated. First, this chapter reinforces the prevalence of various modes of control such as budgeting and BSC in contemporary organizations. It also shows the predominance of budgetary control, and concludes that *budgeting is not dead* and that *budgeting will never die*. The evidence further suggests that MCS is a cyclical process moving through various modes of control, such as budgeting and BSC, as desired by powerful members in the organizational landscape across time. The fate of new control systems is fragile and temporary. They are neither predetermined nor possess any inherent qualities. Thus, remnants of an old technology can be rediscovered and reused after a long dormant period (Vaivio, 2007). Networks integrate, disintegrate and may reappear, when the circumstances change, or when a different set of powerful actors emerges (Chow *et al.*, 2010). A system deemed to have disappeared at a specific point of time might be made to work again. Thus one cannot dismiss the possibility of BSC reappearing in the future as the prime control tool in Bank Omega.

Second, it concludes that the design and operation of control systems are not merely technical phenomena. Instead, they represent broader struggles between various actors, and concentration purely on the technical aspects is inadequate in the quest to understand the functioning of such systems in a given context. The research highlights the importance of discovering the key human and non-human actors behind the process, relationships between various actors and how they come together in building networks of support, as a means to better comprehend the design, operation and the fate of control systems (such as BSC and budgeting) in terms of how and why they become a failure or success. It also illuminates how an organization's MCS become isomorphic with the external institutional environments (DiMaggio & Powell, 1983). Thus, it is concluded that organizational actors and external institutional forces become intertwined in the design and operation of MCS, and that the two theories of ANT and NIS can be brought together to yield a wider and plausible explanation of the functioning of control practices in organizations.

Third, parallel to other public sector accounting research, this study portrays the use of management control information for external legitimacy for SOEs. It also depicts the use of such information for the internal decision making of the top management as a diagnostic and interactive tool in both the public and private sectors. Fourth, it is discerned through this research that the circumstances which produce differences in design, operation and uses in management control, apart from contextual variances between public and private, are also attributable to differences in key actors, their reactions to control systems and the nature of relational networks formed. This reinforces the contention that context matters, and raises doubts as to the universal applicability of a particular control tool, as MCS are phenomena that are economically as well as socially and politically constructed, and cannot be divorced from the context within which they operate. Seen in this light, the insights afforded through this chapter should be interpreted in light of the *contextual ramifications* of the particular banks, but those contextual ramifications may extend well beyond the divergence between *public* and *private*.

Appendix 19.1

Interview questions

1 What does management control mean to you?
2 What are the management control systems used in the bank?
3 What is the role of management control systems?
4 Are there any positive or negative influences from the labour union for the functioning of management controls?
5 What do you think about management control practices of the bank? Are they successful and effective? Give reasons for your answer.
6 What prompts your organization moving towards new managements accounting practices?
7 Does regulation influence your organization's managements accounting practices?
8 Do you have formal procedures for performance measurement and management control? Can you describe the procedures? Are they successful? If yes, how? If no, why not?
9 Who is involved in the process of developing performance measurement and management control?
10 Are you using other organizations' managements accounting practices as a model for your organization? Why?
11 How are the performance measurement and management control reports prepared? Who are involved?
12 Have employees attended training with regard to performance measurement and management control? What type of training have they attended? Who has received training? Is it compulsory?
13 Do you have a separate division/unit to handle the management accounting function? Who is the head of the management accounting function? How many people are there in the division/unit? To whom does this division report to?
14 What are the functions or roles of the members in this division/unit? Does your division/unit need additional expertise?
15 Do you have specific criteria in selecting personnel for this division/unit? What is their educational background? What relevant experience do they have?
16 Are there any members of professional associations in this division/unit? If yes, is it important to have such people?
17 How do you work with other departments in the organization in collecting information on performance measurement and management control?

18 To what extent does the top management use budgetary control and variance analysis as a control mechanism?
19 How are divisional budgets prepared? Are there any influences on this?
20 How do you use budget information for your day-to-day activities?
21 Do you think that it is important to meet budget targets? Why?
22 Has the bank implemented new management accounting practices such as the BSC in the recent past?
23 Who initiated them? Are they successful?
24 What are the factors that have contributed to the success or failure of new management accounting practices?
25 Who supported the practices and who opposed them? How was staff resistance (if any) dealt with?
26 What are the barriers/difficulties faced in the implementation of new management accounting techniques such as BSC?
27 What was the role played by the top management in implementing new management accounting practices?
28 Do you think that the nature of the industry the business is operating in makes particular demands on the management accounting practices?
29 If the bank has adopted new management accounting practices, what is the position of the previous budgetary control system after the implementation of the BSC? Was it replaced or does it form a part of the BSC?
30 What are the factors (internal as well as external) that influence the bank in adoption of new management accounting practices?

Notes

1 This list, although illustrative, is not exhaustive.
2 ANT was pioneered by Michel Callon, Bruno Latour, and John Law (see e.g. Callon, 1986; Latour, 1987; Law, 1991), and subsequently used by several accounting researchers including, Alcouffe, Berland, and Levant (2008) and Briers and Chua (2001).
3 This chapter is premised upon two comparative banks (case studies), related to the private and public sectors in Sri Lanka, and these findings cannot be generalized to a wider population. Generalizability is not the goal of case study research, and it is not a concern of this chapter as well. Thus, insights obtained from these banks are not necessarily relevant to the study of MCS in banks in general.
4 Real names of the banks are not divulged and are designated as Bank Alpha and Bank Omega to preserve their confidentiality.
5 While the BSC has migrated to many countries around the world, it made significant inroads in the Sri Lankan setting from the late 1990s. A large number of local companies had attended seminars where it was attractively packaged and marketed by various consultants and institutions such as CIMA, Sri Lanka Division and Distant Learning Center, Colombo.

References

Abernethy, M., & Lillis, A. (1995). The impact of manufacturing flexibility on management control system design. *Accounting, Organizations and Society, 20*(4), 241–258.
Abernethy, M. A., & Vagnoni, E. (2004). Power, organization design and managerial behavior. *Accounting, Organizations and Society, 29*(3–4), 207–225.
Ahn, H. (2001). Applying the Balanced Scorecard concept: an experience report. *Long Range Planning, 34*(4), 441–461.

Alcouffe, S., Berland, N., & Levant, Y. (2008). Actor-networks and the diffusion of management accounting innovations: a comparative study. *Management Accounting Research, 19*(1), 1–17.
Andon, P., Baxter, J., & Mahama, H. (2005). The Balanced Scorecard: slogans, seduction, and state of play. *Australian Accounting Review, 15*(1), 29–38.
Ansari, S. L., & Euske, K. J. (1987). Rational, rationalising and reifying uses of accounting data in organizations. *Accounting, Organizations and Society, 12*(6), 549–570.
Anthony, R. N. (1965). *Planning and Control Systems: A Framework for Analysis*. Boston, MA: Graduate School of Business Administration, Harvard University.
Aranda, C., & Arellano, J. (2010). Consensus and link structure in strategic performance measurement systems: a field study. *Journal of Management Accounting Research, 22,* 271–299.
Berry, A. J., Capps, T., Cooper, D., Ferguson, P., Hopper, T., & Lowe, E. A. (1985). Management control in an area of the NCB: rationales of accounting practices in a public enterprise. *Accounting, Organization and Society, 10*(1), 3–28.
Berry, A., Loughton, E., & Otley, D. (1991). Control in a financial services company (RIF): a case study. *Management Accounting Research, 2*(2), 109–139.
Braam, G. J. M., & Nijssen, E. J. (2004). Performance effects of using the Balanced Scorecard: a note on the Dutch experience. *Long Range Planning, 37*(4), 335–349.
Briers, M., & Chua, W. F. (2001). The role of actor-networks and boundary objects in management accounting change: a field study of an implementation of activity based costing. *Accounting, Organizations and Society, 26*(3), 237–269.
Callon, M. (1986). Some elements of a sociology of translation: domestication of the scallops and the fishermen of St Brieuc Bay. In J. Law (Ed.), *Power, action and belief a new sociology of knowledge?* (pp. 196–233). London: Routledge & Kegan Paul.
Carpenter, V. L. & Feroz, E. H. (1992). GAAP as a symbol of legitimacy: New York's decision to adopt generally accepted accounting principles. *Accounting, Organizations and Society, 17*(7), 613–644.
Carpenter, V. L., & Feroz, E. H. (2001). Institutional theory and accounting rule choice: an analysis of Four US state governments' decisions to adopt Generally Accepted Accounting Principles. *Accounting, Organizations and Society, 26*(7–8), 565–596.
Chenhall, R. H. (2003). Management control system design within its organizational context: findings from contingency-based research and directions for the future. *Accounting, Organizations and Society, 28*(2–3), 127–168.
Chow, D., Moll, J., & Humphrey, C. (2010). *Networks and the diffusion of accounting technologies: the UK whole of government accounts project*. Paper present at the sixth Asia Pacific Interdisciplinary Research in Accounting (APIRA) Conference, Sydney.
Christiansen, J. K., & Skærbæk, P. (1997). Implementing budgetary control in the performing arts: games in the organizational theatre. *Management Accounting Research, 8*(4), 405–438.
Cobb, I., Helliar, C., & Innes, J. (1995). Management accounting change in a bank. *Management Accounting Research, 6*(2), 155–175.
Covaleski, M. A., & Dirsmith, M. W. (1983). Budgeting as a means for control and loose coupling. *Accounting, Organizations and Society, 8*(4), 323–340.
Covaleski, M. A., & Dirsmith, M. W. (1986). The budgetary process of power and politics. *Accounting, Organizations and Society, 11*(3), 193–214.
Covaleski, M. A., & Dirsmith, M. W. (1988a). The use of budgetary symbols in the political arena: an historically informed field study. *Accounting, Organizations and Society, 13*(1), 1–24.
Covaleski, M. A., & Dirsmith, M. W. (1988b). An institutional perspective on the rise, social transformation, and fall of a university budget category. *Administrative Science Quarterly, 33*(4), 562–587.
Covaleski, M. A., & Dirsmith, M. W. (1991). The management of legitimacy and politics in public sector administration. *Journal of Accountability and Public Policy, 10*(2), 135–156.
Dassanayake, K. (2000). Structure of financial system in Sri Lanka. *Central Bank of Sri Lanka – News Survey, 21*(1), 10–11.
Davis, S., & Albright, T. (2004). An investigation of the effect of Balanced Scorecard implementation on financial performance. *Management Accounting Research, 15*(2), 135–153.
DiMaggio, P. J., & Powell, W. W. (1983). The iron cage revisited: institutional isomorphism and collective rationality in organizational fields. *American Sociological Review, 48*(2), 147–160.
Ekholm, B., & Wallin, J. (2000). Is the annual budget really dead? *European Accounting Review, 9*(4), 519–539.

Helliar, C., Cobb, I., & Innes, J. (2002). A Longitudinal case study of profitability reporting in a bank. *British Accounting Review, 34*(1), 27–53.

Henri, J. F. (2006). Organizational culture and performance measurement systems, *Accounting, Organizations and Society, 31*(1), 77–103.

Hope, J., & Fraser, R. (2000). Beyond budgeting. *Strategic Management, 82*(4), 30–35.

Hopper, T., & Major, M. (2007). Extending institutional analysis through theoretical triangulation: regulation and activity-based costing in Portuguese telecommunications. *European Accounting Review, 16*(1), 59–97.

Hopwood, A. (1987). The archeology of accounting systems. *Accounting, Organizations and Society, 12*(3), 207–234.

Hoque, Z. (2003). Total Quality Management and the Balanced Scorecards approach: a critical analysis of their potential relationships and directions of research. *Critical Perspectives on Accounting, 14*(5), 553–566.

Hoque, Z., Covaleski, M. A., & Gooneratne, T. (2013). Theoretical triangulation and methodological pluralism in management accounting research. *Accounting, Auditing & Accountability Journal*, 26, 1170–1198.

Hoque, Z., & Hopper, T. (1994). Rationality, accounting and politics: a case study of management control in a Bangladeshi jute mill. *Management Accounting Research, 5*(1), 5–30.

Hoque, Z., & James, W. (2000). Linking Balanced Scorecard with Size and market factors: impact on organizational performance. *Journal of Management Accounting Research, 12*, 1–17.

Hussain, M. M., & Hoque, Z. (2002). Understanding non-financial performance measures in Japanese banks: a new institutional sociology perspective. *Accounting, Auditing & Accountability Journal, 15*(2), 162–183.

Innes, J., & Mitchell, F. (1997). The application of activity-based costing in the United Kingdom's largest financial institutions. *The Service Industries Journal, 17*(1), 190–203.

Johanson, U., Skoog, M., Backlund, A., Almqvist, R. (2006). Balancing dilemmas of the balanced scorecard. *Accounting, Auditing & Accountability Journal, 19*(6), 842–857.

Kasurinen, T. (2002). Exploring management accounting change: the case of Balanced Scorecard implementation. *Management Accounting Research, 13*(3), 323–343.

Latour, B. (1987). *Science in action: how to follow scientists and engineers through society*. Milton Keynes, UK: Open University Press.

Latour, B. (1996). *Aramis or the love technology*. Cambridge, MA and London: Harvard University Press.

Law, J. (1991). Introduction: monsters, machines and sociotechnical relations. In J. Law (Ed.), *A sociology of monsters. Essays on power, technology and domination* (pp. 1–23). London: Routledge.

Libby, T., & Lindsay, R. M. (2010). Beyond budgeting or budgeting reconsidered? A survey of North-American budgeting practice. *Management Accounting Research, 21*(1), 56–75.

Lowry, J. F. (1990). Management accounting and service industries: an exploratory account of historical and current economic contexts. *ABACUS, 26*(2), 159–184.

Malmi, T. (2001). Balanced Scorecards in Finnish companies: a research note. *Management Accounting Research, 12*(2), 207–220.

McCunn, P. (1998). The Balanced Scorecard...the eleventh commander. *Management Accounting, 76*(11), 34–36.

McNamara, C., & Mong, S. (2005). Performance measurement and management: some insights from practice. *Australian Accounting Review, 15*(1), 14–28.

Meyer, J. W., & Rowan, B. (1977). Institutionalized organizations: formal structure as myth and ceremony. *American Journal of Sociology, 83*(2), 340–363.

Modell, S. (1996). Management accounting and control in services: structural and behavioural perspectives. *International Journal of Service Industry Management*, 7(2), 57–80.

Nanayakkara, G. (1992). *Culture and management in Sri Lanka*. Sri Lanka: Post Graduate Institute of Management, University of Sri Jayewardenepura.

Nanayakkara, G. (1997). Some reflections on Buddhism on morality in business and management. *Sri Lankan Journal of Management, 2*(3), 217–233.

Neely, A., Bourne, M., & Adams, C. (2003). Better budgeting or beyond budgeting? *Measuring Business Excellence*, 7(3), 22–28.

Nørreklit, H. (2000). The balance on the Balanced Scorecard: a critical analysis of some of its assumptions. *Management Accounting Research, 11*(1), 65–88.

Norris, G. (2002). Chalk and cheese: grounded theory case studies of the introduction and usage of activity-based information in two British banks. *British Accounting Review, 34*(3), 223–255.

Otley, D. T. (1994). Management control in contemporary organizations: towards a wider perspective. *Management Accounting Research, 5*(3–4), 289–299.

Otley, D. (1999). Performance management: a framework for management control research. *Management Accounting Research, 10*(4), 363–382.

Otley, D. (2006). Trends in budgetary control and responsibility accounting. In A. Bhimani (Ed.), *Contemporary issues in management accounting* (pp. 291–307). New York: Oxford University Press.

Rigby, D. (2001). Management tools and techniques: a survey. *California Management Review, 43*(2), 139–160.

Sandhu, R., Baxter, J., & Emsley, D. (2008). Initiating the localisation of a Balanced Scorecard in a Singaporean firm. *Singapore Management Review, 30*(2), 25–41.

Shapiro, B., & Matson, D. (2008). Strategies of resistance to internal control regulation. *Accounting, Organizations and Society, 33*(2–3), 199–228.

Simons, R. (2000). *Performance measurement and control systems for implementing strategy*. Upper Saddle River, NJ: Prentice Hall.

Soin, K., Seal, W., & Cullen, J. (2002). ABC and organizational change: an institutional perspective. *Management Accounting Research, 13*(2), 249–271.

Speckbacher, G., Bischof, J., & Pfeiffer, T. (2003). A descriptive analysis on the implementation of Balanced Scorecards in German-speaking countries. *Management Accounting Research, 14*(4), 361–387.

Tsamenyi, M., Mills, J., & Tauringana, V. (2002). A field study of the budgeting process and the perceived usefulness of the budget in organizations in a developing country – the case of Ghana. *Journal of African Business, 3*(2), 85–103.

Tuomela, T. (2005). The interplay of different levers of control: a case study of introducing a new performance measurement system. *Management Accounting Research, 16*(3), 293–320.

Vaivio, J. (2007). Qualitative research on management accounting: achievements and potential. In T. Hopper, D. Northcott, and R. Scapens (Eds.), *Issues in Management Accounting* (pp. 425–443). London: Pearson.

Wallander, J. (1999). Budgeting – an unnecessary evil. *Scandinavian Journal of Management, 15*(4), 405–421.

Wickramasinghe, D., Hopper, T., & Rathnasiri, C. (2004). Japanese cost management meets Sri Lankan politics: disappearance and reappearance of bureaucratic management controls in a privatized utility. *Accounting, Auditing & Accountability Journal, 17*(1), 85–120.

Widener, S. K. (2007). An empirical analysis of the levers of control framework. *Accounting, Organizations and Society, 32*(7–8), 757–788.

Wildavsky, A. (1979). *The politics of the budgetary process* (3rd ed.). Boston: Little, Brown and Company.

Wildavsky, A. (1986). *Budgeting, a comparative theory of budgetary processes* (2nd ed.). New Brunswick: Transaction Books.

20

Performance measurement in SMEs

Robin Jarvis

Introduction

The aim of this chapter is to examine through the literature the application of performance measurement in Small and Medium Size Entities (SMEs). However, when addressing issues relating to SMEs, it is necessary to consider the important question of the definition of a SME. Conveniently, the European Commission (EC) has defined SME. The EC has needed to adopt a uniform definition across Europe for the consistent application of regulation throughout European Union's internal market. Helpfully, most research literature and policy within Europe, in need of a common definition, also use the EC definition. This consistency in the context of the SME research agenda is important so that we can compare and develop a robust literature. The EC definition includes three metrics which will be described later in the chapter[1] in the context of our study of SMEs and Performance Measurement Systems.

The literature of most business-related subjects until relatively recently has held the misconception that small and medium size entities (SMEs) are smaller versions of large business entities. As Marchini (1995) states (as quoted in Garengo *et al.* 2005), 'the small enterprise is different from the big company: you cannot simply look at the needs of SMEs by turning your binoculars upside down and making small what was big'. This notion of sameness to some extent has gradually been eroded. In terms, however, of financial management and specifically performance management, much of the education literature and 'how to do it books' maintain this misconception of homogeneity in the advocacy and the application of performance management systems. This is particularly evident in financial management books for undergraduates, postgraduates, and professional accounting and finance students. For example, in one of the main management accounting texts used in the UK (Drury, 2015), no reference is made to SMEs or smaller business entities in the index of the book. Many pages in this text are devoted to performance management and measurement but no reference is made to SMEs in that context. It is not therefore surprising that the vast amount of accounting and finance students assume that the applications and tools promoted in their studies are appropriate for both large and small business entities. They have very little perception of this significant gap in our knowledge of how small firms use tools to manage finances or what practices are appropriate to smaller enterprises.

From an accounting and finance research perspective, very little empirical and theoretical research has been carried out focusing on performance management in the context of SMEs (Garengo *et al.*, 2005). Much of the research in the past has concluded that there is a lack of awareness, or application of 'best practice' in SME. These best practice models, however, are almost invariably idealisations of managerial and accounting systems employed in large entities (Jarvis *et al.*, 1996; Taticchi *et al.*, 2010; Tenhunen *et al.*, 2001). Most of these papers focused on subjects such as the application of Activity Based Costing (ABC) and the Balanced Scorecard that arguably may not be appropriate to smaller entities but may be usefully employed in medium size entities. Therefore, significantly this research literature often makes the assumption, as previously mentioned with the text books on the subject, that the models of performance measures that are appropriate for large business entities firms are also suitable for small entities (Taticchi *et al.*, 2010). More recently, those researchers who have examined SMEs and performance management have tended to concentrate on the larger end of the SME definition range that is in the manufacturing sector of the economy where some of these large entity models could be relevant. For example, in a review by Garengo *et al.* (2005) of research into performance measurement systems, the focus of their attention is on independent and manufacturing SMEs that employ more than 20 people.

The main theme running throughout the chapter is the need to differentiate the aims of performance management in the context of the size of the firm. From the above discussion, it can be seen that the subject is complex. The overall aim of the chapter is to provide students and researchers insights into these complexities and explore the application of performance management in SMEs. We begin by examining the business entity landscape and its contribution to the economy of SMEs. This analysis will be influential in examining the appropriateness of performance measurement systems to varying sizes of business entities. Of the utmost importance in this analysis of performance management are the adopted objectives of the firm. This will be examined in the light of myths and realities. The next section addresses the issue that the differing nature and characteristics of varying sizes of business entities require the researcher to carefully choose methods of research that will dictate the appropriate technique for collecting and analysing data. This is followed by the examination of the empirical evidence of performance measurement systems. Finally, the influence of Small and Medium Size Practices of Accountants (SMPs) is examined in the adoption by SMEs of performance measurement systems.

The size of a SME and the adoption of performance management systems

The European Commission's definition of SME referred to earlier details three metrics: employment, total balance sheet value and total turnover. Taking, for convenience, just one of the metrics, the numbers employed, which arguably is a reasonable surrogate collectively for all three metrics, the definitions are in the following ranges: micro-entities 0–9 employees, small entities 10–49 employees and medium size entities 50–249 employees.

Although we may have established an acceptable definition, it becomes apparent that within this range of SMEs the needs and behaviours are likely to be very different. For example, it is extremely likely that a one-employee business entity as compared to a business entity that

Table 20.1 Enterprise size class analysis of key indicators, non-financial business economy, EU-27, 2009

Size of Enterprise	*Percentage (%) of total employment*	*Percentage (%) of total business entities*	*Percentage (%) value added to factor costs*
Micro (0–9 employees)	29.6	92.2	21.6
Small (10–49 employees)	20.8	6.5	18.2
Medium (50–249 employees)	17.2	1.1	18.3
SME in total	67.6	99.8	58.1
Large (≥250 employees)	32.4	0.2	41.9

employs 249 employees will differ greatly in terms of its character and needs. In the context of performance measurement systems, we will later be examining what effect that size plays.

If we now turn to the distribution of SMEs under their defining categories some interesting patterns emerge in terms of their contribution to the EU economy from an employment perspective. Table 20.1 shows the number of business entities as a percentage of the total population, the percentage that each category employs as a total of the total employed, and the value added to factor costs in the European Union.

Table 20.1 demonstrates the significant contribution of the micro-entities in the EU from three perspectives. In examining micro-entities, a little further from other sources of information supplied by the EC, the average number of employees working in a micro-enterprise is 2.1 and a large proportion of these micro-enterprises are one-person enterprises (self-employed). To further illustrate the significance of self-employed enterprises, in the UK around 3.8 million enterprises out of a total of 4.9 million are self-employed; that is two-thirds of the total enterprises. The landscape of the economy, in terms of both the EU and the UK, has not always portrayed this picture of a bias to micro-enterprises. In 2014, for example, there are 40 per cent more micro-enterprises in the UK than in 2000 (Dellot, 2014). The above analysis clearly indicates the significance of the contributions of self-employed and micro-entities which is growing both in the UK and overall in EU economies.

From our perspective in examining performance management systems, it could be argued that much of the education and research literature that we considered earlier should be focused on these smaller entities because of their economic contribution to EU economies. As Debono (2014) argues, the paucity of research

> … would suggest that understanding the management accounting issues within the sector can lead to a positive contribution to management accounting knowledge. In turn, this can lead to the provision of better quality management accounting information to the SMEs and therefore boost their already important economic contribution.

Performance measurement: objectives of the firm – myths and realities

One of the most challenging and at the same time engaging issues in examining performance measurement of SMEs from a research perspective, which will be the driving force for policy and understanding of the sector, is the strategic objective that these business entities pursue. There seems to be two main streams of thinking in this debate. In this section, we explore these streams and the myths and realities that provide the context of the debate.

A business entity performance measure should be designed to evaluate the extent to which the strategic objectives of the entity are being achieved. It is recognised that performance measurement can be very influential in ensuring that a business's corporate strategy is successfully embraced (Berry and Jarvis, 2011; Drury, 2015). Systems are designed to reflect the business's strategy objectives that are linked to various groups of stakeholders' goals (Kaplan and Norton, 1996). From a theoretical finance perspective, which primarily focuses on large companies, the underlying assumptions businesses operate in are unregulated markets and competitive economies. In such economies, companies exist for one overriding purpose; that is, in order to benefit their owners. It is assumed that the maximisation of shareholders' wealth is fundamental in satisfying the owners' objectives (Levy and Sarnat, 1994). It is argued that this objective can be translated, in terms of the business entity, to the maximisation of the profits. It follows, according to this line of thinking, that the tools used for decision making and the indicators to assess the performance of the firm will reflect this objective. In more recent years, a strong argument has been articulated recognising that there are a number of stakeholders other than just shareholders within these large companies which are listed on stock exchanges. They include creditors, customers, employees and society as a whole. In the context of performance measures, it has been argued that these other stakeholders should be reflected in the objectives of the firm (Freeman *et al.*, 2004). The development of this theory has resulted in the advocacy of the Balanced Scorecard, Performance Prism and other performance measures to capture these wider interests of stakeholders (Kaplan and Norton, 1992; Neely *et al.*, 2002). However, authors of major finance texts (e.g. Arnold, 2012) persist in assuming that 'The company should make investment and finance decisions with the aim of maximising long-term shareholder wealth'. This assumption, it is argued, is made mainly on 'practical grounds, but there are respectable theoretical justifications too' (Arnold, 2012, pp. 7–9).

It is likely that stakeholder theory as applied to SMEs is likely to focus more on owner-managers' objectives as they are likely to be very influential as compared to other stakeholders of the firm. As neatly explained by Stokes and Wilson (2010, p. 221), 'As many small businesses are the psychological extension of the owner-manager or entrepreneur, their personal motives and objectives will be crucial in assessing success or failure.' In the case of micro-entities and smaller entities the influence of the objectives of the owner-manager is likely to be more significant as the impact of other stakeholders is likely to be less. In contrast the objectives of larger small entities and medium size entities are likely to be influenced by other stakeholders as they are more important to these business entities and will be reflected in the strategic objectives of these business entities.

Unfortunately, as previously mentioned, there are very few educational texts that differentiate between sizes of business entities. These texts are underpinned and driven by the questionable adherence to classical economic theory, often assuming that profit maximisation is, or should be, the central objective of the firm as previously described. Accordingly, the performance measures used and advocated for SMEs often prioritise profit maximisation, employing indicators such as profit margins and return on investment as key performance measures. However, small business researchers have consistently recorded over the last 40 years that business owner–managers pursue a range of goals other than profit maximisation. The most important appear to be business survival and stability, but these are often interwoven with more esoteric aims such as altruistic goals, status considerations and professional pride (Curran *et al.*, 1997; Scase and Goffee, 1980). This is not to claim profit is unimportant, rather that the owner-managers juggle a range of objectives, continually arranging and rearranging within what they perceive as changing constraints internal and external to the entity. But if owner-managers have a variety of (often changing) objectives, selecting business performance measures to assess the extent to which the firm is achieving its objectives will be difficult. In particular, attempts to reduce the business to a financial singularity measuring success solely by financial indicators will not capture the complexities of the models that owner-managers construct for managing their business.

The influence of the concept of growth

Much of the interest in SMEs, from a government policy perspective, has been driven by SMEs' increasing economic contribution and not surprisingly, the growth prospects of these business entities. In particular, the relationship between accounting practices and growth of the business has been cited as the rationale for much of the accounting research into SMEs (Mitchell and Reid, 2000; Parry, 2015). Growth is invariably measured in terms of employment and profits. Parry (2015) has made an insightful contribution to the literature on growth- and alternative-oriented business entities. His views are worthy of a brief examination in the consideration of performance measurement in SMEs.

Parry (2015) argues that this research perspective of questioning the orthodoxy in respect of the desire for growth has been heavily influenced by the 'narrow focus on the interests of policy makers and practitioners' promoting performance indicators that measure and monitor growth rather than building theory. He further argues that methodologies are adopted that do not investigate alternative non-growth entities, which have been commonly described as 'lifestyle' businesses. There is substantive evidence to support the view that a significant proportion of SMEs are lifestyle businesses and a relatively small proportion of SMEs pursue strategies of growth (Storey, 1998). Lifestyle businesses, of course, will reflect the owner-manager's chosen way to meet their personal requirements including a level of income that satisfies their needs rather than maximising income. Owner-managers of these businesses are in the main concerned about their sustainability. Parry (2015) contends that the lack of focus on growth means that lifestyle businesses are frequently ignored in the literature and by policy makers. To readdress this overemphasis on growth-oriented businesses he calls for 'more research that focuses specifically on lifestyle businesses and addresses the issues of sustainability rather than growth'. This would therefore require the researcher to closely study the owner-managers' range of objectives and the way they monitor and measure if these objectives are being met. Often, the nature of the process of monitoring and measurement will be less formal than those prescribed by texts and pronouncements by trainers and others. This will investigated further when considering the empirical evidence.

SMEs and research methods

The legitimacy of choosing a methodology to investigate the performance measurements used in SMEs will differ depending upon the number of issues. An influential factor will clearly be the objectives of the entity as discussed above. In the case of micro-entities where invariably the owner-manager plays a significant part in the direction of the entity, and particularly if that direction takes the form of a lifestyle business, the approach to the investigation must be sensitive to the personal involvement of the owner-manager (Curran *et al.*, 1997; Parry, 2015). In this context, a number of accounting researchers have adopted grounded theory as it is argued the approach fits the nature of the research.

Debono (2014) in his PhD thesis clearly sets out the advantages of grounded theory in the investigation of accounting practices. He points out that '...the theory is grounded in the data itself' and, quoting Strauss and Corbin (1998), 'This means the theories derived (from the analysis of the data) are more likely to be an accurate representation of reality'. It is argued that the approach will capture the complexities and richness of the activity under investigation. Therefore, the approach lends itself to the investigation of accounting practices but particularly those of micro and smaller entities. Grounded theory can be contrasted with approaches that generate theories from abstract generalisations of the researcher about what practices ought to be (Debono, 2014).

However, financial management practices of SMEs, including performance measurement systems, both in the past and now, have been heavily criticised as hindering the effectiveness of SMEs and contributing to their high failure rates. In drawing upon this conclusion, researchers and other commentators have judged these practices on normative 'best practice' models (Curran *et al.*, 1997). These best practice models have tended to be based on an uncritical application of large firm performance measure practices. Typically, SME financial management practices are examined by identifying the performance gaps between current performance of the company and world-class performance (Ahmad and Alaskari, 2014). These large firm practices may be irrelevant to smaller firms, particularly micro-entities where the owner-managers play such an important strategic role in the well-being of the business entity.

The choice of methodology can therefore be seen as critical to the process of identifying the performance measures employed by SMEs and the false assumption made that 'good practice' fits all (Jarvis *et al.*, 1996).

The impact of cost factors on performance measurement systems

In this section, we will examine the differences in cost structures between small and large firms and their influence on performance measurement systems employed in these sizes of entities.

Costs play a significant part in establishing performance management measures. This is particularly the case with traditional short-term financial measures that are employed as targets for managers and employees to achieve within budgetary control systems (Berry and Jarvis, 2011). These costs include direct and indirect costs. The latter are better known as overhead costs. Characteristically, many large business entities are multi-product and departmentalised. In these cases, both direct and indirect costs need to be allocated to products and departments within the entity. However, invariably, overhead costs are costs that cannot be easily and conveniently identified with a particular product or department. Therefore, to establish, for example, the total cost of a product, which includes overhead costs, it is necessary to introduce a method of allocating and absorbing these costs into the product costs. It is unanimously recognised that the process of allocation and absorbing these costs is problematic. This process may result in some misallocation of overhead costs that are employed in a number of management accounting functions including performance measures. The greater the number of products and departments within an entity, the greater the potential misallocation of overheads. Many would argue that ABC has given greater precision to this allocation process in these large multi-product entities that have numerous departments. With the adoption of ABC, there still remains some level of judgement in determining the legitimate overhead costs to be assigned to products and functions within an organisation.

In contrast, smaller entities, by their very nature, are not likely to produce numerous products nor have many departments. It follows that smaller entities can identify product and departmental costs more accurately than their larger counterparts. This is especially true in the case of micro-entities that may have only one product and are not likely to have departmentalised the entity due to the low numbers of employees.

The problem of allocating overheads in larger entities is amplified as overhead costs tend to be a significantly higher proportion of total costs than in the case of small entities. Often, the overhead element will be greater than 90 per cent of total costs. The majority of costs of smaller entities are likely to be direct costs and the problem of misallocation of overhead costs is therefore not such a problem.

We can therefore conclude that cost-based performance measures in smaller entities are likely to be more accurate than in larger firms due to the relative size of overhead costs and the nature of large firms invariably being multi-product and being departmentalised.

Empirical evidence: performance measurement systems

Following the arguments that performance measurement indicators/systems are likely to differ across the range of SMEs in terms of size, we will examine the evidence of actual practices of performance management from the research literature recognising these differences. It should be re-emphasised that there is a paucity of literature from this perspective and generally about SMEs and performance management. A review of the literature was made, and two papers were selected that are dated but are fittingly cited by most of the more recent literature. The more recent papers tend to be country oriented or focusing on specific performance management indicators and tools such as Total Quality Management (TQM) and Economic Value Added (EVA). The objective of this brief review of the empirical evidence is to gain insights generally into what performance management systems and indicators are employed in practice and to obtain some awareness of the underpinning methodology driving the studies that are portrayed in the papers.

The first paper we will consider (Jarvis *et al.*, 2000) is based on face-to-face interviews conducted with 20 owner-managers of entities employing 5–20 people. Ten of the entities came from the manufacturing sector and ten from the service sector. The research methodology adopted is based on grounded theory.

How well the business is doing

Consistently, the sample of small business owner-managers reported that a variety of indicators were used to measure how well the business was doing. Cash and cash flow indicators, however, were stressed as crucial in this regard. Often, the measure of cash included cash equivalents, which were comprised of investments, and assets, which they considered to be highly liquid. One of the respondents referred to a barometer of the bank balance that is used to judge how well they are doing. The amount drawn for the owner-manager's own consumption during a period of time was also taken into account in establishing the 'bank balance', thus ensuring a consistent measure over time. This owner-manager appeared to fasten on to the almost physical notion of cash which they contrasted with the intangible nature of profits. In the assessment of performance measurement on individual jobs cash was also at the forefront in assessing that the entity was working efficiently. The following quote illustrates this preference: '...and we do that on a pounds per hour basis. That is how much is actually costing us to do the job'.

Cash and survival

An important reason for owner-managers preferring cash indicators rather than profit measures was because it is seen as a more effective short-term measure that is key to the objective of survival. Solvency of a business entity is the ability to pay creditors in a timely fashion, which is linked to availability and access to cash. Accessing cash, other than from the entity's own sources, is much more limited in the case of small entities as compared to their larger counterparts. As the findings from the research assert, '...No matter how it is incorporated into performance measures, it is the survival element of cash flow management that is continually presented as crucial by respondents'.

An important indicator of how well a business entity is performing is generally recognised as turnover. The interviewees, however, were cautious, recognising this measure's limitation to the actions necessary to survive. The more direct action of getting money in was the critical action to surviving. The crucial uncertainties of turnover figures were recognised, and it is the immediacy and physicality of the cash that can be counted which provides a direct indicator of business survival. Related to this point is the evidence that late payment is a much more significant problem in the case of smaller entities as compared to large (Beaver, 2002). The evidence of respondents not only emphasises the importance of cash itself but also the movement of cash into the business – cash flows as the process rather than the outcome.

Measures used by external parties

Cash flow indicators were also perceived by owner-managers as significant from the perspective of the bank and creditors. There was an acknowledgement that others are actively measuring the entities' ability to pay debts and have a healthy working capital position. A quote from one of the respondents exceptionally captures this view:

> ...Without positive cash flow you're weakening your working capital. You're giving the bank areas of grey that you're unable to pay your way. Then you make the bank unhappy. The bank panics and before [long] you're down around the table at the bank discussing the needs of the bank. It's breathing confidence over the bank that counts and that lies in the strength of the business and not by a massive great block of house acting as security.

In such cases, the bank legitimises the use of cash as a measure of the businesses' health reflecting the entities' ability to survive. Therefore, the owner-managers are employing the cash flow indicator as a measure of well-being from two important perspectives, internal and external.

Non-financial measures

There was evidence from respondents that cash indicators by themselves were not sufficient and 'too financially oriented'. This resulted in other non-financial indicators being used to accompany the financial indicators. The non-financial measures tended to be more 'sensitive and fast reacting' than financial measures, but they were often linked. One of the respondents – an owner-manager of a pest control business – used the number of telephone enquiries as an initial guide to business performance then related that to financial measures:

> … The phone ringing basically. When the phone rings it's good because that's how we get our work. And then you're doing work and you get paid for it.

Audibility of the telephone rings gives immediacy to what is going on and is being used as an informal measure of how well the business is doing. The immediacy of the rings is accessible unlike most financial measures. Similar to other examples, this indicator is related to survival. While the work comes in, to a great extent, it measures the future well-being of the business. The concept of busyness is identified here as well, in particular being able to measure non-financial activities that are crucial to the business such as 'whether the phone rings … and whether the job is getting done'. This theme of the importance of busyness as a measure of performance was common to other respondents.

A mixture of measures

It is evident from the research evidence that invariably a mixture of financial and non-financial measures were used to monitor and measure the performance of the entity. Employing these performance measures was often more complex than perhaps expected. The measures tended to be employed from when the owner-manager of the entity committed the firm to the contract through to the contract's conclusion. It was recognised that the monitoring process tended to focus on shortfalls and losses, emphasising the survival theme again rather than potential improvements that would enhance growth of the business and maximise profit.

One of the owner-managers of an entity, a manufacturer of television lighting equipment, whose percentage of trading with just one client was significant, underlined the complexity and the mix of factors employed to monitor and measure business performance. This is demonstrated in the following interview abstract replying to how he monitored and assessed his firm's performance:

> Many, many things. One: you must keep your eye on the cost of raw materials. Two: you must keep your eye on the quality of the parts that you buy from outside. Three: you must keep your eye on the quality of the product you're got in house (*Quality of goods sold*). Many, many things. You're just got to have your wits about you. It's no use in a business such as ours leaving the business to run itself.

This response suggests that the owner-manager uses more measures than he can actually relate to: 'many, many things'. However, the financial measure of controlling costs is clearly seen as important. The parts purchased in this industry tend to be expensive and any increase in cost is likely to have a significant effect on profit margins. But once again this financial measure was balanced by a non-financial measures, in this case the quality of purchased parts and the quality of goods finally sold. Poor quality of both could jeopardise the survival of the business particularly with the entity's reliance on one client. Once again note the heavy emphasis on survival.

From another perspective, the television lighting manufacturer also gave some interesting insights into the motives for selecting the measures. In his case, the motive of choosing and employing performance measures allowed him to control the business in terms of the business environment and markets. The owner-manager, rather than waiting for things to happen, proactively emphasised his ability to make events happen, to control them and measure outcomes. These measures while varied are an interrelated series of goals that tie his own success and abilities closely to the performance of the firm. Noticeably, the owner-manager takes responsibility and delegates little. There was more evidence more generally from the research indicating that owner-managers were personally very proactive in monitoring performance judged in various ways. It is also evident that there are very close links between performance measures and the owner-managers' diverse objectives, whether they be person or business related.

It may seem from the above account of the research that more conventional financial management functions and routines are seen as unimportant by the sample of small business owners. This would be an incorrect conclusion. Much emphasis was given to those financial indicators and actions to ensure the survival of the firm. Flexibility in the use and analysis of financial management for assessing how the business was performing was paramount. This latter point is amply illustrated by one of the sample, a bookshop/stationery owner, who gives emphasis to the importance of profit as an indicator but relates to the importance of other financial indicators:

> The most important thing must be the bottom line on the accounts situation. But it's not just the single indicator. It's got to be linked with the liquidity. So it's sales, costs and therefore net profit and liquidity.

The linking of profit and liquidity (cash) is seen as critical and is stressed by all the informed SME commentators (e.g. Watson, 2010). Often, there has been much criticism of small firms due to their lack of understanding of the importance of the link between profits and cash. Generally, the research threw up no evidence that this was the case.

Cash, however, remains central to most of the measures employed. The tangible nature of cash in terms of its 'countability' can be interpreted as the key element of its attractiveness. Often liquidity is measured through invoices sent or more tangibly to bank balances.

Overall, the analysis of the research questions some commentators' views that stress the lack of financial skills and sophistication of small business owners as compared with the idealisation of large enterprise financial and business performance practices. In fact, in this context, it is interesting to relate how well, generally, small businesses managed the recent 2008/2011 crisis. During this period, there were fewer insolvencies recorded in the UK than expected, and bank balances (i.e. deposits) of SMEs were at the highest ever recorded. This is arguably a strong indicator that small firms are very aware of the importance of cash and their ability to ensure that on rainy days they have sufficient cash for their survival.

The second paper 'Performance measurement systems in SMEs: a review for a research agenda' (Garengo *et al.*, 2005) takes a very different perspective than the previous paper. The paper is a literature review examining performance measurement systems (PMS) in SME manufacturing firms. The review focus is on SMEs that exclude micro-entities and those employing less than 20 employees. So here, we are examining very different types of firms, particularly in terms of size, than the study we previously considered by Jarvis *et al.* where the focus of attention was on small entities that employed less than 20 employees and the sample was equally split between service and manufacturing. With the concentration on manufacturing, the level of capital required to purchase and maintain the plant and machinery necessary to produce products is likely to be reflected in the PMS argue Garengo *et al.* Targets reflecting the return on these assets come to mind. Additionally, the investment in software also seems a prerequisite for successful implementation of PMSs.

A PMS is, adopting Neely *et al.*'s (2002) definition, a balanced and dynamic system that is able to support the decision-making process within a business entity by gathering, elaborating and analysing information. It is claimed that the analysis of the literature '...has highlighted the need for changes in managerial culture and rationalisation of management systems to support the management of increasing complexity in manufacturing SMEs'. Interestingly, it is acknowledged that for these larger SMEs it is the 'entrepreneur-owner' who is critical to the success of the entity and who is personally responsible for decision making within the entity. Important to this success is the entrepreneur's ability to be flexible and to act quickly to meet the demands in the market place and business environment. Primarily, these skills are developed through the process of the entrepreneur 'learning by doing' (Jennings and Beaver, 1997). This is consistent with the findings of Jarvis *et al.* (2000). This study showed that the responsibility of the owner-manager and their ability to be flexible in relation to the market, etc. was also critical to the success in the adoption of performance measures for the smaller entities that were previously studied. More emphasis is, however, given for SMEs, within the PMS approach, to use technology to be innovative and focus on the management of uncertainty and changes in the market. This is perhaps a reflection of the larger size of firms within this sample and the nature of manufacturing industries in which these SMEs operated.

Garengo *et al.* cite four main factors that are influential in promoting the adoption of PMS in manufacturing SMEs. They are as follows:

- the evolution of the competitive environment,
- the predisposition to grow exploiting wider markets,
- the evolution of quality to embrace continuous improvement,
- significant developments in IT.

The point is made that effective PMSs use a balance of both financial and non-financial indicators. However, the non-financial are somewhat more formal and sophisticated than those observed in the case of the previous study (Jarvis *et al.*, 2000). References are made for example to the Balanced Scorecard and ABC.

The review indicated that only a few SMEs employ PMSs. A number of specific characteristics that can be obstacles to the implementation and use of PMS are sourced from the literature. These are as follows:

- Lack of human resources: Typically, in a majority of SMEs, employees and owner-managers are concerned with the day-to-day operations to survive. Invariably, for these sizes of entities, there is not the capacity to consider longer-term strategic issues and to develop and implement new systems.
- Managerial capacity: SMEs, from a managerial perspective, tend to be flat across the organisation. The owner-manager will invariably be in charge and will lead both the operational and managerial functions with the business. Because of the pressure of meeting short-term demands and delivery times the concentration will be on the operational aspects of the business at the cost of managing the business effectively.
- Limited capital resources: This relates to the constraints on financing new technology and software necessary to be innovative and to fully meet markets' demands.
- Reactive approach: SMEs tend not to have formal planning systems and decision processes. This hinders the thought process of thinking strategically in terms of the long term. This often will result in an emphasis given to the short term that may effectively be a barrier to innovation.

- Tacit knowledge and little attention given to the formalisation of processes: Knowledge is often tacit and not explicit. This results in a lack of ability to collect relevant information that is necessary and critical in the decision-making and managerial processes.
- Misconception of performance measurement: This evidence suggests that owner-managers are not convinced that an investment in developing a PMS would have a positive effect on the business in the long term.

A brief reflection indicates that in large companies these obstacles are likely not to exist or to be as prominent as in the case of SMEs. This is perhaps not surprising as the PMS as described in the review were aligned within a business strategy agenda that was developed in the 1990s by Kaplan and Norton and others. The focus of their work was on large manufacturing companies.

The concept of the important role of stakeholders is also an acknowledged part of PMSs. The importance of recognising their objectives within the overall strategy of the business seems to be essential for a PMS. A significant literature emerged in the 1990s emphasising the importance of a stakeholder approach to managing companies. However, at the same time, it was accepted that there is much complexity in capturing all the stakeholders' goals and aligning them with an entity's strategy that is then reflected in a PMS. It is likely that from an SME perspective, as previously argued, the focus on stakeholders is not so relevant when there exists a dominant entrepreneur-owner and where the prime aims reflect the owner.

The paper concludes that although literature stresses the importance of PMS in SMEs, the research indicates that only a few SMEs do employ PMS. It must bring into question whether the PMS as described and implemented by large business entities are appropriate for SMEs. The authors hint that perhaps these large firms' models should be remodelled specifically for SMEs taking account of the obstacles described above and the very nature of SMEs. The paper suggests further research and posing a number of research questions.

It is interesting to examine a more recent paper (Ates *et al.*, 2013), which very much follows the second paper's approach (Garengo *et al.*, 2005) but is not so thorough about the obstacles to SMEs in adopting the authors' perception of good performance management practices. The paper cites Garengo *et al.* (2005) and is similarly concerned with the good practices based on 'theory' derived from the literature that have primarily been advocated for large entities in their pursuit of effective performance management systems, e.g. Kaplan and Norton. Similarly, the authors confirm that SMEs in practice focus on 'internal and short-term planning' and do not spend sufficient time on developing long planning and strategies. However, the paper does recognise that the approach they are advocating is a top-down approach that does not take account of '...the difficulties that SMEs have in managing concepts such as mission and vision'. This paper also demonstrates that the arguments in the earlier paper by Garengo *et al.* (2005) have not dramatically moved on in the application of performance management in the context of SMEs.

Another paper with a distinctive perspective in terms of the information used by SMEs in judging performance management focuses on the statutory financial reports produced by SMEs (Collis and Jarvis, 2000). The report is based on a survey of 385 small companies sourced from the FAME Database. While all the responding companies came within the EU definition, the majority were classified as small but did not include companies with a turnover of below £0.5 million. The FAME Database at the time excluded these smaller companies. The research paper starts from the well-documented evidence that the main users of statutory financial reports are directors of the companies themselves (Carsberg *et al.*,

1985; Collis and Jarvis, 1981, 2000; Dugdale *et al.*, 1997). The paper also recognises that the major difference between large and small companies rests in the financial strategies that they pursue. In general terms, large companies' main aims are focused on shareholders' desires for maximising profits and growth, while smaller firms are more interested in lifestyle strategies in pursuit of survival and stability. Invariably, the financial reports are supplemented by explanations from external accountants who tend to produce the report and a breakdown of the information in the financial report for management purposes once again supplied by the external accountant. This was the case for the sample respondents, over 80 per cent receiving some form of additional annual information from their external accountant. From the owner-managers of the respondent small firms, financial reports were seen to be serving a confirmatory function.

The main uses of the financial reports from the owner-managers' perspectives were as follows:

- for deciding on directors' pay/bonuses/dividends,
- comparing performance with previous periods,
- capital structure decisions,
- long-term planning,
- deciding employees' pay and bonuses.

Although the research recognises this is not the most important source of information for accessing performance, the fact that the information invariably derives from an independent source (the external accountant) and is to be filed at Companies House,[2] gives the owner-manager confidence in making a number of important decisions. In this way the financial report serves as a confirmatory function.

The influence of small and medium size practices of accountants (SMPs) in the adoption by SMEs of performance measurement systems

SMEs, whether they are incorporated or not, are likely to use external accountants to meet their statutory compliance requirements (IFAC, 2008). For those incorporated SMEs, this will include financial reporting requirements and tax computations and returns. In the case of unincorporated entities the service supplied may just be limited to tax. It is likely that if an accountant is employed in such a capacity they are likely to be in the category of Small and Medium Practitioners (SMP). Primarily, SMPs are used because of a gap in the internal resource base of SMEs. This is particularly the case with micro and smaller entities.

Defining SMPs is fraught with difficulties similar to those found with SMEs. However, a definition by IFAC captures the nature of SMPs:

> accounting practices whose clients are mostly SMEs, external sources are used to supplement limited in-house technical resources, and contain a limited number of professional staff.
>
> *(IFAC, 2010)*

Research also shows that the SME-SMP relationship, established through compliance work, will often lead into the provision of non-compliance advice and support (Bennett and Smith,

2004; Blackburn and Jarvis, 2010; Blackburn *et al.*, 2010; Carey *et al.*, 2005). The evidence further indicates that external accountants specifically will advise their clients regarding the financial management of the entity (Berry *et al.*, 2006).

We can conclude that there is a strong likelihood that the performance measures in practice employed in SMEs will be influenced by external accountants. This begs questions as to the nature of the advice delivered. Will it follow, for example, the assumptions regarding the desire for growth as compared to sustainability?

Conclusion

The aim of the chapter was to examine the application of performance measures in SMEs. While perhaps not surprisingly it was found that there are differences in the performance measures between large entities and SMEs; it was however also recognised that from a number of perspectives it was necessary to carefully examine the needs of the varying sizes of business entities within the categorisation of SME which is subsequently reflected in the performance measures adopted by these entities. Owner-managers of smaller entities will follow objectives that reflect their needs. This will often give a greater emphasis to a wider, more informal selection of measures than those adopted by larger entities to determine if the entity has met its objectives. The evidence suggests that the popular emphasis on growth as an important driver is not necessarily well founded with smaller entities. Greater emphasis is given to survival and sustainability.

From a researcher's perspective, there is a need to adopt a methodology, particularly in the case of 'lifestyle' businesses of micro-entities, that is sympathetic to capturing the close involvement of the owner-manager. This includes consideration of the range and definitions of success in 'lifestyle' businesses and the impact of external influences. Another difference between large and smaller entities is their cost structures. The smaller the entity, invariably the less complex the cost structures will be. This is particularly the case with accounting for overheads where, in the case of smaller entities, significantly more of the costs are direct. Although costs and revenues are important in the performance measures of SMEs, cash is given much more emphasis in smaller entities because of their vulnerability in their aim to survive in what may often seem to be a very uncertain economy.

The empirical evidence, although very limited, reflects these differences described above between large and small entities. The danger is the approach in researching these entities. There have been a number of occasions where researchers have adopted a normative approach when investigating small entities. This has resulted in a distortion of reality and can be very dangerous in practice and policy perspective. A number of studies of SMEs have argued for a much more grounded approach in researching these size of entities.

Accountants in practice play a very important role in advising their SME clients in the process of the adoption of performance measures. Therefore, a great deal of responsibility rests with these accountants. This is an area of importance that needs to be investigated robustly by academics, and which may result in some important initiatives by the accounting profession. But perhaps the most significant deficiency in the study of performance measures employed by SMEs is the lack of research of the subject, that will be addressed in the future.

Notes

1 European Commission, 2015: ec.europa. eu/enterprise/policies/sme/files/sme_definition/sme_user.
2 UK Companies House supply free company information including registered office address, filing history, accounts, annual return, officers, charges and business activity.

References

Ahmad, M.M. and Alaskari, O. (2014) Development of assessment methodology for improving performance in SME's. *The International Journal of Productivity and Performance Management*, 63(4), pp. 477–498.

Arnold, G. (2012) *Corporate Financial Management*, 5th Edition. London: Financial Times, Prentice Hall.

Ates, A., Garengo, P., Cocca, P. and Bititci, U. (2013) The development of SME managerial practice for effective performance management. *Journal of Small Business and Enterprise Development*, 20(1), pp. 28–54.

Beaver, G. (2002) *Small Business, Entrepreneurship and Enterprise Development*. London: Financial Times, Prentice Hall.

Bennett, R.J. and Smith, C. (2004) The selection and control of management consultants by small business clients. *International Small Business Journal* 22(5), pp. 435–462.

Berry, A. and Jarvis, R. (2011) *Accounting in a Business Context*, 5th Edition. Hampshire, UK: South Western Cengage Learning.

Berry, T., Sweeting, R.C. and Goto, J. (2006) The effect of business advisers on performance of SMEs. *Journal of Small Business and Enterprise Development*, 13(1), pp. 223–248.

Blackburn, R., Carey, P. and Tanewski, G.A. (2010a) The role of competence, trust and professional ethics in supply of external business advice by accountants to SMEs. A Report for the Association of Chartered Certified Accountants.

Blackburn, R. and Jarvis, R. (2010) The role of small and medium practices in providing business support to small and medium size enterprises. Information Paper. International Federation of Accountants, April.

Carey, P., Simnett, R. and Tanewski, G.A. (2005) Providing business advice to small and medium sized enterprises. Report prepared for CPA Australia, July.

Carsberg, B.V., Page, M.J., Sindall, A.J. and Waring, I.D. (1985) *Small Company Financial Reporting*. London: Prentice Hall International.

Collis, J. and Jarvis, R. (2000) How owner-managers use accounts. Centre for Business Performance, ICAEW.

Curran, J., Jarvis, R., Kitching, J. and Lightfoot, G. (1997) The pricing decision in small firms: complexities and deprioritising of economic determinants. *International Small Business Journal*, 15(2), pp. 17–32.

Debono, F. (2014) Management accounting and sensemaking – A grounded theory study of Maltese manufacturing SMEs. Thesis for the degree of Doctor of Philosophy, Southampton University.

Dellot, T. (2014) Salvation in a start-up? The origins and nature of the self-employment boom, RSA Action and Research Centre.

Drury, C. (2015) *Management and Cost Accounting*, 9th Edition. Andover, UK: Cengage Learning.

Dugdale, D., Hussey, J. and Jarvis, R. (1997) The owner manager and the FRSSE: can less mean more?. *Certified Accountant*, 89(11), pp. 32–33.

Freeman, R.E., Wicks, A.C. and Parmar, B. (2004) Stakeholder theory and 'the corporate objective revisited', *Organization Science*, 15(3), pp. 364–369.

Garengo, P., Biazzo, S. and Bititci, U. (2005) Performance measurement systems in SMEs: A review for a research agenda. *International Journal of Management Reviews*, 7(1), pp. 25–47.

IFAC (2008) The crucial roles of professional accountants in business in mid-sized enterprises. Information Paper, International Federation of Accountants, September.

IFAC (2010) Annual Report 2009, International Federation of Accountants.

Jarvis, R., Curran, J., Kitching, J., and Lightfoot, G. (2000). The use of quantitative and qualitative criteria in the measurement of performance in small firms. *Journal of Small Business and Enterprise Development*, 7, 123–133.

Jarvis, R., Kitching, J., Curran, J. and Lightfoot, G. (1996) The financial management of small firms: an alternative perspective. ACCA Report no. 49, Chartered Association of Certified Accountants, London.

Jennings, P. and Beaver, G. (1997) The performance and competitive advantage of small firms: a management perspective. *International Small Business Journal*, 15, pp. 63–75.

Kaplan, R. and Norton, D. (1992) The balanced scorecard: measures that drive performance, *Harvard Business Review*, Jan–Feb, 71–9.

Kaplan, R and Norton, D. (1996) Using the Balanced Scorecard as a strategic management system, *Harvard Business Review*, January/February, pp. 75–85.

Levy, H. and Sarnat, M. (1994) *Capital Investment and Financial Decisions*. Englewood Cliffs, NJ: Prentice Hall.

Marchini, I. (1995) 'Il governo della piccola impresa', *La gestione delle funzioni*, Vol. 3. Genova: ASPI/INS-EDIT.

Mitchell, F. and Reid, G. (2000) Problems, challenges and opportunities: small business as a setting for management accounting research, *Management Accounting Research*, 11(4), pp. 385–390.

Neely, A.D., Adams, C. and Kennerley, M. (2002), *The Performance Prism: The Scorecard for Measuring and Managing Business Success*. London: Pearson Education Ltd.

Page, M.J. (1884) Corporate financial reporting and the small independent company. *Accounting and Business Research*, 14(55), pp. 271–282.

Parry, S. (2015) The influence of neoliberal economics on small business accounting research: a critical evaluation of agendas and methodologies. *International Small Business Journal*. Forthcoming.

Scase, R. and Goffee, R. (1980) *The Real World of the Small Business Owner*. London: Croom Helm.

Stokes, D. and Wilson, N. (2010) *Small Business Management and Entrepreneurship*. Andover, UK: South Western Cengage Learning.

Storey, D. (1998) The ten percenters. Fourth Report: Fast Growing SMEs in Great Britain. Deloitte and Touche Tohmatsu, London, UK.

Strauss, A. and Corbin, J (1998) *Basics of Qualitative Research Techniques and Procedures for Developing Grounded Theory* (2nd edition). London: Sage Publications.

Taticchi, P., Flavio, T. and Cagnazzo, L. (2010) Performance measurement and management: a literature review and a research agenda. *Measuring Business Excellence*, 14(1), pp. 4–18.

Tenhunen, J., Rananen, H. and Ukko, J. (2001) *SME-Oriented Implementation of a Performance Measurement System*. Lahti, Finland: Department of Industrial Engineering and Management, Lappeenranta University of Technology.

Watson, J. (2010), SME Performance – Separating Myth from Reality. Cheltenham, UK: Edward Elgar, http://ec.europa.eu/eurostat/statistics-explained/index.php/Small_and_medium-sized_enterprises.

21

In search of hospitality

Theoretical and practical issues in performance measurement and management in hotels

Ruth Mattimoe and John Paul Tivnan

Introduction

The purpose of this chapter is to outline the performance measurement and management (PMM) literature on hotels against the background of the generic literature in the same area. The context of hotels is very important, because they are situated within the economically important service sector. Tourism is a service industry of significant importance to the economies of both Ireland and England:

> Tourism in England contributes £106 billion to the British economy (GDP) when direct and indirect impacts are taken into account, supporting 2.6 million jobs. When only direct impacts are taken into account (i.e. excluding aspects such as the supply chain), the contribution is £48bn, with 1.4 million jobs directly supported. In 2011, there were 208,880 VAT registered businesses in England in tourism sectors (this includes categories such as accommodation, food and drink, transport, travel agencies, cultural activities etc).
>
> *(www.visitengland.com/biz/tourism-england/value-tourism-england)*

First, it explains the key operational aspects of the cost structure of hotels and the variability of demand and fixed capacity, that tends to make them revenue-oriented businesses with revenue management as a key driver of their profitability. Then, the role of representative industry bodies such as *Fáilte Ireland* and *Visit Britain* is explained.

Second, the literature is reviewed in two stages, because in this area, there are two groupings – the literature and practices of the practitioner/hotel consultancy firms and tourism industry bodies and the academic literature. As sizeable differences exist between the worldview of academics and that of practitioners, the authors of this chapter put the professional hospitality and tourism industry bodies *and* hotel consultancy firms into one group (called the "consulting to practice" cohort) as they directly represent, advise or are working with the industry. Then, the literature of the hospitality academics is deemed to be a separate constituency (the theoretical cohort), because they only interface indirectly with the practitioners in the industry. Such groupings correspond with the study of Van Helden *et al.* (2010) who classified researchers and consultants as distinct and separate groups, noting differences in the knowledge creation process among them.

The academic literature on PMM is discussed, starting with basic definitions of these concepts and covering all three generations of multi-dimensional Performance Measurement (MDPM) frameworks right up to Strategic Enterprise Management systems. Performance Management is discussed, and the Fitzgerald and Moon (1996) dimensions, standards and rewards framework for implementing any MDPM system is reviewed. Then, against this backdrop, the academic PMM literature *in hospitality* is discussed. The key performance indicators (KPIs) for hotels are explained, and the role of benchmarking as a continuous improvement mechanism in the industry is profiled.

Moving to the hotel consultancy literature, the need for benchmarking as a mechanism for continual improvement in hotels is discussed and the hotel consultancy firm's *Crowe Horwath Annual Hotel Industry Survey* is profiled, highlighting the types of KPIs that are used in this survey. The use of the survey as a tool by which hoteliers can benchmark their operations is explained. The prevalence of financial metrics in this survey is noted. Moving to the importance of trend data within the industry, the use of dashboards and visuals is highlighted as an important characteristic of how the industry KPIs are presented.

Next, the online tools and research reports promulgated by Fáilte Ireland, which is the Irish tourism industry professional body, are deemed to be part of the "consulting to practice" constituency.

The chapter concludes with some recent empirical work on the metrics reported by small and medium-sized three-star hotels (all independent) in the northwest of Ireland, which shows very basic performance measurement systems, mainly financial – namely a focus on profit supplemented by personal knowledge of customers, which was considered more important than service quality. Some uncertainty regarding ways to measure quality was reported, and innovation was implicitly understood, without being formally measured.

Hotels – a profile of their operational characteristics

In this section, an attempt is made to profile a hotel's cost structure as well as the volatility of demand, and the ensuing need for hotels to be revenue focused is discussed.

A hotel is a total market concept, comprising location, facilities, service, image and price. Image is a by-product of location, facilities and service, but is enhanced by such factors as its name, appearance, atmosphere and association (famous movie stars as past guests, etc.).

Price expresses the value given by the hotel through its location, facilities, service and image and the satisfaction derived by its users from these elements of the hotel concept. Location is a fixed entity, but price, image, facilities and service lend themselves to some adaptation with time (Medlik, 1994).

> The individual elements assume greater or lesser importance for different people. One person may put location as paramount and be prepared to accept basic facilities and service, ...ignoring the image, as long as the price is within a limit to which he is willing to go. Another may be more concerned with the image of the hotel, its facilities and service. However, all the five elements are related to each other, and in a situation of choice, most hotel users tend to either accept or reject a hotel as a whole, that is the total concept.
>
> *(Medlik, 1994, p. 15)*

The hospitality industry has been acknowledged as an inspiring industry due to the intrinsic complexity (Berts and Kock, 1995). A restaurant operation within a hotel is pure manufacture, whereas the provision of a room is a pure service activity. A pub or a bar in the hotel operates as a retailer, buying stocks of alcohol that are stored until sale. Some really large hotels in Las Vegas, for example, illustrate the mixed example of manufacturing, service and retail in that they have rooms, entertainment and gambling (pure services), restaurants (manufacturing) and shops and bars (retail) all under one roof (e.g. Caesar's Palace).

The broad range of businesses within the industry also leads to a variety of ownership and management structures. Dittmann *et al.* (2009, p. 1355) give an interesting summary:

> An individual can decide to own and operate his or her own hotel unaffiliated with a brand. Alternatively, the owner can contract with a third party to manage the hotel. Another series of organizational forms begin with a hotel company (brand). They have the option of owning a hotel themselves or franchising. If they choose to franchise, the franchisee has to decide whether to operate the hotel him or herself or to contract with another party for the management of the hotel. If the franchisee opts for a management contract, he or she has to decide whether the hotel company (brand) should run the hotel or contract with some other third party. The final form is when a real estate developer decides to build a hotel. The individual rooms are sold to investors who then choose to live in their room or enter the room into a rental pool. A manager is then hired according to a standard management contract.

The hospitality industry competes a lot on quality as do most service firms, and this can be based on building a brand and sustaining brand value which must be sustained by quality of service, quality of employees and customer satisfaction. In manufacturing industries, rework can correct employee failures such as defective products, but in the hospitality industry, contact with customers is critical once they enter the "service factory" and mistakes cannot be easily corrected, before the customer experiences the service.

As Figure 21.1 shows, the rooms departments (in hotels) have low variable costs – usually they comprise (on the accommodation side) the costs of cleaning and of letting a room. This means that there is price discretion or that discounting is possible, because of minimal variable costs in any hotel whose revenue is derived mainly from selling rooms, rather than being a food and beverage operation. Therefore, it opens up the possibility of using dynamic room rates in pricing rooms. As the variable cost per occupied room is normally very low in relation to the average room rate (ARR) in hotels, even a 50 per cent reduction in the selling price leaves a sizeable contribution per occupied room. It also means that hotels must focus on maximising revenue rather than simply control of costs, as they have high fixed costs to cover, such as the costs of insuring the hotel building, depreciation of fixtures and bedroom furniture and administration costs.

As Figure 21.1 shows, the food and beverage department in a hotel has a lower fixed cost element in the total cost structure than variable cost. The rooms department has a high fixed cost element in the total structure, particularly if it is a luxury (five-star) hotel, and so the break-even point is higher than that of the food and beverage department. A luxury hotel will provide higher quality of facilities, high-specification buildings and stylish furnishings, with less flexibility to employ casual (variable cost) labour, but more permanent, highly skilled employee and management teams, which drives up the fixed cost proportion of total costs in these hotels (Harris, 2011).

Cost structure profile	Food and beverage department	Rooms department-budget hotel-2-star and 3-star	Rooms department-luxury hotel-4-star and 5-star
Variable cost compared to total cost	80%	50%	40%
Fixed cost compared to total cost	20%	50%	60%

Figure 21.1 Cost structure in the hotel industry

Profit-sensitivity analysis and profit-multipliers

Due to the presence of high fixed costs and a high break-even threshold, hotels with a significant rooms operation can be termed market-oriented or revenue-oriented (Harris, 2011). Such a hotel would be sensitive to revenue-based key factors, such as price level and volume of sales.

Harris (2011, p. 138) notes the key factors that profit is influenced by, such as room occupancy, ARR, number of covers[1] (meals), food and beverage prices, food and beverage cost of sales, other variable costs and finally fixed costs. Then, each of the factors is varied individually by say 10 per cent, holding the others constant, and the impact on profit is assessed, using a technique known as profit-sensitivity analysis.

$$\text{The profit-multiplier}(\text{PM}) = \%\ \text{change in net profit} \,/\, \%\ \text{change in the individual key factors}$$

The profit-multipliers for each of the key factors are computed, and a ranking is drawn up. If revenue-based key factors are top ranked, then the hotel is clearly a market-oriented one, whereas if cost-based factors are top ranked, then the business is cost-oriented. Harris (2011, p. 148) notes that "profit-sensitivity analysis provides a basic framework for developing a profit improvement programme". He also gives an interesting example of a luxury hotel as an example of a revenue-oriented business, whereas an airline catering contractor's profit-multiplier profile would represent a cost-oriented business. "The price level will usually be fixed by annual agreement with the airlines and the sales volume will normally be determined by the airlines' needs. Thus, both the revenue-based profit-multipliers are outside the control of the catering contractor. Therefore, the most appropriate control strategy to maintain profitability is to concentrate on cost of sales, variable payroll and to a lesser extent variable overhead" (p. 147).

Volatility of demand and yield (revenue) management

The pursuit of revenue is characterised by high volatility in demand. Hotels do not experience the same level of demand for their rooms each night, each week or each month or each year. The perishability of the room stock means that "you cannot save the room stock for another day; a sale lost is lost forever in these circumstances" (Jones *et al.*, 2012, p. 95). In the early years of the 1980s, following deregulation of the US airline industry and the discounting used by budget airlines, "yield management" was the term used to describe this demand-based flexible approach to pricing. Guilding (2014, p. 308) noted that the price of an air ticket depended on how far in advance the booking was made, whether it coincided with a period of high demand as well as prices offered by competing airlines. A constantly changing market with discounting by competitors and different market demand unfolding day by day, meant that seat pricing was a dynamic exercise. Today, the same mechanism operates in hotels for room rate pricing, but it is called revenue management. Further discussion of the intricacies of revenue management systems is omitted here, as it belongs to the theme of Analytics or Big Data.

Seasonality

Most hotels experience fluctuations in demand for hotel rooms such as peaks and troughs depending on the time of year and the day of the week. Weddings are most popular on Saturdays; business travel is mainly taken Mondays to Thursdays, but slackens in the summer as holidays are taken; short-break travel is mainly at weekends; major local, national and international events impact on demand for hotel rooms in Dublin and other cities – such as the Dublin Horse Show in August. There is a seasonality also in terms of peak holiday season (July–August), then off or low season (October–March) and finally the shoulder months between high and low season (April–June). This assumes the typical Irish or British situation where the high season is the (sunny) summer months, whereas in ski destinations, obviously the above low season could in fact be their high season.

All of these issues provide challenges to the revenue management functions in hotels, whether it be through simply packaging weekend breaks to cover periods of low demand to the sophisticated algorithms of expert systems software – see, for example, the market leading company: www.ideas.com.

Having profiled the operational characteristics of hotels, it is now useful to briefly describe the role of the national tourism industry representative bodies in Ireland and the UK, before proceeding to consider the general performance management and measurement literature.

Tourism industry representative bodies in Ireland and the UK

Fáilte Ireland is the National Tourism Development Authority. Its role is to support the tourism industry and work to sustain Ireland as a high-quality and competitive tourism destination. They provide a range of practical business supports to help tourism businesses better manage and market their products and services. They also work with other state agencies and representative bodies, at local and national levels, to implement and champion positive and practical strategies that will benefit Irish tourism and the Irish economy. They also market Ireland as a holiday destination through a domestic marketing campaign (DiscoverIreland.ie) and manage a network of nationwide tourist information centres that provide help and advice for visitors to Ireland – see more at: www.failteireland.ie/Footer/What-We-Do.aspx#sthash.8xMvK2sJ.dpuf.

The Irish Hotel Federation (IHF), which represents the hotels themselves, offers reports and surveys detailing the issues facing the hospitality industry in Ireland, including items such as budget planning, strategic planning and waste management policy (www.ihf.ie). The Irish Tourist Industry Confederation (ITIC) acts as a representative body for the hotel industry, dealing with issues such as lobbying government on policies impacting on tourism (www.itic.ie).

In addition to their destination promotion activities and grading inspections, etc., tourist boards also try to raise awareness of and prime benchmarking as a way of improving performance (Ogden, 1998). Professional hospitality and tourism industry bodies' literature was deemed to include reports and tools issued by bodies such as Fáilte Ireland, the Irish Hospitality Institute, the IHF, among others and indeed the equivalent in the UK (VisitBritain,[2] British Hospitality Association, etc.).

Performance measurement and management (PMM)

Before measurement, the company's strategy, organisation and processes must be understood and translated into a set of objectives. Then, there are two approaches to performance measurement to monitor that strategy – first, the stakeholder approach which means that companies compete on many dimensions other than financial ones, and so other non-financial measures need to be developed to capture the quality, service and flexibility issues of today's customer-oriented strategies. Second, the shareholder perspective favours a single financial metric such as profit, market share or residual income or economic value added.

The stakeholder perspective has a number of MDPM frameworks, such as the SMART pyramid (Lynch and Cross, 1991), the results and determinants framework (Fitzgerald *et al.*, 1991), the balanced scorecard (Kaplan and Norton, 1992) and the performance prism (Neely and Adams, 2001). These frameworks share some basic features – they must have a link to corporate strategy, include external as well as internal measures, include financial and non-financial measures, and make explicit the trade-offs between the various measures of performance (Fitzgerald, 2007, p. 224).

The frameworks are prescriptive in nature with generic dimensions of performance such as flexibility and customer satisfaction being specified. The actual measures chosen by hotels for these dimensions will depend on the business type and on the competitive strategy adopted by the organisation. Thus, as outlined at the start of this section, the starting point in all of these frameworks must be corporate strategy, cascading down into the specification of the critical success factors (CSF) which must be reflected either directly or indirectly in the set of measures used. Neely *et al.* (2003) discuss three generations of performance measurement frameworks. First-generation ones (balanced scorecard and the Skandia Navigator) supplemented traditional financial measures with non-financial ones. Second-generation ones (the Performance Prism) were a significant advance on first-generation ones, because they required success maps to be developed which required the question of how value was created from the transformation of resources across the perspectives, to be addressed. They also were further refined by the addition of failure or risk maps (Neely *et al.*, 2002). These identify the potentially critical failure points in the organisation that "if unmonitored could lead to excess exposure to risk" (p. 131). The neglect of how free cash flow is created in the latter models, led to third-generation frameworks that required organisations to look at the cash flow consequences of the linkages between the non-financial and intangible dimensions of organisational performance and the cash flow consequences of these (p. 132).

While the balanced scorecard (Kaplan and Norton, 1992) may be the first tangible balance of performance measures, Ridgeway (1956) had first acknowledged that concentration on any single measure of performance would lead to dysfunctional consequences as performance may then be maximised against that measure, to the detriment of overall performance. Research by Ittner and Larcker (1998a) concluded that "by incorporating non-financial indicators into their measurement systems, many firms sought to create a wider set of measures that capture not only firm value, but also the factors leading to the creation of value in the business" (Ittner and Larcker, 1998a, p. 214). It is therefore very important for an organisation to construct an optimal measurement system with a mix of financial and non-financial measures.

In an interesting paper, Bourne *et al.* (2003, p. 15) conducted research with executives in a number of leading European companies and concluded that "the past obsession with pure financial performance is decreasing and there may be a recognition that there is a trade-off between hitting today's financial results and sustaining the capabilities and competencies that allow companies to compete effectively in the future". Companies, they claim, are being asked to explain not only what their profitability is, but also how they achieve it and if they can explain this, it supports their share price. They also observed that many companies (one of the best known being Sears Roebuck and Co.) create a success map, which is a diagram showing the logic of how the objectives of the organisation interact to deliver overall performance; they have a great advantage in communicating both "how" objectives are to be achieved and "why" objectives have been developed (p. 16).

Another change that was observed was that companies (Shell for example) were using their own data to test their assumptions and were finding "counter-intuitive relationships that gave them greater insight into how to better manage their business" (p. 17). Another interesting finding they found was that the innovation and learning perspective was being evaluated in terms of the companies developing their process capabilities, in conjunction with their underpinning resources. So, they were managing their performance in a manner that brought them beyond measuring the indications of innovation (p. 19). Finally, they found that "linking objectives from the success map with process improvement initiatives creates sustainable improvements in performance" (p. 20).

Performance management

Measuring performance will have no impact unless action is taken as a consequence of that performance measure. Performance Management can be achieved using the Fitzgerald and Moon (1996) dimensions, standards and rewards framework, which answer the questions:

- What should be measured?
- How should standards/targets be set for the measures?
- What should be the rewards for meeting the targets/standards?

In particular, the measures should be balanced across the perspectives of whatever MDPM is being used; the targets must be owned, must be achievable and equitable between units and the bases for rewards should be clear, should motivate those concerned and should relate to matters controllable by those affected (Smith, 2007).

Recent research

Brignall and Ballantine (1996) have argued that there are three core elements to the design of any MDPM system:

- a control model (feedforward, feedback or a mix),
- a level/unit of organisational analysis (e.g. corporate, SBU, product),
- multiple dimensions of performance.

Brignall and Ballantine (2000) set out nine aspects to follow in designing and implementing a MDPM—noting the need to identify first of all the key stakeholders and their information needs, the level of the organisation where measurement will take place and ... finally the Fitzgerald and Moon (1996) dimensions, standards and rewards framework to smooth the implementation process. Ittner and Larcker (2003) caution that the selection of non-financial measures should not be chosen simply based on generic performance measurement frameworks and managerial guesswork, but more on "sophisticated quantitative and qualitative inquiries into the factors actually contributing to economic results" (p. 95).

Brignall and Ballantine (2004) explore the interaction between PMM systems and the many ways in which organisations strive to improve performance via organisational change programmes. Strategic Enterprise Management (SEM) systems are computerised enterprise management packages, but are designed to help with strategic change and integrated management processes aligned with strategy. Brignall and Ballantine (2004) argue that the design, implementation and use of SEMs can be studied using a model of "context, content and process" for organisational change (Pettigrew, 2000).

Stringer (2007) carried out a review of 120 field studies of Performance Management research over 15 years, published in the *Accouting Organisations and Society* and the *Management Accounting Research* journals, noting the striking diversity in terms of the performance elements studied, the types of studies, the theoretical development, the research questions, research sites and countries, whether the studies examine the whole organisation or parts of organisations and who is interviewed. This has led to a fragmentary nature of theoretical development in PM, as few studies use the same theoretical base or attempt to build on the theoretical development of prior studies.

A recent special issue of the top rated *Management Accounting Research* journal (Bourne *et al.*, 2014) noted that the last 30 years have seen "a revolution in performance measurement and management". The trend has been for traditional one-dimensional financial-based measurement to be replaced by multi-dimensional performance measurement frameworks (MDPM), which have financial and non-financial KPIs such as the SMART pyramid, balanced scorecard and Performance Prism. A lot of research was carried out over the last 30 years on the development and implementation of measurement systems, but the current focus of research "is concerned with how performance measurement is and should be used to manage the performance of the enterprise" (p. 117).

From an academic perspective, Bourne *et al.* (2014, p. 117) note that published studies "on the impact of performance measurement on performance management are inconsistent in their findings". From a practical perspective, new organisational structures, globalisation and increasing reliance on international supply chains, create additional complexity. The latter draw an interesting conclusion in relation to performance measurement research in general, noting the trend towards "a move away from simple frameworks and processes towards a more nuanced view of the field" (p. 117).

A degree of subtlety is required to use performance measures to manage an organisation. When the environment is changing rapidly, solutions are uncertain and precise measurement infeasible, people must engage with the *intent* of the KPIs and realise that they are just indicators of performance, rather than real performance. Bourne *et al.* (2014, p. 118) note that this may be encountered in many settings, particularly professional and knowledge work and even many service settings. This point is also made by Parmenter (2006), a noted performance improvement consultant and is discussed later.

Next, a brief overview of the PMM in the hospitality literature is discussed, starting with scorecard research in hotels.

Performance measurement in hotels: a review of academic literature

For modern business increasingly dominated by services, such as hotels, with its combination of intangible assets and need to create a consistently good service experience, the measurement of competitive performance becomes increasingly more difficult. It would appear from the literature and from visitor ratings by Fáilte Ireland, for example, that the three criteria of *customer service, quality and price* are vital to the hotel industry. In any service business, there is a complexity attaching to the determinants of competitive success and to the production of the service. As a result, the route to profitability is multi-faceted and differs between hotels even of the same grade. The above summarises the main aspects of hotels that make PMM for them, somewhat different from the generic PMM approach.

It is not surprising, therefore, that the balanced scorecard can be applied to hotels. An interesting diagram from Evans' (2005, p. 381) article shows a very good example of the causal linkages across the financial, customer, internal, learning and growth and innovation perspective using a hotel situation. This can be located at: http://dx.doi.org/10.1108/09596110510604805. Another interesting discussion of the benefits from the application of the balanced scorecard is mentioned in Huckenstein and Duboff (1999) of the Hilton Group's adoption of the scorecard, which was rated very positively.

Evans' (2005) survey found that many hoteliers (in the northeast of England) were using measures from all four scorecard categories and not just financial measures. However, Evans (2005, p. 387) reported that "further research is necessary to understand the relationship between the measures and the strategy and vision of the companies concerned and to understand whether managers fully understand the causal linkages inherent in the Balanced Scorecard".

By contrast, Atkinson and Brander-Brown (2001) suggested that the UK hotel industry appeared to concentrate on past-oriented financial measures, which suffer from such deficiencies as being lagging rather than leading indicators, being short term in focus and not linked to the competitive environment. They used a postal questionnaire of 88 hotel companies – all of the operators listed in *The Hospitality Yearbook 1999,* a mix of large international hotel organisations with multiple brands, regional chains as well as smaller independent operators. Of the non-financial measures that were monitored, it was quality of service and customer satisfaction that was measured, but they tended to be past-oriented measures.

Harris and Mongiello's (2001) survey of European chain hotel property general managers, using a balanced scorecard format, found that although some companies emphasised financial and/or customer measures, there was fairly convincing evidence that companies were using all four scorecard perspectives. Furthermore, through their assessment of managers' performance indicator (PI) choices based on "actions" taken, rather than on choices "listed", even though financial indicators were found to be the most used measures, they were not so prominent as to dominate managers' behaviour.

In a follow-up study comprising a small number of in-depth interviews with general managers who had completed the earlier questionnaire, Harris and Mongiello (2006) identified an interesting decoupling. While the managers interviewed were required to report (mainly) financial PIs to their corporate offices, when given a choice in managing their own properties, they described a significantly broader range of indicators.

Reports of the success of the scorecard in the hospitality literature are largely positive, but Atkinson (2006) concluded that the research is small-scale isolated projects, noting the need for more in-depth research. Another key trend is the separation of hotel investment companies from hotel operating companies, which has implications for corporate objectives and goal congruence, prompting the need for more work to see how in practice scorecard and similar frameworks can mediate the potentially diverging objectives of different stakeholders such as owners and operators. Increasing corporate ownership of hotels may lead investors for example, to set demanding financial targets, while paying little attention to the processes driving the results.

In a study of the association between non-financial performance measures and financial performance measures in a US hotel chain, Banker and Potter (2005) analysed the association between guest satisfaction and the level of complaints with revenue and gross operating profit (GOPPAR) and found that improvements in non-financial measures were followed shortly by increases in revenue and profit. From the results, they suggest that quantifying the relationship between financial and non-financial measures may provide the potential basis for setting targets for non-financial measures.

PricewaterhouseCoopers' (2000, p. 17) study suggests that "the number of rooms in a hotel does affect profitability...". O'Neill and Mattila (2006), who assessed the relationship between hotel revenue indicators and profitability in a sample drawn from published data, supported the PWC study. They found that although profitability was affected by age, scale and brand affiliation of hotel properties, occupancy was ultimately a larger contributor to net operating income. Similarly, Pine and Phillips (2005) undertook a broad comparative study of hotel performance in China using available data. Overall, the findings indicate that the bigger the hotel and the higher the star rating, the better the performance. They suggest that this may be partly due to the fact that the high performers apply international standards and business and management techniques and/or have foreign partners.

Although there has been significant growth of national and international hotel chains in recent decades, independent hotels continue to dominate the market in many countries (Shaw and Williams, 1994). An investigation into performance measurement practice in independent hotels in Northern Cyprus found the emphasis to be on guest satisfaction at the departmental level and financial results at the hotel level. Interestingly, this manifested itself in terms of mainly qualitative "real-time" measures related to the guest experience and quantitative "past" measures for financial results (Haktanir and Harris, 2005).

Phillips (1999), in an article entitled "Hotel performance and competitive advantage: a contingency approach", noted that traditional accounting-based measurement systems are no longer satisfactory for firms seeking competitive advantage (p. 359). In their quest for competitive advantage, existing performance measurement systems are falling short. In this conceptual paper, Phillips argues that a performance measurement system has the potential to deliver competitive advantage "if inputs, processes, outputs, markets and environmental characteristics are congruent with business objectives" (p. 359). He uses a 115-bedroom four-star mid-market hotel, part of a major hotel chain to show how the proposed performance measurement system can assist hoteliers in delivering competitive advantage. The hotel was focused on the business market segment and was located in the southeast of England and included bars, restaurants, a conference suite and a leisure club.

To satisfy rising customer expectations and keep pace with increasing competition, independent hotels will need to place a greater emphasis on the development of their own performance measurement system (PMS). In this regard, insights from consulting can be helpful. One of PWC Dublin's performance improvement partners, Cronin (2009) emphasises the need to provide *insights* rather than just information as vital in a world where, to achieve performance improvement, the business model is being squeezed all the time to generate gains:

> The world has now changed, minimizing revenue loss, cutting cost and conserving cash is what really matters. Analyzing that 0.5% drop in margin, challenging that supplier for cost and service, struggling with that pricing decision, screaming for that cost analysis, and

> reducing headcount have all become the priorities of the day. … Converting to an agile model with the appropriate mix of fixed and variable cost to meet market demands is key.
>
> *(Cronin, 2009, p. 45)*

Cost issues in hotels

Cost metrics such as payroll costs (rooms, food and beverage) as a percentage of the associated departmental revenue (rooms, food and beverage) are also vitally important for monitoring as are utility costs, which form part of undistributed operating expenses (see www.tandfonline.com/doi/pdf/10.1080/10913211.2015.1038196). As noted by Crowe Horwath (2015b, p. 11), these costs include gas/oil, electricity, water and waste removal, and while hotels have implemented conservation programmes to reduce the level of usage, prices have been increased by the utility provider:

> While the hotel sector is operating at 15.7% below [pre-recession] average room rate, the unit costs for utilities have vastly increased over the same period.
>
> *(p. 11)*

Moving next to the first section of the "consulting to practice" literature – namely that of the industry representative bodies, the aim is to explore the websites of these representative bodies to see the wisdom they promulgate regarding PMM.

Fáilte Ireland surveys and reports: professional tourism bodies' literature

Fáilte Ireland provides hoteliers with many surveys and reports containing valuable data on tourism in Ireland (www.failteireland.ie/Research-Insights/Accommodation-Statistics-and-Reports.aspx). For example, it annually conducts a visitor attitude survey, providing hoteliers with pertinent information on Ireland as a tourism destination, such as the importance of destination determinants in the decision of tourists to choose Ireland. Similarly, it annually produces a hotel survey, to monitor hotel performance, particularly with regard to occupancy levels, and to provide summative demand and supply trends in relation to grade, region, size and location (www.failteireland.ie). Fáilte Ireland also makes available information on the current performance of tourism sectors in Ireland, and also provides projections of future performance. The *Tourism Barometer*, provided quarterly by Fáilte Ireland, provides an insight into the performance of all sectors of the tourism industry and provides prospects for the remainder of the year (FI, 2010b).

The *Tourism Barometer* consists of a series of charts and indicates *trends* with regard to occupancy, overseas market performance, concerning issues and employment and perceptions as to factors affecting positive/negative performance, reasons for price increases/decreases and opinion trends as to the current economic situation. The accommodation occupancy survey offers hotels a benchmark for occupancy levels across the various accommodation types: hotels, guesthouses, bed and breakfasts, hostels and self-catering (www.failteireland.ie). Furthermore, the professional body provides overseas market estimates, enabling hoteliers to assess the overall market size.

Other Fáilte Ireland supports – the Business Tools website – KPI templates

The *Business Tools*[3] website provides access to cutting edge thinking, best practice business expertise and solid management advice. It consists of *online benchmarking tools* to increase

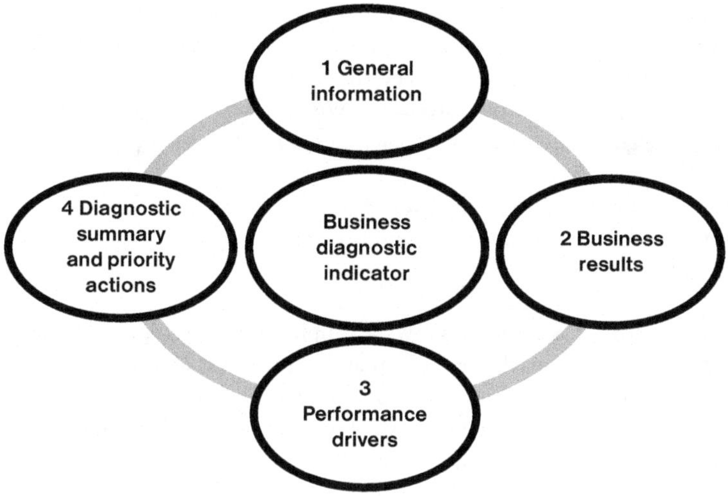

Figure 21.2 Business diagnostic indicator

competitive position and online best practice guides to improve business performance and some online solutions and specialised supports. This diagnostic indicator was developed by Fáilte Ireland and tourism operators to identify support needs within their enterprises. It is an online interactive facility accessed via the main Fáilte Ireland website, where all hoteliers can input their own financial metrics and benchmark their own financial performance with industry averages, so highlighting areas for improvement. Fáilte Ireland advocates adopting a KPIs perspective, and insists KPIs are not generalisable across all hotels in the industry, so each hotel must customise their own set. They also provide a template enabling hotel management to create a marketing budget and action plan specific to their hotel.

As part of the diagnosis, hoteliers are encouraged to enter background information in Stage 1, then at Stage 2, enter "hard" data or business results mostly in percentage terms, which will give a snapshot of the business and can be compared to external benchmarks such as the *Crowe Horwath Annual Hotel Survey* results. At Stage 3 – performance drivers – the 5 Ps – promotions, performance, profitability, people and processes – are highlighted (Figure 21.2).

This section (Stage 3) of the Diagnostic is focused on the *critical business dimensions which drive the results in the business.* It therefore tries to guide the hotelier towards leading indicators and processes, in contrast to the Crowe Horwath Annual Survey. The Diagnostic seeks to analyse current performance across five critical dimensions:

3.1. Promotions: How well do you currently implement your sales and marketing strategy and your customer relations management strategy?
3.2. Performance: How effective are your business planning efforts and how efficiently do you manage your key operational departments?
3.3. Profitability: How effective is your financial management system and how well do you monitor activity and results across all elements of the business?
3.4. People: How effectively do you manage, deploy and measure the impact of your human resources?
3.5. Processes: How well do you manage key supporting processes in your business?

Within each of these five areas, ten key questions are posed, the purpose of which is to prompt a discussion on the relevant area in order to determine whether it is an area of excellence or an area of deficiency and needing attention. For each key question, two sub-questions are provided to help the hotelier answer the key question. A simple three-point scale is used for "scoring" the response to each key question as follows:

- we underperform or are not active in this area,
- we perform well in this area,
- we excel in this area.

When the overall scoring is done, it shows a simple summary representation of where the business stands in relation to each area. Ultimately, the aim is to determine whether a particular area is an area of excellence or an area of deficiency and needing attention. See more at: www.Fáilteireland.ie/Supports/Develop-your-tourism-enterprise/Business-tools/Check-and-compare-your-hotel's-performance.aspx.

Once the performance gaps are identified, then moving to Stage 4, Fáilte Ireland offers best practice advice in the form of templates and questions for the hotelier to ask him/herself. See more at: www.Fáilteireland.ie/Supports/Develop-your-tourism-enterprise.aspx).

To conclude, an examination of the website of Fáilte Ireland shows that this professional body is promoting a practical approach to PMM. As illustrated above, there is an online interactive Business Diagnostic Indicator facility, which guides the hotelier forward –from benchmarking his/her financial metrics – to an examination of the *processes* behind these hard data. A further example of an initiative that encourages process benchmarking is the *Optimus* programme, promoted by Fáilte Ireland.

The Optimus framework

Fáilte Ireland created the *Optimus* framework to overcome the traditional frailties of PM in hotels. This framework is a derivative of total quality management (Ehrlich, 2006) and enables businesses to increase profitability, efficiency and competitiveness. Optimus is rooted in the principles of the European Excellence Framework for Management (EFQM) model. The objective of *Optimus* is to instil a customer-oriented focus throughout a hotel, whereby all procedures and processes are aligned towards the achievement of customer satisfaction. *Optimus* actively promotes excellence in the Irish hotel industry through the provision of awards for achievement of service excellence, best practice and business excellence (www.optimus.ie).

To realise such business excellence, *Optimus* consists of three steps, starting with Step 1, Service Excellence, leading to Step 2, the Mark of Best Practice, where the hotel is benchmarked in its results and processes against leading hotels. Step 3 is Business Excellence and to achieve this award, the standard of the EFQM must be satisfied. Implied characteristics of hotels obtaining this honour include inspirational leadership, strong values, ethics and culture and a focus on continuous learning and innovation among others.

Further to the three steps, level four and five awards can be achieved, which are recognised by EFQM. To achieve level four and five status, a hotel must develop effective partnerships with other hotels and stakeholders, conduct business activities ethically, and balance its commercial and legal responsibilities with its responsibilities to society (www.optimus.ie).

As the final part of the literature review, the hotel consultancy firms and what they promulgate, is next for consideration. These are closer to practitioners, because they actively work with hotel clients. Effectively, this source of literature (along with that of the professional tourism bodies) is viewed as the cohort which consults to practice and to practitioners (practice cohort).

Hotel consultancy literature/practice

Those organisations who wish to embrace change may find that the identification and transfer of *best practices* is key to successful change. Leading organisations in the industry may present best practice which others wish to model or benchmark. By comparing one's organisation to the best in class, performance gaps can be identified and one can seek to improve to the benchmark standard (ICAEW, 2006). Using benchmarking as a tool will support the firm's analysis and business case for continuous improvement. Firms select their own particular areas in need of improvement and benchmark these.

World-class organisations have recognised that to achieve the best results from benchmarking, they must go beyond simple benchmarking of numbers or metrics. They must critically examine their own practices (go behind the figures) and explore how the *process* performs and then understand the enabling factors that allow it to perform in such a manner, that defines it as best practice.

Many types of benchmarking exist – *metric, process, strategic, internal and competitive.* Metric is the initial step in benchmarking and helps identify a performance gap by gathering numerical data. The last type of benchmarking – competitive benchmarking – is useful in mining how your company is, compared to the industry.

It can be difficult for any firm to directly access competitor information. In the case of the hotel industry, a hotel consultancy firm, first founded in New York with the arrival of two brothers from Hungary, began to act as intermediaries, carrying out an annual survey that allowed average data to be collected from the hotel industry. Horwath Hotel, Tourism and Leisure (HTL) Consulting also established the *Uniform System of Accounts for the Lodging Industry* (USALI) – a system so successful, that it has become the international industry standard for hospitality accounting. Chin *et al.* (1995) noted that the widespread use and acceptance of a standard chart of accounts, in the form of the USALI, have helped competitive benchmarking.

Some of the benchmarking firms providing information to the hotel industry are now discussed.

TRI Hospitality (www.trihospitality.com/) is a private consulting firm based in the United Kingdom, of which there is no equivalent in Ireland, due to the considerably smaller market size. The HotStats chain hotels survey is compiled each month by TRI Hospitality Consulting. It collects profit and loss benchmarking data from more than 1,650 properties representing 360,000 rooms from 100 different brands in the UK, Europe and the Middle East, which enables monthly comparison of hotels' performance against their competitors.

It is distinguished by the fact that it provides in excess of 100 performance metric comparisons covering 70 areas of hotel revenue, cost, profit and statistics, providing far deeper insight into the hotel operation than any other tool. The KPI data collected and reported by the firm are divided into three branches: profitability, DataWeek and market intelligence. Over 100 metrics in the profitability branch are provided, focusing on rooms department, market segmentation, restaurants and public houses, conference facilities, sales and marketing department, overheads, expenses, utility costs, payroll and profits. DataWeek provides information updated daily on room KPIs.

Furthermore, HotStats issues monthly surveys and reports, in which an analysis of the hotel industry environment and performance is provided. HotStats describes within its reports the main KPIs for hotels to be: occupancy percentage, ARR, room RevPAR, total RevPAR, payroll percentage of total revenue and total GOPPAR (HotStats 2011a,b). For full-service hotels, HotStats includes two additional indicators, namely food and beverage RevPAR and the GOPPAR percentage of total revenue (HotStats, 2011c).

Benchmarking in hotels and the Crowe Horwath Annual Hotel Industry Survey

Crowe Horwath Ireland is a member of *The Horwath HTL* network comprising over 50 offices in 39 countries and carries out the Ireland Hotel Industry Survey. As specialist hospitality consultants, the *Crowe Horwath Annual Hotel Industry Survey* serves as a hotel consultancy-based benchmarking tool for the sector (Crowe Horwath, 2015a). Detailed information can be extracted, such as illustrated in Table 21.1.

The most recently available one is the *Ireland Hotel Industry Survey 2015*, an adapted extract from which, shown in Table 21.1, shows the typical metrics that would be reported for the Irish hotel industry, providing average figures for each grade of hotel to perform their own benchmarking exercise. Although shown below by grade of hotel, the same metrics are reported elsewhere in the survey, by region and also by size of hotel – hotels of 1–49 rooms, 50–99 rooms and 100+ rooms. The hotelier reading the survey can fill in his/her own metrics on a special table at the back of the survey booklet, called "Analyse your own Operation" (see, for example, Crowe Horwath, 2015b, p. 43).

Crowe Horwath does not provide a multi-dimensional (MDPM) framework per se for the industry; however, extensive discussion and analysis of the overall average industry results by grade, location and size of hotel are provided, and it therefore enables benchmarking (see later).

Table 21.1 Overall performance measurements: Ireland hotel industry survey 2015 (based on the 2014 season)

	All hotels 2014	*Luxury 2014*	*First class 2014*	*Mid-price 2014*	*Economy 2014*
Average room occupancy	67.8%	68.3%	68.7%	68.7%	62.2%
Average room rate	€82.29	€159.04	€81.71	€62.25	€50.01
RevPAR	€55.79	€108.62	€56.13	€42.77	€31.11
Total revenue per available room (*TRevPAR*)	€53,916	€88,121	€57,053	€43,526	€26,346
Gross operating profit per available room (*GOPPAR*)	€11,902	€20,056	€12,570	€9,574	€5,241
Profit before tax and finance per available room	€9,201	€15,548	€9,821	€7,439	€3,301
Profit before tax and finance per room %	17.1%	17.6%	17.2%	17.1%	12.5%
Gross margin %					
Food %	69.1	69.9	69.5	68.4	68.8
Beverage %	66.9	68.9	67.0	66.7	65.3
Profit before tax to room revenue %	44.3	38.2	47.6	46.8	30.0
Profit before tax to total revenue %	17.1	17.6	17.2	17.1	12.5

Source: Adapted from Crowe Horwath (2015b, pp. 6 and 27).

In small hotels, cash flow is essential for survival, as they may experience low turnover and profitability. Ogden (1998) found wide variation in standards of quality and cost control across the small hotel section in Scotland, noting that "one of the main reasons for the disappointing performance was the lack of standard procedures and performance standards with in-built management checks" (p. 189).

Small hotels pride themselves on an ability to offer a specialised service as a key part of their competitive strategy, compared to the more undifferentiated service delivery package of large chains. Ogden (1998, p. 189) clarifies that benchmarking is not about standardisation "but about highlighting critical success factors and developing systems to improve attainment of them which will fit the specific operation".

Taking an overview of the key metrics, the figures in Table 21.2 next (reading from right to left) show that

- occupancy levels grew by 1.9 percentage points to 67.8 per cent,
- ARR increased by €4.80 to €82.29, up 6.2 per cent on 2013,
- total revenue per room (TRevPAR) grew by 9.5 per cent to €53,916,
- profit margins improved by 2.2 percentage points to 17.1 per cent,
- overall profit before tax and finance per room increased by 25 per cent to €9,201,
- note that average room occupancy and ARR are also analysed *per month* in the Survey.

Table 21.2 Key highlights – all hotels

	All hotels 2014[a]	*All hotels 2013*[b]	*All hotels 2012*[c]
Average room occupancy[d]	67.8%	65.9%	63.8%
Average room rate[d]	€82.29	€77.49	€74.72
RevPAR	€55.79	€51.07	€47.67
Total revenue per available room (*TRevPAR*)	*€53,916*	€49,249	€47,145
Gross operating profit per available room (*GOPPAR*)	€11,902	€9,977	€9,094
Profit before tax and finance per available room	*€9,201*	€7,347	€6,497
Profit before tax and finance per available room %	*17.1*	14.9	13.8
Gross margin %			
Food %	69.1	67.9	67.1
Beverage %	66.9	66.7	65.9
Profit before tax to room revenue %	44.3	39.0	36.7
Profit before tax to total revenue %	17.1	14.9	13.8
Other cost-based metrics:			
Departmental payroll and related expenses as % of rooms revenue	24	24.7	25.1
Departmental payroll and related expenses as % of food and beverage revenue	33.4	32.9	34.0
Undistributed payroll and related expenses as % of total revenue	38	37.8	39.4

a Adapted from Crowe Horwath (2015b, pp. 6 and 27).
b Adapted from Crowe Horwath (2014, pp. 34 and 35).
c Adapted from Crowe Horwath (2013, pp. 34 and 35).
d Note that average room occupancy and average room rate are also analysed *per month* in the Survey.

Interestingly, the ARR in 2014 lags the pre-recession (2006) ARR (see Crowe Horwath, 2015b, p. 8). This can be seen in Figure 21.3. Further analysis of this rate *by grade* reveals a lag also. In these highlights (Figure 21.3), there is a clear emphasis on *financial revenue-oriented* measures of performance such as ARR and Occupancy, RevPAR, and TRevPAR.

In addition, one cost metric is reported, namely the ratio of departmental labour cost to rooms revenue and indeed, the equivalent cost metric is reported for food and beverage and total revenue. This labour cost metric in fact measures resource utilisation for a high cost in hotels – that of labour. In the survey, there are some non-financial statistics such as percentage of repeat business, length of stay and number of guests per room. Therefore, benchmarking metrics are available based on *non-financial* as well as financial data such as Average Daily Room Rate and RevPAR. Non-financial metrics are reported, but are not headlined in the survey as much as financial metrics.

Dashboards and the visual

An interesting consulting article by Jonathan Tellis (2010) explains the definition of an information dashboard (based on the book by Stephen Few) and it is used by the business intelligence software industry to convey the idea that it is possible to drive an organisation using constantly adjusted KPIs, in the same way that it is possible to drive a car. A visual display is needed on a single screen to allow the most important information to be monitored at a glance (p. 11). The use of visuals such as the Occupancy and ARR trend in the chart (Figure 21.3) shows the *trend* in these metrics.

Such charts could be done by individual hotels to see how their trend compares to the overall trend for the industry. As Caeman Wall, Head of Research at Fáilte Ireland, says, "after two decades of such reports, Crowe Horwath's analysis of the sector is at this stage a priceless piece in the mosaic of intelligence we have for this industry" (Crowe Horwath, 2015c, p. 4). The results (Figure 21.3) show the drop in occupancy and ARR rates in 2008 and 2009 when the hotel industry hit recession, but a slow recovery in room occupancy, rates, revenue and profits beginning in 2012.

Trend data, as shown in Figure 21.3, can bring figures alive, particularly for non-finance personnel. It is something that is very common in hospitality, particularly in the Crowe Horwath Survey, the Fáilte Ireland Tourism Barometer[4] and other reports as well as Visit

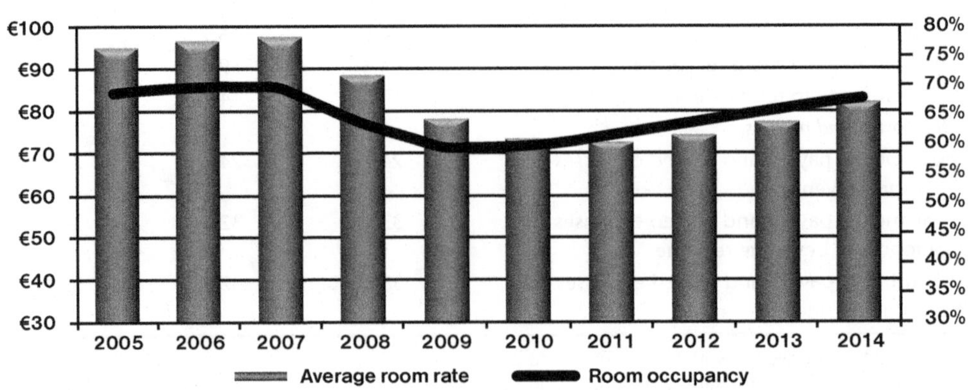

Figure 21.3 Occupancy and ARR trends

Britain, the national tourism body for Britain. For instance, by surfing to VisitBritain at www.visitbritain.org/latest-quarterly-data-uk-overall, anyone can get some charts showing the latest quarterly data for overall visits to the UK, based on the International Passenger Survey. This shows the overall volume and value of visits to the UK by overseas residents. The metrics reported are number of visits, spending and visitor nights from April to June 2015. By surfing on, further charts can be seen, showing for the latest quarter for example, visits to the UK by overseas visitors, the breakdown of visits, nights and spend by market and purpose of visit.

Finally, Parmenter (2006) gives practical advice based on consultancy experience regarding the "new thinking on key performance indicators". He suggests (p. 3) that there are in fact three types of performance measure – KRIs, PIs and KPIs (key results indicators, performance indicators and key performance indicators). He developed the 10/80/10 rule (an organisation should have no more than ten KRIs, up to 80 PIs and ten KPIs).

The common characteristic of KRIs is that they are the result of many actions – they give a clear picture of where you are going, but do not tell management what they need to do to achieve desired outcomes. Only PIs and KPIs can do this. KRIs that have often been mistaken for KPIs include customer satisfaction, net profit before tax etc. The 80 or so PIs that lie between KRIs and KPIs are PIs. They help teams align themselves to the firm's strategy. They include net profit on key product lines, profitability of the top ten customers, etc.

A KPI should tell you what action needs to take place and comprise a set of measures focusing on those aspects of organisational performance most critical for the current and future success of an organisation. They should number less than 10, be measured frequently (daily or 24/7), be non-financial, be understood by all staff and acted upon by the senior management team on a daily or 24/7 basis and be capable of being tied down to individual or team responsibility and have a significant impact on most of the CSF and balanced scorecard perspectives for the organisation (p. 3).

This is valuable clear advice from an acknowledged expert in the field of Performance Measurement consultancy.

Having considered the literature from academia, the tools promoted by Fáilte Ireland to measure and manage performance and the hotel consultancy reports and benchmarking data, it is now appropriate to review empirical work carried out in hotels in the northwest of Ireland. This provides an important check on the *actual practice* of PMM.

Empirical findings from a survey of hotels in the northwest of Ireland

The empirical work was based on a taught master's dissertation carried out over 3 months, which examined what measures were used by management to evaluate performance in three-star hotels, in the northwest region of the Republic of Ireland. The tourism industry in Ireland, particularly in the northwest region, has undergone significant growth since the early 1990s attributable to demand for alternatives to agriculture and fuelled by generous incentives through European Union (EU) grant aid. Using a survey of all three-star hotels in the region, listed in the IHF's *Be Our Guest* guide, a useable response rate of 57 per cent was achieved from the postal questionnaire survey. This was higher than the 20 per cent reported in a postal survey of 88 hotels by Atkinson and Brander-Brown (2001). The questionnaire was divided up into 12 dimensions of performance. These were classified into financial performance, customer service, operations and marketing (this questionnaire is not reproduced here but is available from the authors).

Demographics

Respondents were asked to indicate a profile of their age, position, gender and education.

Owner-managers and managers were evenly split with 50 per cent each. 43.8 per cent of respondents were aged between 31 and 40 years, and a further 43.8 per cent were over 41 years. Only 12.5 per cent of respondents were between 20 and 30 years. 81.3 per cent of respondents were male and 18.8 per cent were female. Regarding education, 43.8 per cent of respondents indicated that they had attained either certificate or diploma. 12.5 per cent indicated that they had attained a master's degree.

Sample selection

The questionnaire was distributed by post to a sample of 28 three-star hotels and guesthouses in the northwest region of the Republic of Ireland, based on the entire listing per the *Be Our Guest* guide. Responses were received from 16 of the 28 surveyed. The sample, while small, was believed to serve as a good approximation of the views of three-star hotel managers.

Financial performance

Respondents to the survey viewed *profitability* as very important to the success of the organisation. It was used extensively in decision making and strategy formulation but not so much in staff performance evaluation. Cost efficiency was not considered as important as profitability, as a determinant of success.

Customer service

Relations with customers and product/service quality are considered in the literature to be one of the most important determinants of success in the hospitality industry (Croston, 1995). Respondents reiterated this suggestion with over 80 per cent agreeing that *customer retention*/satisfaction was a very important driver of long-term success. It was not, however, extensively used in evaluating managerial and staff performance. Respondents also did not believe that service quality was as important as relations with customers for long-term success. Respondents were also unsure as to the quality of their measurement system for assessing product/service quality.

Operations

Operational/divisional performance was not considered very important to long-term success and was not used extensively in evaluation of staff performance. It also emerged that relations with employees were not considered very important. The majority of hotels surveyed were small to medium businesses and as the case findings suggested, relations with employees were considered very good with high levels of communication and were thus not considered an issue. Likewise, relations with suppliers were not considered of paramount importance.

Respondents did not agree that innovation was a crucial area in the success of hotels or service firms. Innovation was identified by Fitzgerald *et al.* (1991) as a good source of competitive advantage, yet respondents were divided over its importance. However, as Fitzgerald *et al.* (1991) suggested, innovation is a naturally occurring phenomenon in service businesses. Perhaps these hotels had an informal system that facilitated innovation, but were neither aware of it nor measured it.

Summary of empirical findings

The results show a lag in the performance measurement framework in use in these hotels – they would appear to belong to the first generation of such frameworks. A significant number of in-depth interviews with some of the respondents to the survey, would complement the questionnaire findings, as would an exploration of the training and qualifications of the hotel owner-managers who replied.

Conclusions

There has been a significant increase in the amount of published work on generic PMM, as noted by the recent *Management Accounting Research* 2014 issue devoted to the topic. Similar work on PMM in the hospitality industry is ongoing and has been discussed. The academic literature is plentiful in the area of generic frameworks that balance financial and non-financial performance measures and indeed has progressed to the third generation of such frameworks. Hotel consultancy firms, however, provide a significant amount of benchmarking data, largely of financial revenue-oriented measures, with fewer non-financial measures.

The industry in the UK is also well served by many sources of benchmarking data from VisitBritain, HotStats, etc. Eminent consultants like Parmenter (2006) warn that there should be no more than ten KPIs and they must be measured daily. When the tools and advice offered by an industry representative body such as Fáilte Ireland are reviewed, benchmarking of financial results is the first stage in diagnosing your business, but interestingly, the other stage is an examination of the processes that contribute to these results with a focus on *people, processes, performance* and *profitability*.

When actual practice by hotels was examined, however, the research was limited in that it was done by means of a postal survey, rather than by using case studies. The short study in this chapter was based on a small sample of owner-managed small- and medium-sized hotels in the northwest of Ireland and has produced similar results to those of Atkinson and Brander-Brown (2001) in the UK, namely a majority of the respondent hotel companies almost exclusively monitor financial dimensions of performance. Also, there was some similarity in the attention and importance paid to customer satisfaction that was monitored more frequently and at more organisational levels in the latter study, than quality of service, in common with the Irish study reported here.

In practice, the empirical work showed a focus on measuring and managing the financial dimensions, especially revenue performance. It is then possible, however, for these hotels to follow up on improving their capabilities and processes using the *Optimus* framework, for example, which is primed and evaluated (through awards and certificates, etc.) by the industry representative body – Fáilte Ireland. This practice can counteract the apparent lack of measurement of the other non-financial aspects of a hotel's business, such as quality of service, customer satisfaction and innovation. If the hotelier does not measure these aspects using their own non-financial measures, they may still intuitively understand them or may rely on the help and support from the industry representative body – in the form of templates, to improve performance in these areas.

When actual practice is assessed using hotels in the northwest of Ireland, it would appear that some of the prescriptions of the academic literature are followed, in that financial performance is measured, but there is a lag in the use of MDPM frameworks. The management and measurement of the non-financial aspects of a hotel's performance can be encouraged through the use of Fáilte Ireland's *Optimus* framework and its various online templates aimed at improving operational as well as financial performance.

Hotel consultancy firms can also provide benchmarking data through the *Crowe Horwath Annual Hotel Industry Survey*, for example. Therefore, the role of the industry bodies is to help the hotel move towards better performance in stages or levels, without implementing an official MDPM approach per the academic literature. Therefore, the SME hotels in this survey displayed a somewhat nuanced approach to PMM, through a combination of basic financial measurements and focus on profitability, supplemented by an awareness (but no measurement) of what else was important in the particular hotel.

Therefore, the lack of non-financial measures *per se* may not be a hindrance to good performance, provided the hotelier is *able to explain* not only what their profitability is, but also how they have achieved it, as Bourne *et al.* (2003) emphasise.

The insights and tools offered by the "consulting to practice" cohort, therefore, are hugely complementary to the prescriptions of the purely academic literature (the "theoretical" cohort), when discussing issues of actual PMM in hotels.

Appendix 21.1

Definition and explanation of KPIs used by hotels

Research by Croston (1995) suggested that "success in hotels is a journey, not a destination". To help understand this journey, some KPIs are now defined and explained.

The Average Daily Room Rate or ARR is defined as follows:

$$\frac{\text{Room sales revenues achieved}}{\text{Total no. of rooms occupied}}$$

and the Average Room Occupancy metric is

$$\frac{\text{No. of rooms sold}}{\text{Total rooms available in the hotel}}$$

Both of these metrics, on their own, are incomplete measures of sales performance. A higher level of room sales revenues will not result from an increased occupancy level, if the room rate has been disproportionately dropped. Similarly, a higher level of total revenue from rooms will not result, if an increase in the ARR coincides with a disproportionate decline in the occupancy rate.

To circumvent this incompleteness problem, the manager can link the ARR to occupancy statistics and this is what RevPAR achieves – it aggregates the two metrics.

If we take a hotel with 100 rooms of which 60 rooms are sold for a given day, generating a total revenue of €4200, we can compute RevPAR in either of two ways:

$$\text{RevPAR} = \text{ADR} * \text{Average Occupancy}$$

By dividing the Total Revenue by the Number of rooms sold (€4200/60), we get the value of €70 as the Average Daily Room Rate. Meanwhile, we find a 60 per cent Occupancy rate (60/100 rooms occupied).

So, aggregating the ARR by the Occupancy per cent, we get (€70 * 0.6) = €42 = RevPAR

An alternative calculation is to divide (€4200/100), where we also arrive at a RevPAR result of €42.

Total revenue per room or *TRevPAR* is an update to the widely used RevPAR – it is the total revenue earned from all of the guest spend – so it includes the revenue earned from letting the room, but also includes food and beverage spend and spend on spa treatments, tours, parking, gifts, etc. *TRevPAR* is the preferred metric for accountants and hotel owners, because it effectively determines the overall financial performance of a property, while *RevPAR* only takes into account revenue from rooms. *TRevPAR* is useful for hotels where rooms are not necessarily the largest component of the business. Outlets such as banquet halls and spas also provide a source of revenue for these hotels.

It is interesting to note that in the adapted extract (Figure 21.3), that *both RevPAR and TRevPAR* are reported.

GOPPAR per available room goes beyond RevPAR by taking total annual hotel revenue after all departmental and undistributed operating expenses and dividing this figure by the number of rooms available. It puts attention on profit at the broader hotel property level but correlates it to rooms, the main driver of hotel business.

The Yield statistic is a measure of room revenue achieved in relation to room capacity and is expressed as a percentage:

Yield percentage = Rooms revenue/Maximum potential rooms revenue

Actual revenue is related to maximum potential revenue on the basis of 100 per cent room occupancy or guest occupancy, or however full capacity is defined for a particular hotel, using the full rack rate and excluding value added tax and breakfast (if included) to give maximum attainable revenue (Harris, 2011, p. 44).

It is the reciprocal of *RevPAR,* which is a monetary value per room. This simple yield statistic provides a single value for measuring the performance of the hotel in revenue management terms, but it does not probe the profitability earned. To do this would mean deducting the cost of servicing the room from the revenue, so computing a contribution-based yield figure. See Adams (2006, p. 112).

The yield statistic above can be maximised by managing both the room rate and the occupancy percentage, "so that when demand exceeds supply, the customer pays more and when demand is low, the price is discounted, while ensuring that each customer pays the maximum possible price" (Adams, 2006, p. 112). "Rate cutting can generate more revenues, but is not always transferred to the bottom line when operating profit per occupied room is falling, owing to expenses increasing at the rate of inflation" (Adams, 2006, p. 110).

Notes

1 In the restaurant industry, the term "cover" refers to a diner who eats or a meal that is served. A cover differs from a table in that it represents only one of the meals served at that table. It differs from a dish in that it includes the extras that a diner orders, such as drinks, appetizers and desserts. When projecting sales, many restaurateurs find that they achieve a greater degree of accuracy by basing their calculations on expected number of covers rather than expected number of tables. See http://yourbusiness.azcentral.com/cover-restaurant-6923.html.

2 As the strategic body for inbound tourism and the national tourism agency – a non-departmental public body funded by the Department for Culture, Media & Sport – Visit Britain has a unique role in raising Britain's profile worldwide, increasing the value of tourism exports and developing

Britain's visitor economy. Its mission is to grow the value of inbound tourism to Britain, working with a wide range of partners in both the UK and overseas. See: https://www.visitbritain.org/.

3 www.failteireland.ie/Supports/Develop-your-tourism-enterprise/Business-tools/Check-and-compare-your-hotel%E2%80%99s-performance.aspx.

4 See for example: www.Fáilteireland.ie/FáilteIreland/media/WebsiteStructure/Documents/3_Research_Insights/3_General_SurveysReports/Fáilte-Ireland-tourism-barometer-October-2015.pdf?ext=.pdf.

References

Adams, D. (2006), *Management Accounting for the Hospitality, Tourism and Leisure Industries: A Strategic Approach*, 2[e], London: Thomson Learning.

Atkinson, H. and Brander-Brown, J. (2001), "Re-thinking performance measures: assessing progress in UK hotels", *International Journal of Contemporary Hospitality Management,* 13(3): 128–135.

Atkinson, H. (2006), "Performance measurement in the international hospitality industry", *In*: Harris, P.J. and Mongiello, M. (eds) *Accounting and Financial Management: Developments in the International Hospitality Industry,* Oxford: Elsevier, pp. 46–70.

Banker, R.D., Potter, G., and Srinivasan, D. (2000), "An empirical investigation of an incentive plan that includes nonfinancial performance measures", *The Accounting Review,* 75(1): 65–92.

Berts, K. and Kock, S. (1995) "Implementation considerations for activity-based cost systems in service firms: the unavoidable challenge," *Management Decision,* 33(6): 57–63.

Bourne, M., Franco, M. and Wilkes, J. (2003), "Corporate performance management", *Measuring Business Excellence,* 7(3): 15–21.

Bourne, M., Melnyk, S.A., Bititci, U., Platts, K. and Andersen, B. (2014) Editorial – Emerging issues in performance measurement, *Management Accounting Research,* 25: 117–118.

Brignall, S. and Ballantine, J. (1996), "Performance measurement in service businesses revisited", *International Journal of Service Industry Management,* 7(1): 6–31.

Brignall, S. and Ballantine, J. (2000), "From performance measurement to performance management: the determinants of performance", Paper presented at the EAA Annual Congres, Munich, March.

Brignall, S. and Ballantine, J. (2004), "Strategic enterprise management systems: new directions for research", *Management Accounting Research,* 15: 225–240.

Brotherton, B. and Wood, R.C. (eds) (2008), *The Sage Handbook of Hospitality Management,* London: Sage Publications Ltd.

Chin, J., Barney, W. and O'Sullivan, H. (1995), "Best accounting practice in hotels: a guide for other industries?", *Management Accounting,* 73: 57.

Cronin, G. (2009), "Cost reduction- what others are doing", *Accountancy Ireland,* 41(4): 45–47.

Croston, F.J. (1995) "Hotel profitability – critical success factors", *In:* P.J. Harris (ed.) *Accounting and Finance for the International Hospitality Industry,* Oxford: Butterworth-Heinemann.

Crowe Horwath (2013), *Ireland Hotel Industry Survey 2013,* Dublin: Bastow Charleton and Horwath HTL.

Crowe Horwath (2014), *Ireland Hotel Industry Survey 2014,* Dublin: Bastow Charleton and Horwath HTL.

Crowe Horwath (2015a), *Benchmarking- How do you measure up?*, Available from: www.crowehorwath.com.au/opportunities/images/Benchmarking_How_do_you_measure_up_AU.pdf [Accessed 20 Sept 2015].

Crowe Horwath (2015b), *Ireland Hotel Industry Survey 2015,* Dublin: Bastow Charleton and Horwath HTL.

Crowe Horwath (2015c), *Ireland Hotel Industry Survey Executive Summary and Highlights 2015,* Dublin: CH, Available from: https://www.crowehorwath.net/uploadedfiles/ie/industries/hotels,_tourism_and_leisure/crowe%20horwath%20hotel%20industry%20report%202015%20-%20executive%20summary.pdf [Accessed 5 November 2015].

Dittmann, D.A., Hesford, J.A. and Potter, G. (2009) "Managerial accounting in the hospitality industry", *In*: Chapman, C.S., Hopwood, A.G. and Shields, M. D. (eds) *Handbook of Management Accounting Research,* London: Elsevier, pp. 1353–1369.

Ehrlich, C. (2006) "The EFQM-model and work motivation", *Total Quality Management and Business Excellence,* 17(2): 131–140.

Evans, N. (2005), "Assessing the balanced scorecard as a management tool for hotels", *International Journal of Contemporary Hospitality Management*, 17(5): 376–390.

FI (2010a), *Tourism Facts 2010 – Preliminary Version*, Available from: www.failteireland.ie/FailteCorp/media/FailteIreland/documents/Research%20and%20Statistics/Tourism%20Facts/2010/2010_Preliminary_Tourism_Facts.pdf.

FI (2010b), *Tourism Barometer 2010: Wave 3 September.* Available from: www.failteireland.ie/FailteCorp/media/FailteIreland/documents/Research%20and%20Statistics/Current%20Tourism%20Performance/Tourism-Barometer-September-2010.pdf.

Fitzgerald, L. (2007), "Performance measurement", *In*: Hopper, T.H, Northcott, D. and Scapens, R.W., *Issues in Management Accounting*, Essex: Pearson Education Limited.

Fitzgerald, L., Johnston, R., Brignall, S., Silvestro, R. and Voss, C. (1991), *Performance Measurement in Service Businesses*, London: CIMA.

Fitzgerald, L. and Moon, P. (1996), *Performance Measurement in Service Businesses: Making It Work*, London: CIMA.

Guilding, C. (2014), *Accounting Essentials for Hospitality Managers*, 3e Abingdon, Oxford: Routledge.

Haktanir, M. and Harris, P. J. (2005), "Performance measurement practice in an independent hotel context", *International Journal of Contemporary Hospitality Management*, 17(1): 39–50.

Harris, P.J. (2011), *Profit Planning*, 3e, Oxford: Goodfellow Publishers Ltd.

Harris, P.J. and Mongiello, M. (2001), "Key performance indicators in European hotel properties: general managers' choices and company profiles", *International Journal of Contemporary Hospitality Management*, 13(3): 120–127.

Harris, P.J. and Mongiello, M. (eds) (2006), *Accounting and Financial Management: Developments in the International Hospitality Industry*, Oxford, UK: Butterworth-Heinemann, Elsevier.

HotStats (2011a), "UK Chain Hotels Market Review March 2011", Available from: www.hotstats.com/USERFILES/FILE/UKCHAINHOTELSREVIEW/HOTSTATS_MONTHLY_PR_UK_MARCH_2011.PDF.

HotStats (2011b) "UK Chain Hotels Market Review April 2011", Available from: www.hotstats.com/USERFILES/FILE/UKCHAINHOTELSREVIEW/HOTSTATS_MONTHLY_PR_UK_APRIL_2011.PDF.

HotStats (2011c) "UK and European Hotel Industry Report March 2011", Available from: www.hotstats.com/USERFILES/FILE/HOTSTATS_2011.PDF.

Huckenstein, D. and Duboff, R. (1999), "Hilton hotels: a comprehensive approach to delivering value for all stakeholders", *Cornell Hotel and Restaurant Administration Quarterly*, 40(4): 28–38.

Institute of Chartered Accountants in England and Wales (ICAEW) Finance and Management Faculty (2006), *Benchmarking finance and accounting, A Finance and Management special report,* [online]. Available from: http: //www. icaew.co.uk/fmfac. [Accessed 20 September 2015].

Ittner, C. and Larcker, D. (1998a), "Innovations in performance measurement: trends and research implications", *Journal of Management Accounting Research*, 10: 205–239.

Ittner, C. and Larcker, D. (1998b), "Are non-financial measures leading indicators of financial performance? An analysis of customer satisfaction", *Journal of Accounting Research*, 36: 1–35.

Ittner, C. and Larcker, D. (2003), "Coming up short on non-financial performance measurement", *Harvard Business Review*, 81: 88–95.

Jones, T., Atkinson, H., Lorenz, A. and Harris, P. J. (2012), *Strategic Managerial Accounting: Hospitality, Tourism and Events Applications*, 6e, Oxford: Goodfellow Publishers Ltd.

Jones, T.A. (1995), *Accounting and Finance for the International Hospitality Industry*, Oxford: Butterworth-Heinemann.

Kaplan, R.S, and Norton, D. P. (1992), "The balanced scorecard – measures that drive performance", *Harvard Business Review* (January–February): 71–79.

Lynch, R.L. and Cross, K.F. (1991), *Measure up! Yardsticks for Continuous Improvements*, Oxford: Blackwell.

Medlik, S. (1994), *The Business of Hotels*, 3e, Oxford: Butterworth-Heinemann.

Neely, A. and Adams, C. (2001), "The performance prism perspective", *Journal of Cost Management*, 15: 7–15.

Neely, A., Adams, C., Kennerly, M. (2002), *The Performance Prism: The Scorecard for Measuring and Managing Business Success*, London.

Neely, A. Marr, B., Roos, G., Pike, S. and Gupta, O. (2003), "Towards the third generation of performance measurement", *Controlling*, (March-April): 129–135.

Ogden, S.M. (1998), "Comment: benchmarking and best practice in the small hotel sector", *International Journal of Contemporary Hospitality Management*, 10(5): 189–190.
O'Neill, J.W. and Mattila, A.S., (2006), "Strategic hotel development and positioning: the effects of revenue drivers on profitability", *Cornell Hotel and Restaurant Administration Quarterly*, 47(2): 146–154.
Parmenter, D. (2006), "The new thinking on key performance indicators", *Finance and Management Magazine* (ICAEW), Issue 133, May, pp. 1–4.
Pettigrew, A.M. (2000), "Linking change processes to outcomes: a commentar on Ghoshal, Barlettt and Weick", *In*: Beer, M. and Norhia, N. (eds) *Breaking the Code of Change*, Boston, MA: Harvard Business School Press, pp. 243–266.
Phillips, P.A. (1999), "Hotel performance and competitive advantage: a contingency approach", *International Journal of Contemporary Hospitality Management*, 11(7): 359–365.
Pine, R. and Phillips, P.A. (2005), "Performance comparison of hotels in China", *International Journal of Hospitality Management*, 24(1): 57–73.
Potter, G. and Schmidgall, R.S. (1999), "Hospitality management accounting: current problems and future opportunities", *International Journal of Hospitality Management*, 18(4): 387–400.
PricewaterhouseCoopers (2000), "Does room count help explain profitability? Is there an optimum room count?", *Hospitality Directions*: US Edition, July, New York, pp. 17–21.
Ridgeway, V.F. (1956), "Dysfunctional consequences of performance measurements", *Administrative Science Quarterly*, September, 1(2): 240–247.
Shaw, G. and Williams, A.M. (1994), *Critical Issues in Tourism: A Critical Perspective*, Oxford: Blackwell Publishing.
Smith, J. (2007), *Handbook of Management Accounting*, 4[e], London: Elsevier and CIMA.
Stringer, C. (2007) "Empirical performance management research: evidence from AOS and MAR", *Qualitative Research in Accounting and Management*, 4(2): 92–114.
Tellis, J. (2010) "Gorgeous dashboards", *Finance and Management Magazine* (ICAEW), June, pp. 11–13.
Van Helden, G.J., Aardema, H., ter Bogt, H.J., and Groot, T.L.C.M. (2010), "Knowledge creation for practice in public sector management accounting by consultants and academics: Preliminary findings and directions for future research", *Management Accounting Research*, 21(2): 83–94.

22

The role of performance management systems in non-government organizations (NGOs)

Robert H. Chenhall, Matthew Hall and David Smith

The role of performance management systems in non-government organizations (NGOs)

The presence of a large third sector, comprising those non-profit organizations that lie between the public and private sectors, is seen as an indicator of a healthy society and economy (Verdier, 2002). Non-government organizations (NGOs) occupy a central position in the delivery of welfare services. Increasingly, governments rely on NGOs to deal with large-scale welfare issues through the provision of social services and the implementation of public policy (Lewis, 2003). In recent years, NGOs have become increasingly important in addressing humanitarian issues relating to welfare and developmental aid. For example, it has been estimated that the value of assets controlled by NGOs in the UK has risen from £12 billion in 1970 to over £50 billion in 2009 (Hilton *et al.*, 2012, p. 229). As a result, NGOs have come to be described as an integral part of civil society (Hadenius & Uggla, 1996; Howell & Pearce, 2001; Lewis, 2005).[1]

Questions of how effective and efficient NGOs are in delivering their outcomes have emerged as funding agencies and government require increased accountability and governance (Gray *et al.*, 2006; Unerman & O'Dwyer, 2006; O'Dwyer & Unerman, 2008). Traditionally, NGOs have tended to focus on shared norms and values, rather than coercive or formalized procedures, to achieve compliance and cooperation. The commitment of workers, volunteers and other organizational members may be facilitated through symbolic actions and rewards, and not primarily through financial control and remuneration based on profit making (Lewis, 2005, p. 21). Anheier (2000, p. 2) noted that '…in the past, "management" was often regarded as a "bad word" in the non-profit world, as a practice at odds with what some regard as the essence of the sector: voluntarism, philanthropy, compassion, and a concern for the public good'. The importance of the role of values and symbolic rewards requires that the management of NGOs extends well beyond the simple transfer or replication of existing public- or private-sector management templates (Lewis, 2003).

Notwithstanding the importance of commitment to values in directing the efforts of NGOs, increasingly, managers of these organizations are developing an interest in how more formal business-like management (new public management) can help to ensure that resources are used efficiently and that organizational objectives are effectively achieved (Dixon *et al.*, 2006; Gray *et al.*, 2006; Unerman & O'Dwyer, 2006). An important aspect of this movement has been the introduction of formal quantitative performance measurement systems (PMS), often expressed in accounting terms (English *et al.*, 2005). This has introduced practices contrary to customary approaches in social welfare organizations where qualitative assessment has been the norm.

A major challenge facing NGOs is to accommodate pressure to adopt more formal PMS in ways that are consistent with the unique character of NGOs and ensure that the primary focus of delivering on welfare objectives is maintained while encouraging a concern with assessing the efficiency of operations and effectiveness in achieving outcomes. These issues are particularly pertinent for larger NGOs where their size is relevant to generated complexity in control. Smaller NGOs, focused on local specific concerns, such as environmental protection for a local parkland, can often be managed with minimal formal systems relying on personal and informal controls of the managers.

In this chapter, we first examine issues concerning the design of PMS in NGOs. We highlight the need for performance measures to be congruent with and precisely related to the desired outcomes of the NGO, to be sensitive to changes in the circumstances of the NGO and to be verifiable. We discuss the suitability of recent developments in integrated PMS, notably the balanced scorecard, to NGOs. In the following section, we use data from three of our published studies to examine several topical issues that are important to the application of PMS in NGOs. First, we discuss the importance of ensuring that PMS are consistent with preserving the social capital of NGOs. Then, we examine how the pluralistic values that are an important part of the culture of NGOs can be preserved when implementing PMS in a business-like way. This involves the use of PMS to achieve compromise, typically between the values of senior management and employees, rather than domination by senior management values. Additionally, we examine how the values of employees can be accommodated and a pluralistic culture maintained by using PMS in an expressive way. In the final section, we draw on our own research and the wider literature to identify and outline the implications for PMS stemming from important characteristics of NGOs.

In the following section, we examine issues concerned with the design of PMS for NGOs.

Design features for PMS in NGOs

PMS are designed to assist in managing performance related to the inputs, throughputs, outputs and outcomes of organizations. Ideally, performance measures should be congruent with, and precisely related to, the desired outcomes of the NGO. Performance measures for inputs, throughputs and outputs should be verifiable and be sensitive to changes in outcomes. These characteristics of PMS have been identified as ensuring that employees' efforts are aligned with those of the organization and to make sure that performance indicators are an authentic representation of events (Moers, 2006; Merchant & Otley, 2007). If PMS do not have these qualities, the NGO may well allocate effort in inefficient ways across relevant tasks, or even worse, pursue tasks that do not lead to achievement of desired outcomes.

Efforts to provide performance measures that are congruent with and precisely related to outcomes provide the first step in linking specific outputs to more general outcomes, such as outputs from programmes related to new low-rent housing to the outcome of a reduction in poverty. Identifying performance measures congruent with outcomes and providing plans to achieve these outcomes have become necessary to attract and maintain external funding, and to bid for projects from government or other funding sources, either independently or as part of consortia of NGOs. More advanced applications of PMS will attempt to assess precisely how inputs, throughputs and outputs assist in the achievement of outcomes, that is, the PMS becomes part of the management of the NGO. An early attempt to provide a management control system (MCS) to link inputs to outcomes was devised by Ramanathan (1985). This approach makes explicit linkages across the activity cycle by identifying the value of social benefits from the NGO's operations, outcomes that portray the social relevance of performance accomplishments, output indicators of the volume of activity, input indicators of real resources and how these resources translate to costs. These data are used for the calculation of cost/benefit ratios for programmes and responsibility centres. The system is designed to ensure that actual outcomes, outputs, throughputs and inputs are compared with plans.

The application of PMS as a management aid has followed the logic of integrated PMS in the business sector (Bititci *et al.*, 1997). However, often the nature of the NGO's work flows presents challenges in identifying and defining precise measures and how they contribute to assessing the efficiency and effectiveness of managing inputs, throughputs and outputs, and how they contribute to the effectiveness of delivering on outcomes. For example, to develop new housing initiatives to help reduce poverty, the NGO may have to match possible sites with the location of those most in need, liaise with other organizations, including other NGOs, to modify existing structures or build new facilities. This will likely require careful co-ordination to ensure that participating bodies agree on the type of housing, the costing and who should have first priorities in occupancy. Precise performance measures at each stage can assist in ensuring that the design, costs and occupancy priorities match the planned outputs. If a combination of NGOs is involved, it is usually efficacious to have a principal NGO to manage the coordinated effort.

Developing precision in PMS at the programme level is also complicated by the difficulty of isolating the effects of individual programmes and how they relate to outcomes. NGO programmes are often highly interdependent with individual projects contributing outputs that combine with other projects to deliver on desired welfare outcomes. For example, improved health for a client group may require programmes to improve water purification, nutrition and waste disposal. It can be difficult to assess the precise impact of each project on overall health outcomes, as the programme outputs depend on interdependencies between the projects. For example, it may be that enhanced health outcomes related to a reduction in gastroenteritis due to effective nutrition improvement programmes are negated by less successful programmes related to poor drinking water quality or unhygienic waste disposal. Moreover, as performance measures often aggregate projects into overall effects, some projects may be successful, while others are not, and aggregate measures do not reveal these differences. Returning to our example, thus, using only a measure of the number of individuals suffering from gastric complaints to assess health of a client group will be inadequate to reveal if the health problem is due to programmes related to nutrition, water quality or waste disposal, or a combination of all these programmes. Clearly, precise, disaggregated measures of these health concerns provide better-quality information to assess client health. An additional issue in using performance measures to assess the contribution of a project to overall outcomes is that many indicators have lagged effects with outcomes not seen for several years. Even within projects, using PMS to evaluate employees can be problematic as it is difficult to determine whose efforts have contributed to outcomes given the collegial nature of the work.

As well as the necessity of performance measures to be congruent with and precisely related to desired outcomes, they should be verifiable. Verifiability of measures is important in circumstances (such as in many NGOs) where there is concern as to the efficacy of formal measures to be an accurate reflection of performance. Informal controls found in NGOs tend to rely on personal assessments and subjective measures. However, it has been shown that subjective measures can be biased and less able to distinguish between variation in performance due to leniency and compression of the measures (Moers, 2004). More verifiable measures can help to assist in overcoming perceptions of bias in the application of informal, subjective measures and as such help gain acceptance for including formal PMS in performance management by operating personnel.

Finally, to maintain congruence, PMS should be sensitive to changes in the circumstances of the NGO. NGOs experience changes that may require adjustments to PMS from the changing profile of stakeholders, particularly funders and other NGOs. Similarly, different client groups and operational locations present differing contexts and the need for additional new measures that relate to local conditions. Engaging in a variety of government contracts requires adoption of official governance measures and for systems to assess progress towards achieving contracted programme outcomes.

Developing more integrated approaches to PMS has followed from work in the private sector on balanced scorecards (Kaplan, 2001). Kaplan highlights the way in which important stakeholders, including employees dedicated to particular social welfare outcomes, donors and government can provide a plethora of preferred outcomes. This can result in a diffusion of organizational energy. To avoid this, NGOs need to develop a clear strategy focused on the mission for the targeted client group (e.g. outcomes of poverty, health), not programmes that service the client group, and base strategy on a realistic assessment of resources and competencies of the NGO. Given sufficient commitment from top management, the application of a balanced scorecard in NGOs provides a basis to think through how the operations of the NGO will deliver programmes in efficient ways and how these relate to delivering on the NGO's strategic mission. It also helps in communicating to employees how their work does (or does not) relate to the main objectives of the NGO. It identifies the financial implications of programs and can help in ensuring an investment in activities that will help development of the NGO.

While the basic logic of the balanced scorecard in NGOs follows from the standard balanced scorecard business model, there are obstacles to its implementation. The balanced scorecard approach to PMS stresses that strategic mission, such as a reduction in poverty, should be centre stage in the framework. For one NGO, this may be quite specific, such as an improvement in new housing to reduce poverty, or for another NGO, to improve vaccinations to improve childhood health. For other NGOs, these missions can become entangled, as homelessness and health may be common interdependent problems for the target clients. In this case, there may have to be trade-offs where decreasing poverty may involve either providing housing or overcoming health issues. Providing housing may divert resources from health initiatives and consequently cause an increase in poverty. These trade-offs may become acute where different donors are supporting different initiatives, either health or housing. While the balanced scorecard may highlight and clarify these difficulties, further developing the balanced scorecard will require potentially difficult choices for the NGO before the framework can be implemented. This type of problem may also be apparent when identifying programs that are competing to deliver on the NGO's mission. Should housing to reduce homelessness involve the provision of low rental self-contained units or more communal housing? Different programmes will receive support from donors and employees who come to the NGO with preferences for an area of work. To gain benefits from the balanced scorecard, strong leadership and belief in the approach will be required that can be at odds with the more democratic and participatory culture of many NGOs, particularly smaller NGOs that rely on their informal procedures to sustain their activities. These obstacles to implementation provide particular challenges to the implementation of balanced scorecards within NGOs.

It is apparent that considerable progress has been made in thinking about how PMS can become an integral part of managing NGOs, including the modification of balanced scorecard-type frameworks that can potentially integrate operations with desired outcomes. However, there are specific challenges to designing PMS in NGOs derived from the ambiguity in NGO outcomes, complications in linking operations to outcomes, measurement issues and resistance from employees to formal performance management.

In the following three sections of this chapter, we focus on three of our studies (Chenhall *et al.*, 2010, 2013, 2015) that examine issues relating to the development and operation of PMS in NGOs. At the time of writing, these three studies are among the only examples of published accounting studies examining performance management issues in NGOs. The three studies relate to two different case organizations, a welfare NGO called the Tennant Centre (Tennant) located in Australia (Chenhall *et al.*, 2010) and a development NGO headquartered in the UK called Voluntary Services Overseas (VSO) (Chenhall *et al.*, 2013, 2015). In the next section, we draw on data from our study of Tennant to explore the interplay between PMS and social capital in an NGO. This is followed by sections that discuss the role of PMS in developing compromise, at VSO, and the expressive role of PMS, also at VSO.

PMS and social capital

Social capital relates to existing and emerging social infrastructures that facilitate individual and collective actions of many kinds (Foley & Edwards, 1999). Social capital can be considered as a property of an organization, where individual and collective actions provide actual or potential benefits for organizations (Adler & Kwon, 2002). There are two forms of social capital: bonding and bridging (Gittell & Vidal, 1998). Bonding involves developing close interpersonal relationships based on shared aims, and bridging to building networks between the NGOs and other parties. NGOs foster bridging social capital to develop contacts and networks to ensure welfare is well funded and delivered to those most in need. NGOs are concerned that those within the organization and its networks interact around common welfare ideals. To ensure this occurs, NGOs attempt to make sure that participating individuals and agencies are bonded by sharing core NGO values. Social capital can substitute for other resources such as financial or human capital by providing strong network connections and social ties (Coleman, 1990), which is particularly important in the NGO context where financial capital can be limited. Of concern is that implementing formal PMS in NGOs can result in a degradation of social capital. This can result as a consequence of the design features of PMS and the way in which they are employed.

To demonstrate connections between PMS and social capital, we draw on our study of an NGO, called Tennant, that cares for people from disadvantaged backgrounds, many of whom have had dealings with the justice system or have been otherwise marginalized (see Chenhall *et al.*, 2010). Its sponsoring organization is Carewell, which is affiliated with a large philanthropic organization.

Tennant had relied on informal, organic controls but had recently introduced a variety of formal PMS in an attempt to develop more business-like approaches to managing the organization. Some of the PMS were supportive of social capital, and some are obstructive. We consider a programme management system and budgets that were employed to plan, monitor and evaluate operations. We also assess the important role of formal belief systems to Tennant.

The programme management system illustrates how the interactive use of formal controls can be consistent with customary organic controls, when they are employed in enabling ways.[2] The programme management systems involved scheduled formal meetings and impromptu gatherings, and discussions that were more consistent with the customary background organic processes at Tennant. The characteristics of these controls supported an enabling approach. They were highly transparent, flexible and provided details of interdependencies between specific programmes and other parts of Tennant's operations.

The programme management system helped build both internal bonding and external bridging social capital. The systems helped in clarifying and communicating Tennant's purpose across the organization, in client selection and in monitoring client treatment. The client information provided by the systems is confidential, privileged and to be used only within the organization. Access to this type of privileged information enhances bonding and feelings of solidarity (Fields *et al.*, 2008, p. 168). The quantification of programme expectations within the programme management system assisted bridging by providing a means by which structural connections between potential alliance partners could be rendered more 'objective' and 'trustworthy' (Free, 2007, p. 5). In bidding for a new contract, a programme would be instigated with detailed information on Tennant's credentials and expertise in providing service delivery, as well as timelines, financial budgets, performance measures and the potential roles of selected partners. This would form the basis for negotiations with potential partners, and if the final project details were acceptable to Tennant, it would then form the basis for a formal proposal to be submitted to funding agencies or government. This form of bridging enhanced Tennant's power and authority in establishing alliances.

In order to attract economic capital, Tennant attempted to promote an attitude of efficiency and cost consciousness among its employees. The government that sponsored welfare programmes to competing NGOs required increased accountability. This had led to a view held at Carewell that financial accountability should be pushed down to the coordinator level. Attempts to achieve this resulted in a clash between pressures to be financially accountable and the belief that this distracted from the core activities of providing welfare services. Apart from the programme management system, budgeting and formal reporting were generally viewed as an impediment to spending time and effort on clients. As part of budgeting, procedures for allocating head office costs to operational divisions were seen at Tennant as being unfair and unnecessary. An erosion of bonding developed between Carewell and Tennant. The budgets did not provide information that might have helped discussions on how tensions between Carewell and Tennant could be repaired. The broader pictures of the local implications of budget cuts on programmes and of the role of organization-wide overheads were not disclosed. The controls were not flexible in decisions linking financial and operational issues. In summary, the budgets did not support an enabling approach to control.

Formal financial control at Tennant had unintended effects of inhibiting bonding and potentially of distracting the organization from its core values of delivering on welfare services. The formal budgetary systems negatively affected bonding because employees lacked identification with the aims underscoring the new formal systems.

The issue of ensuring that particular values of an NGO can be sustained is not restricted to addressing incompatibilities between financial and service delivery concerns. More generally, NGOs face situations where core values related to welfare service delivery can be potentially compromised from sources both within and outside the NGO. This raises the general issue of how formal systems can be employed to reinforce adherence to core organizational values. Here, the role of belief systems is pertinent (Simons, 1995). Belief systems are 'the explicit set of organizational definitions that senior managers communicate formally and reinforce systematically to provide basic values, purposes, and direction for the organization' (Simons, 1995, p. 34). Tennant employed belief systems to communicate core values to potential employees during recruitment, and to reinforce these values to existing employees and to others outside the organization. This involved an array of artefacts including formal documents and posters, photographs, statues and paintings of Tennant's patron in the main offices.

Belief systems can add most values when used actively to influence employee behaviour in specific situations (Dowling, 2001; Mullane, 2002; Mundy, 2009). Importantly, belief systems in action can assist in preserving bonding social capital when there is inherent tension between a caseworker's values and those of the organization. Disagreements deriving from the need to focus on operational and financial matters, and between organic and formal controls, had potential to erode bonding at Tennant. Clark (2006) notes that resolution of this type of conflict cannot rely on the dictums of professionalism and suppression of individual feelings; rather, values need to be continually revisited and reaffirmed. It is here that we observed the application of Tennant's belief systems to provide a focus whereby caseworkers could discuss and come to terms with Tennant's aim to provide welfare and to do this in cost-efficient ways. While derived from a top-down approach, employing belief systems to work through the conflict between employee values and those of senior management enhanced bonding within Tennant.

While belief systems were important in communicating and strengthening specific social justice values that helped to develop and sustain bonding within Tennant, the strength of these systems and their resulting effects on bonding appeared to limit the development of strong alliances with other entities in the welfare sector. Driven by a strong belief in their own values, Tennant's strategy was to structure alliances in such a way as to enable Tennant to gain influence and develop alliances that allowed its values and operational methods to play a prominent role, limiting potential clashes with the values and operational methods of other organizations. This approach limited potential alliance partners to those over which Tennant could exert a dominant role, thereby restricting the bridging aspect of social capital.

Formal controls based around project management, budgets and performance measurement were helpful in establishing perceptions of competence and demonstrating sound operational and financial performance to government. These formal controls provided evidence of Tennant's effectiveness and financial viability. To ensure its dominant role in alliances, programme management and budget systems were used to identify which partners would interact in ways that enabled Tennant to achieve its purposes. This would establish a network of agencies that might provide suitable services. If these arrangements did not suit the partners, or partners presented a unified counter-argument, the alliance would likely be terminated.

Overall, Tennant illustrates how MCS in general, and PMS in particular, can both assist and hinder the development of both bonding and bridging social capital. In many NGOs, there is a need to demonstrate the effective implementation of PMS; however, there can be a reluctance of operational employees to accept formal PMS. By incorporating welfare and economic values into belief systems, these systems can go beyond merely communicating values to employees and outsiders, and form part of the process of managing and maintaining employees' and outsiders' identification with core organizational values. Formal programme management systems were well received when employed to plan and monitor operations. These controls appeared to map well onto the everyday work of employees and clarified objectives and monitored client treatments. In NGOs, this is particularly salient as the proximity of controls to activities can have critical consequences for client welfare. Formal programme management systems were complemented by effective organic decision processes that were employed within loose structures and open communication networks. We see this approach of combining formal programme management systems with informal controls working as complements to facilitate internal bonding.

It is clear from Tennant's experiences that PMS can help manage the work of NGOs, if the PMS relate well to activities of employees and their expectations for their work outcomes. One aspect of PMS is that while they may engage employees in identifying threats and opportunities, they tend to do this within a set of values prescribed from top management. Often, these values are consistent with those of employees; however, it is also apparent that the move to develop more business-like approaches may generate the potential for a misalignment between such approaches and the concern with traditional welfare values. This may occur as the NGO grows and develops with various stakeholders wishing to promote their particular view as to the NGO's purpose.

In the next two sections, we use data from prior case studies to elaborate on the notion of using PMS to develop compromises between competing values and 'views of the world' to overcome conflict, disharmony and potential ineffective operations (Chenhall *et al.*, 2013). We then show how engagement can be enhanced when PMS are implemented in an 'expressive way' (Chenhall *et al.*, 2015). The expressive use of PMS can be advantageous in its own right, and PMS could conceivably be used as a means of developing 'compromising accounts'.

Compromises in the development of PMS

A concern in NGOs is that the values related to delivering on welfare outcomes and those related to a more business-like approach to managing efficiently may generate conflict, typically between employees and management, with consequent negative outcomes to the operations of the NGO. To examine how PMS can be used in ways to ensure that compromises between competing values are sought rather than a dominant view being prescribed and reflected in the PMS, we draw on our study of an NGO called Voluntary Service Overseas (VSO) (see Chenhall *et al.*, 2013). VSO's original aim was to link volunteers with partner organizations in developing countries. More recently, measuring the impact of operational activities has become increasingly important to VSO. Our study focused on VSO's efforts to develop a PMS framework combining different metrics and narrative content into a single report, called the Quality Framework (QF) that would provide a common set of performance measures for each of VSO's country offices.

In developing PMS, it is possible that different modes of evaluation can potentially operate at once, with different modes privileging diverse core beliefs, metrics and measuring instruments. It is within this setting that compromising accounts, that is, accounts of performance that seek to develop a compromise between these differing worldviews, can be developed. Variations in the design and operation of PMS are likely to be important in whether different values are polarized, or can be reconciled and coexist. The different modes of evaluation within a PMS can be viewed as different ways of conceptualizing the representation of performance, that is, through particular types of metrics (e.g. financial vs. non-financial), and narrative content (stories, management reports, disclosures). PMS are critical because it is in discussions over the different metrics, images and words that can be used to represent performance that the actual worth of values is frequently debated, established and contested.

VSO had traditionally operated in a culture where the use of narrative performance reports, to share stories of good practice, key learnings and significant changes, was common. However, such approaches met criticism from some members of the organization due to the inability to 'compare' performance of different country offices, due to a lack of standardization. This led to the development of a performance measurement tool called the Strategic Resource Allocation (SRA). The SRA employed precise quantitative measures on 16 areas of performance to ensure standardization and consistency. This approach was completely at odds with the original evaluation practices based more informally on learning. In effect, the SRA privileged a single mode of evaluation, that is, standardized metrics, such that compromise between the differing worldviews was not possible. As the new system was to be used to evaluate the survival of programmes, managers were encouraged not to reveal poor results, which was at odds with the original PMS where problem areas were used to assist in sharing knowledge and enhance learning. The SRA was dropped after 1 year of operation.

A second attempt at developing a PMS, called the Annual Country Report (ACR), involved maintaining the use of PMS for comparative reporting but was based purely on narrative reporting, that is, no metrics. The ACR thus sought to formalize the traditional focus on narrative performance reports. As a consequence, however, the ACR also privileged a single mode of evaluation (that of learning) such that compromise between the differing worldviews was still not forthcoming.

The next attempt to developing the PMS, the QF, aimed to address compromise between the competing worldviews. A key difficulty in developing the QF was trying to reconcile between the need to standardize, i.e. have indicators that provide a consistent method for measuring success in each programme office, while concurrently respecting the uniqueness of programme offices, and the need for indicators to be 'inspirational' and to provide a mechanism for learning. It is at the specific design level, i.e. making choices about the content of elements, indicators and narrative components in the QF, that the compromise between different modes of evaluation was most acute. Country directors were viewed as central to this task and were given the opportunity to make suggestions for elements and indicators.

A critical concern in developing the QF was to define 'quality' at VSO. It was here that staff with different worldviews were able to advocate for the inclusion and exclusion of particular elements and indicators. This resulted in a set of 14 elements relating to various aspects of programme quality, such as inclusion, volunteer engagement, innovative programming and financial management. Each element had a set of indicators (with one to five indicators per element), with the scores on the indicators, along with country director and regional director judgement, used to determine an overall element score. Local knowledge was considered paramount in that indicators were required to produce results that were 'recognizable' to programme office staff, partners and volunteers. Providing space in the QF report for narrative discussion to reflect the different operating environments in different countries was also critical.

Discussion around the elements of the QF, particularly those related to what was to be included and excluded, represented a rich opportunity for constructive debate over areas of prioritization. Central to this debate was discussion around the 'measurability' of certain aspects of performance, with some staff arguing that certain aspects of performance (for example, indicators for the 'inclusion' element) should not be scored, as their very nature did not afford quantification. To some extent, concern over such issues was alleviated by the ability to 'include' such items in the space devoted to narrative, which country directors felt was a critical component of the QF as it allowed discussion of important issues that they believed were not captured in the indicators. Importantly, while the QF was certainly not perfect, it provided a mechanism for managers to debate issues of importance to the organization.

However, the QF ran into difficulties with headquarters claiming a lack of consistencies in scoring across regions and countries. This resulted in a swing back to emphasizing standardization of scoring. Descriptions of the meaning of various scores (ranging from one to four) on indicators were provided, with a removal of recognition that high performance may differ depending on local programme offices. Scoring of some indicators was done by headquarters using centralized databases. In its first year of operation, all the QF results, without narrative, were compiled in a spreadsheet and distributed to country directors. There was much debate on the scoring processes with little agreement on accommodating regional differences. Thus, while more consistent scores were likely, the initial compromise appeared tenuous, particularly as those whose preferred mode of evaluation was centred on uniqueness and learning expressed concern that fundamental principles associated with their worldview were not being respected.

Reconciliation of the coexisting desires for learning and standardization proved to be a central task in preparing the QF for its second year of operation. Considerable debate about the QF focused on concern from operational managers that the use of competition to 'shame' programme offices into improvements was not only 'horrible', but also fundamentally against the QF's purpose as a learning tool. A compromise between competition and learning, between comparisons and sharing good practice, was addressed through agreeing to differential disclosure, whereby the identity of the top three performing programmes would be made public, whereas the identity of poorer performers would be reported only to headquarters. Disclosure of good performers would allow the sharing of good practice between programme offices without creating a ranking, while disclosure of poor performers to headquarters would allow management action to be taken without 'naming and shaming' programme offices.

However, the desire to highlight poor performance lingered on in the QF, with 11 of the 14 element summaries identifying countries with 'weak' performance, typically with reference to a 'low' score on the element. Thus, despite intentions to enact a compromise between learning and competition, translating this fully into practice proved difficult. An evaluation of the QF by VSO's top management highlighted how the compromises being made in the design and operation of the QF were not final but were ongoing. We see that positive features of the QF that were closely aligned to one worldview inevitably gave rise to suggestions for improvement that sought to address the concerns of those with different preferences. In this way, the coexistence of, as well as reconciliation between, different worldviews can be seen as an enduring feature of a compromising account.

Expressing beliefs and values in the PMS

PMS can be implicated in organizational members' attempts to reveal, or make comprehensible, their preferred value systems for the organization. To do this, the PMS should have the capacity to help individuals express their values and beliefs. We term this the 'expressive role' of PMS whereby PMS can help (or hinder) employees to express their values and beliefs – a key aspect of which is the degree to which a PMS can facilitate the display of a variety of beliefs held by organizational members. This can be contrasted with a more instrumental role that is designed to maintain or create some normative aim (Frumkin, 2005). How, and how well, a PMS can fulfil an expressive role relates to the way its design (e.g. the inclusion and/or exclusion of different indicators in the PMS) and process of development (e.g. engagement) enables the expression of employees' values and beliefs. The expression of values through PMS can help (rather than be disconnected from or conflict with) achieve organizational objectives by mobilizing the energy, motivation and commitment of employees that values expression can create (cf. Huy, 1999; Frumkin, 2005; Dutton *et al.*, 2006). To understand the expressive role of PMS, we draw on our study of the development of a PMS in the mental health programme at VSO Sri Lanka (see Chenhall *et al.*, 2015).

One way in which the expressive role of PMS can enable the emergence of employees' values and beliefs is to facilitate the display of a variety of emotions and feelings. This notion of 'display freedom' can overcome the tendency for more authoritative uses of PMS to suppress the types and intensity of emotions that can be expressed, by way of the oppressive use of power and culture (Huy, 1999, p. 339). Huy's (1999) work suggests that the creation of an environment in which there is freedom from the fear of reprisal for holding 'inappropriate' views, and in which there is 'time' and 'space' to have the ability for reflection, experimentation and expression of new ideas, is likely to support the development of display freedom. This suggests that for a PMS to fulfil an expressive role, it would need to be developed according to these characteristics.

VSO developed a PMS to evaluate the performance of volunteers working in operational facilities, such as a mental health ward within a hospital or rehabilitation centre. The PMS was called LEAP, an acronym representing 'Learning, Evaluation, Assessment for Partners'. The final version of LEAP had four sections: Capacity Building and Service Delivery, Training and Behaviour of Staff, Patient Experiences, and the Impact of Mental Health Services on the Lives of Beneficiaries. Each consisted of a set of indicators, where each indicator was scored on a five-point scale and was accompanied by narrative information.

The first step in establishing LEAP's expressive role was to make the system accessible to staff, volunteers and partner representatives. This was important as many staff had little experience with monitoring and formal evaluation, which inhibited engagement with a formal system like LEAP. LEAP avoided jargon, used non-technical language and expressed indicators in a way that related directly to the activities of the mental health programme. Furthermore, one of the key principles in developing LEAP was that it should be as simple as possible. The development process was also characterized by much experimentation and trial and error, including seven iterations of LEAP, where staff, volunteers and partners were able to offer a wide variety of feedback and suggestions on a regular basis. This is particularly relevant as users were likely to find the PMS more accessible where their experiences were drawn on to develop the measures (Wouters & Wilderom, 2008). Finally, accessibility was also aided by translating some of the documentation from English into the local languages. Clearly, defining accessibility is dependent on the level of expertise of the users of the PMS.

Games and other techniques designed to encourage a sense of playfulness (cf. Huy, 1999) were a feature of the development of an expressive role for LEAP. For example, a playful tone was set for a meeting where LEAP was introduced. At the very start of the activity, all 50 participants were asked to stand up and, then, on the count of three, to jump in the air and shout 'LEAP'. This prompted much laughter from participants. One game involved participants being organized into groups of approximately five people, and then being provided with 20 min to answer five questions concerning the making of rice, where each question was designed to mimic a stage in a typical evaluation process, such as monitoring, evaluation and impact. Responses from each group were collected and placed on a flipchart, and the session ended with analogies being drawn between the stages in the evaluation of making rice and the stages in the evaluation of the mental health programme. The game itself prompted much discussion, joking and laughter throughout.

Several design features assisted in developing an expressive role for LEAP. An important reason for volunteers to join VSO was to 'make a difference' in the lives of staff and patients who they were working with in their placements. LEAP provided the opportunity for volunteers to display how their work had an impact at VSO. For example, indicators were developed concerning patient behaviour (such as whether patients provide input into their treatment), as well as a separate section on 'the impact of mental health services on the lives of beneficiaries', that included indicators such as the length of stay, readmissions, community visits and discharges. LEAP provided a vehicle whereby volunteers could discuss indicators that reflected how they were achieving work related to their values and beliefs.

The need for developing 'congruent' outcome indicators to enable a PMS to be expressive of volunteers' beliefs was apparent with LEAP. For volunteers, the key value was to improve the 'life situation' of patients. This emphasis moved the performance assessment away from just recording the inputs and throughputs of medical treatment (such as recording use of medicines and drugs) to measures related to outcomes such as 'the impact of mental health services on the lives of beneficiaries' that helped target output indicators such as the length of stay, readmissions, community visits and discharges. As many of the indicators concerned beneficiaries, this meant that most of the time spent completing LEAP related to discussions concerning patients. This helped staff and volunteers to express the importance of beneficiaries as it provided the space and freedom to discuss and reflect on patient progress. Importantly, LEAP was seen as most effective when it was modified to be simpler, clearer and more user-friendly. This reduced the feelings that the PMS was an imposition on the work of volunteers and helped in understanding how values and beliefs were translated into performance measures. LEAP also provided the opportunity to discuss positive and negative beneficiary outcomes that enabled volunteers and staff to express a wide range of experiences and emotions without fear of reprisal. This enhanced the expressive role of LEAP compared to more traditional usage that can impose sanctions for failing to meet targets.

While the use of PMS in an expressive way provides opportunities to accommodate employees in the clarification of organizational purpose and can help motivate commitment to the organization, it is possible for the expressive role to also be consistent with more conventional instrumental approaches to PMS. At VSO, the development of indicators for beneficiaries provided a mechanism to enable the exchange of views relating to volunteers' values and beliefs about beneficiary care (expressive role), and also enabled the organization to more accurately capture outputs and outcomes relating to beneficiary care that could help with decision making and resource allocation (instrumental role).

In this chapter, we have provided an overview of the challenges inherent in designing PMS in NGOs. We have discussed the design characteristics of PMS emphasizing the sensitivity of design to the perception of employees that PMS should be consistent with the context and demands of their workplace. We singled out the preservation of social capital as important to NGOs and showed how PMS can both assist and hinder this preservation. Given the importance of developing ways to address competing values from various stakeholders, particularly employees and management, we developed the ideas of compromising PMS and the expressive use of PMS as means of ensuring that values of different stakeholders are considered as part of the dynamic evolution of the NGO.

In the following section, we draw on these ideas and the broader literature to identify four key summary characteristics of NGOs pertinent to the design and implementation of effective PMS in NGOs. These are the dominance of social over financial goals, the diversity of stakeholders, motivation based on social welfare values rather than financial rewards, and an action rather than administrative culture.

Characteristics of NGOs and implications for performance management systems

Drawing on our own research and the wider literature, we identify and outline the implications for PMS stemming from important characteristics of NGOs.

The dominance of social over financial goals

NGOs are formed to achieve social or welfare objectives that are often expressed in general terms. For example, 'Oxfam's vision is a just world without poverty. We envisage a world in which people can influence decisions that affect their lives, enjoy their rights, and assume their responsibilities – a world in which everyone is valued and treated equally'.[3] Working towards these objectives provides a strong central focus for those working within the NGO, and the achievement of these objectives legitimizes the NGO to outside bodies such as beneficiaries, donors and government (Suchman, 1995). This has a consequence that performance of the NGO is assessed by how effectively beneficiaries, serviced by the NGO, are assisted by the NGO's activities (Fowler, 1997). As there are many factors that may influence the well-being of the client group, it can be difficult to attribute success, or failure, solely to the activities of the NGO. For example, efforts by an NGO to provide health services to inhabitants of isolated communities in developing countries could succeed or fail depending on the extent to which the community trusts interventions from outsiders and the level of community resistance, based on culturally sensitive preferences for local treatments.

Given that the NGO's objectives are typically related to a variety of social purposes that are ill-defined, such as poverty reduction, it is difficult to focus on a single 'bottom-line' metric to assess performance (Marsden & Oakley, 1990). As well as determining what to measure, it is challenging to develop standards or expectations for performance. Given that each NGO operates in a distinctive setting bounded by specific activities or regional and national variations, benchmarking may lack relevance. Moreover, given a lack of development in PMS within the NGO sector, there is a lack of standardization of PMS to provide guidance to individual NGO managers.

While most NGOs have social goals as their primary focus, some have divisions that are dedicated to earning profit from commercial operations, such as Oxfam and Salvation Army charity shops, to assist in funding operations. This adds a layer of complexity for the MCS as they will be required to provide the accounting systems to generate financial accounts appropriate for for-profit organizations.

At Tennant, we see a clear reluctance to focus on financial goals and a lack of awareness of financial issues among employees. This suggests that integrating financial metrics into systems such as balanced scorecards and other performance measurement frameworks might prove challenging for many NGOs. A key issue, then, is how NGOs can position financial metrics within the overall approach to performance management. One avenue may be to include financial goals and associated metrics as a supporting element in the performance management process, with social goals still given prominence as the primary focus. At VSO, we observed a variety of measures (including those linked to financial management) in the QF with no single bottom-line metric. This led to a complex PMS and difficulties in tracking social goals over time. Within this PMS, there were also problems in setting performance levels for each indicator, and with comparing performance between different countries. However, having a variety of measures, even if some were considered imprecise or lacking comparability, was important in gaining acceptance of the PMS and engaging staff involved in performance management issues. Also, the lack of an overall bottom-line metric was important in avoiding feelings of comparison and competition that were at odds with social goals and cooperative ways of working that characterize NGOs.

Diversity of stakeholders

While most businesses have a variety of stakeholders such as employees, customers and regulators, it is the owners or shareholders who are usually identified as the key stakeholders. Typically, stakeholders other than shareholders do not have a direct role in formulating the objectives, strategies and operations of the business, whereas the owners have a key role in, at least, accepting the direction and policies of the business. Similarly, it can be argued that NGOs have their client base as their key stakeholder. However, the role of funders, regulators, host governments and other NGOs in enabling NGOs to survive can be significant. The salience of these different bodies and their ability to directly influence NGO policies and procedures can result in tension between competing objectives (Brown & Moore, 2001; Lewis, 2005).

A consequence of these powerful stakeholder groups is that accounts, or multiple accounts, are required to provide information of concern to the different groups. This may result in increased transaction costs and a plethora of different unconnected accounts, or over-accounting, which are often costly and confusing (Edwards & Hume, 1996). Additionally, burgeoning PMS can suffer from poor quality as those providing information lack motivation to spend effort to provide reliable information in areas that they see of little relevance to their activities. These may involve, for example, conventional financial budgets to justify funding to a philanthropic organization and to provide a basis to control expenditure against these budgets. These accounts may be irrelevant to the social worker who is concerned with, for example, assessing the progress of clients in overcoming substance abuse. Often, the social worker will be compelled to account for financial matters, which may require them to make difficult choices on where to concentrate action with a consequence that deserving groups are not provided welfare (Chenhall *et al.*, 2010). This situation can develop tension and problems and cut across core employee values of providing welfare for all deserving individuals. NGOs can face serious challenges in developing PMS that enable managers and operational personnel to provide services within the NGO's resource constraints.

There are additional problems for developing PMS that derive from NGOs having a diversity of stakeholders. Concerning partner NGOs, it is quite likely that each partner NGO will have different PMS developed to suit their needs and desired outcomes. As the activities of the NGOs become interdependent, establishing a common way to assess activities, outputs and outcomes can require considerable effort to modify existing systems or develop new approaches to address the considerations relevant to the partner projects (Tchouakeu *et al.*, 2011). It seems unlikely for most NGOs that major, costly developments to achieve compatible PMS would be forthcoming for one-off partnerships.

Donors are stakeholders with considerable influence over the reporting requirements of NGOs. Increasingly funding is tied to particular projects rather than general funding to the organization (Ebrahim, 2003).[4] This can occur as funders are not convinced that general funding will result in the NGO allocating funding to their preferred projects, and they seek improved PMS to enhance accountability for their preferred project results. Also, an overall effect can be a belief that if the donors influence the PMS, then their interests dominate the NGO's mission and public interest, which may erode the legitimacy of the NGO (Brown & Moore, 2001).

VSO presents a clear case of the need to negotiate performance measures between groups or different stakeholders, each with a different perspective on how to measure performance. Clearly, this can prove challenging with disagreements between stakeholders an inevitable part of the process. However, the ultimate acceptance and use of a performance measurement system in NGOs seem to require negotiation and compromise, with opportunities for stakeholders to discuss and reach a consensus on suitable metrics and how they will be used in performance management processes. The VSO case also illustrates how these negotiations are not a 'one-off' but need to be continued over time, revisiting metrics and continuing discussions among stakeholders in order to maintain and even strengthen the systems. At Tennant, certain PMS practices had varying effects on different stakeholders. For example, informal approaches to PMS were very helpful for internal bonding among employees, but then limited external bonding with external stakeholders like potential alliance partners. In contrast, more formal PMS practices were seen as important to external stakeholders such as the government, but did not resonate with staff such as social workers. In situations of limited resources, these tensions could create something of a dilemma for NGOs in trying to develop different systems for different stakeholders.

Motivation based on social welfare values rather than financial rewards

A significant part of the success of NGOs is the primary motivation of most employees to deliver welfare services, be they professional social workers, ancillary staff or administrators.[5] NGO employees tend to be 'value driven', focusing on the services being provided rather than on maximizing their financial rewards (Lewis, 2005, pp. 15–16). Values based on trust, justice, equity, rights and empowerment form the basis of much of the advocacy roles that NGOs often perform. NGOs have been consistently rated as the most trusted institutions in society by the Edelman Trust Barometer.[6]

Having a highly motivated work force is a much sought after feature for most organizations. In NGOs, it provides for high levels of employee commitment (Clark, 1991). However, it can provide for highly focused attention to the work tasks of the employee, particularly at the operational level. This can result in a molecular, or worse a myopic, view from the employee to the overall work of the NGO (Chenhall *et al.*, 2010). A tendency for a functional, short-term approach to the work of the NGO may inhibit its ability to react to broader, long-term changes in the needs of existing and potential clients, a changing landscape of funding options, the activities and competition from other NGOs and the possibilities for changes in regulations. Clearly, these matters are the purview of strategic planners. In the main, NGOs' operational employees have an ideological rejection of business practices like strategic planning (Billis & MacKeith, 1993). However, as in other organizations, the ability of the NGO to be responsive and agile depends to a large extent on how strategies can emerge from those close to operations who can readily identify the strategic uncertainties of the NGO (Sahley, 1995). Given the committed work force of NGOs, PMS can assist in ensuring successful survival and adaptation if employees can be convinced to engage with the PMS to contribute their insights into the direction and operations of the NGO.

A concern with social welfare values and a reluctance to accommodate financial concerns was apparent in both Tennant and VSO. Employees at Tennant, particularly, were highly suspicious of business-like practices seeing them as an intrusion into their work to attain welfare outcomes. Informal practices were seen to respect the values of solidarity and empowerment. But this outcome may have more to do with the way that business-like practices such as budgeting were implemented at Tennant, as there was insufficient attention to communicating the value of tools like financial planning and accountability for improved service delivery. At VSO, a clash between employee and management values was central to the difficulties in employing PMS. Attempts to ensure that PMS were expressive of social values within LEAP and the QF (e.g. respecting country uniqueness) enabled employees to promote a focus on their primary values. Unlike the for-profit sector where PMS are typically linked to financial incentives or other extrinsic rewards, in NGOs, it appears more important to link PMS to the expression and achievement of social values and goals in ways that can motivate sustained engagement in these processes.

An action rather than administrative culture

A key inhibitor to developing formal PMS in NGOs has been that these organizations have traditionally involved a culture of action and not administration (Korton, 1987). Much of the resistance to the introduction of 'business-like' techniques derives from a view that PMS are time consuming and a distraction from welfare work (Chenhall *et al.*, 2010). In many NGOs, this has resulted in a lack of interest and investment in accounting and more particularly PMS. This negativity towards accepting PMS as a potentially valuable tool is intensified as designing and implementing PMS are complicated and made difficult by diverse values, multiple stakeholders and an emphasis on pursuing social objectives that are difficult to articulate and measure. This refutation of accounting and PMS is exacerbated by a tendency for some NGOs (or their stakeholders) to employ approaches from other sectors such as business or government that may not be suitable (Smillie, 1995).

Given the reliance of NGOs on donor funding, there is pressure to show that contributed money is used to deliver welfare services. NGOs are obliged to show that the percentage of contributed funds going to administration is minimal (Sargeant *et al.*, 2009). NGOs are quick to claim that only a small percentage of funds are used in administration. For example, Medecins sans Frontieres claims that in 2014, 5 per cent of funds were used in administration and 10 per cent on fund raising[7]; World Vision Australia notes that in 2014, 5 per cent of funds were used to support administration and 10 per cent on fund raising.[8] It seems difficult for NGOs to convince donors and the general public that the effective use of administration, including PMS, can enhance the ability of the NGO to deliver its services. Rather, it appears that there is a view that low administration costs signal good performance (Smillie, 1995). This can be at odds with a focus on programmatic impact. This emphasis on minimizing administrative and support costs can encourage NGOs to build in excessively low administrative costs when bidding for projects, which do not allow for recovery of actual costs incurred, which can undermine the eventual delivery of services and, in the extreme, undermine the financial sustainability of the NGO (Smillie, 1997).

Evidence from both Tennant and VSO shows how initiatives to develop more complex administrative structures around formal PMS were not well received by employees, as they believed that they did not have the time or expertise to engage in business-like practices. Employees prioritized direct work related to client welfare over engagement with initiatives related to formal PMS. At Tennant, employees claimed that they were 'social workers not accountants'. At VSO, it was important that LEAP was kept simple and accessible to ensure engagement of staff who were suspicious of elaborate PMS that were akin to bureaucracy. Similarly, the QF also had to avoid getting too big and complicated to avoid being seen as a 'monster'.

Overall, engaging staff who tend to view PMS as administrative work presents challenges to the operation of PMS in NGOs. Avoiding complexity and elaborate systems seems an essential starting point, not only to engage staff but also to manage perceptions regarding spending on administrative costs. A fruitful strategy may be to link the metrics and indicators in the PMS as closely as possible to the operational work of staff in order to break down the idea that working with a PMS is a separate task divorced from helping clients. Where possible, engaging staff directly in the design and operation of PMS, for example, through the joint development of indicators (as seen at VSO) also seems a promising strategy.

Conclusion

The role of PMS in NGOs has become important as pressure for NGOs to operate in more business-like ways has developed due to increased reporting requirements of funding bodies and governments, and heightened competition between NGOs for funds and welfare projects. While much has been written on the potential benefits of PMS to help ensure that NGOs operate in effective and efficient ways, the particular characteristics of NGOs often inhibit the successful implementation of PMS (Sawhill & Williamson, 2001).

In this chapter, we have identified a series of issues that complicate the implementation of PMS in NGOs. These focus on issues related to the ambiguity in the values and goals of NGOs, particularly a lack of clarity of an overarching goal, the difficulty of measuring impact on welfare goals and of the outputs of programmes, and the incompatibility of the values of key stakeholders exacerbated by tension between social and financial goals. Additionally, the culture of NGOs tends to be focused on efforts to attain social rather than financial outcomes, which can work against developing more business-like practices. Maintaining this culture depends, in part, on the preservation of strong social capital that generates challenges to develop PMS that are sensitive to maintaining social capital.

We examined various approaches to the design of PMS for NGOs, noting that it is unlikely that a single ideal system will be appropriate to the diverse goals, strategies and methods of NGOs. In terms of implementation of PMS, we noted that a key is to engage operational employees in ways that will preserve social capital and enable them to have their values and goals, for the NGO, acknowledged by senior management. We discussed how compromising accounts can present opportunities for continual debate on the design and implementation of PMS, thereby avoiding the privileging of any one set of values. Such an approach is consistent with the ethos of NGOs that respect the opinions and beliefs of those within the NGO. To help expedite this process, we discussed an expressive role for PMS and how this might be achieved.

The role of PMS in NGOs has become increasingly important as NGOs are attempting to develop business-like administrative practices. Consequently, research into this area is gaining in significance. Research should continue to explore issues related to both the design of PMS to suit NGOs and the specific circumstances of NGOs that present challenges to implementation. We see research opportunities to examine how more formal PMS can be combined with the customary informal or organic controls that are compatible with the cultures of NGOs. There are considerable concerns with ensuring that measurement issues are explored to ensure that PMS are congruent with NGO goals and that they are precise, verifiable and sensitive to changing circumstances. While such qualities are common to PMS in most settings, they are particularly pertinent to NGOs as they face considerable pressure to demonstrate how they are effective in achieving hard to measure welfare goals in efficient ways, and that the employees who are reluctant to embrace formal PMS have confidence in the measures.

Notes

1 While 'civil society' has been defined in numerous ways, the term is generally taken to mean a realm or space where there are a set of organizational actors who are not part of the household, the market or the state (Lewis, 2005, p. 45). Lewis and Madon (2004, p. 120) define civil society as '...an institutional space between state, market, and household in which citizens could form associations, organize public action, and represent their interests and aspirations'.

2 The term 'interactive use of formal controls' refers to the use of formal controls to involve managers regularly and personally in the decision activities of subordinates by way of face-to-face meetings (Simons, 1995, p. 95) and to motivate information gathering outside routine channels to help identify strategic uncertainties and emerging strategies (Simons, pp. 95–96). Organic controls are informal decision and communication processes (Chenhall & Morris, 1995). The term 'enabling controls' refers to the use of controls that enable employees to repair local situations, and that have the characteristics of internal transparency, global transparency and flexibility (Ahrens & Chapman, 2004).

3 Source: Oxfam Strategic Plan 2013–2019: The Power of People against Poverty, available at Oxfam.org.

4 Governments and large donors tend to have greater access to NGO management than smaller NGOs and as a consequence can influence goals and policies, and make demands on the design of PMS.

5 In addition to highly motivated employees, some NGOs have large numbers of low-skilled, low-paid employees who may be less committed to the ideals of the NGO and be less involved in the PMS.

6 Source: Edelman Trust Barometer (2015), *in Edelman Trust Barometer, Annual Global Survey*. Available at: EDELMEN.COM/TRUST2015.

7 Source: www.msf.org.uk.

8 Source: www.worldvision.org.

References

Adler, P.S. & Kwon, S.W. (2002). Social capital: prospects for a new concept. *Academy of Management Review*, 2, 1, 17–40.

Ahrens, T. & Chapman, C.S. (2004). Accounting for flexibility and efficiency: a field study of management control systems in a restaurant chain. *Contemporary Accounting Research*, 21, 2, 271–301.

Anheier, H.K. (2000). Managing non-profit organisations: towards a new approach. Working paper. London: London School of Economics and Political Science.

Billis, D. & MacKeith, J. (1993). *Organising NGOs: Challenges and Trends in the Management of Overseas Aid*. London: Centre for Voluntary Organisation, London School of Economics.

Bititci, U.S., Carrie A.S & McDevitt, L.G, (1997). Integrated performance measurement systems: A development guide. *International Journal of Operations and Production Management*, 17, 6, 522–535.

Brown, D.L. & Moore, M.H. (2001). Accountability, strategy, and international nongovernmental organizations. *Nonprofit and Voluntary Sector Quarterly*, 30, 3, 569–587.

Chenhall, R.H., Hall, M. & Smith, D. (2010). Social capital and management control systems: a study of a non-government organization. *Accounting, Organizations and Society*, 35, 737–756.

Chenhall, R.H., Hall, M. & Smith, D. (2013). Performance measurement, modes of evaluation and the development of compromising accounts. *Accounting, Organizations and Society*, 38, 4, 268–287.

Chenhall, R.H., Hall, M. & Smith, D. (2015). The expressive role of performance measurement systems: a field study of a mental health development project. *Accounting, Organizations and Society*, forthcoming.

Chenhall, R.H. & Morris, D. (1995). Organic decision and communication processes and management accounting systems in entrepreneurial and conservative business organizations. *Omega, International Journal of Management Science*, 23, 5, 485–497.

Clark, C. (2006). Moral character in social work. *British Journal of Social Work*, 36, 75–89.

Clark, J. (1991). *Democratising Development: The Role of Voluntary Organisations*, London: Earthscan Publications Ltd.

Coleman, J.S. (1990). *Foundations of Social Theory*. Cambridge, MA: The Belknap Press of Harvard University Press.

Dixon, R., Ritchie, J. & Siwale, J. (2006). Microfinance: accountability from the grassroots. *Accounting, Auditing, and Accountability Journal*, 19, 3, 405–427.

Dowling, G.R. (2001). *Creating Corporate Reputations: Identity, Image, and Performance*. New York: Oxford University Press.

Dutton, J.E., Worline, M.C., Frost, P.J. & Lilius, J. (2006). Explaining compassion organizing. *Administrative Science Quarterly*, 51, 59–96.

Ebrahim, A. (2003). Accountability in practice: mechanisms for NGOs. *World Development*, 31, 5, 813–829.

Edwards, M. & Hulme, D. (Eds). (1996). *Nongovernment Organizations – Performance and Accountability: Beyond the Magic Bullet*. London: Earthscan Publications.

English, L., Guthrie, J. & Parker, L.D. (2005). Recent public sector financial management change in Australia: implementing the market model. In Guthrie, J., Humphrey, C. & Jones, L. R. (Eds) *International Public Financial Management Reform: Progress, Contradictions, and Challenges*. Series: Research in public management. Greenwich, CT: Information Age Publishing, pp. 23–54.

Fields, J., Copp, M. & Kleinman, S. (2008). Symbolic interactionism, inequality and emotions. In Stets, J. & Turner, J.H. (Eds), *Handbook of the Sociology of Emotions* (pp. 155–179). New York: Springer.

Foley, M.W. & Edwards, B. (1999). Is it time to disinvest in social capital? *Journal of Public Policy*, 19, 199–231.

Fowler, A. (1997). *Striking a Balance: A Guide to Enhancing the Effectiveness of Non-governmental Organisations in International Development*. London: Earthscan Publications.

Free, C. (2007). Supply chain accounting practices in the UK retail sector: enabling or coercing co-operation? *Contemporary Accounting Research*, 24, 3, 1–24.

Frumkin, P. (2005). *On Being Nonprofit: A Conceptual and Policy Primer*. Boston: Harvard University Press.

Gittell, R. & Vidal, A. (1998). *Community Organizing: Building Social Capital as a Development Strategy*. Thousand Oaks, CA: Sage.

Gray, R., Bebbington, J. & Collison, D. (2006). NGOs, civil society and accountability: making the people accountable to capital. *Accounting, Auditing & Accountability Journal*, 19, 3, 319–348.

Hadenius, A. & Uggla, F. (1996). Making civil society work, promoting democratic development: what can states and donors do? *World Development*, 24, 10, 1621–1639.

Hilton, M., Crowson, N., Mauhot, J-F. & McKay, J. (2012). *A Historical Guide to NGOs in Britain: Charities, Civil Society and the Voluntary Sector since 1945*. London: Palgrave MacMillan.

Howell, J. & Pearce, J. (2001). *Civil Society & Development. A Critical Exploration*. London: Lynne Rienner Publishers.

Huy, Q.N. (1999). Emotional capability, emotional intelligence, and radical change. *Academy of Management Review*, 24, 2, 321–345.

Kaplan, R.S. (2001). Strategic performance measurement and management in nonprofit organizations. *Nonprofit Management & Leadership*, 11, 3, 353–370.

Korton, D.C. (1987). Third generation NGO strategies: a key to people-centred development, *World Development*, 15, (supplement), 145–159.

Lewis, D. (2003). Theorizing the organisation and management of non-governmental development organisations: towards a composite approach. *Public Management Review*, 5, 3, 325–344.

Lewis, D. (2005). *The Management of Non-governmental Development Organisations*. London: Routledge.

Lewis, D. & Madon, S. (2004). Information systems and non-governmental development organisations: advocacy, organisational learning and accountability in a southern NGO. *The Information Society*, 20, 2, 117–126.

Marsden, D. & Oakley, P. (1990). *Evaluating Social Development Projects*. Oxford: Oxfam Publications.

Merchant, K. & Otley, D.T. (2006). A review of the literature on control and accountability. In Chapman, C.S., Hopwood, A.G. & Shields, M.D. (Eds), *Handbook of Management Accounting Research* (pp. 785–802). London, New York and Amsterdam: Elsevier.

Moers, F. (2004). Discretion and bias in performance evaluation: the impact of diversity and subjectivity. *Accounting, Organizations and Society*, 30, 67–80.

Moers, F. (2006). Performance measure properties and delegation. *The Accounting Review*, 81, 4, 897–924.

Mullane, J.V. (2002). The mission statement as a strategic tool: when used properly. *Management Decision*, 4, 5, 448–455.

Mundy, J. (2010). Creating dynamic tensions through a balanced use of management control systems. *Accounting, Organizations and Society*, 35, 5, 499–523

O'Dwyer, B. & Unerman, J. (2008). The paradoxical potential of a quest for greater NGO accountability: the case of Amnesty Ireland. *Accounting, Organizations and Society*, 33, 7–8, 801–824.

Ramanathan, K.V. (1985). A proposed framework for designing management control systems in not-for-profit organizations. *Financial Accountability & Management*, 1, 1, 75–92.

Sahley, C. (1995). *Strengthening the Capacity of NGOs: Cases of Small Enterprise Development Agencies in Africa*. Oxford: INTRAC Management and Policy Series No. 4.

Sargeant, A., Lee, S. & Jay, E. (2009). Communicating the 'realities' of charity costs: an institute of fundraising initiative. *Nonprofit and Voluntary Sector Quarterly*, 38, 333–342.

Sawhill, J.C. & Williamson, D. (2001) Mission impossible? Measuring success in nonprofit organizations. *Nonprofit Management & Leadership*, 11, 3, 371–386.

Simons, R. (1995). *Levers of Control*. Boston: Harvard Business School Press.

Smillie, I. (1995) *The Alms Bazaar: Altruism under Fire in Non-profit Organisations and International Development*. London: Intermediate Technology.

Smillie, I. (1997). NGOs and development assistance: a change in mind-set? *Third World Quarterly*, 18, 563–577.

Suchman, M. (1995). Managing legitimacy and institutional approaches. *Academy of Management Review*, 20, 571–610.

Tchouakeu, L-M.N., Maldonada, E., Zhao, K., Robinson, H., Maitland, K. & Tapia, A.H. (2011). Humanitarian NGOs: a comparative study of NGOs information technology coordinating bodies. *International Journal of Information Systems and Social Change*, 2, 2, 1–25.

Unerman, J. & O'Dwyer, B. (2006). Theorising accountability for NGO advocacy. *Accounting, Auditing and Accountability Journal*, 19, 3, 349–376.

Verdier, D. (2002). *Moving Money: Banking and Finance in the Industrialized World*. Cambridge: Cambridge University Press.

Wouters, M. & Wilderom, C. (2008). Developing performance-measurement systems as enabling formalization: a longitudinal field study of a logistics department. *Accounting, Organizations and Society*, 33, 4–5, 488–516.

23

Performance management in the public sector

The case of the English ambulance service

Geoffrey Heath, James Radcliffe and Paresh Wankhade

Introduction

Management control can be seen as encompassing management attempts to direct and coordinate the activities of organisations towards the achievement of common goals (Coates *et al.*, 1983) while adapting to changes in their environments (Berry *et al.*, 1995). R.N. Anthony, in his pioneering work, located management control at the tactical level in organisations between strategic planning and operational control. The purpose of management control is to implement strategies formulated at the strategic level (Anthony 1965; Anthony and Govindarajan, 1998). Monitoring success through performance evaluation, therefore, inevitably plays an important role in management control.

This chapter contributes to the themes of the volume concerning the use of performance management to support management control in organisations, by exploring the issues with regard to the public sector. It does this by examining in particular the recent, rather controversial, experience in the English ambulance service (a relatively under-researched area) where concerns over perverse incentives and unintended consequences loom large.

New public management

Attempts to measure and manage performance are a long-standing feature of the public services, despite the inherent difficulties. De Bruijn (2002) gives an excellent account of the potential advantages, disadvantages and risks of performance evaluation systems, together with principles for their successful design. Since the 1980s, a number of common aspects and trends in performance measurement, review and verification have been identified in the public sector. For example, Robert Picciotto of the World Bank claimed that

> performance management is a visible component of the public sector reform movement which is spreading throughout the world in response to a wave of democratization, decentralisation and devolution of government services. It is a major tool of the new public management movement.
>
> *(Picciotto, 1999)*

In particular, an enhanced role for performance management is a key feature of the 'New Public Management' (NPM). (See, for example, the celebrated accounts of Pollitt, 1986; Hood, 1991; 1995). Hood (1991) provided seven 'doctrinal components' of the NPM:

1 'Hand on professional management' with an accountable management process that ensured freedom to manage.
2 'Explicit standards and management of performance' through the setting of goals and performance measures which should preferably be quantitative.
3 More emphasis on output controls, with rewards linked to performance, as opposed to a more 'traditional' emphasis on input and process controls.
4 Clearer divisions of roles and units through purchaser/provider splits and the decentralisation of budgets.
5 An increased role for competition in the public sector.
6 A management style that involved greater 'flexibility' and the development of a more commercial orientation.
7 Greater control of resource use through rigorously applying downward pressure on costs.

Doctrinal components 2 and 3, in particular, ensure that explicit standards, targets and measures of performance (of a notably managerial kind) form one of the main pillars of the NPM (Hood, 1995). Similarly, Power (1994; 1999) analysed the parallel development of an 'audit explosion' exemplified by value for money auditing in the public sector, which is heavily dependent on the use of performance indicators.

Performance indicators were, therefore, fundamental to a major change in the nature of public-sector management, which took place in the 1980s and 1990s. This change was international despite variations and exceptions (Pollitt and Bouckaert, 2000), and has persisted in the UK despite changes in government (see, for example, Cutler and Waine, 2000; McLaughlin and Murji, 2001). This has been a somewhat peculiar development, however, as there are well-established difficulties in using performance measurement in the public sector.

There is an extensive academic literature on the topic, much of which points to potential perverse incentives and unintended outcomes. (See Johnsen, 2005, for a thorough and most helpful review of the literature to that date.) Nevertheless, many NPM reforms seem preoccupied with organisational performance measurement despite variations within the reform movement (Carter *et al.*, 1995; Hood, 1995; Pollitt and Bouckaert, 2000; Talbot, 2005). Debates about targets, performance indicators and their unintended consequences, therefore, are an integral part of the NPM literature (Wankhade, 2011).

Heath and Radcliffe (2007) attempted to draw on these critiques in examining the performance measurement regime that then applied to the English ambulance service. This concentrated solely on response times. The paper referred to a number of earlier discussions, which had pointed out the perverse incentives and unintended consequences often associated with performance measurement and reporting regimes, and argued that this applied in the case of the ambulance service.

Public-sector context

In the public sector,

- objectives are difficult to define precisely;
- organisations have many differing and even contradictory objectives;

- outcomes are difficult to measure, and outputs are frequently used as a proxy for outcomes;
- means, as well as ends, are significant in political contexts;
- responsibilities may be shared among many public agencies and partners;
- identifying causality is often difficult because of long time scales and numerous intervening variables.

There are many technical problems that can arise when performance indicators are used misguidedly. These are often associated with cost cutting and/or attempts to assert management control. They include the following:

- concentrating on outputs rather than outcomes, results rather than causes, and economy and efficiency rather than effectiveness, equity or quality;
- focusing on the short term at the expense of the long term;
- using inappropriate but available comparators;
- using a limited range of unrelated indicators or, conversely, too many indicators leading to information overload;
- ignoring issues of controllability;
- treating indicators as definitive rather than as raising issues for exploration ('dials' rather than 'tin openers' in the terminology of Klein and Carter, 1988).

Many of these issues arise in connection with the ambulance service performance measurement regimes we investigated.

Similarly, the behavioural aspects of inappropriate schemes are well established. The indicators can come to be seen as ends in themselves rather than leading to learning and dialogue, with unmeasured or unmeasurable aspects of performance neglected. As we have suggested, schemes may have unintended and even perverse consequences. These dangers are reinforced where single-dimension measures are used, indicators are closely linked to reward and sanction, or there is a crude 'league table' approach. As Picciotto (1999) points out, there is a danger of moral hazard, i.e. efforts being directed towards measured results rather than improving quality. At worst, outright manipulation of results can take place. Again, there is evidence that this applied in the case of the ambulance service, especially with regard to motivating dysfunctional behaviour (see, for example, Heath and Radcliffe, 2007; 2010; Wankhade, 2011). Significantly, a number of papers (Hood, 2006; Radnor, 2008; Bevan and Hamblin, 2009) used the English ambulance service to substantiate their arguments concerning 'gaming' in public services.

Discussions on performance within the wider public sector include controversies concerning top-down, bottom-up or balanced approaches to performance measurement (OECD-PUMA, 1994, 1997); quality and performance (Morgan and Murgatroyd, 1994); and accountability and performance (Power, 1994; Hillison *et al.*, 1995). The critique of performance measurement centres around the complexities of running public services (Talbot, 2005), transaction costs (Hood *et al.*, 1998), manipulation and deception (Bevan and Hood, 2006), unintended consequences (Smith, 1995), and the performance paradox (Meyer and Gupta, 1994). Agreement is also lacking in the literature about a precise definition of performance, methods of measurement, whether performance measurement increases efficiency of services and on issues of accountability (Neely 1999; Neely *et al.*, 1995; Pollitt, 2001; De Bruijn, 2002; Greiling, 2006).

The literature reveals many models of performance, but few offer clear theoretical explanation or empirical validation (Talbot, 2005). The work of Meyer and Gupta (1994) on 'paradoxes of performance' suggests a weak correlation between performance indicators and performance itself over a given period of time. Performance measurement has also come under criticism for its lack of integration within the democratic process and poor implementation (Public Administration Select Committee, 2003).

New public governance

These issues have emerged across a wide range of countries and institutions as part of a more general concern with the impact of NPM and its appropriateness outside the Anglo-Saxon world, which championed the NPM approach. Christensen and Lægard (2007, p. 9) have noted how the post-NPM world is one of 'mixed models and increased complexity'. Denhardt and Denhardt (2000), for example, present a New Public Service (NPS) approach as a viable alternative to old public administration and the NPM, calling for a greater public participation in the delivery of public provisions. The emphasis is not on steering (NPM) or rowing (public administration), but serving. Liddle (2007) argued that a new public governance model (NPG) would strengthen democratic control over decision making and citizen involvement, as well as improving public trust in government institutions and types of services provided. However, governance (like NPM in many ways) lacks a precise definition and has been used in different contexts and applications (Tendler, 1997; Minogue *et al.*, 1998).

Osborne has developed a model of NPG that contrasts the main components of NPG with those of NPM (2006; 2009; 2010). The key features of the NPG model arise out of its emergence from Institutional and Network theory, which places an emphasis on the pluralist nature of the state. He contends that governance has become increasingly problematic:

> It posits both *a plural state*, where multiple interdependent actors contribute to the delivery of public services, and *a pluralist state*, where multiple processes inform the decision-making system.
>
> *(Osborne, 2010, p. 9)*

He argues that this pluralism requires that public services engage more with their environment than has been the case in the past. This includes the idea emerging from policy network theory that engagement with more members of the public though increased networks can reverse the trend towards lower levels of participation in the traditional political process (Guy Peters, 2010). However, Guy Peters does note that such an approach may not resolve the problems of representative democracy as it does not guarantee that those who dominate the present decision-making system will not dominate this new approach.

However, Osborne contends that the focus of NPG would place the organisation within its environment and its emphasis is on 'Negotiation of values, meaning and relationships' (2010, p. 10). For him, this would result in a more sustainable public service model with greater levels of public trust in the decision-making process. However, he does caution that the approach he adopts towards NPG should not be seen as normative, but rather as the development of an analytical tool for future research into public services.

Performance score cards

It has been recognised for some time in the accounting literature that reliance on a single measure of performance, such as Return on Investment, can be misguided and, therefore, multiple models of performance evaluation have been developed. The best known of these is the Balanced Scorecard (BSC), which was introduced by Kaplan and Norton in 1992 and has been developed by them and others through a number of versions since. (See, for example, Kaplan and Norton, 1992; 1996a; Olve *et al.*, 1999.) Other chapters in this volume refer to these developments in more detail (e.g. Dugdale in Chapter 2).

Briefly, the BSC is a framework to assist the design and implementation of strategic performance management in organisations by integrating external and internal perspectives, short-term and long-term objectives, financial and non-financial measures, and leading and lagging indicators. In the original version of the BSC, the dimensions of organisational performance are classified into four perspectives:

- Financial perspective,
- Customer perspective,
- Business process perspective,
- Organisational learning and growth perspective,

The four perspectives are held to be interlinked, and none is pre-eminent (see Figure 23.1). However, as originally formulated, they have proved to be of limited relevance for many organisations. Consequently, the BSC has been adopted flexibly in practice and, subsequently, more perspectives suggested, such as one for corporate social responsibility or sustainability (Olve *et al.*, 1999).

There have been problems of appropriately trading-off and weighting performance on one perspective against that on another (success on other perspectives, for example, may be accompanied by increased cost). Also, the BSC is a strategic instrument, and initially, there were some difficulties in linking the strategic to the tactical and operational levels. Now,

Financial Perspective *How do our investors see us?*		**Customer Perspective** *How do our customers see us?*
	Vision	
Organisational Learning & Growth Perspective *How can we innovate and improve?*		**Business Process Perspective** *What must we excel at?*

Figure 23.1 The balanced scorecard

the use of *strategy maps*, which are 'visualisations' of an organisation's objectives, targets and plans, is advocated to counter difficulties in 'drilling down' from the strategic level (Kaplan and Norton, 1996b).

Intriguingly, although initially less well known elsewhere, a similar approach, called the *Tableau de Bord* (TdB), has been practised in France since the 1920s (Lebas, 1996). The TdB is less formal than the BSC and is intended as a 'piloting' instrument (hence, it is sometimes translated as the 'dashboard'). Any particular dashboard is customised around critical success factors and key performance indicators (financial and physical) specific to the organisation.

There has been considerable debate regarding the merits of the BSC versus those of the TdB (see, for example, Epstein and Manzoni, 1998; Nørreklit, 2003; Bourgignon *et al.*, 2004; Bessire and Baker, 2005; Bukh and Malmi, 2005.) Nevertheless, despite these disagreements and some difficulties in practice, it is generally agreed to be logical to adopt some form of multiple performance evaluation model rather than to rely on a single indicator. However, the previous performance measurement regime in the English ambulance service did not fit with this.

Changing role of paramedic

A major issue affecting the nature and role of performance indicators applying to the ambulance service relates to the changing role of the ambulance service personnel, most notably that of ambulance or community paramedics. Formerly, the role of emergency ambulance staff was seen as concentrating on transporting patients speedily to hospital accident and emergency (A&E) units. It is now accepted, however, that the role of the ambulance paramedic has evolved to encompass a greater range of skills to be applied in a wider variety of situations. The Department of Health has acknowledged that

> Traditionally ambulance services have been perceived as an emergency service ... stabilizing the patient's condition sufficiently for rapid transport to hospital for definitive care ... Ambulance services have changed their traditional approach and are now embedded in urgent care as a whole.
>
> *(Department of Health, 2005)*

Similarly, the Commission for Health Improvement stated that

> Whereas ambulance staff might have been seen in the past as transportation services, they now play a more significant role in emergency care. Paramedics take responsibility for greater clinical decision making and they provide an increasing range of interventions.
>
> *(Commission for Health Improvement, 2003)*

Paramedics are increasingly making use of their skills at the scene of incidents, potentially enhancing the patient experience and impacting on survival rates prior to accessing hospital care. This is a crucial issue as it is part of evolving government policy to promote an enhanced role for paramedical activities at the scene, in terms of both providing care and giving advice.

> Ambulance clinicians should be equipped with a greater range of competencies that enable them to assess, treat, refer or discharge patients.
>
> *(Department of Health, 2005)*

Consequently, it was deemed necessary to develop the skills of ambulance crews and paramedics through an increasingly high level of education and training, providing enhanced triage capability at the scene and a wider range of treatment (Ball, 2005). Paramedic training and education has moved into Higher Education (Till and Marsh, 2015), and new specialist paramedic roles such as the paramedic practitioners (PP), emergency care practitioners (ECP), critical care practitioners (CCP) and community paramedics (CP) have been developed across different ambulance trusts in England. These roles allow paramedics equipped with enhanced knowledge and skills to make complex decisions about patient care. Till and Marsh (2015) argue that this has resulted in better triage and treatment at the scene by crews. The Paramedic Evidence-Based Education Project (PEEP), developed by Allied Health Solutions, was aimed at moving towards standardised education and training to ensure consistency across the profession. However, it highlighted considerable variations in the current education and training models, for example, in the length, content and academic level of the associated educational programmes, which may act as a barrier to the full professionalisation of the workforce (Lovegrove and Davis, 2013).

The development of ECPs, dating from 2000, entailed a major redesign of the paramedic's role (Ball, 2005). Cooper *et al.* (2004) established that the then still emerging role of the ECP focused on advanced assessment and patient management skills. ECPs were significantly more likely to treat patients at the scene than ordinary paramedics and less likely to have them conveyed on to an A&E department. Both ECPs and stakeholders felt that the additional training of the ECP improved their clinical practice. The Treat and Refer approach also entailed staff with enhanced skills using new protocols regarding non-transportation of patients. Compared to routine practice, there were similar conveyance rates to A&E, but more time was spent at the scene with greater assessment. Patient satisfaction ratings were similar or higher (Snooks *et al.*, 2004). However, there were some safety concerns and issues around managing change, while, interestingly, there were difficulties in persuading some patients that they did not need to go to A&E.

Mason *et al.* (2007a) concluded that the use of ECPs was improving ways of working locally and facilitating the reconfiguration of service delivery. It led to reduced attendances at A&E and reduced admissions, shorter episode times and higher levels of satisfaction. Furthermore, it seemed that there were cost savings, particularly with regard to reducing operational costs, although a significant investment in training expenditure was also required. Similarly, Gray and Walker (2008a) found that advanced practitioners who can assess and treat at the point of access are increasingly important and can provide potentially significant cost savings to the NHS. Halter *et al.* (2006) and Hill *et al.* (2014) also concluded that these specialist roles have reduced the conveyance of patients to emergency departments, thus reducing the costs associated with ambulance journeys.

In addition, Halter *et al.* (2006) found that care provided by ECPs was considered equal or considerably better than that provided by traditional ambulance practitioners, especially with regard to 'thoroughness of assessment'. Similarly, Mason *et al.* (2007b) examined a scheme that used extended skills practitioners to assess and, if necessary, treat older people with minor injury or illness in the community. They concluded that the initiative provided a clinically effective alternative to standard ambulance transfer in such cases, although there were some concerns regarding the level of inter-agency cooperation required and the amount of training and operational costs. Snooks *et al.* (2013) noted that the adoption of enhanced telephone triage and Treat and Refer protocols by English ambulance services had been accompanied by a decline in conveyancing rates from 90 per cent in 2000 to 58 per cent in 2012.

The continuing need to develop a professional work force has been highlighted in several policy documents, and workforce development is seen as an integral element of the ambulance modernisation programme (National Audit Office, 2010; 2011; AACE, 2011; NHS

England, 2013; NHS Confederation, 2014; 2015). Blaber and Harris (2014) regard the development of clinical leadership for paramedics as the *sine qua non* of ambulance professionalisation. However, current evidence regarding the implications of new specialist paramedic roles on patient safety and quality of care is rather mixed.

A recent ambulance scoping review (Fisher *et al.* 2015) has demonstrated the lack of quality information available regarding ambulance service patient safety in the UK. The study cautioned that operational pressures including performance targets are still seen as more important than patient safety for ambulance services. There are some concerns about patient safety and quality of care (Fisher *et al.*, 2015; O'Hara *et al.*, 2015; Turner *et al.*, 2015). These include issues around assessment and referral of older people with a fall who were left behind at the scene (Halter *et al.*, 2011), about the safety of patients while making decisions about treating them at the scene (Tohira *et al.*, 2013) and the safety of patents involved in decisions not to convey (Fisher *et al.*, 2015; O'Hara *et al.*, 2015). The National Audit Office expressed a different sort of concern. Although advanced practitioners could potentially reduce transfers of patients to A&E by 30 per cent and some services were fully utilising their greater skills, most ambulance services were simply using them alongside other paramedics without focusing on where they could have most impact on conveyance rates. Moreover, the call categorisation systems in most services were not sophisticated enough to send them to only the most suitable calls (National Audit Office, 2011).

Nevertheless, the Keogh Urgent and Emergency Care Review (NHS England, 2013) emphasised the significant role of the ambulance services in the urgent and emergency care networks, and their contribution towards reducing pressures in A&E has been widely acknowledged (NHS Five Year Forward View, 2014; NHS Confederation, 2014; 2015). Thus, despite some controversy, there have been significant developments in the reconfiguration of ambulance service activity in ways that should add value to the patient. This raises a number of issues. In particular, for performance evaluation, there is the challenge of how to devise a performance measurement regime that reflects the increasingly multifaceted nature of ambulance work. Indeed, these developments were constrained by the contradictory influence of the performance indicators applied to the ambulance service, as we aim to show in the next section. This point is referred to briefly in a number of papers in the literature (e.g. Gray and Walker, 2008a; 2008b), and we have tried to explore it in more depth elsewhere (Heath and Radcliffe, 2007; 2010; Radcliffe and Heath, 2009; Wankhade, 2011; Heath and Wankhade, 2014).

Previous performance evaluation regime

The four key performance indicators that applied were concerned only with response times, as shown in Figure 23.2 (Department of Health, 2005; Healthcare Commission, 2008).

Rapid response times are clearly important (although they can be achieved in ways that create unnecessary risk and stress: see Sanders and Gough, 2003). However, concentrating on the time taken for vehicles to arrive at the scene of an incident ignores what happens subsequently at the scene and meant that ambulance services were not being judged on the total package of care they provided. There were, instead, just a few indicators of output rather than outcome in only one dimension of performance. This contrasts with the tendency towards multi-dimensional models of performance management, exemplified by the BSC and TdB.

Moreover, the effects of the regime were reinforced by the league table approach that was adopted, with notable perverse effects. The focus on results rather than causes and the narrow range of indicators led to the regime becoming notorious for 'gaming', such as distorting activity and manipulating reported results. It fell, therefore, into many of the pitfalls in the academic literature and became highly controversial (Heath and Radcliffe, 2007; 2010; Wankhade, 2011).

STATUS	PERFORMANCE INDICATOR
Immediately life threatening (Category A)	Response within 8 minutes irrespective of location in 75% of cases. Fully equipped ambulance in attendance within 14/19 minutes of initial call in 95% of cases (unless control room decides an ambulance is not required)
Urgent need for hospital care defined by doctor	Patient should arrive at hospital within 15 minutes of arrival time specified by the doctor in 95% of cases
All other patients (Category B/C)	Response within 14 minutes (urban) or 19 minutes (rural)

Figure 23.2 National performance requirements for ambulance services

As we have seen, the Department of Health has promoted an enhanced role for paramedical activities at the scene (Department of Health, 2005), but this wider role was not reflected in the performance measures. Moreover, as the Healthcare Commission stated, most services perform well against national standards; but, not surprisingly, performance is more variable in those aspects that receive less national attention (Healthcare Commission, 2008). Therefore, aspects of performance other than response times tended to be played down.

Consequently, over time a great deal of controversy arose regarding the performance measures, leading to a report from the Commission for Health Improvement (Commission for Health Improvement, 2003). The Commission recognised that measuring outcomes of emergency ambulance care is complicated by the difficulty ambulance trusts may face in obtaining data from acute hospital trusts and in the problems of developing databases across organisational boundaries. Nevertheless, the Commission concluded that

> A priority for ambulance trusts must be to develop credible measures of outcome … (which) should be included among ambulance service key targets in future.
>
> *(op. cit. p. 22)*

Similarly, the Audit Commission (1998), while acknowledging the difficulties, had held that an examination of outcomes was required for the proper evaluation of care. Consequently, the Department of Health (2005, p. 56) proposed that for patients presenting conditions that may be immediately life threatening, the first two performance measures be retained.

> For all other patients, ambulance trusts are to be assessed on the overall quality of care provided…

The proposed wider set of indicators was not forthcoming immediately, although standardisation was attempted through the 'Call to Connect' targets, which defined response times more stringently and reduced the variation in interpretation (Wankhade, 2011) but had further perverse effects (Woollard *et al.*, 2010).

New ambulance performance regime

In December 2010, however, the then new coalition government announced the introduction of a range of 'clinical' quality indicators for ambulance services to take effect in April 2011. Timeliness was still seen as important, but no longer the only important factor (Department of Health, 2010a). The 11 indicators additionally included indicators of outcome or processes relevant to outcome but not cost (in contrast to the BSC perspectives). They were set out initially in broad terms (Department of Health, 2010b – see Figure 23.3)

1	Outcome from acute ST-elevation myocardial infarction (STEMI)
2	Outcome from cardiac arrest – return of spontaneous circulation
3	Outcome from cardiac arrest – survival to discharge
4	Outcome following stroke for ambulance patients
5	Proportion of calls closed with telephone advice or managed without transport to A&E (where clinically appropriate)
6	Re-contact rate following discharge of care (i.e. closure with telephone advice or following treatment at the scene)
7	Call abandonment rate
8	Time to answer calls
9	Service experience
10	The eight minute response time concerning immediately life threatening cases and provision of transport within nineteen minutes where needed
11	Time to treatment by an ambulance-dispatched health professional

Figure 23.3 List of ambulance clinical quality indicators

A paper (Cooke, 2011) by the then National Clinical Director for Urgent and Emergency Care gave more detail. The proposals were based on three principles: the regime should be based on evidence, move from a target culture to one of continuous improvements in clinical care, and provide information to patients and the public to enable them to judge the quality of care provided. The indicators were intended to focus on outcomes where available or otherwise on process measures that have a proven link to outcome (Cooke, 2011). Ambulance services, therefore, are expected to share information and work with others in a whole systems approach.

The results of the indicators are published monthly in the form of a dashboard for each of the ambulance services in England. These were presented as four clinical indicators and eight process or systems indicators. (Calls closed via telephone advice and following treatment at the scene are now shown separately, as are re-contact rates.) From 2012, Category A calls were divided into Red 1, the most time-critical, and Red 2, which are serious but less time-critical (Department of Health, 2012a). The clinical indicators are published after the systems indicators because of the time required for the outcomes of patients transported to A&E by ambulance to be established (Gov. UK, 2013). It was intended that a narrative account of the experience of ambulance service users should also be presented, but patient experience is not currently reported (Heath and Wankhade, 2014).

The new indicators are meant to be considered as a set that forms the basis of patient-centred continuous improvement. It is accepted that each indicator taken individually has weaknesses and there is also the danger that one can be improved at the expense of another, which is not acceptable (Cooke, 2011). The set of indicators is reviewed annually, although it is not clear how this is being done.

The approach underlying the dashboard responded to the debates concerning the previous performance management regime. Criticisms of that regime and research into the role of the ambulance paramedic both seem to have influenced the changes. Thus, Cooke (2011) acknowledged that concentrating on time targets, without examining the quality of care, gave rise to perverse incentives. It is necessary, therefore, to know the outcomes of clinical interventions in order to improve the situation, especially as many patients previously taken to A&E are now dealt with in other ways.

In the new approach, using indicators as targets was rejected as this was held to give no incentive to aim for more than the target. Instead, the indicators were intended to promote a culture of continuous improvement whereby feedback motivates learning and innovation to gain further improvement in a virtuous circle. Such a culture, if indeed implemented effectively, would also act against tendencies to gaming (Heath and Wankhade, 2014).

Moving from a very limited set of indicators to a much broader one, however, while welcome in itself, may also give rise to difficulties. The measures may indeed turn out to be a balanced set of indicators, or they may make assessment of service performance too complex to be meaningful. Issues may arise of trading-off performance on one measure against another. It may be that, in practice, some of the indicators will be stressed (most likely response times), simplifying the issues faced but facilitating gaming.

Quality accounts

More or less contemporaneously with the adoption of the dashboard, the Health Act 2009 required most organisations that provide NHS services in England (including ambulance services) to publish Quality Accounts annually from April 2010 (Department of Health,

2012b). The accounts are intended to promote a number of desirable, but potentially conflicting objectives:

- scrutiny of, debate about and reflection on the performance of NHS organisations;
- accountability of service providers, both upwards and outwards towards stakeholders;
- benchmarking of performance;
- continuous, evidence-based quality improvement programmes;
- engagement of stakeholders.

Some parts of the Quality Accounts are mandatory and set out in guide lines, but most of the content of the report was intended to be determined locally, including the performance indicators reported in them. Quality Accounts were to be developed, and therefore, by engaging stakeholders, including service users, the accounts were intended to be easily understandable and readily accessible (Department of Health, 2010c). Research suggested that prior to the launch of Quality Accounts, representatives of local communities welcomed the idea of increasing accountability for quality improvement via these accounts. However, they were concerned that issues would arise around reliability of information, presentation and understandability, trading-off priorities, and establishing meaningful dialogue and consequent actions (Foot and Ross, 2010).

A subsequent study (Foot *et al.*, 2011) suggested that early-published Quality Accounts justified this caution. There was considerable variation in the contents and presentation of the accounts (e.g. the number of quality measures and the aspects of performance measured), which also had numerous technical limitations (e.g. the measures were often presented without definition, context or discussion). Disappointingly, given the 'philosophy' underlying the approach, involvement of stakeholders was also regarded as weak. There was a lack of comparative data which limited the accounts as instruments of accountability. Foot *et al.* (2011) argued, therefore, for greater consistency and some mandatory content (including some performance measures), while maintaining a local dimension. Reporting of a small set of core indicators was indeed mandated later (Department of Health, 2012c; 2013). The indicators that must be reported by ambulance trusts are shown in Figure 23.4. They are selected from the dashboard indicators, although on what basis is not clear.

1	Percentage of Category A telephone calls resulting in a response at the scene of the emergency within eight minutes.
2	Percentage of Category A telephone calls resulting in an ambulance response at the scene within nineteen minutes.
3	Percentage of patients with pre-existing diagnosis of ST elevation myocardial infarction who received an appropriate care bundle.
4	Percentage of patients with suspected stroke who received an appropriate care bundle.

Figure 23.4 Quality indicators to be included in English Ambulance Service Quality Accounts

The local development of accounts seems desirable in terms of promoting stakeholder engagement, deliberation, reflexivity and accountability, and in responding to specific local requirements for information. However, it does mean that each ambulance service in England could produce markedly different types of reports, hampering comparability and benchmarking. The diverse set of audiences for Quality Accounts means that they are intended to serve potentially contradictory purposes; particularly in terms of how far they can support both internal processes for quality improvement and external accountability (Heath and Wankhade, 2014).

The 'bottom-up philosophy' of Quality Accounts is also at odds with that of the dashboard, which is a standardised set of indicators, imposed 'top-down'. Thus, English ambulance services must now address two performance measurement regimes, both of which seem improvements on the previous regime, but which differ considerably.

Organisational culture

Simons (1999) has identified four 'levers' which organisations may use to implement management control. These are dealt with in more detail elsewhere in this volume (see Chapters 2 and 28 and several in between) and so are discussed here briefly. They are as follows:

- *Belief Systems*
  The explicit sets of definitions that are communicated formally and reinforced systematically by senior managers to provide basic values, purpose and direction for the organisation (cf. organisational culture).
- *Boundary Systems*
  The explicit statements in formal information systems that define specific risks to be avoided and how they are to be avoided (e.g. audit controls).
- *Diagnostic Control Systems*
  The formal information systems which managers use to monitor organisational outcomes and to correct deviations from pre-set standards of performance (e.g. budgeting).
- *Interactive Control Systems*
  The formal information systems which managers use to involve themselves in the decision activities of their subordinates by regular dialogue.

Figure 23.5 shows how the levers are linked in Simons' conceptual framework. Simons argues that organisations need to have a range of control instruments because it is necessary to have the appropriate balance between various factors that affect the performance of the organisation, such as

- freedom and constraint,
- empowerment and accountability,
- bottom-up creativity and top-down direction,
- experimentation and efficiency,
- innovation and stability,
- emergent and intended strategy.

It is more effective, therefore, if management exerts control through the full range of levers rather than a single one, as long as they support and complement each other, rather than

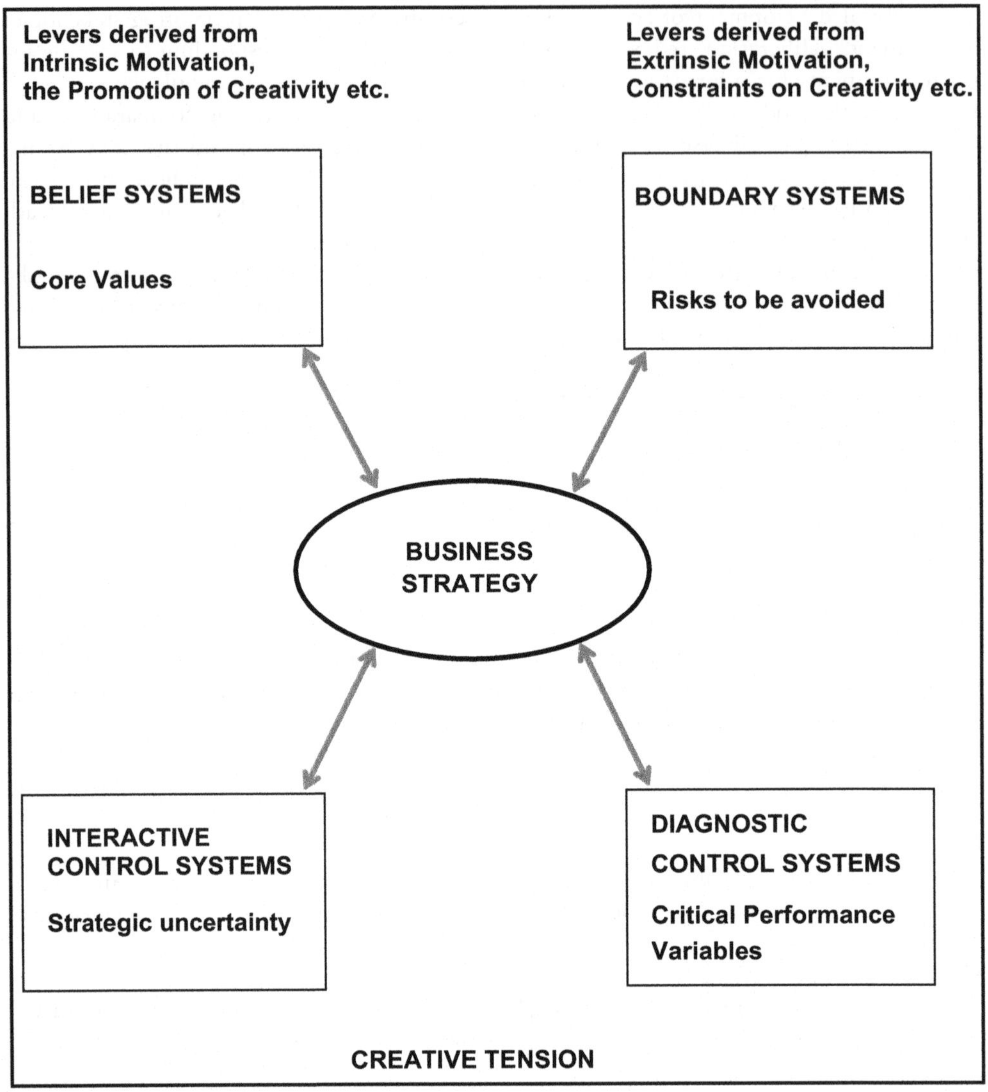

Figure 23.5 Linking the levers

conflict (e.g. where budgetary control might emphasise financial rewards and the organisational culture intrinsic rewards). However, the levers do not automatically align with each other. Also what is the appropriate balance between them will vary from organisation to organisation and from time to time.

Control in organisations can be seen as supporting efforts to achieve corporate objectives, while adjusting to changes in the organisation's environment. Following Simons, therefore, such control by senior management seems most easily exercised where there is a strong unitary organisational culture that encompasses executives' values and is in line with the other levers of control. This does not correspond well to the situation of the English ambulance service.

This is particularly significant because changing organisational cultures rather than structures has become a fashionable prescription for health service reform in the UK. However, changing cultures is not easy as an organisation's culture is subject to various local contingencies (see, for example, Wankhade *et al.*, 2015). Therefore, the issues of how organisational cultures are perpetuated and how organisational cultures and sub-cultures support resistance to attempts at organisational change are important. Ogbonna and Harris (2014) suggest that factors such as historical legacy, sub-cultural dynamics and external influences can, under relevant circumstances, promote a level of cultural perpetuation, which acts as a strong barrier to efforts at culture management and change.

This argument is important for the ambulance service where serious attempts have been made to reform cultural values around the professionalisation of paramedics. The identity of the paramedic as a multi-skilled clinical professional is intended to supersede that associated with the role which concentrates only on rapid transportation to A&E. Similarly, values around the notion of the ambulance service as the 'health arm of the emergency services' are to be replaced by those associated with the 'emergency arm of the health service'.

However, there is evidence that this transformation of culture has not been totally successful (McCann *et al.*, 2013; Wankhade *et al.*, 2015). The tendency for rapid response to be predominantly valued in the existing culture supported resistance to embracing professionalisation wholeheartedly. Wankhade (2012) reported that a variety of assumptions, values and beliefs were held in the sub-cultures of different occupational 'tribes' (i.e. executives, middle managers, paramedics and control room staff) at the ambulance service he researched, rather than a dominant belief system.

Moreover, Radcliffe and Heath (2009) argued that organisational sub-cultures and the performance management regime then in place reinforced each other in countering efforts at reform. Attempts to bring 'top-down' cultural change also come up against the pressing need to deal with issues like increasing demand and declining resources (Wankhade and Brinkman, 2014). However, Radcliffe and Heath also contended that the influence of central government in favour of professionalisation did have some effect. Thus, historical legacy, sub-cultural dynamics and extra-organisational influences all played a part. Notably, however, the views of service users had a limited impact on the culture(s).

The changing role and identity of ambulance personnel and the conflict between professional cultures and management objectives around this, have significant implications for government policy. At the same time, this phenomenon adds to our understanding of management control. The English ambulance service presents an interesting case, therefore, where the senior executives' belief system is countered by both resistant sub-cultural norms *and* the diagnostic lever (i.e. the predominant performance indicator: rapid response times).

Discussion

The ambulance performance management regime has moved from a single measure model to a wider set of indicators, and this has been generally welcomed. The thinking behind the dashboard reflects the debates about the previous performance measurement regime. Both the criticisms of the regime and the research into the changing role of the ambulance service seem to have influenced the reforms. However, within the larger debates between NPM and NPS or NPG, it is important to examine the extent to which the current ambulance performance frameworks exhibit public involvement and patient participation.

It is unclear as to how and to what extent the views of ambulance staff and other stakeholders were accessed and used in setting up the dashboard or how they participate in the revisions promised. Quality Accounts, on the other hand, echo the NPS/NPG literature on participation. However, there are questions about the practical issues that arise and the extent to which they do contribute towards the ambitious objectives of more debate and reflection on performance, greater stakeholder engagement and so on. The extent to which the dashboard and Quality Accounts are based on different approaches to performance reporting and accountability may also prove significant.

An emphasis on the negotiation of values, meaning and relationships is central to NPG (Osborne, 2010). This is also of critical importance when considering the problem of implementation, particularly where such a process involves attempts to modify the prevailing culture. Pressman and Wildavsky (1973) demonstrated that central government policy initiatives are often not implemented fully or as intended when applied locally. Policy implementation studies have now moved away from seeing the process as a top-down management problem, in which any deviation from the original intentions is perceived as being a management failure, to one which is more the end result of a period of negotiation and consensus building (Susskind, 2006; Hill and Hupe, 2014).

Indeed, the idea that policy outcomes are the result of a 'negotiated order', in which those affected by the policy play a part in its implementation by how they respond to that policy, is a key to understanding the nature of policy 'success' and 'failure' (see Barrett and Fudge, 1981). Such an approach is also found in Lipsky's concept of 'street-level bureaucracy' which contains within it concerns 'to recognise the validity of the perspective of low level officials *and* of the public to whom they relate' (Hill and Hupe, 2014, p. 199). It may be argued then that the development of a set of performance measures that involves an awareness and understanding of the perspectives of users and those delivering the service, as well as those of senior managers, will result in a more sustainable and effective regime.

This approach has similarities to that of Crozier and Friedberg (Crozier, 1964; Crozier and Friedberg, 1980). They see organisations as both the setting for conflict and confrontation between organisational 'players', which they characterise as games, and for their resolution. Actors pursue stratagems to meet their own needs or objectives through 'games playing'. However, these games have the paradoxical effect of integrating the actors into the organisation, because the rules of the game are accepted by the players. Power is then 'a bargaining relationship over time within a framework of constraints which the actors cannot easily change. As a bargaining relationship, the power game centres around the predictability of behaviour' (Crozier, 1976, p. 307).

Thus, Crozier and Friedberg do not see the players in their games as being equal. Instead, power is seen as a central feature of organisational life, which cannot be reduced to the formal authority structure. In their model, *uncertainty explains power*, Crozier (1976) argues that 'Regulation is not achieved by command, evaluation and control, but indirectly by the results of games where each partner fights for his own interests … and must cater to the wishes of a stronger partner…' (p. 303). Those in a position to cope with uncertainty have informal power over those who are dependent on their choices. (Thus, skilled manual workers or public-sector professionals, for example, may have sway over those who manage them.) However, social constraints prevent actors taking too much advantage of their power; otherwise, organisations would cease to function. Moreover, they accept their inferiority in one game because they are always part of other games where they may be in a superior position.

Friedberg (2009) explains that the approach is based on 'borrowings' of two key concepts from American social science: Dahl's concept of *the relational theory of power* and Simon's concept of *bounded rationality*. The positional theory of power stresses the interactions between interdependent but partially autonomous individuals pursuing their own personal strategies in terms of their expectations of other actors' likely behaviour. This behaviour is 'rational', therefore, in terms of satisficing under imperfect knowledge. The social order of organisations is the emerging (and possibly temporary) outcome of the boundedly rational but purposeful behaviour of the participants.

Moreover, Crozier (1964) identified a workers' sub-culture in the organisations he studied, which was adopted by all staff except new or marginalised employees, despite all other differences (such as class background or political allegiance). There was, therefore, only a short learning period before new members were socialised into the dominant set of beliefs and attitudes by a process of autonomous group development. The main features of the sub-culture concern demands for independence and autonomy, and oppose the goals of the organisation and the aims of management. However, while this is a rigid system of attitudes and beliefs, derived from the pressure of the group, practical behaviour is not entirely determined by it, but is also affected by other considerations. Management attempts to use both formal authority relationships and informal arrangements to guide group solidarity, the effects of the sub-culture and the power struggle towards a conflictual but stable equilibrium (Crozier, 1964).

Conclusion

The recent history of performance management in the English ambulance service presents an interesting case, where factors like perverse incentives and sub-cultural resistance act to impede top-down management efforts. NPG would suggest that effective performance evaluation regimes require the participation of stakeholders, including service users and employees. Implementation theories suggest that central government policies are unlikely to be implemented effectively without recognising the perspectives of employees in a negotiated order. The work of Crozier and Friedberg suggests that paramedics and control room staff are likely to have strong sub-cultures valuing independence, which support the significant relational power they derive from their specialist expertise. Our case points to the validity of all these suggestions.

The research reviewed broadly supports the policy of expanding the role of ambulance paramedics and the development of a wider range of performance indicators. However, the literature suggests that not involving stakeholders may incur resistance to change. The policy implications resulting from this include the need for government to engage more readily with ambulance paramedics and other professionals in the continuing refinement and implementation of performance measurement tools, especially if attempts to change organisational culture are to be effective.

In addition, the issue of involving users of the service is relevant. Different perspectives may emerge concerning the purpose of the ambulance service when users are increasingly involved. NPG is a response to an era in which governance and implementation have become more difficult and the divorce between user and provider perspectives has continued. Greater user involvement may be a challenge to service providers, and user perspectives on the purpose of the service will need further research. Similarly, there may be an important issue surrounding a generational difference between older ambulance personnel and more recently trained professionals with a wider range of skills, where the traditional view of the ambulance service as simply the emergency transport of patients is challenged.

References

AACE (2011) *Taking Health Care to the Patient 2: A Review of 6 Years' Progress and Recommendations for the Future*, Association of Ambulance Chief Executives, London.

Anthony, R.N. (1965) *Management Planning and Control Systems: A Framework for Analysis*, Harvard University Press, Boston, MA.

Anthony, R.N. and Govindarajan, V. (1998) *Management Control Systems*, Mcgraw-Hill, Boston, MA.

Audit Commission (1998) *A Life in the Fast Lane*, Audit Commission, London.

Ball, L. (2005) 'Setting the scene for the paramedic in primary care: a review of the literature' *Emergency Medicine Journal*, 22, pp. 896–900.

Barrett, S. and Fudge, C. (1981) *Policy and Action: Essays on the Implementation of Public Policy*, Sage, London

Berry, A., Broadbent, J. and Otley, D. (1995) *Management Control*, Palgrave Macmillan, Basingstoke.

Bessire, D. and Baker, C. (2005) 'The French Tableau de Bord and the American Balanced Scorecard: a critical analysis' *Critical Perspectives on Accounting*, 16, 6, pp. 645–664.

Bevan, G. and Hamblin, R. (2009) 'Hitting and missing targets by ambulance services for emergency calls: effects of different systems of performance measurement within the UK' *Journal of the Royal Statistical Society*, 172, Part 1, pp. 161–190.

Bevan, G. and Hood, C. (2006) 'What's measured is what matters: targets and gaming in the English public health care system' *Public Administration*, 84, 3, pp. 517–538.

Blaber, A. and Harris, H. (2014) *Clinical Leadership for Paramedics*, Open University Press, Berkshire.

Bourgignon, A., Mallaret, V. and Nørreklit, H. (2004) 'The American Balanced Scorecard versus the French Tableau de Bord: the ideological dimension' *Management Accounting Research*, 15, 2, pp. 107–134.

Bukh, P.-N. and Malmi, T. (2005) 'Re-examining the Cause-and-Effect Principle of the Balanced Scorecard' in Jönsson, S. and Mouritsen, J, (eds), *Accounting in Scandinavia – The Northern Lights*, Liber and Copenhagen Business School Press, Copenhagen, pp. 87–113.

Carter, N., Klein, R., and Day, P. (1995) *How Organisations Measure Success: The Use of Performance Indicators in Government*, Routledge, London.

Christensen, T. and Lægreid, P. (2007) *Transcending New Public Management: The Transformation of Public Sector Reforms*, Ashgate, Aldershot.

Coates, J., Rickwood, C. and Stacey, R. (1983) *Control and Audit in Management Accountancy*, CIMA, London.

Commission for Health Improvement (2003) Sectoral Report: *What CHI Has Found in Ambulance Trusts*, Commission for Health Improvement, London.

Cooke, M. (2011) 'An introduction to the new ambulance clinical quality indicators' *Ambulance Today*, 8, 1, pp. 35–39.

Cooper, S., Barrett, B., Black, S., Evans, C., Real, C., Williams, S. and Wright, B. (2004) 'The emerging role of the emergency care practitioner' *Emergency Medicine Journal*, 21, pp. 614–618.

Crozier, M. (1964) *The Bureaucratic Phenomenon*, University of Chicago Press, Chicago, IL.

Crozier, M. (1976) 'Comparing Structures and Comparing Games' in Pugh, D. (ed.) (1990) *Organization Theory*, Penguin, Harmondsworth.

Crozier, M. and Friedberg, E. (1980) *Actors and Systems: The Politics of Collective Action*, University of Chicago Press, Chicago, IL.

Cutler, T. and Waine, B. (2000) 'Managerialism reformed? New labour and public sector management' *Social Policy and Administration*, 34, 3, pp. 318–332.

De Bruijn, H. (2002) *Managing Performance in the Public Sector*, Routledge, London.

Denhardt, R.B. and Denhardt, J.V. (2000) 'The New Public Service: Serving Rather than Steering' *Public Administration Review*, 60, 6, pp. 549–559.

Department of Health (2005) *Taking Healthcare to the Patients: Transforming NHS Ambulance Services*, Department of Health, London.

Department of Health (2010a) *Reforming Urgent and Emergency Care Performance Management* www.dh.gov.uk/en/Healthcare/Urgentandemergencycare/DH_121239.

Department of Health (2010b) *Patients to Be at Heart of A&E and Ambulance Care* www.dh.gov.uk/en/MediaCentre/Pressreleases/DH_122877.

Department of Health (2010c) *Quality Accounts Toolkit 2010/11* www.dh.gov.uk/publications.

Department of Health (2012a) *Changes to Ambulance Time Categories* www.gov.uk/government/news/changes-to-ambulance-time-categories.

Department of Health (2012b) *Frequently Asked Questions about Quality Accounts* www.dh.gov.uk/health/2012/02/quality-account-faq/.

Department of Health (2012c) *Quality Account Audit and Future Reporting Changes Advised* www.dh.gov.uk/health/2012/02/quality-account-reporting/.

Department of Health (2013) *Quality Accounts: Reporting Arrangements for 2012/3* www.dh.gov.uk/en/Publications and statistics/Lettersandcirculars/Dearcolleagueletters/DH132725.

Epstein, M. and Manzoni, J.-F. (1998) 'Implementing corporate strategy: from Tableaux de Bord to Balanced Scorecards' *European Management Journal*, 16, 2, pp. 190–203.

Fisher, J.D., Freeman, K., Clarke, A., Spurgeon, P., Smyth, M., Perkins, G., Sujan, M. and Cooke, M. (2015) 'Patient safety in ambulance services: a scoping review' *Health Service and Delivery Research*, 3, 21. doi:10.3310/hsdr03210.

Foot, C. and Ross, S. (2010) *Accounting for Quality to the Local Community*, The King's Fund, London.

Foot, C., Raleigh, V., Ross, S. and Lyscom, T. (2011) *How Do Quality Accounts Measure Up?* The King's Fund, London.

Friedberg, E. (2009) Introduction to Crozier, M. (2010 edition) *The Bureaucratic Phenomenon*, Transaction Publishers, New Brunswick, NJ.

Gov. UK (2013) *Statistical Press Notice: Ambulance Quality Indicators – Monthly Update for England* www.gov.uk/government/news/statistical-press-notice.

Gray, J. and Walker, A. (2008a) 'Avoiding admissions from the ambulance service: a review of elderly patients with falls and patients with breathing difficulties seen by emergency care practitioners in South Yorkshire' *Emergency Medicine Journal*, 25, pp. 168–171.

Gray, J. and Walker, A. (2008b) 'AMPDS categories: are they an appropriate method to select cases for extended role ambulance practitioners?' *Emergency Medicine Journal*, 25, pp. 601–603.

Greiling, D. (2006) 'Performance measurement: a remedy for increasing the efficiency of public services?' *International Journal of Productivity and Performance Management*, 55, 6, pp. 448–465.

Guy Peters, B. (2010) 'Meta-governance and Public Management', in Osborne, S. (ed.) *The New Public Governance? Emerging Perspectives on the Theory and Practice of Public Governance*, Routledge, Abingdon, pp. 36–51.

Halter, M., Marlow, T., Tye, C. and Ellison, G. (2006) 'Patients' experiences of care provided by emergency care practitioners and traditional ambulance practitioners: a survey from the London ambulance service' *Emergency Medicine Journal*, 23, pp. 865–866.

Halter, M., Vernon, S., Snooks, H., Porter, A., Close, J., Moore, F., and Porsz, S. (2011) 'Complexity of the decision-making process of ambulance staff for assessment and referral of older people who have fallen: a qualitative study' *Emergency Medicine Journal*, 28, pp. 44–45.

Healthcare Commission (2008) 'Not just a matter of time: a review of urgent and emergency care services in England', Commission for Healthcare Audit and Inspection.

Heath, G. and Radcliffe, J. (2007) 'Performance measurement and the English ambulance service' *Public Money & Management*, 27, 3, pp. 223–227.

Heath, G. and Radcliffe, J. (2010) 'Exploring the utility of current performance measures for changing roles and practices of ambulance paramedics' *Public Money & Management*, 30, 3, pp. 151–158.

Heath, G. and Wankhade, P. (2014) 'A balanced judgement? Performance indicators, quality and the English ambulance service, some issues, developments and a research agenda' *The Journal of Finance and Management in Public Services*, 13, 1, pp. 1–17 www.Cipfa.org/policy-and-guidance/the-journal-of-finance-and-management-in-public-services.

Hill, H., McMeekin, P. and Price, C. (2014) 'A systematic review of the activity and impact of emergency care practitioners in the NHS' *Emergency Medicine Journal*, 10, pp. 853–860.

Hill, M. and Hupe, P. (2014) *Implementing Public Policy*, Sage, London.

Hillison, W., Hollander, A. Iceman, R. and Welch, J. (1995) *Use and Audit of Performance Measures in the Public Sector*, Institute of Internal Auditors Research Foundation, Altamonte Springs, CA.

Hood, C. (1991) 'A public management for all seasons?' *Public Administration*, 69, 1, pp. 3–19.

Hood, C. (1995) 'The "new public management" in the 1980s' *Accounting, Organisations and Society*, 6, pp. 93–109.

Hood, C. (2006) 'Gaming in Targetworld: the targets approach to managing British public services' *Public Administration Review*, July/August, pp. 515–521.

Hood, C., James, O., Jones, G., Scott, C. and Travers, T. (1998) 'Regulation inside Government: where NPM meets the audit explosion' *Public Money & Management*, 18, 2, pp. 61–68.

Johnsen, Å. (2005) 'What does 25 years of experience tell us about the state of performance measurement in public policy and management?' *Public Money & Management*, 25, 1, pp. 9–17.

Kaplan, R. and Norton, D. (1992) 'The Balanced Scorecard – measures that drive performance' *Harvard Business Review*, 70, 1, pp. 71–79.

Kaplan, R. and Norton, D. (1996a) 'Using the Balanced Scorecard as a strategic management system' *Harvard Business Review*, 74, 1, pp. 75–85.

Kaplan, R. and Norton, D. (1996b) 'Linking the Balanced Scorecard to strategy' *California Management Review*, 39, 1, pp. 53–79.

Klein, R. and Carter, N. (1988) 'Performance Measurement: A Review of Concepts and Issues' in Beeton, D. (ed.) *Performance Measurement: Getting the Concepts Right*, Public Finance Foundation, London.

Lebas, M. (1996). 'Management Accounting Practice in France' in Bhimani, A. (ed.), *Management Accounting: European Perspectives*, Oxford University Press, Oxford, pp. 74–99.

Liddle, J. (2007) 'Challenges to democratic legitimacy, scrutiny, accountability in the UK national and local state' *Public Administrative Quarterly*, 31, 4, pp. 397–428.

Lovegrove, M. and Davis, J. (2013) *Paramedic Evidence Based Education Project (PEEP): End of Study Report*, Allied Health Solutions, UK.

Mason, S., O'Keefe, C., Coleman, P., Edlin, R. and Nicholl, J. (2007a) 'Effectiveness of emergency care practitioners working within existing emergency service models of care' *Emergency Medicine Journal*, 2007, 24, pp. 239–243.

Mason, S., Knowles, E., Colwell, B., Dixon, S., Wardrope, J., Goringe, R., Snooks, H., Perrin, J. and Nicholl, J. (2007b) 'Effectiveness of paramedic practitioners attending 999 calls from elderly people in the community: cluster randomized control trial' *BMJ*, 335, p. 919.

McCann, J., Granter, E., Hyde P. and Hassard, J. (2013) 'Still blue collar after all these years? An ethnography of the professionalization of emergency ambulance work' *Journal of Management Studies*, 50, 5, pp. 750–776.

McLaughlin, E. and Murji, K. (2001) 'Lost Connections and New Directions: Neo-liberalism, New Public Management and the "Modernisation" of the British Police' in Stenson, K. and Sullivan, R. (eds) *Crime, Risk and Justice: The Politics of Crime Control in Liberal Democracies*, Willan Publishing, Cullampton.

Meyer, M.W. and Gupta, V. (1994) 'The performance paradox' *Research in Organizational Behaviour*, 16, 4, pp. 309–369.

Minogue, M., Polidano, C., and Hulme, D. (1998) *Beyond the New Public Management: Changing Ideas and Practices in Governance*, Edward Elgar, Cheltenham.

Morgan, C. and Murgatroyd, S. (1994) *Total Quality Management in the Public Sector*, Open University Press, Buckingham.

National Audit Office (2010) *Major Trauma Care in England*, HC 213, Session 2009–2010, The Stationery Office, London.

National Audit Office (2011) *Transforming NHS Ambulance Services*, The Stationery Office, London.

NHS Five Year Forward View (2014) NHS England, Leeds.

NHS England (2013) *Transforming Urgent and Emergency Care in England: Urgent and Emergency Care Review*, Phase 1 Report, NHS England, Leeds.

NHS Confederation (2014) *Ripping off the Sticking Plaster: Whole-systems Solutions for Urgent and Emergency Care*, NHS Confederation, London.

NHS Confederation (2015) *Rip off the Sticking Plaster Now: Enabling the Local Implementation of Sustainable Urgent and Emergency Care Models in 2015/16*, NHS Confederation, London.

Neely, A. (1999) 'The performance measurement revolution: why now and what next?' *International Journal of Operations and Production Management*, 19, 2, pp. 205–28.

Neely, A., Gregory, M., and Platts, K. (1995) 'Performance measurement system design: a literature review and research agenda' *International Journal of Operations & Production Management*, 15, 4, pp. 80–116.

Nørreklit, H. (2003) 'The Balanced Scorecard: what is the score?' *Accounting Organizations and Society*, 28, 6, pp. 591–619.

OECD-PUMA (1994) *Performance Measurement in the Government: Performance Measurement Results Oriented Management*, OECD, Paris.

OECD-PUMA (1997) *In Search for Results, Performance Management Practices*, OECD, Paris.

Ogbonna, E. and Harris, L.C. (2014) 'Organizational cultural perpetuation: a case study of an English Premier League football club' *British Journal of Management*, 25, pp. 667–686.

O'Hara, R., Johnson, M., Siriwardena, A.N., Weyman, A., Turner, J., Shaw, D., Mortimer, P., Newman, C., Hirst, E., Storey, M., Mason, S., Quinn, I. and Shewan, J. (2015) 'A qualitative study of systemic influences on paramedic decision making: care transitions and patient safety' *Journal of Health Services Research & Policy*, 20 (Supplement 1), pp. 45–53.

Olve, N., Roy, J. and Wetter, M. (1999) *Performance Drivers: A practical Guide to Using the Balanced Scorecard*, John Wiley & Sons, Chichester.

Osborne, S. (2006) 'The New Public Governance?' *Public Management Review*, 8/30, pp. 377–388.

Osborne, S. (2009) 'Delivering public services: are we asking the right questions?' *Public Money and Management*, 29/1, pp. 5–7.

Osborne, S. (2010) *The New Public Governance? Emerging Perspectives on the Theory and Practice of Public Governance*, Routledge, London.

Picciotto, R. (1999) 'Towards an economics of evaluation' *Evaluation*, 5, 1, pp. 7–22.

Pollitt, C. (1986) 'Beyond the managerial model: the case for broadening performance assessment in government and the public services' *Financial Accountability and Management*, 2, pp. 155–170.

Pollitt, C. (2001) 'Convergence: the useful myth?' *Public Administration*, 79, 4, pp. 933–947.

Pollitt, C. and Bouckaert, G. (2000) *Public Management Reform: A Comparative Analysis*, Oxford University Press, Oxford.

Power, M. (1994) *The Audit Explosion*, Demos, London.

Power, M. (1999) *The Audit Society: Rituals of Verification*, Oxford University Press, Oxford.

Pressman, J. and Wildavsky, A. (1973) *Implementation: How Great Expectations in Washington are Dashed in Oakland*, California University Press, Berkeley.

Public Administration Select Committee, House of Commons (2003), *On Target: Government by Measurement*, Vol. 1, Stationery Office, London.

Radcliffe, J. and Heath, G. (2009) 'Ambulance calls and cancellations: policy and implementation issues' *International Journal of Public Sector Management*, 22, 5, pp. 410–422.

Radnor, Z. (2008) 'Muddled, massaging, manoeuvring or manipulated? A typology of organisational gaming' *International Journal of Productivity and Performance Management*, 57, 4, pp. 316–328.

Sanders, G. and Gough, A. (2003) 'Emergency ambulances on the public highway linked with inconvenience and potential danger to road users' *Emergency Medicine Journal*, 20, pp. 277–280.

Simons, R. (1999) *Performance Measurement and Control Systems for Implementing Strategy*, Prentice Hall, Upper Saddle River, NJ.

Smith, P.C. (1995) 'On the unintended consequences of publishing performance data in the public sector' *International Journal of Public Administration*, 18, 2/3, pp. 277–310.

Snooks, H.A., Dale, J., Hartley-Sharpe, C. and Halter, M. (2004) 'On-scene alternatives for emergency ambulance crews attending patients who do not need to travel to the accident and emergency department: a review of the literature' *Emergency Medicine Journal*, 21, pp. 212–215.

Snooks, H., Kingston, M., Anthony, R. and Russell, I. (2013) 'New models of emergency prehospital care that avoid unnecessary conveyance to emergency department: translation of research evidence into practice' *The Scientific World Journal*. doi:10.1155/2013/182102.

Susskind, L. (2006) 'Arguing, Bargaining and Getting Agreement' in Moran, M., Rein, M. and Goodin, R.E. (eds) *The Oxford Handbook of Public Policy*, Oxford University Press, Oxford, pp. 269–295.

Talbot, C. (2005) 'Performance Management' in Ferlie, E., Lynn, L. and Pollitt, C. (eds) *The Oxford Handbook of Public Management*, Oxford University Press, Oxford, pp. 491–517.

Tendler, J. (1997) *Good Governance in the Tropics*, John Hopkins University Press, Baltimore, MD.

Till, R. and Marsh, A. (2015) 'Ambulance Service Modernisation' in Wankhade, P. and Mackway-Jones, K. (eds) *Ambulance Services: Leadership and Management Perspectives*, Springer, New York.

Tohira, H., Williams, T.A., Jacobs, I., Bremner, A. and Finn, J. (2013) 'The impact of new prehospital practitioners on ambulance transportation to the emergency department: a systematic review and meta-analysis' *Emergency Medicine Journal*, 26, pp. 88–94.

Turner, J., Coster, J., Chambers, D., Cantrell, A., Phung, V.-H., Knowles, E., Bradbury, D., and Goyder, E. (2015) 'What evidence is there on the effectiveness of different models of delivering urgent care? A rapid review' *Health Services and Delivery Research*, 3, 43, pp. 1–133.

Wankhade, P. (2011) 'Performance measurement and the UK emergency ambulance service: Unintended Consequences of the ambulance response time targets'. *International Journal of Public Sector Management*, 24, 5, pp. 384–402.
Wankhade, P. (2012) 'Different cultures of management and their relationships with organisational performance: evidence from the UK ambulance service' *Public Money & Management*, 32, 5, pp. 381–388.
Wankhade, P. and Brinkman, J. (2014) 'The negative consequences of culture change management: evidence from a UK NHS ambulance service' *International Journal of Public Sector Management*, 27, 1, pp. 2–25.
Wankhade, P., Radcliffe, J. and Heath, G. (2015) 'Organisational and Professional Cultures: An Ambulance Perspective' in Wankhade, P. and Mackway-Jones, K. (eds.) *Ambulance Services: Leadership and Management Perspectives*, Springer, New York.
Woollard, M., O'Meara, P. and Munro, G. (2010) 'What price 90 seconds: is "Call to Connect" a disservice to 999 callers?' *Emergency Medical Journal*, 27, 10, pp. 729–730.

24

Management control systems research in the public higher education sector

Current status and future research agenda

Chaturika Seneviratne and Zahirul Hoque

Introduction

The modernization of public services is a longstanding objective of many governments across the globe, aimed at providing better services to the citizen (Arnaboldi and Azzone, 2004). In the light of New Public Management (NPM), public sector organizations of most Western countries have encouraged reforms to the procedures and structures in consistence with the principles of economy, efficiency and effectiveness (Arnaboldi *et al.*, 2004). In general terms, NPM refers to the introduction of private sector management styles and instruments to the public sector with the focus of enhancing its efficiency and effectiveness. Hood (1995, p. 95) asserted NPM as 'couched in the language of economic rationalism'. Thus, by claiming the benefits of better measurement of costs and revenue with the greater focus on output/outcome and improved comparability of performance with greater accountability (Venieris and Cohen, 2004), public sector organizations including central government, local governments and other public sector agencies such as hospitals, education institutions and police forces are imperative to adopt such modernized management control concepts and techniques (Cavalluzzo and Ittner, 2004; Hood, 1995; Van Helden, 2005).

Over the past decade, the public sector higher education sector around the world has been confronting tremendous environmental changes such as government funding cuts, competition from private sector providers and introduction of the 'self-management' concept to university affairs (Gumport and Sporn, 1999). These 'winds of change' have exerted enormous pressures on higher education institutions to ensure efficiency and effectiveness of service quality and value for money in provision of their services (Upping and Oliver, 2012) and present new challenges for higher education institutions signifying a clear mandate for change. Being inspired by NPM, for more than two decades, it has been evident that universities are seeking to introduce diverse managerial tools and accounting techniques founded upon the broader notion of Management Control Systems (MCS).

The notion of MCS has evolved over the years attracting a wide range of assertions capturing diverse views with regard to its conceptualization (Anthony, 1965, Lowe, 1971, Abernethy and Chua, 1996, Otley, 1999, Simons, 2013). Preliminary insights into MCS refer to the seminal work of Robert Anthony (1965), who defines management control 'as the process by which managers ensure that resources are obtained and used effectively and efficiently in the achievement of the organization's objectives' (Anthony, 1965, p. 27). Premised on Anthony's conceptualization of management control, one camp of scholars emphasized the technical and passive features of the MCS, defining a set of calculative practices such as budgeting, product costing, and cost-volume-profit analysis that supports management in their decision making and control of the organization (Otley, 1994, 1999). Another camp of scholars emphasized the importance of the human aspect and the need to influence them to behave towards the accomplishment of organizational intended aims (Argyris, 1960, Brownell, 1982, Flamholtz, 1983). Since all these connotations of MCS are presented with scant attention to the actual functioning of control systems in their particular operational settings, the importance of capturing the interplay between the organization and its socio-economic context has been emphasized (Uddin and Hopper, 2001, Wickramasinghe and Hopper, 2005). Thus, in a more contemporary sense, MCS is defined as a set of social practices constructed within the context where they operate being associated by the wider social, economic and political pressures (Burchell *et al.*, 1980, Berry *et al.*, 1985, Hoque and Hopper, 1994).

In this chapter, our aims are (a) to take stock of the existing research on management control practices in the public higher education sector, (b) to highlight gaps in that research and (c) to outline some ideas for future research. This exercise has not been the primary focus of prior public sector management and accounting research literature (for example, see De Vries and Nemec, 2013). Hence, this chapter casts a light on the probable new areas to be explored empirically and novel theoretical perspectives to be drawn on in future research. For our review purpose, MCS is perceived by encompassing all pillars placed from strategic to operational in order to ensure the fulfillment of organizational worthy intentions. The review results indicate that with the adoption of modern managerial philosophy to the traditional higher education sector around the world, there has been a bourgeoning trend in management control research in higher education from the year 2000 onwards.

The remainder of the chapter is organized as follows. We begin by elaborating the review method used. Next we present the outcome of the literature review. By shedding a new light on the findings of the current review, we then present the knowledge gaps in the existing body of literature and suggest some avenues for future research. Concluding remarks are made in the final section.

Review method

In this chapter we include articles from well-reputed international refereed accounting journals that publish quality work in MCS. Further, we also include leading journals in management and organizational fields and some highly ranked public sector and higher education journals. Appendix 24.1 presents the list of journals covering all publications from the commencement of each particular journal to the year 2015.

The articles were mainly searched using the terms 'higher education', 'universities' and 'management controls', and this search was limited to the articles published in the main online databases. In order to ensure the relevance of the journal papers, in addition to the above search terms, each of the key themes of MCS, such as strategy, strategic management, budgeting, and performance measurement, were also searched simultaneously.

Nevertheless, this effort resulted in a considerable number of papers that do not have a meaningful relation to the precise review requirements. While certain online databases identified articles that consisted of words 'higher education', 'universities' and 'controls' individually in the text, the relevant papers were selected manually within the scope of the current review. We have excluded articles on financial accounting and reporting, conceptual papers, commentary, book reviews and editorial introductions, and specifically target on articles that are centered on diverse MCS and the issues pertaining to MCS in higher education institutions. Our effort resulted in 48 studies for the review, and frequency distribution of the articles in these journals is exhibited in Table 24.1.

As depicted in Table 24.1, the largest number of relevant articles (nine) was found in *Financial Accountability & Management* (FAM), being one of the key accounting journals explicitly publishing research on the financial accountability, management and accounting of all types of governmental and other non-profit organizations. This was closely followed by *Critical Perspectives on Accounting* (CPA), a journal vitally focused on articles shaped by non-conventional thoughts published seven articles. Alongside these, *International Journal of Educational Management* (IJEM) published seven papers and *Higher Education* (HE) comprised five relevant papers, a journal purely focused on the research in the domain of higher education. No other journals possessed a considerable number of papers focused on management control practices in the higher education sector. Meanwhile, a leading accounting journal *Australian Accounting Review* (AAR), which interlinks business and academic features, published three relevant articles. Only one paper appeared in *European Accounting Review* (EAR), another international scholarly journal in accounting arena.

Table 24.1 Distribution of the selected papers covered by the review across the journals

Journal	*Number of papers*
Financial Accountability & Management (FAM)	9
Critical Perspectives on Accounting (CPA)	7
International Journal of Educational Management (IJEM)	7
Higher Education (HE)	5
British Journal of Management (BJM)	3
Australian Accounting Review (AAR)	2
Journal of Accounting & Organizational Change (JAOC)	1
Journal of Management Studies (JMS)	2
Organization Studies (OS)	2
International Journal of Public Sector Management (IJPSM)	1
Australian Journal of Public Administration (AJPA)	1
European Accounting Review (EAR)	1
Public Administration (PA)	1
Accounting, Organizations and Society (AOS)	1
Accounting, Auditing & Accountability Journal (AAAJ)	2
Journal of Management Accounting Research (JMAR)	1
Management Accounting Research (MAR)	1
Journal of Accounting Research (JAR)	1
Total	48

Extending the list, other leading management accounting journals, such as *Journal of Management Accounting Research* (JMAR) and *Management Accounting Research* (MAR), contain one paper each in relation to universities' control systems. Additionally, the field of management-oriented journals like *Journal of Management Studies* (JMS) and *Organization Studies* (OS) published two papers each. Moreover, generalist accounting journals such as *Accounting, Organizations and Society* (AOS), *Journal of Accounting Research* (JAR) and *Journal of Accounting & Organizational Change* (JAOC) comprised one article each, and *Accounting, Auditing & Accountability Journal* (AAAJ) consisted of two papers connected to the topic under inquiry. Furthermore, the journals *International Journal of Public Sector Management* (IJPSM), *Australian Journal of Public Administration* (AJPA) and *Public Administration* (PA), which specifically focus on issues pertaining to effective management processes of public sector organizations, contain only one relevant article each.

Findings

The following section presents the results of our review. This exercise displays diverse issues surrounding the topics selected, issues explored, theoretical orientations, research settings, methods of investigation and results analysis.

Topics

Table 24.2 shows the frequency distribution of MCS topics for the 48 articles reviewed.

As presented in Table 24.2, the most commonly occurring MCS topic is performance measurement and management systems with 13 papers, followed by the topics on quality assurance and quality management techniques and strategic management/planning each containing six articles. Management accounting change has also been widely researched, comprising five research papers within the review. Further, contemporary strategy-driven performance management technique, namely Balanced Scorecard (BSC), and performance

Table 24.2 Distribution of topics

Topics	*Number of papers*
Performance measurement systems (PMS)	13
Quality assurance and quality-related techniques (TQM/QM)	6
Management accounting change	5
Strategic management/planning	6
Development and use of Balanced Scorecard (BSC)	4
Performance appraisal	3
Interdependent relations and effectiveness	3
MCS (general)[a]	4
Budgeting	2
Benchmarking	1
Management accounting information	1
Total	48

a Papers classified in this category focused on multiple aspects of management control, used generic management control typologies or discussed MCS in a general sense, rather than focusing on a specific management control tool (e.g. budgeting, performance measurement systems).

appraisal system also received increasing attention within the arena of the higher education sector, being covered in four and three articles each, respectively.

However, while a sizable number of reviewed articles are related to the performance measurement/management/BSC and performance appraisal arena (altogether 20), by and large the performance management-related phenomenon was presented as the most widely researched area within the sampled articles. Among them, however, some were confined to the designing of performance measurement systems for a particular university setting and probing into possible relationships between those measures. Empirically, many of these papers therefore lack in critical examination of concerns pertaining to the development, operation and use of performance management systems (PMS) drawing on pragmatist epistemological viewpoint (Cutt *et al.*, 1993, Jackson, 1999, e.g. Taylor, 1994, Al-Turki and Duffuaa, 2003, Dill and Soo, 2005, McDevitt *et al.*, 2008, Schmulian and Coetzee, 2011) and failed to embrace a sound theoretical framework (e.g. Ball and Wilkinson, 1994, Dill and Soo, 2005). Since many of these studies are presented distant from a researcher, avoiding deeper contextual understanding of the practices that operate, they fail to portray a multi-faceted view of a social phenomenon grounded in performance management practices. In spite of the setting where the phenomenon is entrenched upon, many of these studies were not in-depth by nature and examined issues at a surface level and elucidate more practical insights in relation to diverse performance measures and other related performance evaluation techniques being resulted in a lack of 'thick descriptions' (Geertz, 1973).

Noteworthy among the studies reviewed under PMS, few studies provide 'rich' insights advocated by the sound theoretical debate on the phenomenon being studied (Dyer and Wilkins, 1991, Ahrens and Dent, 1998). More importantly, drawing empirics from Swedish public higher education sector, Modell (2003) explored the issues in relation to the emergence and elaboration of PM practices at the institutional level. Later, Modell (2005) in his study examined political interplay between different constituents who have striven to dominate the representation of the students' interest and how this interplay is conditioned by institutionalized configurations and prevailing power relationships in the Swedish university sector. These two papers (Modell, 2003, 2005) were fundamentally premised on macro-level initiatives and response of the actions of macro-level actors on new PMS by avoiding close scrutiny of the micro-processual actions in implicating the emergence and elaboration of PMS in the particular research setting. Taking a rather different stance, Arnaboldi and Azzone (2010) investigated the challenging role of controversies driven by the relationships between actors and the system during the translation and operationalization process. The studies purely focused on the emergence and adoption of a performance appraisal system, founded upon the UK university sector, by Townley (1993, 1997, 1999), are significant here. All three studies deeply explored organizational as well as institutional level based relational, constitutive and political dimensions attached to the different phases of the performance appraisal system advocated by a sound empirical and theoretical discussion.

Strategic management and planning have been a point of interest for some researchers. In one of these, drawing evidence from a large Australian public university, Holloway (2004) analysed the inconsistencies between traditional and emergent strategic planning, and concluded that in the milieu where high-performing techniques are inspired, university forges such a new strategic direction as a rhetoric rather than reality. Hence, the main emphasis of this study is to bring out the 'richness' of social phenomena driven by the holistic analyses of the context where it operates from a critical viewpoint. In a comparable tone, Hutaibat *et al.* (2011) and Jiang and Carpenter (2013) probed into the application of strategic management and their related issues confronted by the Western universities within the process of university corporatization.

Drawing attention to the modern performance management tools, grounded upon one large Fiji public university, Lawrence and Sharma (2002) showed how new managerial philosophies like BCS are adopted and their interactions with the context where commercial values outperform the academic values. While investigating the use of the BSC in 30 universities around the globe, Sayed (2013) depicted that BSC has not been sufficiently influential to performance measurement in the university context since it is ill-positioned with a lack of understanding, an unclear success rate, slower new adoptions and subsequent abandonment. By further enriching the research on development and application of BSC within the sphere of higher education, McDevitt *et al.* (2008) presented a unique version of BSC by linking long-term strategic objectives with short-term actions specifically for the university divisions. In order to scrutinize the ability of deploying MSC as a strategic management system, Hladchenko (2015) conducted a comparative analysis of BSCs of one Austrian and three German higher education institutions. Whereas the former two studies viewed BSC beyond the narrow, naïve rationalistic approach by depicting a more pragmatic stance, the latter study focused more on the technical aspects of a different model of BSC rooted in a technically rational paradigm.

Among the studies reviewed, seven were founded on quality assurance and other quality-related advanced techniques applied in the higher education institutions (e.g. Brennan and Shah, 2000, Singh, 2002, Blackmur, 2004, Pettersen, 2015). Informed by Habermasian insights, Dillard and Tinker (1996) critically examined the way in which academic atmosphere is implicated by the new total quality management technologies such as continuous improvement in Western universities. Perusing a similar line of enquiry, Singh (2002) made a critical exploration of how students are positioned as consumers within the contemporary educational experience through the adoption of student evaluation of teaching, mandated by the quality assurance framework. On a rather different managerial technique, Arnaboldi and Azzone (2004) examined the technical and behavioural concerns implicated in the adoption of benchmarking technique in the Italian public university sector. Budgeting has been the point of interest for some researchers. Quite apart from the traditional conception of 'external legitimacy', drawing empirics from an Australian university, Moll and Hoque (2011) depicted how the university budgeting process has been internally legitimated due to the demand made by internal constituents instead of so-called external institutional forces. Walker (2000) examined the statutory budget reporting process in New South Wales universities. Even though the two studies above are grounded upon a similar type of controlling phenomena, latter study (Moll and Hoque, 2011) is in depth by nature and entrenched in sound theoretical discussion.

Another array of studies (Chung *et al.*, 2009, e.g. Bresser and Dunbar, 1986) profoundly examine diverse aspects such as strategy, structure and performance measurement systems, and their influence on effectiveness and efficiency in university contexts. Of further significance, management accounting change has also been an interesting theme for some scholars (e.g. Jones, 1994, Parker, 2002, Venieris and Cohen, 2004). In general, all of these articles predominantly focused on the nature and magnitude of change in the public higher educational environment in developed countries and the implications on university identity and their role pertaining to cultural, governance, structural and operational dimensions. Of further significance, Parker (2011) claimed that the manner in which institutional dimensions strive to promote the NPM is supported by private sector philosophies into universities and closely follows the pattern. Parker (2013) conducted an extensive examination of cost-efficiency strategies employed by universities under the competitive international higher education market while being insightful on global strategic context for future accounting research on university and higher education sector generally. Whereas only four articles (Lee and Piper, 1988, Deem, 2004, Ho *et al.*, 2006, Agyemang and Broadbent, 2015) focus on management practices and technologies as a package in the university context, the research founded upon the themes such as management accounting information (Pettersen and Solstad, 2007) has been evident as the least popular areas of management control research in higher education.

Research methods deployed

In terms of the methods used to research the reviewed articles, these generally fall into eight groups, namely qualitative/case study, quantitative/survey, archival/historical analysis, literature review, descriptive/practical insights, grounded theory method, action research and multi-methods. As seen from Table 24.3, the case study/qualitative method has been extensively chosen (22), and it is evident that the case study/qualitative research method is the most popular choice in the area concerned. In contrast to this finding, survey/quantitative methods (six) were applied for a few of the researches in the higher education sector in relation to MCS. These two methods accounted for more than half of the papers reviewed. Further, 13 studies capitalized on descriptive analysis, providing more practical insights rather than being explicitly articulated as a specific research method. Furthermore, three articles opted for multi-method as their research method in order to explore the area under study. Further, it was noted that the remaining five research methods (literature review, grounded theory method, archival/historical analysis, ethnographic study and action research) were used for one article each.

Table 24.3 depicts the articles in terms of the frequency of the research methods used. In the table, it appears that there is dominancy in utilizing qualitative/case study-type articles (22) over the quantitative research methods-driven articles in management control research in the higher education sector. Although the quantitative/survey approach failed to emphasize the meanings people attach to the phenomena, and thus, is not competent in capturing the 'highly context- and time-specific analyses of how people communicate and act in a particular social setting' (Lukka and Modell, 2010, p. 464), one cannot dismiss the existence of functionalism-driven approaches. The survey method has been deployed in some studies to explore the contextual and structural facets affecting the adoption of management control practices. Bresser and Dunbar (1986) deployed a hierarchical multiple regression analysis by

Table 24.3 Distribution of research methods

Research method	*Number of papers*
Qualitative/field/case study/interviews	22
Descriptive/practical insights	13
Quantitative/survey	6
Multi-method	3
Literature review	1
Archival/historical analysis	1
Grounded theory method	1
Action research	1
Total	48

using survey data from 35 UK universities to examine the extent to which contextual and structural contingencies influence university research and teaching effectiveness. Drawing empirics from 85 management schools of UK universities, Taylor (1994) used a multiple regression analysis on three databases to develop quantitative indicators to measure the research input and output. By deploying a survey method, while Venieris and Cohen (2004) explored the interplay between changes in strategy and decision making, 6 years after the inception of accounting reform in Greek universities, Decramer *et al.* (2012) identified institutional factors associated in adopting the PMS in two different higher education institutions. In another instance, Chung *et al.* (2009) replicated and extended the Interdependencies model of organizational design (Abernethy and Lillis, 2001) to understand the interdependent relations among strategy, structure and performance measurement systems in the Australian university context.

Since the quantitative/survey methods measure and observe the phenomenon from a distance, outsider perspective (Lukka and Modell, 2010), it might limit the broader understanding of MCS as a socially constructed practice within the milieu where it operates. This concern is addressed by the case study/qualitative approach. Capitalizing on these features, as the response to a dynamic environment, many scholars utilized the qualitative case study method to gain deeper insight into the subject being studied in the higher education arena. Within the sampled articles, most of the case study-based research is longitudinal in nature and concentrated on the implications that come across in design, translation and operational phases of control systems (Modell, 2003, 2005, Arnaboldi and Azzone, 2010). Among the scholars who carried out single in-depth case studies on management controls in the modern university context, Holloway (2004), Townley (1999), and Lawrence and Sharma (2002) are significant. In another single in-depth case-oriented study, by drawing empirics from a large Australian public university, Moll and Hoque (2011) illustrated the imperative of internal legitimacy in contrast to the so-called external legitimacy enforced by the institutional field. Founded upon the multiple case study approach, Agasisti *et al.* (2008) adopted a study to reflect the need to shift from theoretical to empirical level of strategic management accounting as a valuable management tool in an Italian higher education context. In general, these studies are in-depth by nature and advocated by an intense theoretical base in bringing out the 'richness' of the social phenomena, capturing the interactions between organization, processes and institutional setting which is applied in the situation.

Arnaboldi and Azzone (2004) have undertaken action research to explore the support management activities to convene the use of an intra-organizational benchmarking within an Italian university, aimed at introducing a cost accounting system. Hutaibat *et al.* (2011) used the grounded theory method to study the strategic management accounting practices embedded in an English higher education institution. Whereas grounded theory has the advantage of letting particular themes emerge from data by allowing the uniqueness of the setting to be explored, rather than limiting findings to a pre-determined theory, it entails the danger of losing focus, sustains high levels of judgements and is unable to cope with vastly diverse data.

Further adding to the list, 13 studies were descriptive by nature while shedding more light on practical insights into the contemporary management controls without explicitly stating the research method used (e.g. Cutt *et al.*, 1993, Blackmur, 2004, Deem, 2004, Dill and Soo, 2005). In three instances, scholars opted for mixed method as their research design (Babbar, 1995, Frølich, 2011, Schmulian and Coetzee, 2011) by triangulating both qualitative and quantitative methods to explore the meaning and better understanding of phenomena than either research approach alone.

Theories adopted

Table 24.4 provides the distribution of the theoretical perspectives used in the studies under review. Within this effort, it is necessary to identify the theoretical framework predominantly employed in each study and classify papers accordingly. Within the sampled articles, more than half of the studies (27) did not visibly apply any theory and published in either practitioner-oriented, sector-specific journals or both academic and practitioner-oriented journals. While some articles were single or multiple case studies (Jackson, 1999, Walker, 2000, Pettersen and Solstad, 2007, Ter Bogt and Scapens, 2012, Jiang and Carpenter, 2013), others were either in the form of quantitative/surveys (e.g. Ball and Wilkinson, 1994, Taylor, 1994, Chung *et al.*, 2009) or in the form of mixed methods (e.g. Frølich, 2011). Among them, a further stream of papers was descriptive in nature, offering some practical insights to a reader (e.g. Lockwood, 1972, Cutt *et al.*, 1993, Brennan and Shah, 2000, Deem, 2004, Dill and Soo, 2005, Sayed, 2013). Even if the broader underlying theoretical framework is not explicitly presented, some of the studies (Bresser and Dunbar, 1986, Lee and Piper, 1988, Pettersen and Solstad, 2007) are informed by specific conceptual underpinnings such as accountability, communal values and managerialism.

Perhaps the most noteworthy trend to emerge from an examination of Table 24.4 is the significant growth (starting from early 2000 onwards) in the number of papers employing sociological/institutional/critical theories. Considering the journals in which sampled articles are published, it is apparent that the prominent accounting journals such as AOS, MAR, CPA, AAAJ and FAM pay more attention to the articles that are advocated by intense

Table 24.4 Distribution of theories

Theories adopted	*Number of papers*
No explicit theory	27
Sociological perspectives:	
Neo-institutional sociology (NIS)[a]	5
Actor-Network Theory (ANT)	1
Grounded theory	1
Habermasian informed analysis	4
Foucauldian approach	1
Multiple theories[b]	2
MacIntyre's work	1
Structural contingency theory	1
Pettigrew theory	1
Human resources management	1
Other	3
Total	48

a There were two studies mainly drawn from NIS, and extensive discussion was surrounded by NIS. Hence, these two studies were categorized under the theme of 'Neo Institutional Sociology' rather than categorizing them under the theme of multiple theoretical deployments.

b When a particular article is informed by more than one theoretical framework by devoting fairly similar importance, those studies are categorized as 'multiple theories'. For instance, Holloway (2004) deployed two theoretical frameworks; Habermasian insights and the Decision Assurance theory in a comparable manner to understand the diverse aspects of inconsistencies confronted by the universities in implementing novel strategic planning. Hence, this is categorized under 'multiple theories'.

theoretical insights. Further, many studies published in journals such as IJPSM, IJEM, PA and HE are mostly descriptive in nature and do not clearly articulate any theoretical orientation. Noteworthy is the fact that a journal like CPA published a growing number of articles advocated by intense discussions drawn on a critical theoretical viewpoint with regard to the modern accounting practices and their repercussions on contemporary higher education settings.

By adding to the list, two studies were founded upon multiple theoretical lenses, while another research was built on grounded theory principles. With this focus, it is noteworthy that a large number of papers were drawn on sociological/critical theories as CPA advocates that the sociological perspective is vital to study control systems in their wider organizational and socio-political settings, capturing the complex interactions between accounting systems and context. Being informed by the emic perspective, several scholars have used a wider sociological-based viewpoint in management control research in higher education sector (e.g. Townley, 1997, Modell, 2003, 2005, Arnaboldi and Azzone, 2010, Moll and Hoque, 2011). Remarkably, neo-institutional sociology (NIS) theory has been a popular choice for management control researchers in the higher education sector over the past two decades. Capitalizing on the three isomorphism forces of NIS (DiMaggio and Powell, 1983), Townley (1997) investigates divergence of institutional logic among the UK universities' academic staff in responding to institutionally enforced performance appraisal mechanism. Using the NIS framework, Parker (2011) depicted a deep analysis of underlying trends in corporatization of public sector universities in the developed country context pertinent to the university environments, profiles and structures. The NIS perspective is capable of accommodating the investigations of the effects of changing organizational contexts in terms of both convergent and divergent changes across organizations (Lounsbury, 2008, Scott, 2013). This feature of NIS has particularly facilitated Parker's (2011) analysis in understanding the fundamental drivers of university corporatization in the Western context.

Depicting a comparison of two theoretical viewpoints named as goal-directed (conventional positivism) and process-oriented NIS (post-positivism), Modell (2003) revealed that NIS is embedded with more explanatory power in depicting the evolution of loose couplings between formally stated goals and performance indicators formed to convene complex interplay between conflicting constituent interests. In both of these attempts (Modell, 2003, 2005), theoretical explanations are primarily drawn on the NIS perspective, while being confined to organizational field-level (macro) dynamics. As mentioned before, drawing empirics from an Australian university, Moll and Hoque (2011) investigated the imperative of the internal 'legitimacy' embedded in the micro-level aspects of the budgeting process.

From a rather different theoretical viewpoint, Arnaboldi and Azzone (2010) applied an Actor-Network Theory (ANT), specifically using Latour's work (1987, 1996, 2005), to study the PM translation process in NPM settings, particularly in Italian universities over 11 years, which were subject to the more powerful and weaker voices of the network. In contrast to NIS, ANT assigned a weight to recognize human and non-human facets involved in the translating process of control systems into operational use. In spite of the popularity of ANT in management control research, surprisingly only one study is drawn on ANT to investigate the management control practices in the university sector. Using a rather different theoretical orientation, entrenched in Michel Foucault's knowledge/power, Townley (1993) illustrates the way in which specific managerial activities are articulated in the performance appraisal subject to the forces of power and interests in UK universities. Premised in the human resource management (HRM) perspective, Edgar and Geare (2010) explored the people management approaches and their influences on the performance outcomes advocated by the in-depth interviews in the New Zealand university context.

Another line of study deployed critical theory perspective as a way of analysing the MCS within the contemporary context equipped with the 'business-like' accountabilities and results-oriented management styles. Picking up on this current issue, scholars deviated rather from the 'neutral' stance (Baker and Bettner, 1997) and adopted a critical viewpoint in accounting research. Of further significance is the work by Lawrence and Sharma (2002) who examined the impact of new managerialism and ubiquitous management philosophies on traditional university administration in developing country context, drawing insights from Habermas's critical theory of societal development advocated by Decision Assurance theory. Following a similar theoretical orientation, while Singh (2002) and Dillard and Tinker (1996) made a critical argument on the repercussion of the novel performance management techniques such as teacher evaluation mechanisms and total quality management technologies, Parker (2002), being informed by Habermasian informed analysis, made a critique on organization structure and process changes impacted by the pressures that come along with the globalization of education and funding changes. Holloway (2004) examined the inherent inconsistencies that emerged from the application of modern strategic planning in Australian university settings.

Notwithstanding the singular theoretical stance, researchers in accounting have visibly justified rationales for using multiple theories referred to as 'theoretical triangulation' in order to explain a social phenomenon (see Ansari and Euske, 1987, Hoque and Hopper, 1994, Hopper and Major, 2007). By following the pattern, some studies (e.g. Arnaboldi and Azzone, 2004, Decramer *et al.*, 2012) capitalized on the advantage of the situation where 'no single theory can have a monopoly on explanations of accounting and organizational practices since each theory has its own virtue and collectivity, thus adding to our understanding practice and individuals in their social, economic and cultural context' (Hoque *et al.*, 2013, p. 1).

As discussed in the above sections, the diverse purposes of deploying multiple theoretical perspectives can be identified with regard to the two studies of Modell (2003, 2005). In one instance, Arnaboldi and Azzone (2004) deployed rational and behavioural perspectives entrenched upon two different theoretical paradigms of positivism and post-positivism, respectively, to investigate the results of an intra-organizational benchmarking subject to external environmental conditions and internal top management commitments in an Italian university. The researcher can apply multiple theoretical perspectives to uncover new ways of understanding the data. By adhering to the assertion made by Lukka and Mouritsen (2002), claiming that singular theory approach might lead to interesting issues being unexplored merely because they are not captured by particular theory chosen, some of sampled articles go beyond rather than being confined to theoretical limitations to enrich their research results in the arena of management control grounded in the higher education sector. By and large, these studies featured with an emic (subjective/insider) perspective in contrast to the more detached and neutral etic (outsider) perspective (Headland, 1990) and depicted a multi-faceted view of the phenomena founded on an intense theoretical stance.

Gaps in prior research and directions for future research

By going beyond the current array of studies, there are still opportunities to be capitalized on in future research.

In terms of topics under inquiry, it became apparent that many of the researchers focused on the design and implementation phases of the contemporary MCS imperative to be adopted under the umbrella of NPM. For example, PMS has been a popular research topic (e.g. Modell, 2003, 2005, Arnaboldi and Azzone, 2010). Some studies have been centred on new implementation of strategic management and planning systems in the dynamic higher education sector (e.g. Holloway, 2004, Jiang and Carpenter, 2013). Most of these studies focused on the issues pertaining to the introduction of new managerial concepts to universities inspired by so-called NPM initiatives. From the sampled articles, although it was quite possible to understand problems attached to the design, translation and implementation of MCS, inconsistencies that accompany the subsequent use of such systems have not been the interest point in past research. Future researchers are thus inspired to focus on the issues/challenges confronted in the operation and use (post-implementation) of various control systems encompassing those that have not been captured adequately in prior studies.

By perusing the topics, although performance management gained high popularity, many of the studies depicted on the surface level of practices illuminated further practical insights without probing into its deeper and holistic view (e.g. Jackson, 1999, Al-Turki and Duffuaa, 2003). Even if most of the studies are inspired by the institutional approach to understand the complexities embedded in the management control practices from their broader historical, social, economic, political and cultural perspectives, limited attention has been paid to grasping how management control practices shape and/or are shaped by the micro-processual actions of actors, 'their singularity, and their point of view or position' (Bourdieu and Wacquant, 1992, p. 107) in the field in which they operate. Thus, by moving beyond the broader institutional forces, 'practice diversity, actors and micro processes' of a more comprehensive approach, a crucial yet unexplored area (Lounsbury and Crumley, 2007), particularly in management control research in the context of the higher education sector. Our review also shows that so far little attention has been paid to understanding the impact of the interplay between the internal dynamics (micro) and institutional facets (macro) in the design and operation of management control practices in a single study. Therefore, there are limited insights into the current knowledge about these concepts. This could be a path for future researchers.

In relation to theory, the research in the recent past has witnessed a departure from the conventional mainstream positivism, allowing an alternative post-positivism perspective by recognizing interaction between control practices and context where it operates. Thus, there is a growing trend in utilizing sociological, institutional and critical perspectives in the domain of higher education over the past two decades while being accepting of the fact that the social reality is not easily captured by key variables (Ahrens and Chapman, 2006). In spite of the accessibility to alternative sociological insights, most of the scholars opted for the diverse facets of NIS as their theoretical orientation in management control research in the higher education sector (Townley, 1997, Modell, 2003, 2005, Moll and Hoque, 2011, Parker, 2011, Decramer *et al.*, 2012). As a reflection on past studies under review, many of the articles are monopolized by a single theoretical viewpoint rather than using multiple theoretical lenses (with the exception of Modell, 2003, 2005, Arnaboldi and Azzone, 2004, Holloway, 2004, Decramer *et al.*, 2012). Of further concern, in recent years, without being locked into a myopic view, some of the studies are entrenched in critical arguments advocated by critical theories such as Habermas's thoughts of societal development, to reveal the acute problems confronted by the contemporary higher education sector (e.g. Dillard and Tinker, 1996, Singh, 2002, Holloway, 2004). However, some studies in the sampled articles are silent on the area of theoretical orientation (Ball and Wilkinson, 1994, Buckland, 2009, Ter Bogt and Scapens, 2012, to mention a few, and Brennan and Shah, 2000, Deem, 2004, Dill and Soo, 2005).

Generally, management control research in the higher education sector appears to be stagnant, with researchers either restricted to re-applying existing theories or failing to clearly articulate a new theoretical framework. By adhering to the above line of inquiry, in the future there is an opportunity to open up new directions by capitalizing on similar theories and probing the likelihood of combining them with a different theory. With regard to the application of NIS, there is the possibility of building a bridge between NIS and Bourdieu's practice theory[1] to re-examine the relationship between actors and the institutions and to bring the salience of individuals in understanding the phenomena in holistic point of view (Mangi, 2009, Lawrence *et al.*, 2011). Further, by adhering to the proliferation surrounded by NIS, there is a possibility of extending the social and institutions discussion by adding power dynamics (particularly Clegg's circuits of power[2]) which exert a pressure on shaping/re-shaping rules followed in particular organizational settings (Ribeiro and Scapens, 2006).

Whereas much research conducted in the recent past has witnessed how organizational MCS are shaped by institutional forces (see e.g. Modell, 2003, 2005, Parker, 2011) that reinforce continuity and reward conformity, the relevancy of institutional entrepreneurship in capturing the agency, interests and power into institutional analyses still remains an unexplored area (Garud *et al.*, 2007) particularly in higher education research. Within the milieu where higher education institutions operate, it is interesting to deeply explore who are the institutional entrepreneurs and how they constitute/reconstitute control practices despite the complexities associated with 'rules, norms, and regulations explaining who/what can be acted upon and who/what cannot' (Hoffman, 1999, p. 351).

A further possibility is to depart from existing theories and evaluate the applicability of new theoretical insights that have not been explicitly evident in the literature to date. Being insightful into the growing body of literature on 'practice' (see e.g. Gherardi and Nicolini, 2000, Orlikowski, 2000, Nicolini *et al.*, 2003, Jarzabkowski, 2005, Chia and Holt, 2006), there is a vast opportunity to entrench upon the practice-based perspective to grip the various deeply embedded processes of acting and doing, on the everyday activities performed (Whittington, 2006) within the management control practices in universities. As institutions and their processes are supposed to be 'power laden', the power is perceived as an imperative aspect to understand the society (Clegg, 2010). However, so far 'power' has been lacking in higher education research in understanding the issues, complexities and indeterminacies associated with the MCS practice. This is particularly the case in the public university sector which has a looser corporate ideology that needs to operate alongside concerns drawn from the state that mean it is difficult to quantify and set out clear objectives and enforce a decision (Pettigrew, 2014). Within this context, future studies can explore the underlying truth of complexities embedded in the socially constructed practices in the special setting of a power dynamics-oriented viewpoint.

With regard to the research design, the majority of the research was confined to one particular paradigm being undertaken with methodological limitations that are incapable of enriching the new research results and possibilities. Within the sampled articles, the majority of the studies are descriptive, presented practical insights, commentaries and tend more towards the illustration upon the narrow and superficial features of the control practices in higher education sector. The prevailing gap provides the opportunity to utilize the diverse research methods referred to as 'methodological pluralism' in order to unleash potentiality in providing the 'synergy of being informative that could permit a richer portrayals of the organizational reality revealing unique organizational issues and dynamics' (Hoque *et al.*, 2013, p. 23), which could add more value to the management control research in the higher education sector in the future.

Concluding remarks

In conclusion, this chapter adds to our knowledge by describing an array of theoretical and empirical insights into the emergence, use and the contextual concerns of management control practices in the public sector higher education sector. It is notable that more than 65 per cent of the sampled articles are published after the year 2000, during a time when NPM thoughts flourished in the higher education sector. We believe that our detailed review provides a reflection on the contemporary status and paves a way forward in management control research in the sphere of higher education and the remarkable contribution made to the management accounting literature. Moreover, it identifies some blind spots in the existing body of literature and the ways that future research could be more productive in the area under review. Similar to any other literature review of this kind, our review also encountered difficulty in overcoming the biases and omission that could arise from the selection process of the relevant articles in relation to the management control arena in the higher education sector from their respective journals.

In a more contemporary sense, the activities of universities are sought to be either managing or were 'managed' in a heretical manner (Deem, 1998), within the milieu where 'new managerialism' blossomed. Thus, driven by the pressures of more corporate-biased values, universities are increasingly being required to demonstrate control practices in their organizational settings with some vigorous management. Throughout this chapter, which is built upon the review of the current body of literature, the focus was mostly on management control concepts and techniques at a superficial level. Having acknowledged the significance of the current literature, further empirical work is thus vital to address some other issues which have been paid scant attention in management control research in the domain of higher education as discussed in the previous section.

It is worth noting that the alternative future research avenues identified in this chapter will add holistically to improve the understanding of the future potential for management control research in higher education and to void the gaps identified in the preceding discussion pertaining to their research topics, theories and methodologies. Further, we believe our chapter will prompt researchers to be more insightful on important research topics, best research methods and theoretical perspectives in order to deal with the challenges identified in this chapter in a more successful way.

Appendix 24.1 List of journals reviewed

Journal	*Number of papers*
Financial Accountability & Management (FAM)	9
Critical Perspectives on Accounting (CPA)	7
International Journal of Educational Management (IJEM)	7
Higher Education (HE)	5
British Journal of Management (BJM)	3
Australian Accounting Review (AAR)	2
Organization Studies (OS)	2
Journal of Management Studies (JMS)	2
International Journal of Public Sector Management (IJPSM)	1

Journal	*Number of papers*
Australian Journal of Public Administration (AJPA)	1
European Accounting Review (EAR)	1
Accounting, Auditing & Accountability Journal (AAAJ)	2
Public Administration	1
Accounting, Organizations and Society (AOS)	1
Journal of Accounting & Organizational Change (JAOC)	1
Journal of Management Accounting Research (JMAR)	1
Management Accounting Research (MAR)	1
Journal of Accounting Research (JAR)	1
Accounting and the Public Interest (API)	Nil
Qualitative Research in Accounting and Management (QRAM)	Nil
The Accounting Review (AR)	Nil
The International Journal of Accounting (TIJA)	Nil
Journal of Cost Management (JCM)	Nil
Public Administration Review (PAR)	Nil
Journal of Public Administration Research and Theory (JPART)	Nil
Australian Journal of Management (AJM)	Nil
British Accounting Review (BAR)	Nil
International Public Management Journal (IPMJ)	Nil
Accounting Forum (AFOR)	Nil
Behavioral Research in Accounting (BRA)	Nil
Contemporary Accounting Research (CAR)	Nil
Total	48

Notes

1 Bourdieu's practice framework integrates three main theoretical concepts of habitus, capital and field by fundamentally encapsulating the human interactions in constituting the practices within the social space.

2 Clegg's (1989) circuit of power framework is multifarious expressed in triad perspectives named as episodic, social and systemic at three different levels.

References

Abernethy, M. A. & Chua, W. F. 1996. A field study of control system 'redesign': the impact of institutional processes on strategic choice. *Contemporary Accounting Research*, 13, 569–606.

Abernethy, M. A. & Lillis, A. M. 2001. Interdependencies in organization design: a test in hospitals. *Journal of Management Accounting Research*, 13, 107–129.

Agasisti, T., Arnaboldi, M. & Azzone, G. 2008. Strategic management accounting in universities: the Italian experience. *Higher Education*, 55, 1–15.

Agyemang, G. & Broadbent, J. 2015. Management control systems and research management in universities: an empirical and conceptual exploration. *Accounting, Auditing & Accountability Journal*, 28, 1018–1046.

Ahrens, T. & Chapman, C. S. 2006. Doing qualitative field research in management accounting: positioning data to contribute to theory. *Accounting, Organizations and Society*, 31, 819–841.

Ahrens, T. & Dent, J. F. 1998. Accounting and organizations: realizing the richness of field research. *Journal of Management Accounting Research*, 10, 1–39.

Al-Turki, U. & Duffuaa, S. 2003. Performance measures for academic departments. *International Journal of Educational Management*, 17, 330–338.

Ansari, S. & Euske, K. J. 1987. Rational, rationalizing, and reifying uses of accounting data in organizations. *Accounting, Organizations and Society*, 12, 549–570.
Anthony, R. N. 1965. *Management Planning and Control Systems: A Framework for Analysis*. Harvard Business School Press, Boston, MA.
Argyris, C. 1960. *Understanding Organizational Behavior*. Dorsey Press, Homewood, IL.
Arnaboldi, M. & Azzone, G. 2004. Benchmarking university activities: an Italian case study. *Financial Accountability & Management*, 20, 205–220.
Arnaboldi, M. & Azzone, G. 2010. Constructing performance measurement in the public sector. *Critical Perspectives on Accounting*, 21, 266–282.
Arnaboldi, M., Azzone, G. & Savoldelli, A. 2004. Managing a public sector project: the case of the Italian Treasury Ministry. *International Journal of Project Management*, 22, 213–223.
Babbar, S. 1995. Applying total quality management to educational instruction: a case study from a US public university. *International Journal of Public Sector Management*, 8, 35–55.
Baker, C. R. & Bettner, M. S. 1997. Interpretive and critical research in accounting: a commentary on its absence from mainstream accounting research. *Critical perspectives on Accounting*, 8, 293–310.
Ball, R. & Wilkinson, R. 1994. The use and abuse of performance indicators in UK higher education. *Higher Education*, 27, 417–427.
Berry, A. J., Capps, T., Cooper, D., Ferguson, P., Hopper, T. & Lowe, E. A. 1985. Management control in an area of the NCB: rationales of accounting practices in a public enterprise. *Accounting, Organizations and Society*, 10, 3–28.
Blackmur, D. 2004. Issues in higher education quality assurance. *Australian Journal of Public Administration*, 63, 105–116.
Bourdieu, P. & Wacquant, L. J. 1992. *An Invitation to Reflexive Sociology*, University of Chicago Press, Chicago, IL.
Brennan, J. & Shah, T. 2000. Quality assessment and institutional change: experiences from 14 countries. *Higher Education*, 40, 331–349.
Bresser, R. K. & Dunbar, R. L. 1986. Context, structure, and academic effectiveness: evidence from West Germany. *Organization Studies*, 7, 1–24.
Brownell, P. 1982. The role of accounting data in performance evaluation, budgetary participation, and organizational effectiveness. *Journal of Accounting Research*, 20, 12–27.
Buckland, R. 2009. Private and public sector models for strategies in universities. *British Journal of Management*, 20, 524–536.
Burchell, S., Clubb, C., Hopwood, A., Hughes, J. & Nahapiet, J. 1980. The roles of accounting in organizations and society. *Accounting, Organizations and Society*, 5, 5–27.
Cavalluzzo, K. S. & Ittner, C. D. 2004. Implementing performance measurement innovations: evidence from government. *Accounting, Organizations and Society*, 29, 243–267.
Chia, R. & Holt, R. 2006. Strategy as practical coping: a Heideggerian perspective. *Organization Studies*, 27, 635–655.
Chung, T. K. J., Harrison, G. L. & Reeve, R. C. 2009. Interdependencies in organization design: a test in universities. *Journal of Management Accounting Research*, 21, 55–73.
Clegg, S. 1989. *Frameworks of Power*, Sage, London.
Clegg, S. 2010. The state, power, and agency: missing in action in institutional theory? *Journal of Management Inquiry*, 19, 4–13.
Cutt, J., Trotter, L. & Lee, C. E. 1993. Performance measurement and accountability in Canadian Universities: making a start in the area of teaching. *Financial Accountability & Management*, 9, 255–266.
Decramer, A., Smolders, C., Vanderstraeten, A. & Christiaens, J. 2012. The impact of institutional pressures on employee performance management systems in higher education in the low countries. *British Journal of Management*, 23, S88–S103.
Deem, R. 1998. 'New managerialism' and higher education: the management of performances and cultures in universities in the United Kingdom. *International Studies in Sociology of Education*, 8, 47–70.
Deem, R. 2004. The knowledge worker, the manager-academic and the contemporary UK university: New and old forms of public management? *Financial Accountability & Management*, 20, 107–128.
De Vries, M. & Nemec, J. 2013. Public sector reform: an overview of recent literature and research on NPM and alternative paths, *International Journal of Public Sector Management*, 26, 4–16.
Dill, D. D. & Soo, M. 2005. Academic quality, league tables, and public policy: a cross-national analysis of university ranking systems. *Higher Education*, 49, 495–533.

Dillard, J. F. & Tinker, T. 1996. Commodifying business and accounting education: the implications of accreditation. *Critical Perspectives on Accounting*, 7, 215–225.

DiMaggio, P. J. & Powell, W. W. 1983. The iron cage revisited: institutional isomorphism and collective rationality in organizational fields. *American Sociological Review*, 48, 147–160.

Dyer, W. G. & Wilkins, A. L. 1991. Better stories, not better constructs, to generate better theory: a rejoinder to Eisenhardt. *Academy of Management Review*, 16, 613–619.

Edgar, F. & Geare, A. 2010. Characteristics of high-and low-performing university departments as assessed by the New Zealand performance based research funding (PBRF) exercise. *Australian Accounting Review*, 20, 55–63.

Flamholtz, E. G. 1983. Accounting, budgeting and control systems in their organizational context: theoretical and empirical perspectives. *Accounting, Organizations and Society*, 8, 153–169.

Frølich, N. 2011. Multi-layered accountability. Performance-based funding of universities. *Public Administration*, 89, 840–859.

Garud, R., Hardy, C. & Maguire, S. 2007. Institutional entrepreneurship as embedded agency: an introduction to the special issue. *Organization Studies-Berlin-European Group for Organizational Studies*, 28, 957.

Geertz, C. 1973. *The Interpretation of Cultures*. Basic, New York.

Gherardi, S. & Nicolini, D. 2000. The organizational learning of safety in communities of practice. *Journal of Management Inquiry*, 9, 7–18.

Gumport, P. J. & Sporn, B. 1999. *Institutional Adaptation: Demands for Management Reform and University Administration*, Springer, New York.

Headland, T. N. 1990. Introduction: a dialogue between Kenneth Pike and Marvin Harris on emics and etics. In T. N. Headland, K. L. Pike, & M. Harris (Eds.) *Emics and Etics: The Insider/Outsider Debate* (pp. 13–17), Sage, Newbury Park, CA.

Hladchenko, M. 2015. Balanced Scorecard – a strategic management system of the higher education institution. *International Journal of Educational Management*, 29, 167–176.

Ho, W., Dey, P. K. & Higson, H. E. 2006. Multiple criteria decision-making techniques in higher education. *International Journal of Educational Management*, 20, 319–337.

Hoffman, A. J. 1999. Institutional evolution and change: environmentalism and the US chemical industry. *Academy of Management Journal*, 42, 351–371.

Holloway, D. A. 2004. Strategic planning and Habermasian informed discourse: reality or rhetoric. *Critical Perspectives on Accounting*, 15, 469–483.

Hood, C. 1995. The 'New Public Management' in the 1980s: variations on a theme. *Accounting, Organizations and Society*, 20, 93–109.

Hopper, T. & Major, M. 2007. Extending institutional analysis through theoretical triangulation: regulation and activity-based costing in Portuguese telecommunications. *European Accounting Review*, 16, 59–97.

Hoque, Z., Covaleski, M. A. & Gooneratne, T. N. 2013. Theoretical triangulation and pluralism in research methods in organizational and accounting research. *Accounting, Auditing & Accountability Journal*, 26, 1170–1198.

Hoque, Z. & Hopper, T. 1994. Rationality, accounting and politics: a case study of management control in a Bangladeshi jute mill. *Management Accounting Research*, 5, 5–30.

Hutaibat, K., Von Alberti-Alhtaybat, L. & Al-Htaybat, K. 2011. Strategic management accounting and the strategising mindset in an English higher education institutional context. *Journal of Accounting & Organizational Change*, 7, 358–390.

Jackson, M. P. 1999. The role of the head of department in managing performance in UK universities. *International Journal of Educational Management*, 13, 142–155.

Jarzabkowski, P. 2005. *Strategy as Practice: An Activity Based Approach*, Sage, London.

Jiang, N. & Carpenter, V. 2013. A case study of issues of strategy implementation in internationalization of higher education. *International Journal of Educational Management*, 27, 4–18.

Jones, C.S. 1994. Changes in organizational structures and procedures for resource planning in three British Universities:1985–92. *Financial Accountability and Management*, 10, 237–250.

Latour, B. 1987. *Science in Action: How to Follow Scientists and Engineers through Society*, Harvard University Press, Cambridge, MA.

Latour, B. 1996. *Aramis, or the Love of Technology*, Harvard University Press, Cambridge, MA.

Latour, B. 2005. *Reassembling the Social-An Introduction to Actor-Network-Theory, by Bruno Latour*, pp. 316. Foreword by Bruno Latour. Oxford University Press, Sep 2005, 1.

Lawrence, S. & Sharma, U. 2002. Commodification of education and academic labour—using the balanced scorecard in a university setting. *Critical Perspectives on Accounting*, 13, 661–677.

Lawrence, T., Suddaby, R. & Leca, B. 2011. Institutional work: refocusing institutional studies of organization. *Journal of Management Inquiry*, 20, 52–58.

Lee, R. & Piper, J. 1988. Organisational control, differing perspectives: the management of universities. *Financial Accountability & Management*, 4, 113–128.

Lockwood, G. 1972. Planning in a university. *Higher Education*, 1, 409–434.

Lounsbury, M. 2008. Institutional rationality and practice variation: new directions in the institutional analysis of practice. *Accounting, Organizations and Society*, 33, 349–361.

Lounsbury, M. & Crumley, E. T. 2007. New practice creation: an institutional perspective on innovation. *Organization Studies*, 28, 993–1012.

Lowe, E. A. 1971. On the idea of a management control system: integrating accounting and management control. *Journal of Management Studies*, 8, 1–12.

Lukka, K. & Modell, S. 2010. Validation in interpretive management accounting research. *Accounting, Organizations and Society*, 35, 462–477.

Lukka, K. & Mouritsen, J. 2002. Homogeneity or heterogeneity of research in management accounting? *European Accounting Review*, 11, 805–811.

Mangi, L. C. 2009. Neoinstitutionalism and the appropriation of bourdieu's work: a critical assessment. *Revista de Administração de Empresas*, 49, 323–336.

Mcdevitt, R., Giapponi, C. & Solomon, N. 2008. Strategy revitalization in academe: a balanced scorecard approach. *International Journal of Educational Management*, 22, 32–47.

Modell, S. 2003. Goals versus institutions: the development of performance measurement in the Swedish university sector. *Management Accounting Research*, 14, 333–359.

Modell, S. 2005. Students as consumers? An institutional field-level analysis of the construction of performance measurement practices. *Accounting, Auditing & Accountability Journal*, 18, 537–563.

Moll, J. & Hoque, Z. 2011. Budgeting for legitimacy: the case of an Australian university. *Accounting, Organizations and Society*, 36, 86–101.

Nicolini, D., Gherardi, S. & Yanow, D. 2003. *Knowing in Organizations: A Practice-based Approach*, M.E. Sharpe, Armonk, NY.

Orlikowski, W. J. 2000. Using technology and constituting structures: a practice lens for studying technology in organizations. *Organization Science*, 11, 404–428.

Otley, D. 1994. Management control in contemporary organizations: towards a wider framework. *Management Accounting Research*, 5, 289–299.

Otley, D. 1999. Performance management: a framework for management control systems research. *Management Accounting Research*, 10, 363–382.

Parker, L. 2011. University corporatisation: driving redefinition. *Critical Perspectives on Accounting*, 22, 434–450.

Parker, L. D. 2002. It's been a pleasure doing business with you: a strategic analysis and critique of university change management. *Critical Perspectives on Accounting*, 13, 603–619.

Parker, L. D. 2013. Contemporary university strategising: the financial imperative. *Financial Accountability & Management*, 29, 1–25.

Pettersen, I. J. 2015. From metrics to knowledge? Quality assessment in higher education. *Financial Accountability & Management*, 31, 23–40.

Pettersen, I. J. & Solstad, E. 2007. The role of accounting information in a reforming area: a study of higher education institutions. *Financial Accountability & Management*, 23, 133–154.

Pettigrew, A. M. 2014. *The Politics of Organizational Decision-Making*, Routledge, New York.

Ribeiro, J. A. & Scapens, R. W. 2006. Institutional theories in management accounting change: contributions, issues and paths for development. *Qualitative Research in Accounting & Management*, 3, 94–111.

Sayed, N. 2013. Ratify, reject or revise: balanced scorecard and universities. *International Journal of Educational Management*, 27, 203–220.

Schmulian, A. & Coetzee, S. 2011. Class absenteeism: reasons for non-attendance and the effect on academic performance. *Accounting Research Journal*, 24, 178–194.

Scott, W. W. R. 2013. *Institutions and Organizations: Ideas, Interests, and Identities*, Sage Publications, Thousand Oaks, CA.

Simons, R. 2013. *Levers of Control: How Managers Use Innovative Control Systems to Drive Strategic Renewal*, Harvard Business Press, Boston, MA.

Singh, G. 2002. Educational consumers or educational partners: a critical theory analysis. *Critical Perspectives on Accounting*, 13, 681–700.

Taylor, J. 1994. Measuring research performance in business and management studies in the United Kingdom: The 1992 research assessment exercise. *British Journal of Management*, 5, 275–288.

Ter Bogt, H. J. & Scapens, R. W. 2012. Performance management in universities: effects of the transition to more quantitative measurement systems. *European Accounting Review*, 21, 451–497.

Townley, B. 1993. Performance appraisal and the emergence of management. *Journal of Management Studies*, 30, 221–238.

Townley, B. 1997. The institutional logic of performance appraisal. *Organization Studies*, 18, 261–285.

Townley, B. 1999. Practical reason and performance appraisal. *Journal of Management Studies*, 36, 287–306.

Uddin, S. & Hopper, T. 2001. A Bangladesh soap opera: privatisation, accounting, and regimes of control in a less developed country. *Accounting, Organizations and Society*, 26, 643–672.

Upping, P. & Oliver, J. 2012. Thai public universities: modernisation of accounting practices. *Journal of Accounting & Organizational Change*, 8, 403–430.

Van Helden, G. J. 2005. Researching public sector transformation: the role of management accounting. *Financial Accountability & Management*, 21, 99–133.

Venieris, G. & Cohen, S. 2004. Accounting reform in Greek universities: a slow moving process. *Financial Accountability & Management*, 20, 183–204.

Walker, R. G. 2000. Statutory budgeting and financial reporting by Australian universities. *Australian Accounting Review*, 10, 2–16.

Whittington, R. 2006. Completing the practice turn in strategy research. *Organization Studies*, 27, 613–634.

Wickramasinghe, D. & Hopper, T. 2005. A cultural political economy of management accounting controls: a case study of a textile Mill in a traditional Sinhalese village. *Critical Perspectives on Accounting*, 16, 473–503.

Part IV

PMC research

The lens through which PMC may be viewed

25

Researching performance management

An actor-reality perspective

Will Seal

Introduction

This chapter responds to calls for business research to have practical impact (Bennis and O'Toole, 2005) by proposing an actor-reality perspective (ARP). ARP is a research design based around a particular view of performance management in which organizational reality and success are based on an integration of four dimensions: facts, values, logics/possibilities and communication. In the ARP research design, reality is based on the pragmatic criterion that "what works" is real. With the research focus on the organizational member actor as a purposeful, social human being, performance management is seen as a way of recognizing and constructing organizational reality. The contribution of the ARP as a research design is that it narrows the gap between theory and practice (Nørreklit *et al.*, 2006; Seal, 2012) because it avoids both an excessive focus on one or two dimensions of reality and the naive views of reality sometimes in the mainstream management control literature (Nørreklit *et al.*, 2006). Second, by proposing an actor-based philosophy of performance management, the application of ARP seeks to avoid the pitfall of management control illusion (Dermer and Lucas, 1986) which stems from top-down, mechanistic and uni-rational perspectives on the organization. Developing their suggestions for impactful research, Bennis and O'Toole (2005) argue that business schools should adopt a professional orientation similar to Law and Medical schools. From an accounting perspective, such a call is likely to find some support. Yet in order to promote a professional paradigm, a profession such as accountancy needs a valid concept of truth which can be based on an ARP conceptual framework. Nørreklit *et al.* (2007) argue that

> The accounting profession has a dilemma in this regard. Its traditional paradigm of realism assumes a tangible, real-world, truth substantiation for the performance information that it produces. Such substantiation cannot be found for many components of accounting measurements. Consequently, the profession opens itself to criticism from those who identify these disparities. To assume a defensible position in society, accountants need to base their discipline on a concept of truth consistent with their prevailing paradigm. *(p. 186)*

Although some of the core ideas and philosophies that influence ARP go back hundreds or even thousands of years, the approach is a relative newcomer in the management accounting and performance management literature (Nørreklit *et al.*, 2006; 2007) and is still relatively unfamiliar to many accounting researchers. For those unfamiliar with the basic principles of ARP, the chapter begins in section "What is ARP and what is its distinctive contribution?" by describing the main features of an ARP research design. In section "Applying the actor reality research design: some examples of research on the balanced scorecard and the levers of control", some examples of ARP research are presented, which show how the approach can be applied in research on well-known performance management packages such as the balanced scorecard (BSC) (Seal and Ye, 2014) and the levers of control (LOC) (Seal and Mattimoe, 2014). The final section discusses the approach in the light of possible alternatives.

What is ARP and what is its distinctive contribution?

The fundamental methodological position that underpins all ARP research is an ontology based on the philosophy of pragmatic constructivism (PC). In the PC ontology, reality is based on the German concept of *wirklichkeit* – that is, reality is "that which works" as opposed to illusions or dreams that do not work[1] (Nørreklit, 2011). It is a constructionist perspective that tries to avoid the forms of social constructionism that overemphasize communicative elements of reality. Nørreklit *et al.* (2006, pp. 43–44) argue that

> [...] social constructivism – in the way it is interpreted in management accounting research – supresses (socio-)economic logic and individual values, as a consequence of which any attempt by the organization to apply rational/logical economic calculations in choosing between opportunities and controlling its own future becomes incomprehensible.

ARP rejects extreme forms of social constructivism that deny the existence of an external objective reality. In ARP, facts are a dimension of reality and are constructed though a relationship between the actor and the world as shown in Figure 25.1. In short, ARP has an empirical dimension that offers a way of checking the validity of constructions such as a management control model. In ARP, fictions may play a role in the construction and communication of a management control *topos*, but they must, at least in principle, be checked against a reality that, although a construction, has some basis in (but does not correspond to) an external world (Nørreklit, 2011).

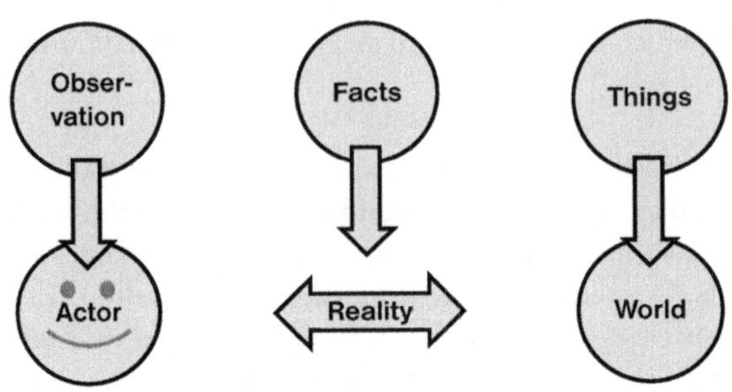

Figure 25.1 The construction of facts as a relation between the actor and the world

In summary, ARP is based on a view of reality constructed through the integration of facts, logics, values and communication. The PC framework can be used to model reality construction by individual actors, by managers and by multi-authoring collectivities. As its name suggests, ARP claims to explicitly confront problems of the management control illusion by arguing that managerial control illusions may be avoided by the construction of a practically valid organizational *topos* (Nørreklit *et al.*, 2006), which for any particular organization is the "result of applying a conceptual framework to a specific historical situation" (Nørreklit *et al.*, 2006, p. 48). In the ARP framework, it is argued that a realistic performance management/management control *topos* depends on the successful integration of four dimensions of reality. On this basis, the theory-practice gap can grow wider if a theory focuses excessively on only one or two dimensions of reality. For example, agency theory is very strong on the logic dimension, while contingency theory combines the logic dimension with a naive view on social facts. Other theoretical traditions such as institutional theory may overemphasize the social constructivist dimension to the neglect of commercial logics and reflexive human agents. From this ontological position, we can try to construct theories that draw on all four dimensions of managerial reality as shown later in the chapter.

An organizational *topos* is necessary but not sufficient for organizational success. If the organizational *topos* is top-down and mechanical, then there may be elements of illusion either in the individual elements or in the integration between the elements. There may be illusions of control because senior managers are perceived by organizational members that they are treated as machines rather than thinking self-motivated actors (Nørreklit, 2011). The organizational *topos* gains practical validity by being constructed in specific business contexts and co-authored by all organizational members. This multi-authoring is important because it implies that by respecting the values and insights of other organizational members, business leaders can potentially tap into the creativity and enthusiasm of all employees. The emphasis on co-authorship and different views of reality enables ARP to shed light on some of the specific ontological and epistemological issues raised in comparisons between management accounting and operational management. Because of its emphasis on the construction of reality, ARP provides us with a framework that enables us to question such assertions avoiding functional prejudices and strives to create a "real" (i.e. illusion-free) management control approach system from an explicit set of ontological assumptions. The ARP framework argues that a successful management control *topos* will succeed because it is based on reality rather than illusions – it has *practical validity*. As Nørreklit explains,

> Practical validity means that the controlling stories and concepts, the topoi, are not embedding hidden illusions. The process of practical validation ensures that the story is realistic, i.e. it can be implemented successfully at every step.
>
> *(2011, p. 16)*

In order to develop a practically valid management control *topos*, an actor-based management (ABM) approach is proposed. Cinquini *et al.* recommend that the following principles should guide the development of a performance management system:

> The design process is initiated from the top. However, the interaction between the various (groups of) employees involved takes place as dialogues. A dialogue is a dynamic and reflective process of conversation between two or more persons during which both parties pose questions and receive answers. Both are creative and logical in the process. Their understanding and concepts of reality get reflected in the dialogue...
>
> *(2013, p. 364)*

How ARP narrows the gap between theory and practice in business research

Seal (2012) argues that the lack of practical impact of business school research, including in performance management, may be attributed to a search for legitimacy within the wider academy. As Bennis and O'Toole (2005) point out, US business schools sought prestige by adopting what they saw as the scientific method – a strategy that could be traced to a form of "physics envy". Yet paradoxically, in disciplines such as physics, the ultimate source of status in the academy is based on practical success. In the physical sciences, the scientific method has prestige because ultimately it has produced theories that have practical application. As mentioned earlier, word reality in Germanic languages is translated as "that which works". However, as Nørreklit (2011) also points out, while realism in the physical world can exist independently of whether actors perceive it, in the social world, reality depends on a conceptually constructed actor-world relationship.

A second problem in the business academy is a preference for management-in-general rather than management-in-context. In Armstrong's (2006) view, management-in-general works at the level of individual career progression (that is, it matches educational market reality) but fails on the criterion of producing managerial knowledge that works. Finally, although interpretive research has recognized the actor-world relationship as a social construction, it has failed to generate much in the way of usable prescriptions for practicing managers because commercial logics are seen as socially constructed rituals or symbols rather than materially significant business models.

In some respects, ARP represents a form of critical performativity (Spicer *et al.*, 2009), in that it is *normative, pragmatic, takes an affirmative stance, provides space for respondents' views* and *seeks out organizational potentialities* (Spicer *et al.*, 2009, p. 546). ARP encourages dialogic between members of the organization and between researchers and the researched (Seal and Mattimoe, 2014). Although it does not take an explicitly critical position by, for example, rejecting the profit motive, ARP supports a style of management that achieves its long-term financial goals through participatory rather than top-down models of management control (Nørreklit, 2011).

Some comparisons with other interpretive approaches

Narrative: people make sense through stories

Overall, it would seem that in terms of the production of management control knowledge, PC and narrative have many overlaps and complementarities. Practitioners/interviewees seem to like stories both in order to make sense of their own roles in their organizations and to develop personal strategic agendas. Field researchers should respect this tendency both in their attitude to interviewing and in their interpretation of data. Yet, venturing another observation, when it comes to the linking of theory and data and the production of valid management control knowledge, the PC approach provides a vital set of criteria against which we can evaluate the stories of practitioners on the basis of "does it work?" Given the ambiguity of what constitutes organizational success, it may be hard to be test whether or not a particular management control framework embeds illusions of control. Thus, although management control researchers may prefer a research framework that urges us to at least try and separate fact from fiction, they should recognize that just as practitioners search for stories that make sense of complex organizational contexts, so academics also need their own stories. The great value of narrative approaches are that they put these issues clearly "on the table" and help to protect us from the illusions and ideologies of a naive scientism. Not only can the data collection process be enhanced by drawing on both narrative and PC methodologies, but the tensions between the two can also enrich the interpretation of management control field data.

Recommendations based on PC derive their power from a holistic approach to managerial problems, with an emphasis on empathy rather than direction. Change comes though greater awareness and understanding by organizational members, which enables better integration between the dimensions of their management control *topoi*. The notion of management change as therapy and empathy is also consistent with a narrative approach. Thus, although the researchers did have a specific research agenda that reflected the interests of their primary funding sponsors, the interviewees were given freedom to tell their own stories, enabling them to "reflect … to select salient aspects, and to order them into a coherent whole" (Elliott, 2005, p. 24). As Elliott and others point out, the construction of any story involves identifying cause-and-effect relationships. In the context of a business interview, it is likely that knowledgeable interviewees will themselves interweave theories into their descriptions of why they did something or why one thing worked while another did not. The process of interviewing provides not just information for the researchers but also a chance for the interviewees to reflect on their experiences, exchange ideas and validate their own interpretations with researchers who were impartial observers of the organizational politics of the hotel. In defence of narrative, it does have a useful role to play in the collection and analysis of field data (Czarniawska, 1997). The approach stimulates awareness of literary aesthetics and recognizes the emotional impact of fieldwork stories. It also validates an approach to interviewing, which allows the interviewees to explain and reflect on their identities and roles within the organization (Chase, 2011).

Another way that narrative thinking can complement ARP is to draw on Boje (2001; 2008) who argues for a distinction between stories and narratives. In Boje's view, *narrative* "aspires to abstraction and generality" (2008, p. 1), while *story* "has retained more grounded interplay with the life world, and its generativity" (2008, p. 1). This distinction is the basis for his proposal for an *antenarrative* perspective (2001) and his advocacy of a storytelling organization (2008). Antenarrative is fragmented, non-linear, incoherent, collective, unplotted and pre-narrative speculation (Boje, 2001). Storytelling or "storying" can be more speculative and forward looking than narrative that imposes a retrospective logic (Boje, 2008). The forward-looking aspect of storying is particularly significant if the organization is trying to re-construct itself through developing and implementing a new strategy or operational model. Boje (2008) does not recommend a rejection of narrative but a synthesis with storytelling via a dialectical approach:

> Narrative analysis combined with antenarrative analysis can be a field that is about multi-voiced ways of telling stories, with even antenarrative and non-linear ones whose linear plot sequence is missing and where no one seems to mind. To tell organization stories differently will, I think, require this more dialectic approach.
>
> *(p. 9)*

As will be shown later in this chapter, the concepts of multi-voicing and dialectics are also characteristic of ARP approaches (Nørreklit, 2011; Seal and Mattimoe, 2014) and constitute the ways that these approaches are related to narrative analysis. If the strength of ARP is its concern to avoid illusions of control that may be harboured by top-down, mechanical modes of governance, then the strength of (ante)narrative is its generative capacity with its openness to speculative stories that imagine alternative organizational futures (Boje, 2001; 2008).

Sensemaking: any map is better than no map

Narrative thinking may be linked to some aspects of sensemaking, particularly in situations of ambiguity and uncertainty as when "people confront something unintelligible and ask 'what's the story here?' their question has the force of bringing an event into existence" (Weick *et al.*, 2005, p. 410). Yet to many, the most evocative image associated with sensemaking is the metaphor of a *map* linked to the intuition than if travellers are overwhelmed by lethargy, then "any map may be better than no map". Swieringa and Weick (1987) argue that management accounting academics can overemphasize the analytical and decision-making aspects of management accounting to the neglect of cognition, motivation and commitment. One result of the traditional focus is that researchers may underestimate the effect on action in creating order. Arguing that order may be constructed by managers if, by acting *on a presumption of order,* "action implants the rationality that was presumed" (1987, p. 304). As Swieringa and Weick argue,

> Biased, incomplete analyses may mobilize strong action which, because of its strength, may often change situations so that they, in fact, eventually validate the incomplete presentation that first stimulated the action. Self-validating action stimulated by relatively crude accounting approaches may be a common though neglected pathway by which management accounting affects organizations.
>
> *(1987, p. 293)*

While PC and sensemaking do have overlaps and complementarities, the PC approach provides a vital set of criteria against which we can evaluate the "maps" of practitioners on the basis of "does it work?" Given the ambiguity of what constitutes organizational success, it may be hard to test that a particular management control framework does not embed illusions of control, we should at least prefer a research framework that urges us to try see that not only does the management control package promote organizational action but also that action should be evaluated according to some notions of organizational success. Any map may work in the sense that it overcomes despair and lethargy, but with PC, we are urged to explore the characteristics of a good map.

If sensemaking focuses on cartography – the process of map making – then PC has a set of concepts with which a specific map can be evaluated in detail. For example, it can be used to ask fine-grained questions concerning the relationship between the actor and the world in the construction of facts. The PC concern with facts can be used to ask critical questions about the completeness of specific performance indicators. The appeal to facts may suggest that PC has a less forgiving attitude to management control packages than sensemaking. In other words, the specific characteristics of the organizational *topos* may be subject to a more careful scrutiny than they might under sensemaking criteria. Or, to reprise the famous story, any map may be better than no map, *but some maps are better than others.* As a way of evaluating management control models/organizational maps, PC proposes a concept of pragmatic truth. For example, the London Tube map may have a very poor correspondence with reality, but it meets the criterion of pragmatic truth (Mitchell *et al.*, 2013) in that it enables millions of passengers to successfully navigate their way around the London Tube system. However, as Mitchell *et al.*, point out,

> A problem with this pragmatic concept of truth is that one can only know the truth after events have proven whether the expectations were met. Since it is absurd to wait

> for ex-post testing of all statements and especially of strategic statements, a concept of preliminary truth, pro-active truth similar to the correspondence notion of truth, is needed to provide a basis for action.
>
> *(2013, p. 21)*

Mitchell *et al.* have set out the processes by which actors create a practical valid reality in terms of a pro-active truth as follows:

> … in order to apply the pragmatic notion of truth one needs an idea of truth based on the present. This is *pro-active truth*. This pro-active truth is then subject to a continuous process of improvement which identifies and diminishes the difference between the pragmatic truth as the outcome and with pro-active truth.
>
> *(2013, pp. 21–22)*

With a pro-active truth perspective on management control, the map metaphor begins to show some limitations as creating a map is not the same as planning a journey. Here, PC is undoubtedly more productive with its stress on integration between values, possibilities, logics and communication. The PC framework for creative governance (Nørreklit, 2011) promises to go beyond retrospective sensemaking by offering a recipe for the future, an approach that enables strategic performance control (Mitchell *et al.*, 2013; Seal and Mattimoe, 2014). In sum, PC proposes ways to develop and test a new strategic map through the concept of pro-active truth.

It would be wrong to present PC and sensemaking in some sort of notional competition. Although they focus on different aspects of management control and accounting, they both share an interest in performativity. In short, both approaches explicitly ask either how is a map used or how does it relate to individual and organization action? In sensemaking, the great fear seems to be inaction induced by organizational paralysis; in PC, the great fear is not organizational inaction but a concern that actors, particulary senior managers, may be suffering from the illusion that the system of control that they impose on an organization necessarily enables a successful outcomes or even a degree of control.

Actor-Network Theory and the sociology of translation

If narrative and sensemaking are compared to ARP because of many conceptual similarities and complementarities, then we cannot say the same about Actor-Network Theory (ANT). This approach is only mentioned in this chapter because the commonality of the word "Actor" may evoke curiosity about the relationship between ANT and ARP.[2] Ironically, the shared use of the word "actor" actually reveals a marked distinction between the two approaches. It is clear that in ARP, the actors are *human* actors. Yet in ANT, actors or actants may be human *and* non-human, that is, artefacts such as computers or texts. Although both ANT and ARP are *constructivist*, the ontological bases of the two approaches are quite distinct especially with respect to their different views on the construction of facts. While in principle in ARP, an individual human actor can "test" some physical facts using pragmatic criteria – e.g. if a cup holds water, then it is a cup – in ANT, "(W)e need others to help us transform a claim into a matter of fact" (Latour, 1987, p. 108). In ANT, a central focus is on the notion of translation, that is, "the interpretation given by the fact-builders of their interests and that of the people they enrol" (Latour, 1987, p. 108). In short, the focus in ANT is on the *relationships* between actants and how it leads to the fabrication (or de-construction) of facts.

In sum, the appeal of ARP is not only constructivist (shared with narrative, sensemaking and ANT in differing degrees), but it is also *pragmatic*. Its explicit claim to be practical, to ask "Does it work?", suggests a shared value system with the many performance management researchers who ultimately hope that their research will have some sort of (positive?) practical impact.

Applying the actor reality research design: some examples of research on the balanced scorecard and the levers of control

The PC framework is very general, emphasizing the weakness of past theories, so it may seem reasonable to ask: What would be an appropriate theory that accommodates all four dimensions of reality? As argued above, the dimension of communication is crucial in integrating the elements within an organization. Yet communication is also the way by which outside influences such as institutionalized logics and values (Lounsbury, 2008; Mattimoe and Seal, 2011) can affect the realities of organizational actors. The dimension of communication is shown as the conduit whereby outside data affect individual elements of reality as well as the way in which these separate elements may be combined within the organization through the practices of management control. These issues are further illustrated below with examples from applications of the ARP framework to specific performance management situations.

Some examples of actor-reality research in performance management

ARP and the balanced scorecard

Although many of the claims about cause-and-effect relationships with the BSC (Kaplan and Norton, 1996) have been questioned on both logical and empirical grounds (Nørreklit, 2000; Ittner *et al.*, 2003), Seal and Ye (2014) report on a case study of a major bank that the BSC was not only enthusiastically implemented but it seemed also that the managers avoided some of the worst excesses of pre-Credit Crunch delinquency. Indeed, an argument could be made that the particular configuration of the bank's BSC helped to reinforce a more risk averse culture and avoided the bad lending decisions that pervaded the finance industry prior to 2008.

The Seal and Ye (2014) paper addresses the research question: How does a management control system based on the BSC affect the behaviour of organizational actors? The paper approaches the problem through a synthesis of two main theoretical/methodological strands. One strand draws on a PC view of management control (Nørreklit *et al.*, 2006), and the other draws on a critical discourse perspective on organizational action (Seal, 2010). These theories are deployed to build a conceptual framework that can be used to interpret the construction of a management control discourse in specific empirical situations. The framework is then deployed to show how, in a particular instance, the BSC can be seen as impacting on organizational action. An important outcome of the interpretive framework and the evidence in the case study is that the paper can propose a re-appraisal of the relationship between the practice of the BSC and the BSC literature.

As the first step in an enquiry into how a management control system based on the BSC can affect the behaviour of organizational actors, the paper developed a theoretical framework for management control based on PC and critical discourse analysis. This framework argued that a management control system based on the BSC can integrate the multidimensional nature of managerial reality.

The framework was then applied to a case study of a BSC implementation in a major multi-national bank. It was found that the bank tailored its BSC to its industry profile by adding risk to the traditional dimensions of performance. This addition to the BSC reinforced and supported the bank's traditional prudence, which allowed it to avoid much of the poor lending that characterized many of its competitors.

In terms of implementation and usage, the BSC was deeply embedded in the organization driven by the support of the CEO and through the mandatory involvement of all employees. Interviewees at all levels of the bank reported that the BSC helped them to construct a personal managerial discourse that linked their own action with wider organizational action. The practitioners in the case are relaxed about constitutive impact of the BSC model and its wider institutionalization. Unlike many of the advocates of the BSC, they accepted the efficacy of the BSC without having to be convinced of specific cause-and-effect relationships. Paradoxically, instead of celebrating the rhetorical triumphs of the BSC and the way that it can mould organizational discourse, academics who are either unfamiliar with or unsympathetic to the discoursal analysis of organizational action are condemned to strain unconvincingly to identify "scientific" relationships between the dimensions of performance set out in the BSC. From a linguistic perspective, the paradox may be resolved simply by accepting the logic of discourse analysis – texts help to create organizational reality, and texts that are characterized by good rhetoric will have more impact than those that are less persuasive. Thus, a wider contribution of the paper suggests a way to reconcile the *practice* of the BSC with the way it has been advocated by its founding fathers in the BSC literature. In a comment on their paper, the leading "founding father" of the BSC, Robert Kaplan, confessed that he did not understand the theory used by Nørreklit *et al.* (2012). He suggested that "(P)erhaps Nørreklit *et al* believe that the BSC may be fine in practice but it doesn't work in theory" (Kaplan, 2012, p. 542). Paradoxically, in this throwaway remark, Kaplan (2012) is actually neatly summarizing the argument in this paper. The BSC affected action in *Trafalgar Bank* in ways that mainstream management control theories struggle to explain because, informed by a naive realist ontology, they fail to appreciate the centrality of communication and the way that reality is constructed in organizations.

The ARP research design and the levers of control model

Seal and Mattimoe (2014) apply the ARP research design to performance management by asking a commonly posed question: How do managers exercise strategic control? Many researchers have noted that an important part of strategic control involves the identification and management of *tensions* in the organization. Focusing on the role of management control systems, some researchers have built on the seminal insights of the LOC model (Simons, 1995; Otley, 1999; Ahrens & Chapman, 2004; Tuömela, 2005; Widener, 2007; Mundy, 2010). The LOC model is usually portrayed as a management system in which organizational tensions are constructed through an *intentional* interplay between different types and levels of control. In short, organizational tensions are seen as being "designed" by senior managers through their use of control systems. Although researchers have been inclined to focus on tensions between performance management systems, Simons himself argued that LOC should be *broadly defined* to include organizational systems such as standard operating procedures and codes of practice (Simons, 1994; 1995). The defining metaphor of the Simons model is based on a mechanical view of management control; management objectives including controlling strategy are achieved by pulling levers. The Simons (1995) framework does discuss the possibility of blending organic and mechanistic control but, as Ahrens and

Chapman point out, concepts such as belief and boundary systems are "very general" (2004, p. 278) and the relationship between mechanistic and organic control remains "relatively unspecified" (2004, p. 278).

In contrast, the paper develops an approach to management informed by an actor-based leadership style that "implies enhanced awareness of the situation and competences of people and the function and power of communicative action" (Nørreklit, 2011, p. 9). Furthermore, it views organizations as places where tensions are not constructed by senior managers through the mobilization of control systems but are pre-existing between different functional areas of the organization. Building on perspectives which see organizations as coalitions (Cyert and March, 1992), the paper shows that tensions can emerge between different organizational and/or functional perspectives (e.g. accounting versus marketing; head office versus business unit). Drawing on fieldwork from the hospitality industry, examples were found of circumstances where overall organizational effectiveness was enhanced rather than damaged by opposing priorities. We term these situations as *dialectical management by design* (DMD) whereby senior managers control and adjust corporate strategy by recognizing and even encouraging conflicts between functional areas of the organization. The DMD approach is not inconsistent with the broader interpretations of the LOC (Simons, 1995) but offers a deeper interpretation of organizational tensions based on the ontological and epistemological properties of dialectical methodology (Arbnor and Bjerke, 2009) and actor-based principles of management (Nørreklit, 2011). Actor-based methodologies can also help to evaluate the success/failure of particular management control frameworks by drawing on the criterion of *practical validity* (Nørreklit, 2011). The paper takes a particular perspective on actor-based research informed by PC, which has a specific concept of reality, which maintains that success is achieved when organizational governance is informed by reality rather than illusions or myths (Nørreklit, 2011; Nørreklit *et al.*, 2012). In contrast to the LOC approach in which organizational tension is seen as a "gift" of senior managers, actor-based approaches are more inclined to favour organizations that are governed by "bottom-up" rather than "top-down" principles (Cinquini *et al.*, 2013).

A second and related contribution of the paper is to show that organizational tensions may not follow conventional expectations. For example, it is not uncommon to cast the accountant in the role of "corporate policemen" as custodians of financial information (Sathe 1982; 1983). Although we found evidence in our fieldwork of accountants acting as custodians of the budgetary system, we also found that accountants may themselves be conflicted between revenue generating and cost saving. Furthermore, it is possible that in some situations, the marketing and/or revenue management functions may seem to be the corporate policemen as they seek to protect the corporate brand against unplanned price discounting or short-term cost-saving tactics. Seal and Mattimoe (2014) presented an actor-based theoretical and methodological framework that has been used to develop an approach to strategic performance management based explicitly on dialectical principles. Adopting a PC methodology, it showed that the tensions that exist between different functional areas of an organization may be mobilized to maintain and develop specific business models. The framework saw the firms as coalitions of functional areas had their own specific values, facts, logics and communications. These could be seen as self-referential systems that related to each other in a dialectical manner.

The theoretical and methodological concepts were illustrated with fieldwork from the hospitality industry. The fieldwork revealed tensions within the various organizations. However, the fieldwork also showed how these tensions could be used creatively to maintain and develop the operating models of the case study firms. Sometimes, the tensions seemed to just emerge from the different organizational and/or functional perspectives (e.g. accounting versus marketing, head office versus business unit). On other occasions, there were examples of circumstances where overall organizational effectiveness was seen to be enhanced by opposing priorities. These situations may be seen as examples of DMD. Although there was evidence of accountants acting as custodians of the budgetary system, in other situations, the marketing or revenue management functions seemed to be the corporate policemen as they sought to protect the corporate brand against unplanned price discounting or short-term cost-saving tactics.

The paper urges practitioners, academics and other interested parties such as consultants to develop and embrace a discourse on the benefits of organizational tensions and conflicts. The LOC made an invaluable start, but its key insights have been left undeveloped and an implicit rather than explicit characteristic of successful organizations. If dialectical management is a "practice that dares not speak its name", then this paper urges the management community to have a fresh look at the dialectical mode of thinking as well as recognizing that the management of conflicts between functional specialities is as much a management package as any of some of the better-known approach such as the BSC.

Conclusions

Building on the ontology of ARP, the chapter proposes an ontological position that argues that managerial reality is constructed through the integration of facts, values, logics and communication. The research design argues for an interpretive theoretical framework that enables an understanding of wider influences on local logics, values and facts. As mentioned in the introduction, in fairness to the academic community, critical perspectives on the relationship between action and discourse also imply that not all of the lack of impact can be attributed to the failings of the message or the messenger. Self-interested executives may be resistant to sound academic concepts because they threaten managerial discretion and power. Yet the message from the business academy to the practitioner could be more persuasive. In particular, although business school research traditions vary across the world, the common problem among different research approaches is a failure to develop research strategies that understand all the dimensions of managerial reality. This chapter has argued that an appropriate combination of methods, methodology and theory can deliver impactful research in management accounting and management control. The challenge for future research is to apply this combination to a set of organizational case studies that can form a body of texts that can help organizational actors understand and construct different organizational futures.

As was pointed out in the introduction, the ARP is a relatively new research framework and requires both further refinement and more demonstrations of its productivity as a research design. This productivity would be validated if it can deliver on its aspirations to develop the sort of *professional* knowledge that will increase the impact of performance management research.

Notes

1 See footnote in Nørreklit, 2011, p. 19.
2 Indeed, after giving a presentation on ARP at a conference, the author was asked by a member of the audience to explain the relationship between ARP and ANT!

References

Ahrens, T., Chapman, C. 2004. Accounting for flexibility and efficiency: a field study of management control systems in a restaurant chain. *Contemporary Accounting Research*, 21(2), 271–301.

Arbnor, I., Bjerke, B., 2009. *Methodology for Creating Business Knowledge*, third ed., Sage, Los Angeles, CA.

Armstrong, P., 2006. Ideology and the grammar of idealism: the Caterpillar controversy revisited. *Critical Perspectives on Accounting*, 17, 529–548.

Bennis, W., O'Toole, J., 2005. How Business Schools lost their way. *Harvard Business Review*, 83(5), 96–104.

Boje, D., 2001. *Narrative Methods for Organizational and Communication Research*, Sage, London.

Boje, D., 2008. *Storytelling Organizations*, Sage, Los Angeles, CA.

Chase, S., 2011. Narrative inquiry: still a field in the making. In: Denzin, N. and Lincoln, Y. (Eds.), *The Sage Handbook of Qualitative Research*. Sage, Thousand Oaks, CA, pp. 421–434.

Cinquini, L., Mitchell, F., Nørreklit, H., Tenucci, A., 2013. Methodologies for managing performance measurement. In: Mitchell, F., Nørreklit, H. and Jakobsen, M. (Eds.), *The Routledge Companion to Cost Management*. Routledge, London, pp. 360–380.

Cyert, R. and MarchJ., 1992. *A Behavioral Theory of the Firm*, Cambridge, MA: Blackwell.

Czarniawska, B., 1997. *Narrating the Organization: Dramas of Institutional Identity*, University of Chicago Press, Chicago, IL.

Dermer, J., Lucas, R., 1986. The illusion of managerial control. *Accounting, Organizations & Society*, 11(6), 471–482.

Elliott, J., 2005. *Using Narrative in Social Research: Qualitative and Quantitative Approaches*, Sage, London.

Ittner,C., Larcker, D., Meyer, M., 2003. Subjectivity and the weighting of performance measures: evidence from the Balanced Scorecard, *The Accounting Review* 78(3), 725–758.

Jakobsen, M., Johansson, I., Nørreklit, H., (Eds.), 2011. *An Actor's Approach to Management*, Djof Publishing, Copenhagen.

Kaplan, R.S., 2012. The balanced scorecard: comments on balanced scorecard commentaries. *Journal of Accounting & Organizational Change*, 8(4), 539–545.

Kaplan, R. and Norton, D., 1996. *The Balanced Scorecard: Translating Strategy into Action*. Boston, MA: Harvard Business School Press.

Latour, B., 1987. *Science in Action*, Harvard University Press, Cambridge, MA.

Lounsbury, M. 2008. Institutional rationality and practice variation: new directions in the institutional analysis of practice, accounting, organizations and society, 33(4–5), 349–361.

Mundy, J., 2010. Creating dynamic tensions through a balanced use of management control systems. *Accounting, Organizations & Society*, 35(5), 499–523.

Nørreklit, L., 2011. Actors and reality: a conceptual framework for creative governance. In: Jakobsen, M., Johansson, I., Nørreklit, H., (Eds.), *An Actor's Approach to Management*. Djof Publishing, Copenhagen, pp. 7–38.

Nørreklit, H., Nørreklit, L., Israelsen, P., 2006. Validity of management control topoi: towards constructivist pragmatism. *Management Accounting Research*, 17(1), 42–71.

Nørreklit, H., Nørreklit, L. and Mitchell, F., 2007. Theoretical conditions for validity in accounting performance measurement. In: Neely, A. (Ed.), *Business Performance Measurement*. Cambridge University Press, Cambridge, pp. 179–217.

Nørreklit, H., Nørreklit, L., Mitchell, F., Bjørnenak, T., 2012. The rise of the balanced scorecard! Relevance regained? *Journal of Accounting & Organizational Change*, 8(4), 490–510.

Mitchell, F., Nielsen, L., Nørreklit, H., Nørreklit, L., 2013. Scoring strategic performance: a pragmatic constructivist approach to strategic performance measurement. *Journal of Management & Governance*, 17, 5–34.

Otley, D.T., 1999. Performance management: a framework for management control systems research. *Management Accounting Research*, 10(4), 363–382.

Sathe, V., 1982. *Controller Involvement in Management*. London: Prentice-Hall.

Sathe, V., 1983. The controller's role in management, *Organizational Dynamics*, 1 (Winter), 31–48.

Seal, W., 2010. Managerial discourse and the link between theory and practice: from ROI to value-based management. *Management Accounting Research*, 21(2), 95–109.

Seal, W., 2012. Some proposals for impactful management control research. *Qualitative Research in Accounting & Management*, 9(3), 228–244.

Seal, W., Mattimoe, R., 2014. Controlling strategy through dialectical management. *Management Accounting Research*, 25(3), 230–243.

Seal, W., Ye, L., 2014. The balanced scorecard and the construction of a management control discourse. *Journal of Accounting & Organizational Change*, 10(4), 466–485.

Simons, R.A., 1994. How new top managers use control systems as levers of strategic renewal. *Strategic Management Journal*, 15(3), 169–189.

Simons, R.A., 1995. *Levers of Control, How Managers Use Innovative Control Systems to Drive Strategic Renewal*, Harvard Business School Press, Boston, MA.

Spicer, A., Alvesson, M., Karreman, D., 2009. Critical performativity: the unfinished business of critical management studies. *Human Relations*, 62(4), 537–560.

Swieringa, R., Weick, K., 1987. Management accounting and action. *Accounting, Organizations and Society*, 12(3), 293–308.

Tuomela, T. 2005. The interplay of different levers of control: a case study of introducing a new performance measurement system. *Management Accounting Research*, 16(3), 293–320.

Weick, K., Sutcliffe, K., Obstfeld, D., 2005. Organizing and the process of sensemaking. *Organizational Science*, 16(4), 409–421.

Widener, S., 2007. An empirical analysis of the levers of control framework. *Accounting, Organizations and Society*, 32(7–8), 757–788.

26

The nature and practice of interpretive accounting research

Ivo De Loo and Alan Lowe

Introduction

In interpretive research, the use of conversations, narratives and stories from 'the field' often provides the basis for researchers' representations. Interviews are frequently seen as an important information source in such research (Ahrens and Chapman, 2006). Some academic authorities have thrown doubt on the reliability of data gained from interviews (Alvesson, 2003, 2010; Silverman, 2011). We argue here that researchers need to be more cognizant of the limitations and constraints of their theoretical, methodological and philosophical frameworks when conducting interpretive research. An example aims to illustrate this.

One of the authors previously worked at a university where he was told by a colleague, sometime after he had joined the organization and had been given management responsibilities, that if he really wanted changes to happen in his department, he should first talk to the dean to introduce his ideas and then to his deputy if he also wanted to obtain support from the university board. Although the dean was officially the person who should contact and negotiate with the board about such issues, and also saw himself as the one in charge of departmental changes, his deputy turned out to be very much involved in matters such as the facilitation of significant organizational change.

Now suppose that this university was included in a research project, and both the dean and the deputy would be interviewed by an academic, from a different university, about large-scale departmental change. It would not be unlikely (but of course far from certain) for both the dean and the deputy to tell the interviewer(s) that the former implemented departmental change on his own without consulting colleagues (Alvesson, 2003, 2010; De Loo and Lowe, 2012).

Quattrone (2006) thinks that every interview constitutes a 'lacuna', in which issues are left out, altered or portrayed differently by an interviewee in whatever way he or she deems fit, for whatever reason. This often happens subconsciously, for instance as an interviewee suddenly gets emotional, or wants to appeal to the interviewer(s). Alvesson (2003, 2010) argues that the research interview may be interpreted along two dominant metaphors: as a research method with which 'true-life data' can be gathered, or as a human encounter where such 'data' are actively created between interviewer(s) and interviewee(s), who are affected by their surroundings, previous experiences, and what happens during the interview. This all leads up to what is stated in the interview encounter.

Later in the contribution, we claim that the brief vignette above, set in a university department, illustrates that *any* research situation may be far from a 'normal' situation in which everyone is inclined to provide 'actual' or 'factual' information. In interpretive research, such as in accounting, the use of conversations, narratives and stories from 'the field' often provides the objects around which representations occur (Ahrens and Chapman, 2006). When conducting interpretive research in accounting, Boland and Pondy (1983) note the central role of focusing '...on action in organizational settings...' and the importance of accepting that the '...perspectives of interest are those of the individual actors' (p. 226). These authors further argue that purely subjective interpretations must be overcome (see also Llewellyn, 1993) in the analysis and writing up phase of the research. How this is to be done, however, remains something of a mystery. We claim, following Lillis (2008), that this issue is often taken for granted or left unexplained when interpretive research (in accounting) is written up and discussed (see also Ahrens and Chapman, 2006; Vaivio, 2008).

When defining interpretive (accounting) research, we personally prefer an ontology that stresses the inter-subjective nature of constructions of the world 'out there' and (what may count as) 'reality', and an epistemology that acknowledges that facts and values are interrelated and cannot be separated in a meaningful way, because a researcher is inevitably part of the research and cannot rise above the research and remain encapsulated by it at the same time (Armstrong, 2008; Walsham, 1995, 2006).[1] Hence, we would claim that in the social sciences, research generally tries to develop understandings about (groups of) subjects and the environments (containing other subjects and objects) in which they live, engage and evolve (see also Ahrens, 2008). Consequently, we argue that it needs to be recognized that in interpretive research, methodology, the orientation of the research, and (especially) the researcher are always intimately bound up with method and the research process and can hardly be studied in isolation (Chua, 1986). In this contribution, we focus on research interviews as the main information source in a qualitative study. Of course, there are other information sources available (such as documents, video materials, photographs and oral accounts) that may be used in an interpretive study, possibly in conjunction with interviews. But since interviews seem to be used so prominently in the management accounting literature (Merchant and van der Stede, 2006; Parker, 2012), we feel that a focus on their role is justified.

We proceed as follows. After giving some indication of how frequently research interviews tend to be used in management accounting research, we discuss several perspectives on the research interview as a way to get insights into human interaction and behaviour in organizations. This is what some authors claim is possible, but which is something upon which we cast doubt. We will chiefly use works by David Silverman as an exemplar of this line of thinking. We then analyse several papers that implicitly or explicitly conduct interpretive management accounting research more deeply in 'Management accounting research', and try to assess how far this research follows the aforementioned line of thinking, or attributes more modesty to its research findings. To conclude, the final section sets out what we personally see as viable avenues for engaging in interpretive management accounting research when using research interviews.

The 'trouble' with interviews

Speklé and Kruis (2014) mention that in 2012 and 2013, 29 papers using qualitative or mixed method research (in which one or more qualitative methods were applied) were published in two leading accounting journals (out of a total of 47 empirical papers): *Management Accounting Research* and *Accounting, Organizations & Society*. We found that of these 29 papers, 26 used interviews as an information source. Seventeen of the 26 papers were published in *Management Accounting Research* and nine in *Accounting, Organizations & Society*. Of the 17 papers published in *Management Accounting Research*, nine used research interviews next to other information sources, such as documents, observation and archival 'data' to obtain information about whatever was studied. Eight papers in *Accounting, Organizations & Society* did the same. Nine papers (eight in *Management Accounting Research* and one in *Accounting, Organizations & Society*) solely used research interviews as an information source. We have summarized this in Table 26.1.

Parker (2012), presenting an overview of management accounting research over the last 40 years, states that it is not unusual to find that '...the researcher repeatedly visits the field site(s), employing interview, observation and documentary evidence gathering methods. This is typical of field based case study research...' (p. 58). He also states that by so doing, over time, an influential 'qualitative tradition' has emerged, focusing on '...the understanding and critiquing of management and accounting processes, as well as having the ability to address the concerns of practitioners and policymakers' (p. 54) (see also Merchant and van der Stede, 2006; Vaivio, 2008). This makes it interesting and also imperative to analyse the role of the research interview in the research act more deeply.

Ahrens and Chapman (2006, 2007) are sometimes regarded as important authors who have endorsed or affected the growth of the 'qualitative tradition' mentioned by Parker (2012). They have also often used interviews in their works themselves (in, for instance, Ahrens and Chapman, 2000). In footnote 1 of Ahrens and Chapman (2006), the authors state that they

> ...draw on Silverman's (1993) usage of the term qualitative in relation to methodology, which, in the management accounting literature, has, with minor variations, also been referred to as naturalistic, holistic, interpretive, and phenomenological. It stands in contrast to a positivistic approach to research.
>
> *(p. 819)*

Thereby, Ahrens and Chapman suggest a direct link between qualitative and/or interpretive (accounting) research and Silverman (1993). Therefore, we use this and additional works by

Table 26.1 Method choices in empirical papers in two leading accounting journals (in 2012 and 2013)

	Management Accounting Research	*Accounting, Organizations & Society*
Qualitative research methods	19	10
... in which interviews are used as an information source	17 (9 of which were mixed method designs. One Paper with such a design contained just a single interview)	9 (8 of which were mixed method designs)
Quantitative research methods	12	6
Total	31	16

Silverman as exemplars of how interpretive research could or ought to be conducted.[2] How does he feel about the use of research interviews in qualitative research?[3]

Silverman (2011) notes that when conducting interviews, it is debatable whether 'quality' information will be gained from respondents. He purports that it is, consequently, uncertain what researchers can distil from interviews. It can never be ascertained how far the information received corresponds to how 'goings on' were perceived by different individuals. In another publication, Silverman (1998) suggests that interviews '...neglect a great deal about how people interact. Put more strongly: [interviews] ... are primarily concerned with the environment around the phenomenon rather than the phenomenon itself' (p. 11). Silverman (1997, 1998, 2011) commends the use of 'naturally occurring data' instead: data that are somehow recorded as they occur in real time.[4] This he finds the most viable way in which statements about human interaction can be made through qualitative research, as it allows the analysis of what people in organizations do, instead of what they say they do. Silverman (1997; see also 1998, 2011) posits that in order for qualitative research in the social sciences to be called 'rigorous', criteria for validation and verification have to be upheld.[5] He argues that such criteria are likely to be hampered when interviews are the primary or sole information source used. For instance, Silverman (1997) states that his '...heart sinks whenever [he] ... read[s] yet another "open-ended" interview study claiming to tell it "like it is"' (p. 249), as '...qualitative researchers who want to use the interview to depict the "personal" have ... been deluded' (p. 249), because '[t]he technology of the interview ... generates a type of encounter in which the agenda of questioning and the formulaic patterns of exchange reveal the predictable, in the guise of a private confession' (p. 248; see also Atkinson and Silverman, 1997).

In spite of these strong reservations, Silverman has continued to use interviews himself (Seale and Silverman, 1997) and describes this method extensively in his books, partly due to its popularity across many domains (Silverman, 2011). In the latter publication, it is asserted that something can be gained from interviews anyway when they are carefully coded and meticulously analysed. Nevertheless, Silverman insists that more suitable approaches may be available when the study of human interaction is the focus of the research.

Alvesson (2003, 2010) lists several metaphors along which the research interview can be interpreted. He first distinguishes two overarching metaphors: an interview can either be regarded as a research instrument to obtain valid, accurate information ('the conventional view'), or as a human encounter that takes place in a more complex social (among others, organizational) setting, from which a whole range of (possibly authentic) responses can follow, the 'truthfulness' of which may be hard to determine as the link with revealing things 'as they are' may be difficult or absent. Alvesson then derives eight more detailed metaphors, which are in line with the latter viewpoint on the research interview. These metaphors sketch pragmatically useful re-conceptualizations of such interviews. Examples include seeing the interview as an instance of identity work or impression management, or as resulting from an attempt, by the interviewee, to establish a clear storyline that might make sense to the interviewer (the interviewer may be 'guilty' of doing this him or herself of course; see also De Loo and Lowe, 2012).

Table 26.2 lists some of the characteristics typically associated with the conventional view of the research interview. An example of this view is provided by Argyris and Schön (1974). They assert that people hold mental maps about the actions they undertake. These differ from the maps they relate to when they tell about what they do, for instance in an interview situation. More specifically, Argyris and Schön believe that there is an 'espoused theory' consistent with what people say and a 'theory-in-use', which is in line with what

Table 26.2 Characteristics of the conventional view of the research interview

Main tenet of the conventional view of the research interview	Research interview as a means to transmit and receive knowledge
Associated assumptions and/or requirements	Gathering responses relevant to research question(s) by the interviewer(s)
	After trust has been established with the interviewee(s), so that honest answers will be produced
	Using large quantities of material
	Following strict analysis protocols (involving detailed coding)
	Leading to 'deep' conceptualizations of the interviewee(s)' inner lives and/or social practices
	While maintaining researcher objectivity and neutrality (as far as possible)

Source: Adapted from Alvesson (2003, pp. 15–16).

they do in a particular situation. They assess the former by talking to someone, and the latter by examining what someone does, either through direct observation or through some form of recording that is made when someone takes action. For example, in one organization, Argyris and Schön noted that a management consultant claimed that no matter how large or small the conflict he may have with a manager during a consulting assignment, he would always first bring forward his understanding of the disagreement, and then negotiate, together with the manager, how the disagreement might be resolved. This was his 'espoused theory'. Analysis by the authors of the consultant's behaviour in an actual conflict situation (which was captured on audiotape) suggested, however, that he solely advocated his own point of view when discussing a problem with a manager. Consequently, the consultant seemed to have a different 'theory-in-use'. This, at least, is an illustration of how people perceive or talk about their own actions can be very different from their actual behaviour.

In line with the 'conventional view' of the research interview, Argyris and Schön (1974) believe that interviewees will be upfront about what they do, but when this differs from what is ostensibly done, it is the difference in mental maps that matters in explaining this. Interestingly, Silverman (1998) seems to think similarly. Interviews can only reveal what people *say* they do, not what they 'actually' *do* when having to deal with others. He argues that interviews can only provide '...decontextualized accounts of meanings [that] are very limited guides to the complexities of … interaction' (p. 19).[6] Although someone might also view an interview as a complex situation involving all kinds of interactions, which can thus lead to contextualized accounts of meanings, we agree with Silverman that an interview situation cannot simply be regarded as a 'data gathering session'. On the other hand, Silverman seems to believe that people will endeavour to be upfront about what they do, only inadvertently misstating this. We claim, on the contrary, that even in an interview situation, people might intentionally conceal what they do, as the complexities of the human encounter may be such that information is deliberately withheld or altered (see also Quattrone, 2006). This is in line with seeing an interview as a human encounter where both interviewee and interviewer are, to some extent, playing out roles to keep the interview acceptable for those involved. Table 26.3 summarizes some of the characteristics associated with this metaphor.

Table 26.3 Characteristics of the research interview as a human encounter

Main tenet of the research interview as a human encounter	Research interview as the production of a situated account
Associated assumptions and/or requirements	Gathering responses relevant to research question(s) by the interviewer(s), through active interaction with the interviewee(s) Whose main goal is to help construct a morally acceptable exchange with the interviewer(s) Thus, the interview encounter itself is a social context that warrants analysis At best, local findings will be produced Each interview situation has its own 'flow', which cannot be completely (re)constructed or somehow separated from what may be called the 'knowledge produced' The interviewer as researcher is directly involved in the creation of the accounts produced and their subsequent analysis

Source: Adapted from Alvesson (2003, pp. 16–18).

Illustrations of how the research interview may be seen as a human encounter in a management accounting context have been provided by De Loo and Lowe (2012). The brief vignette that we started this chapter with is in line with this view as well. When an interview is seen as a human encounter, the occurrence of multiple interpretations of whatever is produced is likely, and it depends on the interviewer as researcher, and writer how a statement is finally perceived and included in the research account. He or she is the one who decides how and which meaning(s) is/are ascribed to particular statements (Riessman, 1993). The researcher having such a role is inevitable, in any research project (Armstrong, 2008).

An example highlighting this approach of the research interview would be the following interview quote taken from a UK-based female junior auditor who had recently entered the profession. The auditor had been interviewed by phone by a female colleague of the authors to share her views on an undergraduate course she had recently followed at her university. This was done for an unrelated research project that the female colleague was then engaged in. Near the end of the interview, after a lengthy intervention from the colleague/interviewer, the interviewee suddenly started to talk about her deeper feelings about her current work experience (see also De Loo, Cooper and Manochin, 2015):

> It's quite difficult because they [the interviewee's managers] do actually encourage you to actually, you know, being a team as a whole, stay social together as well, but people have different interests like me. I don't actually ... I prefer after work to sit in my room and read some books, that's my social life ... But the expectations the firm has ... They probably prefer people doing things together so that's why I think it's quite difficult for, shall I say, certain types of people.

This statement may be seen as an instance of identity work, where the interviewee pitches her own views on how she would like to run her private life (which she prefers to be quiet) against what she believes her managers desire (hanging out together with other junior auditors after work). Although this may well be a truthful account, it is likely that it would never have been told if the interviewer had not shared some of her own experiences on how she tried to balance her professional and private lives before.[7] Consequently, the interviewee's statement may also be regarded as an attempt to please or accommodate the interviewer by putting forward a personal account. It is impossible to tell which interpretation is to be preferred or to be taken as more truthful or relevant. Both interpretations could apply, and in this instance, elements of both may apply at the same time.

Although Silverman (1997) acknowledges the researcher's role in the conduct and writing up of a research project, he seems to take the view that it is not very useful to go into great lengths analysing it. He suggests that while this may lead to interesting discussions among researchers, it will not likely be of interest to others. Silverman argues that he strives for a 'minimalist aesthetic' in the research act, focusing on clarity and rigor in its conduct, with a 'passionate commitment' to beauty and truth (see ibid., p. 240/244 for more detailed statements about this). In particular, a focus on research method can help to evaluate the quality of someone's research, using, for instance, conversation or discourse analysis techniques (Benwell and Stokoe, 2006). By so doing, a '... kind of social science which seeks to make practical interventions which might make social institutions more efficient or effective' can be advocated (Silverman, 1997, p. 246). Silverman's argument, therefore, seems to be that rigor in research can be reached by a focus on research method, and by the effectuation of the research outcomes through their correspondence to what 'really' goes on when people interact.

In so doing, Silverman (1998, 2011) decides to use terminology that is commensurate with positivism when setting out his point of view (Kalekin-Fishman, 2001; see also ten Have, 2008), but decides to adapt their definition as he goes (Seale and Silverman, 1997). For example, expressions like validity, verification, reliability and generalizability are all present in his work. Positivism (and also certain stances on realism) draws its appeal, in part, from its determination to ignore '... the ontological discontinuity between natural and social phenomena [and] leave its representations unreflexive and unproblematical' (Knights, 1995, p. 248). Although Silverman (1998) states that he does not regard himself as a positivist, and acknowledges that there is no generally accepted 'doctrine' supporting qualitative research, he does choose to adopt positivist or realist epithets (the ones mentioned above). In the case of Silverman (1998), this suggests that somewhere down the line, he believes that unreflexive and unproblematical representations of research can be made. If not, his use of these expressions is at the very least misleading (see also Kalekin-Fishman, 2001).

As Silverman (1998, 2011) spends a lot of time on describing approaches to meticulously transcribe and analyse 'data', it is clear that he sees this as an important element of how to achieve less problematical research outcomes. He also asserts that engaging in these analytical methods can give rise to more effective and/or efficient working practices in the research process (Silverman, 1997). We disagree with such a view. Methods do not contain some neutral observational language, and observations made by a researcher are imbued by his or her assumptions and values and cannot be 'superimposed' on working practices to make them more effective ... just like that. A researcher is an epistemic subject by definition (Johnson, 1995). Acknowledging this makes Silverman's (1997) adherence to 'truth', which is to be reached through verification and validation by a succinct application of research methods unattainable. It has been argued that researchers could try to assess their role in the research act by engaging in reflexive practices (Alvesson and Sköldberg, 2000). But this would still not lead to the purging of the definitive and necessarily partial role played by the researcher in the research that has been conducted (Dambrin and Lambert, 2012).

Nevertheless, if someone decides to engage in reflexive practices, '... it is important to consider what kind of ... self-reflection might form a basis...' of this (Johnson, 1995, p. 487). Kilduff and Mehra (1997) address five aspects, which they call 'problematics', that we believe could help researchers in determining their own position in such a debate. Kilduff and Mehra think that these 'problematics' are not often covered in research papers for they do not conform to generally accepted publication standards. The 'problematics' the authors distinguish are as follows[8]:

- The plausibility of meta-narratives (Lyotard, 1984). Do overall conceptual schemes, describing how 'the world' 'works', exist or not? If they exist, under which circumstances can they be established?
- The relation between truth and fiction (Weick, 1995; see also Knorr-Cetina, 1999; Latour, 2005). Is truth fixed, or rather, dependent on social conventions, context and/or language?
- The relation between object and subject (Clifford and Marcus, 1986; see also Ahrens, 2008; Cunliffe, 2011). Is someone willing to view scientific work as involving interpretation, which is laden with conventions and taken-for-granted assumptions? If so, (how) can such conventions and assumptions be scrutinized?
- The effect of writing style on how scientific endeavours are perceived (Riessman, 1993; see also De Loo and Lowe, 2012; Latour, 2005). How far is someone willing to accept that aesthetical considerations can affect the value of the empirical work that is done, and how it is viewed by others?
- The possibilities of having progress in science (Kuhn, 1970; see also Flyvbjerg, 2001). Is empirical generalizability feasible or is this, rather, a myth, as more research only leads to more questions?

Kilduff and Mehra (1997) claim that the implicit or explicit stances researchers take on the 'problematics' influence the way they conduct and relate to research. These stances are, however, hardly ever discussed or written about. We feel that opening up these debates (perhaps in a way similar to Ahrens *et al.*, 2008) could foster better understandings about what research might achieve, given that researchers are always necessarily actively involved in the research process.

Management accounting research

Defining interpretive research

At this point of our contribution, we would like to analyse some contributions to the interpretive management accounting literature more closely. Following Chua (1986), we accept that the 'interpretive' label relates to a specific paradigm, setting out particular takes on the ontological, epistemological and methodological viewpoints used in a research project. We discuss these issues in detail below with particular reference to the role of the research interview in interpretive research.

Furthermore, we would like to emphasize that the 'qualitative' label operates at the level of research methodologies (see also Myers, 2009; Richardson, 2012). Hence, the expressions 'interpretive' and 'qualitative' play a role at different levels of abstraction (when discussing paradigms), contrary to what Ahrens and Chapman (2006) think. Among others, this view is reinforced by Lee and Lings (2008), who note in distinguishing methodology that '... it is important to never confuse *interpretive* with *qualitative*, as is often done. Simply saying a piece of research is qualitative does not imply it is also interpretive, and conversely saying you are an interpretive researcher is not the same as saying you use only qualitative data. Never make that mistake …' (p. 65, emphasis in original).

In the management accounting literature, one of the most prominent papers that aimed to describe what interpretive research in accounting entails is Ahrens *et al.* (2008). Alas, the paper failed to come up with a description that all the authors involved endorsed. The information systems (IS) literature, which regularly addresses aspects of management control, offers several influential papers on an acceptable conception of interpretive research (Klein and Myers, 1999; Walsham, 1995, 2006).[9] We accept that these papers focus on case research and field studies, which do not comprise all research methods that may be used in (interpretive) research (Myers, 2009). The authors of the papers acknowledge that what someone decides to call 'knowledge' and/or 'reality' in interpretive research is one's own construction. It is neither necessary nor likely that what is concluded on the basis of such research is some direct manifestation of the world 'out there'. Walsham (1995) formulates this as follows: '[i]nterpretive researchers are not saying to the reader that they are reporting facts; instead, they are reporting their interpretations of other people's interpretations' (p. 78). This basic principle of interpretive research also informs the evaluation criteria for interpretive field studies that Klein and Myers (2009) present (based on an application of hermeneutic methods). The involvement of the researcher in the research act, as well as the impossibility of describing exactly what this involvement looks like, is evident from their criteria. They carefully address key interactions that exist between researcher(s) and subject(s) of the research; that these interactions may affect subjects' subsequent interpretations and interactions; and that there may be multiple interpretations of the same situation and materials, which a researcher can only try to make sense of (see also Alvesson, 2003).

Walsham (1995, 2006) argues that despite much effort to clarify the role of the researcher in interpretive research, it remains difficult to pin down exactly what it entails. There are many research methods that can be applied (in fact, no method is deemed unacceptable). Interpretive research is likely to use some form of research interviews as an information source at some stage of the research. Walsham (1995) does say that interpretive research clearly deviates from positivistic research. He also states that if someone wishes to describe it in its broadest terms, he or she has to combine specific views on ontology, epistemology, the role of the researcher in the research act (which is chiefly part of a study's methodology), and what may count as 'valuable' research deliverables. In short, one needs to adhere to a (broadly defined) paradigm (see also Chua, 1986; Guba, 1990). Although, as we have indicated, Walsham (1995, 2006) is very specific about the role of the researcher in the research act, and also turns out to be specific about what may count as deliverables from such research, he is much less specific about the combination(s) of ontology and epistemology that interpretive researchers can apply.

Let us consider first what Walsham (1995) sees as potentially valuable contributions from interpretive research. He lists four possible contributions: the development of concepts, the generation of theories, the drawing of specific implications (from specific settings) and the contribution of 'rich' insights (in a phenomenon or situation). It is argued that all of these contributions are provisional at best. They are constructions that are based on insights from the researcher(s) that they have distilled from information gathered in specific contexts during a specific period. One cannot say that these insights are stable or applicable across multiple contexts and/or time periods. Hence, they do not possess predictive qualities (these can only be attributed retrospectively), but summarize what a researcher thinks he or she has

Table 26.4 Tenets of interpretive research

Tenet	*Description*
Ontology	Many possibilities, but certainly *not* a reality that exists independently of constructions from the researcher(s)
Epistemology	Many possibilities, but certainly *not* one that allows facts to be distinguished from values
Role of the researcher	A researcher is very much involved in the research. His or her interpretations cannot be fully removed from the research at any stage
Research deliverables	The (provisional) development of concepts, the generation of theories, the drawing of specific implications, and/or the contribution of rich insights

Source: Adapted from Walsham (1995, 2006).

witnessed and/or concluded in a particular situation. Others may endorse these insights and combine them with their own, or not. In Walsham (2006), suggestions are provided on how to write up and report on interpretive research.

As indicated above, Walsham (1995) is much less specific about the combination(s) of ontology and epistemology that, he thinks, are useful or warranted in interpretive research. He does point out that various different combinations are possible. He argues that the only combination that is not allowed in interpretive research is an ontology that regards the world 'out there' as something concrete that can be apprehended directly through research, without constructions by the researcher(s), and an epistemology that asserts that facts and values can be derived with certainty. Hence, Walsham (1995) questions whether research contributions must be based on facts. However, this is exactly what authors such as Silverman (2011) suggest is possible as long as the analysis has been carried out meticulously.

We have summarized Walsham's (1995, 2006) definition of interpretive research in Table 26.4.

How far are the notions depicted in Table 26.4 reflected in several well-known management accounting papers that are said to be 'interpretive'? We examine this below.

Assessing interpretive accounting research

We took the tenets of interpretive research listed in Table 26.4 and tried to assess the extent to which several sample papers conformed to/applied these tenets.

We have selected, and discuss below, two interpretive accounting papers that we regard as good illustrations of how these tenets might be best understood. Both look at the consequences of national policy reforms, but at different levels of analysis: Chiwamit, Modell and Yang (2014) and Ezzamel, Robson and Stapleton (2012). The former paper analyses how attempts were made by various key agents to get Economic Value Added (EVA™) institutionalized as a governance mechanism in state-owned organizations (SOEs) in China and Thailand; the latter contains empirical research on the introduction of specific budgeting practices in situations of competing institutional logics in educational organizations in the UK. The Ezzamel, Robson and Stapleton paper was chosen from among the sample papers reported in Table 26.1. The Chiwamit, Modell and Yang (2014) paper was selected since it focused on a similar topic as the Ezzamel, Robson and Stapleton (2012) paper, but at a different level of analysis. The paper, as we will demonstrate, also takes a very different view of what constitutes interpretive research. Our summary analysis is provided below.

Chiwamit, Modell and Yang (2014)

As stated by Chiwamit, Modell and Yang (2014), their paper seeks to explain how EVA™ came to be promoted by both the Chinese and Thai governments as an important governance mechanism for their SOEs ... and how the related (contestable and fragile) institutionalization processes unfolded. The authors study the political, technical and cultural (institutional) works involved in these processes, at what they describe as the field (country) level. An earlier paper (Yang and Modell, 2013), as well as a later one (Yang and Modell, 2015), focuses on the associated institutionalization process in a local, Chinese governmental organization.

The authors see EVA™ as being part of a larger, social movement on shareholder value, which they link up with broader, neo-liberal concerns about deregulation. Through their research, Chiwamit, Modell and Yang (2014) wish to give some indication of the societal relevance of management accounting innovations (which they perceive EVA™ to be), and how it came to be involved in the generation and maintenance of field cohesiveness in the two countries.[10] Clearly, this is no small claim.

In their empirical analysis, the authors emphasize field-level differences, commonalities, and challenges related to the institutionalization of EVA™. Country-specific variations in political systems, capital market developments and the influence of consulting firms, including Stern Stewart, are singled out in the research. The analysis is chiefly based on interview material collected between 2009 and 2012 in the course of two unnamed and apparently expansive projects. Especially in Thailand, a broad range of interviewees was selected, as more actors turned out to be relevant in shaping and changing the institutional field than in China (where mainly government officials were interviewed). Documents and other working materials were used to corroborate findings that predate the periods of the research. 'Key' interviewees (in the eyes of the researchers) were interviewed more than once. A loosely structured interview guide was used, focusing on specific themes Chiwamit, Modell and Yang wished to examine. In Thailand, most interviews were recorded and transcribed. In China, in order to make interviewees feel comfortable, the researchers decided upfront to take only notes/summaries. These were subsequently compiled into records of individual interviews.

Two extensive narratives are presented in the paper, immediately after the research design has been described, addressing the institutional work involved in embedding EVA™ in Chinese and Thai SOEs. These narratives are written up with great certainty, even though it is not indicated at all how they emerged so specifically from the (chiefly interview) material. The same holds for the conclusions that are drawn. Just one example of the level of certainty involved in the writing up of the research appears in the following sentence: '[s]imilarly, in the Thai field, EVA™ was initially mobilised as a means of facilitating large-scale privatization by a group of dominant political actors with strongly vested, economic interests in pursuing such a reform programme rather than favouring global, capital markets' interests' (Chiwamit, Modell and Yang, 2014, p. 170). There are many similar sentences throughout the analysis.

By writing up the narratives in this way, and (implicitly) suggesting that these comprise unequivocal interpretations of the materials collected,[11] Chiwamit, Modell and Yang seem to be mixing elements of the two metaphors on how to view the research interview from

Alvesson (2003, 2010). On the one hand, they did not indulge in excessive coding, or used strict interview guides. This is in line with the view of the research interview set out in Table 26.3. In addition, they decided not to record some interviews, which suggests that they treated these as human encounters in a complex setting. This also supports the views in Table 26.3. However, by presenting their findings without further elaboration on the interpretation process, and by doing this in an uncompromising manner, there is an implication that the interviews yielded a transmission of knowledge, and that any researcher (certainly those involved in this particular project) would have come up with the same narrative (which would imply researcher neutrality and invest him or her with substantial perceptive powers). This would be in line with the take on the research interview in Table 26.2. It also suggests that the authors believe that somewhere down the line, (partially) unproblematic representations of research findings can be made. This does not gel very well with the fleeting and value-imbued nature of the materials that form the basis of the research findings from interpretive research. This notion of the construction of interpretive research findings is among its principal tenets (as shown in Table 26.4).

Even though we find the narratives presented by Chiwamit, Modell and Yang (2014) compelling, we think that through their research design, they (inadvertently) suggest that they somehow have the 'power' to combine particular elements of interpretive research (that they choose) with a positivist or realist take on methodology. We find this rather doubtful, and would not be inclined to follow this kind of reasoning ourselves, or recommend it – as part of an interpretive research design … despite the paper's strengths.

Ezzamel, Robson and Stapleton (2012)

Ezzamel, Robson and Stapleton (2012) contains a case study carried out across a number of educational institutions in the UK, in which the implementation of specific budgeting practices is studied. The authors report the context as reflecting competing institutional logics. The paper ends with the identification of four theoretical insights on how logics (may) affect budget practices. We find the theory section convincing and well written. The authors take some liberties in regard to the selling of somewhat dated empirical material. More specifically, they say that '[t]he empirical cases, studied in two phases in the 1990s and in 2011, explore tensions that emerged between the new business logic, prevailing professional logic, and governance logic in the education field' (Ezzamel, Robson and Stapleton, 2012, p. 281). The phases the authors mention cover the 1993–2011 period: from 1993 to 1999 and the year 2011. It is argued that these phases needed to be discerned in order to study '… the intervention of budgetary techniques in the field of school education in the UK occasioned by the 1988 Education Reform Act' (p. 300). But exactly why *these* phases had to be examined remains unclear.

This deficiency, however, does not affect the broad appeal of the paper. It may reasonably be seen as an exemplar of 'good practice' in interpretive (and qualitative) research. The authors are very clear about the fact that they study meanings, which may be volatile and fleeting. Several interviews with a variety of staff members (including in finance, education and treasury) in the institutions were conducted to find these. Thereby, Ezzamel, Robson and Stapleton (2012) seem to adhere to Alvesson's (2003) second metaphor as to how to interpret the (outcomes of the) research interview (summarized in Table 26.3). In addition, to corroborate their findings, the authors note that several meetings were attended to see how discussions about budget practices evolved. The interviews were fully transcribed and analysed using CAQDAS. In the paper, reference is made to Silverman (1993) in passing, when the coding process is described, and the authors say that they derived some unique codes based purely on the interview material.

A coding list was developed iteratively (using base codes drawn from previous literature, theoretical insights and insights gained during the interview process), after which each interview was coded separately by each researcher. A meeting was held to overcome differences in coding and interpretation. The authors say that the changes that had to be made during the meeting were minimal. Thereafter, themes were developed that superseded the codes that had been developed, using grounded theory principles.

The reference to grounded theory principles may be a little surprising in an interpretive context since they include an emphasis on verification (Alvesson and Sköldberg, 2000). Goulding (1998) asserts that grounded theory does fit interpretive research, as the meaning of the materials that are collected in 'the field' (for example through research interviews) tends to be analysed by researchers. Verification should, she believes, consequently not be seen as correspondence to some concrete reality 'out there', but correspondence to at least some opinions of the respondents who are part of the research. Partially therefore, Goulding argues that researchers should refrain from excessive coding and 'forcing' codes on selected pieces of text. The interpretations involved in grounded theory go much further than that. For example, researchers have an active role in how codes come about and interpretations unfold. In addition, interpretations may change as the research progresses.

What Ezzamel, Robson and Stapleton (2012) present are clearly their shared interpretations of the budgeting practices at hand, resulting in the (also, shared) theoretical propositions with which the paper ends. The interpretations presented also take a prominent place in the writing style of the paper, in which the 'we'-form is used often. A telling example of this is when the authors say that '[o]ur study highlighted what *we saw* as the prevalence of three key institutional logics operating in the key organizations we studied in the field of education' (Ezzamel, Robson and Stapleton, ibid., p. 299, emphasis added). Hence, we feel they indicate that their findings and propositions are firmly their own. All this serves to indicate that the main tenets of interpretive research listed in Table 26.4 seem to be followed.

Differences in interpretation, however minimal they may have been, are not fleshed out further in the paper. Even though the interviews are coded, the authors indicate that the coding list came about iteratively, which highlights that this also involved interpretation … despite the link with Silverman (1993). Of course, coding cannot precede interpretation in interpretive research, and Ezzamel, Robson and Stapleton certainly do not suggest this.[12]

To conclude, we have the impression that the Ezzamel, Robson and Stapleton (2012) paper 'breathes' interpretive research throughout, in which the role of the researcher in the research act shines through very clearly. We would like to offer this paper as an example of interpretive research that fits our own views.

To conclude

In this chapter, we argue that researchers need to be more cognisant of the limitations and constraints of their theoretical, methodological and philosophical frameworks when conducting interpretive research. We also put the view that the use of particular (qualitative) methods or information sources alone does not define whether an interpretive research project has been carried out. Other factors must be present to make this determination. For instance, Schutz (1972) asserts that researchers, when conducting interpretive research, are often seeking to uncover innate structures guiding human behaviour by being attentive and engaging in 'deep' probing. These structures may be temporary and may differ between research settings, but they can be distilled nevertheless (Vaivio, 2008). This is a view that can also be found in Ahrens and Chapman (2006). Such research can allegedly help to build a bridge between 'theory' and 'practice' (Baldvinsdottir, Mitchell and Nørreklit, 2010; Malmi and Granlund, 2009). The position adopted by researchers supporting this stance is close to that of authors such as Silverman (1997, 1998, 2011), who supports similar aims for qualitative research. Therefore, not surprisingly, Silverman is invoked directly by some management accounting researchers, including Ahrens and Chapman (2006). In contrast, we have argued that using positivist epithets to describe interpretive research practices and aims (which is very much lurking in the background when this position is adopted) is confusing (see also Armstrong, 2008; Lillis, 2008; Richardson, 2012).

Sandelands (1998) asserts that since the 'world' is 'eternally' unfinished and incomplete, it follows that it is better to have theories and/or research findings that are unfinished, possibly ambiguous, and alive with questions than finished, dead theories that presume to provide answers to questions which invalidate it. Theories are, we believe, constructions generated by the subjectivity of human meanings (see also Bernstein, 1983). In ethnographic research,[13] passing judgement on which practices are worthy of exploration, and the interpretation and framing of these in terms of a 'theory', are a reflection of an ethnographer's observation of daily conventions. Thus, the values and ideology of the observer implicitly become part of the selection of views and insights for the production of an ethnographic account. The subjective representations that result from such processes have been the object of censure by those preoccupied with the search for scientific 'truth', suggesting that such social facts are mere human fabrications. Yet, few would claim that (even) positivist methodologies have been entirely successful in eliminating bias from experimentation and research design (Bonoma, 1985). Smith (1991), for instance, argues that while scientific inquiry claims to '… annihilate the scientist's viewpoint through the separation of the producer of the statement and the procedure whereby it is produced..., [there is] no magic trick that may bypass the act of interpretation' (p. 147). Gouldner (1970) argues that '… positivism premises that [the] self is treacherous and that, so long as it remains in contact with the information system, its primary effect is to bias or distort it' (p. 495). He goes on to claim that '… the assumption that the self can be sealed off from information systems is mythological' (ibid.). Indeed, this analogy is embraced by ethnographers, who argue that the human world can only be known in subjective human terms. We would claim that an argument such as this deserves wider recognition in the management accounting literature.

Knights (1995) recommends researchers to dispense with the illusion of neutrality that many academics seek to cultivate around their activities. A number of writers have discussed how greater modesty might be brought into the execution and reporting of research. In so doing, some authors emphasize the significance of narrative styles of writing (Czarniawska, 1998; Deetz, 1996; Van Maanen, 1996), while others introduce aspects of multivocality (Linstead, 1993; see also Hopper and Bui, 2015) or problematize the boundaries between theory and method (Burrell, 1997; Jacques, 1992). We would suggest that such issues might be brought to the fore more explicitly in interpretive accounting research. We firmly believe that the entanglement (Geertz, 1988; Weick, 1995) of the researcher in the research act cannot be circumvented. It makes all research inherently subjective (Armstrong, 2008). Neither by an appeal on method nor by an appeal to someone's skills or insights, is there any way that it can be ascertained that research outcomes correspond to some reality that is 'out there', or can make such a correspondence with this reality more effective or efficient. The brief vignette we provided at the beginning of this chapter may therefore be illustrative to the present discussion. For most, if not all research in the social sciences it may be that instead of distilling 'hard facts' that are somewhere 'out there', distilling interpretations, partly based on someone else's interpretations, that can be shared with others, is the best researchers can do when engaging in research and constructing our research stories (Geertz, 1988; Knights, 1995; Weick, 1995).

Notes

1 In section 'Management accounting research', we will see that this view on interpretive research is aligned with broader views on what this research entails. Since Walsham (1995) finds it valuable to set out one's views on interpretive research at the beginning of a research contribution, we decided to follow his approach.
2 We could also have referred to works from other authors, like Eisenhardt (1989, 1991) and Yin (1989), even though these do not focus on the research interview per se.
3 Later in this contribution, we will argue that the expressions 'qualitative' and 'interpretive' ought not to be mixed in the way that Ahrens and Chapman (2006) suggest.
4 In doing so, Silverman seems to neglect that what is called 'data' is determined by the researcher.
5 Silverman (1998) positions himself as an interpretive sociologist. In interpretive sociology (Schutz, 1972), it is often argued that experiences are labelled as such and are infused with subjective meanings through the self-interpretation of the person who lives them. At the time that they occur, experiences do not represent distinct events. They are arranged as such retrospectively. The associated meanings may then be used prospectively for interpretation purposes in the research process or indeed in everyday life. Silverman has a specific take on what this may (ultimately) yield. This take will be addressed at the end of section 'The "trouble" with interviews'.
6 In this particular segment, Silverman talks about human-computer interaction.
7 This is what the interviewer said right before the interviewee expressed the quote above: "... [E]specially sometimes, you know, it is in the early career steps that everything becomes so intense, but do not change, be who you are and then you could make a difference from where you are. Sometimes, we try to adjust ourselves to the conditions, but when things are like the jungle, what do you have to adjust yourself into? Just be yourself and keep your eyes open and you can make a difference I think". This rather personal statement may have prompted the interviewee to state her own ideas on the matter.
8 Alvesson (2003) notes that Silverman, on almost all of Kilduff and Mehra's (1997) 'problematics', tends to emphasize '... ideals such as accumulation of knowledge, objectivity, the possibility of and very precise demands for representation, a clear writing style, and the possibility of generalization' (Alvesson, 2003, p. 17).
9 To our knowledge, such overview papers on interpretive accounting research are pretty much absent, with the possible exception of Hopper and Bui (2015). However, they do not explicitly define the term. Parker (2012) contains an overview of what he calls the 'qualitative tradition' in accounting research, but as stated earlier, the expressions 'interpretive' and 'qualitative' ought not to be mixed.
10 Note that this involves two different connotations of what may be called 'social' or 'society'.
11 The authors do indicate that they applied a 'comparative case logic' to see if their theoretical framework, which is based on neo-institutional theories, was sufficiently extensive, but make a reference to Eisenhardt (1989) in doing so. She is not known to be a great supporter of interpretive research.
12 Otherwise, we would fall back into the danger of believing that 'facts' are revealed in the research, which would contrast Table 26.4.
13 Because of its engagement with '...how society gets put together...' (Garfinkel, 1974, p. 16), ethnography is a process of analytical description and interpretation by an observer constructing meanings of how a group of people order their lives.

References

Ahrens, T., 2008. Overcoming the subjective-objective divide in interpretive management accounting research. *Accounting, Organizations and Society*. 33, 2, 292–297.
Ahrens, T., Becker, A., Burns, J., Chapman, C., Granlund, M., Habersam, M., Hansen, A., Malmi, T., Rihab, K., Mennicken, A., Mikes, A., Panozzo, F., Piber, M., Quattrone, P., Scheytt, T., 2008.

The future of interpretive accounting research: a polyphonic debate. *Critical Perspectives on Accounting*. 19, 8, 840–866.
Ahrens, T., Chapman, C.S., 2000. Occupational identity of management accountants in Britain and Germany. *European Accounting Review*. 9, 4, 477–498.
Ahrens, T., Chapman, C.S., 2006. Doing qualitative field research in management accounting: positioning data to contribute to theory. *Accounting, Organizations and Society*. 31, 8, 819–841.
Ahrens, T., Chapman, C.S., 2007. Management accounting as practice. *Accounting, Organizations and Society*. 32, 1, 1–27.
Alvesson, M., 2003. Beyond neo-positivists, romantics and localists: a reflexive approach to organizational research. *Academy of Management Review*. 28, 1, 13–33.
Alvesson, M., 2010. *Interpreting interviews*. London: Sage.
Alvesson, M., Sköldberg, K., 2000. *Reflexive methodology: new vistas for qualitative research*. Los Angeles: Sage.
Argyris, C., Schön, D., 1974. *Theory in practice: increasing professional effectiveness*. San Francisco: Jossey-Bass.
Armstrong, P., 2008. Calling out for more: comment on the future of interpretive accounting research. *Critical Perspectives on Accounting*. 19, 8, 867–879.
Atkinson, P., Silverman, D., 1997. Kundera's immortality: the interview society and the invention of the self. *Qualitative Inquiry*. 3, 3, 304–325.
Baldvinsdottir, G., Mitchell, F., Nørreklit, H., 2010. Issues in the relationship between theory and practice in management accounting. *Management Accounting Research*. 21, 2, 79–82.
Benwell, B., Stokoe, E., 2006. *Discourse and identity*. Edinburgh: Edinburgh University Press.
Bernstein, R.J., 1983. *Beyond objectivism and relativism: science, hermeneutics, and praxis*. Philadelphia: University of Pennsylvania Press.
Boland, R.J., Pondy, L.R., 1983. Accounting in organizations: toward a union of rational and natural perspectives. *Accounting, Organizations and Society*. 8, 2/3, 223–234.
Bonoma, T.V., 1985. Case research in marketing: opportunities, problems and a process. *Journal of Marketing Research*. XXII, 199–208.
Burns, R., 1994. *Introduction to research methods*. Melbourne: Longman (2nd edition).
Burns, J., Vaivio, J., 2001. Management accounting change. *Management Accounting Research*. 12, 4, 389–402.
Burrell, G., 1997. *Pandemonium: towards a retro-organization theory*. London: Sage.
Chiwamit, P., Modell, S., Yang, C., 2014. The societal relevance of management accounting innovations: economic value added and institutional work in the fields of Chinese and Thai state-owned enterprises. *Accounting and Business Research*. 44, 2, 144–180.
Chua, W.F., 1986. Radical developments in accounting thought. *The Accounting Review*. 61, 4, 601–632.
Clifford, J., Marcus, G., 1986. *Writing culture: the poetics and politics of ethnography*. Berkeley: University of California Press.
Cunliffe, A.L., 2011. Crafting qualitative research: Morgan and Smircich 30 years on. *Organizational Research Methods*. 14, 4, 647–673.
Czarniawska, B., 1998. *A narrative approach to organization studies*. Thousand Oaks: Sage (Qualitative Research Methods Series, No. 43).
Dambrin, C., Lambert, C., 2012. Who is she and who are we? A reflexive journey in research into the rarity of women in the highest ranks of accountancy. *Critical Perspectives on Accounting*. 23, 1, 1–16.
De Loo, I., Cooper, S., Manochin, M., 2015. Enhancing the transparency of accounting research: the case of narrative analysis. *Qualitative Research in Accounting and Management*. 12, 1, 34–54.
De Loo, I., Lowe, A., 2012. Author-itative interpretation in understanding accounting practice through case research. *Management Accounting Research*. 23, 1, 3–16.
Deetz, S., 1996. Crossroads: describing differences in approaches to organization science. Rethinking Burrell and Morgan and their legacy. *Organization Science*. 7, 2, 191–207.
Eisenhardt, K.M., 1989. Building theories from case research. *Academy of Management Review*. 14, 4, 532–550.
Eisenhardt K.M., 1991. Better stories and better constructs: the case for rigor and Academy of Management. *The Academy of Management Review*. 16, 3; 620–627.
Ezzamel, M., Robson, K., Stapleton, P., 2012. The logics of budgeting: theorization and practice variation in the educational field. *Accounting, Organizations & Society*. 37, 5, 281–303.
Flyvbjerg, B., 2001. *Making social science matter*. Cambridge: Cambridge University Press.

Garfinkel, H., 1974. The origins of the term ethnomethodology. In: R. Turner (Ed.). *Ethnomethodology: selected readings*. Harmondsworth: Penguin, 69–81.

Geertz, C., 1988. *Works and lives: the anthropologist as an author*. Stanford: Stanford University Press.

Goulding, C., 1998. Grounded theory: the missing methodology on the interpretivist agenda. *Qualitative Market Research: An International Journal*. 1, 1, 50–57.

Gouldner, A.W., 1970. *The coming crisis of Western sociology*. New York: Basic Books.

Guba, E.G., 1990. The alternative paradigm dialog. In: Guba. E.G. (Ed.). *The paradigm dialog*. London: Sage, 17–27.

Hopper, T., Bui, B., 2015. Has management accounting research been critical? (Paper presented at the 25th anniversary of management accounting research. London School of Economics, London, April 17, 2015).

Jacques, R., 1992. Critique and theory building: producing knowledge 'from the kitchen'. *Academy of Management Review*. 17, 3, 582–606.

Johnson, P., 1995. Towards an epistemology for radical accounting: beyond objectivism and relativism. *Critical Perspectives on Accounting*. 6, 6, 485–509.

Kalekin-Fishman, D., 2001. Review: David Silverman 2001. Interpreting qualitative data: methods for analysing talk, text and interaction. *Forum Qualitative Sozialforschung/Forum: Qualitative Social Research*. 2, 3, Art. 6. (Refer to www.qualitativeresearch.net/fqs-texte/3-01/3-01review-kalekin-e.htm).

Kilduff, M., Mehra, A., 1997. Postmodernism and organisational research. *Academy of Management Review*. 22, 2, 453–481.

Klein, H.K., Myers, M.D., 1999. A set of principles for conducting and evaluating interpretive field studies in information systems. *MIS Quarterly*. 23, 1, 67–93.

Knights, D., 1995. Refocusing the case study: the politics of research and researching politics in IT management. *Technology Studies*. 2, 2, 230–254.

Knorr-Cetina, K., 1999. *Epistemic cultures: how the sciences make knowledge*. Cambridge: Harvard University Press.

Kuhn, T.S., 1970. *The structure of scientific revolutions*. Chicago: The University of Chicago Press (2nd edition).

Latour, B., 2005. *Reassembling the social: an introduction to actor-network-theory*. Oxford: Oxford University Press.

Lee, N., Lings, I., 2008. *Doing business research*. London: Sage.

Lillis, A., 2008. Qualitative management accounting research: rationale, pitfalls and potential. A comment on Vaivio (2008). *Qualitative Research in Accounting & Management*. 5, 3, 239–246.

Linstead, S., 1993. From postmodern anthropology to deconstructive ethnography. *Human Relations*. 46, 1, 97–120.

Llewellyn, S., 1993. Working in hermeneutic circles in management accounting research: some implications and applications. *Management Accounting Research*. 4, 3, 231–249.

Lyotard, J., 1984. *The postmodern condition: a report on knowledge*. Minneapolis: University of Minnesota Press.

Malmi, T., Granlund, M., 2009. In search of management accounting theory. *European Accounting Review*. 18, 3, 597–620.

Merchant, K.A., van der Stede, W.A., 2006. Field-based research in accounting: accomplishments and prospects. *Behavioural Research in Accounting*. 18, 117–134.

Mounce, H.O., 1997. *The two pragmatisms: from Peirce to Rorty*. London: Routledge.

Myers, M.D., 2009. *Qualitative research in business and management*. Los Angeles: Sage.

Parker, L.D., 2012. Qualitative management accounting research: assessing deliverables and relevance. *Critical Perspectives on Accounting*. 23, 1, 54–70.

Quattrone, P., 2006. The possibility of the testimony: a case for case study research. *Organization*. 13, 1, 143–157.

Richardson, A.J., 2012. Paradigms, theory and management accounting practice. *Critical Perspectives on Accounting*. 23, 1, 83–88.

Riessman, C.K., 1993. *Narrative analysis*. Thousand Oaks: Sage (Qualitative Research Methods, No. 30).

Rorty, R., 1979. *Philosophy and the mirror of nature*. Princeton: Princeton University Press.

Sandelands, L., 1998. *Feeling the form in social life*. Lanham: Rowman and Littlefield.

Schutz, A., 1972. *The phenomenology of the social world*. London: Heinemann.

Seale, C., Silverman, D., 1997. Ensuring rigor in qualitative research. *European Journal of Public Health*. 7, 4, 379–384.
Silverman, D., 1993. *Interpreting qualitative data: methods for analysing talk, text and interaction*. London: Sage.
Silverman, D., 1997. *Qualitative research: theory, method and practice*. London: Sage.
Silverman, D., 1998. Qualitative research: meanings or practices? *Information Systems Journal*. 8, 1, 3–20.
Silverman D., 2011. *Interpreting qualitative data: methods for analysing talk, text and interaction* (3rd edition). London: Sage.
Smith, N.C., 1991. The case-study: a vital yet misunderstood research method for management. In: N.C. Smith, Dainty, P. (Eds.). *The management research handbook*. London: Routledge, 145–158.
Søberg, M., 2005. The Duhem-Quine thesis and experimental economics: a reinterpretation. *Journal of Economic Methodology*. 12, 4, 581–597.
Speklé, R.F., Kruis, A., 2014. Management control research: a review of current developments. In: Otley, D.T., Soin, K. (Eds.). *Management control and uncertainty*. London: Palgrave, 30–46.
ten Have, P., 2008. Review: David Silverman (2006). Interpreting qualitative data: methods for analysing talk, text and interaction (3rd edition). *Forum Qualitative Sozialforschung/Forum: Qualitative Social Research*. 9, 1, Art. 16. (Refer to http://nbn-resolving.de/urn:nbn:de:0114-fqs0801160).
Vaivio, J., 2008. Qualitative management accounting research: rationale, pitfalls and potential. *Qualitative Research in Accounting & Management*. 5, 1, 64–86.
Van Maanen, J., 1996. Commentary: on the matter of voice. *Journal of Management Inquiry*. 5, 4, 375–381.
Walsham, G., 1995. Interpretive case studies in IS research: nature and method. *European Journal of Information Systems*. 4, 2, 74–81.
Walsham, G., 2006. Doing interpretive research. *European Journal of Information Systems*. 15, 3, 320–330.
Weick, K.E., 1995. *Sensemaking in organizations*. London: Sage.
Yang, C., Modell, S., 2013. Power and performance: institutional embeddedness and performance management in a Chinese local government organization. *Accounting, Auditing & Accountability Journal*. 26, 1, 101–132.
Yang, C., Modell, S., 2015. Shareholder orientation and the framing of management control practices: a field study in a Chinese state-owned enterprise. *Accounting, Organizations & Society*. 45, 5, 1–23.
Yin, R.K., 1989. *Case study research: design and methods*. Newbury Park: Sage (2nd edition).

27

Research in performance management and control

The impact of research and the measurement of impact

Jane Broadbent

Overview

Systems of performance management and control (PMC) are ubiquitous. This chapter aims to look at a specific approach to PMC that considers how to build 'better' performance management and control (PMC) systems. The assumption is made that where resources are scarce, it is important and indeed ethical to make best use of them. Thus, systems of PMC are important, and the research undertaken in PMC should impact on policy and practice. A model of how best to achieve systems of PMC that are not dysfunctional is offered. It is not, however, enough to design 'better' systems of PMC; they also need to be adopted in practice. The chapter goes on to consider the manner in which it is possible to engage with policy makers and practitioners to adopt these systems – how impact of research can be achieved. To provide an example, finally, the chapter considers the impact of one particular PMC-the impact of the assessment of research impact which was one element in the UK Research Excellence Framework (REF) that took place in 2014.

I must highlight that the chapter is not one based on prior research but instead is a polemical commentary based on my experience in the REF exercise itself. A lengthier and more comprehensive consideration of the issues of PMC in the context of REF is already published in the paper by Agyemang and Broadbent (2015).

Prior assumptions and a conceptual framework

Before addressing the aims of the chapter, I will briefly highlight the prior assumptions and the conceptual framework that underlies my thinking.

If we take the view that PMC are legitimate activities – and some may not do so, especially when these activities are seen as the prerogative of management – then a serious approach to impact is essential, in my view. This is an especially important outcome in the context of academic research in the area of PMC. There is little sense in using systems of control if they do not achieve their aims to achieve the desired ends, or if indeed they simply cause dysfunctional outcomes. This approach of course assumes that the ends are desirable, and in making this statement, I am aware that the desired outcomes in any situation can be highly contested. In order to judge the legitimacy of the outcomes, some criteria are needed. The criteria used in this respect are ones that I have adopted in the long-standing research agenda that I have operationalised with Richard Laughlin over a period of 25 years (see Broadbent and Laughlin, 2013, for more details). Where the desired ends are, in the eyes of society, amenable to substantive justification and regulative of practice, rather than legitimated by procedure and constitutive (Broadbent, Laughlin and Read, 1991; Broadbent and Laughlin, 2013), then the assumption in this chapter is that this is a desirable and not a colonising change. A desirable change is one that reflects the values and culture of the organisation or society, and is thus part of the societal or organisational lifeworld (Laughlin, 1991). A colonising change is one that forces changes in the societal or organisational lifeworld.

If we are to have impact as researchers and thus advocate PMC systems that achieve desired outcomes, arguably we need to take a conceptual approach that Broadbent and Laughlin (2009) describe as 'relational' approaches. Relational approaches are processual and reflexive; they acknowledge complexity and involve all parties in the development and construction of appropriate systems. These are seen to create the environment for the development of positive change that is regulative and amenable to substantive justification. Thus, I wish to argue against a transactional and instrumental approach that is far more likely to lead to negative outcomes and dysfunctional consequences because this imposes solutions and is constitutive and legitimated by procedure.

Conceptual priors and a potential solution to achieving positive impact: relational not transactional control systems

In a society, and indeed in organisations, where we arguably have a moral and ethical imperative to use the scarce resources of the world in an effective and efficient manner, it seems appropriate to use systems of PMC to ensure that we do not waste these resources. What is more contestable is where the decisions are to be made about the nature of the PMC and in essence where the power to make decisions about their nature lies.

Misquoting Karl Marx, my assumption in approaching academic work is that it is not sufficient to understand the world; it is also important to change that world. Post-modern thinking advises caution about assuming universal solutions and seeing them as 'progress', Bauman (1989) for example pointing to the horrors of the holocaust as an example of the imposition of a single 'solution'. Thus, modernist projects that see some notion of a 'better' world are both feared and unfashionable. While there is undoubtedly a need to guard against all encompassing visions of instrumental rationality, as the introduction to this chapter has noted, I would wish to argue that there is a way to assess what is change for the better. My worry about abdicating the possibility to make such choices is that this leaves us neutered and only able to offer criticism rather than critique. I would like to suggest that there is a need to move beyond the stark juxtaposition of modern and post-modern thinking and look to reflexive approaches that do not eschew the need to make choices and work towards them. In this way, choices will be contestable and will be mutable, being created and recreated in the context of open organisational discourse. Nevertheless, the need to make choices is recognised. Arguably, in the context of control, this can be achieved when the nature of the PMC enables the development of reflexive systems of PMC, and this, as noted earlier, might be achieved by the adoption of relational approaches to PMC (Broadbent and Laughlin, 2009).

Management accounting research has over many years demonstrated that the use of performance measurement, particularly when accompanied by incentives for achieving the desired outcomes, will affect the behaviour of individuals and groups. We have learned that humankind is adept at achieving targets that are set, but that in achieving those targets, there may well be dysfunctional effects on other parts of an organisation. David Otley tells the story of the baggage handlers who were expected to deliver the first bag to the baggage collection belt within a set time. While the first bag did make that target, a lone baggage handler sprinting across to the baggage hall with a single bag, other bags might be quite some time behind! This has led to the argument that we need to think about developing systems of performance management rather than performance measurement. Arguably, even the latter are far too reliant on the use of performance measurement and therein lies the problem. The ingenuity of humankind is such that it can be said that as soon as a system of PMC that relies on performance measurement is implemented, because of the ability of humankind to achieve targets whatever, it is already of limited use. It is also clear that systems of PMC are least easy to implement in contexts where they are needed most, in complex and uncertain situations. This led Broadbent and Laughlin (2014) to argue for the use of a middle-range approach to management control and for the adoption of relational forms of control.

The analysis by Broadbent and Laughlin (2009) provides a conceptual framework that identifies the two conceptual approaches to management control – 'relational' and 'transactional' discussed above. Relational approaches to control are ones that are developed interactively in the context of discourse and recognise the need for both controllers and those subject to the controls to engage in developing meaningful measures. They are reflective of the need for longer-term relationships to be built and are built on a communicative rationality and systems of reflexive law (Teubner, 1983, 1984, 1986). The latter is important as it advocates an approach that does not define the inputs or outputs in an authoritative fashion. Instead, it advocates systems that provide for reflexive development of the inputs and how systems are developed to provide reflexively agreed outcomes. *Thus, the processes are focussed on agreeing the nature of the processes themselves rather than simply specifying how particular outputs should be achieved.* Systems development is embedded in organisational process and is a sustained rather than 'one-off' activity. This reflexive and sustained approach to developing PMC is arguably better equipped to lead to effective and positive modes of PMC.

In contrast, transactional approaches are ones that are imposed, are very tightly specified in terms of the inputs provided, the outputs expected and the process of how to achieve them. They are perhaps based on an 'accounting logic' (Broadbent and Laughlin, 2013, p. 14) which assumes the linear relationship between inputs and outputs. This approach works best in simple situations where there is agreement as to what are appropriate outcomes. Sadly, it is also an approach that is being adopted more widely, in more complex situations where there is ambiguity about the processes and dissension or ambiguity of the required outcomes due to incompatible desired outcomes for a variety of stakeholders. In this case, there is a likelihood that the outcomes will be negative and dysfunctional.

In Broadbent and Laughlin (2014), we argued in more detail for the use of a middle-range approach to management control in complex situations. Here, more specifically, I argue that, given the propensity of a target culture to lead to dysfunctional effects in any complex system, it is at least sensible and probably essential to turn to relational systems of control. This assertion recognises that the reflexive process that is foundational to this approach must also be embedded in the monitoring of the performance. Thus, not only must the results of PMC be fed back into the cycle of performance, but also they must be fed forward, so where necessary, there is a development of the systems for controlling and monitoring outcomes.

In this way, a continuing reflexive cycle is set up, which recognises that PMC is enacted on an ongoing basis.

While one should not underestimate the difficulty of dealing with complex situations where there may be multiple stakeholders often with conflicting aims, an approach that seeks to engage is arguably more likely to achieve desired outcomes than might be the case where given solutions are imposed. In positions where the power differential is substantial, then brute force may well be able to impose given solutions for some time; but in most societies and organisations, some level of co-operation is required to ensure action.

An example might help illustrate the problems. Perhaps more relational approaches would find a means of defining the PMC that would best help us assess the efficacy of our English accident and emergency (A&E) departments for example. Over 20 years ago, George, Read and Broadbent (1994) demonstrated how systems of triage in A&E departments tended to lead to more patients waiting the same length of time. The use of systems of triage was intended to ensure that urgent cases were given priority. We argued that the reason for this dysfunction was the potential for blame to be allocated to triage nurses making wrong decisions. Thus, the severity of some cases was overestimated to ensure that nurses were not held accountable if wrong decisions were made and the spread of estimations of urgency was narrowed. More recently, we have seen that A&E departments struggle to meet waiting time targets for reasons that are beyond their control – such as lack of hospital beds to move patients on to. These two examples demonstrate that over a period of 20 years, imposed methods of dealing with A&E waiting times have not been successful. It has often been commented that we are seeing simple solutions for complex problems and they do not work.

Adopting reflexive relational systems of PMC is, however, quite difficult for managers who are to be held accountable. The difficulty is that what this approach gives us is not a solution that defines what must be measured and controlled. Instead, it suggests how such a system might be developed. This approach is akin to what Teubner (1983, p. 275) calls 'reflexive law' an approach that does not define inputs, process or output, but instead will 'foster mechanisms that systematically further the reflexion structures' within organisations. For those who see management or leadership as a heroic activity leading from the front, the Grand Old Duke of York approach (as per the children's rhyme where he marched them up to the top of the hill and then back down again), this might be anathema. I would argue that it is an approach that reflects the inducements and contributions model of control (Barnard, 1938). Here, the role of a manager is to provide sufficient inducements to obtain the contributions necessary to maintain the feasible set of activities that will sustain the organisation in question. This model of management is more that of conductor than heroic leader but is one that I argue is much more fruitful, especially in complex situations where the processes to achieve outcomes are not well understood. Sadly, in my experience, there is more affinity to the heroic leader model in modern management programmes, and consequently, the approach is more common in practice.

To summarise my argument so far, I have argued that to build systems of PMC that achieve desired outcomes, i.e. change that is amenable to substantive justification and regulative of behaviour, a relational approach to building systems of PMC is required. I have also suggested that whatever the approach to control, the PMC adopted will lead to behavioural change and that transactional approaches to control are more likely to lead to negative outcomes and dysfunctional systems. I have further argued that the relational approach is perhaps not likely to be popular in a society where the heroic manager is the predominant model of management.

The nature of relationships between researchers, and practitioners and policy makers

It is of course no use academics having good ideas if they are not used. The relationship between academics and both policy makers and practitioners is enormously important and has been the focus of some debate that has highlighted a dichotomy between those who see a 'gap' between practitioners and academics (e.g. Tucker and Lowe, 2014) and those who see a different relationship rather than a gap (Laughlin, 2011). The prescription offered is that reflexive discourse between academics and policy makers or practitioners is necessary.

My contention is that those researching PMC should be concerned about the need for their research in the area to achieve positive impact insofar as this is conducive to achieving change that is deemed amenable to substantive justification and is regulative of accepted behaviour. One of the barriers to impact is claimed by academics to be the fact that practitioners and policy makers do not engage with research. This argument is substantiated by the complaints of the latter that academics spend too much time offering criticism of the actions of practitioners and policy makers without offering any solutions to how things might be fixed. It is for this reason that the reflexive approach as described above is offered as a way of achieving impact for our academic endeavours. However, there is no doubt that the idea of a practitioner-academic 'gap' has been accepted into the discourse of the academic community (Tucker and Lowe, 2014). Arguably, this is a discourse that we should seek to dispel. This is because we are, by now, clear that the discourses with which we engage do not simply reflect our reality, but they also create them. Turning again to the work of Laughlin (2011), we can seek a solution. Laughlin argues that we should see the accounting profession not simply as comprising the practitioners who are then set in opposition to academics. Instead, we should see practitioners, academics and professional bodies as separable but interrelated, each taking different roles. In this sense, despite the different roles, we are *all* part of that professional community. If we see the world in this fashion, then we have a basis for engaging in our different roles instead of constructing fissures within the profession. Thus, by changing our discourses and by engaging reflexively with practitioners and policy makers, we can start to build ways of developing impact. The key issue for impact must be building trust and engagement. This must mean engaging with users.

Just as a relational approach is required to develop control systems that engage stakeholders both in the definition of relevant outcomes and also the development of systems to achieve those ends, then it is arguable that for researchers to achieve impact with their research they must also adopt relational approaches with users. In short, it is not sufficient for researchers to have good ideas in isolation and expect policy makers and practitioners to pick them up; instead, they must recognise the need to engage reflexively with practitioners and policy makers in a relational manner. Achieving impact is, in my view, linked to the development of relationships and trust between academics and practitioners. This aspect of the argument will be returned to, but first of all consideration will be given to the methods which build research approaches that adopt a relational approach.

Reflexive engagement can take place at a number of different levels. Laughlin (1987) describes a three-stage mode of research that we have used successfully over a number of research projects (see Broadbent and Laughlin, 2013, for a synopsis of the relevant research). This approach is longitudinal and, in the first stage, is led by researchers who engage with the organisation in question to gather their insights into the organisational aspect that is the subject of the research. At the second stage, the insights are taken back to the members of the organisation in question and are discussed in depth to refine the insights of the researchers. In the final stage, the members of the organisation themselves must lead, moving from the mutually developed understanding of issues that have been the subject of the research, through to an organisational solution.

While this is a very specific approach, it is not unique in recognising the need to engage users. For example, other researchers have discussed the importance of the co-production of knowledge (see a collection of papers discussing this in the journal *Public Money and Management*, 30(4)). Just as any one of us would be wary of a manager or an outsider, without meaningful consultation, imposing a solution to control processes in organisations that we have understood well, so policy makers and practitioners will be wary of researchers' solutions.

Engagement must also mean adopting broader approaches to communication that address the practical difficulties that emerge from developing academic discourses within academic journals and eschewing other venues for delivering our research findings. Thus, we should value the opportunity to publish in practitioner journals and in books. These locations will not appear on the various dean's rankings of prestigious journals that are to be found across the world and which consequently distort the communicative processes, but will enable practitioners to access research findings.

We should also be aware that one of the very best ways of developing understandings between researchers and practitioners and policy makers is also in the context of the relationships we build with future holders of these roles – our students. Thus, research-led teaching is important, and the very best researchers should not eschew this activity if they are serious about their research having impact.

The latter two elements of engagement are not ones that are encouraged by the strictures of the UK REF, and it is to the impact of this more specifically that I now turn.

The impact of the UK research excellence framework: adopting a transactional approach

In the UK, researchers or at least their institutions are now taking notice of impact but perhaps for reasons that are not commendable. HM Treasury decided that it is important that the public funds that are provided for research should be allocated with some attention to the impact of research on practice. This perhaps is based on the assumption that research should be 'useful' in what might be seen as a rather instrumental way. This instrumental rationality meant that the Higher Educational Funding Council for England (HEFCE) in turn had to address this concern and this led to the development of a system of PMC that measures impact as an element in the Research Assessment Exercise (REF). The UK REF is currently undertaken every 6 years. A complex set of general and subject specific criteria defines who can be submitted and the criteria for evaluating their submissions. Panels and sub-panels comprised mainly of academics with some expert users make judgements about the quality of research as submitted by institutions. Details of the 2014 UK REF may be found in Pidd and Broadbent (2015) and in the relevant documentation on the HEFCE website.

The REF allocates financial resources and also reputation. Reputation is itself a driver for resource accumulation as it influences student choice and thus income from student fees. This linkage between PMC and resource allocation makes the former a significant driver of behaviour, especially in what is considered by the institutions to be a resource-rationed environment. While some level of consultation was undertaken before the element was added to REF, the system is basically a top-down system imposed on universities. It is a transactional management control system. It is also a system that drives institutions to achieve highly rated outcomes, and in turn this might be argued to lead to games-playing. An example of this more generally is in the competition among institutions to hire scholars who have successful publishing records. In the last REF, this led to the fractional appointments of overseas scholars who also have full-time positions in their home institutions. Some of these scholars have longstanding mentoring and research relationships in the UK, but others appeared on the books shortly before the census date for recognition of staff in the REF. While this may simply be a coincidence, it does have a sense of gamesmanship about it.

Returning to impact more specifically, assessment of the impact cases was undertaken by academic members of the assessment sub-panel with the help of a number of user assessors. The REF exercise demonstrated that UK research is providing impact. This is good news for the sector and for society as a whole. Impact was found in a variety of different sectors, affecting large- as well as small- and medium-sized enterprises. Some impact stories described models that have been implemented across companies or sectors. Others looked at specific interventions in particular companies or groups. Policy impacts were also described. Those involved in the assessment of the exercise were challenged as this was a first time that impact has been considered and consultation has already been started to consider the success of the approach.

As noted at the outset, it is clear that the imposition of any PMC that cannot be avoided will influence behaviour; the question is whether this will result in dysfunctional impacts alongside the desired results. There is some limited evidence at this stage of the exercise. REF submissions relating to impact required that an impact template and one case study describing impact be provided by each institution submitting, added to that a further case study for every ten researchers in the submission was also required. Thus, a submission of ten researchers required two case studies, and a submission of 20 required three case studies. Whether this level of submission makes sense in the context of what a fair expectation of impact activity might be is an open question, although the cases provided were generally of a good quality. However, anecdotal stories have suggested that in some institutions, researchers who might have been submitted to the REF were omitted in order to ensure that only impact cases considered to be of high quality were provided for assessment. Given the impact on the individual of non-submission to REF, loss of self-esteem and possible career disadvantages, then there is a possibility that dysfunctions have already set in.

We can see now that institutions are building bureaucratic structures to seek to maximise the measurement of the impact of research as defined by the criteria set by the regulatory bodies. Research Impact Managers, Deans and Deputy Deans of Impact (or people with similar titles) have been appointed. Systems for gathering evidence of impact are being built, and systems for disseminating research, with the hope that this will generate impact, are all emerging in our institutions. This all seems a shame. It reflects the need to react and respond to the PMC and not to the needs of society. The bureaucracy that is being created will have a material cost and will use a good deal of the resources that it is designed to generate. Moreover, the approach has raised some generalised resistance. For example, questions have been asked about the extent to which blue-sky research can be valued if all we are doing is responding to instrumental needs.

A series of dysfunctional reactions and resistance to the use of a PMC relating to research impact have therefore emerged. Thus, the aims of the PMC are being subverted. This is the result of a PMC that has been imposed with little reflexive involvement with the academics who are subject to the controls.

Finally

This short polemic argues that if research is to be undertaken, at some stage, impact is important and achieving impact is a meaningful ambition for a researcher, although not the only potential ambition. Blue-sky research is also an important part of the academic agenda. More specifically in the context of this volume that is concerned with PMC, academic researchers who are interested in the development of such systems need to engage with users to develop systems that help make the best use of scarce resources in society and organisations. The argument presented is that this is best achieved by researchers playing their part in building relational systems of PMC in organisations and society. These systems are best equipped to deal with complex situations where multiple stakeholders may have competing goals. They recognise the need to embed the development of control in organisational discourses and to see the issue of system development as processual and not project based.

I also argue that a reflexive and relational engagement with practitioners and policy makers is the basis both for developing effective systems of PMC and for their adoption in organisations and society, thus ensuring impact. Academics have a responsibility for engagement. This does not rule out the responsibilities of users themselves, and in a society where the 'heroic' manager leading a group to achieve specific goals is predominant, then I recognise the difficulty of engagement.

In making these arguments, I am arguing for the notion that we can aim for change to make society 'better'. Recognising the critique from post-modern perspectives rejecting the notion of 'better', I nevertheless maintain that if a reflexive engagement is undertaken to the development of desirable aims, then the possibility of emancipation remains a possibility. It may not be achieved; indeed, this may be a counterfactual, but the adoption of a relational and reflexive approach remains an aim to work towards.

In conclusion, I briefly examined the example of the UK REF 2014 that provides an example of a transactional PMC system which not only can create outcomes, but can also have dysfunctional effects. My hope is that, notwithstanding the dysfunctional imperatives the system seems to be creating, academic colleagues will instead embrace the impact agenda, where appropriate, in a positive manner. That they will seek to develop relational and reflexive approaches, embedded in academic and user discourse, that will define and redefine positive outcomes and the systems used to monitor them in order to achieve positive outcomes.

Perhaps then, the best place to finish is to reprise the exhortation to remember that it is not enough to understand the world, we must also seek to change it. To do so will ensure our academic activities will have impact.

References

Agyemang, G. and Broadbent, J. (2015) Management Control Systems and Research Management in Universities: An Empirical and Conceptual Exploration, *Accounting Auditing and Accountability Journal*, 28(7), 1–28.

Barnard, C. (1938) *The Functions of the Executive*, Cambridge MA, Harvard University Press.

Bauman, Z. (1989) *Modernity and the Holocaust*, Ithaca, NY, Cornell University Press.

Broadbent, J. and Laughlin, R. (2009) Performance Management Systems: A Conceptual Model, *Management Accounting Research*, 20(4), 283–295.

Broadbent, J. and Laughlin, R. (2013) *Accounting Control and Controlling Accounting: Interdisciplinary and Critical Perspectives*, Bingley, Emerald Group Publishing.

Broadbent, J. and Laughlin, R. (2014) Middle Range Thinking and Management Control Systems. In Otley, D. and Soin, K. (Eds) *Management Control and Uncertainty*, Basingstoke: Palgrave Macmillan, pp. 255–268. doi:10.1057/9781137392121.

Broadbent, J., Laughlin, R. and Read, S. (1991) Recent Financial and Administrative Changes in the NHS: A Critical Theory Analysis, *Critical Perspectives on Accounting*, 2(1), 1–29.

George, S., Read, S. and Broadbent, J. (1994) Do Formal Controls Always Achieve Control, *Health Services Management Research*, 7(1) 31–42.

Laughlin, R. (1987) Accounting Systems in Organisational Contexts: A Case for Critical Theory, *Accounting, Organizations and Society*, 12(5), 479–502.

Laughlin, R. (1991) Environmental Disturbances and Organisational Transitions and Transformations: Some Alternative Models, *Organization Studies*, 12(2), 209–232.

Laughlin, R. (2011) Accounting Research Policy and Practice: Worlds Together or Worlds Apart? In Evans, E., Burritt, R. and Guthrie, J. (Eds) *Bridging the Gap Between Academic Research and Professional Practice*, Sydney: Centre for Accounting, Governance and Sustainability, University of South Australia and Institute of Chartered Accountants of Australia, pp. 22–30.

Pidd, M. and Broadbent, J. (2015) Business and Management Studies in the 2014 Research Excellence Framework. *British Journal of Management*, 26(4), 569–581. doi:10.1111/1467-8551.12122.

Teubner, G. (1983) Substantive and Reflexive Elements in Modern Law, *Law and Society Review*, 17(2), 239–285.

Teubner, G. (1984) Autopoiesis in Law and Society: A Rejoinder to Blankenburg, *Law and Society Review*, 18(2), 291–301.

Teubner, G. (ed.) (1986) *Dilemmas of Law in the Welfare State*, Berlin, Walter de Gruyter.

Tucker, B.P. and Lowe, A.D. (2014) Practitioners are from Mars; Academics are from Venus? An investigation of the Research-Practice Gap in Management Accounting, *Accounting, Auditing and Accountability Journal*, 27(3), 394–425.

28
PMC
Entering a developing field

Tony Berry and Elaine Harris

Introduction

In this final chapter, our aim is to provide a useful guide to researchers entering (or re-entering) the field of performance management and control (PMC). The approach taken was to request contributing authors and members of the Management Control Association (MCA)[1] to share some words of wisdom based on their experience as scholars in the field and to weave these in with our own observations and recommendations. The chapter is divided into two main sections. First, we summarise key developments in the field of PMC, identifying what we and our fellow authors consider as the seminal works or milestones in PMC research. The references for this section are collected together in Appendix 28.2 and presented in chronological order to follow the historical account.

Then, we take the reader on a journey through a field-based study, offering tips and advice along the way from our collective experience. We are grateful to those authors and colleagues from the wider academic community who agreed to share their recommendations with us to fulfil our aim of guiding researchers in this challenging and complex arena. Finally, we conclude with some words of encouragement that we hope will inspire and motivate new and seasoned researchers alike to enter and continue working in this fascinating field.

The field

In chapter 2 of this volume, David Dugdale reviewed the major developments in the literature of management control. In this the final chapter of the volume, we have reiterated and built from his themes. He noted that Berry *et al.* (2009: 6) identified " …three models of integrated performance management systems [that] have emerged in the literature: strategic performance measurement systems (SPMS) like Kaplan and Norton's balanced scorecard; Simons' levers of control; and Ferreira and Otley's performance management and control framework" (see Figure 9.1, p. 160). However, the earliest formal work was that of Robert Anthony (1965).

Planning and Control Systems; Strategic, Managerial and Operational were distinguished by Anthony (1965) as three levels of purpose which taken together provided a basis for analysis and design of control systems. This is a somewhat hierarchical ordering, but does helpfully separate out three different kinds of problems. Each of these has been taken forward in a variety of literatures, as this volume attests. As the concept of corporate strategy came to replace the older idea of business policy strategic control became a dominant idea, echoed in the work of Simon and Otley. While much criticised for its functionalist stance, the limitations of his model as an ideal type and the lack of research to establish it as explanatory, Anthony's seminal work repays a critical reading.

In parallel to Anthony was an emerging approach to performance management systems (PMS) via cybernetics. Otley and Berry (1980) suggested that there were four necessary conditions for control: (1) an objective for the system being controlled, (2) a means of measuring results along the dimensions defined by the objective, (3) a predictive model of the system being controlled and (4) a choice of relevant alternative actions available to the controller. (The literature of control engineering has developed similar models with very considerable sophistication in modelling, measurement, information flows and decision-taking.) These authors noted the acute limitations of the accounting model of control, the problems of having adequate predictive models of complex organisations in fluid environments (see Ashby, 1956) and the need for feed-forward as well as feedback control processes.

The author of Chapter 2 (Dugdale) recommends Burns and Stalker (1961) as a "book that had a major impact by demonstrating that a logical, rational, hierarchical structure might not always be as good as an organic structure … emphasises the possible importance of culture (long before Ouchi and Simons talked about values and beliefs)" (Dugdale, personal communication, 22 February 2016).

> … the emptying out of significance from the hierarchic command system, by which co-operation is ensured and which serves to monitor the working organization under a mechanistic system, is countered by the development of shared beliefs about the values and goals of the concern.
>
> *(Burns and Stalker, 1961: 122)*

He also recommends Lukes' (1975, 2005) work on the dimensions of power, with its notions of coercion and resistance, silencing of objections and the controlling power of persuasion that a particular course of action is in the other person's best interests. This work is not as widely cited in the PMC literature as that of Anthony Giddens (1979, 1984), but it points to the social complexities of the organisational context within which PMC takes place. As context is of vital concern to case study researchers, such a revelation is important, especially to those entering the field from a professional practice background, for whom these theories may otherwise lay undiscovered.

The MCA published works on New Perspectives (Lowe and Machin, 1983) and (following Chua, 1986) Critical Perspectives (Puxty and Chua, 1989) on management control. MCA also published a review and extension by collaborating authors (Berry, Broadbent and Otley, 1995, 2005). The text by MCA members (Emmanuel, Otley and Merchant, 1985) made a major contribution to the teaching of management accounting in context, which placed importance on the behavioural aspects of PMC. A further useful review of the development of the management control may be found in the volume of papers edited by Berry, Broadbent and Otley (1998), which grouped papers along the themes of control as goal directed and integrative, control as adaptation, the social structure of control in organisations and the organisation in its environment. Some of the tensions in approaches to studying control systems, especially those between technical and social control studies, were illustrated together with issues arising from critical social theory.

A more complex development followed from the work of Williamson (1973) who contrasted economic coordination by hierarchy and by markets (from considerations of transaction costs) and that of Ouchi (1980) who considered the influence of culture via an idea of control through clan membership and identity. These three highly contested ideas of control, via hierarchy, markets and culture continue to resonate through the literature of PMS as do the ideas of closed and open systems.

We presume Robert Simons (1995) named his "Levers of Control" by thinking of a mechanical metaphor most likely taken from railway signalling mechanisms. Based on a 10-year study of control systems in US businesses, Simons (1995, p. ix) observed that " … the most innovative companies used their profit planning and control systems more intensively than did their less innovative counterparts". He expanded control theorising in his conclusion that successful organisations had achieved balance between four modes of control that he characterised as diagnostic, interactive, boundary and beliefs systems. Diagnostic systems " …are the backbone of traditional management control … Three features distinguished diagnostic control systems: (1) the ability to measure the outputs of a process, (2) the existence of predetermined standards against which actual results can be compared, and (3) the ability to correct deviations from standards" (p. 59). Note that these three constitute three of the four elements identified by Otley and Berry (1980) but exclude the need for a predictive model, although it may be readily conceded that Simons would see that as implicit in his model as a necessary precursor to establishing predetermined standards. It is important to note that the four modes of control proposed include both technical and social controls.

The widespread acceptance of the problems and limitations of financial and accounting reporting led to two contrasting responses, both concerned with the need for a rich reporting of a wide array of information. In France, this led to the development of the Tableau de Bord, a French description of a car dashboard or an aircraft cockpit, with its array of information; hence, the term "Pilotage" is used commonly and frequently. French scholars (e.g. Daum, 2005) applied this train of thought to the enterprise control area decades ago. A definition was offered (Daum, 2005, p. 2):

> The Tableau de Bord is a management tool that is comprised of both a set of indicators that are related (not by deterministic, algebraic operations but) by causal relationships and links, and the process of selection, documentation, and interpretation of these indicators. Each one of these indicators is chosen to measure the status of a part of the business to be managed, so that all indicators, taken together, offer a model the general functioning of the business (system) in achieving its objective.

Again note the common core idea of a model with causal relationships.

The most known approach to "information integration" was the balanced scorecard. Kaplan and Norton's (1992) balanced scorecard introduced three non-financial dimensions of performance: customers, internal processes, and learning and growth that "balanced" the financial dimension. Kaplan and Norton (1992) set out a template that linked vision and strategy to actions in each of the dimensions through the identification of objectives, measures, targets and initiatives. Kaplan and Norton (1996a) recommended that the vision and mission should be translated into " …an integrated set of objectives and measures" (p. 4) with "ambitious goals" that guide resource allocation and priorities so as to further long-term strategic objectives. Feedback and learning then encourage "strategic learning" across all four dimensions of the scorecard. The development of the balanced scorecard followed in the tradition of feedback control but included non-financial as well as financial measures and emphasises the importance of leading indicators such as market share and product innovation as well as lagging indicators such as financial results. This approach appears to be a pragmatic enrichment of organisation information flows, with the value of pulling it all together in one place around an implicit or explicit causal model; much as did the Tableau de Bord. But it also derived from, the perhaps rare, 1960s corporate practice where information rooms contained updated charts of all the major factors of performance.

Daum (2005) offered a comparison of the Tableau de Bord and the balanced scorecard (Current authors' tabulation of the principal differences):

The balanced scorecard concept has the following main contributions	*Major contribution of the Tableau de Bord*
Its allusion to the importance of strategic control and strategic, enterprise-wide change management in today's dynamic business environment, and the tools (strategy maps, etc.) it provides for this	A clearly, explicitly defined "enterprise framework" that ensures that intentions (mission, vision, values) are compatible with procedure (strategy) and the measurement of the achieved or achievable results (measurement system)
Its explicitly proposed four perspectives, which provide a measure of explicit, general logic as a starting point for defining the company-specific causal model (in contrast to the strictly generic approach of the Tableau de Bord concept)	Development of a refined concept for operative control of the value-creating processes at a company, based on a causal model
	A standardised approach for its implementation, based on a rich base of experience from business practice that has become integrated in general business practice and in the teachings at universities, grandes écoles and business schools

Economic Value Added (EVA, copyright Stern Stewart) promulgated by Stern Stewart set out to focus each part of the organisation's contribution to value added. It was based on the concept of residual income measured as "economic value added", a single, clear (financial) measure that, they claimed, would align the interests of managers with those of shareholders. They argued that the first duty of a company is to create value for its shareholders, and in so doing, it would also serve wider society. The EVA calculation is more comprehensive than other financial metrics such as the price/earnings ratio and, mathematically, was held to be consistent with the net present value calculation recommended for the appraisal of investment opportunities. This single measure is perhaps the ultimate application of the reduction of variety (Ashby, 1956).

Ferreira and Otley's (2009) performance management framework built on Otley's (1999) framework that comprised five key questions relating to (1) organisational objectives and their evaluation; (2) strategies, plans and activities, and how they are assessed and measured; (3) performance targets for the areas raised in (1) and (2); (4) rewards and penalties for achievement or failure to achieve the targets; and (5) feedback and feed-forward loops so that the organisation can learn from experience and adapt behaviour in the light of that experience. Dugdale (op. cit.) noted that Otley (1999) "tested" the framework against three control systems: budgeting, the balanced scorecard and EVA. He concluded that none of these provide a *comprehensive* PMS. Budgetary control concentrates only on financial objectives, does not consider links between means and ends, and does not explicitly consider rewards (although bonuses are often linked to budget-based targets). EVA has just a single financial objective and does not consider the link between means and ends, although appropriate incentive schemes are central to the method. The balanced scorecard considers both financial and non-financial performance measures that emerge from strategy but does not address how targets or reward structures should be set.

Otley's analysis implicitly presumes that a management control system (MCS) "should" address all the relevant issues: objectives, strategies, targets, feedback and rewards/penalties. While budgeting, EVA and the balanced scorecard provide valuable insights, none delivers a *comprehensive* system of control. Otley found the framework useful when investigating PMS and, with Ferreira, developed it further, expanding the number of questions to four contextual and eight functional (Ferreira and Otley, 2009). This extension to a more complex framework seems to follow Ashby's idea that as only variety can destroy variety, then the model for PMS must match the variety in the domain to be managed. This pattern is seen in Anthony, Kaplan and Norton, the Tableau de Bord and Simons. An interesting question arises for research: Are the approaches to PMS by increasing variety in the models more effective than the EVA model that essentially eliminates variety? In what circumstances might such research find different answers? However, it should be noted that early attempts to test the effectiveness of Anthony's model were unsatisfactory.

The technical basis of or for control systems has been in endemic conflict with approaches arising from sociological and psychological theories (see, for example, Burns and Stalker, 1961). People are individuals and members of social groups; they are not naive mechanisms, are not replaceable bits of kit or computer programmes, are not without intelligence, feelings, values and experience, and are sceptical in their response to managers and to control systems. All of these affect how people respond to and use controls, including how people build models of their masters in order to exercise some countervailing control. Equally, people may be self-interested (as individuals and group members), so will cooperate with technical controls as well as be in conflict with them where behaviour may sometimes be seen as devious compliance. A parallel here are the complex interactions, well explored in the leadership literature, of leaders and followers.

Dugdale (op. cit.) observed that Simons emphasised that interactive "systems" are actually *uses* of the control system, and Tessier and Otley (2012) continued the analysis by pointing out that diagnostic and interactive "systems" are *uses*, boundary "systems" are a *purpose* and beliefs systems are a *type* of control system. This led Tessier and Otley to reframe Simons' analysis differentiating purpose into performance and compliance, use into strategic and operational issues and type into social and technical controls. Simons' classification has the merit of having being inductively derived by *empirical* study of how managers actually use their "levers of control", but, Dugdale argued, Tessier and Otley force a more rigorous conceptualisation of Simons' ideas. However, Tessier and Otley draw attention to two *types* of management control and organisation theory that has long recognised a major distinction between *technical* and *social* controls. Technical systems are linked to "scientific" management, emphasising process analysis, specialisation, standardisation, clear job descriptions and lines of authority. This contrasts with the "human relations" school that relies on human interaction for coordination and control.

Simons' diagnostic and beliefs systems are readily categorised as technical and social systems, respectively (though organisational theory sees "social controls" as more wide-ranging, including social norms, culture and shared values as well as top-management-driven vision and mission statements). Both technical, diagnostic systems and social, beliefs systems can be used interactively to foster interaction and communication. Similarly, both technical and social control systems can be used to set boundaries: technical systems can make acceptable/unacceptable behaviour more explicit (for example through budgetary and authorisation limits), while social controls can help to shape a culture that is acceptable to wider society.

Broadbent and Laughlin (2009) provided a further interesting categorisation of PMS, noting that too much attention in the management, management control and management accounting literatures had been given to ex post performance measurement as distinct from ex ante performance management. They developed a conceptual model of PMS building on the work and insights primarily of Otley (1999) and Ferreira and Otley (2009) who share similar concerns. Particular attention was given to analysing the underlying factors that influence the nature of any PMS, which led Broadbent and Laughlin to the development of Ferreira and Otley's conceptualisation into a "middle-range" model of PMS lying on a continuum from "transactional" at one end to "relational" at the other, the spectrum being built on, respectively, underlying instrumental and communicative rationalities and guided by a range of contextual factors. Broadbent's Chapter 27 in this volume on research impact demonstrates the significance of relational systems and gives a deeper meaning to the ideas of social controls.

The development of the control of railways via the use of signal and related systems (Rolt, 1955) was largely a product of appalling accidents. These led to accident enquiries and recommendations to have systems in place to have a good likelihood of preventing any similar accident. Of course, the various parties to this, the injured and their relatives, campaign groups, governments, insurance companies, engineers, scientists and the directors of the railway companies, did not share the same enthusiasm for the recommendations, especially where significant costs were to be borne. The actual changes were always, it appeared, to be more than the companies wanted and less than the campaigners wanted. But this error-driven approach does seem to be endemic in building control systems as variety "creeps" in to the models and systems. This became more pronounced as analysis of high-profile accidents (Three Mile Island, Chernobyl, Deepwater Horizon, etc.) demonstrated that the variety in any social and technical domain is almost impossible to capture. This brings us to the topic of risk in PMC (covered by Mikes and Zhivitskaya in Chapter 9 of this volume) and the MCA publication edited by Otley and Soin (2014) on control and uncertainty.

For the journey (some guidance for new or returning researchers in the field)

It is clear from this brief review that control and PMS have been approached in similar ways from the mixed standpoints of experience of practice leading to progressive model building (Ashby, Anthony, Kaplan and Norton, Tableau de Bord, Otley, Ferreira and Tessier) and by theorising prior to and from empirical studies (Otley, Simon, Broadbent and Laughlin). In this volume, Seneviratne and Hoque (Chapter 24) and Mai and Hoque (Chapter 12) provide reviews of how some MCS research is developing. We also note that most of the empirical chapters in this volume were based on single case studies (with two studies using multiple cases) and two chapters on qualitative research methods. This reflects the research philosophy of the editor and many (but by no means all) of the members of MCA.

It is with this in mind that we offer tips and advice for researchers working in this paradigm. Sticking with our railway theme, the next section is structured (more or less) in the order a typical journey into the field for a research study in PMC might be experienced. We also present extracts from the tips and advice given by the Faculty (plenary speakers) at the MCA2016 doctoral colloquium held in Antwerp in Appendix 28.1. Other tips contributed by colleagues showed considerable overlap, so these have been woven into the journey in our own words.

a The grounding; always go back to the source literature and read it for yourself. It really is important that you understand how other scholars have viewed, interpreted, understood and misunderstood source literature. While survey papers are very valuable starting points, beware of simply accepting the judgements of other authors, however distinguished they may be. Do not "name-drop" key authors without reading their work.

b Be clear about your philosophical methodological position; but be flexible; do not get trapped in methodological purity. The basic books on method and methodology are probably in your library, but Paul Feyerabend's book *Against Method* (2010) is refreshing.

c You as the Researcher are a research instrument, especially in your mental processes. To think critically is crucial, that is to form a well-grounded appreciation of a piece of literature. Chapter 26 by Lowe and de Loo in this volume is an exemplar. You are often encouraged to reflect upon your work and its development. To think reflexively is to go further into your own underlying assumptions about knowledge and how it is developed. This will enable you to read others' work both more critically and more kindly as you discover how difficult research is.

d When you consider a proposed Research Design, set out to see if the conclusion of your work will permit you to answer the following five key questions:

   1 What is the Knowledge debate to which you seek to make a contribution?
   2 What is (a) the contribution you seek to make, (b) the argument that supports it and (c) why is that an important contribution?
   3 What were the evidence gathering processes and the nature and extent of evidence that you will have obtained?
   4 What are the evidenced conclusions regarding the argument for your contribution?
   5 What are the implications for knowledge (debate, practice, further research)? The latter includes an assessment of impact.

   If you can answer these questions clearly and effectively, you will have the basis of a good academic paper in a high-quality journal. These five questions interestingly also provide a nice template for your abstract and for analysing other research papers.

e It is easier to contribute to an existing domain of knowledge than to create a new one; but if you can create a new one, then the developing research programme will be a substantial reward. Be careful to consider the context of your study and how you will put boundaries to the object of your study. Most novice researchers (and some more experienced ones) are too ambitious in terms of what might be done in a reasonable time, especially within the constraints of a degree programme or research contract.

f Research Skill building seems to be an endless process as research quality requirements tighten up what is acceptable. It is an achievement to become proficient in the methods you choose to use, but it is also necessary to become proficient in a variety of evidence-gathering methods and analytic processes. PMC involves complex ideas that require a variety of research approaches, and you need to be able to read and understand contemporary published research (utilising methods other than your own).

g You will have noticed that in this volume that case study methods are very common, mostly single case studies with only a couple of chapters using multiple case studies. You could reread the review chapters by Hoque and his colleagues to get an insight into the difficulty of conducting research on PM systems before you enter the field.

h Prepare for interviews meticulously; you may only have one chance to speak with that busy company executive, so make the most of it. Not only should you prepare a structured interview plan (with lead and supplementary questions) and be clear about how you plan to analyse the responses, but you should also do your homework on the organisation, industry and individual you plan to interview, so that you can present yourself as reasonably knowledgeable. Being well prepared also gives you confidence, and you will appear more competent. You never know when you might want to speak with that contact again, or be recommended to their colleagues.

i When in the field, whether in a one-to-one interview or attending a meeting, listen carefully and concentrate hard immediately afterwards to make notes that will help you to view the data reflexively. Do not just rely on digital recordings of interviews; also keep a personal research log to note non-verbal clues. Even if you have a research assistant to type up transcripts, listen to the recordings yourself. You should immerse yourself in the data to make sure that you don't miss key insights in the analysis.

j Being a doctoral candidate in this field seems to require you to be a "sole trader" who is doing an individual piece of research making your unique contribution. But this may not be wise. Being a participant contributing to a much larger study might improve the quality of the research outcomes, of your research training, of the impact of the project. The conundrum is that while the academic reward systems favour sole traders, the complexity of this field and the requirements for the quality and significance of research require research partnerships. One of us was a party to a multiple case study design across six organisations that involved six researchers, one of whom was a doctoral candidate. All of the six studies and multiple member teams led to organisational learning and published academic contributions, and the award of a well-merited doctorate! It would be a stretch to claim that the six studies were well integrated, but there was a team ethos.

k It is becoming crucial to both seek and achieve impact. Jane Broadbent's chapter illuminates the task, its difficulty and the need for a relational process. The notion that all research needs to have high-level policy implications is noted as an aspiration of government funders. For our discipline, especially for early career researchers, a more feasible aim is that some practitioners (if only those who agree to participate in field studies) will be impacted by our work in the sense of seeing their own practice differently as a result of engaging with us.

At the risk of raising academic hackles, we suggest that researchers also need to consider impact from the perspective of "a knowledge intermediation role" where persons gather expertise in facilitating understanding, communication and assessment of impact. You might learn here from the work of the leading management consultants (who may in your view be less academic) but are surely very experienced in entering the world of organisations with the intent of making an impact. The very gifted consultants also make seminal knowledge contributions. So, even this idea might lead to a significant shift in how knowledge is developed. Of course, this idea has been in circulation for some years in the form of a shift from only academic led research to include problem and practice centred research partnerships.

l The myth of stability; it is a cliché that we work in changing worlds, but it is important to note that some parts change faster than others. However, all field research takes place in changing political, economic, social and environmental contexts across nations, regions and the globe. So, the systems that you might study will be changing as you study them.

m Accessing data; the original field study is a common first research project; but access to important and interesting organisations can be very difficult.

It may be possible to use published material. For example, one of us was involved in a study based on the published reports of the UK Board of Trade (as it then was) inspections of corporate failures to build a model of how corporate reporting requirements were changed over 20 years. The banking crisis of 2008 has spawned many studies. There are reports of public enquiries, commissions, etc. that provide an array of evidence.

To end our journey, we reiterate Otley's (2008) eight "desirable attributes of a research project in this area: …

Incremental – builds on what we know already.
Interpretative – includes individual perceptions that drive behaviour.
Integrated – keeps an holistic focus.
Inclusive – considers all stakeholders.
International – not confined to a single culture.
Imaginative – not formulaic.
Interesting – or why do it?
Influential – relevant to practice".

Together with the tips provided in Appendix 28.1, we hope that these recommendations will help researchers, especially those new to academia, to embark on their journey with the awareness that others who travelled before them will have made mistakes along the way. Publishing can be a humbling experience, but a worthwhile one.

Concluding comments

As this volume demonstrates, the study of PMS is a very complex and dynamic field. There is a need for more and better empirical studies of PMS. We have noted how the approaches to theorising PMC have developed in variety and in more complex models and frameworks. Much of the reported research has been conducted in a kind of cottage industry in a community of academic practice. Is this tradition a sufficiently fruitful process or, in the face of the need to study large complex systems, should the academy take the lead in seeking to build bigger research teams from wider communities of practice? This second approach might enable PMS researchers to attain a higher impact (economic and social benefits) for their work.

Appendix 28.1: Top tips for PhD students

Alexandra Van den Abbeele, Professor of Management Accounting and Control and Head of Research Centre for Accountancy, KU Leuven, Belgium

- It's YOUR PhD – Take ownership.
- Academics need you – Find a mentor!
- Love to hate your thesis – Take a break!
- Focus only on the next step or hurdle as you work.
- Write up as you are going.
- KISS (keep it simple and short) – see Faff (2015) for how to pitch a research project (communicate your ideas).
- Finished is better than perfect.
- The written thesis is just part of the PhD.
- Build a good reputation (go to conferences, be friendly and helpful).
- Have a plan for life post PhD.

Anne-Marie Kruis, Associate Professor of Management Accounting and Control, Nyenrode Business University, The Netherlands

- Don't be afraid to present your ideas right from the start.
- Don't wait for your perfect idea, just get out there and start presenting your proposal.
- Don't do your research in isolation – join your discipline/community and discuss your work (that way you get feedback).
- Learn from the ideas of others and be inspired by your colleagues.
- Your PhD study should be fun, so get out there and enjoy it.

Eddy Cardinaels, Professor of Accounting, KU Leuven, Belgium and Tilburg University, The Netherlands

- Think in core concepts to define and motivate the theory.
- Read outside your discipline; often parallels with other related fields → economics, psychology, HRM, etc. → we can borrow theory and design from these fields.
- Be prepared for the tension question. Why should we care? What is new? Has this been done?
- Do the "spouse test" by explaining your ideas in non-technical language to see if they fall asleep or listen and understand.
- Narrow down the research question (after starting broad).
- Going from theory to actual design further thought – recommend the use of Libby boxes, see, for example, Bloomfield *et al.*, 2016; helps with structure and construct validity.

Kari Lukka, Professor and Head of Department of Accounting and Finance, Turku School of Economics, University of Turku, Finland

- Anchor questions (of any piece of research), e.g. what, why, how:
  - What is getting examined? (Clarity of the research question is the basis for everything.)
  - Why is the research question important? (i.e. Motivation for the question, positioning in relation to literature/theory and gap in prior knowledge.)
  - How will the study be carried out? (Methodology, methods, data sets, plans for analysing the data.)
  - What are the results? (Findings, conclusions, contribution and learning.)
- Research question and theory.
  - Theoretical level (how does the research question relate to theory?)
  - Empirical level (plays only secondary role in principle).
  - Frequent mistake to mix these two levels together.

- Domain vs. Method theory.
  - Domain theory is about our discipline (management accounting/control).
  - Method theory is a theoretical lens or tool to use to contribute to domain (see Lukka and Vinnari, 2014).

Source: These tips have been extracted with permission from Faculty presentations at the MCA doctoral colloquium in Antwerp, 6 September 2016.

Appendix 28.2: Recommended reading in chronological order

Ashby W R (1956) *An Introduction to Cybernetics,* Chapman and Hall, London.

Burns T and Stalker G M (1961) *The Management of Innovation,* Tavistock Publications, London.

Anthony R N (1965) *Planning and Control Systems: A Framework for Analysis,* Harvard University, Graduate School of Business Administration, Boston.

Lukes S (1975, 2005) *Power: A Radical View,* Palgrave Macmillan, Basingstoke.

Otley D T and Berry A J (1980) Control, Organisation and Accounting. *Accounting, Organisations and Society,* 5 (2), 231–244.

Ouchi W G (1980) Markets, Hierarchies and Clans. *Administrative Science Quarterly* 25 (1), 129–141.

Lowe E A and Machin J (1983) *New Perspectives on Management Control.* Macmillan, London.

Emmanuel C, Otley D and Merchant K (1985, 1990) *Accounting for Management Control,* Chapman and Hall, London.

Chua Y F (1986) Radical Developments in Accounting Thought. *The Accounting Review,* 61 (4), 601–632.

Puxty A and Chua Y F (1989) *Critical Perspectives on Management Control.* Macmillan, London.

Kaplan R S and Norton D P (1992) The Balanced Scorecard: Measures that Drive Performance, *Harvard Business Review,* (January–February), 71–79.

Simons R (1995) *Levers of Control: How Managers Use Innovative Control Systems to Drive Strategic Renewal,* Harvard Business School Press, Boston, MA.

Berry A J, Broadbent J and Otley D T (1995, 2005) *Management Control: Theories, Issues and Practices.* Palgrave Macmillan, Basingstoke.

Kaplan R S and Norton D (1996a) Putting the Balanced Scorecard to Work, *Harvard Business Review,* (January–February), 3–13.

Kaplan R S and Norton D (1996b) *The Balanced Scorecard,* Harvard Business School Press, Boston.

Berry A J, Broadbent J and Otley D T Eds. (1998) *Management Control Theory.* Dartmouth Publishing Company Ltd., Aldershot.

Kaplan R S and Norton D (2001) *The Strategy-Focused Organization,* Harvard Business School Press, Boston.

Pettit J (2001) EVA and Strategy, Stern Stewart & Co. Research, downloaded 14/2/2015 from www.sternstewart.com.br/publicacoes/pdfs/EVA_and_strategy.pdf.

Kaplan R S and Norton D (2004) *Strategy Maps,* Harvard Business School Press, Boston.

Daum J H (2005) Tableau de Bord: Besser als die Balanced Scorecard?, *Der Controlling Berater,* issue 7, pp. 459–502 (French Tableau de Bord: Better than the Balanced Scorecard?).

Berry A J, Coad A F, Harris E P, Otley D T and Stringer C (2009) Emerging Themes in Management control: a review of recent literature, *The British Accounting Review,* 41, 2–20.

Ferreira A and Otley D A (2009) The Design and Use of Management Control Systems: An Extended Framework for Analysis, *Management Accounting Research,* 20, 263–282.

Broadbent J and Laughlin R (2009) Performance Management Systems: A Conceptual model, *Management Accounting Research,* 20, 283–295.

Bischof B, Essex S and Furtaw P. (2010) Participating in Opportunities and Risks. Long Live the Bonus Bank! Stern Stewart Research// Volume 40 downloaded 14/02/2015 from www.sternstewart.com/files/ssco_studie40_en.pdf/.

Tessier S and Otley D (2012) A Conceptual Development of Simons' Levers of control framework, *Management Accounting Research,* 23 (3), 171–185

Broadbent J and Laughlin R (2013) *Accounting Control and Controlling Accounting: Interdisciplinary and Critical Perspectives,* Emerald Group Publishing, Bingley.

Notes

1 The MCA is a network of researchers who are interested in the broad area of control in organisations. The ethos of the MCA is to develop critical insights into control processes and encourage research that recognises the organisational, personal and social contexts of control. www.managementcontrolassociation.ac.uk/.

2 Excluding those presented in chronological order in Appendix 28.2.

References[2]

Bloomfield R, Nelson M W and Solties E (2016) Gathering Data for Archival, Field, Survey, and Experimental Accounting Research, *Journal of Accounting Research*, 54 (2), 341–395.

Faff R W (2015) A Simple Template for Pitching Research, *Accounting and Finance*, 55 (2), 311–336.

Feyerabend P (2010) *Against Method*. 4th Edition, Verso Books, New York.

Giddens, A (1979) *Central Problems in Social Theory: Action, Structure and Contradiction in Social Analysis*. London, Macmillan.

Giddens, A (1984) *The Constitution of Society: Outline of the Theory of Structuration*. Cambridge, Polity Press.

Lukka K and Vinnari E (2014) Domain Theory and Method Theory in Management Accounting Research, *Accounting, Auditing & Accountability Journal*, 27 (8), 1308–1338.

Otley, D (1999) Performance Management: A Framework for Management Control Systems Research. *Management Accounting Research*, 10 (4), 363–382.

Otley D T (2008) Did Kaplan and Johnson Get it Right? *Accounting, Auditing & Accountability Journal*, 21 (2), 229–239.

Otley D and Soin, K (eds) (2014) *Management Control and Uncertainty*. Basingstoke, Palgrave Macmillan.

Rolt L T C (1955). *Red for Danger*. Bodley Head, London; (1986 Pan Books).

Williamson O E (1973) Markets and Hierarchies: Some Elementary Considerations. *American\Economic Association*, 63 (2), 316–325.

Index